CW00766307

CHARLES HUBER

CHARLES HUBER
FRANCE'S GREATEST ARABIAN EXPLORER

WITH A TRANSLATION OF HUBER'S FIRST JOURNEY IN CENTRAL ARABIA, 1880–1881

William Facey

In collaboration with
Michael C.A. Macdonald

Foreword by
Christian Julien Robin

Arabian Publishing

Charles Huber: France's Greatest Arabian Explorer
With a translation of Huber's First Journey in Central Arabia, 1880–1881
By William Facey

Introduction, Translation and Appendices 1, 3–13: © William Facey
Appendix 2: 'Concordance of the inscriptions recorded by Huber on his 1880–81 Arabian journey': © Michael C.A. Macdonald

Produced and published in 2022 by
Arabian Publishing Ltd
a division of Medina Publishing Ltd
www.medinapublishing.com

Arabian Publishing

Medina Publishing

Published under the auspices of the
International Association for the Study of Arabia (IASA)
and the Académie des Inscriptions et Belles-Lettres, Institut de France

IASA
International Association for the Study of Arabia
الرابطة الدولية لدراسة الجزيرة العربية

ACADÉMIE DES INSCRIPTIONS ET BELLES-LETTRES
INSTITUT DE FRANCE

Design and digital artwork: Sherif Dhaimish, Alexandra Lawson and Luke Pajak

Printed and bound in Great Britain by Clays Ltd, Elcograf S.p.A.

The TranslitLSU font used in this work is available from Linguist's Software, Inc.
Tel +1 (425) 775-1130. www.linguistsoftware.com

All rights reserved. No part of this publication may be reproduced, stored in a retrieval system, or transmitted in any form or by any means, electronic, mechanical, photocopying, recording, or otherwise, without the prior permission of the copyright holders

A catalogue record for this publication is available from the British Library

ISBN: 978-1-911487-67-8

Frontispiece: Portrait of Charles Huber taken from his *carte de visite*. This photograph was taken in Strasbourg in the studio of Gerschel Frères (4th floor, 3 rue de la Meisengasse) in 1882 or early 1883.

In memoriam

Dr Alasdair Livingstone
1954–2021

Assyriologist, teacher and friend who, as Archaeological Adviser to the Department of Antiquities and Museums in Saudi Arabia during 1981–85, travelled in search of inscriptions and rock art through the regions traversed by Charles Huber

Ch. Huber
Juillet 1884. Mort pour la science

Epitaph on the tomb of Charles Huber (1847–1884), set up at the expense of the French government in the non-Muslim cemetery in Ğiddah.

Raoul Jolly, 'Les missions françaises. Voyages de Charles Huber, Arabie.' *Journal des Voyages et des Aventures de Terre et de Mer*, no. 856, 3 décembre 1893, pp. 362–3

The greatest of all French explorers of Arabia

Harry St J. B. Philby, *Arabian Days: An Autobiography*, p. 3

Except for the observations of Huber in the region south of the Nefûd, no other explorer's data were of use to me in the construction of my map of Northern Arabia.

Alois Musil, *Arabia Deserta: A Topographical Itinerary*, p. xv

No man can live this life and emerge unchanged. He will carry, however faint, the imprint of the desert, the brand which marks the nomad; and he will have within him the yearning to return.

Wilfred Thesiger, *Arabian Sands*, p. 1

Contents

Illustrations

Frontispiece

Studio portrait of Charles Huber, as used on his *carte de visite*. Taken in Strasbourg by Gerschel Frères, 1882 or early 1883. By kind permission of the Société de Géographie, Paris.

Between pp. 58 and 59

1. Charles Huber's *carte de visite*, using the portrait taken in Strasbourg by Gerschel Frères, 1882 or early 1883. By kind permission of the Société de Géographie, Paris.
2. Charles Huber in Arab dress. Studio photograph taken in Strasbourg by Gerschel Frères, 1882 or early 1883. By kind permission of the Bibliothèque nationale et universitaire, Strasbourg.
3. Maḥmūd, Huber's servant and travelling companion, photographed in October 1884 by Snouck Hurgronje. With thanks to Prof. Jan Just Witkam.
4. Huber's name carved in Arabic at al-Āyy, at the southern tip of Ǧabal Mismāʾ. With thanks to Florent Égal.
5. Huber and Euting's graffiti signatures at Ǧabal Mismāʾ. With thanks to Florent Égal.
6. Huber's name carved at al-Maḥaǧǧah. With thanks to Florent Égal.
7. The Huber-hunters: Abdulrahman al-Shaya, founder of Horizons Tours, Riyadh; Mohammed al-Maʿrek, specialist on Huber and Euting's routes in Arabia; Florent Égal, author of the website https://www.saudiarabiatourismguide.com. With thanks to Florent Égal.
8. The Taymāʾ Stele, front and side. By kind permission of the Musée du Louvre/Scala.
9. Euting's first drawing of the Taymāʾ Stele, from his Notebook V, 17 February 1884 (Tagbuch 15.2.84 to 20.4.84. Md676-22). By kind permission of the Manuscript Department, Library of Eberhard Karls Universität, Tübingen.
10. Euting's drawing of the Taymāʾ Stele published in Nöldeke 1884.
11. Euting's drawing of the Taymāʾ Stele published in Huber 1891: 319.
12. Portrait of Julius Euting in Arab dress, 1885, by Adolf Meckel von Hemsbach. Frontispiece to Euting's *Tagbuch einer Reise in Inner-Arabien*, vol. 2 (1914).

13. Sī ʿAzīz bin Shaykh al-Ḥaddād, photographed in 1884 by Snouck Hurgronje. With thanks to Prof. Jan Just Witkam.
14. Charles Huber's tomb in the non-Muslim cemetery at Ǧiddah, photographed by Fr Raphaël Savignac in 1917. By kind permission of the École biblique et archéologique française, Jerusalem.
15. The cover of Huber 1885. By kind permission of the Société de Géographie, Paris.
16. Page 119 from Huber's handwritten manuscript of his 1880–81 Arabian journey. Copyright Bibliothèque nationale de France, Paris.
17. Huber's letter from Paris to Ibn Rashīd in Ḥāʾil, dated *ca.* 10 April 1883. Copyright Académie des Inscriptions et Belles-Lettres (AIBL), Institut de France, Paris.
18. A letter from Huber in Damascus to Charles Maunoir in Paris, dated 24 September 1883. Copyright Académie des Inscriptions et Belles-Lettres (AIBL), Institut de France, Paris.

Page 68

Euting's sketch of the Taymāʾ Stele as discovered *in situ* in the Ṭlayḥān, February 1884. From Euting's letter to Nöldeke dated 8 July 1884 from Beirut. By kind permission of the Manuscript Department, Library of Eberhard Karls Universität, Tübingen.

Page 205

Euting's two sketches of Khaybar oasis, published on Huber's map of his Arabian journey (see end of this volume).

Appendix 1

11 pages of drawings of inscriptions and graffiti recorded by Huber and published in the *Bulletin* de la Société de Géographie, Paris (Huber 1884a). By kind permission of the Société de Géographie, Paris.

At end of volume

Fold-out map reproduced from Huber 1884b. By kind permission of the Société de Géographie, Paris.

Foreword

The French geographer and explorer Charles Huber (1847–84) achieved distinction through his two memorable expeditions in Arabia. The first, in 1880–81, was the subject of a detailed report, published in three issues of the *Bulletin de la Société de Géographie* in 1884 and 1885, under the title 'Voyage dans l'Arabie centrale (1878–1882): Hamâd, Shammar, Qaçîm, Hedjâz'. The second, in 1883–84, which culminated in Huber's tragic murder, is known only in the form of the bare data that he recorded in his notebooks, and which were published by the Société de Géographie in 1891 under the title *Journal d'un voyage en Arabie (1883–1884)*.

The present volume is primarily the first English translation of the 'Voyage dans l'Arabie centrale', the only connected exploration narrative that Huber ever wrote. But it is also much more than that, in two ways. First, it includes a methodical commentary on every matter in the text requiring clarification. Secondly, it offers the first-ever biography of Huber, with a particular focus on two aspects of the second expedition: the relationship with the German Semitist Julius Euting, who had joined forces with Huber, and the discovery and acquisition of the celebrated Taymā Stele.

Were it not for a few recurrent allusions to these two latter topics in the scholarly literature, one might say that Charles Huber had sunk without trace. A few details aside, he is hardly mentioned at all by historians of 19th-century European exploration. Specialist articles devoted to him can be counted on the fingers of one hand, and tell us little about his life and travels. Although he was murdered in Arabia towards the end of an officially sponsored mission aimed at continuing the exploration of Arabia and acquiring ancient stone inscriptions, his memory was honoured neither by official recognition nor by obituaries in the press and specialist journals. The French Republic confined itself to funding a tomb in the non-Muslim cemetery at Ǧiddah, adorned with the terse inscription 'Mort pour la science', 'Dead in the cause of science'.

At odds with this neglect, Huber's expeditions were innovative and rich in discoveries of all kinds. In geographical terms, he opened up hitherto completely unknown areas of central Arabia, identified the watershed between the Ḥiǧāz and Naǧd, and used instruments to establish the precise locations of the places he visited. His travels were productive in terms of antiquities too: national collections benefited from his acquisition of stone inscriptions of the first importance, most notably the famous Taymāʾ Stele preserved in the Louvre, inscribed in the Aramaic language and script and dating perhaps to 500 BC.

In the end Huber's tragic death, at the hands of his own guides in July 1884 when he was just thirty-six, a victim apparently of pure avarice, could have made him a martyr for science (like the Austrian Siegfried Langer, killed in Yemen in 1882), or even a romantic hero. He was destined to be neither.

A few explanations can be offered for this intriguing descent into obscurity. Chief among them is undoubtedly Huber's instinctive reluctance to thrust himself into the limelight, as his publications show. Unlike other explorers who were raconteurs skilled at seducing their extensive readerships with colourful accounts of their exploits, he leaves himself out of his own story, and almost never describes the innumerable difficulties and challenges that he had to surmount. If Arabia had become relatively easy of access since the Ottomans had extended their dominion over its coastal areas, their authority was reduced or non-existent in the interior, where a fierce conflict raged between two tribal chiefs. Moving around was thus extremely difficult and dangerous by reason of the climate, poverty, war and anarchy, to say nothing of undercurrents resulting from rivalries between European powers. Huber, however, has hardly anything to say about such obstacles. This is especially true of the notebooks of his second journey, which are a dry repository of factual data. But it is no less true of his narrative style in the 'Voyage dans l'Arabie centrale'. Huber, in short, sought recognition above all else as a leading geographer and explorer among his fellow-professionals, and had no ambitions for literary success or public admiration.

Another explanation as to why Huber was not as celebrated as he should have been is that he had committed various indiscretions in his youth, which inclined the authorities to treat him with a certain wariness. Finally, it is also probable that Huber, despite evidence that he could be sociable enough when required, was by nature a lone wolf.

The primary source on Huber, an Alsatian who had opted for French nationality in 1871 on the annexation of Alsace-Lorraine by Germany, is of course the narrative of his first journey and the notes that he took during his second. But these are usefully complemented by the diary compiled by the German Semitist, Julius Euting, on his own journey of exploration in 1883–84, since for the major part of this venture Euting accompanied Huber, who possessed the topographical knowledge they needed but lacked Euting's financial means and epigraphic expertise. Euting's notes allow us to trace the progressive deterioration of the two men's relationship, made all the more inevitable by the French authorities' hostility to their association.

At the same time there are numerous archive collections available, despite some having been destroyed in successive wars, notably in Strasbourg. These vast deposits have not yet been exploited to the full. A great merit of William Facey's work is that it presents in translation a large number of unpublished documents, in particular those preserved in the Cabinet du *Corpus Inscriptionum Semiticarum* of the Académie des Inscriptions et Belles-Lettres. In this work, involving the decipherment of handwritten texts and the identification of individuals, he has benefited from the highly efficient help given him by Mme Maria Gorea, *auxiliaire* of the Académie, especially with the archives of the Cabinet du *Corpus* that have been digitized.

Thanks to these new sources, the British scholar has been able to piece together the first-ever biography of Huber, a landmark event. Facey's translation of Huber's first expedition brings this work back into the spotlight after a long period of quasi-inaccessibility and as such is a most useful exercise. His translation is enriched by all the research required to clarify the text. This is embodied in notes explaining the topography, pinpointing locations and accurately establishing Huber's Arabian itineraries. To give just one example of this project, Huber, who was not a philologist, transcribed Arabic place names in a very idiosyncratic fashion. It was thus necessary to identify the places and transliterate their spellings according to a proper system. Facey has successfully addressed this enormous task, the difficulty of which all specialists will recognize.

Facey's work makes a decisive contribution to the history of Arabian exploration and to many hitherto unknown aspects of Charles Huber's life. On the more debatable issues such as the relationship between Huber and Euting, or the affair of the Taymāʾ Stele, he has marshalled all the available evidence and cautiously puts forward plausible interpretations, which will be susceptible to evolution as and when new documents come to light.

Christian Julien Robin

Member, Académie des Inscriptions et Belles-Lettres (Institut de France)
Président de la Commission du *Corpus Inscriptionum Semiticarum*

Preface and Acknowledgements

Charles Huber's two journeys between 1880 and 1884 have ensured his place among the foremost Arabian explorers of the 19th century. Tragically, his early death supervened before he could set about publishing a wholly satisfactory account of either of them.

Of the two, the second journey, undertaken in 1883–84 and cut short by his murder north of Ǧiddah, has been the more accessible, as it was published in book form in 1891 under the title *Journal d'un voyage en Arabie (1883–1884)*. Even so, this was far from a coherent thematic narrative, being merely a faithful reproduction of his surviving diary notes and lists of observations. As such, it is a very useful document, but too dry and disconnected to merit publication in translation.

The first journey, in 1880–81, is a different matter. Huber did publish this as a continuous narrative, albeit a hurried one that caused him various misgivings. This is the travelogue that is offered in translation here. It first appeared not as a monograph but serially, in successive issues of the *Bulletin de la Société de Géographie* in Paris (see Huber 1884a, 1884b and 1885a). Though the Société republished the parts together almost immediately in a single volume (Huber 1885b), neither version has been easily accessible to readers, and the latter monograph in particular seems to be all but unobtainable these days. Since then, Huber's first Arabian journey has never to my knowledge been republished, with the exception of an Arabic translation in 2003 (Huber 2003).

The lack of a proper, critical English edition of this highly significant journey has for long represented a gap in the literature on the exploration of Arabia. Covid-19 isolation during 2020 offered a golden opportunity to remedy this. We now have a fully annotated translation which, among other things, clearly identifies the places that he travelled through and the inscriptions that he recorded (for the latter, see Appendices 1 and 2). As almost nothing has ever been written about Huber himself, this is preceded by a substantial biographical introduction that takes the story up to his death in July 1884, and then focuses on the Franco-German imbroglio over the Taymāʾ Stele. Appendices 3–12 present a selection of correspondence relevant to Huber's travels and, in some cases, to his character and friendships. Huber's 1880–81 journey through the Nafūd desert to Naǧd, the Ḥiǧāz, and back to Damascus via north-east Arabia, Iraq and the Ḥamād, can now take its place as one of the significant landmarks of 19th-century travel alongside those of the other great 19th-century Arabian explorers.

THE TRANSLATION: PRESENTATION OF HUBER'S TEXT

The Translation presented here is of the articles first published serially in successive issues of the *Bulletin de la Société de Géographie* in 1884–85 (see Huber 1884a, 1884b and 1885a). The page numbers of the original articles are shown in the English text between square brackets, e.g. [305].

A major difficulty in Huber's travel writing is posed by his outdated and, to modern eyes, eccentric transliteration of Arabic names. Readers can be forgiven for being nonplussed by such nomenclature as El-Uscevuasce, Dheraghrath, Ešeqah,'Ašbîbïah and Āmâdzeñ, to take just five egregious examples. I have taken the bull by the horns and imposed a modern system of transliteration throughout the work, so presenting Arabic words and names in a correct and recognizable form – in these instances, as al-Washwāsh, Zarghaṭ, al-Shuqqah, al-Shibībiyyah, and Umm Ādhan.

As I embarked on the translation I feared that many such names might defy identification. However, by dint of much poring over maps and the works of other travellers in the region who had taken the trouble to record names in a properly transliterated form – such as Doughty, Euting, Musil, Jaussen and Savignac, and al-Rāshid – it has happily been possible to identify very nearly all of them. In addition, the Bibliothèque nationale de France kindly provided me with a digital copy of Huber's original handwritten manuscript of the 1880–81 journey, in the margin of which he had written an Arabic version of many of the names. Huber's account of his 1883–84 journey (Huber 1891) has also been useful, as there too he recorded many spellings in Arabic script. I have also consulted the useful GeoNames website. Unfortunately I have not been able personally to consult the comprehensive *Mawsūʿat ismāʾ al-amākin fīʾl-Mamlakah al-ʿArabiyyah al-Suʿūdiyyah* (The Encyclopaedia of Saudi Arabian Place Names), but I am very grateful to Dr Laïla Nehmé for her kindness in offering to check a number of items for me. In the rare instances where I have finally been unable to identify a correct spelling, I have retained Huber's version and placed an asterisk in front, thus for example *Dheïeth 'Aïaš, *Ourdemy.

Some sticklers for correct orthography, particularly Saudi Arabians from the regions through which Huber travelled, may wish to challenge some of my versions of Arabic names and words. For their sake, I have included Appendix 13, which sets out the transliteration system used followed by the full list of my spellings, each one matched to Huber's own version.

This translation is liberally supplied with explanatory footnotes, intended to make this the definitive edition of Huber's journey. I hope that French readers too will find them a useful companion to Huber's original text. A few footnotes by Huber himself, and by the editorial staff ('La Rédaction') at the Société de Géographie, appeared in the original articles; these are identified in our translation by (CH) and (The Editors). The vast majority, however, have been added by myself and Michael Macdonald; these are shown between square brackets [] and where appropriate attributed to (MCAM), or very occasionally to (MCAM/WF). Elsewhere, a few footnotes in Appendix 4 were kindly supplied by Prof. Maria Gorea, identified as (MG). Otherwise, all unattributed footnotes in the Translation and throughout the rest of the work are mine.

I have thought it worth including extensive appendices, as they make available in translation much source material that is otherwise difficult of access to scholars. They are by no means comprehensive and are far from representing the full extent of the source material to which future researchers will need to gain access. For example, there is much further digging to be done in the archives of the Académie des Inscriptions et Belles-Lettres (AIBL) of the Institut de France to establish the full extent of correspondence between Huber and Ernest Renan. There are also discoveries yet to be made in the archives of the Ministère de l'Instruction publique et des Beaux-Arts, held in the national archives at Pierrefitte-sur-Seine, as well as in the archives of the Staatsbibliothek in Berlin (notably Nachlass Dillmann).

Acknowledgements

I am above all grateful to Michael Macdonald not only for encouraging me to undertake the Translation but also for agreeing to participate editorially. Michael, as all those scholars who know him as M.C.A. Macdonald are aware, is a formidable authority on the languages, scripts and inscriptions of ancient northern Arabia, Jordan and Syria, the very region that Huber did so much to open up to European awareness. Michael has given much sage advice on the text, and has contributed a multitude of useful notes as well as the comprehensive concordance of inscriptions recorded by Huber that forms Appendix 2.

As so little has been written until now about Huber, it was essential to gain access to a document that is in effect the foundation of Huber studies in English. This is Helen Pearson's unpublished MA thesis 'Relations between Julius Euting and Charles Huber in Arabia', submitted to the University of Manchester in 1993. I am grateful to Helen's supervisor, Prof. John Healey, for facilitating my contact with her, and especially to Helen herself for lending me the only surviving copy of her work, which is a monument to her diligence in tracking down a great deal of original archive material on Huber in France and Germany, some of which I have been unable to consult at first hand.

It was the realization that there existed a little-known archive of Huber's correspondence in Paris, in the Archives du Cabinet du *Corpus Inscriptionum Semiticarum*, part of the AIBL, that led me to direct my enquiries there. I am extremely grateful for the kind permission of the AIBL's Secrétaire perpétuel, Michel Zink, and its Secrétaire général, Hervé Danesi, to translate and publish the many documents in its rich holdings which have made a key contribution to this work. At the outset of my research, it was the kind suggestion of Prof. Christian Robin, Président de la Commission du *Corpus Inscriptionum Semiticarum* (*CIS*), that directed me to Prof. Maria Gorea, a professor of Aramaic epigraphy and philology at Université Paris 8 and Université Sorbonne Nouvelle. Among her roles is that of Auxiliaire de l'AIBL, in charge of the Cabinet du *CIS*, in which capacity she has been more than generous with her time in seeking and making available correspondence and other documents relating to Huber, not just in the Archives du Cabinet but in the French national archives at Pierrefitte-sur-Seine and La Courneuve as well – institutions to which I am also grateful. Her enthusiastic collaboration has been greatly appreciated, and without her vital input this edition of Huber's first Arabian journey would have been much the poorer. My warm thanks also go to Prof. Christian Robin for his ready support for my work, and for contributing the foreword.

Vital too has been the generous co-operation of the institution that holds Julius Euting's diaries and other archives: the Manuscript Department of the Library of Eberhard Karls Universität Tübingen, first under its head Dr Wilfried Lagler, who retired in 2019, and then under its present head, Dr Kristina Stöbener, who has kindly continued the Department's support.

In addition, special mention must be made of the help given me by Prof. Jan Just Witkam in Leiden. He generously gave me access to his three articles in the forthcoming *Scholarship in Action: Studies on the Life and Work of Christiaan Snouck Hurgronje (1857–1936)*, to be published by Brill, which shine a new and unprecedented light on the latter's activities in the Ḥiǧāz in 1884–85. He also made various useful comments on my account of Huber's time in the Ḥiǧāz. Citations of these unpublished articles (Witkam, forthcoming/a, /b and /c), refer to his typescript (TS) and therefore the page references will not correspond with the published version.

I am grateful to Michael Crawford for his perceptive suggestions and comments on the Introduction, which inspired various improvements. I have also been lucky enough to benefit from the comprehensive translation (as yet unpublished) of Julius Euting's *Tagbuch einer Reise in Inner-Arabien* (Euting 1896 and 1914) by Dr Christopher Metcalf, Lobel Fellow in Classics at The Queen's College, Oxford. Further thanks go to two more friends, Barbara Newton and Marion Unia, for help with the translation of archive sources in both French and German.

As ever I am in the debt of the staff of the Foyle Reading Room at the Royal Geographical Society, London, in particular Eugene Rae, Julie Carrington, David McNeill and Jan Turner, for keeping the works of Huber and Euting on reserve for me and for their good humour in fulfilling my tiresomely frequent requests for maps of Arabia and other materials. I am grateful to Peter Harrigan, Sherif Dhaimish, Alexandra Lawson and Emma Dacre of Medina Publishing; to Tony Plews for his meticulous work in making clean digital versions of Huber's map and Euting's portrait; and to Luke Pajak for designing the jacket. My thanks also go to the following for responding helpfully to my queries: Yousef al-Bassam (of ʿUnayzah); Louis Blin; James Budd; Prof. Rachel Chrastil; Florent Égal, author of the website www.saudiarabiatourismguide.com; Prof. Ulrike Freitag; Prof. John Healey; Alexandra Hirst; Jean-Baptiste Humbert; Benoît Jordan of the Strasbourg City Archives; Dr Marcel Kurpershoek; Claude Lorentz and Maryline Simler at the Bibliothèque nationale et universitaire (BNU), Strasbourg; Mohammed al-Maʿrek, follower in Huber's footsteps; Dr Laïla Nehmé; Prof. Benjamin Reilly; Sylvie Rivet at the Société de Géographie in Paris; Abdulrahman al-Shaya, founder of Horizons Tours, Riyadh; Fr Jean-Michel de Tarragon of the École biblique et archéologique française, Jerusalem; Frances Topp; Richard Wilding; François Wyn and Marta Bardaro at the Bibliothèque nationale de France, Paris.

Finally, I would like to record my appreciation of the keen interest my wife Marsha has taken in Charles Huber, and for the many conversations we have enjoyed about his personality, his background in Strasbourg, and especially his relations with Julius Euting and their Franco-German context.

William Facey

INTRODUCTION

CHARLES HUBER
FRANCE'S GREATEST ARABIAN EXPLORER

IN THE FIVE YEARS from 1880 to 1884, the French-Alsatian geographer Charles Huber (1847–84) made two remarkable desert journeys, either one of which would have entitled him to the recognition he enjoys as one of the pioneering 19th-century explorers of Arabia.[1]

Their chief importance lay in the wealth of new geographical information he was able to collect on a region that, despite its adjacency to the Fertile Crescent, had remained stubbornly inaccessible to Europeans. Their timing adds extra interest, for Huber embarked on them very shortly after the Arabian ordeal of Charles Doughty in 1876–78, and the more stately progress of Wilfrid and Lady Anne Blunt through some of the same territory in 1878–79. For much of Huber's second great journey, in 1883–84, he was travelling with Julius Euting (1839–1913), the eminent German Semitist whose vivid account of his own part in it was not published until years later, in 1896 and 1914. Taken together, the disparate narratives of these five travellers shine a light of unprecedented clarity on social and political conditions in central Arabia over a very brief time span, during which the Second Saudi State,

[1] These 19th-century pioneers in northern and central Arabia include, in chronological order of journeys: Ulrich Seetzen (1809–11); John Lewis Burckhardt (1814–15); George Forster Sadleir (1819); Maurice Tamisier (1833–34); Georg August Wallin (1845 and 1848); Richard Burton (1853 and 1877–78); James Hamilton (1854); Charles Didier (1854); William Gifford Palgrave (1862–63); Carlo Guarmani (1864); Lewis Pelly (1865); Joseph Halévy (1869–70); Charles Doughty (1876–78); Wilfrid and Lady Anne Blunt (1878–79); Julius Euting (1883–84); Snouck Hurgronje (1884–85); and Eduard Nolde (1893).

ruled from Riyadh, was being eclipsed by the Shammar tribal state centred on Ḥāʾil.

Despite Huber's great posthumous reputation, however, very little has been written about him. There has been no biography nor even, apparently, any obituaries. He spent more time in Arabia and covered more ground than any of the other 19th-century French travellers such as Maurice Tamisier, Charles Didier, Thomas-Joseph Arnaud and Joseph Halévy.[2] In France his fame has rested mainly on his alleged discovery in 1880 of a celebrated ancient Aramaic inscription, the Taymāʾ Stele, during his first and solo Arabian journey in 1880–81 which is translated in this volume – a claim subjected to a critical examination below. The histories of Arabian exploration published in English give his travels due recognition, but the emphasis in these has been chiefly on his 1883–84 journey in the company of Euting.

This relatively low profile has endured in part because Huber himself published little, having lost his life at the young age of thirty-six without fulfilling his potential as either explorer or writer. His first Arabian venture, from his departure from southern Syria in May 1880 to his arrival in Iraq nine months later, covered some 5,000 kilometres on camelback through the Great Nafūd, northern Naǧd and the northern Ḥiǧāz.[3] This epic quest was the subject of the only continuous narrative that he ever published. It appeared just after his death, in the form of articles in three quarterly issues of the *Bulletin de la Société de Géographie* of 1884–85,[4] which were then rapidly collated in monograph form by the Société in 1885.[5] Apart from an Arabic translation published in 2003, the English translation presented here is the only subsequent republication of this highly significant document of Arabian exploration.

By the time the first of these articles was being prepared for publication in 1884, Huber was on his second journey in Arabia. Unable to supervise their printing, he expresses misgivings in his surviving correspondence about their

---

[2] He makes no appearance in the classic account in French of Arabian exploration, Jacqueline Pirenne's *À la découverte de l'Arabie*, but that is because Pirenne's cut-off date was 1870 (Pirenne 1958: 309).

[3] Henri Duveyrier's (1883: 215) estimate of Huber's entire journey, including the final leg from Baghdad to Damascus.

[4] Huber 1884a, 1884b, 1885a. The title of the latter two articles, 'Voyage dans l'Arabie centrale (1878–1882)', is misleading, as the Arabian journey that they describe took place only from May 1880 to February 1881.

[5] Huber 1885b.

quality.[6] His hesitancy was not unjustified, as they do indeed exhibit occasional inconsistency and signs of hurried composition. The narrative is plain and unadorned, with a narrow focus on geographical matters. Occasionally it breaks down into little more than disconnected jottings about the route and journey times. There are few sustained descriptions or reflections, and none of the comparing and contrasting that one might expect from a writer who had travelled in Syria and North Africa. In one passage, he excuses himself by promising to write at a later date about the history, customs and statistics of the places he passed through,[7] but his murder on 29 July 1884 forestalled the production of any such work, which would undoubtedly have been of the utmost historical value.

In no sense, therefore, is his narrative an example of the sensational literary travel-writing that was so popular with the 19th-century reading public. Huber's style is undramatic and matter-of-fact, and he tends to leave himself out of his story. He evinces neither the taste for drama nor the literary pretensions of British travellers in Arabia such as Richard Burton, William Gifford Palgrave and Charles Doughty. As on any such journey, there were many moments of danger and narrow escapes from disaster, but Huber preferred not to dwell on such colourful misadventures. A single incident at Khaybar perfectly illustrates his impersonal approach. He ends a letter from there with an afterthought: 'I only just managed to avoid being robbed by bedouin 200 metres from the gardens of Khaybar. Luckily I lost nothing. I killed one of my assailants and wounded another.'[8] A British traveller such as Burton would have revelled in playing up this hair-raising confrontation. But Huber, despite a Burtonesque disregard for

---

[6] See Appendix 4, Letter no. 2 dated 28 March 1882, to Charles Maunoir, third paragraph from the end. Huber's Letter no. 3 in Appendix 4, dated 18 May 1882 to Charles Maunoir, reveals that he realized on his return to France that his longitudes were inaccurate because his chronometer was faulty. In his letter to Weisgerber from Ḥāʾil dated 30 November 1883 (Letter no. 25 in Appendix 4) he also says: 'You will also tell me if they have decided at the Société de Géographie to publish my article on my first journey, but do not insist on it with anyone because once again I am not satisfied with this work.'

[7] Having crossed the Nafūd and reached Ḥāʾil in 1880, he writes: 'From now on I intend to give no more than a broad geographical outline of the regions I travelled through, and so I shall postpone till another time the chapter on their customs, history and statistical data.' See Translation Part I, p. 136 (Huber 1884b: 354); also Translation Part II, p. 173 and note 74 (Huber 1884b: 495–6).

[8] Huber 1881: 270 (letter to M. de Quatrefages).

his own safety, makes no mention whatsoever of it in his published account presented here. Just occasionally, he does give us a tantalizing glimpse of the kind of travelogue that he was capable of writing, for example his vivid descriptions of dervishes in the last stages of thirst in the Wādī al-Sirḥān (p. 96), his first meeting with the Emir Muḥammad al-Rashīd on the edge of the Nafūd (pp. 131–4), or the brutal stage-management of his escort out of ʿUnayzah (pp. 173–4). In general, though, his sober reporting stands in striking contrast to two British works covering much the same ground at almost exactly the same time: Doughty's *Travels in Arabia Deserta* and Lady Anne Blunt's *A Pilgrimage to Nejd*. Huber's writing entirely lacks the literary aspirations of Doughty's extraordinary tale of tribulations in northern Arabia, just two years before his own explorations there. Nor is there much of the skilful narration that typifies the Blunts' account of their 1878–79 trek through northern Arabia to Ḥāʾil. Yet, as his correspondence presented in the Appendices shows, he could be as fluent and expressive as a writer as he seems to have been in conversation.

It is clear that Huber was consciously trying to mark himself out as a purely scientific explorer, and so to set his travelogue apart from the exaggerations and sensationalism in other Victorian bestsellers such as Palgrave's *Narrative of a Year's Journey through Central and Eastern Arabia* (1865). The British consul in Ǧiddah, Thomas Jago, an acquaintance from Syria days, referred to him as 'Dr Huber, a French scientific gentleman',[9] a description that would surely have found favour with him. The coasts of Arabia had been more or less accurately charted by British maritime surveyors during the first half of the 19th century. With his sextant and barometer, Huber bravely extended this project into inland Arabia, a pioneering effort that was continued by his scientific successors such as Alois Musil and Harry St John Philby, and brought to completion by the meticulous mapmaking of the United States Geologic Survey (USGS) in the later 20th century. After Huber, the use of instruments in central Arabia became *de rigueur* among serious travellers, for example the Britons Douglas Carruthers, Gertrude Bell, Gerard Leachman and William Shakespear. For these reasons, Huber's account, matter-of-fact and unpolished though it may be, has a status of its own, made all the more significant by being the sole sustained narrative ever published by one of Arabia's great explorers.

[9] Jago to Granville, letter dated 2 July 1884, in Burdett 2013 iii: 409.

Particularly striking is the lack of any tone of supposed European superiority as Huber moves among the tribespeople of northern Arabia. This lack of cultural snobbery can perhaps best be explained by his working-class background, and is a quality he shares with other Arabian travellers of modest origin, such as Eldon Rutter and Alan Villiers. It stands in sharp contrast to the disdain and impatience that occasionally mar Euting's colourful journal of the 1883–84 expedition. Huber's fervent patriotism was never in doubt and he was always concerned to promote the political interests of France,[10] but this does not seem to have translated into a personal feeling of superiority when dealing with Arabs, with whom his relations were refreshingly egalitarian. Inevitably, as a representative of a European country intent on discovering as much as he could about a little-known region of the Arab East, he is vulnerable to the charge of Orientalism, in the pejorative sense made fashionable by Edward Said:[11] that he must somehow, in the very act of studying the East, be tainted by a European sense of supremacy and detachment, and unavoidably engaged in a project of appropriation, devaluation and subjugation – in short, of intellectual colonization. It is a universal truth that every observer approaches the object of study with a point of view and a set of prejudices. The salient question is whether these are fixed or, preferably, open to adjustment and evolution. Naturally a reader should be aware of such attitudes, especially if they are impervious to change, but it is also important to look beyond them and to take a nuanced view, since they may be far from the most interesting aspect of the travelogue in question. And in any case, not all travellers approach their subject with a fixed sense of superiority. Many are open to change, and many are actually respectful and even admiring of the so-called Other. To dismiss travel accounts solely on the grounds that their authors can only be guilty of colonial attitudes and cultural imperialism is to indulge in lazy determinism. It leaves no room to appreciate and explore the rich and varied range of authorial voices, for example, in an Arabian context, avowed anti-imperialists such as Wilfrid Scawen Blunt or Harry St John Philby. Likewise, to analyse Huber's work solely as an expression of an Orientalist mindset would be a reductionist exercise blinding the reader to almost everything of value in his writing.

---

[10] See for example his analysis of French policy in the Near East and the machinations of the British in Appendix 4, Letter no. 13 dated 20 May 1883 from Huber to Charles Maunoir.

[11] Said 1991 (first published 1978). Said sidesteps any discussion of anti-imperialists such as Wilfrid Blunt and St John Philby (Said 1991: 237, 246).

Huber did not live to publish a connected account of his second great Arabian journey in 1883–84, about half of it made in Euting's company, which covered at least 3,700 kilometres in northern Arabia, Nağd and the Ḥiğāz. His diaries and notebooks were saved, however, and the decision was taken by the Société de Géographie and the Académie des Inscriptions et Belles-lettres (AIBL) to publish them exactly as they were, without editorial expansion or improvement. This work was undertaken by three grandees of the French Orientalist and geographical establishment: Ernest Renan, Charles Barbier de Meynard and Charles Maunoir. The result, published in 1891 under the title *Journal d'un voyage en Arabie (1883–1884)*, was intended only to be a faithful rendering of Huber's notes and sketches and, while of exceptional value as the detailed record of his journey and observations, is very far from being a literary work of exploration.[12]

Despite this patchy publication record, Huber's achievement has always been acknowledged by other European travellers, and he was hailed by an Englishman, Harry St John Philby, as the 'greatest of all French explorers of Arabia'.[13] Philby with characteristic self-regard rated himself as the greatest of all,[14] but held Huber in almost equal estimation. Both men were obsessive observers and compilers of detail, and the memorial to Huber in Ğiddah funded by the French government – 'Mort pour la science'– struck a chord of familiarity in the Englishman. With a fatuous pride smacking of narcissism, he seems to have genuinely believed that something of the great Arabian explorer's spirit had passed into him at birth, when he wrote:

> In the little European cemetery at Jidda there is to be seen a massive block of granite, placed there by the French government in commemoration of the greatest of all French explorers of Arabia. And on that stone is recorded the startling fact that Charles Huber perished, at the hands of his Arab guides, in the service of science on 29th July, 1884. It was surely then no mere coincidence that I was born almost exactly nine months later, on 3rd April, 1885, to assume the mantle of the great Frenchman …[15]

[12] Huber 1891. For more on this, see pp. 39 and 44–5 below.
[13] Philby 1948: 3. Winstone (1976: 77; 1978: 126) even rated Huber as the greatest Arabian explorer of all.
[14] For Philby's estimation of himself as Arabia's greatest explorer, see Facey 2013: 128.
[15] Philby 1948: 3; Ryckmans 1952: 503.

The story of Huber's short life inevitably centres on his dedication to the scientific exploration of Arabia. But to fully understand what drove him, we also have to glean what little we can about his personality from his letters and other writings, and to take into account his background as a French patriot coming of age in Alsace during a time of Franco-German conflict. The latter was a formative experience that not only contributed much to his uneasy relationship with Julius Euting, but also created the personal and political context for the colourful affair of the Taymāʾ Stele. These are the themes that will be explored in what follows.

French patriot and geographer

Auguste Hugues Charles Huber was born on 19 December 1847 in Strasbourg, capital of Alsace, into very modest circumstances. His father Georges was a railwayman who had previously been a shoemaker, and his mother worked as a washerwoman.[16] His father would be crushed to death between two train carriages in the mid-1870s, while his mother, to whom Charles was said to be devoted, lived until about 1887. He had two younger brothers, one of whom became a mechanic who later moved to Nancy in the French part of Lorraine, and a sister married to a German employed at the Strasbourg arsenal.[17]

The young Huber underwent a Catholic education in Strasbourg, attending a municipal school in the Fossé des Tanneurs before going on to a school of Christian doctrine in the rue des Soeurs. Though wayward in his attendance, he was an inquisitive boy with a taste for science. When his working life began with a humdrum job as a clerk and bookkeeper at a bailiff's, he used his wages to pursue courses in physics, chemistry and anatomy at the Strasbourg Academy. He was also helped by priests at the Trappist church in the rue Ste Elisabeth, where he was a regular congregant. He was clever, ambitious, and determined to transcend his social origins.

[16] The biographical details given here are summarized from Appendix 3, Letter no. 3 dated 12 April 1879; Appendix 4, Letter no. 10 dated 25 November 1882; and the biographical notice presented as Items nos. 1 and 2 in Appendix 12. Other sources are Weyl 1987; Pearson 1993: 37–40; Lozachmeur and Briquel-Chatonnet 2013; Kurpershoek and Lorentz 2018: 109; and fr.wikipedia.org: entry Charles Huber (explorateur), consulted September 2020. An official record confirms his birth date as 19 December (not October) 1847, and names his mother as Elisabeth Stapfer.

[17] For Huber's family, see Appendix 12, item no. 2. One brother, Émile, a mechanic, was living in Nancy in 1884 (Appendix 9, Letter no. 5 dated 15 September 1884 from de Lostalot to Maunoir).

Like many autodidacts, he felt that his freelance studies lacked direction and consistency, though they did lead him to acquire some medical expertise – a very useful skill for a prospective explorer.

Though physically not especially prepossessing, he seems to have been a compelling companion who had no trouble finding ready listeners. This side of his character would come into play when he was seeking sponsorship for his journeys, and also on his Arabian travels when much tact and persuasiveness would be needed in his dealings with people along the way, from emirs to tribesmen. His efforts to drum up backing for his expeditions would demonstrate a knack for attracting influential people to his cause: prominent supporters included Xavier Charmes, paymaster at the Ministry of Public Education, Charles Adolphe Wurtz, a member of the Institut de France, Jean Louis de Quatrefages,[18] chairman of the Musée d'histoire naturelle in Paris, and G.A. Le Bel, a businessman engaged in the extraction of oil from the Alsatian tar-sands.[19] These and others were genuine supporters who were prepared to come to Huber's defence against his detractors.

By temperament enthusiastic and courageous to the point of recklessness, Huber pursued his projects with a single-minded zeal that could blind him to consequences and occasionally lure him into deceit to further his ends. Some of his youthful escapades had unwelcome outcomes. One friend spoke of unspecified romantic entanglements that ended badly,[20] but more serious is evidence that in 1868 he was convicted of theft, for which he served six months in jail.[21] The prison records were destroyed in the siege of Strasbourg, so we have no details of the charge, but one can speculate that the crime related to money and perhaps involved embezzlement. Later, in Algeria in 1874, he seems to have been a misfit in the government department to which

[18] Jean Louis Armand de Quatrefages de Bréau (1810–92), with whom Huber would correspond during his Arabian journey, was a prominent French biologist who had been educated at Strasbourg University. See also Appendix 3, note 1 (p. 306).

[19] For Xavier Charmes, see Appendix 3, Letter no. 17 dated 13 May 1882; no. 19 dated 11 May 1882; no. 22 dated 8 August 1882; no. 23 dated 20 October 1882; no. 24 dated 28 October 1882; and no. 25 dated 30 October 1882. For Charles Adolphe Wurtz, see Appendix 3, Letter no. 1 dated 3 September 1878. For G.A. Le Bel, see Appendix 3, Letter no. 4 dated 8 August 1879, and no. 8 dated 22 September 1879.

[20] Appendix 12, Item no. 3 dated 20 April 1891.

[21] For Huber's jail sentence imposed on 27 March 1868, see Appendix 3, Letter no. 3 dated 12 April 1879; no. 5 dated 21 August 1879; no. 7 dated 8 September 1879; and no. 8 dated 22 September 1879. Letter no. 11 dated 7 October 1880 states that Huber served his sentence in 1869, not 1868, but this may be an error.

he was attached and to have made an enemy there. As his friend G.A. Le Bel wrote: 'As far as his position is concerned, he was probably not very well suited to it; his unusual penchant for adventure, and for anthropology and gynaecology, would be more than enough to explain how he came to leave his employment.' Allegations of dishonesty, some untrue, tended to dog him throughout his short life, and a streak of self-pity sometimes showed itself in his claims that fate held a grudge against him. Self-aggrandizing though this may sound, it points to a pattern of tempting fate that can be recognized in the extreme risks that he took on his travels in Arabia, culminating in the tragic dénouement that cut them short.

He was twenty-two in 1870 on the outbreak of the brief but brutal Franco-Prussian war. The French had opened hostilities in July of that year and their rapid defeat over the following six months came as an unexpected hammer-blow to national pride. One of its major results, besides the occupation of Paris, was the annexation by the newly unified Germany of Alsace, which had been part of France since 1681. This war manifested ominous portents of the mechanized destruction that would lay waste swathes of Europe in the following century, including much-improved long-range artillery and military transport, and a new willingness to undermine enemy morale by terrorizing civilian targets. Strasbourg became one of the first victims of this barbarous descent into total war when, in August 1870, it was surrounded by German artillery and subjected to a prolonged bombardment that killed hundreds, made thousands homeless and reduced areas of the historic city to rubble. The world-famous Municipal Library, home to many priceless manuscripts and Renaissance printed books, was totally destroyed. An unspeakable humiliation had been inflicted on French-speaking Strasbourgeois such as the Huber family.[22]

France had imposed universal conscription in 1870 and Huber would undoubtedly either have volunteered or been enlisted, though no evidence has yet come to light for his war service. However, it is known that he was wounded in the leg, and that he walked with a slight limp as a result. One of his friends commented that the war of 1870 made a *franc-tireur* or maverick of him, implying that it had reinforced Huber's natural instinct to go his own

[22] Macgregor 2014: 73: 'In Paris … the loss of Strasbourg in 1871 became the symbol of a monstrous wrong. … Strasbourg had been transformed into *the* totemic object of Franco-German enmity.' See also Chrastil 1914 for a full account of the siege of Strasbourg and its consequences.

way. But the choice of words is interesting, as it perhaps implies that Huber had joined Strasbourg's *francs-tireurs*, a volunteer force of marksmen formed to serve as sharpshooters in the defensive works around the city.[23] In early 1871, Huber went to live in Nancy, in Lorraine but outside the German sphere of control, and returned from there to Strasbourg towards the end of 1873.[24]

In 1871, in the wake of the French defeat, the Treaty of Frankfurt reorganized the border territory by formally annexing to Germany the region of Alsace and the Moselle department of Lorraine. It imposed a deadline of 31 October 1872 by which the citizens of what was now to be known as Elsass-Lothringen were either to declare themselves loyal to France and leave the country, or else, should they choose to remain, to be regarded as German subjects. Despite dual citizenship not being an option, the Huber family chose to stay put, maintaining their residence in Strasbourg while defiantly refusing to renounce their French nationality. Like many Strasbourgeois, they clung to their identity with a fervour reflecting the trauma inflicted upon French national feeling generally. For a time, Huber himself seems to have been torn. Moving frequently between Strasbourg and Paris during the 1870s, he could be a Frenchman in France but this served to aggravate his difficulties with the German authorities when he returned to Alsace. His sister was married to a German at the Strasbourg arsenal, and there is some indication that while at home he did at one point opt for German nationality.[25] In this he was no different from many French people returning to Alsace to resume their livelihoods who, in so doing, incurred the scorn of their own compatriots for being Frenchmen in France but Germans in Germany. Like many of them, Huber would have refused to relinquish his French nationality, in defiance of the German rules. This would continue to cause him problems, as it did for his brothers, who were imprisoned for doing their national service in France – perhaps the reason why one of them moved to Nancy. Whatever Huber's

[23] Appendix 12, item no. 2. On the volunteer National Guard and *francs-tireurs* of Strasbourg, see Chrastil 2014: 28–30. G.A. Henty, the famous war correspondent and writer of improving adventure novels for Victorian boys, paints a graphic picture of life as a *franc-tireur* during the 1870–71 conflict which is full of authentic detail, as he was correspondent for the *Standard* during the Franco-Prussian War (Henty 1872). Hesba Stretton's fictional account of the siege of Strasbourg is likewise based on personal experience (Stretton 1871).

[24] Appendix 3, Letter no. 3 dated 12 April 1879, from the government of Algeria to the Minister of Public Education, Paris.

[25] Appendix 3, Letter no. 4 dated 8 August 1879 and Letter no. 8 dated 22 September 1879 from G.A. Le Bel to the Minister of Public Education.

reasons for compromising over his nationality, there is no question about his ardent French patriotism, which would soon come to have not just civil but also personal repercussions during his second journey in northern and central Arabia in 1883–84. In this, as will be seen, he became the ambivalent companion of the German scholar, Julius Euting. In 1871 Euting had chosen, with what to Huber and his fellow-countrymen would have seemed indecent haste, to make his career in Huber's home city, a place that true French patriots now regarded as occupied territory.

By 1874, Huber had added physical anthropology to his range of interests, espousing the late 19th-century obsession with classifying and measuring human populations that accompanied European colonization of the globe. As was typical of many Frenchmen with a sense of adventure and an urge to widen their horizons, he decided to go to Algeria. Arriving in January 1874, he found employment in the French administration, in the directorate-general of civil affairs.[26] Here he was exposed for the first time to Arab society and the Arabic language, perhaps not yet suspecting the significance that this would one day hold for him. But, once again, he was dogged by scandal, and by questions over his nationality. There was perhaps another sexual entanglement, but graver still was 'the affair of the Arab skulls that he tried to remove from a cemetery near Algiers and which had to be hushed up'.[27] His employment lasted several months, during which he had ample opportunity for travel and anthropological research, and the mid-1870s seem to have been for him a time when his interests became focused not just on science but on Arab culture too. It was also a period during which another passion, book collecting, came to dominate his life.

On Huber's return to Strasbourg, conditions for a French patriot would have been far from welcoming, and he prudently opted for a life of quiet obscurity, supporting himself once more as an account-keeper. Meanwhile, already a voracious reader, he was quickly becoming an obsessive bibliophile. He began to amass an important collection of fine volumes, most of them relating to his beloved Alsace but many too on the Middle East, including some Arabic and Syriac manuscripts. His acquisitiveness was often compulsive. Even a sedate occupation such as book-collecting could stir the

[26] Appendix 3, Letter no. 3 dated 12 April 1879, from the government of Algeria to the Minister of Public Education, Paris.

[27] Appendix 3, Letter no. 8 dated 22 September 1879 from G.A. Le Bel to the Minister of Public Education, Paris.

risk-taking side of his personality and he would sometimes commit himself to the purchase of books without actually being able to pay for them, hoping for the best in the devil-may-care style that would characterize his travels.

During this time, his feelings led him to join Léon Gambetta's Ligue d'Alsace, an anti-German organization urging Alsace-Lorrainers to retain their French citizenship – a move that served to exhaust the patience of the German authorities. It was now, in 1878, that he was expelled by them, and left Alsace once again. He headed for Paris, adopted a fake identity – first as M. Paul, then as M. Rémond – and secured a job at a chemical company at Nogent-le-Rotrou, south-west of the capital. No reasons are given for the adoption of these aliases, but one may surmise that his criminal record and problems over his nationality may have inspired a need to lie low for a time. Thus far, it is evident that his background had schooled him in a certain deviousness, to which he would continue to resort in pursuit of his ambitions, as occasion demanded.

Meanwhile, it seems that he was carrying on with his studies in Arabic and anthropology. Even before 1878, he was beginning seriously to plan a feat of eastern travel that would make his name. His first prospectus is preserved in the archives of the Société de Géographie in Paris. It focuses on the Arab hinterlands of the Levant and Arabia, and sets out his aims and proposed *modus operandi*.[28] Besides his plan to collect geographical data, he listed his objectives as being 'to use every opportunity to inspect ruins and old monuments in order to describe them and copy the inscriptions', to collect anthropological data, and to acquire manuscripts.[29] He envisaged adopting a Muslim identity and living in Egypt before setting out, in order to remove all trace of European origin. He foresaw a major difficulty in the anthropological aspect of his task, which involved measuring the heads of suspicious Muslims, but thought he could overcome this if he made his measurements while performing minor surgery on them, as they would be unable to refuse! He planned to investigate the area around al-Madīnah to see whether 'early Arabs' of the tribes of ʿAws and Khazraj, contemporaries of

[28] Note sur son projet de voyage en Arabie, n.d. (before 1878), a 6-page document in the archives, Département des Cartes et plans de la Bibliothèque nationale de France, les collections de la Société de Géographie. See Kurpershoek 2018: 104.

[29] Huber is known to have acquired at least two manuscripts of so-called Nabaṭī (Arabic oral) poetry in Ḥāʾil. These are now held in the Strasbourg National and University Library (the BNU). It is not known whether Huber acquired them on this first Arabian journey in 1880 or on the 1883–84 journey. See Kurpershoek 2018.

the Prophet Muḥammad, were still living there. This first prospectus came to nothing, but he would very soon try again.

Huber's first journey in Arabia, 1880–81

In 1878, just as the Englishman Charles Doughty was coming to the end of his eccentric Arabian odyssey, Huber dreamed up his next proposal. This time his plan was to undertake a geographical survey not only of Arabia but also of regions farther east, in Persia, Afghanistan, and even as far as Tibet.

Huber's prospectus for such an absurdly far-reaching enterprise, submitted to the Ministry of Public Education in Paris, was at best sketchy, at worst laughably unrealistic.[30] In three short handwritten pages, he set out a hazily formulated plan for a journey that would take him south from Gaza through the Ḥiǧāz to Naǧrān and the Yemen. From there he would travel through southern Naǧd to al-Qaṣīm and Ǧabal Shammar, and thence to Iraq. From Baghdad he would head to Tehran and Khurasān and, should his health allow, continue from there to Kafiristan, Dardistan and Tibet. In addition to geographical data, he would collect information on languages, ethnography and natural history. He planned to take three years, and asked the ministry to cover just part of the cost, by awarding a grant of 8,000 francs – in today's money, a little less than £20,000. He does not say where the rest of the money was coming from, which suggests that he intended to fund it from his own resources. He claimed to have the support of the various learned societies, and his letter includes a note recommending the project to the ministry by Charles Adolphe Wurtz, an eminent scientist from Alsace and member of the Institut de France. Possibly to Huber's surprise, the Expeditions Committee of the ministry was quickly persuaded, and awarded him the 8,000 francs he had asked for.[31]

Huber's first travels in the Levant and northern Arabia would begin in early 1879 and end with his return to Damascus in December 1881 – a journey that represented a mere fraction of his original, over-ambitious proposal. It

---

[30] Appendix 3, Letter no. 1 with itinerary, dated 3 December 1878.

[31] Appendix 3, Letter no. 2 dated 17 December 1878 from the Ministry of Public Education to Huber. For Huber's plan to go to Tibet, see also Huber 1879: 195; Appendix 12, item no. 2. For his intention to go on from Iraq into Persia and Afghanistan once he had completed his second Arabian venture, see also Appendix 5, Letter no. 4 dated April 1883 from Huber to Muḥammad ibn Ḥāǧ Raḥīm Shayrawānī in Naǧaf.

is not clear what prompted him to shift his attention from North Africa to Arabia. There is evidence that he knew nothing of the journeys of Doughty and the Blunts until after he had already set out,[32] so it is possible that his interest was first kindled by the two most recent published accounts of Arabian travel, which both appeared in 1865: William Palgrave's *Narrative of a Year's Journey through Central and Eastern Arabia (1862–63)*, and Carlo Guarmani's Itinéraire de Jérusalem au Neged septentrional, published in the *Bulletin de la Société de Géographie*.[33] Huber's interest was not in Arabian horses, as Guarmani's had been, but in mapping a region of which Europe had almost no geographical conception, a project of which Guarmani can also be said to have been a pioneer, albeit a lesser one.

Huber began his mission by visiting Algiers again: he spent a month there to test his scientific instruments, on the grounds that the skies over Paris were continuously overcast.[34] He was still there on 5 April 1879, when he presented himself to the directorate of the interior and, on the strength of his diplomatic passport, was given a free first-class passage to Tunis and whatever official publications he might find of use.[35] He then seems to have gone back to France, as he was in Marseille again in mid-April 1879.[36] As he tells it, he had various tasks to carry out at the Montsouris Observatory and the Museum of Natural History, and did not set out for the Levant until May.[37]

Little did he know that his past was slowly catching up with him. On 12 April, the government in Algiers sent a letter to the minister in Paris alerting him to Huber's criminal record, based on information received from Strasbourg. At least one of Huber's friends, G.A. Le Bel, sprang to his defence, ascribing the claim to unfounded rumour-mongering, and the minister himself was incredulous enough to suspect that it might be a matter

[32] Huber 1881: 269–70, letter to Quatrefages, in which the mysterious English traveller 'Khalil' (i.e. Doughty) is misidentified as Wilfrid Scawen Blunt; Guarmani 1865.

[33] Palgrave 1865; Guarmani 1865.

[34] Appendix 3, Letter no. 6 dated 28 July 1879 from Charles Huber in Lebanon to the Minister of Public Education, Paris.

[35] Appendix 3, Letter no. 3 dated 12 April 1879, from the Division of the Interior, Government of Algeria, to the Minister of Public Education, Paris.

[36] fr.wikipedia.org: entry Charles Huber (explorateur), consulted September 2020. Pearson (1993: 40) shows that he was still in France on 14 April 1879, when he was about to depart from Marseille for the Orient.

[37] Appendix 3, Letter no. 6 dated 28 July 1879 from Huber to the Minister of Public Education, Paris.

of mistaken identity, but further checks in officialdom would eventually substantiate the charge.[38]

Meanwhile Huber, happily unaware, arrived in Lebanon towards the end of May. At the end of July he wrote confidently from Beirut to the minister telling him that he was studying Arabic in a *madrasah* in Lebanon, and also negotiating with tribes in the Syrian desert to provide him with guides and protection as far as al-Ǧawf. He had already started making collections of insects, fish fossils and geological samples, as well as twenty-five Maronite skulls to be sent to de Quatrefages in Paris. The French consul in Beirut did everything he could to dissuade him from pursuing his foolhardy venture into Arabia, but Huber carried on with his preparations in blithe disregard.[39]

In an extraordinary piece of luck, he made the acquaintance of the Abbé Pierre Géraigiry. This man had been Palgrave's companion Barakat on his journey through central and eastern Arabia in 1862–63, a feat that entitles him to an important place in the history of Arabian travel.[40] He would have been a fount of first-hand information and advice on the perils and pitfalls of penetrating Naǧd. Most interestingly, he confirmed Huber in his skepticism of Palgrave's reliability. Huber was hopeful that he had persuaded Géraigiry

[38] Appendix 3, Letter no. 3 dated 12 April 1879 from the Government of Algeria to the Minister of Public Education, Paris; no. 4 dated 8 August 1879 from G.A. Le Bel to the Minister of Public Education; no. 5 dated 21 August 1879 from the Minister of Public Education to the French consul, Strasbourg; no. 7 dated 8 September from the Ministry of Justice, Paris to the Minister of Public Education; no. 8 dated 22 September 1879 from G.A. Le Bel to the Minister of Public Education, Paris; no. 11, a note dated 7 October 1880 from the minister's office confirming Huber's imprisonment.

[39] The narrative of Huber's year in Lebanon and Syria up till May 1880 is based on the following sources: Appendix 3, Letter no. 6 dated 28 July 1879 from Huber in Lebanon to the Minister of Public Education, Paris; no. 9 dated 29 October 1879 from T. Gilbert, with enclosure by Huber, to Charles Maunoir at the Société de Géographie in Paris; no. 16 dated 27 March 1882, enclosing his report on his expedition, from Huber to the Minister of Public Education, Paris.

[40] Appendix 3, Letter no. 9 and enclosure dated 29 October 1879. The Abbé Pierre Barakat Géraigiry (1841–1902) features prominently in Palgrave's Victorian best-seller, *Narrative of a Year's Journey through Central and Eastern Arabia (1862–63)*, with which Huber was familiar. Géraigiry was born in Zahleh, Lebanon, where Palgrave, then known as Father Michael Cohen, met him as a young priest and chose him as his travelling companion for the great Arabian journey. He studied in France and became bishop of Baniyas in 1886, later becoming well known as Peter IV Barakat Géraigiry, patriarch of the Melkite Greek Catholic Church from 1898 until 1902. (Allan 1972: 161–3.)

to write his own account of the journey to set the record straight. Alas, there is no evidence that the priest ever did so, but how tantalizing a thought it is that there may somewhere be a manuscript, lying unrecognized.[41]

Huber seems to have stayed in Lebanon until the end of September, when at last he went to Damascus. At the end of October, he extolled the help given him by the French consul there, T. Gilbert, who had undertaken to put him in touch with the main tribal chiefs in the Syrian desert, as well as with Ibn Rashīd in Ḥāʾil. He was planning a trip to Palmyra, where he hoped to collect some more skulls from the ancient tombs. He sounded upbeat, but he soon ran into a succession of delays and difficulties which would have unnerved a less tenacious man. He was made to waste two and a half months fruitlessly roaming the desert purlieus between Damascus, Qaryatayn and Palmyra in anticipation of a promise of safe conduct to al-Ğawf made by Saṭṭām ibn Shaʿlān, chief of the Ruwalah, which turned out to be empty. His only achievement was to reach Palmyra in November, as noted on the folding map at the end of this volume.[42] The Druze uprising of 1879 was blocking the routes to the south through the Ḥawrān, and then he was further thwarted by the terrible winter of 1879–80, which blanketed the desert in two feet of snow and rendered the routes impassable for weeks. He fell ill with a fever, and took refuge in the convent of the Lazarite Fathers in Damascus, where he received medical care.[43] It was not until early March 1880 that he was able to set out once more. This time he headed south for the camp of Muḥammad Ṭūkhī, one of the great shaykhs of the Wuld ʿAlī, who was looking after his camels and who had also offered him protection as far as al-Ğawf. When he caught up with this shaykh at Ğarash, the great Roman site east of the Jordan river, he found that his camels were sick or else too weak to march, and that they could not be replaced for at least a month. Visiting the Druze shaykhs in the Ḥawrān, he made arrangements to be supplied with camels and guides as soon as possible, and made his disconsolate way back to Damascus, cursing his ill-luck. When he received news from his Druze friends that the routes were now open and the animals ready, he finally set off for the third time from Damascus on 28 April 1880, only to find that the Banī Ṣakhr shaykh

[41] Huber was right to regard Palgrave's book as unreliable, or 'fantaisiste' as he calls it. For a critique of Palgrave's veracity, see Facey 1992: 137–61.

[42] See also Appendix 4, Letter no. 8, where he lists his journey to Palmyra as the subject of his first sketch map.

[43] For the Lazarite convent, see Appendix 3, Letter no. 21 dated 17 July 1882 from Huber to Xavier Charmes.

who had promised to provide the guides had gone back on his word. By this time, Huber could have claimed with justice that this seemingly malevolent concatenation of setbacks proved that the hand of fate was indeed against him. But he rose above it. Determined not to retreat to Damascus yet again, he now bravely decided to find his own guides. He went to Boṣra in the southern Ḥawrān, where he at last found two men prepared to accompany him. As they were ne'er-do-wells, outcasts from their tribe, he was risking his life, but he threw himself upon fortune. So far, through no fault of his own, he had been forced to squander eight months, almost 2,000 francs and the greater part of his gifts just to reach his starting point for Arabia.[44]

That Arabia was at the core of his ambition is demonstrated by the fact that his travelogue does not begin until this point, as he leaves Boṣra: see the Translation, Part I, p. 88. The specifically Arabian part of his journey would occupy about nine months, from mid-May 1880 to February 1881.

Seemingly still unaware, as he set off from Boṣra, of the vexation caused in Paris by the revelation of his criminal conviction, he made for the little oasis of Kāf (one of the 'Salt Villages', Qurayyāt al-Milḥ) at the northern end of the great depression known as Wādī al-Sirḥān, just inside present-day Saudi Arabia.[45] Rightly judging that he would need powerful protection during his travels, he was aiming for Ḥā'il, the political capital of northern Naǧd, where the Rashīdī dynasty held sway, having established itself in the 1830s as the paramount clan of the Shammar group of tribes. Such was the influence of its current emir, Muḥammad al-Rashīd, that he now had the backing of the Ottoman Turks in their manoeuvres to counter the encroachment of the British into the affairs of the Gulf shaykhdoms and the Red Sea. The expansion of Ḥā'il's power and influence in northern and central Arabia was coming at the

[44] For the narrative presented here, see Appendix 3, Letter no. 9 and enclosure dated 29 October 1879; no. 16 and report dated 27 March 1882 from Huber to the Minister of Public Education. See also Duveyrier 1883: 213; fr.wikipedia.org: entry Charles Huber (explorateur), consulted September 2020. Maunoir 1880: 201; Maunoir 1883: 55: '… M. Huber, chargé en 1879 d'une Mission du Ministère de l'Instruction publique. Ayant accompli d'abord diverses courses soit en compagnie des Bédouins Rouala, jusqu'à 170 kilomètres au sud de Palmyre, soit seul dans le désert à l'est du Jourdain, dans le Hauran, le Djebel Druse, le Ledja, M. Huber quittait Damas pur la troisième fois le 28 avril 1880.'

[45] He reached Kāf on 17 May 1880 and al-Ǧawf on 26 May 1880 (Huber 1884b: 307, 311, 315) and not, as stated by Ward (1983: 389) and al-Sudairī (1995: 143), in May 1878, an error that can be traced back to Hogarth's *The Penetration of Arabia* (1904: 252–3).

expense of the Second Saudi State, centred on Riyadh to the south, where a damaging civil war had led to a shrinking sphere of influence.[46]

From Kāf, Huber followed the Wādī al-Sirḥān to the oasis of al-Ǧawf and its chief settlement, Dūmat al-Ǧandal. From there he set off across the Great Nafūd, the formidable desert of towering pink sand dunes, by the well-worn route to the little oasis of Ǧubbah. Hearing that the Emir Muḥammad al-Rashīd was installed not far away at the wells of Umm al-Qulbān, Huber went there to meet him and then accompanied him to Ḥāʾil, which he reached on 13 June 1880. The emir, despite an avowed attachment to the Wahhābī creed, accorded Huber a gratifyingly warm reception. This can be taken in part as evidence of Huber's magnetic ability to turn on the charm. But the emir too was politically astute, and alive to the possibilities of cultivating relations with outside powers other than his Ottoman allies. He was thus open to receiving foreign visitors, having welcomed Wilfrid and Lady Anne Blunt in similar fashion just eighteen months before. Huber on his side showed a desire to be helpful. He would later undertake to procure firearms for Ibn Rashīd, and even to explore diplomatic channels to bring about the return of the oasis of Khaybar, now under Ottoman occupation, to Rashīdī control.[47] Having established the friendly relations with the emir and other members of the ruling family that were to stand him in good stead on both this and on the 1883–84 journey, Huber proceeded to use Ḥāʾil as a base for six pioneering forays around northern Naǧd and the northern Ḥiǧāz.[48]

On 1 July, just as he was embarking on this programme of excursions, Huber sent, via Damascus, a 20-page report to the Minister of Public Education in Paris requesting an extension and an additional 15,000 francs, as well as some more instruments, so that he could extend his explorations into central and southern Arabia.[49] The plea would fall on deaf ears, and Huber would remain in the dark as to why. No more support would be forthcoming. A terse ministerial note dated 7 October 1880 explains the new *froideur*:

---

[46] Çiçek 2017: 105–16.

[47] See Appendix 5, Letter no. 2 dated April 1883 from Huber to the Emir Muḥammad ibn ʿAbd Allāh al-Rashīd.

[48] Huber's routes are shown on the folding map after Huber 1884b: 416: see the folding map bound with this volume.

[49] See Appendix 3, note 18 (p. 320) for the gist of Huber's letter of 1 July 1880 to the minister (Item no. 53 in Dossier F/17/2976/1:1, French National Archives, Pierrefitte-sur-Seine).

> M. Huber had been recommended by the professors at the museum, who were unaware of his past. Later we received the proof, from the Ministry of Justice, that in 1869 [*sic*; 1868] M. Huber had served six months in jail for theft. The Expeditions Committee furthermore has found M. Huber's first report to be pitiful.[50]

Huber's first excursion from Ḥā'il was to nearby ʿUqdah, the little oasis close to Ḥā'il in the rugged gorges of Ǧabal Aǧā.[51] His second was to Ǧabal Sarrā', a rich inscription site to the south-west of Ḥā'il.[52] Both of these were locations that he would later visit with Euting.[53] The third trip was a wider exploration of Ǧabal Aǧā in the vicinity of Ḥā'il.[54] On 31 July 1880, he set out south-eastwards on a more dangerous venture outside Ibn Rashīd's sphere of control to the reputedly fanatical territory of al-Qaṣīm, where he could not be assured of the emir's protection.[55] Visiting Buraydah and its environs (where he had been preceded in 1862 by Palgrave, in 1864 by Guarmani and in 1878 by Doughty), he met its emir, Ḥasan walad Muhannā, whose semi-subjection to Ibn Rashīd was symbolized by the payment of a tax, and whom he and Euting would entertain in Ḥā'il in January 1884.[56] He then stayed for a while at ʿUnayzah, an independent town with a more cosmopolitan ambience which had also been visited by Guarmani. It was the place where Doughty had sought refuge in April–July 1878 and which features so vividly in his *Travels in Arabia Deserta*, though Huber could not yet know that.[57] This excursion was followed in September by a fifth round-trip, to Ǧabal Ǧildiyyah east of Ḥā'il, another rich source of ancient rock art and graffiti to which he would later take Euting.[58]

[50] Appendix 3, Letter no. 11 dated 7 October 1880 from the Office of the Minister of Public Education to unidentified recipient(s).
[51] Huber 1884b: 355–9.
[52] Huber 1884b: 359–63. See also Appendix 3, Letter no. 10 dated 11 July 1880 from Huber to the Minister of Public Education, Paris, enclosing a transcription of the Ǧabal Sarrā' inscriptions.
[53] Euting 1914: 114–17 (Chapter X, entries for 27–28 January 1884).
[54] Huber 1884b: 468–73.
[55] Huber 1884b: 473–502.
[56] Euting 1914: 65–6, 80–2 (Chapter IX, entries for 21 and 29 December 1883); For Buraydah see Doughty 1936 ii: 339–56; Guarmani 1938: 42–3, 94.
[57] For ʿUnayzah see Doughty 1936 ii: 357–486; Guarmani 1938: 39–42, 92–3.
[58] Huber 1884b: 502–4; 1891: 78–103; Euting 1896: 227–40 (Chapter VIII, entries for 9–16 November 1883).

In October, Huber was still living in hopes of receiving the funds and instruments he had requested in his letter of 1 July, and was planning to go to Ǧiddah to collect them on completion of his sixth round-trip from Ḥāʾil.[59] The latter, by far the longest of his six excursions, would take about nine weeks. It is of particular relevance to the story of his later relations with Euting, as it took him westwards along the southern fringe of the Nafūd sands, via Ǧabal Mismāʾ and Ǧabal ʿIrnān, to Taymāʾ, Madāʾin Ṣāliḥ and al-ʿUlā in the northern Ḥijāz. He would revisit these places, all of vital significance for Aramaic and Ancient North Arabian epigraphy, with Euting in early 1884.[60] Huber then returned via the forbidding basalt-strewn landscape of Khaybar and al-Ḥāʾiṭ, reaching Ḥāʾil on 1 January 1881. There he was met by a letter from the French consul in Ǧiddah that filled him with anxiety. Writing to the minister on 2 January 1881, he enquired:

> I am without news from the ministry, our consul in Ǧiddah not having handed to the messenger that I had sent to him before my departure for the west, a ministerial envelope in his possession, fearing that it would not reach me. But he does write that M. le Ministre has charged him to tell me to return to Paris on my arrival in Ǧiddah. So is my expedition to be terminated? And does the Expeditions Committee no longer wish to continue lending me its support? Yet I was sure of success and of being the first Christian to cross Arabia as such from side to side, and to do so not as an amateur like my predecessors, but as a professional explorer.[61]

Unsure as to the cause of this withdrawal of ministerial favour, he included with this letter a second one reporting on his 64-day round-trip to Taymāʾ, Madāʾin Ṣāliḥ, al-ʿUlā, Khaybar and al-Ḥāʾiṭ.[62] In this he made sure to highlight what he regarded as his major geographical discovery: the identification of a north–south line running from Taymāʾ to a range of

---

[59] Appendix 3, Letter no. 12 dated 12 October 1880 from Huber to the Minister of Public Education, Paris.

[60] Huber 1884b: 504–30; 1885: 92–104.

[61] Appendix 3, Letter no. 13 dated 2 January 1881 from Huber to the Minister of Public Education, Paris; no. 14 dated 2 January 1881, ditto. Huber was unaware that he had been preceded by G.F. Sadleir in 1819 as 'the first Christian to cross Arabia'.

[62] Appendix 3, Letter no. 14 dated 2 January 1881 from Huber to the Minister of Public Education, Paris.

extinct volcanoes in the Ḥarrat Khaybar centred on Ra'̓s al-Abyaḍ as the watershed of northern Arabia. He had established the extent of the granite uplift of Ǧabal Aǧā (also known as Ǧabal Shammar), made some interesting anthropological observations about the people of al-ʿUlā and Khaybar, and recorded many of the tomb inscriptions at Madāʾin Ṣāliḥ. Though he could not know it at the time, these discoveries would redeem his reputation in Paris and lead to his being taken seriously again.

For now, short of funds but able to draw on a little money from his mother, he was anxious to head homewards. Heeding news from the desert that the route to Ǧiddah was infested by vengeful parties of ʿUtaybah and Hutaym tribesmen in the wake of raids by Ibn Rashīd, he took the prudent decision to go instead to Baghdad. Conveniently, the Persian Ḥajj caravan was preparing to leave Ḥāʾil on its way back to Iraq, and he decided to join it.

Leaving on the 17th, the caravan followed a circuitous route round the southern edge of the Nafūd to join the Darb Zubaydah running northwards to Baghdad.[63] After exploring ancient sites and taking part in British Museum archaeological investigations at Sippar in Babylonia, and also spending time at Ḥillah, the site of ancient Babylon,[64] he made his eighth and final journey, from Baghdad to Damascus, later in the year. Having reached the latter on 14 December 1881,[65] he returned to Paris via Egypt and Istanbul.[66]

So ends the travelogue published here in translation. In it, Huber sticks to facts of objective exploration and observation. He was clearly uninterested in appealing to a wider readership, and a consequence of playing down anything that might lend his account a colourful tone of dangerous desert adventure is that he reveals almost nothing about himself. Nevertheless, such a lone ordeal

[63] Huber 1885a: 104–25. The Darb Zubaydah was the pilgrimage route from Baghdad to Mecca. It was named after Zubaydah bint Ǧaʿfar, wife of Caliph Ḥarūn al-Rashīd, in recognition of the numerous wells, cisterns and resting places she had sponsored along its entire length.

[64] For Huber's travels in Iraq, see Appendix 3, Letter no. 17 dated 13 May 1882 from Huber in Strasbourg to Xavier Charmes. See also Appendix 5, Letter no. 3 dated April 1883 to Ḥamūd ibn ʿUbayd in Ḥāʾil: Huber writes that he was also ordered by the French government to study the plague ravaging Mesopotamia. The excavations at Sippar were directed by Hormuzd Rassam, an Assyrian Christian born in Mosul who became a protégé of Layard's and was eventually naturalized British; as well as his archaeological work he served as a British diplomat. See Wikipedia, entry Hormuzd Rassam, consulted 12 January 2020. (MCAM/WF)

[65] Huber 1885a: 126–39.

[66] Appendix 5, Letter no. 2 to the Emir Muḥammad ibn ʿAbd Allāh al-Rashīd.

could only have been brought to a successful conclusion by a confident and single-minded man of steely ambition and determination, not to mention resourcefulness and physical stamina. It is obvious that he combined courage and stoicism to a remarkable degree.[67] Described by one contemporary as 'quelque peu bizarre et misanthrope', Huber was like many explorers in being a self-reliant loner who could declare that 'il y a longtemps que je doute que l'homme ait été créé pour vivre en société'.[68] But this represented only one side of this complex character. His letters to Dr Weisgerber, and the testimony of other friends such as A. Sauval, demonstrate not only that he was supremely determined to fulfil his ambitions and make a name for himself, but also that he was eloquent, persuasive and capable of warm reciprocal attachments.[69]

As is clear from the letters he wrote during 1882 to Charles Maunoir at the Société de Géographie on completion of this journey, his interest in the region was first and foremost scientific, and focused on its geology, topography and mapping.[70] Huber's explorations and the scientific data he collected were recognized immediately by the French geographical establishment as a major contribution to knowledge. For the first time, it was possible to envisage the compilation of a credible map of northern Nağd, building on Guarmani's data. His most significant topographical discovery, the pinpointing of the watershed of northern Arabia in the Ḥarrat Khaybar, was new to science.[71] Huber had also given rein to his interest in the written

[67] Pearson 1993: 44–51.

[68] 'For a long time I have doubted that man was created to live in society': see Pearson 1993: 48, quoting from an article by 'G.E.' in the *Journal d'Alsace et de Lorraine*, 14 August 1931, p. 1. G.E. was possibly Jules Ernest Gérock (1859–1934), a Strasbourgeois pharmacist and man of letters with an interest in geography, who was a frequent contributor to this journal in the 1920s and '30s (with thanks to Prof. Maria Gorea for this suggestion).

[69] See Appendix 4 for letters to Dr Weisgerber: Letter no. 16 from Beirut dated 3 July 1883; no. 19 from Damascus dated 17 August 1883; and no. 24 from Ğiddah dated 6 July 1884. See also Appendix 12, item no. 1, letter from A. Sauval.

[70] Appendix 4, Letters nos. 1–11.

[71] For the importance of Guarmani and Huber's pioneering contribution to the mapping of northern Nağd, see Duveyrier 1883; Hogarth 1904: 252, 268, 270; Kiernan 1937: 264–6; Pearson 1993: 42–3. See also the unpublished map *Travellers' Routes in the Country around Teima, 1876–1914* (1914), scale 1:270,000, on which the Royal Geographical Society plotted Huber's 1880 and 1883–84 routes between the longitudes of Qalʿat al-Akhḍar and Ğabal Mismāʾ (Kiernan 1937: 266), as well as those of Doughty, Carruthers and Bell. Unfortunately other sheets seem to be missing. Doughty's travels too were important in establishing the watershed of north-west

word, taking pains to record 146 inscriptions and graffiti en route.[72] The results restored him to favour with the ministry and established his reputation as an explorer, winning him the gold medal of the Société de Géographie in Paris.[73] Maunoir's resounding endorsement was that 'the publication of the results of this journey will show M. Huber to be a worthy emulator of Guarmani, Palgrave, Pelly, the Blunts, and Doughty'.[74]

On this first Arabian venture, Huber made Arab friends and amassed experience and skills that would prove to be of great practical value when he returned in the company of Euting to many of the same places in 1883–84. The network of contacts that he had built up, and his familiarity with the landscape, language and culture of northern Arabia would inevitably place him, tacitly or otherwise, in a position of superior knowledge and authority to his German counterpart despite being the younger man by some eight years. Arguably too, and perhaps of even greater significance for his relationship with Euting, there was a psychological legacy of this first journey: it seems to have imbued him with a heightened sense of proprietary entitlement, on behalf of France,[75] to all the discoveries that both of them would make on their joint expedition.

A deniable partnership with Julius Euting, 1882–83

Back home in Strasbourg in early 1882, Huber immediately set about writing up his travels, and submitted his report to the ministry on 27 March.[76] He then relieved his frustration at having realized only a small part of his initial ambition by applying himself straight away to raising funds for a second

---

Arabia, but his compass bearings and rough route distances were not regarded by the Royal Geographical Society as sufficiently accurate or systematic to be included on the map (Hogarth 1928: 157–9).

72 Huber 1884a. Many of these were recopied more accurately by Euting on the later journey. See Appendix 12, item no. 2 for the insight that Huber's attraction to epigraphy could be seen as an extension of his bibliophilia. Nonetheless, Huber's Letters nos. 1–11 of 1882, in Appendix 4, demonstrate that his overriding interest was in the accurate mapping of Arabia, for which see also Duveyrier 1883. (MCAM/WF)

73 Duveyrier 1883 details Huber's contributions to the geography and mapping of northern Arabia. The gold medal was awarded in early 1883: see Appendix 3, Letter no. 28 dated 17 February 1883 from Maunoir to the Minister of Public Education.

74 Maunoir 1883: 56.

75 Appendix 11, Letter no. 1 dated 8 July 1885 from Ernest Renan to Julius Euting.

76 For Huber's first complete report on his first Arabian journey, see Appendix 3, Letter no. 16 and report of March 1882. The full 65-page handwritten report is part of Item no. 66 in Dossier F/17/2976/1:1, French National Archives, Pierrefitte-sur-Seine.

expedition, not only to cover the same ground over again, but also if possible to extend his travels into central and south-western Arabia. His desire to return to Arabia was compounded by a concern that his longitude calculations might have been inaccurate,[77] and by a wish to collect more precise records of ancient inscriptions by making paper squeezes.

Encouraged by Charles Maunoir, he submitted his proposal for a second Arabian journey to Xavier Charmes at the Ministry of Public Education as soon as 11 May.[78] His itinerary would once again begin at Damascus, from where he would proceed straight to the northern Ḥiğāz, visiting Taymāʾ, Madāʾin Ṣāliḥ, al-ʿUlā and Khaybar. He would then go south to al-Madīnah before turning north-east towards Wadi Rimah and Ḥāʾil. Here he would avail himself of the Emir Muḥammad ibn Rashīd's friendship to penetrate southwards into the settled districts of Nağd, specifically al-Washm, al-Sudayr, Riyadh and al-Aflāğ. He would go on from there to Wadi al-Dawāsir and Nağrān, explore the ancient kingdoms of Yemen, and go east to Ḥaḍramawt. Crossing Mahra territory, he would reach Oman before following the Gulf coast back through eastern Arabia. His aim was to be the first scientific explorer of Arabia as a whole, and this time there was no talk of Persia or Tibet. In the covering letter addressed to Xavier Charmes he wrote:

> I have the honour to enclose for you my official request for the continuation of my mission to explore Arabia. I do not need to tell you that you can have every confidence in me for the success and sound results of the expedition. I shall perhaps appear presumptuous to some members of the [Expeditions] Committee for proposing my project to explore Nağd, Nağrān, Māʾrib and the Mahra country, but I am nonetheless very sure of my business. I have spent five years doing nothing but studying the [Arabian] Peninsula, I know all the literature on it almost by heart, and I can say that I am almost as familiar with it as I am with my own apartment. Besides, I do not need to plead my case before you, as you know what motivates me and that success must be mine, and

[77] Appendix 4, Letter no. 3 dated 18 May 1882 from Huber to Maunoir.

[78] Appendix 3, Letter no. 18 dated 11 May 1882 from Huber to the Minister of Public Education; no. 19 dated 11 May 1882 from Huber to Xavier Charmes. See also Appendix 4, Letter no. 2 dated 28 March 1882 from Huber to Maunoir; no. 3 dated 18 May 1882 from Huber to Maunoir; no. 6 dated 6 July 1882 from Huber to Maunoir.

> that I could never be content with the empty glory of just crossing Arabia, but that I must bring back serious, precise and complete documentation.

He was emboldened to make such a confident approach by the high regard in which he knew he was held by Charmes, who he was sure would promote his cause. The confidence extended to the scale of funding he requested: this time, no less than 35,000 francs over a period of two years – perhaps about £75,000 in today's money. But there were other calls on the ministry budget and, while Charmes was warmly supportive, its response was frustratingly slow: Huber would have to wait until the following year for his grant, and then, disappointingly, it would be set at no more than 10,000 francs. In the meantime, he had to make do with a refund by the ministry of 2,900 francs, representing the overspend on his first expedition.[79]

In Strasbourg, Huber was finding himself in challenging circumstances. During the summer and autumn of 1882, he was assailed by imputations of dishonesty of the kind that tended to follow him around. These dented his morale. The first was a false allegation that he owed money in Damascus to the Lazarite Fathers for accommodation and medical care during the bitter winter of 1879–80. As Huber had proof that the payment had been made, he was able to brush this aside. The second canard came from a Paris lawyer, by the unimprovable name of M. Bastard, claiming that a certain Huber, now resident in Larnaca, Cyprus, had stolen a valuable piece of furniture from his client in France. As Huber had no connection with Cyprus, he was easily able to dismiss this one as a case of mistaken identity. A third allegation, this time unspecified, was deemed serious enough to be made the subject of a ministry enquiry. Huber was naturally overwhelmed with anxiety that an unfavourable verdict would spell the end of his dream of exploration.[80] Fortunately the matter was quickly resolved, and Charmes wrote a fulsome note to Huber reporting that the

[79] Appendix 3, Letter no. 19 dated 11 May 1882 from Huber to Xavier Charmes; no. 25 dated 30 October 1882 from Huber to Charmes; no. 26 dated 6 November 1882 from Charmes to Huber; no. 27 dated 11 November 1882 from Huber to Charmes. For Charmes' supportive attitude towards Huber, see Appendix 3, Letter no. 23 dated 20 October 1882 from Huber to Charmes; no. 24 dated 28 October 1882 from Charmes to Huber; no. 25 dated 30 October 1882 from Huber to Charmes.

[80] Appendix 3, Letter no. 21 dated 17 July 1882 from Huber to Charmes; no. 22 dated 8 August 1882 from Huber to Charmes or Maunoir; no. 23 dated 20 October 1882 from Huber to Charmes.

enquiry had completely cleared him and assuring him of the ministry's continuing support.[81]

More serious than these irritants were the restrictions under which Huber and his family were forced to live in Strasbourg. Residency and travel permits were hard to obtain, and he was required to report to the police every week. He describes to Maunoir how he was interrogated on his return from a visit to Paris. His two brothers had been imprisoned and fined for having performed their military service in France, his family's property was under compulsory administration, and he was feeling it necessary to keep a low profile if he wanted to stay in Strasbourg while he prepared for his next Arabian expedition.[82] On the positive side, his exploits in Arabia were causing a stir among scholars in France and Germany interested in the Middle East, and Julius Euting would have been immediately alerted to Huber's return from there.

Euting's privileged background was very different from Huber's.[83] He was born on 11 July 1839 in the Swabian city of Stuttgart, at that time capital of the independent Kingdom of Württemberg. His father, a senior civil servant, was a prominent member of the Baden-Württemberg establishment. Unlike the Catholic Hubers, the Eutings were Protestants. Academically successful as a boy, Euting's natural linguistic talent turned him towards the study of Arabic and ancient Near Eastern languages. From early on he nursed an ambition to travel in Arabia, but had to put it aside for lack of funds. In 1866, he secured his first academic appointment as librarian of his old Protestant seminary, moving two years later to Tübingen University Library. He was to remain a librarian for the whole of his career, but this proved no bar to extramural scholarly pursuits. A keen interest in Semitic epigraphy, a love of nature and a sense of adventure combined to make a traveller of him. Though he could not claim Huber's level of fortitude when it came to pioneering exploration, he was physically fit and a passionate hiker despite being a heavy smoker.[84] A great added advantage was his outstanding artistic

[81] Appendix 3, Letter no. 24 dated 28 October 1882 from Charmes to Huber; Appendix 4, Letter no. 9 dated 14 November 1882 from Huber to Maunoir.

[82] Appendix 4, Letter no. 10 dated 25 November 1882; Lozachmeur and Briquel-Chatonnet 2013: 2, paragraphs 6–10.

[83] The sources for this biographical sketch are Hunziger-Rodewald 2020; Lyall 1913; Pearson 1993: 18–32; Pfullmann 1993; and Healey 2004. Lyall (1913: 505) seems to be in error in placing his birthday on 17 July.

[84] For Huber's self-presentation as a tougher traveller than Euting, see Appendix 8, letter dated 3 September 1883 from Huber to Theodor Nöldeke.

talent. In 1869, he visited Sicily and then Tunis to study the Punic inscriptions of Carthage, which resulted in scholarly publications that have stood the test of time. In 1870, he went again to Sicily and then on to Greece, Asia Minor and Constantinople.

Directly on conclusion of the Franco-Prussian war of 1870–71, Euting moved to Strasbourg to take up a post in Rohan Palace as under-librarian in the newly founded Kaiser-Wilhelms-Universität. Here he would quickly rise to senior librarian and then in 1900 to director. He was joined at the university in 1872 by the eminent Semitist Theodor Nöldeke (1836–1930), a man known for his Prussian nationalist leanings,[85] with whom he established a warm lifelong friendship. In addition to his library duties, Euting took up a parallel appointment in 1880 as honorary professor in the Strasbourg philosophy faculty, where he was a popular and entertaining lecturer. His passion for epigraphy led to his becoming a leading authority on Phoenician, Punic, Aramaic, Nabataean, Syriac and Mandaic, and he also made occasional forays into Hebrew and Samaritan. His publication of the squeezes and copies he would make of the Nabataean inscriptions in Arabia during his journey with Huber in 1883–84 provided the first reliable records of the largest number of the tomb inscriptions then known at Madāʾin Ṣāliḥ, only some of which Doughty had been able to record.[86]

Euting's scholarly eminence is shown by the fact that his is the most cited name in the literature of Semitic epigraphy between *ca.* 1875 and 1920.[87] In the course of his career, during which he was showered with academic honours, he associated with the élite of European Semitic studies, including Ernest Renan and Joseph Halévy in France. He was also friendly with Christiaan Snouck Hurgronje (1857–1936), the influential Dutch colonial adviser, student of Islam and scholar of Arabic and Indonesian languages, who had studied under Nöldeke in Strasbourg in 1881. Euting's younger friend and former pupil, Enno Littmann (1875–1956), would succeed Nöldeke as Professor of Oriental Languages at Strasbourg in 1906.

Not only did Euting's social background and academic attainments stand in contrast to Huber's, but his colourful personality and whimsical nature

---

[85] Irwin 2006: 197–8.

[86] Euting made excellent squeezes of 27 out of the 38 Nabataean inscriptions on the façades and interiors of the tombs. These were published in Euting 1885a. Doughty, who did not have the advantage of a ladder, had made squeezes of 20 of these inscriptions, plus copies (Doughty 1884). (MCAM)

[87] Healey 2004: 327.

were also at variance with Huber's earnest single-mindedness. Diminutive in stature and extrovert by temperament, Euting had an omnivorous curiosity and revelled in a wide range of interests. He was, to apply Isaiah Berlin's famous distinction, a fox to Huber's hedgehog. His many friends testified to his sociability, his boyish character and impish sense of humour, his love of storytelling and mimicry, his talent for entertaining children, and his penchant for idiosyncratic dress.

By the time Huber returned to Strasbourg in early 1882, Euting's early ambition to go to Arabia had already been rekindled by the news of Doughty's travels there during 1876–78, in particular his discoveries at the great Nabataean site of Madāʾin Ṣāliḥ (ancient Ḥegrā). Doughty had been the first European to visit and report on this sensational site – modern Saudi Arabia's counterpart to Jordan's Petra – and to bring back squeezes and copies of many of the Nabataean inscriptions there.[88] Having been cold-shouldered in London by the British Museum and the Royal Geographical Society, Doughty managed to interest German and French scholars in his discoveries, in particular Halévy and Renan. He was also persuaded by the prestigious German geographical journal *Globus* to publish the first articles about his travels in Arabia.[89] It was thus German and French Orientalists who were the first to appreciate the significance of Doughty's discoveries and, according to David Hogarth, it was Nöldeke who encouraged Euting to revive his plan for an expedition to Arabia.[90]

So Huber's return home to Strasbourg at the start of 1882 merely inflamed an existing desire in Euting to mount an Arabian expedition. The Frenchman's familiarity with inscription sites and his working knowledge of everyday Naǧdī Arabic would have been irresistible to the German, whose Arabic was classical rather than colloquial. We do not know how they first met but, as they were both living in the same small city, it was all but inevitable that their paths would cross and that they would discuss their respective plans for Arabian investigations. Huber quickly found that Euting was eager to join forces. Euting had formulated a plan to travel through northern Arabia

[88] Doughty 1884; 1936 i: 121–223. Renan's notes on Doughty's copies and squeezes of the Nabataean inscriptions: Doughty 1884: 37–54; 1936 i: 224–9.

[89] Doughty 1880, 1881a, 1881b, 1882. *Globus* was a prestigious fortnightly German geographical magazine, published in Braunschweig. Its editor, Richard Kiepert, was responsible for first bringing Doughty's geographical and epigraphic discoveries to the notice of the world and to German academia in particular (Hogarth 1928: 99–101).

[90] Hogarth 1928: 60.

and revisit Doughty's sites, and in May 1882, at exactly the time that Huber was applying for French support for his own expedition, he set about trying to find official German support for a joint effort. He records how he sought the permission of 'His Highness' (*viz*. King Karl of Württemberg) to recruit Huber's services,[91] and pressed ahead with raising funds. It is hard to believe that Euting would have made such approaches without Huber's explicit agreement to work together. In his application to the Imperial Permanent Secretary in Berlin, von Hoffmann, he was open and notably upbeat about the proposed collaboration:

> For M. Huber's aims and areas of expertise do not lie in the field of epigraphy: while he has no difficulty in recording and calculating the geographical location of a given place with the sextant and theodolite, or in making other scientific observations, he has no understanding of the inscriptions that he himself copied in inner Arabia. Since I on the other hand lack all expertise in the sciences, and e.g. can rely only on individually noted estimates in making maps, our aims in the course of our shared journey would not be in competition, but could rather, assuming goodwill, complement each other in the most welcome way.[92]

Euting had initially estimated the cost at 12,000 marks, but soon revised it upwards.[93] When this application to the central German government was rejected,[94] he turned to the governor of Alsace-Lorraine, Edwin Freiherr von Manteuffel, who had been one of the successful German generals in the 1870–71 Franco-Prussian war, requesting financial support and two years' paid leave from his employment as university professor. Von Manteuffel, who was known for his conciliatory instincts and no doubt welcomed an

[91] Pearson 1993: 12.

[92] Pfullmann 1993: 148–9, quoting Euting to von Hoffmann, 19 May 1882 (Federal archive, Potsdam division, Imperial Ministry of the Interior (RMdI), No. 16 056, pp. 7 and 7 verso).

[93] Pfullmann 1993: 148, quoting von Hoffmann to von Bismarck, 8 July 1882 (Federal archive, Potsdam division, Imperial Ministry of the Interior (RMdI), No. 16 056, p. 2 verso): '[Euting] has in the meantime arrived at the conviction that this sum is insufficient, particularly if he is to be able to assert his independence in relation to his travel companion Huber, who is in the service of the French government.'

[94] The rejection was allegedly only because the new German government had not allocated any funds for exploration: see Appendix 12, Letter no. 1 dated 1 October 1884 from A. Sauval to the Minister of Foreign Affairs in Paris.

opportunity to support a Franco-German collaboration, duly obliged with a grant of 17,800 marks.[95] King Karl of Württemberg himself made a lavish contribution in the form of firearms and other weapons to be distributed during the expedition as gifts, chiefly intended for the emir of Ḥāʾil. With sponsors such as this, Euting's joint venture had the stamp of an official German expedition.[96]

Huber meanwhile was finding Euting not only enthusiastic but positively useful, and at this stage there is no evidence of the antipathy that later came to mar their relationship. Euting records how Huber 'once showed me in the diary of his first Arabian journey' an 'ancient Aramaic inscription' which, he says, he dated for Huber for the latter's report to the French Minister of Public Education.[97] Euting also did the drawings of Khaybar, the calligraphic Arabic title and the transliteration chart for Huber's large map of his first journey published in the *Bulletin* of the Société de Géographie in 1884 (Huber 1884b; see folding map at the end of this volume).[98] Nöldeke was recommending to Huber that he and Euting should travel together.[99] Further pressure on Huber may have come from Renan who, as a great admirer of German scholarship,[100] was well known to Euting and his circle of German Semitists and would certainly have given such a collaboration his blessing and encouragement, particularly in view of Euting's epigraphic expertise.

[95] 17,800 German marks was equivalent in 1883 to 22,250 francs, as Euting confirms in Appendix 10, Letter no. 6 dated January 1886 to Renan. This was equivalent at the time to *ca.* 870 pounds sterling, or 100,000 euro or more at 2015 prices (Historia.se).

[96] It should be borne in mind that the 1883–84 Arabian journey pre-dated Germany's enthusiastic embrace of Ottoman Turkey after the accession of Kaiser Wilhelm II in 1888, which the Turks hoped would help to counteract British influence in Arabia (McMeekin 2010: 7–10). There is thus no evidence that ulterior political considerations were behind the German decision to finance Euting's journey.

[97] Euting 1914: 154: Chapter XI, entry for 16 February 1884. This inscription was not the Taymāʾ Stele: see notes 181 and 227 below. In his report of 27 March 1882, to which Euting must be referring, Huber merely mentioned the three inscriptions ('trois belles inscriptions') that he found at Taymāʾ in November 1880 without trying to identify them, so did not use the information that Euting had given him. See report dated 27 March 1882, Dossier F/17/2976/1:1, 'M. Huber (Charles), Mission au Thibet et dans l'Asie centrale', French National Archives, Pierrefitte-sur-Seine, p. 49).

[98] Euting also drew the sketch map of ʿUqdah at the end of Huber 1891. See Appendix 5, Letter no. 4 dated April 1883 from Huber to Muḥammad Shayrawānī, paragraph 3; Appendix 10, Letters no. 4 and 5 dated 1 August and 2 November 1885 from Euting to Philippe Berger.

[99] Lorentz in Kurpershoek 2018: 109.

[100] Irwin 2006: 169.

Later, in April 1883, shortly before their departure together, Euting would help Huber to write Arabic letters to the Emir Muḥammad ibn Rashīd and other contacts in Ḥāʾil.[101] In these, Huber was happy to advertise his intention to travel to Arabia with Euting and was entirely positive about it:

> I shall not leave for Naǧd on my own. My friend [*viz.* Julius Euting], who is a better man than I, will accompany me. He has spent his whole life studying everything to do with the Arabs and like me he loves them greatly.

Thus, by April 1883, there was a firm plan for the two men to travel together. As Huber explained in an important letter to Ernest Renan at the AIBL dated 8 April 1883, the aims were specific: to refine and amplify his geographical data, and to make more epigraphic discoveries. Huber was open with Renan about collaborating with Euting, even stating that 'un compagnon m'est indispensable'.[102] In Huber's mind there were strict conditions, however: Euting would have no official standing; he himself would be the superior partner as the representative of France; and in the division of spoils Euting would be entitled to just a single inscription. As he stated in the letter:[103]

> Having M. Euting as companion should pose no obstacle because, since for his part he has no official assignment, we had made special arrangements that completely protect my rights and as a consequence those of France, and it has been agreed that the Académie des Inscriptions [AIBL] in Paris will take exclusive delivery of all the squeezes, even in the case of my not receiving any financial aid.
>
> The same goes for the dressed stones bearing inscriptions that are at Taymāʾ, which I plan to remove and arrange to transport to France. M. Euting has only asked me for a single one for his personal collection. The others will come to the Académie.

[101] Appendix 5, Letters nos. 1, 2 and 4 dated April 1883.

[102] Pearson 1993: 11–14. There is even some suggestion that Huber neglected to tell Euting about all the funds that he had been granted by the French government: see Appendix 11, Letter no. 1 dated 8 July 1885 from Renan to Euting, implying that Euting had not known about Huber's initial grant of 2,500 francs from the AIBL, which had reached him in Marseille; see also Trüper 2019: 67.

[103] See Appendix 7, Letter no. 2 dated 8 April 1883 from Huber to Renan. See also Pearson 1993: 10–11, 41–3, 93.

From Huber's point of view, however, there was one problem. Instead of the 35,000 francs he had requested from the ministry, the decision had been taken to award him just 10,000. A further 5,000 francs awarded by the AIBL helped to soften the blow.[104] Even so, these funds amounted in total to only about two-thirds of those awarded to Euting.[105] To make matters worse, the ministry grant could not be made available immediately, and Huber would have to start the journey without it.

Nonetheless, with funds agreed, both men were now ready to set forth. Ominously, Euting's understanding of his status on the expedition did not accord with Huber's, for he makes it clear in the preface to Vol. I of his published *Tagbuch* that Huber 'had been my guest from Strasbourg onwards'.[106] They left Strasbourg together on 22 May 1883, boarding a train for Marseille. That they were in Marseille together is proven by a letter to Euting in which Renan records that he had sent Huber 2,500 francs, half the AIBL subsidy, and that Huber had collected the money there – a fact that Huber apparently concealed from Euting.[107]

This concealment is the first sign we have of any unease that Huber might have felt in relation to Euting. From Huber's point of view, there were still unresolved issues. First, and in contrast to Euting, he was anxious about money. Not only had he been awarded one-third less than Euting's grant, but so far he had only a fraction of the money in his hand. He would not receive the 10,000 francs due to him from the ministry until the end of August in Damascus. By that time he had been travelling with Euting for three

[104] For the 10,000 francs awarded by the Ministry of Public Education, and the 5,000 francs by the AIBL: see Appendix 4, Letter no. 21, penultimate paragraph (p. 388); and Letter no. 24, note 154 (p. 401).

[105] 15,000 francs was equivalent in 1884 to *ca.* 480 pounds sterling, equivalent to about 56,000 euros in 2015 (Historia.se). See Appendix 4, Letter no. 21, where Huber states that he had already spent 9,600 francs of the 10,000 awarded him by the Ministry of Public Education before he had even left Damascus.

[106] Euting 1896: v–vi. Pearson 1993: 13. The journey from Strasbourg to Damascus is recorded by Euting in Notebook I (22 May–24 August 1883). His first mention of Huber comes in Alexandria on 30 May 1883 (Notebook I, p. 9r). Euting's original notebooks, sketchbooks and surviving correspondence are held by Tübingen University Library archives, Md 676 and Md 782 A 65. The original notebooks and sketchbooks (see the References) comprising the diary, preserved in Tübingen University Library, can be consulted online at http://idb.ub.uni-tuebingen.de/diglit/Md676.

[107] Appendix 11, Letter no. 1 dated 8 July 1885 from Renan to Euting; Appendix 10, Letter no. 6 dated 6 January 1886 from Euting to the Minister of Education, Paris.

months, entirely at the latter's expense.[108] Even subsequently, throughout the remainder of his time with Euting, he would continue to be dependent on the German's more generous resources.

The second problem for Huber was that while he had been open with his friends in Alsace and with Renan at the AIBL about his collaboration with Euting, he had been less than candid about it with his main sponsor, the Ministry of Public Education in Paris, and in particular with his chief supporter, Charles Maunoir at the Société de Géographie. When he had first reported to Maunoir some months previously that he was intending to travel with Euting, Maunoir had been vehemently against the idea of him co-operating with a German, and had strongly advised him to travel alone.[109] Clearly, Huber was ignoring this admonition. But at the same time he did not want to jeopardize the support he was receiving from the ministry, at Maunoir's recommendation. So from then on he seems to have decided that the best policy was just to keep quiet about his plan to travel with Euting. The price he paid was a constant anxiety that the ministry would find out, and withdraw its funding. And he appears to have prevailed on Euting to play the game, as will be seen.

By 2 June, the two men were in Cairo, where they spent a week before leaving for Port Said. On 12 June they put in at Jaffa, and next day disembarked at Beirut. Then, back in France, a bombshell landed, in the form of an article in the *Journal d'Alsace Lorraine* publicizing Euting's role in the expedition and implying that he was the prime mover and leader:[110]

> Professor Euting, accompanied by M. Charles Huber, has just set off via Marseille on a two-year journey of exploration in the Syrian and Arabian desert. Professor Euting, whose expertise is well known, has been long preparing himself for this expedition, for which the necessary resources have been granted by His Excellency the Governor (Général de Manteuffel, Governor of Alsace Lorraine), from the funds of Alsace Lorraine. His

[108] Appendix 10, Letter no. 6 dated 6 January 1886 from Euting to the Minister of Education, Paris.

[109] Appendix 6, Letter no. 1 dated 12 June 1883 from Maunoir to the Minister of Public Education. For additional evidence of French suspicion of Germans, see Appendix 12, Letter no. 1 dated 1 October 1884 from A. Sauval to the Minister of Foreign Affairs, Paris.

[110] Appendix 6, Letter no. 1 dated 12 June 1883 from Maunoir to the Minister of Public Education, including an excerpt from the *Journal d'Alsace Lorraine*.

> companion, M. Huber, is a Strasbourgeois who has studied medicine and natural sciences; having opted for France after the events of 1870, M. Huber has already made, at the expense of the French government, several journeys in Syria and North Africa.

Maunoir, who until then had been genuinely in the dark about Euting, was incandescent:

> It emerges from this article that M. Huber would be in subordination to M. Euting, who is funded by the German authorities. There are three points in all this that pain me. First, that M. Huber, having himself been commissioned by the Ministry of Public Education, has set out with a German, whatever merits the latter may possess; secondly, that he is considered to be a subordinate of his travelling companion; and third that he forewarned nobody of this part of his plan. On this last point, M. Huber had indeed broached it with me a few months ago, but I had responded with the very formal advice that he should travel alone. Since then, he had not spoken with me again about his plans for a companion.

Maunoir wrote Huber a stiff letter and instituted enquiries in Cairo and Damascus into the relationship between Huber and Euting. Meanwhile Huber quickly managed to mollify him by admitting that Euting was indeed present, but in the capacity not of collaborator but as an importunate hanger-on, who kept following him around and getting under his feet:

> Professor Euting is a great scholar, one of the best authorities on Semitic languages, but he is as much a wild enthusiast[111] as a scholar, and before he suggested travelling with me to Arabia, a plan which he had long been contemplating but which grew much stronger on the news of my epigraphic discoveries in the Ḥiǧāz, he had already announced to the whole world that he would go with me. However, I had never offered him much hope, for the simple reason that I saw more advantage in it for him than for me, and when last January I spoke with you about it in Paris and

[111] It should be noted that in 19th-century French the term 'enthusiaste' had distinctly negative connotations, suggesting fanaticism, zealotry, lack of judgement, etc. (Littré 1873). (MCAM)

> you expressed your disapproval of it, I told him straight away on returning to my country, where he had come to find me, to contemplate it no further. ... What I can affirm is that I have no closer relationship with him than with anyone else, that we are not travelling together and that, as a consequence, there can be no question of being travelling companions or of one being subordinate to the other.[112]

A few days later, Huber was quick to confect some more outrage and disgust at the idea that he and Euting might be travelling together, and showed in doing so that he was not above deceiving even his close friend Weisgerber who, as it happened, was a member of the Société de Géographie and thus in potential contact with Maunoir: [113]

> You will have seen, concerning Euting ... that Maunoir had written to me on the subject and that I replied that there is no question and there has never been any question of an association between Euting and me, and that nothing is more ridiculous than to suppose that I, who have been appointed by the French government, should make myself subordinate to a German appointed by his government. Where would be the advantage, what benefit would there be for me? – I would understand if it were the other way round because I do not need anyone with whom to go to Arabia whereas anybody else would need me. I am surprised that this has not been taken into consideration and that Maunoir swallowed such a ridiculous story so easily. ... On receiving his letter I was ready to have nothing more to do with the Ministry or Maunoir, and that is still not beyond the bounds of possibility. I shall take up again my initial idea of setting off on my own account.[114]

---

[112] Appendix 4, Letter no. 14 dated 25 June 1883 from Huber in Beirut to Maunoir. See also Appendix 6, Letter no. 3 dated 7 July 1883 from Maunoir to the Minister of Public Education.

[113] Appendix 4, Letter no. 14 dated 25 June 1883 to Maunoir; Letter no. 16 dated 3 July 1883 to Weisgerber; and Letter no. 17 dated 13 July 1883 to Maunoir. Huber's friend Weisgerber, a doctor of medicine, was admitted into membership of the Société de Géographie in early 1883 (*Comptes-rendus des séances de la Société de géographie et de la commission centrale*, séance du 8 January 1883, p. 12).

[114] Appendix 4, Letter no. 16 dated 3 July 1883, Huber to Weisgerber from Beirut. See also Letter no. 17 dated 13 July 1883, Huber to Maunoir from Damascus; Letter no. 20 dated 24 September 1883, Huber to Maunoir from Damascus; and Letter no. 21

The impression of Euting being merely an acquaintance and occasional nuisance was later corroborated by Gilbert, the French consul in Damascus who, surprisingly, was unable to observe any actual connection between the two men.[115] By mid-July Maunoir had been completely won round by Huber's display of injured innocence, and was committing himself once again to giving him all the help he needed. But Huber remained on edge, writing to Xavier Charmes, his paymaster at the education ministry, seeking reassurance that he believed the story![116] It does not seem to have occurred to Charmes that Huber might be protesting too much, and his suspicions appear not to have been aroused. At the end of August, the 10,000 francs duly arrived in Damascus, and Huber was able to relax somewhat.[117]

It is clear that Huber, for both financial and political reasons, was desperate to avoid his journey being reported back to Paris as a joint venture with a German.[118] The Franco-German duo meanwhile were touring around archaeological sites in Lebanon and Syria in an ostentatiously deniable kind of way. In Lebanon they spent three weeks making parallel but independent excursions until, on 6 July, they set off for Damascus. They then went on an archaeological tour of the Anti-Lebanon, returning five days later to the city, where they spent the following two weeks. All this time they took great pains not to associate with each other in public. Next, on 27 July, Euting set out on a twelve-day round trip to Palmyra, followed by Huber a day and a half later.[119] Huber had been tasked by the AIBL with making a squeeze of the inscription embodying the Tax Law of Palmyra, a mission that he successfully accomplished.[120]

This charade was designed to keep any suggestion of collaboration under wraps, or at least render it deniable. Euting willingly played his part

dated 30 November 1883, Huber to Maunoir from Ḥāʾil: 'I take the liberty of begging you to excuse my bad temper in my last letter.'

115 Appendix 6, Letter no. 3 dated 7 July 1883 and Letter no. 7 dated 24 September 1883 from Maunoir to the Minister of Public Education.

116 Appendix 6, Letter no. 5 dated 19 July 1883 from Huber to Charmes.

117 Or 9,500 francs: see Appendix 6, Letter no. 6 dated 1 September from Huber to the Minister of Public Education.

118 See Pearson 1993: 142–3 for their semi-detached travel style. In 1886, Euting stated openly that 'Huber felt so compromised by associating with a German that he sought partly to conceal our travelling together' (Pearson 1993: 142, quoting Euting's letter of 17 November 1886 to 'Your Highness').

119 Euting's Notebook II opens on 27 July 1883 with the trip to Palmyra.

120 Appendix 4, Letter no. 19 dated 17 August 1883 to Weisgerber from Damascus.

in it, good-naturedly making allowances for Huber's need to disown him in public, and airily describing it in letters to Nöldeke in Strasbourg. 'In France,' he wrote, 'the current news is that Huber is playing a subordinate role in a big German expedition; he is asking me now not to let anything about him get out into the newspapers.' Again, he asked Nöldeke not to 'divulge publicly the news that I (just today) am off to Palmyra. I am not meeting up with Huber until tomorrow evening, *as if by chance* [my italics].' In another letter he wrote that 'Huber was not allowed to travel with me openly but just remained half a day behind me in Damascus.' And, as they were on the point of leaving Damascus for Arabia, Euting told Nöldeke that 'I shall (in order to keep up the pretence) go on the day after tomorrow, and in two days' time he [Huber] will follow me and we shall then go to the south. Do not however put anything about our plan in the newspaper.'[121]

In contrast to his protestations for French consumption about wanting nothing to do with Euting, Huber was concerned to claim the credit in other quarters for organizing their joint expedition into Arabia. He had not hesitated to advertise his association with Euting farther afield when it suited him to do so, for example in the letters sent to his contacts in northern Arabia in April 1883, not long before their departure.[122] And on 3 September 1883 he wrote to Nöldeke from Damascus:

> I hope that Dr Euting will have passed on the greetings that I asked him to add to each of his letters, and that he will also have told you how busy I was with our preparations, for which I had sole responsibility.
>
> You will probably have been told of our trip to Palmyra and its results. It is there that M. Euting had his initiation to life in the desert, but still with a certain amount of comfort such as tents, a bed, good food, etc. He suffered a great deal from the heat and the fatigue of the forced marches, but what he found hardest to bear on this trip was the lack of sleep.[123]

[121] Excerpts taken from the following four letters from Euting to Nöldeke: dated 4 July 1883 from Beirut, paragraph 2; dated 27 July 1883 from Damascus, paragraph 1; dated 16 August 1883 from Damascus, paragraph 2; dated 28 August 1883 from Damascus, paragraph 2 (Euting Archiv, Tübingen University Library, Md 782 A 65).

[122] Appendix 5, Letter no. 2 dated *ca.* 10 April 1883 from Huber in Paris. See also Letter no. 4 dated April 1883 from Huber to Muḥammad al-Shayrawānī in Nağaf.

[123] Appendix 8, letter dated 3 September 1883 from Huber in Damascus to Theodor Nöldeke.

In the same letter to Nöldeke, Huber envisaged that he and Euting would both travel together as far as Ǧiddah: ‘We are going in the first instance as far as the Djouf [al-Ǧawf], and there we shall take the circumstances into consideration before going farther. In any case, we think we shall be at Djeddah [Ǧiddah] towards the end of the year.’[124] What Huber would do next was still for him an open question. He did not regard himself as tied to Euting, and Euting's own aim was confined to recording inscriptions all the way to Madāʾin Ṣāliḥ and al-ʿUlā, at which point he would be ready to leave Arabia. Huber, as we know, was nursing more far-flung ambitions. In various letters he was still stating his aim to travel right into Naǧd, via Sudayr, al-Washm, Sadūs, Riyadh and beyond as far as Wādī al-Dawāsir, and from there to Naǧrān and even into Yemen as far as Aden. As time went by, he would continually adjust his plans according to the availability of funds and the political situation in central Arabia.[125] As will be seen, he was not destined to reach anywhere in Naǧd south of al-Qaṣīm. But it was a given that at some stage he and Euting would have to part company, and the most natural point for that to happen would be once they had reached Madāʾin Ṣāliḥ.

Up to the start of the Arabian journey, Huber had had understandable practical reasons for appearing to shun Euting, regardless of any personal antipathy towards the German that might by then have been brewing. But now that he had made so convincing a case to his ministry sponsors that he was travelling on his own, he would have to maintain the pretence. At the very least, in the inevitable event that the news would at some stage leak out, he would have to minimize Euting's presence. One medium over which he did have complete control was his diary. In his *Journal d'un voyage en Arabie, (1883–1884)*, published posthumously in 1891, he took the extreme measure of omitting all mention of Euting: there is not a single hint that he was travelling with a European companion. We do not know how he planned to explain this once he was back in Europe. As things turned out, he would never be called upon to do so, because he was fated not to return: he would be murdered by his guides at Rabigh, north of Ǧiddah, on 29 July 1884, four months after he and Euting had parted company.

---

[124] Ibid.

[125] On Huber's various travel plans in Arabia, see Appendix 4: Letter no. 2 dated 28 March 1882 to Maunoir; Letter no. 14 dated 25 June 1883 to Maunoir; Letter no. 19 dated 17 August 1883 to Weisgerber; Letter no. 21 dated 30 November 1883 to Maunoir; Letter no. 22 dated 20 June 1884 to the French Consulate in Baghdad; Letter no. 24 dated 6 July 1884 to Weisgerber.

But now, as they set off for Arabia, in addition to Huber's need to wish Euting away for political reasons, there are signs that on a personal level too all was not well between the two men.[126] Unfortunately for him, Huber was short of money again, having spent almost all of his 10,000 francs on expedition preparations. There was thus a strong financial incentive to stay with Euting, even though by now Huber might have been beginning to regret the association. Once their journey had begun, it is fairly clear that Huber felt little or no commitment to working together, as is shown by numerous instances in Euting's account of the 1883–84 journey. Huber's chagrin at having saddled himself with a fellow-traveller would culminate in his efforts at Ḥāʾil and later at al-ʿUlā to rid himself of Euting altogether, as described in what follows.

THE 1883–84 JOINT ARABIAN ITINERARY

Huber's account of the expedition through northern Arabia, *Journal d'un voyage en Arabie, (1883–1884)* (Paris 1891), opens with a terse account of his own desert trip to Palmyra, a prelude to the great Arabian adventure that was to follow.[127] The laconic recital of route data, lists of wells and other observations sets the tone for the remainder of the work. Brevity and discretion are the order of the day: the alert reader will begin to note the absence of any trace of Euting.

Huber returned to Damascus on 9 August, while Euting set off on a trip to Maʿarrah and Baʿalbak, returning four days later. Euting then stayed in Damascus until 31 August, when at last the time came to embark on the journey into Arabia. It is at this point, as he mounts his horse for the first day's march to Brāq, that he opens his published *Tagbuch einer Reise in Inner-Arabien.*[128] Huber, in line with his game-plan of semi-detachment from Euting, did not leave Damascus with him. Ten days before, on 21 August, he had gone ahead to ʿUrmān in order to check the most recent news from Nağd, which turned out to be far from auspicious for travellers because of ongoing Rashīdī–Saʿūdī raids and counter-raids. Even so, on his return to Damascus

[126] Appendix 12, Item no. 1, Letter dated 1 October from A. Sauval to the Minister of Public Education: 'When I received the first letter, dated 1 September 1883, I was very grieved to learn of annoyances having arisen in connexion with Euting, as he wrote.'
[127] Huber 1891: 1–15, 28 July– 9 August.
[128] Euting 1896 and 1914.

on the 27th, he went ahead regardless with final preparations and on 31 August, the day of Euting's departure, he sent the baggage on to ʿUrmān with Maḥmūd, a man from Maʿān in today's southern Jordan whom he had taken on as his assistant.[129] He himself hung back until 4 September before setting off for Brāq, where Euting was waiting for him at the fort.[130] Euting was perfectly happy to acknowledge Huber's logistical efforts:

> M. Huber has had to complete all kinds of preparations for our trip to Inner Arabia. His plan was to send our luggage ahead (my luggage, actually) straight to ʿOrmān by camel and to collect me at Fort Brāq once all the arrangements had been completed.[131]

Moving on to ʿUrmān, the party exchanged horses for camels and, on 7 September 1883, hurried to join a salt caravan making for Kāf, which they reached three days later. On 12 September their future guide, a Shammarī by the name of Ḥamūd al-Miqrād who had assisted Huber in 1880, arrived in Kāf from the south with two other men from Ḥāʾil. Huber already knew this man well from his previous journey.[132] Now he had been assigned to meet up with Huber by the Emir Muḥammad al-Rashīd but had been sent out too late to escort them from Damascus. Though it was both Huber and Euting who had collaborated in writing to the emir from Paris telling him of their plans and proposing Ḥamūd as guide,[133] Huber records that the party had been 'tous envoyé par l'emir pour *me* chercher à Damas', as if Euting did not exist – a further instance of the erasure of the German that Huber would maintain throughout his *Journal*.[134] Ḥamūd al-Miqrād had other errands to perform in Damascus, and Huber decided to accompany him back there to see whether the firearms he had been awaiting had arrived,[135]

---

129 Huber had hired Maḥmūd in Damascus: see notes 182, 183, 184, 185 and 207 below (pp. 55–6). See also Witkam, forthcoming/a, TS p. 9, note 41.

130 Huber 1891: 15–21.

131 Euting 1896: 15 (Chapter I, entry for 3 September 1883).

132 For Ḥamūd al-Ibrāhīm al-Miqrād in 1880, see p. 136 below, note 144.

133 Appendix 5, Letter no. 1 dated 10 April 1883 from Huber in Paris to Ḥamūd al-Miqrād, and Letter no. 2 of the same date from Huber to Muḥammad al-Rashīd. For Euting's collaboration in writing these letters in Arabic, see Appendix 5, Letter no. 4, paragraph 3.

134 Huber 1891: 24. Huber's notes on his round trip back to Damascus from 15 September to 1 October 1883 are in Huber 1891: 25–34.

135 Huber had promised to supply the Emir Muḥammad ibn Rashīd with four Gras rifles, the latest standard-issue firearms for the French army. See Appendix 4, Letters nos. 14, 15 and 17 dated 25 and 27 June 1883 and 13 July 1883 from Huber to Maunoir;

forcing Euting and Maḥmūd to kick their heels in Kāf for more than three weeks.

Reunited, the party left Kāf on 3 October to make the journey along Wādī al-Sirḥān to the historic oasis of al-Ǧawf, reaching Dūmat al-Ǧandal on 9 October.[136] Huber then went off on a lone reconnaissance of Sakākā, Qārā and al-Ṭuwayr while the saddle-sore Euting stayed in Dūmat al-Ǧandal as guest of Ibn Rashīd's jovial and hospitable governor, Ǧawhar.[137] On 14 October, the party embarked on Huber's second crossing of the great Nafūd sand desert, along the route well worn by previous European travellers,[138] and reached the little oasis of Ǧubbah on the 18th.[139]

Ǧabal Umm al-Silmān, which for millennia has sheltered Ǧubbah from the encroaching sands, provided Euting with his first taste of the richness of Arabia's ancient rock art and inscription sites. He and Huber spent the day recording as much as they could of its prolific drawings and graffiti, but did so independently of each other – the detached mode of investigation that came to typify their entire journey together.[140] This mode of proceeding could have had the advantage that for the most part they would not both have had to copy the same texts and would thus have been able to double their coverage. However, what actually happened was that in a very large number of cases they *did* copy the same texts, so that neither could claim the only record of a particular inscription – thus furnishing proof that by now both men were acting in a spirit of competition.

Passing the village of Qanāʾ and the eastern end of Ǧabal Aǧā, they reached Ḥāʾil on 21 October just as the skies darkened and a prolonged period of torrential rainfall set in. While they met the local notables and waited for permission from the emir to proceed westwards to Taymāʾ and Madāʾin

---

Letter no. 24 dated 6 July 1884 from Huber to Weisgerber; Appendix 5, Letters no. 1 dated April 1883 from Huber to Muḥammad ibn Rashīd; Appendix 6, Letters nos. 3 and 4 dated 7 and 16 July 1883 from Maunoir to the Minister of Public Education. The rifles did not reach Huber.

[136] Huber 1891: 42–9; Euting 1896, Chapter V.

[137] 10–11 October: Huber 1891: 42–8. Euting 1896: 130 (Chapter V, entry for 10 October 1883).

[138] Wallin (1845), Palgrave (1862), Guarmani (1864), and Wilfrid and Lady Anne Blunt (1879).

[139] For the crossing of the Nafūd and the visit to Ǧubbah, see Huber 1891: 49–60; Euting 1896: 141–53 Chapter VI, entries for 14–18 October 1883.

[140] See Huber 1891: 55–9 for Huber's examples, and Euting 1896: 137 and Notebook III, pp. 42r–45r for Euting's.

Ṣāliḥ, they set about exploring the locality, making a day trip to Ǧabal Samrā' (30 October) and two more extended joint excursions: first to ʿUqdah and the highest point of Ǧabal Aǧā (31 October – 3 November 1883); and then eastwards to Ǧildiyyah and Baqʿā' (9–16 November 1883). Ǧabal Ǧildiyyah, which Huber had visited in 1880, was confirmed as another rich source of ancient graffiti. As things turned out, they were to be detained in Ḥā'il for more than three months until the emir, who was engaged in raiding and campaigning against Riyadh and its tribal allies, judged conditions safe enough for them to set out. Euting by this time was seething with impatience to move on. He and Huber were sharing a house but, although it is never explicitly stated, Euting's diary conveys the impression that they preferred to avoid each other. After the trip to Ǧildiyyah and Baqʿā',[141] Euting spent much of the rest of the time in solo encounters with local people, going on solitary rambles outside the city, sketching, and making lone, daredevil attempts to find ibex among the crags of Ǧabal Aǧā. One would have expected two Europeans far from home to celebrate Christmas and New Year's Day together, but this they contrived not to do. Huber's Catholic background may have helped to intensify his alienation from the Protestant Euting, though this is nowhere mentioned.

As January 1884 wore on, they were able to start preparations to leave the waterlogged town and, on the 23rd, Huber, Euting, their assistant Maḥmūd and guide Ḥaylān rode off on four camels south-westwards towards Ǧabal Aǧā and the village of Mawqaq. From there they first made an excursion south-eastwards to Ǧabal Sarrā',[142] the rich site of ancient graffiti visited by Huber in 1880, before retracing their steps and turning westwards to skirt the southern fringe of the Great Nafūd towards Taymā'. Having reached Ǧabal Mismā', they followed a route parallel with and to the south of that followed by Huber in October–November 1880.[143] Euting was of course chiefly intent on fulfilling his ambition to record the Nabataean inscriptions at Madā'in Ṣāliḥ and the pre-Islamic inscriptions at Taymā',[144] but the discovery and

[141] Huber 1884b: 502–4; 1891: 78–103; Euting 1896: 227–40 (Chapter VIII, entries for 9–16 November 1883).

[142] Huber 1891: 220–4; Euting 1914: 114–17 (Chapter X, entries for 27–28 January 1884). See note 52 above.

[143] Huber 1884b: folding map; 504–11.

[144] See, for example Appendix 10, Euting's Letter no. 1 dated 21 November 1884 to Philippe Berger, and Letter no. 2 dated 2 February 1885 to Charles Clermont-Ganneau; Euting 1914: 154–61, 216 (Chapter XI, entries for 16–18 February 1884; Chapter XIV, entry for 15 March 1884).

recording of the five very rich sites of pre-Islamic inscriptions and graffiti in Ancient North Arabian scripts along this Ḥāʾil–Taymā leg of their journey was also a significant achievement of this joint expedition.

They reached Taymāʾ on 15 February 1884. This oasis, mentioned in cuneiform inscriptions and the Bible, was already known to be of great antiquity. Taymāʾ had been visited by Wallin in 1848, Guarmani in 1864 and Doughty in 1877, and Huber himself had passed through it in November 1880,[145] but Euting was the first professional Semitic epigraphist to visit it, and he made a number of important discoveries of Aramaic and Nabataean inscriptions. His story of how the celebrated Taymāʾ Stele was discovered, and an account of the imbroglio that ensued, are presented below.

The two men left Taymāʾ on 21 February for a two-week return trip to Tabūk, arranged while they were in Ḥāʾil. This excursion was chiefly of interest to Huber for reasons of geography and mapping, and epigraphic discoveries were minimal. Returning to Taymāʾ on 6 March, they made preparations to depart for Euting's main goal, Madāʾin Ṣāliḥ and al-ʿUlā, and left on the 13th, arriving two days later. Euting set about copying and making squeezes of many of the pre-Islamic inscriptions at al-ʿUlā and al-Khuraybah (ancient Dadan).

Here they parted company, not once but twice: first at al-ʿUlā on 19 March 1884 and, for the last time, on 27 March at Madāʾin Ṣāliḥ. There, with Huber finally gone, Euting achieved his main goal when he managed to record almost all the Nabataean tomb inscriptions. His rapid publication of these in 1885[146] would consolidate his reputation, and also annoy the French, who felt that Huber's prior claim had been perfidiously pre-empted.[147] On 30 March, his work done, Euting and four Balī tribesmen set off from al-ʿUlāʾ for the Red Sea coast at al-Wağh, and on the first night out he very nearly came to the same sticky end at the hands of brigands as would befall Huber four months later. He was lucky to reach al-Wağh in safety on 5 April 1884, his Arabian journey having covered some 1,750 kilometres. There, instead

[145] For Huber's visit in 1880, see below pp. 188–92. See also Wallin 1850: 330–4; Guarmani 1938: 23–24, 79–81; Doughty 1936 i: 328–44, 566–88; Huber 1884b: 511–14.

[146] Euting 1885a.

[147] Hogarth 1904: 281, quoting a letter from Renan to Nöldeke: Huber had been 'deprived of the fruits of his labours by a series of circumstances that, for my part, I find extremely regrettable'. See also note 170 below.

of going to Ǧiddah to collect his mail and meet up with Huber again,[148] he boarded a dhow coasting northwards to al-Dumayghah before crossing the Red Sea to the Egyptian port of al-Quṣayr. From al-Quṣayr, a five-day journey on camelback brought him to the Nile at Qena, where he boarded a train to Cairo. By June he was in Jerusalem where, in fulfilment of Huber's fears, he dispatched a letter on 12 June to Nöldeke containing his squeeze and transcription of the Taymāʾ Stele. His route home to Strasbourg, which he reached in August 1884, took him via Beirut and Smyrna to Athens and Patras and then through Italy.[149]

HUBER AND EUTING: A FRAUGHT RELATIONSHIP

Euting's frightening experience on the way to al-Wağh may help to explain his hurried departure from Arabia. However, his overriding desire was to get to work arranging the publication of the Taymāʾ Stele and the Nabataean inscriptions from Madāʾin Ṣāliḥ before the French could do so.[150] There is no question that beneath Euting's frequent expressions of friendship and concern for Huber, there ran an undercurrent of fierce competition.

Nor can any discussion of the two men's relationship sidestep the omission by Huber, in his *Journal d'un voyage en Arabie (1883–1884)* (Huber 1891), of even a hint at the existence of a European companion. This resolute effacement is all the more bizarre given the extent and detail of

[148] See Pearson 1993: 122 for the unrealized plan for Euting to go to Ǧiddah. Euting's hurried and risky journey to al-Wağh and then Egypt in April 1884 came to the ears of the British consul in Ǧiddah, Thomas Jago, in September: 'Professor Euting, a Prussian "savant" who visited Nejd and who finally left Haïl last spring on his return to Europe, was attacked by bedouins near Ala [al-ʿUlā], a place about half-way [*sic*] between Haïl and El Wedj on the Red Sea. By killing three [*sic*] with his revolver he escaped and arrived safely at El Wedj and thence by dow to Egypt.' Huber, who had been interviewed by Jago, had evidently said nothing to him about his association with Euting. (Jago to Lord Granville, letter dated 3 September 1884: Burdett 2013 iii: 422–3.) See also Euting's account: Euting 1914: 265–84.

[149] Pearson 1993: 14; Pfullmann 1993: 150–1.

[150] Euting, letter dated 10 April 1884 to Nöldeke from al-Wağh: 'If I send you a tentative drawing [of the Taymāʾ Stele], please would you kindly place it before the Berlin Academy so that the French don't get in first.' See also Euting, letter dated 12 June 1884 to Nöldeke from Jerusalem: 'Do not hesitate to publish it [drawing and text of the Taymāʾ Stele] in the monthly report of the Berlin Academy so that the French do not get in ahead of us, because Huber will by now also have sent off his squeeze from Ǧiddah.' (Euting Archiv, Tübingen, Md 782 A 65). For Nöldeke's publication of the Taymāʾ Stele, see Nöldeke 1884.

Huber's journal, an unwieldy tome running to some 778 printed pages, as well as an Atlas of maps and sketches. Huber's anxiety not to be publicly associated with Euting is not quite adequate on its own to explain why he so painstakingly avoided all mention of him in his private travel diary, because he must have known that the whole story would come out as soon as Euting returned to Europe. For this omission, therefore, additional personal and psychological reasons have to be sought.

Granted, Huber's *Journal* is a very different work from both Euting's published *Tagbuch* and also the unpublished notebooks on which the *Tagbuch* is so closely based.[151] Huber's *Journal*, as published, purports to be a faithful rendering of his original notes with no editorial enhancement at all, and is as dry as dust by comparison with the anecdotal style of Euting's diary. The reader has to negotiate multitudinous lists of compass bearings, barometric readings, local place names, word lists, topographical features, and the durations, no matter how short, of journey stages measured to the nearest minute. Just occasionally one is treated to a more extended account of local events: meetings with the Emir Muḥammad al-Rashīd, Ḥamūd al-ʿUbayd and other local notables are described, and Arab guides and companions such as Ḥamūd al-Miqrād crop up in the daily record. He records his bouts of sickness but otherwise there is almost no personal reaction, whether humorous or negative, to the unforeseen dangers, irritations, delays and comic reversals inherent in desert travel. It is a meticulous repository of data testifying to a courageous and self-disciplined author stoically fixated on his goals.[152] In short, it is the opposite of Euting's lively, coherent, personalized and sometimes emotional narrative. Its plain, factual and fastidious presentation would tempt the reader to accept it as the whole truth and nothing but the truth, were it not for the colossal omission by the Frenchman of any mention of his German counterpart.

Having allowed himself to be drawn into a joint expedition, Huber maintained his deceptions about Euting's participation to the end. From Ǧiddah on 6 July 1884, just three weeks before his murder, he wrote to his friend Weisgerber:

[151] Euting's original notebooks and sketchbooks: Euting Archiv, Tübingen University Library, Md 676. They can be consulted online at http://idb.ub.uni-tuebingen.de/diglit/Md676.

[152] Huber's meticulousness, self-confidence and courage are admirably summarized in Pearson 1993: 44–7.

> You will be happy to hear that Euting succeeded in reaching the town of Ḥāʾil, but that once there I was able, with the help of the emir, to make him go off towards [*le faire filer par*] the west. He must have taken ship in al-Waǧh on the Red Sea. I knew he was intending to call in at Ǧiddah, to where he had his mail forwarded, but on my arrival here I found that he had not shown up. I was unable to prevent him reaching Ḥāʾil, any more than I could have prevented anyone else! Please could you pass this on to those entitled to know. But once arrived, I could do no more than send him onwards, and that was not easy to accomplish, as he was not commissioned by France and had very different means at his disposal from mine.[153]

Huber's wording is vague, doubtless by design: his use of the verbal phrase *faire filer par* ('to make go off towards') is clearly intended to convey the impression to his friend, and to people back in France, that he had not made the journey westwards from Ḥāʾil in the company of Euting. This is a blatant falsehood transcending mere omission: proof is provided by the adjacent graffiti signatures that the two men scratched on a rock at Ǧabal Mismāʾ, and in any case it is incontrovertibly clear from Euting's diary that the two men travelled together from Ḥāʾil, via Taymāʾ, to Madāʾin Ṣāliḥ and al-ʿUlā. Huber must have resorted to the deceit in order to reinforce the fiction back home that he was travelling alone. If so, it was effective, as Renan for example still believed it in 1885 and would use it against Euting.[154]

Huber's lack of a collaborative streak and need to be in sole charge suited Euting up to a point, as he readily acquiesced in it where practical matters were concerned. Though he was perfectly happy to concede that he had handed over all travel arrangements to the Frenchman, however, that did not mean that he regarded himself as the subordinate partner in the enterprise. Euting makes his sense of seniority very clear from the start with this firm statement in the Preface to Vol. I of his *Tagbuch*:

> Even though he was travelling under official instructions from the French government, and had indeed been assigned various funds

[153] Appendix 4, Letter no. 24 dated 6 July 1884, Huber to Weisgerber from Ǧiddah.

[154] Appendix 11: Letter no. 1 dated 8 July 1885 from Renan to Euting. For a photograph by Florent Égal of Huber and Euting's adjacent graffiti signatures at Ǧabal Mismāʾ, see Égal 2018: 1303, and this volume, Illustration no. 5.

> for this purpose, he [Huber] was nevertheless my guest from Strasbourg onwards (22 May 1883) until we parted amicably on 19 March 1884 at el-ʿÖla.[155]

The absence of any proper written agreement between the two men setting out their respective roles, rights and responsibilities means that neither could claim seniority as the rightful expedition leader.[156] The only clue we have relates to Huber's conception of their formal relationship, as set out in the letter quoted above (p. 31) from Huber in Strasbourg to Ernest Renan on 8 April 1883, stating that Euting 'has no official assignment'.[157] Whether Euting would have agreed that he had no official assignment from his own government is a moot point: he had after all received ample support from official German sources. The other point to note is the confirmation that Euting would be entitled to a single inscription, as he would later claim. But there appears to have been no explicit agreement as to which of the two men was the expedition leader or senior partner.

As events unfolded, it boiled down to personalities, and a complex picture emerges. In practice, Euting may have assumed his own precedence, but the tone of Huber's *Journal* as well as various instances in Euting's *Tagbuch* suggest that it was the confident and self-reliant Huber, with his command of colloquial Arabic, who was really the dominant personality. It was Huber who got on better with their bedouin guides and issued their instructions, who made the decisions as to when they should move on and by what route, and who took the lead in negotiations with local shaykhs and governors.[158] In particular, Huber enjoyed much closer relations than Euting with the Emir Muḥammad al-Rashīd, on whose protection they depended on the entire route between al-Ǧawf and al-ʿUlā. He also got on very well with Ḥamūd al-ʿUbayd, the next most powerful figure in Ḥāʾil. Between the latter and Euting, by contrast, a festering mutual detestation developed. Huber, by his own account, was held in warm fraternal regard by the emir, who once told him: 'You are one of us; we will protect you as we would

[155] Euting 1896: v–vi (Preface to Vol. I of the *Tagbuch*).
[156] Pearson 1993: 12.
[157] Appendix 7, Letter no. 2 dated 8 April 1883 from Huber to Renan.
[158] See e.g. Euting 1896: 113 (Chapter IV, entry for 3 October 1883); Euting 1914: 105–6 (Chapter IX, entry for 22 January 1884); Pearson 1993: 99–103. For Huber's *de facto* leadership role, linguistic competence and good relations with guides, see Pearson 1993: 86–9, 102–6, 138.

ourselves; I have never heard anything but good about you; whenever you return you will be welcomed like my brother.'[159] It is certainly the case that Huber spent much more time than Euting in the Qaṣr hobnobbing with the emir and his court, and seems to have felt free to call in there whenever he pleased without waiting to be summoned for an audience. Important matters such as desert politics and the safest routes were discussed with Huber rather than Euting, and Huber took the initiative in inviting distinguished guests, such as the emir of Buraydah, to their house.[160] Even so, there is no sign that Euting was actually unpopular with the Emir Muḥammad, with whom he appears to have been on cordial enough terms and who, as will be seen below, was concerned to forewarn him of Huber's machinations against him.

The sociable and spontaneous Euting revelled in mixing with merchants, craftsmen and the general populace in Ḥāʾil, sketching people and places, dressing up and devising entertainments, while there are hints that the serious-minded Huber disapproved of Euting's antics and confined himself to medical practice and data collection. Huber was careful to respect local manners and customs, and cultivated contacts that he thought would be useful.[161] His only purely social relationship seems to have been with ʿAbdullah al-Muslimānī, an engaging Baghdadi Jew who had settled in Ḥāʾil and converted to Islam, with whom he had made friends on his first journey. Wisely enough, in view of Huber's more diplomatic approach and nexus of useful contacts, Euting seems to have been content to defer to his companion in dealings with their Arab hosts.

The trusting side of Euting's nature predisposed him to maintain his faith in Huber even when the evidence that the Frenchman was trying to get rid of him seems obvious, at least to the reader of the published *Tagbuch*. Euting showed genuine concern for Huber's wellbeing, and generously drew many graffiti and maps in Huber's journals. He also deferred to Huber when it came to sharing out the inscriptions collected on the journey, insisting in retrospect on his claim to no more than a single item of his choice – this would turn out to be the Taymāʾ Stele – and raising no objection to Huber having all the others for France, as stipulated by the latter's agreement with the AIBL.

[159] Huber 1891: 634 (7 May 1884).
[160] Pearson 1993: 68–9; 119 for Huber's greater popularity among the Arabs.
[161] Pearson 1993: 71–3; Huber's greater influence at Taymāʾ: Pearson 1993: 103–5; Euting enjoys mixing with the common people at Taymāʾ: Pearson 1993: 97.

As against all such indications of apparent subordination to Huber, Euting was in much the stronger financial position. Euting's sponsors, as seen above, had put up considerably more money than Huber's. Furthermore, Huber's ministry funds arrived only after the pair had reached Damascus; Euting had thus to foot all expenses between May and August 1883, as they made their way via Cairo and Beirut to Damascus and Palmyra.[162] Even in Damascus, Huber was initially planning to take just half of the 10,000 francs due from the ministry, agreeing with Euting that the remainder would be made available only when they reached Ǧiddah, though in the event he was unable to arrange for the money to be sent there.[163] Again, Euting brought along a large consignment of twenty-four valuable firearms, generously donated by King Karl of Württemberg, as gifts for the Emir Muḥammad, whereas Huber had little comparable largesse to dispense. What is certain is that Huber was plagued by worries about his lack of funds throughout his travels, and was, in a financial sense at least, Euting's dependent on this expedition.

Euting records various instances where Huber was not just acting independently of him but actively trying to place obstacles in his way, and even on two occasions to get rid of him. He was alerted to the first attempt, in Ḥāʾil on 21 January, by the emir himself, who seems to have felt uneasy that Huber was not playing fair:

> In the evening, the Emir summoned me via a slave, who expressly said that no one else should come along. He was alone in the reception hall with Ḥamūd al-ʿUbayd, Sulaymān and Ṣāliḥ al-Rakhīṣ. After the coffee had been prepared, … the chief began to explain that Huber was trying to reach el-Ḥegr and el-ʿÖla without me, and that I ought to be on my guard. … I replied to the chief, in a state of great agitation, that I could not understand what he meant. Thinking that I had not understood the sense of the Arabic words, Ḥamūd repeated or paraphrased what the chief had just said. I responded:
>
> 'I have understood perfectly what you told me, but I cannot believe it! How could Huber possibly entertain such an idea? Have

[162] Huber 1891: 15; Pearson 1993: 12–13.

[163] Pearson 1993: 13. But see Appendix 4, Letter no. 18 dated 19 July 1883 from Huber to Maunoir, stating that arrangements could not be made for delivery to Ǧiddah.

> I not embarked on this whole trip with him with the sole aim of visiting those places? Has he not been my travelling companion, indeed my guest, from the very beginning? That's how he'll remain until the end!'
>
> The chief shrugged his shoulders. I left the castle in a bad temper.[164]

On Euting's return to their house, Huber, allegedly pale with trepidation, asked him what the chief had wanted. Euting, employing considerable delicacy, told him exactly what had been said but stressed that the Qaṣr would not succeed in sowing suspicion and discord between them. Either it was beyond him to suspect Huber of skulduggery, or else he was sending a subtle signal to the Frenchman that he knew precisely what he was up to.

Having thus tried without success to prevent Euting journeying with him from Ḥāʾil to Madāʾin Ṣāliḥ and al-ʿUlā, Huber went on to hamper his efforts to make squeezes of inscriptions at al-ʿUlā by insisting that their eight-metre ladder be left at Madāʾin Ṣāliḥ.[165] A further suspicion must be that Huber was planning to return to Madāʾin Ṣāliḥ before Euting, so that he could use the ladder to steal a march in recording the Nabataean inscriptions himself – as indeed turned out to be the case.

Once they reached al-ʿUlā, Huber suddenly announced that Euting would not be able to return to Ḥāʾil, on the grounds that he would be *persona non grata* there.[166] It was true that Euting was *persona non grata* with Ḥamūd al-

---

164 See Euting 1914: 104–5 (Chapter IX, entry for 21 January 1884). In his manuscript diary for this date Euting states specifically that he suspected only Ḥamūd al-ʿUbayd of plotting to get rid of him (Pearson 1993: 83 note 53). See also the entry for 27 December 1883 (Euting 1914: 74), when Euting first expresses suspicion about a plot to get him to leave.

165 On the ladder, see Euting 1914: 217, 228, 234, 242 (Chapter XIV, entries for 16 March 1884; 18 March 1884; 20 March 1884; and 25 March 1884). Pearson (1993: 130) casts suspicion on Huber's motive in leaving the ladder at Madāʾin Ṣāliḥ.

166 See Euting 1914: 222–3 (Chapter XIV, entry for 16 March 1884). Huber's announcement is described as unexpected in both Euting's handwritten diary and his published *Tagbuch*. However, in his letter to Nöldeke from al-Wağh dated 10 April 1884 (Euting Archiv, Tübingen University, Correspondence, Md 782 A 65), Euting actually states that they parted by agreement and at his suggestion. He seems to have agreed to it quickly enough, and he was confident at that time that the Taymāʾ Stele would be delivered by the Emir Muḥammad al-Rashīd to Baghdad for onward transport to Europe, though he does not specify whether Germany or France. Pearson (1993: 120–6) usefully analyses the discrepancies in Euting's various accounts of the decision to separate from Huber: the handwritten diary; the published *Tagbuch*;

ʿUbayd, but he had still been expecting to return to Ḥāʾil because the bulk of his luggage had been left there. The claim that he would not be able to return was very possibly spurious and, at such a distance from the Shammar capital, Huber must have calculated that Euting had no way of verifying it. If this was true, Euting asks, then why on earth had Huber not told him about it before, in Ḥāʾil? But he quickly accepted the situation, attributing it to his poor personal relations with Ḥamūd. He was either determined not to think the worst of his companion, or else he was not so sorry to part company. It would, after all, give him an early opportunity to return to Europe and see to the urgent publication of his finds.

Huber next told Euting that he was planning to go via Khaybar and past al-Madīnah to Ǧiddah. He said that Euting should copy the Madāʾin Ṣāliḥ inscriptions, return to al-ʿUlā and then go on to al-Wağh, from where he would be able to find a steamboat for Ǧiddah (where he would meet Huber again), or else return directly to Beirut via Suez; Huber himself would travel back from Ǧiddah to Ḥāʾil, and thence to Damascus via Iraq.[167] Huber's ensuing movements did not follow this plan, as will emerge below. He was prone to changing his plans at short notice in response to circumstances, but at this juncture one does wonder whether he was deliberately trying to obfuscate his intentions.

The two men bade each other farewell on 19 March. Though by now Euting was aware that Huber was going back to Madāʾin Ṣāliḥ for a short visit, he was not expecting to see him again, and so was surprised when he himself returned to Madāʾin Ṣāliḥ six days later (on 25 March) and found Huber still there, using the ladder and assiduously making his own squeezes of the Nabataean inscriptions.[168] Huber had completed the job and was ready to leave, making not for Ǧiddah but for Ḥāʾil. Doughty's squeezes and copies of twenty out of the thirty-eight inscriptions had just been published by the AIBL (Doughty 1884), though Huber may not have known this and was in any case keen to establish French priority over the Germans in the publication of new squeezes of them. However, returning to Ḥāʾil would delay this, and he was not able to send his notebooks and the

his letter from al-Wağh of 10 April 1884 to Nöldeke; and his report of 17 November 1886 to 'Euer Durchlaucht'/Your Serene Highness.

[167] Euting 1914: 223 (Chapter XIV, entry for 16 March 1884).

[168] Huber records his work at Madāʾin Ṣāliḥ in impressive detail (Huber 1891: 409–44).

remainder of his squeezes to Renan in Paris until 20 June from Ğiddah.[169] His anxiety about Euting's head start is evident from a letter he wrote to Renan from Ḥā'il on 18 April 1884:

> It is all the more regrettable that Dr Euting has made the same squeezes, and from al-ʿUlā has taken himself off to al-Wağh, from where he will return to Europe.

And:

> I hope nonetheless that nobody will contest the rights of priority [stemming from] my first expedition.[170]

It is clear from this that the matter of who should have the right of first publication of the Taymā' Stele and squeezes of the Nabataean inscriptions from Madā'in Ṣāliḥ had not been settled, or perhaps even discussed, by the two men. Huber was absolutely certain that the entitlement was his, based on his previous travels in the region and his firm sense that the expedition was an official French enterprise, and that Euting was tagging along as a mere 'travelling companion';[171]

---

[169] See Euting 1914: 246–56 (Chapter XIV, entry for 25 March 1884). For Huber sending his squeezes and diaries to Paris from Ğiddah on 20 June 1884, see Huber 1884c; 1891: 753, entry for 22–27 June; Pearson 1993: 124–5, 131–2. Readings of ten new inscriptions from Madā'in Ṣāliḥ, which Doughty had not been able to record, were published from Huber's squeezes for the AIBL late in 1884 by Philippe Berger. He noted, however, that Huber's squeezes 'were greatly inferior to Doughty's and it has been almost impossible to decipher the inscriptions from these impressions': 'Les estampages de M. Huber sont très inférieurs à ceux de M. Doughty, et il eût été presque impossible avec ses empreintes d'établir le déchiffrement' (Berger 1884: 377). Judging from the two squeezes of which photographs were published in the article, no. 32 (pls I–II, = Healey 1993, H 20) and 34 (pl. III, = Healey 1993: H 29), this is perhaps a slightly harsh judgement, but it is possible that these were the best of them. (MCAM/WF)

[170] Pearson 1993: 124–5 quotes Huber's letter to Renan dated 18 April 1884 (Nachlass Dillmann 132): 'Tout cela est d'autant plus regrettable que le Dr Euting a pris les mêmes estampages, et de El 'Ala s'est rendu à El Ouegeh dans la Mer Rouge, d'oû il se rendra en Europe par Geddah'; and: 'J'espère néanmoins que personne ne me contestera les droits de priorité de ma première mission.' Huber does not mention this letter on 18 April in his *Journal*. According to Pearson (1993: 131–2), it was one of two that Huber wrote to Renan from Ḥā'il, enclosing with both of them copies and squeezes of various inscriptions from Taymā' and Madā'in Ṣāliḥ. Pearson (1993: 131–2, 134 n. 34, 135 n. 63) gives no date or reference for Huber's second letter from Ḥā'il, but Huber's *Journal* (1891: 593) does record one sent on 27 April 1884. It is probable that Huber wrote just a single letter to Renan, dated 18 April 1884, but had to wait until 27 April for a courier to take it to Ğiddah; hence the confusion.

[171] Appendix 11, Letter no. 1 dated 8 July 1885 from Renan to Euting.

that being so, he was correct to be suspicious of Euting's intentions. Euting, as the professional epigraphist and the man who had contributed most of the funds, felt the priority to be rightfully his, and seems to have felt no qualms about pursuing first publication himself. As for the expedition being officially French, Euting could have argued with equal force that it had the backing of the King of Württemberg and so was officially German too – though we have no evidence yet that he ever actually put forward that argument.

Hence both men had reason to be suspicious of one another. As Helen Pearson has convincingly shown, instances of surface cordiality and co-operation mask the fact that they were really 'silent adversaries'.[172] But she argues cogently that, of the two, Huber was the one guiltier of deceit, particularly in relation to his claim to the Taymāʾ Stele.[173] Euting emerges as the more open and honest of the two men, a certain innocent streak in his nature rendering him less prone to suspicion. In his handwritten diary, he appears temperamentally resistant to thinking the worst of Huber and persisted, at least during the course of the journey, in suspending his judgement of Huber's behaviour, prey though he must have been to niggling doubts. Such doubts rarely surface explicitly in his diary, the most overt being the plaintive comment in his entry for 27 December 1883: 'There seems to be some kind of plot afoot to make me leave the country on my own and to prevent me visiting al-Ḥijr and al-ʿUlā.'[174]

Even though Euting later came to accept that his companion had made serious efforts to undermine him that far eclipsed any minor aggravations, during the journey itself he refrained from fierce adverse comment in his notebooks. It can be argued that Euting pulls his punches even in the published version of the *Tagbuch*, perhaps in the light of Huber's untimely demise, and that it is Littmann's editorial interventions in Vol. II that really play up Huber's deviousness. An awareness that he himself had very nearly suffered the same fate as Huber may have called forth Euting's charitable instincts. Another factor may have been a reluctance on Euting's part to exacerbate Franco-German relations, especially in the aftermath of the diplomatic incident surrounding the Taymāʾ Stele, and to jeopardize his own friendly relations with colleagues at the AIBL, in particular Ernest Renan and Philippe Berger.

---

[172] Pearson 1993: 129.
[173] Pearson 1993: 145–6.
[174] See Euting 1914: 74 (Chapter IX, entry for 27 December 1883).

Huber, by contrast, eventually proved unable to bottle up his animosity towards Euting. In his last personal letter to Weisgerber, he finally let indiscretion get the better of him and allowed his real feelings to erupt: 'At last he [Euting] is far away, may the devil break his neck for the annoyances he has caused me.'[175]

Whatever hopes Euting and his patrons might have entertained for a fruitful Franco-German collaboration in Arabia had gone sadly unrealized.[176] The explanation must be twofold. First was the Franco-German political context to Euting and Huber's lives, which inevitably did much to poison the relationship between the two men. The second was Huber's deep-seated psychological reluctance to be associated with any partner in his great Arabian enterprise. The irresistible conclusion is not only that Huber was inwardly boiling with political resentment and bent on claiming as much as he could for France, but also that he was possessed to an extreme degree by classic 'explorer's syndrome': the ambition of the pioneer in unknown lands to claim 'firsts' for himself.[177] Differences of class, temperament, scholarly attainment and religious affiliation would merely have served to accentuate these fundamental tensions between the two men.

Huber's final Arabian travels and death in the Ḥiǧāz, 1884

Having finally parted company with Euting at Madāʾin Ṣāliḥ on 27 March 1884, Huber was now truly his own master. But so far from heading to Ǧiddah via Khaybar, as he had at first told Euting he would, he made his way back to Ḥāʾil by a route he had not previously mentioned.

He first headed north to Qalʿat Dār al-Ḥamrāʾ, the fine pilgrim fort on the route from Damascus situated roughly halfway between Madāʾin Ṣāliḥ and Qalʿat al-Muʿaẓẓam. Having searched for inscriptions in the area north of the fort, he turned east and made a rapid transit towards Ḥāʾil, following a direct line passing south of Taymāʾ, which he did not revisit. He was making for Ǧabal Mismāʾ along a route parallel to the one he had taken with Euting, past Ǧabal Kabad/Ḥalwān and Ǧabal ʿIrnān. From the Mismāʾ area he followed

175 Appendix 4, Letter no. 24 dated 6 July 1884 from Huber in Ǧiddah to Weisgerber.

176 Pfullmann 1993: 149; Pearson 1993: 141–3.

177 Pearson 1993: 46. For 19th-century examples of explorer's syndrome, compare for example the quarrel between James Silk Buckingham and William Bankes (Boyer 2017), and the famous row between Richard Burton and John Hanning Speke over the true source of the Nile.

a course very similar to that of his first journey in 1880, along the southern fringe of the Nafūd to the little oasis of al-Ṭuwayyah and then Ǧabal al-Raʿīlah, and reached Ḥāʾil on 7 April.[178]

His first thought on arrival was to send into the desert to recover the camel that was to carry 'la stèle du roi Šazab' from Taymāʾ. Then, settling back into his 'belle maison' in Ḥāʾil, he set about updating his journal.[179] On 18 April, as noted above, he wrote a letter to Renan enclosing copies and squeezes of inscriptions he had recorded at Taymāʾ and Madāʾin Ṣāliḥ, decrying the fact that Euting had made squeezes of the same texts, and insisting on his prior right to them all.[180]

On 19 April, his guide Nuʿmān brought in the camel that was 'to have the honour of going to Taymāʾ' to collect what he persistently calls the 'Phoenician Stele', and on 22 April all was ready for the expedition.[181] His assistant Maḥmūd set off with Nuʿmān on two camels; one was to carry the Stele back while the two men took turns to drive it on foot.[182]

The capable Maḥmūd deserves a place in the fertile corner of subaltern studies devoted to those indigenous individuals who served European explorers so well and who have gone undeservedly unsung in histories of exploration. A native of Maʿān, Maḥmūd was taken on at the start of the 1883–84 journey by Huber, who called him 'mon majordome' or steward. Euting refers to him throughout as a 'servant', which does him scant justice; he turned out to be a highly able assistant comparable to Palgrave's

---

178 For Huber's journey from Madāʾin Ṣāliḥ to Ḥāʾil, see Huber 1891: 451–550; Atlas flles 9, 10 and 11.

179 Huber 1891: 550.

180 Huber in his letter to Renan dated 18 April 1884 (Nachlass Dillmann 132): see note 170 above. See also Pearson 1993: 65, 82 note 25, 124–5, 131–2.

181 The fact that Huber continued to call the Taymāʾ Stele 'Phoenician' is very curious. Euting on first seeing it had instantly thought it to be Phoenician, but realized the next day that it was Aramaic as soon as he started to study it: see Appendix 10, Letter no. 4 dated 1 August 1885 to Philippe Berger. Euting's handwritten diary confirms this (Notebook V, p. 7v). See also Euting 1914: 157–8 (Chapter XI, entry for 17 February 1884). He must have told Huber, especially since he agreed to copy it into Huber's notebook (ibid., Chapter XI, entry for 19 February 1884), but Huber preferred the story that it was Phoenician: see Appendix 4, notes 102, 103 and 106. (MCAM/WF)

182 Huber 1891: 165, 583, 587. On Maḥmūd, see for example Euting 1914, Chapter IX, entries for 18 and 19 November 1883, 6, 14, 16, 27 and 29 December 1883, and 2, 3, 6, 9, 15, 17 and 21 January 1884. See also Witkam (forthcoming/a: TS p. 9, note 41) on Maḥmūd being far more than a servant and more akin to an able assistant. (MCAM/WF)

Barakat. Judging from the Arabic of the letter he wrote to Jacques Félix de Lostalot-Bachoué, the French vice-consul in Ǧiddah, declaring his willingness to come to Ǧiddah to make a statement about Huber's murder, he was a literate and educated man, and he also knew French.[183] He had served for seven pilgrimages as secretary to Muḥammad Saʿīd Pāshā, the Syrian *Amīr al-Ḥaǧǧ* or commander of the annual pilgrim caravan from Damascus, and had also worked with the pasha's two predecessors. Euting's *Tagbuch* abounds with references to Maḥmūd's secretarial functions for both travellers and to his skills as cook and barber.[184] He proved invaluable, to the extent of taking on the responsibility of fetching the Taymāʾ Stele to Ḥāʾil in May 1884 and even recording inscriptions en route. Unlike Euting, he does get various mentions in Huber's *Journal*, though perhaps not as many as he deserves.[185] He caused trouble only when he went on strike for more pay in Ḥāʾil on the grounds that Huber had not told him in Damascus that he would be serving two masters rather than one,[186] and also when on occasion he refused to serve Euting, whom he seems to have come to resent. He appears to have been wholly loyal to Huber, though as the only witness to his master's murder on 29 July 1884 he fell under suspicion of complicity, as related below.

On 27 April, Huber sent couriers to Ǧiddah with his letter to Renan enclosing squeezes, and another to the French vice-consul there, de Lostalot. His letter to de Lostalot does not appear to have survived, nor does Huber explain in the *Journal* what it was about. Probably it was to alert the vice-consul to the arrangements he was making to send the inscriptions to France; and to inform him that he intended to travel to Ǧiddah to collect his correspondence forwarded there from Damascus and France, as well as

[183] Maḥmūd's letter is quoted in Witkam forthcoming/a: TS Appendix 1. A photographic portrait of Maḥmūd by Snouck Hurgronje taken in the courtyard of the Dutch consulate in Jeddah on 11 October 1884 is held in MS Leiden Or. 12.288 P (Nos. 6 and 15): see Illustration no. 3 in this volume. For Maḥmūd's knowledge of French, see Euting 1914: 86, footnote (Chapter IX, entry for 3 January 1884).

[184] Euting 1914: 41, 56–7, 59, 75, 101, 225–6. Maḥmūd's work as a cook, kitchen help and barber is documented in Euting 1914: 80–2, 93, 114, 125, 127, 129, 162, 176, 202 and 204. He dictates poetry about Taymāʾ in Euting 1914: 203, and can be a jolly travel companion (Euting 1896: 80; 1914: 184; Witkam (forthcoming/a: TS p. 9, note 41).

[185] Maḥmūd is mentioned a dozen or so times in Huber's *Journal* (See e.g. Huber 1891: 61, 165, 248, 288, 318, 321–2, 349, 368, 587, 592, 631, 641, 672, and 747–9).

[186] Euting 1914: 9–10 (Chapter IX, entry for 18 November 1883).

the consignment of rifles that he wanted to take back to Ḥā'il as a gift for the emir.[187]

While his men were away, Huber had decided to make an excursion to the wells of al-Ṣulayliyyah, south-east of Ḥā'il towards al-Qaṣīm. He set off on 28 April heading for Ǧabal Salma, and reached the wells on 1 May. He seems to have decided on this trip because he had heard there were inscriptions, but all he found was a single line of signs.[188] He returned by a more westerly route, via Ǧabal Rummān,[189] and reached Ḥā'il on 5 May to find that Maḥmūd and Nu'mān had arrived there just two hours before him, together with a third man, 'rapportant la stèle phénicienne et les autres pierres avec inscriptions'. One would like to know just how the 150-kg Stele had been secured onto the back of a camel, and how these men had managed to load and unload it each day, but on this Huber is silent. The men had passed two places, one with a single inscription and the other with many, of which Maḥmūd had made a number of copies.[190] The 'other stones' must have been the four listed nos. 13–16 on p. 651 of Huber's *Journal*.[191]

On 12 May, a caravan of several hundred camels arrived from al-Madīnah. With it came a letter from de Lostalot in Ǧiddah asking for news. Though

---

[187] Huber 1891: 593; Pearson 1993: 131–2. See note 170 above on Huber's letter to Renan dated 18 April 1884. On the firearms (Gras rifles) for Ḥā'il as a gift for the emir, see Huber 1883: 152; Pearson 1993: 59–60; also Appendix 4 below: Letter no. 14 dated 25 June 1883 and note 64; Letter no. 20 dated 24 September 1883 and note 87; Letter no. 21 dated 30 November 1883; Letter no. 24 dated 6 July 1884. For more on de Lostalot (1842–94) and his background and life, particularly on the intriguing possibility that he and Sī 'Azīz ibn al-Shaykh al-Ḥaddād may have already known each other in New Caledonia in the 1870s, see Witkam forthcoming/a: TS p. 10.

[188] These were probably *wusūm* (camel brands), though they were read as a Thamudic inscription (HU 787) by van den Branden 1950: 118. On the way, at Ghadīr Hasū 'Aliyyā, Huber copied two Ḥismaic inscriptions (HU 788, 786) drawn with charcoal under an overhanging rock (Huber 1891: 604). (MCAM)

[189] For the journey to al-Ṣulayliyyah and back, see Huber 1891: 594–631; Atlas flle 12. For the group of *wusūm* (singular *wasm*) at al-Ṣulayliyyah see Huber 1891: 609–10. (MCAM/WF)

[190] Huber 1891: 641–8. The inscriptions are HU 790 (at al-Ktīb) and HU 791–814 (at al-Khubū). (MCAM/WF)

[191] In his entry for 15 May, Huber (1891: 651–9) lists all 110 Aramaic, Nabataean, 'Phoenician' and Hebrew inscriptions he had copied, including those from Madā'in Ṣāliḥ and Taymā'. Of those from Taymā', he identifies the ones of which he possesses the stone itself ('Je possède la pierre'): nos. 13, 14, 15, 16; the Taymā' Stele is no. 109. See also Pearson 1993: 98 for the stones purchased by Euting and Huber in Taymā'.

disappointingly brief, it was the first letter Huber, now ill and despondent, had received since the previous September, and it brought him some cheer.[192] By 18 May he had finished cataloguing the 110 Aramaic, Nabataean, 'Phoenician' and Hebrew inscriptions of which he had made copies and squeezes, and bringing his journal up to date. He was now ready to leave for Ğiddah.[193] The emir told Huber that Emir Zāmil of ʿUnayzah should be able to arrange his onward passage to the Red Sea port. He also advised him that when he left Shammar territory (i.e. the land under Rashīdī control) he should curb his habitual impatience, resist all temptation to deviate from the route, and put it about that he was a Muslim from Iraq.[194] After some dilly-dallying and fond farewells, Huber left Ḥā'il with Maḥmūd on 25 May. He had decided to leave the inscriptions in Ḥā'il for safekeeping, and so would have to return there from Ğiddah to collect them; he would later plan to take them back to Europe with him via Baghdad.[195]

The emir had furnished him with a bedouin passport and letters for Zāmil of ʿUnayzah, Ḥasan of Buraydah, and ʿAbdullah ibn ʿAbd al-Raḥmān al-Bassam, his representative in Mecca. Going by the route he had taken in 1880 via Ğabal Salma, Fayd, al-Kahfah, al-Quwārah and ʿUyūn al-Ğawa, Huber reached Buraydah on 30 May.[196] He then had to leave in haste on 1 June to catch up with a *samn* (clarified butter) caravan that was just then leaving ʿUnayzah for Mecca.[197] A rushed dinner with Zāmil in ʿUnayzah was followed by an evening march to al-Shibībiyyah, farther west along the great Wādī Rimah, where the caravan was waiting for him. Leaving the wadi at al-Ḥağnāwī, the caravan moved south to Dukhnah and the wells of Shubayrimah. By 6 June they were in the vicinity of Ğabal Nīr and the wells of al-Qāʿiyyah. They were now in the potentially dangerous territory of the ʿUtaybah tribe, for long at enmity with Ibn Rashīd and thus hostile to anyone perceived as

192 Huber 1891: 649.
193 Ibid.: 651–9, 670.
194 Ibid.: 672–3.
195 Appendix 4, Letter no. 24 dated 6 July 1884 from Huber to Weisgerber. Huber had originally wanted to take the inscriptions and luggage with him to Ğiddah, but changed his mind due to reports of danger en route: see Huber's letter to the Ministry of Public Education dated 20 June 1884 (Appendix 4; see also Pearson 1993: 125, 130). In the same letter, Huber confirms his intention to send all the stones, including the Taymā' Stele, to Paris.
196 For the journey from Ḥā'il to al-Qaṣīm, see Huber 1891: 677–707.
197 On butter caravans, see Euting 1914: 273 (Chapter XV, entry for 2 April 1884). The al-Qaṣīm–Mecca route is described in Huber 1891: 707–45. (MCAM/WF)

his friend.[198] Here they joined the Darb al-Ḥiǧāz that runs between Mecca and the towns of lower Naǧd. From this point it was a matter of following the well-worn route via ʿAfīf and al-Muwayh, which they reached on 12 June. On 15 June, in Wādī ʿAqīq, the news came from local bedouin that the road between Mecca and Ǧiddah was closed.

On the 16th, they reached al-Sayl in the fertile Wādī al-Yamaniyyah, forming one of the borders of Mecca's sacred territory where pilgrims were obliged to don the *iḥrām*. Word got about that Huber was no Muslim, and the people in al-Sayl turned hostile, declaring that if they had known him to be a Naṣrānī they would have taken the whole caravan.[199] Pressing on, thirty miles and a few hours later they reached ʿAyn al-Zaymah, about forty kilometres east-north-east of Mecca, where, 'from fear of God', nobody could be found who was willing to act as Huber's *rafīq* (guide and guarantor) on the way to Ǧiddah. Eventually an ʿUtaybah tribesman was persuaded, and Huber and Maḥmūd were 'escorted by thirteen individuals from a kind of urban guard and led forcibly' to the outskirts of Mecca to pick up the road to Ǧiddah. True to form, Huber once again ignores every opportunity to spice up his tale, telling us nothing in his diary about the risks of this journey, and it is only in his letter to Weisgerber that he hints at the dangers he was exposed to: 'In my last trip here across the territory of the ʿUtaybah I risked my life ten times a day.'[200] Sharīf ʿAlī, the local representative of the Sharīf of Mecca based in al-Ṭāʾif, was now informed of their presence and intentions and, after some misunderstanding, they were provided with an official escort. Having spent

[198] The ʿUtaybah tended to side with the Āl Saʿūd ruler Imām ʿAbd Allāh ibn Fayṣal against Ibn Rashīd, though tribal allegiances were notoriously elastic. A British dispatch from Ǧiddah of 19 June 1883 records a recent battle east of ʿUnayzah (letter of Consul Lynedoch Moncrieff to George Wyndham, HM Chargé d'Affaires, Constantinople, dated 19 June 1883, in Burdett 2013 iii: 395–8). The ʿUtaybah were also hostile to the troublesome Ḥarb tribe of the region between Mecca and Madīnah, and were more likely than the latter to support the Ottoman authorities in the Ḥiǧāz. See letter dated 2 July 1884 from Thomas Jago, British consul at Ǧiddah, to Lord Granville, in Burdett 1996 iv: 145–62.

[199] Huber 1891: 745. Carruthers's statement (1935: 111) that Huber 'was travelling as a Muslim' should not be taken to mean that Huber was disguised as a Muslim for the whole Arabian journey. Huber was travelling as a Muslim on this part of his journey only as a temporary expedient, on the recommendation of the emir but, given that it was common knowledge that he and Euting were known and accepted as Christians in Ḥāʾil (see Euting 1914: 86–7: Chapter IX, entry for 3 January 1884), it was hardly a ruse that was likely to succeed.

[200] Appendix 4, Letter no. 24 dated 6 July 1884 to Weisgerber.

the day of 18 June encamped at the foot of Ǧabal al-Qubays, they left the same evening for Ǧiddah, passing within view of the holy city and through its outskirts on the road to Haddah. They had had a lucky escape, though in his *Journal* Huber plays it down in his usual prosaic fashion. Twenty-four hours later they reached the Mecca Gate of the port city, and Huber sent a note to de Lostalot, who offered him hospitality in his own house.[201]

Huber wrote letters dated 20 June to Renan, Maunoir, the Ministry of Public Education and his mother, packed up his squeezes and the first four notebooks of his diary in a chest, and dispatched them by steamer to France on 22 June.[202] He was trying to arrange his return to Ḥāʾil with the *samn* caravan from Mecca, but this was proving difficult. He explained why to Thomas Jago, the British consul in Ǧiddah, who had known Huber since Damascus days and who now found his news from Naǧd of sufficient interest to report it home to Lord Granville, the Foreign Secretary. Ibn Rashīd had been coming off best in campaigns against Ibn Saʿūd and the latter's ʿUtaybah allies during the winter, and ʿUtaybah territory was closed to Huber because, having just made his perilous journey through there, he was now well-known as a Christian and friend of Ibn Rashīd. He was therefore deciding to abandon all thoughts of returning to Ḥāʾil via Riyadh and Sadūs, and to go instead by a 'more westerly course'.[203]

Huber's journal ends abruptly on 28 June 1884, but he was to stay in Ǧiddah for another month. He was short of money and, as he makes clear in the letter of 6 July 1884 to his friend Weisgerber, he had to draw another bill

[201] Huber 1891: 745–51. The ʿUtaybī was called Murayzīq ibn Hayyāl, of the Shiyābīn section of the tribe (Huber 1891: 746). Three days later, Huber wrote in a letter dated 20 June from Ǧiddah to Charles Maunoir in Paris that he was fearful of being robbed and killed by the ʿUtaybah who, though at the time subject to Ibn Rashīd, were resentful of his rule and disinclined to help anyone associated with him (Kurpershoek 2018: 106). See also Appendix 4, Huber's Letter no. 23 to Maunoir of 3 July 1884, saying that ʿUtaybah territory was closed to him. Snouck Hurgronje records that Huber was accompanied from Mecca to Ǧiddah by Ṣāliḥ al-Bassām of ʿUnayzah (Witkam forthcoming/a: TS p. 24).

[202] Huber 1891: 753. He gave a fifth notebook to de Lostalot to take to France (Appendix 4, Letter no. 23 dated 3 July 1884 from Huber to Maunoir; Letter no. 24 dated 6 July 1884 from Huber to Weisgerber). See Appendix 4, Letter no. 22 dated 20 June 1884, for the full letter that Huber wrote from Ǧiddah to the Ministry of Public Education.

[203] Jago to Granville, letter dated 2 July 1884, in Burdett 2013 iii: 409–20, quotation at pp. 419–20. For Huber's unrealized plan to go to Mecca disguised as a woman in the company of Sī ʿAzīz, see Witkam forthcoming/a: p. 8, and Appendix 3 letter no. 2.

of exchange on his mother.[204] Despite his words to Jago, he told Weisgerber that his plan was still to cross Arabia to Baghdad via Sadūs in lower Naǧd, presumably intending to go from there to Ḥā'il, where he could arrange for the Taymā' Stele to be transported to Baghdad:

> If I arrive there [i.e. Baghdad] with no more money in my pocket, then you [Weisgerber] will start a fund-raising drive in Alsace to repatriate me. I am certain that it will succeed.[205]

So great was his enthusiasm that he was dreaming of returning one day to excavate in Taymā':

> If I were rich, so deep is my love for Arabia and science that I would undertake these excavations at my own expense, but I am not.[206]

In the event, downhearted and aware of the risk, he came to the decision to embark on his return to Ḥā'il neither via Mecca nor via lower Naǧd, but by the coastal track to al-Madīnah. This was ostensibly a more prudent course and, to help Huber, de Lostalot had put him in touch with an Algerian merchant who knew this area and the Ḥarb tribe controlling it, and who procured two bedouin guides for him.[207] Unfortunately, in 1884 this route was even more unsafe than usual, there having been a spate of robberies perpetrated by Ḥarbīs preying on pilgrims, especially in the area of the little port of Rābigh.[208] And this is exactly where, on 29 July, Huber met his end aged just thirty-six, murdered by one or both of his guides; or else, as one of them alleged, by the other guide in league with Huber's companion, Maḥmūd. The motive was either plunder or anti-Christian fanaticism, or a combination of the two.[209] The sole eye-witness report was provided by Maḥmūd who,

[204] Appendix 4, Letter no. 24 dated 6 July 1884 from Ǧiddah to Weisgerber.

[205] Ibid.

[206] Ibid.

[207] Lostalot 1885: 442, 446–7. It is possible that 'the Algerian merchant' was Sī ʿAzīz ibn al-Shaykh al-Ḥaddād, though Lostalot does not name him here. See Lostalot 1885 for the French vice-consul's own detailed account of Huber's death, the investigation of who was responsible, the possible guilt of Maḥmūd, and the recovery by Sī ʿAzīz of Huber's belongings and the Taymā' Stele from Ḥā'il.

[208] Letter dated 22 November 1884 from British consul Thomas Jago in Ǧiddah to George Wyndham, HM Chargé d'Affaires, Constantinople (Burdett 1996 iv: 343–8).

[209] Lostalot 1885: 443. Hogarth speculates that perhaps a blood-feud with the ʿUtaybah tribe was a cause (Hogarth 1904: 281). However, though Huber was known to fear the ʿUtaybah (see note 201 above), the tribe controlling this area was the Ḥarb, and

by his own account having had the good fortune to escape with his life to al-Madīnah and then Ḥāʾil, had first sent a letter to the French consulate, which forwarded the news to Paris, and then later amplified this with the statement he gave on arriving at the French consulate in early October 1884.

According to Christiaan Snouck Hurgronje, news of the murder reached Ǧiddah shortly before his own arrival there on 29 August; it had in fact arrived at the French consulate about two weeks before that.[210] Based on Maḥmūd's statement, the 'sole source of the few details about the mysterious curtailment of this life, the dominant characteristic of which was bravery verging on foolhardiness', Huber's editors, Renan and his colleagues, printed the following summary of the incident in the foreword ('Avertissement des éditeurs') to their 1891 edition of Huber's *Journal*:

> M. Huber was murdered, on 29 July 1884, in the course of a scientific journey, by the guides whom he had chosen to conduct him along the route. A desire to seize his weapons and valuables was the motive for the crime. He had left Ǧiddah during the night of 26–27 July last, accompanied by his servant Maḥmūd and his two guides. Maḥmūd was following the route leading the camels loaded with the baggage, while M. Huber and his guides made continual detours to right and left, whether to record ancient inscriptions or to make a sketch or a scientific observation. They met up with each other at the place designated for the day's halt, to refresh themselves with some food and a little rest. The days of 27 and 28 July passed without incident.
>
> On the 29th, just as Maḥmūd reached the halting place, he found that everyone was there, the two guides were praying and M. Huber was stretched out some distance away, beneath an Arab cloak. He thought his master was sleeping and began to unload the camels. Suddenly he realized that two gun barrels were aimed at his chest and heard the voice of one of the guides saying to

T.E. Lawrence later confirmed that Huber's killer was a Ḥarbī (Lawrence 1935: 77–8).

[210] Snouck Hurgronje 1923: 4. See Appendix 9, Letter no. 2 dated 16 August from de Lostalot (in France) to Maunoir, reporting that he had just received news by telegram of Huber's death. For details on Snouck Hurgronje and his activities in the Ḥiǧāz in 1884–85, see Witkam forthcoming/a and b. For Snouck Hurgronje's first hearing about Huber's death and the circumstances surrounding it, see Witkam forthcoming/a: Appendix 3 letter no. 2.

> him: 'Be very careful! Throw down your weapons. If you don't do so, at the slightest hostile movement we will treat you in the same way as your master, who is over there.' He looked that way and saw M. Charles Huber stretched out on his left side, with the whole of the right side of his face covered in blood, but with his features calm and at rest, as if he were sleeping. A pistol shot fired at close range while he was asleep was very probably the cause of death.
>
> Maḥmūd remained a prisoner of the murderers for two days before managing to escape. He went to al-Madīnah, thence to Ḥā'il, before finally returning to Ǧiddah and placing himself at the disposal of the French vice-consulate, with the job of bringing about the punishment of the murderers. He is still there.
>
> M. Charles Huber's body remained exposed to the elements for some days. Eventually, it is said, some passers-by dug a trench and interred him in it.[211]

De Lostalot had left Ǧiddah for Paris and four months' leave on 5 July,[212] some three weeks before Huber set out. Various garbled reports of Huber's tragic end reached him at his home in the Pyrenées.[213] Immediately on his return to Ǧiddah on or just before 24 October 1884, he set about organizing the recovery of Huber's body and possessions.[214] When Huber's remains were eventually delivered to the French consulate in the following March, his skeleton was found to be complete except for the hands and feet, and there was a bullet hole in the

---

[211] Huber 1891: vi–vii. For a letter from Maḥmūd, in both the original Arabic and an English translation, saying that he would be prepared to come to the Dutch consulate to reveal all he knew about Huber's death, and for Maḥmūd's intention to make a statement to the French consulate, see now Witkam forthcoming/a: TS pp. 26–7 and Appendix 1. See also a letter from Christiaan Snouck Hurgronje, who arrived in Ǧiddah shortly after, which records Maḥmūd's story of his lucky escape from his captors (Witkam forthcoming/a, Appendix 3 letter no. 2). Naturally this testimony paints its author, Maḥmūd, in a favourable light. For other possible versions of the circumstances of Huber's murder and Maḥmūd's role, v. Lostalot 1885: 44–7. (MCAM/WF)

[212] 5 July: see Appendix 4, Letter no. 24 dated 6 July 1884 from Huber to Weisgerber, note 155.

[213] See Appendix 9 for letters from de Lostalot to Charles Maunoir and Philippe Berger dated between 12 August 1884 and 20 November 1885 on the topic of Huber's death.

[214] For de Lostalot's arrival back in Ǧiddah, see Appendix 9, Letter no. 6 dated 24 October 1884.

right temple. Instructions eventually arrived for them to be buried at Ǧiddah.[215] The recovery of his remains was just part of a larger effort by the French vice-consul and his agent to rescue the Taymāʾ Stele and other inscriptions from Ḥāʾil along with the remnants of Huber and Euting's possessions, and to this we shall now turn.

THE TAYMĀʾ STELE IMBROGLIO

No episode illustrates the undercurrent of Franco-German rivalry in the 1883–84 expedition more vividly than the affair of the Taymāʾ Stele. Having been acquired in February 1884 by Euting and Huber, this celebrated inscription had arrived in Ḥāʾil on 5 May to await Huber's return to arrange its shipment to Europe. How, after Huber's untimely demise, it was recovered thanks to the efforts of de Lostalot and his agent, taken to Ǧiddah, and escorted to Paris to be deposited at the Musée du Louvre where it remains to this day, is the story told in this section.

The investigation opens with the questions of who saw it first, and which man and thus which country had prior entitlement to it. These issues have never been definitively settled. The official French version was that Huber saw the Stele on his first visit to Taymāʾ, which he passed through during 10–13 November 1880. According to the editors of his 1883–84 journal:

> What he had seen during the course of this journey served merely to kindle an ardent desire to undertake it over again. The Teïma Inscription, above all, which he had discovered as early as 1880, allowed him no sleep.[216]

[215] Lostalot 1885: 444. According to a letter from Sī ʿAzīz b. al-Shaykh al-Ḥaddād (quoted in Witkam forthcoming/a: Appendix 4 letter no. 1), Huber's 'limbs were lying spread out because the birds and wild animals had eaten from them'. According to Augustus Ralli (1909: 243), Huber's remains stayed in Ǧiddah until they were given to Snouck Hurgronje when he left the Ḥiǧāz (i.e. on 20 September 1885); allegedly, Snouck Hurgronje 'took with him Huber's skeleton, except the bones of the hands, which were never recovered. The skull, in the left temple of which was a perforation from a bullet, was buried at Ǧiddah.' Ralli gives no source for this information.

[216] Huber 1891: Avertissement des éditeurs by Ernest Renan, Charles Barbier de Meynard and Charles Maunoir, p. v: 'Ce qu'il avait vu dans ce voyage ne fit qu'exciter chez lui un ardent désir de recommencer. L'inscription de Teïma, surtout, qu'il avait découverte dès 1880, ne le laissait pas dormir.'

In his influential book *The Penetration of Arabia* (1904), David Hogarth pointed not to Huber but to Charles Doughty as the Stele's original discoverer. In 1877, Doughty saw an Aramaic inscription built into the wall of the great Haddāğ well, and Hogarth assumed this to be the Taymā' Stele. But he seems not to have noticed that Doughty himself had immediately withdrawn this identification. This is unambiguously stated in his magisterial index to *Travels in Arabia Deserta* where, under the entry Euting, Doughty writes:

> Correction: the here-mentioned inscription [*viz.* the inscription seen by Doughty on one of the walls of the Haddāğ well] is not that found by Euting and Huber who visited Teyma some years later. Prof. Euting found there another inscribed stone [*viz.* the Taymā' Stele], not mentioned in this work, which the brother of Seydān (531) showed them. The inscription of 24 lines which has been deciphered by Professors Euting and Nöldeke (*Sitzungsber. der k. Ak. der Wiss. zu Berlin* 1884 (No. XXXV), p. 813–820 [= Nöldeke 1884]) is of great antiquity and of the highest value. This inscription has been likewise translated by M. E. Renan: the stone is now in Paris.[217]

So the claim that Doughty saw it can be definitely ruled out. Since then, Huber's alleged primacy as discoverer of the Stele has seldom been seriously questioned.[218] However, it is clear in the passage quoted above that Doughty

[217] Doughty 1888 i: 531–2; ii: 577. This correction appears in all subsequent editions of Doughty's *Travels in Arabia Deserta*. In i: 532 Doughty states of the Haddāğ inscription, in parenthesis: 'Since writing these words in 1879 the haddàj inscription has been seen by Huber and the learned epigraphist Euting some years after me. Euting supposes the inscription, which is dedicatory, and in the same Aramaic letters as the other inscriptions which I found at Teyma, may be of four or five centuries before Jesus Christ.' It is this passage that has caused confusion and led readers such as Hogarth to identify Doughty's Haddāğ inscription erroneously with the Taymā' Stele (Hogarth 1904: 280–1). Hogarth himself perpetuated this error in his biography of Doughty (1928: 60), and it was further perpetuated by Kiernan (1937: 270), Taylor (1999: 148, 327–8), and Trüper (2019: 67–8). Only Pesce (1986: 10–11) dismisses it. The inscription that Doughty saw may have been the one that Euting (1914: 162: Chapter XI, entry for 19 February 1884) and Huber (1891: 324) were told had been pulled out of al-Haddāğ some years earlier, the owner of which refused to sell it to them. (MCAM/WF)

[218] For example, Philby (1957: 82) repeats Huber's claim that he bought the Stele, having first seen it in 1880.

ascribed its discovery to Euting. For this and other reasons that will now be set forth, the case needs to be re-opened.

Most tellingly, in his own account of his visit to Taymāʾ in 1880, Huber makes no specific mention of the Stele. Here is all that he says when describing the ruins known locally as Toumâ, regarded locally as the most recent of the ancient towns that had once existed in the oasis, situated a kilometre south-west of the current town of Taymāʾ:

> The inscriptions that I collected there are not numerous, but they are of enormous interest, as much for their antiquity as for the archaic form of their characters. One of them is Nabataean, a second is Aramaic, and a third remains to be determined. I draw Toumâ to the attention of the next explorer so that excavations can be carried out there, as I am quite certain that he will unearth archaeological treasures.[219]

He goes on to say that Toumâ was constructed from black basalt stone like the ruined settlements of the Ḥawrān and Ǧabal Druze, from which it is clear that he was looking at the area of ruins that includes the extant building known variously as Qaṣr Ẓallum, Qaṣr Raḍm and Qaṣr al-Dāʾir.[220] However, he makes no mention of the building nearby to the south known as the Ṭlayḥān, in a doorway of which the Stele was incorporated when Euting first saw it on 17 February 1884.[221] The Aramaic inscription that Huber saw in 1880 was a short one (no. 85, 86 or 87 in Huber 1884b: 298) and therefore cannot have been the Stele. Whatever it was that kept him awake at night, as his editors maintained, it cannot have been this. The only other possible scenario is that he did see the Stele but so completely failed to ascribe any

---

[219] See Translation, Part II, p. 189 below. Huber 1884b: 511–12: 'Les inscriptions que j'y ai recueillies ne sont pas nombreuses, mais elles sont excessivement intéressantes, tant par leur ancienneté que par la forme archaïque de leurs caractères. L'une d'elles est nabatéenne, une deuxième araméenne et une troisième reste à determiner. Je signale Toumâ au prochain explorateur pour y faire des fouilles, certain qu'on y trouvera des trésors archéologiques.' The three Taymāʾ inscriptions that he recorded are nos. 85, 86 and 87 referred to in Huber 1884a: 291, and reproduced on p. 298 (see Appendix 1 below, pp. 279 and 286).

[220] See Euting 1914: 156–7 (Chapter XI, entry for 17 February 1884).

[221] See Euting's map of Taymāʾ: Euting 1914: 148 (Chapter XI, entry for 15 February 1884; see also Notebook V, p. 34r). According to Philby (1957: 82, 101) this building, which he calls Tulaihan, was demolished by ʿAbd al-Karīm al-Rummān some years before his visit in 1951.

importance to it that he not only omitted it from his journal (published posthumously), but never even mentioned it to Euting.

The latter is the maximal claim that can be made. Even if true, which is highly unlikely, it would hardly be sufficient to qualify Huber as the Stele's 'discoverer'. Nonetheless, however bizarre it may appear, it is at first sight corroborated by his belated claim to have seen it on his 1880 journey, a claim that he made only when he returned to Taymāʾ in February 1884 and was shown the Stele by Euting, who recorded the sequence of events as follows. When, on 17 February, Euting was taken on his own by Zaydān the armourer to the Ṭlayḥān, the German scholar could hardly contain himself:

> Its head was pointing down and the narrow side, depicting the god or king and the priest, was not visible at first. When I saw the letters, I could barely disguise my excitement; feigning calm, I made a paper squeeze. When the owner of the house pressed me for something, I gladly gave him some money. Having ordered Zeidān for next morning, I then rushed home, tired but still highly excited, to tell Huber about the new discovery and to enlighten him about the importance of the inscription.

It was Euting who then tossed and turned as he contemplated the magnitude of the discovery: 'Thoughts of the Stele kept me awake all night.' Later that morning, when Euting says the Stele had been delivered to their house and he had paid the owner and the porters, 'Huber now remembered that he had seen the stone on his first trip (1880) but had failed to recognize its significance'.[222] Even acknowledging that this account by Euting in the published *Tagbuch* of the Stele's discovery singles himself out as its discoverer and is much more detailed than the one in his handwritten diary, and thus may have been retrospectively manipulated,[223] one can draw from it at least one incontrovertible conclusion: that Huber had never once previously mentioned the Stele to Euting.

As for Huber 'now remembering that he had seen the stone', one wonders how Euting could have been taken in by so tardy and opportunistic a claim. It is typical of his naivety that he does appear to have given credence to it, for he repeats it in his letter dated 10 April 1884 to Nöldeke from al-Wağh: 'Huber saw it of course four years ago but he had no idea of the importance

[222] Euting 1914: 158 (Chapter XI, entry for 18 February 1884).
[223] Trüper 2019: 72–3.

and age of the monument.'[224] There is no sign in Huber's narrative of his 1880 visit that he went to the Ṭlayḥān and, even if he had, he would not necessarily have noticed what Euting saw there, as the Stele was not only upside down but partly buried. In his letter to Nöldeke of 8 July 1884 from Beirut, Euting provides an excellent and revealing little sketch of the doorway in the Ṭlayḥān showing the position of the Taymāʾ Stele in the jamb[225] – a sketch that does not appear in either his MS notebooks or his published *Tagbuch*.

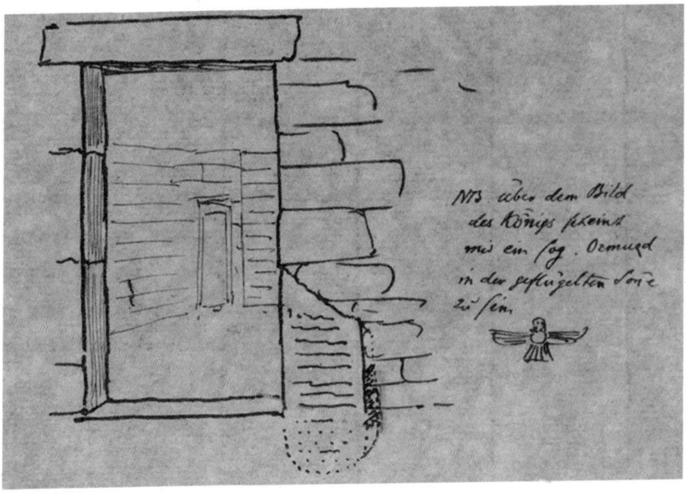

Euting's sketch of the Taymāʾ Stele as found in the Ṭlayḥān, from Euting's letter to Nöldeke dated 8 July 1884 from Beirut (see note 225 below).

Euting immediately carried out a careful examination of the Stele and made a transcription and translation of it: it is Euting's drawing that appears

[224] Euting, letter to Nöldeke dated 10 April 1884 from al-Waǧh (Euting Archiv, Tübingen University, Md 782 A 65); Pearson 1993: 100: manuscript letter from Euting to Nöldeke dated 10 April 1884: 'Huber hat die Inschrift zwar schon vor 4 Jahren gesehen aber keine Ahnung von der Wichtigkeit und dem Alter des Denkmales'; and 'der zwar von Herr Huber schon vor 4 Jahren gesehen, aber in seine Bedeutung nicht erkannt worden war' 'which had actually been seen four years ago by Huber, though he did not realize its importance'. See also Hogarth 1904: 281.

[225] Euting, letter to Nöldeke dated 8 July 1884 from Beirut (Euting Archiv, Tübingen University, Md 782 A 65): 'The stone during its time in Tleḥân طليحان [Ṭlayḥān] had been left with its head (rounded part) downwards in the ground and to the right side of the gateway. Because of this the portrait of the king which could be seen on the left edge of the stele, stood in the mortar of the wall and because it couldn't be seen (it was hidden) it was protected from being destroyed.'

in Huber's published journal.[226] Huber's entry for 18 February 1884 of course says nothing about Euting's role in the discovery of what he oddly calls 'la pierre avec la grande inscription phénicienne',[227] and claims that he himself paid the owner and the porters:

> I have just arranged for ʿAbd al-ʿAzīz [al-ʿAnqarī] ... to go and find the owner of the stone with the great Phoenician inscription, under orders to close with him and bring the stone to me at any price. Whatever the baksheesh may be, I shall pay it. Let us hope they succeed.
>
> At 10.30, my people returned with the stone, *al-ḥamdu lillah*! Two teams, each of four men, have carried it here. I have settled up at 2 reals to the owner and 2 for the porters.
>
> It is a beautiful stele, alas broken at the base, but still measuring [BLANK] high. The characters are carved in relief; but the upper third has unfortunately suffered much damage. Now I possess it; but how to transport it? It weighs at least 150 kg, hence too heavy for a half load [one side of a camel], and to load it onto a single camel, how can that be managed?[228]

Euting would later complain that the money Huber handed over in exchange for the Stele was in any case his, Euting's: Huber, he protests, had paid 'from *my* money'.[229]

---

[226] Huber 1891: 319. See Appendix 10, Letter no. 4 dated 1 August 1885 from Euting to Philippe Berger, in which he forcefully points out that the drawing of the Stele was his, not Huber's. The AIBL seems not to have been fully persuaded of this until 1891: see Appendix 11, Letter no. 5 dated 24 March 1891 from Berger to Renan.

[227] It is extraordinary that Huber continued throughout his *Journal* to describe the Stele as 'phénicienne' (see note 181 above, and Appendix 4, notes 102, 103 and 106). Note also that in his *Tagbuch* (Euting 1914: 154: Chapter XI, entry for 16 February 1884), Euting says that Huber 'once showed me in the diary of his first Arabian journey' an 'ancient Aramaic inscription' which Euting had dated for Huber for the latter's report to the French Secretary of Education. This is almost certainly Huber 1884a: 291, no. 87 on the plates; Doughty (1891: pl. XXVII) was the first to have seen this one, in 1877. Euting made a much better copy in Notebook V, p. 5v. It too found its way to the Musée du Louvre where it has the number AO 27196. It was published as *CIS* ii 114 (see now Macdonald and Al-Najem forthcoming). If Huber had found the Taymāʾ Stele on his first journey, it is inconceivable that he would not have mentioned it to Euting and got him to date that as well. It is equally inconceivable that he would not have mentioned it in the narrative of his journey (Huber 1884b). (MCAM)

[228] Huber 1891: 318.

[229] 'Vom meinem Geld' (Healey 2004: 320). See also Pearson 1993: 107, 110.

Above all, it is significant that Huber himself nowhere mentions that this is the stone he saw in 1880. One may go further: in calling it 'Phoenician', he seems rather to differentiate it from any 'Aramaic' inscription he may have seen in 1880, thus undermining further his claim to priority, as he makes no mention of any 'Phoenician' inscription during his 1880 visit. He did not mention it in his 65-page report to the Ministry of his 1880 visit to Taymāʾ dated 27 March 1882,[230] and made no reference to it in his letter to Renan dated 8 April 1883 written before his departure for Arabia.[231] Nor did he hurry to locate it on his arrival in Taymāʾ in February 1884, as one would expect if he really had seen it before.[232] One is driven to conclude that it was Euting, not Huber, who was the true discoverer of the Taymāʾ Stele. Euting himself certainly thought so, and lost no time in laying claim to the Stele for himself. He, or possibly his editor Littmann, chooses this juncture in his published diary (18 February 1884) to record the prior agreement he had made with Huber about the division of epigraphic spoils:

> Before departing on our journey, Huber and I had agreed in Strasbourg that I would be able to select as my personal property for my collection, which would pass at that time to the state, *one* inscribed stone among all the transportable antiquities that he had discovered or that we might discover together in the future, whereas all other finds were to remain with him. Thus, we now concluded an agreement that he would leave the stele of Ṭlēḥān to me.[233]

On their return to Taymāʾ from their excursion to Tabūk, Euting witnessed the Stele and other items being packed up for transport in the courtyard of their house (10 March 1884):

---

[230] Appendix 3, Letter no. 16 dated 27 March 1882 and report of March 1882.

[231] Appendix 7, Letter no. 2 dated 8 April 1883 from Huber to Renan.

[232] These clinching arguments are set out in Pearson 1993: 145–6. There is no mention of having seen the Stele in 1880 in Huber's unpublished letters translated in Appendices 3 and 4 below.

[233] Euting 1914: 161 (Chapter XI, entry for 18 February 1884). That this was in fact a definite arrangement is clear from Huber's letter to Renan of 8 April 1883 (Letter no. 2, Appendix 7 below), and from Euting's letters to Nöldeke from al-Wağh (10 April 1884) and Jerusalem (12 June 1884); from a report written for an as yet unidentified person of importance dated 17 November 1886; and from a letter to August Dillmann of 16 July 1884 (Trüper 2019: 68, citing Euting's correspondence with Dillmann, Staatsbibliothek Berlin, Nachlass Dillmann). See p. 82 below.

> The negro domestic, Naṣṣār, helped to wrap the large Aramaic stone in palm fibre, cloth and a bedouin rug, for which I paid 4 *megīdī*. The other stones have been standing in the courtyard since yesterday, tied up for their onward transport.

Three days later, on 13 March, just before leaving Taymāʾ for Madāʾin Ṣāliḥ and al-ʿUlā, he says: 'We stuck firmly to our decision to leave the stones here for now, and purchased no further animals.' So rich was the haul of inscriptions that Huber and Euting had already decided not to try to carry them on their onward journey to the Ḥiǧāz, but to leave them in Taymāʾ for possible transport back to Ḥāʾil. As Euting had recorded on 18 February: 'The best plan is perhaps not to drag all these stones along with us on our trip through the Ḥigāz, but to send them first through safe territory to Ḥāʾil.' It is hard to say for certain that this was a ploy by Huber to separate Euting from these valuable artefacts: at that point Euting's understanding was still that he would accompany Huber back to Ḥāʾil once they had completed their investigations at Madāʾin Ṣāliḥ and al-ʿUlā. However, suspicion is aroused. As we have seen, Huber had already tried once to get rid of Euting, and would actually succeed in doing so once they reached al-ʿUlā. So if he did have a plan to deprive Euting of the epigraphic fruits of their travels, this latest development would certainly have suited his agenda.[234] After almost two and a half millennia of undisturbed obscurity in a north-west Arabian oasis, the Stele was suddenly on the brink of becoming the focus of a colourful Franco-German diplomatic tussle – a contretemps that would bring it to international attention.[235]

Euting's arrival in al-Waǧh on 5 April 1884 came just two days before Huber's return to Ḥāʾil. On 10 April, Euting wrote to Nöldeke from the Red Sea port describing his discovery of the Stele on 17 February and saying that it was destined for Europe via Baghdad.[236] In this he declares explicitly that he is anxious to beat Huber and the French to first publication of the Stele.[237] On 12 June he sent another letter to Nöldeke, this time from Jerusalem, enclosing his squeeze and transcription, from which Nöldeke promptly made

[234] On Huber's possible duplicity in arranging for the inscriptions to be left at Taymāʾ for the time being, see Pearson 1993: 112.

[235] Pesce (1986: 10–15) gives a useful summary of this affair.

[236] Euting, letter dated 10 April 1884 to Nöldeke from al-Waǧh (Euting Archiv, Tübingen University, Md 782/A65). He does not specify whether it was to go to Germany or France, though see Trüper 2019: 68, where it is suggested that Euting was expecting it to be delivered to Strasbourg.

[237] Euting, ibid.; Healey 2004: 321.

a provisional publication.[238] On 3 July, Renan received Huber's squeeze from Ǧiddah, and wrote bitterly that his protégé, who was then still alive, had been 'deprived of the fruits of his labours by a series of circumstances that, for my part, I find extremely regrettable'.[239] In the matter of publication at least, German scholars had pipped the French at the post, which must have shaken Renan's favourable opinion of them.

On his return to Ḥā'il on 7 April 1884, as we have seen, Huber had immediately set about arranging for the Stele and other inscriptions to be brought there from Taymā'. After their arrival on 5 May, he left them there while he set off on his journey to Ǧiddah, planning to return to Ḥā'il and take the stones on to Baghdad. His absolute resolve to keep the Taymā' Stele for France is declared unequivocally in the letter of 6 July 1884 to his friend Weisgerber:

> Unfortunately the top third of it is slightly damaged; were this not so, it would represent the most significant (Phoenician) text that we know today. … I must mention the enormous difficulty we had in transporting this very large stone from Taymā' to Ḥā'il, and then the difficulty we face in transporting it on camelback to Baghdad. But I will not be deterred by the effort and hardships, as I am only too delighted to be handing over this beautiful stone to France.[240]

News of Huber's murder on 29 July 1884 reached Muḥammad Ibn Rashīd by means of Maḥmūd, who had escaped his captors and made his way via al-Madīnah to the Shammar capital. The emir had taken care to safeguard the stones and some of the two Europeans' other belongings. He sent Maḥmūd back with the pilgrim caravan to Mecca bearing a letter of condolence to the French consulate in Ǧiddah, in which he asked what he should do with them. De Lostalot, still in France, was informed of Maḥmūd's presence in Mecca by telegraph; the sender enquired whether Maḥmūd should be arrested as a possible accomplice in Huber's death, or else treated humanely as a man who had undergone a severe ordeal. De Lostalot felt his authority to be insufficient to treat him as a criminal, and requested that Maḥmūd be sent to the consulate in Ǧiddah to await instructions and further investigation.[241]

---

238 Euting, ibid. First publication of the Taymā' Stele: Nöldeke 1884; see Illustration no. 10 in this volume.

239 Hogarth 1904: 281.

240 Appendix 4, Letter no. 24 dated 6 July 1884 from Huber in Ǧiddah to Weisgerber.

241 This is the version of events as told by de Lostalot himself (Lostalot 1885: 443). According to his own testimony, Maḥmūd arrived in Mecca on 27 September 1884

Meanwhile on 29 August, a couple of weeks after news of Huber's death had reached the city, Snouck Hurgronje arrived in Ǧiddah.[242] He was embarking on his great project to study Islam, Mecca and the Meccans at first hand and, while making preparations, took up residence in the house of the Dutch consul in Ǧiddah, Johannes Adrianus Kruyt, in whose company he had arrived at the port. Kruyt was in temporary charge of French affairs, as not only was de Lostalot still away in Paris but his assistant and translator, Bertrand, was in Aden.

Maḥmūd's arrival in Mecca on 27 September 1884 was the cue for the intervention of Sī ʿAzīz bin al-Shaykh al-Ḥaddād, a worldly Algerian Berber refugee who was resident in the holy city and a pensioner of France.[243] Eager to provide any service that would ingratiate him with the French government, he was a man who 'misses no opportunity to give its representatives proof of his attachment'. This individual would go on to play the central role in the rescue of the Taymāʾ Stele. But, at the present juncture, as the Ottoman authorities wished to prevent Maḥmūd from going to Ǧiddah, and Maḥmūd himself was genuinely fearful that the Turkish authorities might suspect

and took up residence in the house of Sī ʿAzīz ibn al-Shaykh al-Ḥaddād (Witkam forthcoming/a: Appendix 1, letter from Maḥmūd to the French consulate in Ǧiddah).

[242] Snouck Hurgronje arrived in Ǧiddah with the Dutch consul J. A. Kruyt, who had recommended to the Dutch government that Snouck Hurgronje be awarded a grant to carry out research in Arabia (Vrolijk 2013: 206). The following narrative of the circumstances surrounding the transport of the Taymāʾ Stele and Euting and Huber's other effects from Ḥāʾil to Ǧiddah is drawn from de Lostalot's own account (Lostalot 1885) and from Snouck Hurgronje's important article in German entitled 'Aus Arabien', published in the *Münchener Allgemeine Zeitung* of 16 November 1885 (Snouck Hurgronje 1923). The latter formed the basis for Ralli's abbreviated account (Ralli 1909: 238–43). An almost identical version was published in Dutch entitled 'Mijne reis naar Arabië' ('My Journey to Arabia') in the *Nieuwe Rotterdamsche Courant* of 26 and 27 November 1885, and dated Leiden 15 November 1885. Because of the treatment he received from him, Snouck Hurgronje was naturally unlikely to present de Lostalot in a positive light, and this bias should be borne in mind when reading his version of events.

[243] For an account of Sī ʿAzīz's colourful career, see Witkam forthcoming/a: TS pp. 7–9. Of Sī ʿAzīz, Snouck Hurgronje (1923: 5) tells us: '[He] had taken part in revolts during the Franco-Prussian war; after their suppression he had led a varied life and was finally settled by the French government in Mecca, with a monthly pension of 400 francs. … Sī ʿAzīz knows that his only prospect of mercy and return to his beloved homeland is by convincing the French government that he has carried out important services for it.' For more on Sī ʿAzīz and his credibility, and for the story that he and Huber had concocted a plan to go to Mecca with Huber disguised as a woman, see Witkam forthcoming/a: TS p. 8.

him of complicity in Huber's death, Sī ʿAzīz spotted an opportunity: taking Maḥmūd under his wing, he contacted the Dutch consulate with an offer to conduct him there in safety and in secrecy. Then, at the beginning of October, the French consular assistant, Bertrand, returned from Aden, and sent a telegram, drafted by Snouck Hurgronje, to the Wālī of Mecca, requesting that Maḥmūd now be sent to Ǧiddah.[244] Bertrand was followed on the 24th of the month by de Lostalot from France. De Lostalot was now under official instructions to recover Huber's remains, to ensure that Huber's murderers were found and punished, and to arrange for his and Euting's belongings to be fetched from Ḥāʾil and sent to Paris. First, he arranged for Maḥmūd to be kept at the French vice-consulate pending investigations into Huber's murder.

French urgency was all the greater now that the text of the Taymāʾ Stele had been published by Nöldeke and its importance recognized. The first published French reaction to Nöldeke's article had come from Joseph Halévy who, inadvertently but revealingly, referred to the Stele as having been discovered by both Euting and Huber – thus in 1884, not in 1880.[245] Hence Euting's possible entitlement to the Stele was by now a real fear, and every effort was to be made to thwart a German claim to it.

Identifying and punishing Huber's killers meant involving the Ottoman authorities in the Ḥiǧāz, a process that de Lostalot, a man who, according to Snouck Hurgronje, could be rude and arrogant and who knew neither Turkish nor Arabic, seems to have mishandled. Arranging the recovery of the property in Ḥāʾil would require even greater tact and diplomacy: the Ottoman authorities had been fiercely against Huber's return to Ǧabal Shammar and

[244] Snouck Hurgronje 1923: 5; Witkam forthcoming/a: TS pp. 26–7 and Appendix 1, letter from Maḥmūd to the French consulate. Sī ʿAzīz had a personal interest in Huber, as he may have met him before the latter's death. Huber writes: 'De Lostalot has been notified by an Algerian shaykh in exile in Mecca, a pensioner and on the best of terms with the authorities of the holy city, that the governor of the Ḥiǧāz, who is at the moment staying on vacation in al-Ṭāʾif with the Grand Sharif, had just sent the order to the governor of Ǧiddah to have me watched and, if I wanted to return to the interior, to prevent me by force. The shaykh, Sī ʿAzīz, came here himself to communicate this information' (Appendix 4, Letter no. 23 dated 3 July 1884, Huber to Maunoir).

[245] Halévy 1884: 332: Report of a lecture by Joseph Halévy entitled 'Une inscription araméenne': 'M. Halévy fait une lecture sur une inscription araméenne publiée par M. Nölde [*sic*; Nöldeke]. La stèle a été découverte par MM Euting et Huber dans l'oasis de Teima.'

could not be expected to co-operate.[246] Hence covert means involving local Arabs would have to be employed – as Snouck Hurgronje tells it, a delicate task peculiarly unsuited to the allegedly maladroit French consul. Not surprisingly, this would turn out to be another opportunity for the resourceful Sī ʿAzīz.

Meanwhile Snouck Hurgronje had been helping the consulate from time to time with the translation of Arabic letters connected with this matter. He also wrote to his 'old friend, Prof. Euting', who he was sure would wish to know what was happening to his property, to tell him that everything was going to be delivered to Ǧiddah. Though he did so openly, having discussed it with de Lostalot, the latter jumped to the conclusion that this was an attempt by Snouck Hurgronje to seize the Stele, or at least to further Euting's claim to it. Snouck Hurgronje, a famously pugnacious individual whose withering contempt for de Lostalot should be taken with a pinch of salt, was furious:

> In order to facilitate my confession, the scoundrel told me that in his opinion no scholar would hesitate to steal discoveries or results from a colleague; he said that he knew the 'savants', they were all the same, and so on. Once (towards the end of 1884) he expressed his suspicion all but openly and generally threatened to take to court for 'misappropriation of estate' anyone who took possession of any of the mentioned items.[247]

Snouck Hurgronje was naturally nervous that this brouhaha might undermine his plans to take up residence in Mecca. In the interest of his studies and his personal safety, therefore, he felt obliged to declare formally, in a letter to the vice-consul dated February 1885, that he had no designs on the Stele on either his own or anyone else's behalf. Ostensibly this was graciously received by de Lostalot, who for his part promised not to breathe a word in Europe of Snouck Hurgronje's sojourn in Mecca. Snouck Hurgronje, thus reassured, then made his way to the holy city on 21–22 February 1885.

By now de Lostalot had formally engaged Sī ʿAzīz to carry out further investigations on the ground and to recover Huber's remains. On 16 March

[246] For the Ottoman authorities wishing to prevent Huber's return to the interior of Arabia, see note 244 above. The Ottomans were very against foreigners penetrating inner Arabia. Not only were they angry with Ibn Rashīd for facilitating Huber's travels, but they even regarded Huber's murder as 'an act of merit' (Witkam forthcoming/a: TS pp. 26, 36, and Appendix 4 letter no. 2 from Sī ʿAzīz).

[247] Snouck Hurgronje 1923: 7–8.

1885, eight or ten days after Sī ʿAzīz's departure, a chest containing Huber's remains was delivered to the French vice-consulate.[248] Sī ʿAzīz went on to track down one of Huber's guides, a Ḥarbī named Ḥusayn ibn ʿAdī, to a place on the outskirts of al-Madīnah. This man had fled from his village in disgrace but was unrepentant about murdering 'the Christian dog' and indeed proud of what he had done. He had taken the belongings that Huber had with him and sold them in al-Madīnah.[249]

Having fulfilled his mission to recover Huber's remains, Sī ʿAzīz struck a deal with de Lostalot to recover Huber and Euting's belongings from Ḥāʾil, including the Taymāʾ Stele and other inscriptions, and deliver them to the French in Ǧiddah. A fee of 5,000 francs was agreed, and de Lostalot conferred on Sī ʿAzīz official accreditation as a representative of France in the performance of his mission.

Shortly afterwards, towards the end of March 1885, Sī ʿAzīz set off from Mecca for al-Madīnah and Ḥāʾil. Before leaving, he complained privately to Snouck Hurgronje that de Lostalot was not paying him enough for the job. The Dutchman did his best to reassure him that the French government would deal fairly with his travel costs provided he made honest efforts and, since Sī ʿAzīz had done him some small favours in the past, lent him 200 francs, a modest sum that was later repaid.

On 26 May 1885, having endured considerable hardships and indignities en route from Ḥāʾil to al-Madīnah and then Rābigh, Sī ʿAzīz brought his mission to a successful close by having Huber and Euting's possessions delivered by roundabout means from al-Madīnah to the French vice-consulate in Ǧiddah.[250] Snouck Hurgronje next met him in June 1885 in Mecca, when the Algerian was full of praise for the lord of Ǧabal Shammar, extolling the emir's integrity in having kept Huber and Euting's house secure and in handing over everything to him as the emissary of France. He complained again about de Lostalot's alleged stinginess: the Frenchman was now trying to pay him less than the 5,000 francs agreed. Snouck Hurgronje endeavoured again to reassure him, and claimed to have said not another word about the matter to anyone in Mecca.

Meanwhile, further testimony had reached de Lostalot seeming to implicate Maḥmūd in Huber's murder. The second Ḥarbī guide, Musallam

[248] Appendix 9, Letter no. 9 dated 16 March 1885 from de Lostalot to Maunoir.
[249] Lostalot 1885: 443–5.
[250] For a full account of Sī ʿAzīz's adventures, see Lostalot 1885: 444–6; see also Appendix 9 below, Letter no. 10 from de Lostalot to Maunoir dated 28 May 1885.

al-ʿAwfī, keen to exculpate himself, had contacted him with a tale of joint enterprise: according to him, Huber had put up a fight while Ḥusayn shot him first in the chest and then, when Maḥmūd seized him by the legs and knocked him over, in the head. Nonetheless, in de Lostalot's considered view, the case remained open.[251]

He now accompanied Huber and Euting's effects, together with the Taymāʾ Stele, to Paris and reported to the Académie des Inscriptions et Belles-Lettres. Whatever Snouck Hurgronje might have thought of him, he had successfully carried out his instructions on behalf of France, and was duly fêted. In reporting his arrival to the AIBL, Renan led the chorus of praise: 'In order to acquire this monument, M. de Lostalot has exerted a zeal and intelligence that cannot be sufficiently lauded.'[252] On 30 June 1885, the Stele was accessioned into the Louvre (no. AO 1505), where it stands to this day. The remainder of Huber and Euting's personal belongings was sent on to Huber's mother in Strasbourg.[253]

A sensational article on Huber's death and the Stele then appeared in the newspaper *Le Temps*, dated 5 July 1885. A shocked Snouck Hurgronje jumped to the conclusion that de Lostalot was the instigator: 'It would be giving it too much credit,' he fumes, 'to say that only half of it is lies.'[254] The article made de Lostalot the hero of the affair when most credit belonged to Sī ʿAzīz. More ludicrously, it continued:

[251] Lostalot 1885: 447.

[252] Renan 1885: 107: 'M. de Lostalot est débarqué à Marseille le 16 juin, ayant avec lui les objets recueillis au cours de la mission dont il a été chargé par l'Académie. Il rapporte, en particulier, la célèbre stele araméenne de Teïma, qui mérite la seconde place parmi les monuments d'épigraphie orientale connus jusqu'ici. La stèle du roi Moabite Mésa mérite seule de lui être preferée. La stèle de Teïma est une acte d'éclecticisme religieux, une sorte de concordat, par lequel un individu étranger à la tribu des Teïmistes élève la pretention que le culte qu'il rendra à son dieu particulier soit agréable aux dieux des Teïmistes, et que ceux-ci le protègent. Une part sur ce qu'on peut appeler le budget des cultes de la tribu de Teïma, consistant en vingt-neuf palmiers, est prélevée au profit du dieu nouveau. La stele de Teïma peut être rapportée, dit M. Renan, au Ve siècle avant J.-C. Une très curieuse sculpture en relève singulièrement la valeur. M. de Lostalot a déployé, pour acquérir ce monument à la France, un zèle et une intelligence qui ne sauraient être assez loués.' For the depleted condition in which Huber's crates and suitcases arrived at the AIBL in Paris, see Appendix 11 below, draft of a letter from Berger to Renan dated 10 July 1885.

[253] Hogarth 1904: 282; Ralli 1909: 238–43; Lozachmeur and Briquel-Chatonnet 2013: 5, paragraph 30. On personal effects being sent to Huber's mother in Strasbourg, see Appendix 11, Letter no. 1 dated 8 July 1885 from Renan to Euting.

[254] Snouck Hurgronje 1923: 9.

> The Teima Stele had been targeted: it was pursued from Damascus by a German explorer, Prof. Euting, acting under the name Abdul-Réahib [*sic*]; from Mecca by another scholar, Dr Snouk Busyrouse [*sic*; *sc*. Snouck Hurgronje] under the name Abdul-Ghaffar since his conversion to Islam; from everywhere by the Ottoman government which, informed by the indiscretions of these two individuals, tried to seize it. … The whole country was in turmoil, the people up in arms.

And so it went on, depicting the affair as a contest between antiquities thieves and the allegedly omnipresent Ottoman authorities, with no one but de Lostalot to point the finger at the miscreants.[255] Snouck Hurgronje immediately challenged de Lostalot in writing, declaring that he had never had any designs on the Stele. Was he perhaps protesting too much? It is quite possible that he did arrive in the Ḥiǧāz with the intention of helping his friend Euting to pursue his claim to the Stele, but was forced to deny it once he sensed that such action would jeopardize his project in Mecca. He also accused de Lostalot of breaking his word to keep his presence in Mecca secret, thereby placing his research and safety at risk. But at the beginning of August, before he could receive a reply, he was summarily banished from Mecca by the Ottoman authorities. When he reached Ǧiddah he found out the reason why: the article in *Le Temps* had been published in Arabic and Turkish translation. Although he has nothing but praise for his treatment at the hands of the Ottoman officials, who were inclined to accept his explanations, he realized that public attitudes in the Ḥiǧāz towards foreigners living under cover in Mecca, even though he had undergone conversion in the prescribed manner, placed his life at risk.[256]

A few days later, in Ǧiddah, Snouck Hurgronje received de Lostalot's reply. The latter understandably tried to exonerate himself from involvement in the *Le Temps* article, but his letter contained further serious misrepresentations. Gravest was the extraordinary charge that Snouck Hurgronje had 'promised a

[255] Snouck Hurgronje 1923: 9–10.

[256] On the question of Snouck Hurgronje's conversion and circumcision, see Appendix 9, Letter no. 8 dated 25 January 1885 from de Lostalot to Maunoir; Witkam 2007a: xvii–xviii; Witkam 2020: 358 n. 25; Witkam forthcoming/a: TS pp. 14–15, 41–2, Appendix 3, Appendix 4 letter no. 5; Witkam forthcoming/b: TS pp. 7–9; Vrolijk 2013: 206. For de Lostalot's defence of himself against Snouck Hurgronje's accusations, and his own interpretation of Snouck Hurgronje's role in the Taymāʾ Stele affair and banishment from Mecca, see Appendix 9, Letter no. 14 dated 12 November 1885.

cheque of ten thousand francs, payable in cash by M. van der Chys [*sic*; van der Chijs], on the day that the Stele is deposited in your house'. This information had come from de Lostalot's 'agents', *viz.* Sī ʿAzīz. According to Snouck Hurgronje, when he confronted Sī ʿAzīz, the Algerian confessed that he had indeed played on de Lostalot's mistrust of the Dutch scholar as a means of squeezing more money out of the Frenchman. He had made the whole story up – the age-old ploy of inventing a better offer from a third party. Snouck Hurgronje, who seems to have liked the Algerian, was surprisingly charitable about what he calls this 'white lie', and showed magnanimity even when Sī ʿAzīz refused to retract it in writing. After all, the latter was a dependent of the French government and loth to risk his pension by confessing to false testimony. He had in every other way behaved as a good friend to the Dutchman, and had never imagined that his action might place him in jeopardy.

Snouck Hurgronje now realized that the false allegation had rendered his residence not just in Mecca but anywhere in the Ḥiǧāz untenable. Almost three weeks later, on the 'main day of the great pilgrim festival [i.e. the Standing at ʿArafāt on 20 September 1885] in which I had so dearly wished to participate', he took his departure from Ǧiddah. He ends:

> Thus ended my scientific journey, which had started so auspiciously, thanks to the ignorance and bigotry of a consular official. Fortunately, I had already achieved much of what I had intended. … But my self-defence against severe accusations can no longer be withheld. At the same time, I have considered it appropriate to inform the public how pathetically the great powers are sometimes represented in the East, notably in such places where there is hardly any serious work for their officials.[257]

The accession of the Taymāʾ Stele into the Louvre was not quite the end of the affair. However keen Euting may later have become to maintain good relations with the AIBL, at the outset he felt that his rightful entitlement to the Stele had been thwarted. He wrote to Renan, probably in June 1885, stating his claim. Though we have been unable to find Euting's letter, we do have Renan's long reply to it.[258] From this it is clear that Euting had asked for his agreement with Huber to be honoured: that he was entitled to a single inscription, which they had later agreed should be the Taymāʾ Stele; by way

[257] Snouck Hurgronje 1923: 13.
[258] Appendix 11, Letter no. 1 dated 8 July 1885 from Renan to Euting.

of recompense, Euting was offering to pay half of the costs of recovering and transporting the Stele to Europe.

Renan's reply is as noteworthy for the misconceptions it contains as for its firm though not unfriendly refusal. Renan insists that the expedition had been an official one conducted under the auspices of the French government, which thereby had the sole rights to all its scientific results and acquisitions; Euting had been no more than a travelling companion, with no rights over any of the expedition's discoveries; and this was how Huber had consistently presented the expedition to his sponsors in writing. In this distortion of the facts, Huber had completely ignored not only the substantial funds at Euting's disposal but also the fact that they had been provided by the German administration of Alsace, and had omitted to mention that all the arms that they had been able to distribute as gifts had been generously provided by King Karl of Württemberg himself.

Renan then addresses the question of the Taymāʾ Stele. Huber, he says, had made a sketch of this during his first expedition in 1880 which had been published by the Société de Géographie, and had repeatedly told Renan that the Stele had been the principal discovery of his first journey and the main reason why he wanted to return to Arabia. In fact, there is no evidence of the existence of such a sketch by Huber, let alone one published by the Société de Géographie, and Renan seems to have confused the supposed sketch with the three sketches of Taymāʾ inscriptions that Huber did publish in the *Bulletin* of the Société in 1884 (Huber 1884a; Appendix I below). Nor, as argued above, is there any evidence that Huber ever mentioned the Stele to Renan or to anybody else before Euting saw it on 17 February 1884.

As for Euting's offer to pay half the costs of bringing the Stele to France, Renan is on firmer ground, making the valid point that the trouble and expense of that operation would far outstrip any amount that Euting would be able to offer. Here the unspoken implication was that French entitlement to the Stele was based on the very considerable efforts it had made to bring it to France, which would trump any claim to it that Euting might put forward.

The latter point was developed further in a letter that Renan wrote shortly after, on 18 July 1885, to his AIBL colleague Philippe Berger.[259] In addressing the question of an inscription being reserved for Euting, he distinguishes between an entitlement to the Stele arising from first discovery

[259] Appendix 11, Letter no. 3 dated 18 July 1885 from Renan to Berger.

of it, and one arising from the pains taken by the French to bring it to France. This is a valid point; Euting would doubtless have conceded that Germany's diplomatic representation in Arabia and the Ottoman Empire at large was feeble in comparison with that of France and that German diplomats would not have been able to arrange the recovery of the Stele.[260] However, the fact that Renan felt it necessary to foreground this argument could be interpreted as a sign that by now he was perhaps not quite so sure that Huber had really been the Stele's original discoverer:[261]

> Let us get a tight grip on the Euting question. The reserving of 'one inscription' is of course only valid if the Huber–Euting partnership had lasted. The break at Hail put an end to their agreement ('*pacte*'). Euting was so conscious of this that he freed himself from the obligations contained in his letter by sending the copies of the inscriptions to Nöldeke alone. Lastly, in Palmyra Euting acted completely outside the agreement because he took everything for himself. In good conscience, I do not think that this clause of a reserved inscription should be taken into consideration. What we have to do is to avoid scandal. In any case the question of State ownership and the credit for the discovery must be kept completely separate. We scarcely need to bother about the first of these. As for the question of who discovered the Teima inscription, there are abundant proofs apart from Huber's letter.

Whatever the merits of the argument for French ownership put forward here, it is obvious that Renan had been taken in by the falsehood promulgated by Huber for French consumption that he and Euting had separated in Ḥāʾil, before either of them went to Taymāʾ and Madāʾin Ṣāliḥ. Even had this been true, it was a specious basis for arguing that any agreement between Huber and Euting was thereby rendered null and void.

Renan's brush-off was not the end of the matter. In a report written for an as yet unidentified person of importance dated 17 November 1886 (addressed to 'Euer Durchlaucht'/Your Serene Highness), Euting requested

[260] As McMeekin points out (2010: 8–10), the newly unified Germany under Bismarck was far from interested in engaging with the Ottoman Empire. That posture persisted until 1888 and the accession of Kaiser Wilhelm II, who enthusiastically courted Sultan Abdülhamid II and developed a near-obsession with the Islamic Orient.

[261] Appendix 11, Letter no. 3 dated 18 July 1885 from Renan to Berger.

help in making a plea to the French authorities to return the Stele ('welchen er ohne meine Belehrung NB gar nicht der Mitnahme werth erachtet hätte!' 'which he [Huber] would not have thought worthy of taking without my instruction!') and the reimbursement of some expenses. On page 6 of the document, Euting quotes the letter written by Huber to Renan on 8 April 1883 in which Huber confirms the arrangement that Euting would be entitled to an inscription.[262] That Euting genuinely believed in the validity of that agreement and expected the Taymāʾ Stele to be delivered to Strasbourg is further demonstrated by a letter to August Dillmann of 16 July 1884.[263]

We do not know whether this final plea by Euting was ever submitted to the French. If it was, it created no stir, and the affair seems to have fizzled out. Very possibly it was extinguished by larger political considerations to do with Franco-German relations in the aftermath of the annexation of Alsace-Lorraine. Nonetheless, as Hogarth implies in *The Penetration of Arabia*, a whiff of festering injustice was still hanging about it twenty years on, and it continues to do so:[264]

> It [the Stele] is now in the Louvre, and rightfully, since the enterprise and trouble expended in recovering it constitute the only valid title to its possession. But when one recalls Huber's subordinate relation to Euting in matters of archaeology, one must doubt whether the original purchase was not really made at Teima for Berlin rather than Paris.

It is now more than ever timely, even at a distance of 135 years, to revive controversies such as this, as the rightful ownership of important antiquities has recently become very much a matter of global debate and re-evaluation. President Macron himself has been heard to advocate the return of significant items of national heritage to their countries of origin.[265] Jordan, for example, has requested the return of the famous Mesha Stone.[266] Perhaps larger political

---

[262] Appendix 7, Letter no. 2 dated 8 April 1883 from Huber to Renan. See also Pearson 1993: 100–1, 110–12; Healey 2004: 320–1.

[263] Trüper 2019: 68, citing Euting's correspondence with Dillmann, held in the Staatsbibliothek Berlin, Nachlass Dillmann.

[264] Hogarth 1904: 282n.

[265] See e.g *The Guardian*, 18 November 2018, article by Ruth Maclean: 'France urged to change heritage law and return looted art to Africa: report commissioned by Macron recommends restitution of artworks taken during colonial era'.

[266] *The Jordan Times*, 12 April 2016. The Mesha Stele, also known as the Moabite Stone, is an inscription discovered in 1868 among the ruins of the Moabite capital,

considerations may supervene in the context of EU–Arab relations, to bring about the return of the Taymāʾ Stele to the land in which it was created, now part of Saudi Arabia – so achieving belated closure of this intriguing 19th-century Franco-German imbroglio.

Publication history

Since publication in three quarterly issues of the *Bulletin* of the Société de Géographie in 1884–85 (Huber 1884b and 1885a), Huber's account of his first Arabian journey has been reprinted only once, in 1885, as a monograph published by the Société under the same title, *Voyage dans l'Arabie centrale. Hamâd, Šammar, Qaçîm, Hedjâz. 1878–82* (Huber 1885b). The reason why this single-volume edition was issued so hurriedly after the publication of the original articles is unclear, but its timing suggests that it was done in order to honour the memory of a great French explorer as soon as possible after his untimely death. This volume is held by only a few libraries, and seems otherwise impossible to obtain. It should be noted that it does not include the first article in the series, which was devoted to Huber's epigraphic finds (Huber 1884a; see Appendix 1 in this volume).

It is also possibly significant that its publication more or less coincided with the arrival in Paris in June 1885 of the Taymāʾ Stele and the remnants of Huber and Euting's belongings and other finds. However, any suspicion that the text might have been adjusted in order to corroborate a claim that Huber saw the Stele in 1880 can be dismissed: there is no unwarranted insertion of a reference to him seeing the Stele in Taymāʾ at that time. The text is an exact copy of the original articles, even it seems to the extent of using the same letterpress.

Since that time, there has been no French re-edition of Huber's travelogue, nor any English translation. The sole subsequent edition has been an Arabic translation by Elissar Saadeh, published in Beirut in 2003 under the title *Riḥlah fī al-Ğazīrah al-ʿArabiyyah al-Wusṭa, 1878–1882: al-Ḥamād, al-Shammar,*

Dhiban, in modern Jordan. It dates to the 9th century BC, is in a script close to that of Old Hebrew inscriptions but with certain peculiarities, and is the chief extant evidence for the Moabite language. It describes the building projects of the Moabite king, Mesha, and records how he threw off the yoke of Israel. News of its discovery set off a race between France, Britain and Germany to acquire it. Before it could be obtained, some local people smashed it to pieces, but fortunately a squeeze had already been made. The surviving pieces of the stone went to the Musée du Louvre in Paris.

al-Qaṣīm, al-Ḥiǧāz (Huber 2003). This takes the single-volume reprint as its textual source, and thus likewise omits the first article in the series devoted to Huber's epigraphic finds (Huber 1884a). Aspects of this publication are significantly misleading. For example, the publisher's introduction states unequivocally that Huber came across the Taymāʾ Stele on this journey and that he deserves the credit for its discovery. Among other unsubstantiated assertions is the claim that the Emir Muḥammad Ibn Rashīd ordered Huber's assassination, and that this took place not near Rābigh but in al-ʿUlā. The edition includes a number of drawings of rock art and graffiti which are taken from Huber's account of his *second* journey, in 1883–84 (Huber 1891). These include the transcription of the Stele which we now know to have been drawn not by Huber but by Julius Euting in 1884, as well as other drawings by Euting (Huber included no drawings in the travelogue of his first journey in 1880–81). Aside from these deficiencies, which can probably be laid at the publisher's door rather than the translator's, the translation itself contains some useful attempts to transliterate Huber's place names back into Arabic, though not always correctly.

The present edition has been undertaken in order to correct misconceptions and clarify terminology, and to place before readers for the first time a comprehensive and critical English translation of an important record of Arabian travel, so remedying the neglect into which it has fallen since 1885. Time now to turn to Huber's narrative of his first great Arabian journey.

THE TRANSLATION

Charles Huber's First Journey in Central Arabia, 1880–1881

PART I

A Journey in Central Arabia: al-Ḥamād, Shammar, al-Qaṣīm and al-Ḥiǧāz[1]

Bulletin de la Société de Géographie 7th series, no. 5, 1884, 3rd trimester, pp. 304–63

By Charles Huber

Commissioned by the Minister of Public Education 1878–1882

---

1 See the map bound in at the end of this issue. The Editors of the *Bulletin* believe it necessary to warn the reader that, in the system of transliteration adopted by M. Charles Huber:

> ç renders the sound of *ṣād* in Arabic; q that of *qāf*; ghr and rh that of *ghayn*. These three consonants have no equivalents in French.
> š is to be pronounced *ch* [anglice *sh*].
> ÿ is to be pronounced *ī*.
> g before a vowel is to be pronounced *dj* [anglice *ǧ*] (Gebel = Djebel, Gobbah = Djobbah etc.)
> ň, m̆, ř, simply indicate that *n*, *m* and *r*, even when they are found at the end of a syllable, must always preserve the sound that they have in Italian, English and German, i.e. *enne*, *emme*, *ère* [anglice *en*, *em* and *ar*].
> The apostrophe before a vowel represents the Arabic consonant *'aïn* [*'ayn*], a phoneme that occurs in no European language.
> *ah*, *at*, is the silent final *a* [*sic* actually *h*], or *ta marbouta* [*tā' marbūṭah*] of feminine nouns.

[See the preamble to Appendix 13 for further information about Huber's system of transliteration.]

Having been entrusted in 1878 with a scientific mission in Arabia, I met with various delays and difficulties from the start which I have detailed in my report to the minister.[2]

A first attempt to reach al-Ǧawf, with Shaykh Muḥammad Ṭūkhī,[3] was aborted because of the Druze insurrection;[4] the agreement I made subsequently with Saṭṭām ibn Shaʿlān, shaykh of the Ruwalah, did not come to anything because I received no word from him. Nor did an agreement that I concluded with Shaykh ʿAlī al-Qurayshī.

[305] In the end I found the guides essential for my onward progress at the house of Muḥammad al-Khalīl, shaykh of Boṣra, whose guests they were at the time. These men were two *bawwāq*s[5] and two denizens of Kāf. I came to an arrangement with them against the advice of the shaykh of Boṣra, who declared himself unable to vouchsafe me any guarantee that they would abide by their word, insisting that at best I was risking robbery at their hands and being abandoned in the desert. I was in too much of a hurry to heed such wise counsel and left Boṣra next day with my new companions. This was on 14 May [1880], and this first stage of our journey took us only as far as ʿAnz, after we had crossed Umm al-Rummān.[6]

---

[2] [i.e. the Minister of Public Education (Ministre d'Instruction publique). Huber's handwritten report of March 1882 describes these delays in detail (French national archives, Pierrefitte-sur-Seine, Dossier F/17/2976/1:1 entitled 'M. Huber, Charles, Mission au Thibet et dans l'Asie centrale', 1878–82, item 79, 65-page report dated 27 March 1882, pp. 1–10): see Appendix 3, Letter no. 16 and report of March 1882; see also Introduction pp. 16–17). The date given, 1878, refers to the award of Huber's commission, rather than the actual start of his expedition. Lorentz (in Kurpershoek 2018: 109) correctly specifies that Huber spent a year in the region, from May 1879 to April 1880, familiarizing himself with Arabic dialects and customs. As a result, he did not reach Kāf till 17 May 1880 and al-Ǧawf till 26 May 1880 (Huber 1884b: 307, 311, 315).]

[3] [For Muḥammad Ṭūkhī, shaykh of the Wuld ʿAlī, a tribe of the northern ʿAnizah, see Introduction p. 16; also Appendix 3, Letter no. 16 and report of March 1882. This is the 'Mohammed Dukhi ibn Smeyr' known to the Blunts, whom the Emir Muḥammad ibn Rashīd raided on his campaign into the Ḥawrān in April 1880 (Blunt 1879: 319–20; 1881 i: 272–3).]

[4] [This is probably a reference to recent efforts by Midḥat Pasha to subdue the Druze in late 1878 (Blunt 1881 i: 18). Huber refers in one of his letters to a Druze uprising in 1879 (Appendix 4, Letter no. 13 dated 20 May 1883 from Huber to Maunoir, note 42; see also Blunt 1881 i: 18). For Midḥat Pasha, see also note 136 below.]

[5] A *baouwak* [*bawwāq*] is an Arab who, convicted of a felony or other honour crime, has been cast out of his tribe and condemned to permanent exile, in whose word no one can any longer place any trust, and who usually carries out the most menial jobs on the borders of the desert where he still takes refuge. (CH)

[6] [ʿAnz is situated about 35 km south-east of Boṣra at approx. 36° 00' N 040° 45' E.]

ʿAnz, a village of 300 people on a little hill, is the last settled habitation before one reaches the desert. It is noteworthy that despite its situation as an outpost, that is to say between the Druze and the Muslim nomads, ʿAnz is populated entirely by Christians.

There we met five Arabs encamped outside the walls who wanted to go either to Kāf itself or its vicinity, and were waiting for other travellers to join them to form a small caravan. They left with us the next day.

Being a small party, we had to try to avoid any encounters, which are always dangerous on this outer edge of the desert. So, from 15 May, we travelled in a more or less zigzag fashion because the information we had received in Boṣra and ʿAnz on the various encampments scattered about made us apprehensive about the presence of bedouin.

On the morning of 16 May, we made camp three kilometres north-east of Qaṣr al-Azraq.[7] Unfortunately I was unable [306] to approach any closer, because the ground around the *qaṣr*, which is built in a depression, was still all swampy after the winter rains. As far as I was able to discern from afar, it is a completely isolated square tower constructed of dressed masonry, with its upper storeys apparently in ruins. The *qaṣr* has probably been in existence since early antiquity, and must be one of the stations on the route leading into central Arabia through Dūmat al-Ǧandal.

The territory around it is called ʿAmrī or ʿAmarī by the early Arab authors. The anonymous dervish, author of an itinerary of the *ḥaǧǧ* route from Constantinople to Mecca,[8] mentions this point and adds that, during his expedition to the north, the Prophet Muḥammad advanced as far as this *qaṣr* and its stream, probably a reference to the Wādī al-Rayal.[9] The place is of interest because it is here that the Wādī al-Sirḥān begins, extending

---

[7] 'The Blue Castle'. (CH) [Although Huber could not have known it, this is a mistranslation. The adjective *azraq* (feminine *zarqāʾ*) means a bluey-grey and is used of blue eyes, but also of the grey cataract of the eye, of highly polished spear- or arrow-heads, and of clear water. The oasis where the castle is located is called al-Azraq, which may literally mean 'The bluey-grey, or clear, one', possibly referring to the large permanent lake which was its major feature until excessive piping of the water to conurbations virtually drained it in the late 20th century. Thus, *azraq* here is a place name not an adjective, and Qaṣr al-Azraq simply means 'the castle of al-Azraq'. (MCAM)]

[8] [I have been unable to identify this author. Musil (1927: 337–40) describes al-Azraq and cites various earlier authors who mention it: al-Muqaddasī, Yāqūt and Abu-l-Fedaʾ.]

[9] [Actually Wādī Rāǧil. (MCAM)]

to the south all the way to the wells of al-Ğarāwī, at two days' march from al-Ğawf.

I came upon the Wādī al-Rayal in the afternoon of the same day. It still contained water in a few hollows despite the season already being well advanced.

We halted within sight of Qaṣr Azraq just for the midday meal and left straight afterwards. Normally weak and vulnerable caravans such as ours never halt so close to this place, which has the most fearsome reputation; as a place of transit, Qaṣr Azraq is a constant target of marauders.

The plain of Azraq is several kilometres in extent. The soil everywhere is good, lying over a substrate of clay, and there is a thick and vigorous growth of the desert shrubs on which camels depend.

Scarcely had we left this place than the terrain once more turned rugged, with much evidence of volcanic origin. From time to time we traversed tracts of desert entirely covered with rocks that increased enormously in size the closer we drew to Kāf, which we reached [307] towards evening on the next day, 17 May. We had been on the move for most of the night.

The traveller Seetzen[10] reports a route that places Kāf at five days' march from Boṣrah; this was according to one of his guides, Yūsuf al-Milkī. But the error of this becomes immediately obvious when one finds him mentioning Ithrah and al-Qarqar[11] before Kāf.

On the other hand, Seetzen does give us the first information we possess on this place. Kāf, he says, is a ruined castle on top of a hill, completely surrounded by a swamp making it difficult of access. There are a few wells and wild date palms that bear no fruit.

When I arrived among the Druze, I had already learnt that present-day Kāf was a small inhabited village, and Nağm al-Aṭrash, shaykh of the Druze, even gave me a letter for its shaykh.[12]

---

[10] [Ulrich Jasper Seetzen (1767–1811) was a German scholar and traveller. Having made journeys in Turkey, Syria, Jordan, Palestine and Egypt, he arrived in Jiddah in 1809, converted to Islam and performed the pilgrimage to Mecca. He travelled extensively in Arabia, visiting al-Madīnah and going on to Yemen. In September 1811, he left Mukhā' planning to go to Muscat, but was murdered by his guides allegedly on the orders of the Imām in Ṣan'ā'. Most of his papers were lost, but those that survived were published in four volumes (Seetzen 1854), and also as individual items in Zach's *Monatliche Correspondenz*.]

[11] [Huber's rendering of this place name as Korâkir appears to be erroneous. Al-Qarqar is situated a few miles south-west of Ithrah.]

[12] [Nağm al-Aṭrash was still paramount shaykh of the Druze when Huber and Euting

When we reached the oasis, it would have been normal for me to be the guest of my guide, Muḥammad. But as he was a poor man, and his parents likewise, he volunteered to find me accommodation from the next day at the house of the shaykh, who had in any case already laid claim to me.[13]

ʿAbd Allāh al-Khamīs,[14] shaykh of Kāf, is a man of about fifty (he himself does not know his precise age) whose non-existent musculature and weak and prominent history are proof of his bedouin origin.[15] On the history of the village, ʿAbd Allāh told me that his father, Dughayrī al-Khamīs, had been the first to establish himself there fifty or so years ago when he, ʿAbd Allāh, was no more than a child. Whether the numerous little springs of the place formed a marsh at the base of the hill, as Yūsuf al-Milkī recounted, ʿAbd Allāh could no longer recall; it had always been the case that every one of the twelve springs to be found here had [308] been confined within little reservoirs. Having taken the temperature of ten of them at four o'clock in the morning, I found that it was 24.5° on average for those exposed to the sun, and 21.1° for those in the shade of the palms. The average temperature of this region would thus be very high; ʿAbd Allāh assured me that in fact the heat is greater in summer at Kāf than at al-Ǧawf, and that it rains only very seldom in winter. Another indication of the high temperature at Kāf is given by the existence of date palms, which grow very well here. The water is slightly brackish but none the less pleasant to drink.

The village, which is elliptical in shape, extends from east to west and comprises two clusters, one of eight and the other of nine houses, separated by the springs and the 450 palm trees. Other than the palms there are a couple

---

visited him in September 1883 (Euting 1896: 24, 28–30).]

[13] [Kāf is one of several villages in the Wādī al-Sirḥān known as *Qurayyāt al-Milḥ* (nowadays, simply Qurayyāt) on account of the salt deposits in the area (see the aerial photograph of Kāf and the salt-pans in Philby 1923: opposite p. 245). Guarmani visited it in 1864 (1938: 105–6), but Huber, in the description of his own visit presented here, is very sceptical of Guarmani's account (see below, pp. 94–5). For an interesting description of these villages in the 1960s, with photographs, see Winnett and Reed 1970: 56–64. (MCAM)].

[14] Lady Anne Blunt calls him Abdallah el Khamir. (CH) [See Euting 1896: 51–5 for a lengthy description of Kāf and its shaykh, ʿAbd Allāh al-Khamīs, in September–October 1883. Euting stayed there for about three weeks while Huber made a round-trip to Damascus and back.]

[15] [This is a literal translation of Huber's phrase 'dont la musculature nulle et l'histoire faible et saillante prouvent l'origine bédouine.' I have been unable to fathom what he really means by this bizarre statement.]

of pomegranate trees to be found and a few *ithl*.[16] The timber of the latter is used in construction, to make the frames and joists for the doors and roofs of the houses. The inhabitants, about ninety in number, own thirty or so camels, as well as goats and about fifty sheep, plus a few chickens. They possess neither cattle nor horses.

This little oasis owes its existence to the presence in the first place of its springs, and secondly of a salt mine, the revenue of which is the exclusive preserve of the shaykh. This product comes from a small mountain situated five kilometres to the south of Kāf. It is carried on camels close to the village and dumped in troughs containing two-fifths or half a cubic metre of water. The salt dissolves and then crystallizes by evaporation. It is bright white but has a very bitter taste. It is sold to the desert tribes and smuggled into the Ḥawrān and to Ǧabal Druze on camels belonging to the shaykh of Boṣra.[17]

Though their exteriors are clean, the houses are filthy inside. Everyone wears bedouin dress. Nobody can [309] read or write. As always, eye ailments are commonplace.

On the morning of the 19th, ʿAbd Allāh al-Khamīs, who has three wives, brought his only son to see me, a child aged ten who was suffering from a stomach problem. At the same time he brought me a coffee cup full of water, and asked me to enunciate over it the words required to cure the little patient.

I shall be the first European to have climbed the rock upon which stands the Qaṣr al-Sayyid.[18] It is a true isolated outcrop, along with two others

[16] *Ithel* or *ethel*, a species of tamarisk. (CH) [Specifically, *Tamarix aphylla*, the ubiquitous tree of the Arabian oases, grown as wind- and sand-breaks. Its light, strong wood was universally used in inland areas where mangrove poles were not available, as rafters and general building timber (Facey 1997: 60, 120–2). A fine photograph taken in 1921–22 by Maj. A. L. Holt shows the village, oasis and forts of Kāf with Qaṣr Ṣaʿīdī to the right (Facey and Grant 1996: 90).]

[17] The editors have left the responsibility for this spelling [*viz.* Haourân] with the author. The Arabs used to call it Djebel Deroûz, 'the mountain of the Druzes'. (The Editors.) [This is Ǧabal Ḥawrān, known as *Auranitis* in antiquity and Ǧabal al-ʿArab today. The name was changed unofficially from Ǧabal al-Drūz to Ǧabal al-ʿArab apparently in 1937 by some Arab nationalist Druzes meeting in Jordan, and officially in 1948 by the newly independent Syrian nationalist government. (MCAM)]

[18] 'The lord's castle'. (CH) [Huber's translation of the name, 'le château du seigneur' and his transliteration of the Arabic, Qaçr e' Seïed, shows that he interpreted the name as Qaṣr al-Sayyid. His Arabic spelling in his report of March 1882 confirms this (French national archives, Pierrefitte-sur-Seine, Dossier F/17/2976/1:1, entitled 'Mission au Thibet et dans l'Asie centrale', 1878–82, item 79, 65-page report dated 27 March 1882, p. 15). Euting gives a lengthy description of this *ǧabal* in his journal entry for 16 September 1883 (Euting 1896: 71–3) and records the name as Qaṣr

like it but smaller on the plain of Kāf. It rises possibly eighty metres above the level of the plain. Its summit, in the form of a table-top, is about 3,000 metres in circumference. It is formed entirely of great black volcanic rocks, very hard and embedded in an earthy gangue, with some layers of beautiful limestone, also very hard but completely white, of the kind that I had already encountered en route from Azraq to Kāf.

The ruins crowning the upper plateau consist of a wall of three or four metres in height and half a metre to a metre thick, which follows the contours of the eastern mountain crest. The three other aspects lack walls and probably always have, as their rock faces are vertical. The path leading up to the plateau, which has completely collapsed, is likewise on the eastern side and starts at the cemetery of Kāf, which is situated at the base of the massif.

The gateway of this defensive wall was closed by means of a double-leafed gate of black stone, like those one sees in large numbers in all the ruined towns of the Leǧā, Ǧabal Druze and the Ḥawrān, and which I have even seen being used in some of the gardens at Palmyra. One of the door-leaves is lying on the ground below the entrance.

Also on the plateau are two small roofless rooms [310] backing onto the circuit wall, and to the north too are visible the walls of a small building likewise enclosing two rooms. Towards the gateway of the circuit wall is a circular walled basin, four metres in diameter and a metre deep; a little farther on there is a natural hole in the ground in the form of a cave. These two concavities would probably have served as water reservoirs. Between the two reservoirs lies a great block of lava, of irregular shape and about a cubic metre in size, on which are carved various signs identical to those used to this day by the bedouin to mark their camels, and which are called *wasm*.[19]

As the outcrop had no further building traces to offer, I think that it has only ever served as a fortified post making use of a natural position. It could easily be made even more impregnable today.

The full horror of this terrain and these naked and deserted mountains is revealed from the summit of the plateau of Qaṣr al-Sayyid. The view is made all the more desolate by the vividness of the black rocks scattered all over it. Also, the eye comes to rest with pleasure on the oasis spread out at the base of

Ṣaʿīdī. Other travellers, myself included in 1985, have since recorded it as Qaṣr Saʿīdī.]

[19] [*wasm*, pl. *wusūm*, camel brands signifying tribal ownership. (MCAM)]

the southern rock face. In the distance, six miles[20] away, one can see a point on the Wadi al-Sirḥān.[21]

At six miles south by 70° east of Kāf lies another little oasis called Ithrah.[22] Its houses are built not of mud as in Kāf but of black rubble, like those of the Ḥawrān. It is an ancient place which, having like Kāf been abandoned, was repopulated ten years after the latter. Today it comprises twenty houses with about 100 inhabitants, who benefit like the people of Kāf from water supplied by perennial springs [311]. Yūsuf al-Milkī called this place Ittra in his itinerary.

On 20 May 1880, in the shade of the palms at Kāf, I recorded the air temperature from hour to hour. Here are my observations.

4 a.m.	13.5°	10 a.m.	28.7°	4 p.m.	33.1°
5 a.m.	15.1°	11 a.m.	30.8°	5 p.m.	32°
6 a.m.	16.9°	noon	31.6°	6 p.m.	30.9°
7 a.m.	19.8°	1 p.m.	32.5°	7 p.m.	26.4°
8 a.m.	22°	2 p.m.	32.7°	8 p.m.	26.2°
9 a.m.	26.4°	3 p.m.	33.8°	9 p.m.	25.8°

This Kāf/Ithrah region is interesting by reason of being the lowest point between the Ḥawrān and al-Ǧawf. It is the destination as much for the streams flowing down from the Ḥawrān, as for the *shaʿīb*s (ravines) coming from the south that flow into the Ḥamād and Wadi al-Sirḥān. It is that which also explains how the springs remain constant in their rate of flow despite rainfall being so scarce. Besides, as we saw above, this rate of flow is not very considerable, since 450 palms, on their own and unaided by any other crops, are sufficient to absorb it all.

The average of the barometric pressure readings taken at Kāf gave me an altitude of 498 m for this location.

I cannot leave this oasis without mentioning a traveller who passed through here in 1864 and correcting what he said. It is M. C[arlo] Guarmani

[20] I always employ the geographical mile of 1,852 metres. (CH)

[21] That is the same spot where we had crossed it to reach Kāf, a crossing we had achieved in 1 hour 32 minutes and which, at the pace at which we were then marching, would make the valley about 5 km in width. (CH)

[22] Lady Anne Blunt calls it Ithery or Ethra, with the English *th*. (CH) [Lady Anne actually calls it Itheri. See Blunt 1881 i: 82–9 for her description of Kāf and Ithrah.]

of whom I wish to speak.[23] Ruined in the 15th century and rebuilt in the 18th, Kāf, he says, was in former times a station on the caravan route between Damascus and al-Madīnah. Besides Kāf, to which he ascribes 250 inhabitants, and Ithrah, which he calls Etera, with 300 inhabitants, this traveller also mentions ʿAqaylah, with 15 inhabitants; [312] Ghaṭṭī with 150; and al-Washwāsh with 200.[24]

As for the time when Kāf supposedly fell into ruin, since to my knowledge no author mentions this, it is as difficult to deny as to affirm that it took place in the 15th century. And as to the date of its reconstruction, I have already mentioned the account of its revival given by the founder's own son. Finally, as for it having been a station for caravans, I do not believe that such a route between Damascus and al-Madīnah, passing through Kāf, ever existed. A caravan moves too slowly to be able to negotiate a route in this direction along which, for two stretches, it is necessary to go five days without finding water. As for the four other localities mentioned by M. Guarmani, I heard nobody speak of them, and as for the numbers of inhabitants, I hold to my own figures, the head-counts having been too easy to carry out for me to have been mistaken.[25]

I had agreed a price with shaykh ʿAbd Allāh al-Khamīs to serve me as guide himself as far as al-Ǧawf, and we fixed our departure for 21 May.

We were joined by two inhabitants of al-Ǧawf who had been waiting for some time for companions on this journey, and we left Kāf at sunrise,

[23] Guarmani 1865. (CH) [Carlo Claudio Camillo Guarmani (1828–84) was an Arabic-speaking Italian horse enthusiast and traveller who was commissioned by the French army and by the Italian king Vittorio Emmanuele II to seek out pure-bred Arabian horses for their respective cavalry regiments. Starting from Jerusalem, Guarmani travelled through northern Arabia during January–May 1864. His route took him to Taymāʾ, Khaybar, the southern fringe of the Nafūd, Ḥāʾil, Mustaǧiddah, Buraydah and ʿUnayzah in al-Qaṣīm, and finally across the Nafūd by a zigzag route via al-Ḥayāniyyah and Ǧubbah to Dūmat al-Ǧandal, Wadi al-Sirḥān and al-Azraq. His account of the journey (Guarmani 1865, 1866) was much consulted by later explorers.]

[24] The Editors consider it useful to recall that M. Guarmani has rendered Arabic names, as far as he was able, in Italian spelling, which has been retained by M. Huber in this citation. (The Editors.) [Huber spells them Akeile, El-Gotti, El-Ekder, El-Uscevuasce. For an excursion to El-Uscevuasce/al-Washwāsh in 1883, see Euting 1896: 58, 65.]

[25] [Huber is perhaps being a little hard on Guarmani. Euting in September 1883 (entries for 10, 12 and 28 September) mentions localities named Nebts waʿaqēleh and Ghúṭṭī (though admittedly neither of these were villages) and actually visited the village of al-Washwāsh/el-Uscevuasce. See Euting 1896: 51, 58, 92; Musil 1927: 323–7 gives a full list of these 'Salt Villages'.]

accompanied by the entire male population for a quite a distance outside the oasis.

Although the going was over level ground, we were nonetheless in a mountainous region, albeit one of a very specific nature. It is an immense plateau with a stony surface from which arise several completely isolated outcrops in the form of ellipses, cones and spikes, all detached from one other and most of them flat-topped. Nor do they follow any regular arrangement, running from north to south as much as from east to west, with their heights varying from twenty to a hundred metres.

[313] It is curious to note that all these outcrops are composed of a white limestone that produces a very beautiful sand of the same colour, and that they look as though a rain of coarse, calcined black rubble had fallen upon them. It is, in short, the same as the type of terrain that I had already encountered a day before reaching Kāf. All these distinctive outcrops, especially those between Ithrah, Kāf and Wadi al-Sirḥān strictly so called, are known by the generic name al-Qudayr[26] or al-Wurayk.[27]

At midday, there took place an episode that alas still occurs all too frequently in the desert. Just as we entered the bed of Wadi al-Sirḥān, we came across first one, then three dying men and, a little farther on, a corpse. These were four dervishes who had been foolhardy enough to set out from al-Ǧawf eight days before, alone and on foot, aiming for Kāf and then Damascus, without water bottles or provisions. They were counting on coming across bedouin encampments, and thus making their way from one to another to their destination. They were no more than skin and bone, as the saying goes. The dead man, more or less parched and scorched by the sun, was completely naked. His companions, though themselves likewise at death's door, had already shared out his rags.

I had each man given about two litres of water and a little flour, which they consumed on the spot.

I noticed that ʿAbd Allāh, instead of pointing them in the direction of Kāf, which was the nearest point, directed them towards Ithrah. This was to spare his household the troublesome obligation of feeding them.

[26] El Qedeir: 'the little cauldron'. (The Editors.) [*Qudayr* being the diminutive of *qidr*, the general word for a cooking pot.]

[27] There exists also a Ǧabal Wurayk (Oueraïk) to the north of Mawqaq. (CH) [For this Ǧabal al-Wurayk, see e.g. Huber 1891: 246–7, 'Ouréîtz'; Euting 1914: 127.]

At midday, as I said above, we joined the bed of Wadi al-Sirḥān and marched along it for about three hours. Then, leaving it to the west, we again entered a mountainous tract completely covered with black stones [314] called al-Mismā', a name that it takes from the principal mountain in this area, which I was indeed able to make out next morning twelve miles to the east. It is a long range running from north-east to south-west.[28]

On the same day we went back down onto the Wadi al-Sirḥān, and there I was witness to a magnificent spectacle. The ground, which was totally flat, was covered as far as the eye could see with a light layer of dazzling white salt. Leaving this to our left, we marched round it for three hours. It was out of the question to contemplate crossing it because beneath the layer of salt the ground stays damp and exceedingly slippery, and camels are unable to walk over it. A narrow path skirted this *sabkhah*; in some places rocks to our right even forced us to cross some parts of it, but this was done only with the utmost caution and by leaving complete discretion to the camel, which took great care not to stray from either the path or the footsteps of the man in front urging it along.

As well as the peril of slipping and falling, always a hazard when riding a camel, there is the risk of sliding into one of the muddy holes covered with a layer of very fine salt that are widespread in these boggy areas. This area is called Ḥaẓawẓā.[29]

In the evening, we made camp close to four wells called al-Milḥāt. They are well named because their water, which is only 1.5 m below ground, is very salty.[30]

Two days later, on 23 May,[31] we watered at the wells of Qudayr al-

---

[28] This range is also called al-Mismā' al-Sirḥān to distinguish it from the Ǧabal Mismā' that lies roughly halfway between Ǧabal Aǧā and Taymā'. M. Guarmani calls it erroneously Nesma-el-Serhani, and the map of Mme Blunt gives it the name Mizmeh. (CH) [For Ǧabal Mismā' between Ǧabal Aǧā and Taymā', see e.g. Huber 1891: 250–61; Euting 1914: 131–2.]

[29] [Huber's name for this large *sabkhah* is El Haçotah. In his handwritten manuscript, he calls it Hazotah and writes *khaztah* in Arabic in the margin. It undoubtedly corresponds to that named Ḥaẓawẓā on the 1:2,000,000 map entitled *Arabian Peninsula* (1973).]

[30] [The saltiness suggests that Huber's spelling of the name, El Melkhhât, must be an attempt to reproduce al-Milḥāt, *milḥ* being the Arabic for salt.]

[31] [The French text says 13 May, but this is clearly a misprint given that Huber left Kāf on 21 May. Huber's handwritten 65-page report of March 1882 confirms this (French national archives, Pierrefitte-sur-Seine, Dossier F/17/2976/1:1, entitled 'Mission au Thibet et dans l'Asie centrale', 1878–82, item 79, p. 23).]

Maʿāṣir,[32] and in the evening at those of al-Qudayr in the territory of al-Maysarī.[33] Our encampment that night [315] was at al-Nibāǧ,[34] which is the name of the whole area beyond Qudayr al-Maʿāṣir.

The name al-Nibāǧ comes from a little ruined fort that stands about a kilometre south-west of the wells of al-Qudayr.

The wells that I had encountered thus far usually have water all year round but, as M. Guarmani has also observed, it is brackish with a strong and unpleasant odour. Furthermore these wells are nothing more than simple, unlined holes.

The itinerary of Yūsuf al-Milkī also mentions the wells of Qudayr al-Maʿāṣir, but under the name Kadeïr.

On the morning of 24 May, we reached the wells of Qāsayyim and, in the evening, the three wells of al-Ǧarāwī.[35] The latter had already run dry, and we had been counting on them!

From Kāf as far as al-Nibāǧ the way, which often goes along the bed of Wadi al-Sirḥān, is very pleasant to follow because the ground is sandy and well covered with vegetation. Beyond al-Nibāǧ the vegetation begins to grow sparser, the ground becomes stony and the landscape monotonous. The bedrock is sometimes exposed and we were often marching over patches of rounded pebbles. After al-Ǧarāwī the vegetation peters out completely, to be replaced by sand and gravel.

Having found no water at the wells of al-Ǧarāwī, we set off on a forced march and only camped after midnight at Walmā.[36]

25 May was a hard day as we only had enough water to make bread. Because there are no more wells after al-Ǧarāwī, we had to make straight for al-Ǧawf non-stop. We went twenty-two hours in the saddle. Leaving at 4 a.m., we reached our destination on 26 May at 2 o'clock in the morning. I was suffering seriously from thirst.

---

[32] [Spelt thus on the 1:2,000,000 map entitled *Arabian Peninsula* (1973). For Huber's Gedeir al Mâzer. In the margin of his handwritten manuscript, he writes it in Arabic as al-Māshshir.]

[33] Called El-Mueisari by M. Guarmani, and Maazreh by Mme Blunt. (CH)

[34] [Spelt thus on the 1:2,000,000 map entitled *Arabian Peninsula* (1973). For Huber's E' Nebay, which he spells in the margin of his handwritten manuscript al-Nibayy.]

[35] Called El-Gerani by M. Guarmani, and Ierani by Mme Blunt. (CH)

[36] [Walmā, for Huber's Ouelmâ. In the margin of his handwritten manuscript he spells it in Arabic Walmah. I have been unable to identify this well.]

Since morning the ground had become totally stony. It is [316] covered with little shiny pellets like rifle bullets, dark in colour and gleaming as if varnished, making the sight of them very tiring on the eyes. The terrain is completely devoid of vegetation. At 8 o'clock in the evening, a very strong easterly gale blew for two hours and pushed the temperature up to 42°. The heat was stifling and the sky became completely overcast towards nine o'clock. But despite a few drops of rain, the atmosphere remained sweltering all night.

The line of march in the desert never depends on how favourable or otherwise the terrain may be nor on the availability of grazing, however essential that may be for the camels; it depends on the availability of water along the way. Route directions are therefore just lines of wells and nothing more.

These wells have been dug, for the most part, by the bedouin on their grazing grounds. When commercial, political or religious considerations have made it necessary to traverse the various territories of the Arab tribes, which generally do not possess wells on their borders so as to impede hostile incursions, one or two more have been dug to link them together. Apart from that, it is evident that the less labour was required to dig a well, the more they were liable to multiply; such is the case with those to be found in the Wadi al-Sirḥān. It is that which explains why, whenever one compares the routes known up to the present day between the Ḥawrān and al-Ǧawf, one comes across new names every time.

So as to demonstrate more clearly their convergences and differences, I set out here the ones that have been recorded up until the present day:[37]

Itinerary of Yūsuf al-Milkī	*Route of M. Guarmani*	*Route of M. and Mme Blunt*	*My route*
Bosra	Kaf	Melakh	Boṣrah
Hâbbekah	El-Breda	Kaf	ʿAnz
Esrak	Kseba	Itheri	Wadi al-Rayal
		Shadjbeh	Azraq
Ittra	Abu-Terifian	Kuraghiz	Kāf
Korâker	El-Adeimat	Mahiyeh	al-Milḥāt
[317]			

[37] [In this list, spellings of place names have been retained as given by Huber from the information of Yūsuf al-Milkī, Guarmani and the Blunts, for ease of reference.]

Kaf	El-Meheder	Maazreh	Qudayr al-Maʿāṣir
Kadeïr	Weset	Schaybeh	al-Maysarī
Umm el Phenadschir	El-Meiasari	Kasr	al-Qudayr
Kléïah	El-Nebach	Jerawi	Qāsayyim
Dschôf	El-Sceba		al-Ğarāwī
	El-Uescece		
	El-Nebsce		
	El-Gerani		
	Sbeha		
	El-Scegar		

To these four lines of wells I shall add a fifth, told to me by Ghānim the armourer, a native of al-Ğawf these days established at Ḥā'il:[38]

> Al-Azraq – al-Ḥarīm – al-ʿAmrī – Ğabal al-ʿArabī – al-Maʿāṣir – al-Mushāsh – Uwaysiṭ – al-Bayḍah – al-Tiyāq – Shighār – Shaqīr – al-Nabk Abū Qaṣr – Ṣubayḥah

It is easy enough to find the points on a map where these various routes touch, where they intersect and, as a result, the directions they follow.

Miqwaʿ is another famous well in the Wadi.[39]

At al-Ğawf I was accommodated in the house of Shaykh Sulṭān ibn Ḥabūb, a nephew of the Ghāfil who once gave hospitality to Palgrave and his companion.[40] Ghāfil died ten years ago. Sulṭān is brother-in-law to ʿAbd Allāh ibn Khamīs, shaykh of Kāf.

I received a very warm welcome from Ğawhar, a slave, who governs al-Ğawf on behalf of the Emir Muḥammad Ibn Rashīd.[41] A handsome black man, he is 1.75 metres tall and about fifty years of age, with an intelligent face. A smile forever plays about his lips, his manners are distinguished, and he unfailingly received me with the utmost cordiality. He always insisted on

[38] [Euting had extensive dealings with this man in 1883–84, see Euting 1896: 182, 188–90, 196, 205, 210, 212, 227; 1914: 7–10, 13, 15, 27, 42, 47–8, 68, 73, 98, 102, 105.]

[39] [This important well, a favourite watering place of the Sharārāt tribe, was visited by Palgrave on his route along Wadi al-Sirḥān towards the end of June 1862. He refers to it as Magooa' and Magowa' (Palgrave 1865 i: 41, 47).]

[40] [For Ghāfil al-Ḥabūb, see Palgrave 1865 i: 47–9. Palgrave and his companion Barakat (Ğurayğirī) went through al-Ğawf at the end of June 1862.]

[41] [In the margin of his handwritten manuscript, Huber gives this man's name in Arabic as Ğawʿar, and must have corrected it to Ğawhar later. For a vivid description and portrait of Ğawhar in late 1883, when Huber returned to al-Ğawf with Euting, see Euting 1896: 127–9, 137–9.]

me taking the place of honour not just in his own *qahwah*,[42] but even when he came to visit me.

[318] On each of my visits he served me with hot sugared water (the tea of the bedouin) and plenty of coffee, and then had the best dates brought in, mixed with butter. Above all he prepared his own narghileh for me. He is in fact a smoker, but in permitting himself this single grave infraction of puritan Wahhabi principles, he atones for it by an all-the-more-strict observance of those that proscribe music and singing. Al-Ǧawf, once so jolly according to Palgrave, can today boast not a single *rabāb*.[43] During our first interview he pushed his friendliness to the extent of telling me: 'Muslim or Christian, *sawa sawa*', that is to say 'Muslims and Christians are all one'.

Al-Ǧawf,[44] one of the most ancient oases in Arabia, is mentioned as such by Ptolemy and before that still by numerous Arab authors.[45] Ptolemy attaches the name Dumaitha to it, and the Arab writers Dūmat al-Ǧandal,[46] which is also familiar to the Arabs of the present day. One of the Assyrian texts quoted by Mr Rawlinson even leads us to suppose that this place existed in the 7th century BC under the name Dumāte, with a king named Akbarou[47] who was conquered in an expedition conducted by the Assyrian forces of Assurhiddin (680–69 BC).[48]

---

[42] Literally, 'café', 'room in which one takes coffee'. (CH)

[43] A type of violoncello with two strings. (CH) [See Palgrave 1865 i: 46–86 for his eighteen days in al-Ǧawf. He left for Ḥāʾil on 18 July 1862.]

[44] [For a detailed description of al-Ǧawf almost four decades earlier see Wallin 1854: 139–58, and for another of almost twenty years earlier, see Palgrave 1865, i: 56–60. Wallin was the first European traveller to visit it. (MCAM)]

[45] [Huber's sentence is: 'Le Djawf, l'une des plus anciennes oases de l'Arabie, est citée comme telle par Ptolémée et plus anciennement encore par un grand nombre d'auteurs arabes.' This is surely just a careless error overlooked by his editors, as Ptolemy wrote in *ca.* AD 150, many centuries before any Arab authors.]

[46] The name Ǧawf ʿAmīr which it bears in some authors, would be attributable to the Banī ʿAmīr tribe, who would have raised it from the ruins of the old Dūmat al-Ǧandal. (CH)

[47] In Arabic *akbaru* means 'very great'. (The Editors.)

[48] Halévy 1882: 306. (CH) [In fact, Dumate is mentioned in the form Adumatu in the Assyrian Annals, see Ephʿal 1982: 118–24, whereas the name Dumāte in the source referred to by Huber is now read *Il-pi-a-tu/te*, said by Esarhaddon (Huber's Assurahiddin) to be located in the 'distant land of Bâzu, a forgotten part of the mainland, a salty region, a place of thirst': see Borger 1956: 56–57 (A, IV 53–77) and *Reallexikon der Assyriologie und vorderasiatischen Archäologie s.v.* Ilpi'atu. Huber's reference to Henry Rawlinson's work on the Assyrian inscriptions is to Rawlinson

But we hardly know any more than the name of this place, and to see it emerge from its obscurity we have to move all the way forward to the Hiğrah. At this juncture, it had a ruler from the tribe of Kindah, Ukaydir,[49] a Christian against whom Muḥammad sent a force of 420 horsemen to [319] subdue and convert him. These few men laid siege and forced him to surrender, which gives a rather puny idea of the power or valour of this prince, or perhaps of the loyalty of his subjects. He ransomed his precious person for 2,800 camels, 400 cuirasses and as many lances, and appeared in person before the Prophet in al-Madīnah wearing a robe of silk and gold with a golden cross on his chest. He converted to Islam along with his people, and retained his throne on payment of tribute.

According to some authors, the people of al-Ğawf would already have changed their religious beliefs several times: before becoming Christian they would have been Jews, and before that, as pagans, they would have worshipped the goddess Woudd (Love) as their principal idol.[50]

From this time on al-Ğawf, which was then a much more substantial place, faded back into obscurity, and is no more than a name mentioned by the Arab geographers al-Idrīsī, Yāqūt and al-Hamdānī.

Towards the end of the last century al-Ğawf, which was in a permanent state of civil strife, was subdued by the Wahhābīs and made tributary. Ibn Saʿūd sent a governor there to quell the troubles, as well as *khaṭīb*s charged with promulgating the new doctrines.[51]

The destruction of the Wahhābī empire by Muḥammad ʿAlī, pasha of

---

1861. See also Huber 1891: 42–9 and Euting 1896: 123–40 for further descriptions of al-Ğawf in 1883. (MCAM/WF]

[49] These Kindah, allies of Ğudhām, the Lakhmids and the Ṭāʾiyy, came originally from the south. [Ukaydir's full name was Ukaydir ibn ʿAbd al-Malik al-Kindī. The expedition against him took place in October 630 or March 631.]

[50] [Wadd is one of the attested deities of the pagan pantheon of pre-Islamic Arabia. Like most pre-Islamic deities he had grammatical gender but it is not at all clear whether he was conceived of in human form and therefore as a male or a female (see Macdonald 2012a: 291). He was the principal god of the people of Maʿīn in ancient Yemen, and is also attested as a god worshipped by Minaeans in Dadan (modern-day al-ʿUlā). Huber is clearly in error in describing him as a goddess of love based on the meaning of the Arabic word *wudd* 'love, affection'. (MCAM)]

[51] *Khaṭīb*: that is to say, 'he who knows how to perform the worship'. (CH) [*Khaṭīb*: preacher. Al-Ğawf fell to a force from al-Dirʿiyyah in early 1794 (Philby 1955: 84–5). The Ibn Saʿūd referred to was ʿAbd al-ʿAzīz ibn Muḥammad Āl Saʿūd (r. 1765–1803).]

Egypt,[52] restored freedom to al-Ǧawf, which immediately took advantage of it by relapsing into its inter-village and inter-quarter hostilities. This state of affairs lasted until 1838, when ʿAbd Allāh Ibn Rashīd came to the aid of his Shammar compatriots in their struggle against the people of Sūq[53] al-Dalhāmiyyah. They lived in the al-Kharāwī quarter and were just at that point finding themselves [320] the underdogs. He reconquered al-Ǧawf on his own account, so imposing universal concord.

This new yoke weighed heavily upon the people of al-Ǧawf who, when they sensed a loosening of Ibn Saʿūd's governance,[54] thought to take advantage of it to re-establish their independence. So they rose up and chased out the Shammar governor. Some of the impetus to do this probably came from the Ruwalah, whose tribal sections of Nāyif and Shaʿlān had for a long time extracted a small tribute from al-Ǧawf and who also, as inveterate enemies of the Shammar, had never been friends of the Wahhābīs even during their most glorious epoch.

In any case, the Shammar emir in power at that time, Ṭalāl ibn Rashīd, was not a man to countenance such expressions of independence. The Nafūd is difficult, but it is not an obstacle; while for the Arabs, when a campaign is at stake, it is of no account at all.

All that took place in 1853. Scarcely a month after the insurrection, Ṭalāl ibn Rashīd was to be found with his Shammar warriors before the oasis. So as to target the morale of the besieged with greater effect, he had had two small cannon dragged from Ḥāʾil which actually fired a few shots. The heart of the resistance was located in the two *sūq*s[55] of al-Dirʿ Mārid and ʿAyn Umm Sālim, the population of which were al-Ruhaymāt[56] Arabs, originally from the environs of Naǧaf in Mesopotamia.

52 [Muḥammad ʿAli's son, Ibrāhīm Pasha, led a campaign into Naǧd in 1816 and in 1818 laid siege to al-Dirʿiyyah, destroying it and bringing to an end the First Saudi State.]

53 *Sūq* here means a quarter and, in a general sense, a market, or the cluster of buildings around a market. (CH)

54 [*Sic*. Huber must have meant to write 'Ibn Rashīd's government'.]

55 [The quarters of al-Ǧawf were commonly known as *sūq*s or *ḥārah*s. The word *sūq* (pl. *aswāq*) literally means 'market' and because each population group in a town had its own market and its members would seldom if ever go to others, the word came to mean 'quarter'. Al-Sudairī (1995: 163–5) gives a full list of the *suq*s in the 20th century, which bears little resemblance to the list given here by Huber.]

56 [Huber spells these Erhéïmât in his published text and his handwritten manuscript, but in the margin of the latter helpfully writes the name in Arabic as al-Ruhaymāt. They are not mentioned by al-Sudairī (1995: 164–5).]

After twenty days under siege, the two *sūq*s were taken by assault and comprehensively sacked. I could still see the ruins. Only the famous Mārid tower, recently rebuilt and reroofed, is lived in. As for the seething inhabitants, those who had not been killed during the assault had to go into exile and leave the oasis for good. Since then, nothing has occurred to breach the peace.

The explanation for these internal divisions is that al-Ǧawf is not a single entity but is composed of fifteen small towns, built adjacent to one another but each surrounded by a wall, [321] access through which is given by a single gateway. Each settlement was founded by a different tribe and possesses its own particular shaykh.

Here is the list of them:

- Al-Wādī, situated two miles north-east of Mārid.
- Qarāthīn, in the lowest part of the oasis.
- ʿAyn Umm Sālim,[57] in ruins, previously inhabited by Ruwalah bedouin (ʿAnizah).
- Al-Dirʿ Mārid, below the previous quarter, in ruins. Its inhabitants were originally from Shaqrāʾ, to the south of al-Qaṣīm.[58] This *sūq*, which other writers call simply al-Dirʿ, is the most famous one by reason of the Mārid tower which is situated within it and which was probably constructed entirely from large, dressed stones. Also, as I mentioned above, this tower has been recently restored; the upper part has been rebuilt in mud.
- Al-Qaʿīd,[59] towards the west.
- Al-Saʿīdīn, which Wallin calls e'Seidijìn.[60] With a strong tower, al-Quṣayr. Its population, drawn from five sections of different tribes, were at enmity with Sūq al-Dirʿ Mārid.

[57] [As Huber observes below, this quarter was also known as al-Gharb, 'the West', which is also the name for it used by al-Sudairī (1995: 164).]

[58] [Al-Sudairī (1995: 164) names this quarter al-Sūq. Shaqrāʾ, historically an important trading centre, is the chief town of the Washm district of lower Naǧd, about 160 km north-west of Riyadh,]

[59] [Probably the al-Qaʿayyid quarter mentioned by al-Sudairī (1995: 164).]

[60] [See Wallin 1854: 143. Wallin was in al-Ǧawf in 1845.]

- Al-Silmān,[61] just about at the centre of the oasis.
- Ḥabūb[62] (al-Ḥabbuh) of Guarmani.
- Al-Saʿīdān,[63] in the same situation and with the same population as Ghaṭṭī.
- Al-Arḥābiyyīn,[64] once inhabited by bedouin of the Tamīm, but nowadays by immigrants from Ruḥaybah in Syria.
- ʿAlâq, founded and populated by the Ṭafîlah.
- Ashhīb.[65]
- Al-Khadhmāʾ,[66] populated by the Sirḥān bedouin of whom part are still wandering with the Shammar in Mesopotamia; they possess a well that yields the best water in al-Ǧawf. They also include the Mutawalladīn, negro descendants of slaves who once came from Mecca.
- Al-Dalhāmiyyah, destroyed by the Shammar emir during the conquest of 1838. It is in this quarter that the Shammar governor has built his residence, a true stronghold.[67]
- Ghaṭṭī,[68] in the lower part of the oasis, is almost exclusively inhabited by labourers who, as they come originally from Ǧubbah, are Shammar.

Slight differences are noticeable between this list of *sūq*s when compared with those of Wallin and Guarmani.[69] This is because all these *sūq*s also go by alternative names; for example, ʿAyn Umm Sālim is also known as Gharb ('West').

[61] [Or al-Salmān: see al-Sudairī 1995: 164).]

[62] [The rendering Ḥārat Ḥabūb, for Huber's El Heboub, was recorded by me on a visit to Dūmat al-Ǧandal in January 1985. See Guarmani 1938: 101, where he calls it El-Habbub, not al-Ḥabbuh as stated by Huber. Named al-Ḥabūb by al-Sudairī (1995: 164).]

[63] [See al-Sudairī 1995: 164.]

[64] [This rendering, of Huber's É'Rahêbîñ, was recorded by me on a visit to Dūmat al-Ǧandal in January 1985. Also al-Ruḥaybīn (al-Sudairī 1995: 164).]

[65] [I have been unable to identify this quarter, which is not mentioned by al-Sudairī (1995: 163–5).]

[66] [See al-Sudairī 1995: 163 for this rendering of Huber's Khadzmà.]

[67] [For Huber and Euting's visit to this castle in 1883 and Euting's paintings of it, see Euting 1896: 126–30.]

[68] [Named thus also by al-Sudairī (1995: 163).]

[69] [For their lists of the various quarters, see Wallin 1854: 140–4; Guarmani 1938: 103.]

Ever since the Shammar emir became the absolute sovereign of al-Ǧawf, contacts between the oasis and the Ruwalah have become less frequent than previously – especially as the latter [322] have no problem in selling the products of their flocks and herds (wool and butter) elsewhere. Besides, the Ǧawfis have no lack of these commodities, which today they obtain from the Sharārāt, who are all subject to the Shammar and pay tribute to them.

The Ruwalah have always had closer relations with Syria than with al-Ǧawf. It is there that they sell their produce and buy the few essential articles they need, such as their clothes, rice and wheat. They also sell their camels in Syria at much better prices.

During the last century and before the conquest of al-Ǧawf by the Wahhābīs, the oasis was also frequented by bedouin of the Ḥsinnah[70] and Banī Ṣakhr.

The Sharārāt, on the other hand, have cause only to congratulate themselves for having been forced to desist from their pillaging in the area between al-Ǧawf and Palestine and between Taymā' and Ǧabal Shammar, because, entirely surrounded as they are by desert and with no contact with any important centre, they were unable to dispose of either their wool or their camels, which are an exceedingly fine breed. Whereas nowadays it is they who supply al-Ǧawf with wool, butter and even, when they are not more than a day or two's march away, with milk. In exchange they obtain dates, blue and white coarse cotton cloth, and *ʿabā*s,[71] as well as various items essential for life in camp and which they cannot make themselves, such as camel saddles, tanned hides, and so forth.

Al-Ǧawf produces nothing but dates, though these can rival the best varieties in Arabia, and a little wheat, though not enough. Industry is confined

[70] [Huber writes Hesseré, probably a misprint for Hessené, intended to denote the Ḥsinnah, a tribe of the northern ʿAnizah (belonging to the Wuld ʿAlī of the Ẓana Muslim division) originating in Khaybar who, along with the Fadʿān, were among the first of the ʿAnizah to immigrate from the northern Ḥiǧāz into the Syrian desert, perhaps in the 17th century (see Blunt 1879: 374, 382 for the Hesénneh). In Huber's time the Wuld ʿAlī roamed the area to the south-east of Ǧabal Ḥawrān (see Huber's folding map). Huber also gives a breakdown of the tribal sections of the 'Hséneh' (Huber 1891: 660–1). Musil (1928b: 57, 272, 552) calls them al-Ḥsene; Dickson (1949: 575) H'sinna; Ingham (1986: 12) Ḥṣina. Burckhardt (1822: 663) gives an early mention of them: 'Before the time of the Wahabi, the El Hessene and the Bani Szakher [Ṣakhr] likewise visited the Djof.' Burckhardt (1831 ii: 1, 385) provides the spelling: 'Hessenne, or Ahsenne (الاحسنة)' i.e al-Ḥsinnah or al-Aḥsinnah.]

[71] *ʿaba* or *abā*, a cloak worn by men throughout Arabia and as far as the Fezzan in Africa. (CH)

to the manufacture of light-weight brown *ʿabā*s which are sold for between one and 2 *meǧīdī*s[72] according to quality, sandals and other leather artefacts, saddles, and a few crude iron items.

[323] Currency being practically unknown in al-Ǧawf, barter is the basis of all transactions. During my arrival there, I stopped at the first houses in order to record the time from my watch and note it down in pencil; it was two o'clock in the morning. Despite this early hour a young woman came out of a neighbouring house and offered the men with me a bowl of water. These, being well-mannered fellows, told her to offer it to me first, which she did. Having drunk and passed the bowl to my companions, and wanting to acknowledge her kindness, I gave her a quarter-*meǧīdī* coin. She took it, but asked what it was; and, having found out, was greatly astonished. ʿAbd Allāh then asked her if she had never seen money. '*Abadan* [never]', came the reply.

Water, the *raison d'être* of an oasis, the resource that sustains the palms and thus the people, is supplied here by springs, wells and reservoirs; naturally the latter receive water seldom enough, as rainfall is infrequent here. The water is bland or else it tastes bad and is indigestible. The only exception is the well of Radhmā,[73] in the *suq* of the same name, the water of which is less unpleasant.

Many of the inhabitants assured me that the water was diminishing and that in former times there had been much more of it. This would be a natural explanation for the dwindling of the population, which is no longer what it once was.

In the East, where there is no such thing as a census, the population estimate of a particular locality is based either on the number of hearths, or on the number of adults capable of bearing arms, or else on whatever other information can be gleaned. All these methods, when it is possible to use them, enable an approximation to be arrived at, and this can generally be done everywhere except in the Arab countries, where questioning on this topic never fails to arouse suspicion.

One rather original method of reaching an estimate which is very precise and which I have never seen mentioned by any other traveller, but [324] which in any case can hardly be applied with certitude except in Naǧd proper, is to find out how many places there are in the main mosque, or *ǧāmiʿ*.

---

[72] The *meǧīdī*: a silver coin worth 4 francs and 44 centimes. (CH)

[73] [*Sic*. This is presumably a misprint for Khadhmāʾ, as no *suq* named Radhmā occurs in Huber's list of the quarters of Dūmat al-Ǧandal above.]

One of the fundamental precepts of the Islamic reform movement of ʿAbd al-Wahhāb[74] is the obligation to attend the Friday midday prayer, which takes place at the *ǧāmiʿ*. The four other prayers on this day, along with the ones on every other day of the week, can be performed in the local mosques to be found in every *sūq* – or rather, as we might say at home, in the parish churches; while the Friday noon prayer must be performed in the cathedral. Now, the construction of every mosque in central Arabia takes this obligation into account by making the building large enough to accommodate all the adult males obliged to attend the prayer, and their number is generally common knowledge. Moreover, it would be perfectly possible to arrive at an estimate oneself, since we know that for the prayer the worshippers line up side by side, in rows about 1.7 metres apart. Thus, in the mosque, one man takes up the amount of space he would need to lie down. Dividing the total surface area of the mosque by a rectangle of that size is a good method for arriving at the population figure.

However, this method is not applicable to al-Ǧawf specifically, because, though the governor's castle does contain a mosque, no obligation exists nor ever has done to perform the second Friday prayer there. This is because some of the people of the oasis, which is more than five kilometres long, would have to travel too great a distance to get there.

The first traveller to estimate al-Ǧawf's population was Burckhardt, although he never visited it. He lists seven *sūq*s, each comprising an average of 100 houses, that is to say a maximum of 6,000 souls. Palgrave in 1862 ascribed 34,000 souls to it, and Guarmani, two years later in 1864, 6,000 in thirteen *sūq*s.[75]

---

[74] [*Sic*; Huber of course is referring to Shaykh Muḥammad ibn ʿAbd al-Wahhāb and the reform movement instigated by him at al-Dirʿiyyah.]

[75] [Burckhardt 1822, Appendix IV: 662–4 states: 'The Djof is a collection of seven or eight villages, built at a distance of ten minutes or a quarter of an hour from each other, in an easterly line. The ground is pure sand. These villages are called Souk (or markets), the principal of them are: Souk Ain Um Salim (سوق عين ام سالم), Souk Eddourra (سوق الذرع), Souk Esseiddeiin (سوق السيديين), Souk Douma (سوق دوما), Souk Mared (سوق مارد). These villages are all built alike: the houses are built round the inside of a large square mud wall, which has but one entrance. This wall therefore serves as a common back wall to all the houses, which amount in some of the souks to one hundred and twenty, in others from eighty to one hundred.' He makes no attempt to estimate the population. See also Guarmani 1938: 101; Palgrave 1865 i: 61. Guarmani's figure was for Dūmat al-Ǧandal alone, while Palgrave's was for the entire Ǧawf depression including Sakākā. Even so, Palgrave was notorious for exaggeration. (MCAM/WF)]

According to what I learned during my stay in al-Ǧawf [325] and later in the Ǧabal,[76] there would be about 1,500 rifles there. However, I do not believe that the population of al-Ǧawf can be put at more than 12,000.

Here are the names of localities situated in the neighbourhood of al-Ǧawf properly so-called:

- Sakākā, more or less 45 km north-east of al-Ǧawf at the foot of the mountain of Ḥammāmiyyah, with around 8,000 inhabitants. This place has existed for only about a century. Although the most recent of the towns of al-Ǧawf, it is a very thriving place. It has been draining people away from the other settlements, especially since its annexation to the Shammar domain. Its water is very plentiful and is found at less depth than in al-Ǧawf itself.
- Qārā, at about 32 km north by 70° east of al-Ǧawf, with around 1,000 inhabitants.
- Saḥārā, 10 km north-west of al-Ǧawf, with 50 inhabitants.
- Ḥasiyyah, 7 km north by 35° west of al-Ǧawf, with 50 inhabitants.

These two latter places, as ancient as al-Ǧawf itself, were once considerable but have withered away.

- Ǧāwā, on the route to Sakākā, 21 km from al-Ǧawf.
- Muwaysin, a little farther on than Ǧāwā, is exactly half way between al-Ǧawf and Sakākā.[77] Muwaysin and Ǧāwā are as old as al-Ǧawf, Saḥārā and Ḥasiyā, but nowadays stand abandoned and in ruins.

From my first interview with Ǧawhar, the governor of al-Ǧawf, I had been open with him about my plan to make my way to Ḥā'il. He at once gave me to understand that the journey was impossible, painting a graphic picture of the dangers of the Nafūd for me and the impossibility of crossing it in summer.

[76] [i.e. Ǧabal Shammar.]

[77] [Muwaysin, actually situated 12 km north-east of Dūmat al-Ǧandal and 30 km south-west of Sakākā, was the site of an ancient fort (al-Sudairī 1995: 88).]

'The Nafūd at this time of year,' he told me, 'is a sea of fire which will swallow you up, and no one will be willing to act as your guide.' I replied that I knew for certain that bedouin sometimes used to cross it at the height of summer, and that I would be able to do the same.

[326] I insisted no further on that occasion, but the next day, having given him my presents, I raised the matter again, and this time he did not actually raise so many objections. The matter of the guide was his only stumbling-block, but when I put it to him that, in my desire to make my way to the presence of his master, the Emir Muḥammad ibn Rashīd, I was counting on him, Ǧawhar, to find me a guide, he gladly undertook to fulfil my request.[78]

On the last day of the month of May the guide was found, and our departure fixed for the next day. This man was Muḥārib,[79] a little wizened old man with a face like Mr Punch. With him was his son-in-law, Sayil. Both of them are Ǧawfis and they had already made numerous crossings of the Nafūd.

On 1 June, we were all up well before dawn, but the filling of water-skins, the bagging up of our provisions, the last-minute exhortations and farewells to friends and relatives, and most of all the thousand indecisions that afflict every Arab on the point of setting out on a long journey, meant that we only got on the move at 6.30 in the morning.

Hardly had we left the Ǧawf depression, that is to say about a quarter of an hour later, than we reached a stony plateau which is just the continuation of the one that stretches from the north of the oasis as far as the wells of al-Ǧarāwī. After half-an-hour's progress over this plateau, there manifests itself in the distance ahead a long line, whitish at first and then, as one draws nearer, pale pink. It is the Nafūd! After another hour and a half we had reached it.

All those who have read the description of the Nafūd penned by Gifford Palgrave will recall the despairing picture that the Englishman paints of this

[78] [In his 65-page handwritten report dated 27 March 1882, Huber adds a detail: 'I had given him [Ǧawhar] two revolvers and a silk *kufiyyah*, with which he was obviously delighted. Later in Ḥā'il the emir, having learnt this fact, one day chided me saying: "Ǧawhar is my slave and you don't owe him anything."' (French national archives, Pierrefitte-sur-Seine, Dossier F/17/2976/1:1, entitled 'Mission au Thibet et dans l'Asie centrale', 1878–82, item 79, pp. 26–7.)]

[79] [Huber seems to have formed a good relationship with this man, as on his return to al-Ǧawf with Julius Euting in October 1883 he would engage him again, for a trip to al-Ṭuwayr and Sakākā (Euting 1896: 130).]

desert. 'Much had we heard of them [*viz.* the Nafūd sands],' says he, 'from Bedouins and countrymen, so that we had made up our minds to something very terrible and very impracticable. But the reality, especially in these dog-days, proved worse than [327] aught heard or imagined.'[80] He goes on to give the most fantastical description of this desert. According to his account, it would consist entirely of moving sand-hills 200 to 300 feet high, from the tops of which the eye can discern nothing but a boundless sea of fire. 'We were now traversing,' he writes, 'an immense ocean of loose reddish sand, unlimited to the eye, and heaped up in enormous ridges running parallel to each other from north to south, undulation after undulation, each swell two or three hundred feet in average height, with slant sides and rounded crests furrowed in every direction by the capricious gales of the desert. In the depths between the traveller finds himself as it were imprisoned in a suffocating sand-pit, hemmed in by burning walls on every side; while at other times, while labouring up the slope, he overlooks what seems a vast sea of fire, swelling under a heavy monsoon wind, and ruffled by a cross-blast into little red-hot waves.'[81]

I was therefore agreeably surprised to find that all this was at the very least greatly exaggerated, and that crossing the Nafūd was at worst perhaps exhausting for camels. But apart from this inconvenience, the Nafūd has so many positive qualities that I doubt whether a single bedouin would not prefer it to every other desert in the world.

The distinctive character of the Nafūd, besides that of being an absolutely pure desert of sand with no admixture of earth, gravel or any other extraneous material, is provided by its *fulūǧ*.[82]

---

[80] Palgrave 1865 i: 91. (CH) [Huber quotes from the first French translation, for which see Palgrave 1866 i: 87.]

[81] [Palgrave 1865 i: 91–2.]

[82] Here we have respected the orthography (*foûldj*) of M. Huber. He should have written *fouldj*, with a short vowel. *Fouldj*, with the plural *El Aflâdj*, is the name of a province of Naǧd; it is an Arabic word which is also found in the form *feldja*, applicable to the same geological formation, in the topographical nomenclature of the Arabs of the Constantine Sahara. (The Editors.) [Huber's editors are correct about the short vowel, but seem to have confused the roots *flǧ* and *flq*. *Falq* (pl. *fulūq*), or *foûldj* as Huber presents it, means, in the context of the Nafūd, a long, curved dune enclosing a deep horseshoe-shaped depression (*qaʿr*, pl. *quʿūr*) on the leeward side, as described and illustrated in 1883 by Euting (1896: 143–5). In local dialect this was pronounced *falǧ* or *fulǧ*, pl. *fulūǧ* (see e.g. Blunt i: 158) thus creating the confusion. In describing his second journey (with Euting) across the Nafūd in October 1883, Huber confirms the Arabic spelling of what he calls a *fouldj* as فلق, with a *qāf* not a *ǧīm* (Huber 1891: 51).

The *fulǧ* in the Nafūd is a hollow in the shape of a half-oval, with the curve deeply embedded in the sand. It more or less resembles the print of a gigantic horse's hoof.[83] This hoofprint, slightly scooped out [328] in a concave arc, would be about 300 to 400 metres in diameter and, just at its forward point, would sink up to fifty, sixty, seventy or even eighty metres into the sand. Its orientation is what it would be were the horse to be heading in a north-westerly direction. The incline of the interior surface of the horseshoe is astonishing, by reason of the fineness of the sand: it is 50°–60°. Also, the slightest object thrown onto this slope goes rolling down to the bottom, snowballing and setting off quite an avalanche of sand. Despite this unstable equilibrium, however, which would lead one to expect no end of landslides, the *fulǧ* remains unchanging and the Nafūd maintains the same surface configuration. Some of these *fulūǧ* go right down through the thickness of the sand bed, sometimes exposing a clayey soil at the base, and sometimes the bedrock scattered with limestone, quartz and flint – in short, the ground surface of the Ḥamād. The *fulūǧ* of ʿUyūn al-Qafīʿa and al-Bayḍah, marked on the map,[84] are of precisely this type, as well as being among the deepest such formations.

This account enables one to appreciate the inaccuracy of Palgrave's description. There is never any question of going down these *fulūǧ* and climbing up them again, because the incline of the internal surfaces prevents either ascent or descent. The path one follows goes around them or crosses their rear side, as it were along the line of the bowstring.

A large number of the *fulūǧ*, but generally the biggest, are crowned to the west and more often to the south-west by a high hill of sand, itself topped by a crest three or four metres in height, at a very steep angle. As Lady Anne Blunt too has remarked, the whitish colour of these crests contrasts with the

---

See also Groom 1983: 82–3, where a *falq* is defined as a horse-shoe-shaped trough in the sand dunes, and *falaj/fulj* as a stream or water channel. The district of southern Naǧd which, as Huber's French editors rightly point out, is known as al-Aflāǧ, bears this name not because of its dunes but because of its underground water channels, known in southern Arabia and elsewhere as *aflāǧ* (sing. *falaǧ*) – a manifestation of the root *flǧ* – or *qanāt* (sing. *qanāh*). See also Blunt 1881 i: 158–62, for an extended description of these dunes, which they crossed eighteen months before Huber.]

83 [Huber is describing what would now be called barchan dunes. The scientific study of dune formation was in its infancy in his time, and the work of investigators such as R.A. Bagnold (Bagnold 1941) and H.S. Edgell (Edgell 2006) lay in the future.]

84 [The reference is to the folding map at the end of the 3e trimestre 1884 issue of the *Bulletin de la Société de Géographie*, and reproduced at the end of this volume.]

colour of the rest of the Nafūd. But that is simply an optical illusion, because a sample I brought back and compared with others from the Nafūd exhibited exactly the same composition and colour tone.

Apart from the *fulūǧ* and the elevated crests such as these by which they are sometimes overlooked, [329] there is one final distinguishing characteristic of the Nafūd to be described. These are the great billows of sand that cut across it in certain places, ranged from east to west, and overtopping the general level by ten, fifteen and even twenty metres. Their summits too appear whitish. Three or four of them are to be found on the way from al-Ǧawf to the Ǧabal [*viz.* Shammar].

One might well imagine that such a desert of nothing but sand must be the most terrifying void in existence. It is, however, no such thing, thanks to its relatively bushy and vigorous vegetation, which affords camels their sustenance along almost the entire route.

When one has only experienced the Ḥamād with its emaciated little shrubs such as the *ʿādhir* and the *ghaḍā*[85] which grow no taller than two feet, it is a pleasant surprise to find these same species in the Nafūd growing to as much as three or four metres high. The Nafūd is the camels' paradise.

As well as the two shrubs above, which the Nafūd shares in common with the Ḥamād and other deserts, it possesses two shrubs of its own, the *arṭā*[86] and the *ḥamḍ armash*.[87] The first of these is very tasty and the other attains quite a height. Among the herbaceous plants, the best in order of quality are: the *nuṣī*, the *sabaṭ*, the *ʿarfaǧ*, and the *ḥamrā*.[88]

---

[85] [*ʿĀdhir*: *Artemisia monosperma* (Huber 1891: 581; Mandaville 1990: 305, 449; 2011: 141); *ghaḍā*: *Haloxylon persicum*, a large shrub or small tree important for camel grazing.]

[86] [Huber renders this as *yertâ*; *arṭā*, *Calligonum comosum*, must be meant. It is probably identical to the *arta* of the Sahara, a plentiful shrub with many uses including camel grazing, firewood, medicine and tanning (Mandaville 2011: 256–7).]

[87] [*Ḥamḍ*: the generic name for saltbushes of various species, including *ghaḍā*, camels requiring plenty of salt in their diet. The most valued grazing species is *rimth* (*Haloxylon salicornicum*). See Mandaville 2011: 93–4; 192–3. *Ḥamḍ armash* (for Huber's *hamedh ârmaš*): the adjective *armash* perhaps derives from the root R-M-SH meaning 'to be leafy'. (MCAM/WF)]

[88] *Noçy*, certainly identical to the Saharan *neci*, is *Arthratherum plumosum*. *Çobath*, or better *sebot* (v. Kazimirski, *Dictionnaire arabe*, i: 1044), is *Arthratherum pungens*. *'Arfadj* or *'arfej* is *Anvillea radiata*. All these plants form part of the flora of the Sahara zone, as do *ghadâ* and *hamrâ*, of which we are unable to give exact scientific equivalents. (The Editors.) [Not surprisingly, most of these identifications are out of date. *Nuṣī* is *Stipagrostis plumosa*, a common perennial grass growing in thick stands.

All these plants, though chiefly the herbaceous ones, like to congregate, and sometimes considerable areas are covered in the same species.

But above all it is a wet winter that causes the Nafūd [330] to reveal the excellence of its pasture.[89] A few hours of rainfall are enough to germinate the seeds that abound in its sands and, fifteen days later, the ground will be covered as if with a carpet of greenery from a range of species, all with fat leaves and full of sap. This moment is the *ʿushūb*.[90] The camels can be let loose in the Nafūd along with the sheep, with no need for watering. They will not need to be watered for as long as the *ʿushūb* lasts.

The first notion to spring to mind about the origin of the Nafūd's topography may be that the *fulūǧ* are formed by the hurricanes or rainstorms which must sweep through the region from time to time. But the frequency and uniformity of the *fulūǧ* will soon persuade one to abandon this theory. Besides, having been created by the wind, they would be destroyed by it over and over again; but no such thing has taken place. A bedouin will assure you that not only are there never any violent winds in the Nafūd, but also that during the twenty, thirty or forty years that he has been crossing it, there has never been any change in the condition or position of a dune. However, there are certainly some which have specially impressed the bedouin by their huge size, shape, or the colour of their base; among this number are those of ʿUyūn al-Qafīʿa and al-Bayḍah, mentioned above, which have been familiar for generations.

Despite that, I would not venture so far as the Arabs or my guide in claiming that the Nafūd remains for ever immutable in its formation; I shall even argue the contrary, and base my case on the following facts.

Sabaṭ is *Stipagrostis drarii*, another perennial grass well-known as a grazing species in dune country. *ʿArfaǧ* is *Rhanterium epapposum*, a very common shrublet and one of the most important grazing plants. *Ḥamrā* is *Cymbopogon commutatus*, a perennial aromatic grass with a lemony scent, used mainly for medicinal and aromatic purposes. (Mandaville 1990: 339–40; 2011: 259, 262–3, 276–7.)]

89 Rainfall is not very frequent in the Nafūd, but can sometimes be very abundant. M. Guarmani reports that during his crossing it rained for thirty-six hours on the 11th and 12th of May. (CH) [Guarmani crossed the Nafūd from south to north in May 1864 (Guarmani 1938: 54–9).]

90 *'Ašoûb* or *'achoub*: the grazing season. (The Editors) [*ʿushb* or *ʿishb*, pl. *ʿushūb*, is actually the general word for annual plants that spring up after rain and die away in the summer heat, as opposed to *shaǧar*, trees and perennial plants (Mandaville 2011: 337).]

First, I several times came across great open, level spaces of forty, fifty and sixty hectares, the existence of which can only be explained by the [*sc.* progressive] aggregation of the *fulūǧ*. On two of these wide open [331] spaces I could even still follow, to the west, the previous outlines of the sides of the former *fulǧ*.

Second, the prevailing winds in the Nafūd are the westerlies.[91] The proofs of this are, first, the fact that all the plants are bent towards the east; then, the tail or line of sand trailing to the east of every bush or shrub; and, finally, the denudation of their roots on their western sides. This observation provides immediate proof that the Nafūd is on the move from west to east. If it is on the move, it is also obvious that not every part of it is so affected, that the wind only ever causes the surface layers to move, and that the greater part of the transported sand falls onto the *fulūǧ*. It can be deduced from this that the shifting of the Nafūd is in fact an extremely slow process, as a result of all the obstacles encountered in the form of the hills and high dunes, and that the greater part of the sand, if not all of it, is absorbed by the existing *fulūǧ*. If this theory is correct, there should only be a few or even no *fulūǧ* at all on the western edge of the Nafūd, since those would have been the first to aggregate; but I cannot cite any secure data on this matter. The bedouin whom I interrogated for information could only give me contradictory reports.

Likewise no light can be shed on the situation of the Nafūd on its eastern side, because the few landmarks to be found there have been known about for too short a time to provide any clarification.

There still remains one question to answer. This is the most important of all, and I did not deal with it at the beginning simply because I do not have the facts to provide an answer. So I wish to do no more than pose it here. It is, how did the Nafūd originate? I have thought for some time that this colossal mass of sand could be the product [332] of the erosion of the sandstone rocks situated to the west and particularly to the south-west of the Nafūd, and of

[91] To compare identical phenomena, see the report of M. Duveyrier on the sands and winds of the Sahara, in the volume of the *Commission supérieure pour l'examen du projet de mer intérieure de M. le commandant Roudaire*, 1882, pp. 279–95, and plates on pp. 313–18. (The Editors.)

which the mountains of Mismāʾ, ʿAwǧā,[92] al-Khanẓuwah,[93] ʿIrnān, Ḥalwān,[94] Khālah[95] etc. are the relics. But, besides the colossal volume of the Nafūd sands, which seems to me to far exceed the capacity of the rocks that may have existed in the above-mentioned areas, it would also be necessary to posit a regime of prevailing winds different from that today. Finally, there is a more serious objection: how the *fulūǧ* were formed still remains unexplained. In the circumstances, it seems to me wise to await fresh evidence in order to continue the search for an explanation of the Nafūd's formation.[96]

The early Arab geographers knew the Nafūd by the names al-Daḥī and Ṭuʿūs,[97] and list its distinctive features as these same tells or hills of sand, the lack of water, the *ghaḍā* bush and the *nuṣī*. Today these names al-Daḥī and Ṭuʿūs are scarcely known at all. On the contrary, the bedouin often now use the name Raml ʿAlī,[98] while the townsfolk of the Ǧabal always call it al-Nafūd.

Immediately after having left al-Ǧawf, while continuing on across the stony plateau, there becomes visible about twenty kilometres to the south-

92 [Huber would go through these mountains in November 1880, on his way from Ḥāʾil to Taymāʾ and the Ḥiǧāz. Ǧabal al-ʿAwǧā is a continuation to the north of Ǧabal Mismāʾ.]

93 [Huber writes 'Kheñlouah', but Khanẓuwah, an outcrop to the south-west of the Mismāʾ forming a south-easterly extension of Ǧibāl ʿIrnān, must be meant.]

94 [ʿIrnān and Ḥalwān are two sandstone ranges at the south-western corner of the Nafūd.]

95 [Huber would encounter the rock outcrops of Khālah after he passed Ḥalwān on 8 November 1880.]

96 [Huber's deductions about the Nafūd are valid as far as they go, and he was the first to make such observations. The Nafūd sands, eroded from ancient sandstone outcrops to the west and north-west, accumulated over several geological epochs going back to the Pliocene. Most dune formation dates to phases in the Early and Late Pleistocene epochs, with activity continuing throughout the Holocene. See Edgell 2006: 143–9, 248–51.]

97 [Al-Ḍāḥī and Ṭuʿūs: Huber is here quoting Burckhardt 1822: 664: 'To the E. and somewhat to the S. from Djof, three hours, begins the plain called Eddhahi or Taous (الضاحي طعوس), a sandy desert full of small hills or Tels, from which it derives the name of (طعوس).' Al-Ḍāḥī is the name used by Ḥaǧǧī Khalfa for the Nafūd (Musil 1927: 553; 1928a: 2). Nafūd al-Daḥī is today the name for the strip of sand dunes running north–south to the west of the Ṭuwayq escarpment in southern Naǧd, between the latitudes of al-Ḥawṭah and Wādī al-Dawāsir (Edgell 2006: 254–5). Groom (1983: 282) defines *ṭuʿūs* as the pl. of *ṭaʿas*: 'High sand-dunes, usually horseshoe shaped; a sand hill'; whereas Kurpershoek (2005: 189) rather charmingly translates *ṭiʿs* (pl. *aṭʿas, ṭuʿūs*) as 'a smooth drift of rosy sand, conical sand hills' (based on Musil). (MCAM/WF)]

98 Meaning, 'high sand'. (The Editors.)

south-west the summit of a mountain chain running from north-east to south-west and about forty kilometres in length. This is Ǧabal al-Ṭawīl.[99] It is surrounded by the Nafūd and never retains any water after rain.

Should this desert be identified with the one that Arab authors have designated Dahnā or al-Dahnā, which would be a great territory belonging to Banī Tamīm situated to the north-east of Shammar?[100] Elsewhere, Hamaker describes it as follows, according to an old Arabic lexicon:[101]

> Dahnā, situated [333] in the territory of the Tamīm, extends from Ḥaran as far as Raml Yabrīn.[102] It is one of the most productive grazing grounds of Allāh, despite its lack of water. But when it is covered in greenery in spring, a great gathering of Arabs takes place there. These people say that the air is very pure, and no one suffers from fever, etc.

This is a question that I shall keep in reserve to be dealt with later.

As we were in no hurry, we did not push our camels hard, and on this first day we covered a mere twenty-two miles in ten hours on the move. Despite the east wind the temperature was very bearable, chiefly thanks to a light breeze that kept up all day. The sight of the Nafūd was as novel as it was strange, and I found it enchanting.

Next day, having got going from half past three so as to take advantage of the cool of early morning, we reached Wadi Shaqīq at nine o'clock.[103]

---

[99] [Huber writes 'Theouï', but this is surely erroneous, perhaps arising from mishearing the name. The extent and location of Ǧabal al-Ṭawīl is exactly as Huber describes 'Theouï' (see the 1:2,000,000 map entitled *Arabian Peninsula*, 1973).]

[100] Rommel in Abulféda, *Arab. descr.*, p. 82. (CH) [Huber seems to be unaware of the great longitudinal sand dunes known as the Dahnāʾ, which run from the south-eastern corner of the Nafūd in a great arc some 1,200 km in length to the Rubʿ al-Khālī, and effectively demarcate Naǧd from the Eastern Province of Saudi Arabia. Palgrave uses the term erroneously also to denote the Rubʿ al-Khālī (Palgrave 1865 i: frontispiece map, 90, 329.]

[101] [Hamaker 1820.]

[102] Hamaker 1820: 101. (CH) [I cannot identify Ḥaran. Yabrīn oasis is situated about 100 km south of Ḥaraḍ, on the northern edge of the Rubʿ al-Khālī. Dahnāʾ was a name sometimes given to the Nafūd by early writers. However, this old Arabic lexicon was also correct in describing the Dahnāʾ as extending down to the Yabrīn area: it comprises a longitudinal band of sand strips that runs more than 1,200 km from the south-eastern corner of the Nafūd and divides Naǧd from the Eastern Province.]

[103] [For Shaqīq, see Wallin 1854: 160–1; Blunt 1881 i: 164–9; Huber 1891: 50; Euting 1896: 139, 145.]

Wadi Shaqīq is a valley from one to two kilometres in width formed of very broken undulating ground. Its bottom is stony and lies from forty to fifty metres below the level of the Nafūd. The bedrock breaks through the surface at certain points on the wadi bed, while at others the ground is formed of small pellets (flint tubercles). Rocky outcrops alternate with others formed of Nafūd sand. As far as the landscape enables me to judge, Wadi Shaqīq must receive a large portion of its water from the surrounding Nafūd, and must serve as a kind of funnel to the wells of the same name, and perhaps also to those of al-Zuhayrī.[104]

We reached the two wells of al-Zuhayrī at 11 o'clock. Despite their diameter of more than two metres, daylight failed to reach all the way down to the bottom, which we were unable to make out. Having unloaded the bucket and ropes, Muḥārib, wanting to make sure that there was water in the well, dropped a stone down it. It landed with a dull thud. A second, a third and a fourth stone met with [334] the same result in both wells. The wind had blown sand into them. Once we had made sure of this, we abandoned them and marched west, reaching the two wells of al-Shaqīq two hours later.

The wells of al-Zuhayrī, which are the same depth as those of al-Shaqīq, go down through the same ground and probably date to the same period. Yet we are aware only of the latter name; that of the former has never been mentioned before, as far as I know.

M. Guarmani, always so particular about desert place names, did not see them, and also only mentioned a single well, 'Sceghik';[105] and, furthermore, he says that it had been destroyed by Ṭalāl ibn Rashīd in order to deter incursions by the Ruwalah. All the other travellers describe these wells as stone-lined. The truth is that the well walls are constructed of dressed masonry, laid dry with no mortar, through the surface layer of sand, which is seven or eight metres thick. But the rest of the well has been crudely hewn down through the rock. The rims of the wells have been worn and polished by the ropes pulling up the buckets over the centuries.

Near the well were scattered a few rags, about which Muḥārib told me a very sad tale. During the few days at the end of this last April, a dervish left Ǧubbah making for al-Ǧawf completely on his own, on foot, and with a small skin containing a few litres of water and a little flour. It seems that he got as

[104] [Al-Zuhayrī: Huber here spells this El Zhéry, but gives the Arabic spelling in Huber 1891: 50, and in the margin of his handwritten manuscript.]

[105] [Guarmani 1938: 98.]

far as the wells of Shaqīq, but then, having probably run out of water a day or two before, and with neither ropes nor bucket to draw it up from the well, died a miserable death. Some horsemen who had left Ḥā'il ten or so days before came across his corpse.

Could it be that no one had drawn any water from the well for so long that, having become stagnant, it had gone putrid? Or, I asked Muḥārib, was it perhaps that the dervish's corpse had been thrown [335] down the well? The fact is that the water in both the wells reeked with so unbearable a stench of hydrogen sulphide that even the camels recoiled. Notwithstanding, we had to fill the water-skin, which we had already exhausted since our departure from al-Ǧawf.

The temperature of the water in the last buckets that we drew from the well was 23.1°.

If in general parlance in Arabia the Nafūd is sometimes equated with waterless desert, in actual fact this only begins at the wells of Shaqīq and Zuhayrī, and comes to an end at Ǧubbah. The lack of water is the only inconvenient aspect of the Nafūd, and it is this shortcoming alone that renders it difficult. In every other way it is appreciated by people and animals, because of the abundance of forage and wood.

Burckhardt was, I believe, the first person to observe that, other than in the great southern desert of the Rubʿ al-Khālī, and in the Nafūd between the wells of Shaqīq and Ǧubbah, there exists no route in Arabia of comparable length without water.[106] He could have added the line of march from al-Ǧawf towards ʿIrāq, which is longer still, in fact so long that it is not even practicable, and that, in order to make the journey, one has to make a great detour via the wells of al-Ḥazil and Lawqah to reach those of Shubaykah on the Darb Zubaydah (Darb al-Ḥaǧǧ, the route of the Persian pilgrimage).[107]

Once we had supplied ourselves with water, we quickly resumed our march. Next day, i.e. 3 June, we espied from our evening camp, from the summit of a

---

106 [Burckhardt 1829 ii: 405–6.]

107 [al-Ḥazil/al-Ḥuzūl: wells at 29° 50' N 042° 15' E. Lawqah: wells about 60 km east and slightly south of Ḥazil. The Darb Zubaydah ran between Kūfah/al-Naǧaf in ʿIrāq via Fayd (80 km south-east of Ḥā'il) to al-Madīnah, and was named after Zubaydah (d. AD 831), wife of the ʿAbbāsid Caliph Harūn al-Rashīd, who supplied it with stations and cisterns, many of which survive to this day. See the Translation Part III, pp. 225–47 for Huber's journey along it in early 1881.]

great *fulǧ*, one of the peaks of the two famous outcrops of al-ʿAlaym.[108] And on the 4th, at 11 o'clock in the morning, we made camp next to it.

Part of the day of 3 June and of the morning of the 4th was spent in crossing the area of the Nafūd known as al-Falūḥ, which is the most troublesome section of the entire route from al-Ǧawf to Ǧubbah. It boasts the deepest *fulūǧ* and the highest dunes and is, as a result, [336] the most arduous to cross. For the Arabs too it is the most difficult. This is because the numerous detours they are forced to make in order to circumnavigate the *fulūǧ*, as well as the need to choose accessible places by which to cross the craters, often confuse their sense of direction and put them on the wrong track, thus causing loss of time and a great deal of unnecessary fatigue.[109]

Al-Falūḥ is preceded by the area known as Muǧiyān,[110] which is more extensive than al-Falūḥ. It takes its name from a huge hill which is outlined by a white line on the horizon from east to west for several hours' march, and borders al-Falūḥ to the north.

My guide, Muḥārib, was spared embarrassment, at least on this occasion. Directly on leaving al-Ǧawf he had asked me whether I had a compass, and every time he found himself at a loss as to our direction he would turn to me and ask laconically, '*Al-darb*?' ('Which way?'). Having consulted my instrument, I would reply still more tersely by indicating our goal in the Arab fashion, that is, by slicing the horizon with a vertical stroke, hand open and arm outstretched.

The outcrops of ʿAlaym al-Saʿd (little landmark of happiness), or ʿAlaym al-Nafūd, ordinarily known simply as ʿAlaym, are two sandstone[111] peaks about 200 metres apart. They tower over the sand sea, the southern one by some forty metres, the one to its north by about twice that amount. From a distance, and even from fairly close to, their pointed peaks are reminiscent of the pyramids seen from Cairo. Their slopes, at a 45° angle from the

---

108 [For al-ʿAlaym, properly al-ʿUlaym, see also Blunt 1881 i: 176–8; Euting 1896: 148.]

109 'El-Feluh (or, better, el-Feloûh), is the hilliest part of the Nefut, and the most difficult to traverse. It is a succession of steep hills and deep hollows, and it is necessary to twist and turn in all directions, and often to deviate considerably from the true line of march, which is often most difficult to trace.' (C. Guarmani.) (CH) [Guarmani 1938: 98. Huber spells this Feloûh here, as he does in Huber 1891: 50–1, but in the latter he renders the Arabic erroneously as *al-Fulūq*. He gives the correct Arabic spelling in the margin of his handwritten manuscript: al-Falūḥ.]

110 [A name possibly derived from the root *māǧa* (*mawǧ*), with the basic meaning of heave, swell or billow. [WF)]

111 Palgrave states erroneously that they are of granite. (CH) [Palgrave 1865 i: 94.]

horizontal, are [337] difficult to climb, covered as they are by rocky debris, which gives them almost the appearance of rubble heaps. Four kilometres to the north-east of the ʿAlaym rocks stands yet another hill about a kilometre in length, a few peaks of which overtop the sand by ten or so metres.

This beacon in the ocean of sand is a sight to delight the eye because, as well as proving that he is on the right track, it shows the traveller coming from al-Ğawf that, just as soon as he catches sight of it, he has completed one-third of his journey.

At the ʿAlaym rocks this route, which from al-Ğawf has so far been following a south-easterly course, now takes a turn to the southward, even inclining a few degrees to the west.

After an hour's halt we resumed our way. For the whole of the remainder of today the going was relatively easy, but the vegetation grew sparser than before. *Ghaḍā* is almost completely absent, while *arṭā* by contrast, which is seldom found north of ʿAlaym, becomes common to the south of it. But the camel's two favourite plants, *nuṣī* and *ḥamḍ armash*, are always readily available.

On the evening of this day, seeing how very clear the sky was, I took up position to measure the altitude of the Pole Star, and this gave me the chance to observe a curious phenomenon. I was still setting my horizon glass when a slight breeze arose from the west. Once I had the star in my sights, it was impossible to fix on the tangents of the star's edge because they were blurred. The alidade of my sextant, for its part, as well as the stop screw, would only function with a grinding sound. I stopped straight away and then observed that even the slightest breeze was transporting dust particles of such extreme fineness that, when they settled on the glass horizon, they would interfere with the reflected image and at the same time infiltrate every part of the instrument.

To take advantage of the cool night air, we set off on [338] the next day (5 June) at two o'clock in the morning, but after half an hour we had to come to a halt. It was black night; all trace of a track had suddenly vanished and we even had to give up marching by compass direction. We lay on the sand and waited for the first glimmer of dawn while our camels, which we did not let out of our sight, browsed while fully laden.

By around six-thirty in the morning, we had skirted a large *fulğ* known as ʿUyūn Qafīʿa because its rocky bottom is in the form of a huge elongated eye.[112] A quarter of an hour later there appeared a second *fulğ* of the same

[112] [ʿUyūn, the plural of *ʿayn* meaning a spring of water or an eye, is used to denote a 'hollow in the ground where water collects' (Groom 1983: 52). (MCAM)]

dimensions as the first, but it bears no name. Its bottom is likewise of bare rock. Towards eight o'clock our path led by a heap of dead wood called Sumayḥah, to which Muḥārib added a few branches.[113] My guide explained that it is associated with a love story going back a thousand years. This monument of wood, raised in commemoration of that episode, has since served as a lookout point for the crossing of the Nafūd.[114]

About an hour and a half after noon we skirted a large *fulǧ*, the bottom of which was distinguished by two huge white patches – outcrops of marl, which is the bedrock here. It has the same appearance as the ground around the wells of al-Zuhayri and al-Shaqīq. This *fulǧ* is known as al-Bayḍā.[115]

For the benefit of future explorers, let me draw attention here to an interesting detail. This is that between Sumayḥah and the *fulǧ* of al-Bayḍā the route passes a sand hill from the top of which can be seen both the summit of the mountain at Ǧubbah, and that of the higher of the two ʿAlaym.

Today our path traversed one of the quietest areas of the Nafūd. The shrubs have no train of sand on their eastern sides, nor are they bent by the wind in one direction or another. But still more characteristic of this area was that all day we could see plentiful tracks of camels, gazelle and [339] *baqr al-waḥsh*,[116] even though the wind erases them so quickly. These numerous tracks removed any doubt about the direction to take: one had but to follow them.

---

[113] [This name is perhaps derived from the root *s-m-ḥ*, connoting magnanimity or generosity. Alternatively, there may a connection with the widespread desert plant *samḥ* (*Mesembryanthemum forsskalei*), the nutritious seeds of which formed an important part of the bedouin diet (Mandaville 2011: 314–15).]

[114] [Guarmani (1938: 97) describes this place as follows: 'Eighteen hours from Gobbah there is a dune covered with bushes, called Smeha, after a young Sciammarie woman who was violated there; only Arab eyes can recognise it amongst the thousands of others exactly like it all along the track.' (MCAM)]

[115] [i.e. 'the white one'.]

[116] *Alcelaphus bubalus*, the *bubalus* of Pliny. (The Editors.) [Huber's editors are in error here in suggesting that what Huber saw was a hartebeest, specifically the bovid-like bubal hartebeest, once widespread in North Africa. What Huber undoubtedly saw, without realizing it, were the tracks of an Arabian Oryx (*Oryx leucoryx*, also known as the Beatrix antelope, *Oryx beatrix*). The name Huber records, *baqrat el-ouahas*, confirms this: it is the bedouin term for this animal, more correctly *baqr al-waḥsh* (literally 'the wild cow'). Douglas Carruthers, who went in search of the Oryx in the Nafūd and north-west Arabia in 1909, records the same term: *baqr al-wahsh*. Other names for it are *al-mahā* and *al-wuḍīhī*. The Oryx is considered to be extinct in northern Arabia today, not having survived the onslaught of firearms and motor vehicles from the 1930s on. Musil 1928b: 26; Carruthers 1935: 24; Harrison and Bates 1991: 188–9. (MCAM/WF)]

The sixth and final day since our departure from al-Ǧawf was the counterpart of the one preceding my arrival at that place. Despite my boiling it up over coals and mixing it with some tea, the water from the well of al-Shaqīq had made me ill. So I was beginning to fall prey to fatigue and the heat, and was thoroughly content to be coming out of the Nafūd. It was the same with my companions, who had suddenly fallen very silent.

We moved on again an hour after midnight and, because the night was so completely black, Muḥārib asked for my lantern. I lit it and he set off in the lead, on foot. The track now carried on without a break and all we had to do was to follow it. The vegetation continued to dwindle just like the day before, and there were likewise plenty of camel tracks.

At half past noon, we suddenly found ourselves with the mountain of Ǧubbah in front of us. A little beyond, to the left, in a depression in the ground, I could see a wide plain of dazzling whiteness; it looked like a *sabkhah*. It is in this depression that the village of Ǧubbah is situated, though it was not yet visible, hidden as it was by rocky outcrops. Another hour of marching and then, suddenly, from the top of the last sand hill, the whole depression revealed itself. In the valley bottom emerged a long line of palms surrounded by walls concealing the village. When, having had the uniform roseate hue of the Nafūd before your eyes for several days, you suddenly find yourself looking out over this immense bowl with matt silver reflections cut through by the beautiful green of the palm trees, and when the whole scene is lit by the midday sun, you stand dazzled by a picture that seems conjured up by magic.

[340] Before entering Ǧubbah I shall allow myself a few further reflections on the Nafūd.

The line of the route to be followed across the Nafūd is very difficult to trace because one is almost constantly skirting around the *fulūǧ*: it is all zigzags, ascents and descents. There is no such thing as a track in any real sense or a fixed path to be followed, such as those that often constitute desert routes. One simply follows a particular direction. While agreeing that this direction 'carries the inappropriate name of a path', M. Guarmani nonetheless recounts that 'the road from al-Ǧawf is the work of the Banī Hilāl. To make it they filled valleys, flattened hills and as far as possible levelled the sandy ground of the Nafūd, as rough as a stormy sea.'[117]

[117] Guarmani 1865: 504. 'Le chemin du Giof-Amer est l'oeuvre des Benî-Hilâl. Pour le faire on a comblé des vallées, aplani des collines et nivelé autant que possible le sol

Rāḍī, the guide of Wilfrid and Lady Anne Blunt, told them the story that beneath the sand lies a metalled road constructed of stones brought from Ǧabal Shammar.[118] The travellers could have asked him why these stones should have been brought from Ǧabal Shammar when those of Ǧabal Ǧubbah were two days nearer. But this information is obviously erroneous.

To cross the Nafūd, there exists a single track no wider than the steps of a camel, that is twenty-five to thirty centimetres, and, what is more, this track disappears in those areas exposed to the wind. While I was crossing al-Falūḥ, I saw the footprints of my camel erased straight away, and that was with a relatively gentle wind. Just two metres behind us, the sand was once again as flat as a sheet of water.

On this arduous crossing the best and, one may say, the only guide is afforded by camel droppings.

Without interrupting their stride, camels snatch a bite from [341] all the plants they happen across along the way. Thus they chew, ruminate and digest continuously, keeping on the move all the time. It is their droppings that have marked the route across the Nafūd. These are like dates or large olives in shape and size. They are cylindrical, very compact, dry quickly and become very hard, and will last for a considerable number of years under the clement Arabian sky. In the rough areas of the Nafūd exposed to the wind they easily get buried by sand, as one can easily imagine, but the next breeze will uncover them again just as readily.

The direction of the route across Nafūd is known as the Khaṭṭ Abū Zayid, and also the *Dheïeth 'Aïaš.[119] The first name is current north of the Nafūd, and the other to the south.

Wallin took sixty hours to cover the distance between al-Ǧawf and Ǧubbah, while Guarmani took forty-nine and a half. I have calculated that Palgrave must have taken at least eighty-five hours. As for myself, I made the crossing in seventy-six hours. This illustrates how difficult it is to establish itineraries or the map of a region when a traveller omits to specify his rate of progress.

---

sablonneux du Nefut, agité comme une mer orageuse.' (CH) [Guarmani 1938: 97 states: 'The road to Giof-Amer is the work of the Beni-Helal. ... The "road", as it is wrongly called, is merely a levelling of hills, filling up of the hollows, and smoothing out the Nefut sands as much as possible; although it is still as uneven as the sea in a storm, and it is difficult for the European eye to follow its wandering course.']

[118] [Blunt 1881 i: 169–71, 184.]

[119] [Khaṭṭ Abū Zayid: according to the Blunts' guide Rāḍī, Abū Zayid was shaykh of the Banī Hilāl who built the legendary 'road' across the Nafūd (Blunt 1881 i: 169, 184).]

In my own case, although I had a good mount, I had sound reasons not to hurry. My wish was to see and observe the Nafūd at my leisure. So I marched on foot almost the entire way, doing about four kilometres per hour. But for Palgrave to have taken eighty-five hours, when he was suffering so much in this desert and in such a hurry to get out of it, he must certainly have had very mediocre camels. The explanation of Wallin's speed is that he had no baggage and was riding a *dhalūl Sharārī*, that is to say a camel of the finest breed in northern Arabia. As for Guarmani, we know that he crossed the Nafūd on horseback and in haste.

[342] When all is said and done, on a good *dhalūl* one can easily make this crossing in three days without tiring one's mount.

Descending the slope of the last hill in the Nafūd brings one straight onto the plain of Ǧubbah, which is no more than 500 metres farther on. Its completely novel aspect is the most agreeable experience. A few *ithl* trees, already grown old, add life to the countryside outside the walls.

Just like al-Ǧawf, Ǧubbah is built of sun-dried mud bricks, though the walls of a few houses are constructed of rough stones. The first impression is the finest. The enclosure walls and flanking turrets are well-maintained and present a cheerful scene. The interior, as is the case almost everywhere in the East, fails to live up to the exterior.

The basin in which Ǧubbah lies is of a rather distinctive topographical form. It is in the shape of a bowl eight to nine kilometres in length from east to west, and five kilometres wide from north to south. The bottom of the valley, which is 835 metres above sea level, is thus about sixty metres lower than the level of the Nafūd.

Ǧubbah has been identified with the Aïna of Ptolemy,[120] which is proof of its great antiquity. Furthermore the two names have the same meaning, signifying a well or spring.[121] The people have preserved a memory of a spring with an abundant output that once flowed from the mountain of Ǧubbah.

The population of about 800 souls descends from the Armāl section of the Shammar tribe.[122] They are a people of small size and scant physical

[120] Sprenger 1865: 171. (CH) [Ptolemy 6.7.29. However, it should be noted that Sprenger's identification seems to have been made simply on the basis of the rough similarity in the meaning of the two names. See the next note. (MCAM)]

[121] [*ʿAyn* is a common Arabic term for a spring, and *ǧubb* can mean a well pit (Groom 1983: 131).]

[122] [The Armāl are a division of the Sinǧara sub-tribe of the Shammar inhabiting the villages of Ǧubbah and Qanāʾ (Wallin 1854/1979: 74; Oppenheim 1952 iii: 49; Steen 2009: 128).]

development. They are not much liked in the Ǧabal because of their unsociable ways and their avaricious treatment of guests. Lady Anne Blunt enumerates the complaints she felt compelled to make about them.[123]

There is no other cultivation than that of the date palm, for which they make use of forty or so wells. The water in these [343] is about twelve or fifteen metres down, and the water level, they assured me, never changes. It is bland to the taste, but I nevertheless prefer it to the water of al-Ǧawf. Some of the wells only supply water that is brackish and thus undrinkable. The temperature recorded in some of them, from which water was being drawn for several hours, gave a consistent reading of 22.9°.

The dates are small and mediocre, which the people ascribe to the salinity of the water. But in my opinion they themselves are to blame, because their palm trees are not properly looked after. The little rice and wheat they need is brought from Ḥāʾil. Fortunately, their location in the midst of the Nafūd enables them to maintain some herds of camels.

Three kilometres west of the village rise some sandstone outcrops, the highest of which is Umm al-Silmān.[124] I made the ascent the day after my arrival in Ǧubbah, against the advice of the inhabitants, who told me that there was no path, which indeed I found to be the case. The first two-thirds of the ascent presented no difficulty but, farther up, the slope is not only very steep but is also covered in sandstone scree that looks charred, the stones resembling broken tiles. It looks as if the mountain had been covered with a crust three to four centimetres thick that had been smashed to pieces where it lay. Because of the steep gradient of the mountainside, this scree is in such an unstable equilibrium that the slightest touch makes it fall away, bringing down an entire avalanche of stones. One can appreciate that in such conditions feet alone are not equal to the task of reaching the summit, and that they are even less suited to the descent.

Having reached the top a little after sunrise, I was able to enjoy a spectacle as beautiful as it was thrilling. The peak [344] of Umm al-Silmān, the slope of which is precipitous on the east face that I had just clambered up, abruptly falls away again on its western side. The summit, about two metres in length,

[123] [Blunt 1881 i: 189–90, 192–3.]

[124] Wallin calls it Muslimān. Guarmani says that Em-Senman and Umm e'Selmâñ, in the same way as Gebel Gobbah, denotes the whole of the massif, which may cover three to four square kilometres. The highest summit is always referred to as Rāʾs Silmān, 'the head of Silmān'. (CH)

is no more than a metre wide. There is no room for more than two people to sit there. A strong south wind was making it impossible to stand, so I sat down with my back against the rock.

The happy reward for my effort and hardship (for my hands and especially my feet had been well and truly flayed) was the magnificent view of the landscape, and particularly the sight of the highest point of the two ʿAlaym outcrops, which had been the main aim of my climb. Taking the bearing of this point indeed enabled me to verify the direction of my route. I was also able to take bearings on Ǧabal al-Ṭawīl, close to al-Ǧawf, Ǧabal Shammar to the south, and Ǧabal ʿAwthat, ten kilometres east of Ǧubbah.[125]

Ǧabal Umm al-Silmān looks to me to be part of a crater, only the eastern wall of which is still standing. This theory would explain the steepness of the peak's external slope – the one on its eastern side – and the verticality of its western face. My abrupt departure from Ǧubbah prevented me from pursuing further research on this topic. But I will allow myself to flag it up for explorers in years to come, and at the same time recommend the climb to thrill-seekers of the future.

For the summit of Rā's al-Silmān, my aneroid barometer indicated a height of 370 metres above the ground level of Ǧubbah.[126]

For the sake of completeness in setting down what I learned about the mountain of [345] Ǧubbah, I should add that, according to the inhabitants

[125] [Ǧabal al-Ṭawīl: a WNW–ESE range of hills, the eastern end of which is about 50 km south of Dūmat al-Ǧandal. See note 99 above. In his 65-page handwritten report dated 27 March 1882, Huber adds that he also took bearings on Ǧabal Ramīḍ and Ǧabal Aswad, presumably in the Aǧā/Ǧabal Shammar range (French national archives, Pierrefitte-sur-Seine, Dossier F/17/2976/1:1 entitled 'Mission au Thibet et dans l'Asie centrale', 1878–82, item 79, p. 30).]

[126] Lady Anne Blunt speculates that an ancient sea once existed here. Without wishing to dismiss this out of hand, I should point out that the wear on the rocks to the west of Ǧubbah, which could have given rise to this idea, could also be attributed to a completely different cause. During the course of my travels, deep horizontal grooves in rock strata have often come to my notice. These, especially from afar, immediately lead one to suppose that they were produced by floodwaters, even though such a cause is completely impossible to accept. Most often, then, these grooves must be attributed to the friability of an intermediate layer crumbling away through the effects of all the weather phenomena. I can only ascribe a very secondary role to the wind, the influence of which, I believe, has often been much exaggerated. (CH) [Blunt 1881 i: 187–8. In this passage, Lady Anne speculates about the existence of an ancient lake, not a sea as Huber mentions. In recent decades, abundant archaeological evidence has confirmed the existence of an ancient lake here during the Neolithic period. See for instance Petraglia 2012. (MCAM/WF)]

(for I have been unable to find any trace of it in the Arabic sources), its name was once al-Kutayfah.[127] Furthermore its desolate aspect and debris-covered slopes have given it an evil reputation, the blame for much of which resides with the demons who once possessed a castle and buried treasure on top of this mountain. So you must refrain from insisting that the inhabitants provide you with a guide or companion for the ascent. It is already no small thing for them to have allowed you to go up it and then to welcome you back amongst them on your return, for you must definitely have been smelling of sulphur.

On my return to the *qahwah* of Shaykh ʿAqīl, whose guest I was, I found a bedouin there telling us that the Emir Muḥammad Ibn Rashīd had already departed from Ḥāʾil, his capital, several days before and was now at Umm al-Qulbān,[128] a village in the Nafūd a day's march east-south-east of Ǧubbah, from where the bedouin himself had come. I asked whether the emir would be staying for a while in that place and whether he would then return to Ḥāʾil or leave for an excursion into the desert, but the man was unable to provide an answer.

It was of the utmost importance for me to meet the Shammar emir. Though I by no means shared the anxieties on this matter to which my guide was increasingly giving vent the nearer we drew to the Ǧabal, I was still uncertain of the welcome that I might receive from this prince; but I preferred nonetheless to be received by him in person. For one thing, any fanaticism or malevolence that I might encounter at the hands of a subordinate might lead to an unfriendly reception that the emir would feel unable to disavow, so as not to offend one of his loyal followers.

[346] Later on, having become better acquainted with the men and affairs of these parts, I saw that I had divined aright. And since my return to Europe, what has come to my knowledge about the trials and tribulations of Charles Doughty in similar circumstances has confirmed me even more strongly in my opinion.[129]

---

127 [Huber writes El Keteifa. This is perhaps *kutayfah*, the diminutive of *katif*, meaning a mountain bluff (Groom 1983: 137.]

128 [*Qulbān* (sing. *qalīb*): unlined wells (Groom 1983: 225). Umm al-Qulbān lies just to the north-east of the village of Qanāʾ, which nestles beneath the eastern end of the Aǧā range.]

129 M. Charles Doughty, having arrived in Ḥāʾil while the emir was away, was received by 'Anber [*sic*; Huber means ʿAnaybar], one of his slaves whom he had appointed governor until his return. 'Anber, with the self-conceit typical of him and which I was to experience in the same way later, issued Doughty with the order to leave Shammar

So I decided to leave forthwith for Umm al-Qulbān. Having applied elastic dressings to all the grazes sustained during my ascent and descent of Rā'ʾs al-Silmān, I got back in the saddle and left Ǧubbah after three o'clock in the afternoon. Two hours later we were camping near the rocks of ʿAwthat to make bread. An hour after that we moved off again to take advantage of the cool night air, and went on for another two hours. With the Nafūd once again becoming difficult at that point, we made camp for the night. The ground is clear of sand from Ǧubbah all the way to the rocks of ʿAwthat, but by the same token is completely devoid of vegetation. Its whiteness makes it very painful to cross by day, as the glare is extraordinarily tiring on the eyes.

Next day, the 8th of June, we started out at 3 o'clock in the morning. Although the regular *fulūǧ* became sparser and sparser, the Nafūd was hard-going even so, being very hilly with bare rock frequently showing through.

That morning we halted for just an hour for breakfast and then resumed our way, urging our camels on [347] so as to reach our destination before nightfall. The nearer we approached, the more and more visibly anxious Muḥārib became about the reception that might await us there. Were it to be hostile, then perhaps he too, like me, would feel the wrath of the emir. Furthermore he was a regular performer of his prayers, so he was a true believer, and as a consequence it was no small thing for him to be conducting an unbeliever into the presence of the emir. During this final day, he enquired two or three times rather anxiously whether I was absolutely sure of a friendly reception. I reassured him and, in the end, almost managed to convince him.

Already before midday we were beginning to encounter bedouin, either on their own or with herds of camels or flocks of goats or sheep. From these shepherds we learned that the emir was at Umm al-Qulbān to inspect part of his herds, and thus would have to stay there for a few days.

Two hours before reaching our destination, Muḥārib told me that it would be appropriate for him to go ahead so as to herald my arrival to the emir. To do me more honour, and at the same time to speed him on his way, he asked

territory immediately, and threatened the two Hutaymīs who had brought him there with death unless they went back with him whence they had come. However, M. Doughty had been provided with a letter of recommendation to the emir by the *wālī* of al-Madīnah (Doughty 1882: 250). (CH) [Huber, who by the time he wrote up this journey had read Doughty's 1882 article in *Globus*, is referring to Doughty's reception by ʿAnaybar, who was deputizing for his master Ibn Rashīd in Ḥāʾil when Doughty made his way back to the Shammar capital in the spring of 1878 (Doughty 1936 ii: 271–9).]

as a favour if he could ride my *dhalūl*. At that time, as on all my excursions, I was riding a magnificent animal in whose veins flowed Sharārī blood, a seven-year-old female the elegance of whose points aroused the admiration of the bedouin. We swapped animals and he went off at a gallop, happy on so splendid a mount.

The closer we drew, the more numerous the herds became and the more frequent the comings and goings, and it was rather a novel spectacle for us to see the Nafūd suddenly so full of life when for several days we had been experiencing the total solitude of the desert. Otherwise, it continued to present the same appearance as it had since our departure from Ǧubbah, that is to say [348] the *fulūǧ* were becoming sparser and seemed to be being replaced by hills, some of which, fortunately, ran parallel to our route so that, instead of having to cross them, we had only to proceed alongside them.

A few minutes before my arrival, Muḥārib reappeared before me, his face all lit up, announcing that he had seen the emir, who had seemed pleased and desired to see me forthwith. My guide now would not desist from his happy and joyous chatter, interspersed every second with cries of '*al-ḥamdu li'llāh*',[130] a sentiment that I piously repeated each time he uttered it.

At that point we were making our way down an enormous *fulǧ*, one of the biggest I had seen in the Nafūd. At its base lies Umm al-Qulbān, its green palms pleasantly scattered over the pink sands. It was an extraordinarily lively scene. Endless lines of camels, all bellowing as they do when making their evening return from pasture, were coming and going. Over all the noise could be heard the creaking and grinding of the pulleys carrying the well ropes as the herds were being watered.

In front of us stood a vast enclosure which we passed halfway along before seeing, facing north, a big main gate with a single door. Around it were several men wearing robes of a dazzling whiteness that startled me, as I had become unaccustomed to the luxury of clean laundry since leaving Syria. These men, sporting bright red *kūfiyyah*s,[131] were armed with long canes about 1.6 metres in length made from the branches of palm trees, and with these, on my approach, they very unceremoniously chased off the bedouin sitting or lounging around the gateway.

[130] '*Al-ḥamdu li'llāh*': 'Glory be to God'. (CH)

[131] [*kūfiyyah*: the headcloth typical of male Arabian dress, kept in place by an *ʿiqāl*, the double circlet of rope.]

One of these men took my camel by the bridle and led it through a long alleyway into a large courtyard. [349] There yet another gate was opened giving onto a second courtyard, where I dismounted. Waiting for me stood a personage clad in a magnificent *kūfiyyah* in yellow silk topped with an *ʿiqāl* of gold thread, wearing over his shoulders a beautiful black *ʿabāʾ*[132] with a gold-embroidered collar, and holding in his hand a sabre with a handle and fittings of solid silver. He received me with a '*salām ʿalayk*',[133] to which I cordially replied '*ʿalayk al-salām*'.[134] Greeting me on behalf of the emir, he announced that he was charged with bringing me before him.

Taking my right hand to show that I was under protection, he took me through a little doorway, and we found ourselves in front of a basin fed with running water. Beyond stretched a beautiful garden almost entirely planted with pomegranate trees, full of shade and suffused with a delicious freshness.

We rounded the basin and I found myself amidst some forty men arranged in a circle and all squatting on the ground. One section of the circle, covered with rugs, was in front of a house. It was occupied by the emir, seated on his own, his back leaning against his saddle. On my arrival, two of the attendants rose to their feet to let me into the circle. I uttered my salutation, and then the emir rose and in response to my greeting added '*marḥabah*', 'you are welcome'. He gave me his hand Arab-style, that is to say without shaking it but kissing his index finger afterwards, and then bade me sit next to him.

He enquired with much interest whether my journey had gone well, whether I had suffered any hardships and whether I was at all tired. Then he wanted to know all about the purpose of my journey, returning to this topic several times not just on this evening but also on later occasions. He found it very hard to believe that science alone could provide an adequate motive for someone to traverse the deserts of [350] Arabia, where he personally was unable to see anything at all of scientific interest. He then asked me for political news, especially about what had been said in Damascus and the Ḥawrān on the subject of the *ghazū*[135] he had led, two months before, into Wadi al-Sirḥān and right up to Qaṣr al-Azraq and beyond, at least as far as a

[132] For the meaning of this word, see note 71 above. (CH)

[133] *Salām ʿalayk*: 'Peace (be) upon you'. (CH)

[134] *ʿAlayk al-salām*: 'Upon you (be) peace'. (CH)

[135] *Ghazū*: a campaign of war and plunder. In Algeria we call it *razzia* or *ghezzi*. (CH) [This is the raid of April 1880 described in detail in Blunt 1881 i: 272–3.]

day's journey from Ǧabal Druze. Midḥat Pasha,[136] then Wali of Damascus, had indeed been extremely perturbed by it. He spoke also of Mr and Lady Anne Blunt, who had passed through Ḥāʾil eighteen months before.[137] He had retained a pleasant memory of the visit, but found it very strange that Mr Blunt had only ever accepted the cup of coffee after his wife, had always let her go in front, and always sat in the background, etc. etc. He asked me whether it was like that amongst all the Christians. What most astonished the emir, along with every other Arab, was to see Lady Anne mounting a horse and, what is more, doing so very capably.

The Emir Muḥammad Ibn Rashīd is forty-six years old and about 1.65 metres tall.[138] He has a lively and expressive face. His keen eye is penetrating and restless, and his glance constantly darts from one person to another,

---

[136] [Ahmed Şefik Midḥat Pasha (1822–83) was a leading Ottoman statesman who had been governor of Niš in Serbia in the early 1860s. He was an enthusiastic modernizer and a central figure in the reforming Tanzimat movement. Appointed governor of Baghdad in 1869, he re-established Ottoman rule in al-Ḥasāʾ in 1871. Back at the centre of power, Midḥat was appointed Grand Vizier by Sultan Abdülaziz in 1872 and led the constitutional reforms of 1876. A man of liberal and democratic views, he fell foul of Sultan Abdülhamid, and was sent into exile, only to return as a result of British pressure as governor of Syria, a post he held from November 1878 till August 1881. Exiled again by the Ottoman government on the possibly trumped-up charge of having been involved in the death of Sultan Abdülaziz in 1876, he was imprisoned and assassinated in al-Ṭāʾif in 1883. The Blunts met him in Damascus in December 1878 and give a somewhat unflattering account of his character. (Blunt 1881 i: 16–20.)]

[137] [Wilfrid Scawen Blunt (1840–1922) was an English poet and writer of strong anti-imperialist and pro-Arab views. His wife, Lady Anne Blunt (1837–1917), was daughter of the celebrated mathematician Ada Lovelace and granddaughter of the poet Lord Byron. The couple travelled widely in the Middle East and were instrumental in recording and preserving the Arabian horse bloodlines through their farm, the Crabbet Arabian Stud, in Sussex. They travelled through northern Arabia in 1878–79, meeting the emir Muḥammad Ibn Rashīd in Ḥāʾil in January 1879 (Blunt 1881 i: 216–17). Lady Anne's book, *Pilgrimage to Nejd* (Blunt 1881), was extensively edited by her husband and became a bestseller of Victorian travel.]

[138] [Muḥammad al-Rashīd ruled from 1872 to 1897, during which time he established Ḥāʾil as the foremost power in central Arabia. The rise of Ḥāʾil came at the expense of Riyadh, as the Second Saʿūdī State slipped into civil war leading eventually to the exile of the Āl Saʿūd in 1891. Emir Muḥammad ruled a distinctive version of the Arabian tribal state, imposed law and order, and entered into diplomatic relations with the Ottoman Empire and Egypt. He had no children, and after his death the polity was riven by dynastic squabbles and threatened by the recovery of Saudi power in Naǧd after 1902. See Musil 1928a: 240–4; Winder 1965: 242–4; Al-Rasheed 1991: 59–62; Vassiliev 1998: 196–8; Çicek 2017.]

giving him the air of being permanently on guard. In contrast he has a ready smile of great sweetness. His sparse black beard shows him to be a true bedouin. He is a natural conversationalist and enjoys a joke.

I found him to be most attentive to his guest at all times, taking care that I was comfortably seated, put at ease and not discommoded in any way. On the subject of how to conduct myself personally, he always encouraged me to behave as if I was at home and not to adopt the ways of his own people, assuring me that this would cause him no offence.

I had very quickly found complete favour with him, and before reaching Ḥāʾil I was quite certain that he would place no obstacles in the way of me accomplishing my mission. However, as far as my project to go to al-Qaṣīm and beyond was concerned, he urged me from the very first day to refrain from embarking upon it. These regions, [351] he said, were by all accounts in a state of unrest. 'You will stay with us,' he added. And then, to familiarize me with the new milieu that would henceforth be mine, he set about telling me the names of his chief functionaries, who were sitting before us in the circle.

However, here is a trait that conveys a true picture of the Muslim and which, however cordial and affable his exterior may be, affords a glimpse of the Wahhābī within.

From the very first moments of our interview, once compliments had been exchanged and he had become aware of my plan to sojourn in the land of the Arabs, he doubtless felt a qualm about spending so long in the company of an infidel. But his mind, so enlightened in other respects, persuaded him to keep such scruples to himself. Then, to soothe his conscience, he asked me point-blank whether I knew the Muslim profession of faith. To this I replied in the affirmative. 'Say it,' he responded. I recited it straight away with all possible solemnity: '*Lā ilāha illa 'Llāh, Muḥammad rasūl Allāh.*' That is to say: 'There is no deity but God, Muḥammad is the messenger of God.'

Orthodoxy would normally demand that this ritual form of words be prefaced with the word '*ashhadu*', 'I testify', but he was willing to overlook this omission. No sooner had I finished reciting the formula so dear to believers, which was received with a murmur of approval from the whole gathering, than the emir cried out delightedly: '*Wallāh! Anta Muslim ʿindī.*' 'By God! You are a Muslim here with me!' From this moment on he was no longer in the least troubled by his conscience. Freed thus from all restraint, he treated me as a co-religionist – in other words, as an equal.

To conclude this little study of manners, I shall add that during the entire time of my stay in the Ǧabal, apart from having once or twice been under a slight cloud due to the jealously of others, I basked in the unbroken sunshine of the emir's favour, as well as that of his cousin Ḥamūd[139] and of all their family. Nowhere was barred to me [352] and everyone called me their brother and friend. Towards the end of my stay, the emir often even told me that I was now one of them, that I was a Shammarī.

Being in a more fortunate position than Palgrave and Lady Anne Blunt, I never had to hide myself away in order to take notes and write up my journal. It frequently even happened that when I wanted to know the exact spelling of geographical names, the emir himself would write them down for me. The numerous letters that I have received from the emir and my friends in the Ǧabal since my departure from Arabia are proof of the positive impression I left there. Everything that I was able to achieve on my expedition I owe to the emir, and I shall be for ever grateful to him.

He constantly strove to divert me from my plans to go to al-Qaṣīm and travel in the Ḥiǧāz, because the dangers, as I later came to recognize, were real. But once he had given his consent he did everything in his power to ensure my success. Even though there was a risk of appearing unorthodox and besmirching his prestige as a Muslim prince and a Wahhābī one at that – for such he was – he always gave me letters of recommendation when he judged them necessary.

Four days after my arrival, the whole court left Umm al-Qulbān to return to Ḥā'il.

On 12 June, with the dawn, everyone was in the saddle and we marched for a full three hours at a continuous trot in a south-easterly direction. At the

---

139 [Ḥamūd al-ʿUbayd was the most powerful man in Ḥā'il after his cousin, Emir Muḥammad. He was the son of the famous ʿUbayd ibn ʿAlī ibn Rashīd (d. 1869), nicknamed 'The Wolf', who had helped his brother, Emir ʿAbd Allāh, to establish the Rashīdī dynasty in Ḥā'il in the 1830s and remained a much-feared power behind the throne until ʿAbd Allāh's death in 1847 and, after that, during the reign of his successor, Ṭalāl (d. 1868). (Winder 1965: 68–9, 154–6, 240; Al-Rasheed 1991: 40–8.) Doughty was in Ḥā'il in October 1877 and again in April 1878, and describes Ḥamūd al-ʿUbayd in great detail (Doughty 1936 i: 642, 647–52, 655–7, 664–5; ii: 17–18, 24–32, 36, 41–5, 51, 56, 58, 61–3, 68–75). Euting, who had many dealings with Ḥamūd al-ʿUbayd in December 1883 and January 1884, suffered from his avarice and developed a strong antipathy to him (Euting 1896 i: 187–8). For a much more favourable description of Ḥamūd, and a less favourable one of the Emir Muḥammad, see Blunt 1881 i: 228–30. (MCAM/WF)]

end of that time we tackled one of the spurs of Ǧabal Shammar called al-Aswar.[140] The emir's kitchens, which had left far in advance of us, had already prepared the midday meal. This was followed by a long siesta, after which a paper target was set up on a nearby rock, and we did an hour's target practice. On this occasion, I observed that the emir was one of the Ǧabal's proficient marksmen.

Al-Aswar is a watering point where rainfall collects in a granite cleft at [353] a particular point on the mountain. There was still some water left after we had gone.

An hour's journey from Umm al-Qulbān, the Nafūd ended as abruptly as it had begun. The edge is so clear-cut that one can almost have one foot in the Nafūd and the other on the adjacent granite terrain.

At three o'clock in the afternoon we remounted our *dhalūl*s and left al-Aswar. A two-hour trot without a break brought us to al-Laqīṭah,[141] a pretty village where the emir owns a magnificent estate of date palms and fruit trees, and here we spent the night.

We were served upon arrival with a snack of fruits and dairy products. The fruits included delicious melons and watermelons, but the grapes were not yet entirely ripe.

Next day, having left at 4.30 in the morning, it took us two hours to reach the Shammar capital, Ḥāʾil.[142]

When one approaches it from the north, Ḥāʾil is hidden behind a basaltic ridge with a maximum height of 100 metres, running between Ǧabal Aǧā and Ǧabal Samrā, which stands to the east of Ḥāʾil. This little range can be crossed by a pass rising to about twenty metres above ground level. From the top of this pass the cheerful spectacle of Ḥāʾil opens out before one, with its green gardens surrounded by pink walls. To the left, very close to the town, the black mass of Samrā completely dominates it. To the right, at a distance of several kilometres, can be seen the line of the Aǧā range falling away to the south until it disappears from sight. To the north and west, some fifty tents of all the Shammar tribes lie scattered about. These visitors come for a few days to dispose of their produce and make a few purchases before

---

[140] [Huber's El Asouar. However, in the margin of his handwritten manuscript he gives the Arabic spelling as al-Zawar.]

[141] Wallin calls it Laqita; Guarmani, Lechite; Mme Blunt, El Akeyt. (CH) [Al-Laqīṭah was about 18 km north of Ḥāʾil.]

[142] Guarmani, Kaïl; Palgrave, Hâ'yel. (CH)

returning to the desert. They [354] enliven the area outside the town in a very picturesque manner.

As I have wanted to present an overview of the route from Syria as far as Ǧabal Shammar, I have spread myself up to this point by devoting a detailed account to it. But from now on I intend to give no more than a broad geographical outline of the regions I travelled through, and so I shall postpone till another time the chapter on their customs, history and statistical data.[143] What follows for now is a brief description of my various itineraries. After that I shall list the places that currently comprise the two emirates of Shammar and al-Qaṣīm that I travelled through.

***

So as to be able more easily to undertake journeys that were often very long, I made Ḥāʾil my centre of operations. This allowed me to minimize my baggage so that I never had to take along more than a rug and a couple of blankets, besides my weapons and scientific instruments. Food and water were brought by the bedouin or bedouins accompanying me as guides.

My trunks during these absences stayed in my house in Ḥāʾil, and the keys were entrusted into the hands of one of the emir's principal officers, named Ḥamūd al-Ibrāhīm al-Miqrād.[144]

---

[143] [Huber sets out some statistical data about the regions through which he travelled in Huber 1885a: 139–48 – see Translation Part III below, pp. 263–73. But he gives no account of their customs and history, so he must have been planning to publish these separately. It is unfortunate that his untimely demise on 29 July 1884 prevented this.]

[144] The army of the Shammar emir is obviously not an army in the European sense of the word. There are neither conscription nor barracks. It comprises around 500 men, the majority of whom are from the settlements of the Ǧabal, and whom the emir employs specially to carry out his raids, the imposition and payment of tax among the nomadic tribes, and finally to serve as escorts for the Persians making the pilgrimage from Baghdad to Mecca and back. They receive no fixed salary and are given whatever they need for their subsistence. Some twenty of them who have distinguished themselves through services rendered or rather by their intelligence, and who dance constant attendance on the emir at the castle, are better treated. Among this number is Ḥamūd, whom the emir has already several times sent on extraordinary missions to the Khedive in Egypt. (CH) [On the composition of the 'army' at Ḥāʾil, see Rosenfeld 1965. Ḥamūd al-Ibrāhīm ibn Ǧawād al-Miqrād came to play an important role in Huber's Arabian explorations, as he would be assigned by the emir to assist Huber and Euting in their 1883–84 journey through northern Arabia. See e.g. Euting 1896: 60–1, 64, 66; see also Appendix 5, Letter no. 1 dated 10 April 1883 from Huber in Paris to Ḥamūd al-Ibrāhīm ibn Ǧawād.]

Here is the list of my various excursions, in the order in which I made them:
[355]

1. Excursion into ʿUqdah, a valley in the Shammar mountain range (30 June).
2. To Ǧabal Sarrāʾ (9 July).
3. In Ǧabal Shammar (17 July).
4. Journey to al-Qaṣīm, to ʿUnayzah and back (31 July).
5. Excursion to Ǧabal Ǧildiyyah (22 September).
6. Journey in the Ḥiǧāz, to Taymāʾ, al-Ḥiǧr or Madāʾin Ṣāliḥ, al-ʿUlā, and back via Khaybar and al-Ḥāʾiṭ (30 October).
7. From Ḥāʾil to Baghdad.
8. From Baghdad to Damascus across the Ḥamād.

ʿUQDAH

ʿUqdah[145] is a series of little ravines in the interior of Ǧabal Shammar. The extremely narrow pass giving sole access to it is situated about nine kilometres south by 70° west of Ḥāʾil.

The name ʿUqdah appears for the first time as a place name in Arabia in the history of the Wahhābīs by Corancez,[146] in his list of locations in the Ǧabal. However, as I shall show below, this must have been the first and probably for a very long time the only place to be inhabited by the Ṭāʾiyy[147] during their migration from the south towards the Ǧabal.

It is probably in ʿUqdah itself that the place of residence of Ḥātim al-Ṭāʾiyy,[148] the most generous of the ancient Arabs, should be sought.

---

[145] Ukdé in Ritter 1847, *Arabien* ii: 353; Ekede in Guarmani; Agde in Blunt. (CH) [Al-ʿUqdah is in the Aǧā range some 5 km west of the westernmost suburbs of modern Ḥāʾil. It comprises a series of hemmed-in valleys in Ǧabal Aǧā which were accessible only by a single, very narrow fortified defile. Its fort and villages were used as an armoury and refuge by the emirs of Ḥāʾil. It was visited by Guarmani in 1864 (Guarmani 1938: 53–4, 89) and again by Huber, with Euting, in December 1883 (Euting 1896: 192–6). (MCAM/WF)]

[146] Corancez 1810: 118. (CH)

[147] Ṭāʾiyy: the pre-Islamic name of the Shammar. (CH)

[148] [Ḥātim al-Ṭāʾiyy was the byword in oral literature for the tribal virtue of generosity, and his name remains current and much quoted to this day. He died in AD 578.]

When coming from the plain of Ḥā'il, the access to ʿUqdah is through a gorge on the same level as the plain. This passage, about 100 metres across at its mouth, narrows until it is no more than twenty-five or thirty metres in width. It is at this point in the ravine that the emir has caused a wall about three metres high and a metre thick to be built, intended to completely bar [356] the way. To allow coming and going, there is no more than an opening a metre and a half wide at the wall's southern end.

On passing through this wall one immediately finds oneself in a small valley containing the village of al-Qanī with its 150 inhabitants. From this point the valleys open out more or less on all sides, but all of them at heights above the first and thus also above the level of the Ḥā'il plain.

The valley following that of al-Qanī encloses a second village bigger than the first, with 300 inhabitants, called al-Waybār.

These first two communities are the largest in both population and area. In the others there are distributed eight more little groups of dwellings housing about 500 souls altogether. Here are their names:[149] al-Nabaytah – al-Sāqah – Huṣnā – al-Maʿā – al-Ghaḍyān[150] – al-Ḥā'iṭ[151] – Ramīḍ[152] – al-ʿAliyyā.

It is in the village of al-Ḥā'iṭ, to the south of al-Qanī and al-Waybār, that part of Ibn Rashīd's arsenal is located. It is an adobe building, like all the buildings in the Ğabal, covering about eighty square metres in area, but flanked by some more recent structures built by the present emir.

The main building was erected by Emir Ṭalāl to replace another that he had had demolished, and it is probable that when the Ṭā'iyy occupied the Ğabal during their migration from the south, they set up their first establishment on this spot. Up until the accession of Muḥammad, the present emir, this building was the only arsenal of the Shammar dynasty. But Muḥammad, having considerably enlarged the fortress[153] built by Emir

[149] [These names, with the exception of al-Nabaytah and al-Maʿā, are written in Arabic, along with several others, on the sketch map by Huber: item no. 3 in the section entitled Cartes et Croquis included at the back of Huber 1891.]

[150] [Al-Ghaḍyān: an area where *ghaḍā* trees (*Haloxylon persicum*, Mandaville 2011: 249) grow; rough ground (Groom 1983: 90–1).]

[151] Not to be confused with al-Ḥā'iṭ in the Ḥarrat Hutaym, to the east-north-east of Khaybar. (CH)

[152] [Ramīḍ, perhaps Rumayḍ: from *ramḍ*, meaning ground that is very hot from the sun (Groom 1983: 238).]

[153] [i.e Qaṣr Bārzān, the great fortified palace in the centre of Ḥā'il, which reached its greatest extent and most imposing appearance during the reign of Emir Ṭalāl Ibn Rashīd (r. 1847–68). See Blunt 1881 i: 212 for an engraving of it in January 1879.

Ṭalāl which is the equivalent of the Tuileries[154] of Ḥāʾil, has since removed thither the larger part of the weapons stored up till then at ʿUqdah. [357] So today this fort, with its great gate covered in metal sheets, is just a food store containing no more than plentiful supplies of dates, plus a few swords and some matchlocks of little value. The palms of al-Ḥāʾiṭ are the special property of Emir Muḥammad Ibn Rashīd.

A unique feature of ʿUqdah is its palm trees, which have no need to be watered thanks to the configuration of the valleys, the granite substrates of which are overlaid by four or five metres of *baṭḥāʾ*, or granitic gravel,[155] forming the ground surface. The bottoms are all bowl-shaped, so that the rainwater that falls on ʿUqdah remains contained in these little natural basins, into which the roots of the date palms then descend.[156]

Everywhere else, when the water is at too great a depth for the roots to be able to reach it, very large wells have to be dug, and the water has to be drawn up for ten months out of twelve and then for fifteen hours a day. Camels have to be purchased and kept for the job, and then a man has to be employed to manage them. Of all this the fortunate inhabitants of ʿUqdah know little and care less; they have only to put themselves to the trouble of praying for winter rains. They even abuse their good fortune by their idleness, for they take absolutely no care of their palms, which could be much more handsome and productive. Furthermore, the weak state of their palms was fatal during the winter of 1879–80, the harshness of which was felt throughout Arabia. Many trees died, and for a long time even more of them will fail to produce any significant harvest.

[358] Ḥamūd al-Miqrād assured me that ʿUqdah possesses seventy thousand palm trees, which could be an accurate figure. About one-fifth of

---

(Musil 1928a: 240; Winder 1965: 105.)]

[154] [Tuileries: lit. 'tile kilns', the historic royal palace in Paris which was the usual residence of French monarchs from Henri IV in the 16th century until 1871, when it was burnt by the Paris Commune.]

[155] This is probably an error. The Arabic word *baṭḥāʾ* (*bathhâ* in the transcription adopted by M. Huber) literally means in that language 'a broad, dry torrent bed full of stones'. It has kept this meaning among the Arabs of Wadai. In Arabia, M. Huber has thus confused the contents with the container. (The Editors.) [This is also the meaning in Naǧd. It was for example used for the torrent bed running past the eastern side of the old city of Riyadh (Facey 1992: 14–15).]

[156] [This seems oddly at variance with what Huber says about ʿUqdah in November 1883, when he observes that because they have no camels of their own to lift the water, the people of ʿUqdah have to rent them from the bedouin (Huber 1891: 74).]

them belong to the emir and two-fifths to the settled Arabs who live there all year round, the remainder being the property of Shammar nomads.

The latter come in from the desert in the month of May to see to the fertilization of the female palms. They build palm-frond huts and stay there until the harvest in September. A member of the family remains behind in the desert with the herds. Some of them take advantage of their enforced sojourn to sow a few watermelons and other types of melon which they irrigate with water from the wells. The proximity of Ḥāʾil assures them of a ready market for these fruits.

Since part of its population is bedouin, the customs of the desert prevail in ʿUqdah too. For a stranger arriving there, this is expressed in hospitality. During the three days that I spent there, I counted nineteen houses or tents that I had to enter to enjoy the experience of being served with the daily coffee, along with an immense dish of watermelon and diced melons. I say 'had to', because my host of the moment would actually leave off his lounging in the sun as soon as he spotted me to run up and grab my camel's halter and, paying no heed whatsoever to my protestations, lead me to his home. True, what he set before me amounted to very little, and this little was handsomely compensated for by the honour of receiving the French shaykh and friend of the emir, whom he would henceforth have the right to call his brother. Even so, I have to concede that the bedouin who spotted me on the evening that we were looking for accommodation was no less keen to hang on to me despite knowing that it would cost him a sheep – his own share of which would be paltry, as I had two of the emir's men with me.

In the light of my description of the topography of ʿUqdah, which has just a single access artificially barricaded by a wall and [359] which is completely hemmed in by granite crags inaccessible from outside, one can see why this place, if well provisioned and defended by a stalwart garrison, is regarded by the court at Ḥāʾil as a citadel and an impregnable refuge in case of invasion. I would concur with that assessment, but only on condition that the invaders were not European troops, and that there were no cannon to force a breach.

Ǧabal Sarrāʾ

It was during one of my first evenings with the emir that I learned of the existence of ancient inscriptions in the Ǧabal. He directed me to Ǧabal Sarrāʾ, a full day's march to the south of Ḥāʾil, where he said I would find one. He even had the chief Shammar religious authority, Shaykh ʿAwaḍ, summoned, because he had copied it one day onto the flyleaf of a book, which he showed me.[157]

I saw straight away that it was a Himyaritic[158] inscription, and that I could allow myself to expect that there must be more of them, and that I would be able to find them.

On 9 July, the emir assigned two men as guides to accompany me to Ǧabal Sarrāʾ.

Leaving Ḥāʾil at seven o'clock in the morning by the western gate, we soon bent our way to the left, leaving Ǧabal Samrā to the east. Our direction was more or less south by 10° west, without taking into account the variations of the compass needle.

Two hours after leaving Ḥāʾil we had reached the latitude of Qufār, which we left to our right. At noon we halted to eat a few dates in front of Ǧabal Arkān,[159] an outcrop affording a little shade on its northern side, and an hour later we resumed our journey.

Ever since making my way out of Ḥāʾil, I had had Ǧabal Aǧā constantly on my right and always at more or less the same distance. Only to the south of Qufār did my route diverge a little from the Ǧabal. I make this observation in passing in order to [360] justify the direction I give to this mountain on my map, which is a new and noticeably different one from that marked on the most recent maps.

---

157 [Shaykh ʿAwaḍ was not the only local cleric to take an interest in ancient inscriptions. In January 1884 Huber and Euting were given a drawing of this inscription by another one, the *khaṭīb* ʿAbdullah (Euting 1914: 52–3; see also note 161 below). (MCAM/WF)]

158 [Huber is using 'Himyaritic' incorrectly here since it refers to Ḥimyar, the last kingdom in pre-Islamic South Arabia (*ca.* AD 300–570), and was thence applied by mediaeval Arab and 19th-century Western scholars to the script used throughout Ancient South Arabia's 1,500-year history. It is now known as the Ancient South Arabian script (ASA). However, the inscription he is referring to, and the others he and Euting copied on their journeys, are in Ancient *North* Arabian (ANA) scripts which belong to the same script family as ASA but are the result of separate developments. The graffiti Huber is describing here are in the Thamudic B script, except for the first two lines which may be in Thamudic D (see Macdonald 2009 III: 34, 43–4). At the time Huber was writing, the ANA scripts had not been fully deciphered. The first major breakthrough on Thamudic was made twenty years later by E. Littmann in 1904. This was refined by Winnett in 1937 and the decipherment of some of the scripts continues today. (MCAM)]

159 [Huber spells this Ergâñ, and in the margin of his handwritten manuscript in Arabic as Arǧān. This is probably the mountain known as Arkān, some 16 km north of Ǧabal Sarrāʾ at approx. 27° 13' N 041° 34' E (GeoNames).]

Up to a few kilometres to the north of Ǧabal Sarrāʾ, our path took us uninterruptedly over the coarse granite gravel known as *baṭḥāʾ*, which I have described above, and which is completely uncultivated. The gravel layer is not everywhere of equal depth and from time to time one is afforded a glimpse of the subsoil beneath, which is yellowish-grey and consists of a compacted clay marl. In such places the thin tuft of a shrub sometimes appears, or the rampant stalk of a colocynth.[160]

The sun was going down very close to the horizon when I arrived in front of the inscription on Ǧabal Sarrāʾ. It is located in a pass about eighty metres wide, giving access to the route towards Mustaǧiddah and the Ḥiǧāz. The inscription was carved into the rock on the southern face of the pass, six metres from the ground and facing north. Thanks to the scree it is possible to get within about two metres of it. I immediately set about getting into position to make a copy, and noted that Shaykh ʿAwaḍ had accurately reproduced nearly half of the characters. I consider this a satisfactory result for a literate Shammarī, especially in view of the rough state of the inscription and the optical effects of the light on this coarse granite with its multi-coloured granules, the rainbow shades of which quickly tire the eyes. Later, I congratulated myself for having taken the utmost pains in copying this one, as of all the Himyaritic inscriptions I came across on the excursions that followed, none turned out to be so substantial. It consisted of ninety-eight characters.[161]

---

[160] [Colocynth: the ubiquitous desert gourd, *ḥanḍal*, *Citrullus colocynthis*.]

[161] [From a photograph taken almost a century after Huber's first visit (Winnett & Reed 1973: 113) it is now clear that there are actually 111 characters. Moreover, it is not a single inscription but at least six short graffiti. Huber published the copy mentioned here as no. 1 in Huber 1884a: 293 (see Appendices 1 and 2 in this volume), and subsequently copied these inscriptions three more times on his journey in 1883–84: on 27 and 28 January 1884 when he was with Euting (1891: 221–2, = HU 187+188) and on 4 May 1884 (1891: 626 = HU 789) after they had parted company. Euting copied them twice on 27 January (1914: 114–17, where E. Littmann provided readings and translations). Note that both these copies are confusingly numbered as Eut 226 (Jamme 1974: pls 10A and 11A). Both Huber (1891: 136) and Euting (1914: 52) also reproduced copies made by a *khaṭīb*. Huber here and in 1891: 136 calls him 'the S[haykh] ʿAwāḍ the Khaṭīb' but Euting (1914: 52) refers to 'the Khaṭīb ʿAbdullah'. These copies differ considerably from each other so it seems probable that ʿAwāḍ and ʿAbdullah were two different *khaṭīb*s who had copied the inscriptions independently. Littmann was the first to edit them (1904: 66–7) from Euting's copies. They were later studied by H. Grimme (1926: cols 13–25, 1934: 87–90) who treated them as a single 'Felspsalm' ('rock psalm'), and then by van den Branden (1950:

As I said, this inscription is *in situ* on the cliff-face of the mountain itself. I found five more smaller ones on some great granite rocks several cubic metres in size that had tumbled to the side and in front of the inscription.[162] One of these blocks also carried [361] a drawing of an animal which must be either a large greyhound or a gazelle.[163] The line of this drawing is bold and well defined, indicating an artist. Of the hundreds of animal representations carved into the rock that I later came across, this one is the finest.

Night came on as I was finishing my copies. We remounted our camels, which we had left loaded with our camel-bags (*kharǧ*),[164] and approached the wells lying half a kilometre to the east. A number of bedouin, whose tents were located farther to the south, were there to water some camels and sheep. While my animals drank, I took the temperature of the water, which was +21°; it was bland-tasting, and the water table was seven metres down. As it is never wise to camp close to water, even in Shammar territory, I moved on again for another hour to the north-west, and finally came to a halt in a fold in the ground.[165] There my men made bread which we ate with butter, and then we rolled ourselves up in our cloaks to enjoy a well-earned rest. We had spent eleven hours in the saddle and had covered 92 kilometres.

Next morning, having risen with the dawn, we made our way due north, and an hour and half's march brought us to Ǧabal Wallah, where we halted near some wells for over an hour in order to eat.

113–16, no. HU 789, but see Ryckmans 1951: 154–5). Finally, a reading of the texts from their photograph and tracing was published by Winnett and Reed (1973: 86–9, 112–13). (MCAM)]

[162] [These are nos. 2–6 in Huber 1884a: 289, 293 (see Appendices 1 and 2 below). Van den Branden (1950) numbered them as HU 190–3, 197. Huber recopied these inscriptions, with some others from the same place, on the journey in 1883–84 (1891: 223–4). Unfortunately, because the copies are extremely bad, it is often difficult to identify those made on the 1880 journey with those made in 1883–84. However, see the concordance in Appendix 2. (MCAM)]

[163] [Huber does not seem to have copied this drawing either on this journey or in 1884. Euting copied what is clearly an oryx (and certainly not a greyhound or gazelle) between Eut 228 and 229 and the original can be seen, along with crude drawings of other animals, in the photograph in Winnett and Reed 1973: 113 next to their no. 201 a–f. (MCAM)]

[164] *Kharǧ* means large panniers. (The Editors.) [The large tasselled camel bag typical of Arabian bedouin is known as a *khurǧ*, as recorded by me in Dūmat al-Ǧandal and Taymāʾ in January 1985, rather than as *kharǧ* as rendered by Huber (Hilden 2010: 165–6).]

[165] M. Huber here articulates a rule that is observed everywhere in nomad country, notably in the Sahara. (The Editors.)

The water of the wells of Wallah, which number four, is seven metres down. Three of them are dug into the *baṭḥā'* and the fourth into the granite bedrock. At 9 a.m. we resumed our march and reached Qufār towards four o'clock in the evening.

The route we followed from Ǧabal Wallah all the way to Qufār runs to the west of the one I took to go [362] from Ḥā'il to Ǧabal Sarrā' and is almost parallel to it. It also runs more or less half way between my first route and Ǧabal Aǧā, the dark granite masses of which loomed constantly two or three kilometres off to my left. The terrain is formed of *baṭḥā'* all the way, but the proximity of the mountain causes a slight bulge in the ground to appear beneath our feet from time to time, which suggests that the rock lies not far below the surface. It is visible several times and, in ten or so places, long ridges of white veined marble running east–west even break through, as if there was an uplift in a direction contrary to that of Ǧabal Aǧā. In addition, the ground is gullied from time to time by the little torrents that pour down from the mountain to issue a little way off to our right, in Wadi Ḥā'il.

On leaving the emir the day before, his cousin Ḥamūd al-ʿUbayd, who had already previously spoken to me about a large property he owned at Qufār, invited me to stop off there on my return from Ǧabal Sarrā', and undertook to send the necessary instructions there for my reception. This property was the last one to the south of Ḥā'il, and as a result the first to come into our view as we approached the town. From afar I was able to make out a white dot standing out from the pink crenellated walls of Qufār. It was obviously a man wearing just his *thawb*[166] who was waiting for us. In fact he remained standing right up to the moment when, having come right up to him, we made our camels kneel and set our feet on the ground. It was ʿAnbar,[167] Ḥamūd's favourite slave, whom the latter had sent here specially to receive me. He bade me welcome and led me into the garden, where he had prepared a bed of rugs and cushions for me near a little pool.

[363] Having performed my ablutions I took a walk around the garden, which is very beautiful, containing about two hundred palm trees, some vines, peach and fig trees and, in the corners next to the walls, *ithl* or tamarisk trees.

166 Tsoûb, which is pronounced *thoûb* (with the English *th*) means 'shirt'. It is the word for the long robe worn throughout the whole of Arabia, and means the same as the garment called *meslah* in Syria and Palestine. (CH)

167 [ʿAnbar: possibly Huber means ʿAnaybar again, see note 129 above.]

Then I returned to my spot near the pool, where coffee and my narghileh had been prepared during my promenade. I stayed there to enjoy a good rest until sunset, when the mosquitoes announced their presence. So then I went up to the terraces of the buildings, where my companions and I were served with an immense dish of rice and mutton. Like true bedouin, we chose to spend the night outside the village, in the desert.

We left at five o'clock next morning and were back in Ḥāʾil three hours later.

I shall return in another work to Qufār and the important role this town has played in Shammar history.[168] It is still today the largest settlement in area, and in terms of population the second largest in the whole emirate.

[To be continued]

[168] [Qufār (27° 24' 57" N 041° 37' 35" E), had been the largest historic settlement in the extensive agricultural area lying between Ǧabal Aǧā and Ǧabal Salmā before the rise of Ḥāʾil in the early 19th century. It was chiefly inhabited by the Banī Tamīm, the ancient settled tribespeople of Central Arabia. See Wallin 1850: 335; 1854: 201–2; Guarmani 1938: 53, 89–90.]

PART II

A JOURNEY IN CENTRAL ARABIA: AL-ḤAMĀD, SHAMMAR, AL-QAṢĪM AND AL-ḤIǦĀZ (continued)

Bulletin de la Société de Géographie 7th series, no. 5, 1884, 4th trimester, pp. 468–530

By Charles Huber

Commissioned by the Minister of Public Education 1878–1882

ǦABAL AǦĀ

ON 17 JULY, I set off on an excursion into the mountain range that has lent its name to the whole region. Once it was called Ṭā'iyy, later it took the name Ramīḍ, and today it is generally known as Aǧā or Ǧabal Shammar; or also simply as the Ǧabal, that is to say, the Mountain.

This time I started from the northern part of Ḥā'il, turning my steps northwards by 10° east to al-Laqīṭah,[1] a village that I reached after a two-hour trot with the two new horsemen assigned to me by the emir, named ʿAlī al-Miqrād and ʿĪsa.

Two miles before reaching al-Laqīṭah we passed two villages to our right, al-Waṣīd[2] and al-Ǧithāmiyyah.

[1] [Al-Laqīṭah was about 18 km north of Ḥā'il.]

[2] [Huber writes El Oueçīd for this place, and in the margin of his handwritten manuscript gives it in Arabic as al-Waṣīd. It is possible that he means the village named al-Waqīd just to the south-east of al-Laqīṭah.]

We halted in the gardens of the emir at al-Laqīṭah until after two o'clock. Then we set off again, but this time in a westerly direction. We soon found ourselves amidst the first tumbled rocks of the mountain, and after a full hour we made our way into it via the gully of Ghalghal.[3] This ravine widens little by [469] little and soon transforms into a series of very picturesque little valleys, all full of palm trees growing without irrigation as at ʿUqdah, and belonging to the nomads. After following the Ghalghal for an hour and a half, we came up close to a cluster of nine tents, and made camp at a little distance from them.

The palm trees of this area are well-grown. Water is at a depth of six metres.

Leaving next day at four o'clock in the morning, heading southwards by 80° east, we soon left the Ghalghal to enter the valley of Ḥaql,[4] which is no more than a few kilometres long. By half past five we had followed its entire course and, resuming our westward march, we entered the valley of Tuwārin,[5] which lies at the same level as the previous one.

Near the start of this valley, on the left, is the little spring of Utraymiyyah,[6] which emerges from the rock twenty or so metres above ground and is not easy to reach. It flows at a rate of barely three litres per minute into a small basin dug in front of it, which is shaded by three palm trees. Its temperature was 24.1°.

We encamped four kilometres farther on, near the ruins of a small fort called Qaṣr al-Aṣfar.[7] This occupies the summit of a prominent spur jutting out from the mountain and protruding into the valley in a north-easterly direction, a quarter north, to the south-west, a quarter south.[8] The building occupies the entire available surface of the plateau, which is forty metres

[3] Better still, Ghalghala, Arabic for 'the flow'. (The Editors.) [Huber names it Ghalghalah in his handwritten manuscript and gives the Arabic thus in the margin. Possibly related to *ghāll*, a floodbed where trees grow (Groom 1983: 92). The little oasis of Ghalghalah is located at the northern extremity of Ǧabal Aǧā, at approx. 27° 43' N 041° 32' E (GeoNames).

[4] [Ḥaql: probably the valley just to the east of the Tuwārin valley, on the north side of Ǧabal Aǧā. Huber spells it Haql in Arabic in the margin of his handwritten manuscript. However, the derivation is probably from *ḥaql*, lit. a field (Groom 1983: 103).]

[5] [Tuwārin, a small village on the north side of Ǧabal Aǧā giving access to a wide valley in the mountains. It stands just south-east of Ǧibāl al-Nihādah at 27° 39' 51" N 041° 24' 44" E (GeoNames).]

[6] [Utraymiyyah, for Huber's Outreïmïah, is spelt thus in Arabic in the margin of his handwritten manuscript.]

[7] [Qaṣr al-Aṣfar: I have not been able to identify this location in the Tuwārin valley.]

[8] [It is not clear what Huber means by these directions.]

above ground level. It is shaped like a regular parallelogram, with two solid turrets at its eastern angles, and is twenty metres long by twelve wide. The walls, built of rubble, are no more than one or two metres high.

On the southern slope of the spur carrying this fort there are a few palms, traces of fields and water channels, a well with water at a depth of ten metres, [470] and some remains of houses. ʿAlī al-Miqrād told me that it had been five years since these fields were cultivated.

In the valley 500 metres to the west of Qaṣr al-Aṣfar lie the remains of a large square building with sides about twenty-five metres in length, built of pisé or rammed earth. Its walls, flanked by turrets, still stand up to eight metres in height. There are also a well and fields with the remains of fencing. The whole place has been abandoned for a very long time.

A kilometre farther on, a small circular valley opens out containing ruined mud houses, wells and abandoned fields. This place is called Masǧid. It is there, on the rocks to the left, that I was gratified to discover Himyaritic inscriptions for the second time.[9] There were nine of them.

Towards ten o'clock we made camp beneath an enormous block of granite which, when it fell, had stayed lodged above two others, so affording us a little shade. For long centuries past this place has served to provide a few hours' shelter to passing travellers. Some Himyaritic characters are proof of this, as are the numerous rock drawings, in a more than primitive style, of horsemen brandishing a sword or a lance. These, at a distance of two millennia and more, are absolutely identical to the ones that Prince Māǧid drew for me in my notebook at Ḥāʾil.[10]

Once this valley of Tuwārin must undoubtedly have been quite an important population centre. In their migration from the south, just as they did at ʿUqdah, the first Himyarites would surely have established themselves here in these valleys that are so easily defensible and well supplied with water.[11] The inhabitants must have felt the after-effects of the revolutions that have always convulsed Arabia, and the districts of the Ǧabal must have been depopulated many times. The current abandonment of the Tuwārin valley

[9] [On Huber's use of the term Himyaritic, see Translation Part I note 158 above. These inscriptions are nos. 7–15 (= HuIR 7–15) in Appendices 1 and 2. (MCAM)]

[10] [Prince Māǧid was the son of Ḥamūd al-ʿUbayd. It seems that Prince Māǧid made similar drawings for Euting in 1883 which are reproduced in Euting 1914: 25. (MCAM/WF)]

[11] [This theory that north and central Arabia were populated by invasions of pre-Islamic tribes from the south has long been shown to be incorrect. (MCAM)]

probably dates back to the troubles ensuing from the reform movement of ʿAbd al-Wahhāb,[12] a hundred or so years ago.

[471] The Tuwārin valley comes to a dead-end on its southern side, so we did not explore all of it. It must be about thirty-five miles long from north-east to south-west, but we saw only half of it before retracing our steps.

Three o'clock in the afternoon found us once more in the Ḥaql valley. Half an hour later we passed by a cone-shaped block of granite about five cubic metres in size. In its fall from the peaks it had tumbled plumb onto another rock upon which it impinged at just three points. Its underside was a little concave, so that when struck with a stick or stone it rang like a bell with very thick sides. This rock is called al-Dinān[13] and, as ever according to the Arabs, the metallic sound signifies that the block must conceal treasures.

Eight miles farther on we made camp close to a palm trunk that a deluge of rain had one day carried down to that spot. It served as fuel for cooking our supper.

Our campsite afforded a spectacular prospect. It was a valley of a uniform width of 500 metres, flanked by granite cliffs rising to heights of about 300 metres, with the sun suffusing their summits with pinks, reds, and purple-browns that I had never seen before. The ground was perfectly flat and formed of pink *baṭḥāʾ*. It gave one the impression of being in a gigantic street laid out with a mason's line, and freshly sanded and raked.

Next morning, we left this beautiful campsite while our palm trunk, which by now was very dry, carried on burning. After a short walk to the east we found ourselves emerging from the Ḥaql valley into that of Ǧaww,[14] which extends parallel to the Tuwārin valley, that is, from north-east to south-west.

The entrance to the Ǧaww valley is by a very narrow ravine eroded into the granite by the torrent, and which is overshadowed on both sides by high cliffs of rock. The bed of the ravine is [472] encumbered by enormous boulders which sometimes even obstruct the passage of a saddled camel. In shady parts there still remained a few puddles of water. The path goes ahead like this for about a mile, rising all the way. Little by little the gorge widens

---

[12] [The reference is to Shaykh Muḥammad ibn ʿAbd al-Wahhāb (1703/4–1792), founder of the Islamic reform movement known as Wahhabism that gave impetus to the expansion of the First Saudi State from al-Dirʿiyyah (Rentz 2004; Crawford 2014).]

[13] [Huber's Addenañ, possibly *al-dinān*, a clay jug.]

[14] [*Ǧaww*: a *sayl*-bed; a wide, hollow valley or depression in which water collects (Groom 1983: 129). The valley of al-Ǧaww is situated about 5 km north-west of ʿUqdah, at approx. 27° 33' N 041° 33' E (GeoNames).]

out and soon leads one to a high plateau which is a veritable earthly paradise. The palms grow luxuriantly and in abundance, and the other vegetation is very beautiful. Birds were flitting about all over the place and their twittering, which I had not heard for ages, brought a singular gladness to the landscape. A little spring, issuing forth at about eight litres per minute, put the finishing touch to this extraordinarily agreeable spot. Its temperature was 27.5°.

After this plateau, which is circular in shape, the valley runs on through a long avenue entirely planted with magnificent palms, the majority of which, alas, are ailing following a fire that ravaged them the previous year.

At the end of this valley the ground again rises gently to a second plateau of about two square kilometres, which is a watershed. Once there, we turned to the left and, marching south by 67° east, we embarked straight away on a gentle descent. Then we found ourselves in the valley of Bulṭiyyah.[15]

After half an hour's march we reached the little spring of Bulṭiyyah. It is shaded by a hundred or so palms, and we halted there for three hours to wait for a scorching, slightly sand-laden wind to die down.

We resumed our journey at three o'clock in the afternoon. From this point on our route was as follows: 1 mile south-west, seven miles south-east, and three miles north by 65° east, as far as Qufār.[16] The way sloped consistently downwards to Wadi Ḥā'il.

At Qufār, which I was seeing for the second time, I dismounted at the residence of Shaykh Manṣūr, one of the emir's men, who accorded me a magnificent welcome. Next morning, at four [473] o'clock, I left this town which has always received me so hospitably, and three hours later found myself back in Ḥā'il.

On all my excursions in Ǧabal Ṭā'iyy, I was constantly coming across granite of a grey, pink or reddish-brown hue, but always coarse-grained. It is composed of quartz with granules of pink and white feldspar as well as granules of pegmatite. The mountain slopes are everywhere very steep and most often sheer. The granite strata generally lie at an angle of 55° to the horizon. Nowhere are there any foothills properly so-called: the mountains

[15] Or Boultiya. (The Editors.) [Huber spells this Boulthīt here, but gives its Arabic spelling as Bulṭiyyah in the margin of his handwritten manuscript. I have been unable to identify this place, but Huber's description of his route possibly places it at the spring known today as Bi'r Shaghāh, at 27° 28' 15" N 041° 29' 16" E (GeoNames).]

[16] [This route description makes it almost certain that Huber was following the Sha'īb (or Rī'at) al-Salf out of Ǧabal Aǧā and into Wādī Ḥā'il a short distance south-west of Qufār.]

rear up from the ground to their full height, and it is that which makes climbing them so difficult, and indeed practicable in only a very few places.

Al-Qaṣīm

I was unable to leave for al-Qaṣīm until 31 July.[17] That day I left Ḥā'il towards midday, marching south by 50° east. Five hours later, after a journey of sixteen miles, I stood at the foot of Ǧabal Fataq,[18] a completely isolated granite range of the same age as Ǧabal Aǧā and Ǧabal Salmā, but only about twenty miles long from north to south. Twenty minutes later, as we crossed the mountain, we passed in front of the little spring of al-ʿAdwah which, at this time of year, issues forth at scarcely more than a litre per minute.

Once over the Fataq, we immediately found ourselves on a vast plain several leagues[19] in width, bordered on the east along its whole length by the sombre masses of Ǧabal Salmā. The sun was going down as we emerged onto it, and we made camp.

---

[17] [The emir had tried his best to discourage Huber from going to al-Qaṣīm. In his 65-page handwritten report dated 27 March 1882, Huber expands on this, writing that the emir used to paint such a grim picture of it that he was unable to stifle a laugh. Laughing too, the emir had added: 'Stay with us. It is better so.' Huber replied, as he had on other occasions: 'You seem to be scared of those people.' 'My fear is for you,' replied the emir. Huber goes on: 'Finally he told me that an emissary from the Emir Ḥasan of Buraydah was due to arrive in two days' time, and that he would entrust me to him on his departure. This emissary duly arrived two days later and the emir kept to his word by telling him about me straight away. But this man refused point blank to serve as the conduit for the Christian into al-Qaṣīm; he said that he did not want to be responsible for what might befall, and even added that there was much talk of me down there, and astonishment at the favour I enjoyed in the Ǧabal. Seeing the affair taking on a religious aspect, and not wishing to cause the emir embarrassment, I avoided speaking to him about my upcoming visit. But I could well see that he was piqued by the Buraydah emissary's refusal and especially by what was being said about my stay in Ḥā'il. And it was he who broached the subject with me. "Do you want to go to Buraydah?" "You know perfectly well that I do," I replied, "Buraydah and ʿUnayzah too." "God willing," said he, "tomorrow morning I shall give you letters for the emir of Buraydah and of ʿUnayzah, and have no fear."' (French national archives, Pierrefitte-sur-Seine, Dossier F/17/2976/1:1, entitled 'Mission au Thibet et dans l'Asie centrale', 1878–82, item 79, pp. 37–9.)]

[18] [Ǧabal Fataq: Huber spells this Fetet, but on 30 October 1884, when he revisited the mountain with Euting, he records the Arabic spelling as Fataq (Huber 1891: 66). Euting on the same day (1896: 215) records it as both Feteq and Fetets, reflecting the local pronunciation. Also known as Fitik, it is south-east of Ḥā'il at approx. 27° 23' N 041° 58' E.]

[19] [The metric league in 19th-century France measured 4,000 metres, i.e. 4 kilometres.]

Long before sunrise next morning we were on the move again, keeping to the same direction as the day before. We reached Ǧabal Salmā shortly before eight o'clock. It had taken us a little more than four [474] hours at a trot to cross the valley dividing the Fataq and Salmā ranges, which bears the name Wadi al-ʿAdwah like the little spring mentioned above. The whole of this valley is covered in *baṭḥāʾ*, beneath which lies the same clay marl as in the Wadi Ḥāʾil. In just a few places it is pierced through by the bedrock, and sometimes also by the delicately red-, grey- or black-veined white marble. The vegetation is sparse. The prevailing winds in this part of Arabia are invariably the westerlies.

After an hour and a half along the way through Ǧabal Salmā, the terrain begins little by little to take on an increasingly volcanic character, basalt becomes more frequent, and soon the route crosses an ancient crater called al-Niʿayy.[20] This is about 800 metres in diameter and on its south-western side possesses a little spring of the same name, flowing at around a litre and a half per minute. The temperature of its water was 26.2°.

The walls of the crater adjacent to this spring are formed of a gravel conglomerate, together with blocks of basalt and granite embedded in a gangue of earthy ashes, all as hard as rock. A few paces farther on the wall is composed of red basaltic shale.

To the east of the crater, at the point where the route crosses it to go towards Fayd, the going is difficult and dangerous and can only be negotiated by a single camel at a time.

A second crater named al-Radiyyah[21] is situated half an hour farther on, with a very narrow and difficult pass that widens out on the eastern side. The path follows the torrent bed. From time to time this part of the route has been much dreaded by travellers as a lair for brigands to lie in ambush behind the rocks so as to kill and plunder passers-by. These days, thanks to the government of Ibn Rashīd, complete security reigns here, as it does throughout the Shammar domain.

Beyond al-Radiyyah the ground becomes increasingly [475] tumbled, leading one to suspect the proximity of the epicentre of volcanic upheaval.

---

[20] [Al-Niʿayy, which Huber cryptically calls 'Anéaï, is at 27° 10' 25" N 042° 17' 32" (GeoNames). He spells it Aniʿayy in Arabic in the margin of his handwritten manuscript.]

[21] [Huber's E'Redeïah: he spells this in Arabic as al-Radiyyah in the margin of his handwritten manuscript.]

We did in fact come across it an hour and half farther on, a little off to the right of our route, in the form of a recent crater. The ground all around is covered with black basalt rocks. This area and its crater are known as Ǧahannam,[22] appropriately enough, because everything is hellish, but most especially the path itself.

After al-Radiyyah the path inclines more to the east.

All of a sudden, towards three o'clock in the afternoon, we spotted the tops of the palm trees of Fayd about three kilometres ahead, and half an hour later we made our entry into the little town.

Just a few minutes before one reaches Fayd the basalt rocks dwindle away, and the sandstone reappears here and there.

Ancient Fayd, to the identification of which the scholar Ritter devoted some thirty pages without success, is today thoroughly fallen from its former splendour and now comprises no more than forty houses.[23]

Fayd consists of a small group of houses, and also nine homesteads separated from each other by several kilometres. The latter are known by the following names: ʿAyn, al-Ḥamrāʾ, Abū Shaqrah, al-Ṣaʿaynīn,[24] al-Ghuzayzah, al-Ḥuwaymil, al-Ghatār, al-Mālayk, and Bārzān. Among these diverse properties, which all possess palm trees, are still to be found ten or so wells with water and the ruins of former dwellings.

---

[22] Gehennem̆, hell. (CH)

[23] [Ritter 1847: vols. XII and XIII are on Arabia. Huber must have been aware that Fayd was the main station on the mediaeval pilgrim route from Iraq to Mecca and al-Madīnah, though he does not allude to the fact here. It was roughly half way between Kūfah and al-Madīnah, and was lavishly provided with facilities for the pilgrims including a town wall, a large fort, mosque, rest houses and several water catchment cisterns. The most famous benefactor of the road was Zubaydah bint Ǧaʿfar, wife of the ʿAbbāsid Caliph Harūn al-Rashīd, in the late 8th and early 9th centuries AD. Way stations were built all along the route at intervals of a day's march, and it came to be named the Darb Zubaydah after her. Visited by Ibn Ǧubayr in AD 1185, Ibn Baṭṭūtah in AD 1327 and al-Ǧazāʾirī in AD 1572, Fayd flourished until the 17th century, when its role as a pilgrim station was usurped first by Qufār and then Ḥāʾil. Today the site of Fayd has been much excavated and restored, and a museum has been installed. See Musil 1928a: 216–20 for a useful round-up of information about Fayd given by the Muslim travellers, geographers and historians; al-Rāshid 1980: 90–3, 119–20. Mackenzie et al. 1980: 47–9 gives a description of the site.]

[24] [Huber (1891: 686) records Ǧabal Ṣiʿaynīn in 1884 and gives the Arabic spelling. Musil (1928a: 66) refers to al-Ṣaʿaynīn as the name of a volcano in Ǧ. Salmā. Ǧ. Ṣiʿaynīn stands just to the west of al-Shinān, at 27° 04' 57" N 042° 24' 22" E (GeoNames).]

600 metres south of ʿAyn stands a hill of black lava with the remains of buildings, of which the most remarkable are the circular foundations of a tower or a well, ten metres in diameter.[25] Its name is Kharāsh.

To the north by 10° east of this point stands a ruined circular tower which is still eight metres tall and a section of wall [476] known as the *qaṣr*. These, together with a square ruined building 800 metres to the south-west of ʿAyn, which must once have been a mosque, are all that remain to testify to the extent and importance of ancient Fayd.

A few kilometres south-west of the town stands Ǧabal Qufayl. It is about seventy metres high and is the only part of a former crater still extant. From its summit I was able to take compass bearings of the various parts of Fayd mentioned above, along with the following mountains:

- Ǧabal Khuwayt, south by 74° east, where there must be water all year round.
- Ǧabal Ghumayz al-Ǧaww.[26]
- Ǧabal Umm al-Rūǧ, an ancient crater where there are wells.
- Ǧabal Bawṣ al-Thuʿaylibī,[27] with water almost all year round.
- Ǧabal al-Haḍab, with plenty of water.

I also took bearings on points north and south of Ǧabal Salmā, as well as the summit of Ǧildiyyah, which I had to visit later.

The desert around Fayd is known as Abā al-Krūsh.[28]

The wells of Fayd go down first through a layer of sand and gravel varying from five to ten metres in thickness according to location, then two metres of very hard black basalt. Below this is the water, which is of excellent quality. According to the inhabitants this water, which is so far down and so laborious to lift to irrigate the palm trees, is in the process of dwindling away, and it is to this that the withering of the district must be attributed. It is a very curious fact that the wells of Fayd are interconnected by subterranean passages.

---

[25] [This structure was most probably a cistern for the use of pilgrims, on the pattern of all the way stations along the Darb Zubaydah.]

[26] [Ǧabal Ghumayz: see also Huber 1891: 682, 684–6, 688.]

[27] [Bawṣ al-Thuʿaylibī, which Huber spells Bouç e'S'aïleb, is a *ḥarrah* or lava field about 20 km south by west of Fayd, at 26° 57' 19" N 042° 28' 37" E (GeoNames).]

[28] [Abā al-Krūsh: see Musil 1928a: 66, where a major wadi in this area is called Ab-al-Krūš.]

I set off again at four o'clock in the afternoon on the day after my arrival at Fayd to continue my journey towards al-Qaṣīm. Up to that point I had been accompanied by one of the emir's horsemen, but from now on I no longer had anyone with me except for a Shammar bedouin. I myself had wished it so, in view of the emir's doubts about letting me go to al-Qaṣīm, an ultra-Wahhābī region where he had great fears for my safety, especially during the holy month of Ramaḍān which was almost upon us.

[477] On leaving Fayd, we went nine more miles to the east and then to the north-west before making camp. After six hours' rest we resumed our march, all the time heading north-eastwards but bending little by little towards the east. An hour after noon we reached al-Kahfah, the tops of its palms having been visible for two hours.

From Fayd to al-Kahfah the track crosses an unbroken desert tract of volcanic sandstone. The sample that I have brought back is a yellowish quartz sand with fragments of limestone dotted with quartz grains, and containing a lot of magnetic granules. Naked rock of singular aspect appears everywhere. It is as if all of this once liquid and boiling mass had suddenly become solidified, and one is led to believe this by the large, slightly domed sandstone 'bubbles', eight to ten metres in diameter, that one comes across at every step of the way. From time to time one encounters a little sand in a dip in the ground, where there grows a little scrub. But apart from that, this is an extreme example of a stony desert, a desolation beyond words. It is a corner of the true Arabia Petraea. The name of this waste is al-Sharāfah.

Al-Kahfah, with about 200 inhabitants, enjoys a reputation as a healthy place.[29] The prevailing winds appear to be northerlies. According to the people and to Shaykh ʿAmr, whose guest I was, it rained for a mere ten days at the start of winter, and for the rest of the year there has been not a drop.

The shaykh of al-Kahfah being a poor man, it is not he who plies passing strangers with hospitality, but the wealthiest property-owner, ʿAmr, upon whom this responsibility has devolved and who has now been granted the title of shaykh, even though he is not actually such. This ʿAmr is also the *khaṭīb*[30] of the place. It is obvious from this that [478] our mutual situation was a rather

[29] [Huber gives more information on al-Kahfah, which he spells phonetically 'Etzhafeh', in 1884, including a list of its *qulbān* or plantations. Later he uses the more conventional 'El-Kehafeh'. (Huber 1891: 689–70, 698).]

[30] *Khaṭîb*: the name given by the Wahhābīs to their *mullah*s who conduct the public prayers and recite the Qur'ān in the mosques. (CH)

delicate one because, though I might have been worried about being the guest of a Wahhābī cleric, he had even greater qualms about seeing the sanctity of his home defiled by the presence of an infidel. Besides, his diminutive, lean and bony person, his pursed lips, his deep-set, anxious eyes and his bald head all combined to lend him a far from welcoming air. What is more, he had the reputation of being very stingy with his guests. But I heard the people who had come to greet me in the *qahwah* whispering among themselves, saying that I was on the best of terms with the Emir Muḥammad, and that I was his guest and friend. Thus did I experience, for the first time, the wide-ranging protective influence of this revered name. The reception given me by ʿAmr left nothing to be desired. He was, in truth, neither as kind nor as considerate as people had been with me hitherto in the Ǧabal, but kindness and consideration cannot be demanded from a Wahhābī cleric, least of all by a Christian. He treated me well and strongly urged me, for my own good, to give up the idea of going on to al-Qaṣīm. Al-Kahfah being the last location within the Shammar domain, he feared that I might come to grief, because beyond this point security no longer prevailed. By the time I departed we were firm friends and, once in the saddle, I was delighted to hear him wish me '*Allāh maʿk*', 'God be with you', the usual formula for wishing someone '*Bon voyage*' in Naǧd.

Six kilometres south of al-Kahfah there is a group of four homesteads, with date palms and barley fields, called al-Ghumaysah.[31] The water there is better than at al-Kahfah, and there we replenished our water-skins.

One hour farther on lies Umm al-Khashabah, comprising four large properties abandoned following the disappearance of water. During very rainy winters the people of al-Kahfah come there to plant barley, as the soil is very good.

Between al-Kahfah and al-Ghumaysah there are sand dunes.

The site of this oasis is a geological phenomenon that I was seeing for the first time, though I later came across it more [479] frequently. It is situated in a depression in the form of an elliptical bowl, aligned from north-west to south-east, with the long axis measuring about twenty-four kilometres and the short one twelve. The rim of this bowl is about ten to twelve metres high and sharply defined. The whole basin appeared to me to slope downwards from south to north. Al-Kahfah is situated almost on the line of the long axis, towards the northern end.

---

[31] [Also known as al-Quraymiṣah (Geonames).]

I left al-Kahfah on the day after my arrival towards three o'clock in the afternoon, passed successively by al-Ghumaysah and Umm al-Khashabah and then, having crossed the rest of the bowl, made camp on its south-eastern edge at sundown.

At two o'clock next morning, as the first star of the lovely Orion constellation rose above the horizon, I set off once again and ten hours later reached al-Quwārah, the first locality in the district of al-Qaṣīm.

Al-Quwārah is a small village of a dozen houses whose extremely poor inhabitants are all servants working in eight large *qulbān*[32] 600 to 1,000 metres apart, on an area of about five square kilometres. All of them are in a basin of the same origin as the one containing al-Kahfah, but smaller.

The palms of al-Quwārah are mediocre and not much to look at, and bear only three or four, or at most five, bunches of dates. The inhabitants attribute the meagreness of this yield to the shallowness of the soil. In fact while examining the wells, I could see that below the soil layer, which is only two metres thick, the sandstone[33] stratum of two or three metres' thickness begins straight away; beneath it flows the water table, which is very abundant [480] and does not fluctuate at any season. Alas this water, though so lovely and limpid, is too bitter to be drinkable. There are only four wells supplying potable water. The one belonging to my host is not one of them, and he drinks water from a neighbour's well.

Just as at al-Kahfah, the shaykh of al-Quwārah is a poor man, and it is Rubāḥ, owner of one of the eight *qulbān*, who received me. As he had no room to accommodate a guest of quality, he put me up in the little mosque that he had built in his garden, immediately to the left of the large entrance gate. Once I was installed, my thoughts turned to the Emir Muḥammad Ibn Rashīd, who had found it so difficult to reach a decision on my leaving for al-Qaṣīm due to his fears of me falling victim to the religious fanaticism of the local people; and here was I, a Christian taking my very first steps in so intolerant a country, being lodged in the mosque.

---

[32] *Qulbān*: estate of palm-trees with wells, usually a little distant from other habitations, and almost always containing a number of households from the same family. (CH) [*Qulbān* (sing. *qalīb*): unlined wells (Groom 1983: 225). These isolated plantations were usually walled. Huber gives a long list of the *qulbān* of al-Quwārah in 1884 in Huber 1891: 695–6.]

[33] Very fine-grained quartz sandstone. (CH)

Al-Quwārah may be the first locality in the district of al-Qaṣīm and may always have been regarded as such, but its people trace their descent from Ṭā'iyy.[34]

At the house of my host Rubāḥ I had found an inhabitant of Ṭābah, a town in Ǧabal Salmā, who, on his way back from Buraydah accompanied by his sixteen-year-old son with two camels loaded with rice, had been attacked the day before between al-ʿUyūn[35] and al-Quwārah by five prowlers mounted on three *dhalūl*s. In defending himself he had been wounded on his head and shoulder, and his son had been killed. The brigands had then made off to the west with his camels and their loads. He thought he had recognized ʿUtaybah[36] Arabs among them. I bandaged his wounds and gave him the necessary replacement dressings. But his story had made the most deplorable impact on the morale of Ṭrād, the Shammari accompanying me, who despite his height of 1.8 metres was far from [481] belligerent by nature, and had not the slightest desire to get into a fight with those born enemies of the Shammar, the ʿUtaybah.

Happily there were still three travellers at al-Quwārah who had been accommodated among the inhabitants for several days, one of them from the *qawm* of the Emir Ḥasan of Buraydah,[37] and who were waiting for others to join with them before making so perilous a journey from al-Quwārah to al-ʿUyūn. Thanks to this I was able to depart the next day.

So we set off at two hours after midnight. The four Arabs kept their matchlock fuses alight. Just as between al-Kahfah and al-Quwārah, the route went across a stony desert where the bedrock everywhere broke through to the surface. For the first thirty-two kilometres we marched over yellow sandstone and, for the last eight, over red. But all of it is very fine-grained quartz sandstone.

After six hours on the move, we came across two hills to the left of our route. They looked to me to be artificial and, as my men told me, they marked the territorial boundary between al-Quwārah and al-ʿUyūn. A quarter of an hour later two turrets came into view in front of us; below them is situated

[34] Ṭā'iyy: the name of a pre-Islamic Shammar tribe. (CH)

[35] [This is ʿUyūn al-Ǧawā', a few kilometres north-west of al-Qarʿā', and just south of Palgrave's 'Arabian Stonehenge' (Palgrave 1865 i: 251–2). Palgrave travelled from Ḥā'il to Buraydah in 1862, via Fayd, al-Kahfah, Quṣaybā', al-Quwārah and ʿUyūn, but his account is full of exaggerations (Palgrave 1865 i: 216–72).]

[36] [ʿUtaybah: one of the great bedouin tribes of western and central Naǧd.]

[37] [A *qawm* (pronounced *gōm*) is a group of warriors or raiders under a particular leader (Kurpershoek 2005: 279). (MCAM)]

al-ʿUyūn, not yet visible because it is situated in a basin similar to the one enclosing al-Kahfah.

These turrets dominating the heights around al-ʿUyūn are observation posts intended to watch over the surroundings in times of trouble and to guard against surprise attack by signalling the approach of any suspect force. I came across such towers again at other places, especially at Quṣaybāʾ, and even in the Ḥiğāz, at Khaybar.

From the point close to al-ʿUyūn at which these turrets become visible, and thus about two kilometres beyond the frontier hillocks, the ground is very disturbed and signs of numerous craters can be seen everywhere.

At last, eight hours after we had left al-Quwārah, we found ourselves on the rim of the basin that encloses both al-ʿUyūn and [482] Rawḍah,[38] the palms of which we could see in the distance. We would need another two hours to reach it.

Immediately on going down into the depression, one leaves to the right an isolated sandstone rock, the shape of which will catch the attention of anyone who has seen the Sphinx in front of the Pyramids near Cairo, which it closely resembles. I saw traces of Himyaritic and Arabic characters on it, but they were almost entirely obliterated and illegible. Ten minutes later, again to the right of the path, stands a second but much larger rock bearing a large number of partly effaced Himyaritic inscriptions. I was able to copy a few of them.[39] This second rock goes by the name of al-Harashī.[40]

Twenty minutes after our descent into the basin of al-ʿUyūn we arrived before al-Ghāf, a palm grove that is vast but totally invaded by the sand. I trotted along beside this beautiful plantation for twenty-five minutes. One hour later, at exactly midday, I found myself before al-ʿUyūn itself.

To the west, on the side from which we were approaching it, al-ʿUyūn is completely hidden by an enormous sand dune, retained on the town side by a wall of pisé or rammed earth which is continually increased in height as the sand rises.

Al-ʿUyūn, the most considerable place between Ḥāʾil and Buraydah, has a population of about 2,500 souls. In extent too it is very large: from east to west it measures roughly five kilometres, and it is 1,000 to 1,500

[38] [Rawḍah: actually al-Rawḍ, north-west of al-ʿUyūn.]

[39] [It is probable that these are nos. 16–19 in Appendices I and 2. (MCAM)]

[40] [In the margin of his handwritten manuscript, Huber writes this name in Arabic as al-Ḥarashī. These two mushroom-shaped rocks are known locally as Ḥaṣāt al-Naṣlah.]

metres in width. Its palms are beautiful and their produce passes for the best in al-Qaṣīm. Its water, not everywhere of consistent quality but nonetheless drinkable, is very plentiful. It lies immediately beneath the rock, which outcrops all over the town and which is eight to twelve metres thick. As in all other places where the wells are hewn through the rock, here too they are very large in section, from four to eight and even ten metres in diameter. I found the temperature of the water to be 24.1°, but although I took this after a whole day of drawing up water, it [483] can still not be considered an exact measurement in view of the large surface area in contact with the air.

What most strikes travellers like me arriving at al-ʿUyūn from the Ǧabal, where the human race is so handsome, is the frailty of its people. The men especially seem underdeveloped: they are small, ill-favoured and thin with a delicate and emaciated cast of features. With their hollow eyes and prominent cheekbones, their heads covered Wahhābī-style by a red *kūfiyyah* with no *ʿiqāl*, they manage to convey the same appearance and demeanour that renders those sectarians so unappealing in their manner.

The fair sex seem to me to have had a better share. The few women I saw were pretty and slender. As throughout the East, they had very beautiful eyes, despite their pale and sickly complexion.

The shaykh of al-ʿUyūn, ʿAbd Allāh, whom the inhabitants have also dubbed emir, is a man of about thirty who gave me a warm welcome.

Ten kilometres west of al-ʿUyūn lies Rawḍah,[41] another very important place with about 1,500 inhabitants.

I left al-ʿUyūn at three o'clock in the morning on the day after my arrival, and four hours later reached al-Qarʿāʾ, which consists of two sections 1,500 metres apart. One encloses the palm plantations, the other the village of about 800 souls. There are also a few properties scattered around, among them that of the shaykh, which is new and well-organized.

As far as al-Qarʿāʾ my men were still going along with their matchlock fuses lit, but from this point on that precaution was no longer necessary, because the proximity of Buraydah suffices to make the environs safe.

At about three kilometres from al-Qarʿāʾ on the route that I was following lies a saline lake of about two square kilometres in area. It was dry and covered by a thick layer of salt.

---

[41] [See note 38 above. At this point in his handwritten manuscript Huber gives the Arabic spelling as Ghawdah, but this must be an error stemming from the French pronunciation of *r*.]

[484] An hour after leaving al-Qarʿāʾ we reached al-Shuqqah, which lies in a basin about fifteen kilometres long and consists of 200 houses with perhaps 1,000 or 1,100 inhabitants. It is a poor village where the water has been on the decline for some years. Also, except in four of its *qulbān*, it is salty to the point of being undrinkable. However it lies at no great depth, being at most four to six metres down.

Besides the main village, al-Shuqqah possesses six *qulbān*. I give their names here because they are all agreed to be very ancient, in fact more so than the village itself. They are: Rafīʿah, Ghārī, Ǧawā, al-Aṣafāt, al-Safābī, and al-Khabb.[42]

From al-Shuqqah, a full two hours (seven miles) brought me to Buraydah, which I reached just at the time of the *ʿaṣr* prayer.[43] The town is enclosed by walls four metres high built of mud and chopped straw, and their pink hue gives them a completely new-built look. A great gate with two leaves and a stone threshold gives access to the town. The walls are flanked at intervals by round or square towers rising a couple of metres higher than the walls themselves. Neither walls or towers are equipped with earth platforms behind them.[44]

I made straight for the castle. There I found the Emir Ḥasan, who was coming out of the mosque where he had been performing the *ʿaṣr* prayer and who gave me a very cordial welcome. Rugs were brought out into the courtyard, where we sat and exchanged the customary greetings. Then I handed him the letter of recommendation that his suzerain, the emir of Ǧabal Shammar, had given me for him.

Ḥasan[45] being illiterate, it was his secretary who read the letter out to him,

---

[42] [Some of these spellings are uncertain. Huber spells them as follows: Rafîah, Râry, Gouâ, El Açefât, Asefeby, El Khab. He gives Arabic spellings accordingly in his handwritten manuscript.]

[43] [*Ṣalāt al-ʿaṣr*, the afternoon prayer, coming between the midday and sunset prayers. It was now 7 August 1880.]

[44] [i.e. the ramparts lacked firing platforms for defence.]

[45] [Ḥasan b. Muhannā Abā al-Khayl, also known as Ḥasan walad Muhannā, was emir of Buraydah between 1876 and 1891, having allied himself with the Rashīdī rulers of Ḥāʾil in the 1870s against the Āl Saʿūd (Musil 1928a: 277; Philby 1930: 148). Indeed, according to Doughty, who calls him 'that usurping peasant *Weled Mahanna* tyrant of Boreyda' (1936 ii: 37), his sister was one of the wives of Muḥammad Ibn Rashīd (ibid. 39–40). In December 1883, he visited Ḥāʾil, where he was entertained by Huber and Euting (Euting 1914: 65–8, 75, 80–2). In 1890–1, he defected to the pro-Saudi coalition organized by Zāmil of ʿUnayzah against Muḥammad Ibn Rashīd. This was heavily defeated in January 1891 at the Battle of Mulaydah in al-Qaṣīm, which effectively extinguished the Second Saudi State. Ḥasan b. Muhannā lost his left hand

doing so in a low voice so that those present were unable to hear anything. He straight away repeated what he had said to me before this recitation, that he was happy to treat me as well as the Emir Muḥammad had done, that his house was my house, and that I had only to ask for whatever I desired. He also advised me never to go outside the castle without two of [485] his men for company and to carry my sword at all times, after the fashion of shaykhs in Arabia.

The Emir Ḥasan succeeded his father Muhannā, who was assassinated in the middle of the street six years ago. He is a man of fifty-two of vulgar appearance and conveys no impression of superior intelligence. He has a large white speck in his left eye which hampers his vision on that side. He enjoys a certain independence and only pays a tax to Ḥāʾil, part in money and part in kind.[46]

The Emir Muhannā had reigned for ten years and, before him, a man named ʿAbd al-ʿAzīz al-Muḥammad had fulfilled the role of emir for about forty years, that is, since the fall of the Wahhābīs.[47]

Buraydah has existed for barely eighty years, but it succeeded an older town lying two miles to the north of the present-day location, which was called Shamās. The latter was itself founded three and a half centuries ago. The mosque, on which Palgrave bestowed an age of four centuries, was built less than a hundred years ago.[48] The town possesses four schools and six mosques, including the main congregational one. The population, which is all of ʿAnizah stock, amounts to some 10,000 souls.

Buraydah is a great commercial centre, but its trade only reaches its greatest volume during the four months of the year that follow the date harvest. At that season there are often as many as 1,000 tents pitched outside Buraydah as the nomads come to replenish their supplies of dates, wheat, rice, and the few textiles they need.

---

and was taken into captivity in Ḥāʾil, where he died (Musil 1928a: 243, 277, 279–80; Winder 1965: 264, 267, 276–7).]

[46] [Only pays a tax: Huber means that Muḥammad Ibn Rashīd had not replaced Ḥasan with a governor from Ḥāʾil, nor installed a garrison.]

[47] [The Wahhābī 'empire' in Arabia, aka the First Saudi State, came to an end in 1818–19 with the invasion of Naǧd and destruction of their capital al-Dirʿiyyah, near present-day Riyadh, by an Ottoman-Egyptian force led by Ibrāhīm Pasha (see Facey 1997a).]

[48] [Palgrave's lengthy description of Buraydah is in Palgrave 1865 i: 273–322. Palgrave (p. 301) actually wrote that the mosque was nearly two (not four) centuries old.]

Outside those four months, two-thirds of the shops are shut, which led Palgrave to believe that the town was in decline.[49] But I think I can affirm the contrary, that there are more and greater fortunes at Buraydah than at Ḥāʾil itself. The Emir Ḥasan gave me plenty of information in the same vein.

The water at Buraydah is neither good nor sweet; in almost [486] all the wells it is too salty to be potable, and everywhere it is very cloudy. The water table is from five to ten metres below ground and, to reach it, it is generally necessary to penetrate through three layers of sandstone, each of them one to two metres thick.

Ever since Buraydah was built it has suffered from sand invasion, and on this occasion I was once again able to observe that the sands are on the move from west to east. The gardens situated to the west of the town are threatened on their western sides by dunes from six to eight metres high, which the people try to stabilize with *ithl* plantations.[50]

The day after my arrival in Buraydah was 8 August [1880], coinciding with the 1st of the month of Ramaḍān. The evening before, while I was in the *qahwah* with the emir, he asked me whether I would fast and, when I replied in the affirmative, laughed out loud; he assured me that there would be none of that, that he would not allow it, and that in any case my status as a traveller relieved me of the obligation to abstain. Indeed, food was cooked both for me and for my companion as usual, and coffee into the bargain.

Four days after my arrival, I made an excursion to ʿAyn Ibn Fuhayd[51] to the north of Buraydah, a very ancient place, where the palms are irrigated from five springs but where the water, though clear and looking very nice, is undrinkable, as it is saturated with salts of lime and magnesium.

About half way between ʿAyn Ibn Fuhayd and Buraydah, I halted for an hour outside a poor village of sixty inhabitants called al-Ṭarfiyyah. Because its water gave out four years ago, most of its people have dispersed to other places. All the palms are dead and their trunks, bereft of leaves, rise sadly into the air like a forest of broomsticks. They were all a hundred to a hundred and twenty years old, and were once beautiful.

---

[49] [Palgrave 1865 i: 303.]

[50] [*Ithl*: *Tamarix aphylla*, the ubiquitous tree of the Naǧdī oases, with many uses in carpentry and construction.]

[51] [Huber writes 'Ayn Ebn Feyd, but this is properly ʿAyn Ibn Fuhayd, about 50 km north-east of Buraydah.]

With the little water that remains, and which is undrinkable except that from a single well, the people grow [487] melons and watermelons. Aside from that they busy themselves with collecting wood from the desert, which they sell at Buraydah along with their melons.

ʿAyn Ibn Fuhayd, in contrast, is well on its way to prosperity. I saw several plantations of young palms there, including one belonging to the Emir Ḥasan himself.

Three kilometres north by 76° east of ʿAyn Ibn Fuhayd stands an old ruin called Qaṣr Mārid. It is a large, square and very massive structure built of rubble and mud mortar, with sides measuring about forty metres externally, and thirty metres inside the courtyard. The entrance gate faces west, that is to say on the village side, and it is sited on top of a small hill that effectively dominates the country around.

A few yards from the northern side of the *qaṣr* stands a rock in the form of a table, forty to fifty metres long and two metres high. On it are numerous Himyaritic inscriptions, but almost all are worn away. I was only able to copy a few of them.[52]

More or less on the opposite side of the village, two kilometres to the north-west, is an ancient crater marked by large blocks of sandstone scattered over an area about 500 metres square, some of them completely covered in inscriptions. But these inscriptions, about which I had been told a lot in Buraydah, and likewise already at Ḥāʾil, are of relatively recent age and almost all written in Arabic. I inspected almost all the blocks, around 150 of them, and never found anything other than proper names or the formula '*Lā ilaha illa Allāh*'.[53] Nonetheless, a few traces of Kufic, and ten or so Himyaritic ones,[54] proved that more ancient artists had passed that way.

Just like many other places in Arabia, and above all in Nağd, ʿAyn Ibn Fuhayd must have suffered the consequences of all the revolutions that have caused upheaval in this country, and [488] endured a cycle of depopulation and resettlement at various times. The present settlement dates to eighty years ago. Not surprisingly, none of the present-day inhabitants knows anything at all about their predecessors there.

[52] [These are nos. 20–23 (= HuIR 20–23) in Appendices 1 and 2. They are, of course, not 'Himyaritic' but 'Thamudic'. (MCAM)]

[53] 'There is no deity but God.' (CH)

[54] [He appears to have copied only one, which is no. 24 (= HuIR 24) in Appendices I and 2. (MCAM)]

In support of the antiquity of ʿAyn Ibn Fuhayd, I forgot to mention the existence of two contiguous vaulted caves at the north-eastern extremity of the village, which I was unable to examine more thoroughly because they were crammed with debris of all kinds. They are a rather curious phenomenon that is worth mentioning, because between Damascus and ʿUnayzah, and between al-Ḥasāʾ and the Red Sea, I have seen no other example and I do not believe that any such thing exists.[55]

The sands extending to the east of ʿAyn Ibn Fuhayd, according to some Ṣulubī[56] nomads camping near the village when I passed through, are about sixty-five miles wide.

On 13 August, two days after my arrival, I left ʿAyn Ibn Fuhayd well before dawn, and a ride of ten kilometres south by 10° east brought us two hours later to the wells of Wusayṭah. These are important because they supply ʿAyn Ibn Fuhayd with potable water. Every night towards midnight, two men leading fifteen or so donkeys set out from the village with the inhabitants' water-skins to refill them at these wells. Thus every day they make a round-trip of twenty kilometres to fulfil their daily water needs. And what is more, what water it is! Never have I seen such muddy stuff. As for its taste, apart from the water of Shaqīq in the Nafūd I cannot recall ever having drunk anything more foul-smelling. Meanwhile, by a cruel irony, the water from the springs in the village itself, which is used to irrigate the palms, flows as crystal-clear as our streams at home.

The water in the wells lies at a depth of four to five metres beneath a layer of clay soil. The walls of the wells, being earthen, are prone to collapse.

The precarious state of this place and of al-Ṭarfiyyah in relation to so vital a resource as water illustrates how much more bitter is the struggle for survival in some [489] countries of the East than it is for us.

Moving on from the wells of Wusayṭah and veering a little to the right, we went south by 10° west and reached al-Ṣarīf, a valley extending about

[55] [Huber was not familiar with the sinkhole caverns, or *duḥūl* (sing. *daḥl*), which are quite a common feature in the desert of north-eastern Arabia and used to act as vital natural reservoirs for many months after the winter rains.]

[56] [Ṣulubah or Ṣulayb, sing. Ṣulubī: the wandering tinkers, trackers and hunters of the north Arabian and Syrian deserts. Huber (1891: 193–8, 203–4) gives much information about the Ṣulayb; Euting 1914: 101 gives more; and see also Oppenheim 1939–68 iv: 131–53; Dickson 1949: 515–25. See also Translation Part III note 159. (MCAM/WF)]

eight kilometres north–south by two kilometres wide.[57] In its northern part can be seen more evidence of the volcanic nature of the region.

At the very beginning of the valley, level with the ground, one comes upon the ruins of a fort built, in part at least, of dressed masonry. A little farther on, separated from one another by about a kilometre and a half, there are three forts still standing, but these are built of mud. Plenty of greenery can be seen all around, as well as fields of wheat and barley lying fallow. Water in the wells is only two to three metres down. The mud forts consist of just four large walls with a strong gate. Their interiors are divided into a few miserable huts serving as accommodation. The forts, wells and fields are the property of some Ṣulubī families that have their grazing grounds south-east of here, in the dunes beyond Wādī Rimah.[58] From time to time, especially after a rainy winter, they come to al-Ṣarīf to sow barley and maize, and sometimes even wheat.

Continuing our southward course, at an hour after midday we came to the fort of al-Rakiyyah,[59] situated at the centre of a crater two miles in diameter. This fort, also built of mud, has a very handsome exterior even though it actually consists of nothing but walls. Two wretched hovels serve as accommodation for the guardian-cultivators.

The well is inside the fort, and is one of the finest I have seen in the East. Its mouth is twenty-four square metres in area and it is twenty-two metres deep. The upper nine metres are dug through the sand and earth, the

---

[57] [Al-Ṣarīf was to be be the site of a battle in February 1901 between the emir of Ḥā'il and a coalition of Shaykh Mubārak of Kuwait with the Āl Saʿūd, who were then living as refugees at Kuwait. It was a defeat for Kuwait and its ally, but the tide would begin to turn a year later when the young ʿAbd al-ʿAzīz ibn ʿAbd al-Raḥmān Āl Saʿūd recaptured al-Riyāḍ, his ancestral seat, from Ibn Rashīd's governor.]

[58] [Huber calls this Ouâdy Ermek, but it is clear that what he means is Wādī Rimah, the main artery of the great drainage system of central Naǧd that rises in the Arabian watershed in the vicinity of the Ḥarrat Hutaym, and runs eastwards through al-Qaṣīm, before losing itself in the Dahnā' sands east of Buraydah. It then re-emerges as the Wādī al-Bāṭin and turns north-east towards Baṣrah. There is often confusion over the spelling of Rimah, with variants including Rimāḥ, Rumāḥ, and Rummāḥ, with and without the definite article, and Huber may have heard, or misheard, one of the latter. I have opted for the simplest rendering, Rimah, which is used on the 1973 1:2,000,000 map entitled *The Arabian Peninsula* and seems to be generally accepted nowadays. For Huber's defence of his spelling 'Ermek', see Translation Part III, p. 217 and notes 15 and 17. According to Hogarth (1904: 291): 'Ermek [i.e. *ırmak*] is merely the Turkish for "river". Huber must have heard this name in the mouth of some member of the Ottoman garrison in Kheibar.']

[59] [Al-Rakiyyah means a lined well of medium depth, especially one containing water (Groom 1983: 238).]

remainder through the sandstone. In good years the water level generally rises by fifteen or even twenty metres; but as last winter there was only a little rain, the level [490] is correspondingly low. The water is raised from the well by camels using the usual method in the Ǧabal and al-Qaṣīm, and flows through a channel outside the fort to irrigate the fields of barley, maize and wheat, which are very shrunken this year for lack of it. Melons and watermelons were planted along the little irrigation channels.

This fine estate, which belongs to the Emir Ḥasan, was established by his father Muhannā twenty years ago.

The little hamlet of al-Nabqiyyah,[60] with its thirty-five inhabitants, is situated north-east of al-Rakiyyah. From al-Rakiyyah to al-Nabqiyyah stretches a stony desert and then, at a little distance from the latter, the sands begin again.

After a two-hour halt at al-Rakiyyah we resumed our march, going south by about 15° east, and two hours later came to al-Rawḍah,[61] a village of 150 inhabitants where Ibrāhīm Abū Muhannā, brother of the Emir Ḥasan, resides. Each of them possesses a large palm plantation here. The fort that Ibrāhīm has raised for himself, though built of mud, has the more imposing appearance, especially from afar. One might take it for some vast Babylonian construction.

Ibrāhīm is even less intelligent than his brother Ḥasan, and at first sight there is nothing to distinguish him from his servants, among whom he sleeps on his stomach in the sand and dust. In my own case, of course, I was very well received by him.

I was intending to stay a day at al-Rawḍah in order to investigate the local geology, which is interesting, but that proved not to be possible. Since my departure from Buraydah an incredibly hot wind had been blowing, with the sky constantly overcast and the air as heavy as lead. When the wind was blowing, the thermometer rose right up to 50° in the shade. However, I was better able to endure all that [491] outdoors in the countryside than in a house or under the palms. Thus at ten o'clock in the morning on the day after my arrival, when I saw the thermometer rising faster than on the previous day, and feeling as if my head were being crushed in a circlet of iron, I gave the

[60] The local people pronounce this name 'Nebtsïe'. (CH)

[61] [This is perhaps the Rawḍat Muhannā that would be the site of the famous night attack in 1906, in which the Emir ʿAbd al-ʿAzīz Ibn Rashīd was killed by Saudi raiders under ʿAbd al-ʿAzīz Ibn Saʿūd.]

order to depart. Half an hour later, with my head and whole body swathed as if for a journey to the North Pole so as to insulate them from the effects of the sun and the scorching wind, we were on the march southwards. At the end of an hour in this direction, I joined the Wadi Rimah on its course from the west. I went down onto its bed and marched up it for three hours, only then to climb out of it again and pick up my route a little farther to the north. An hour and a half later I re-entered Buraydah.

Three kilometres to the south of the point where I joined the wadi on my way from al-Rawḍah, and thus beyond it, lies the little village of al-Shamāsiyyah with 250 inhabitants. This place, which I was told is poor, was already in existence in the last century.

Some ten kilometres north-west of al-Shamāsiyyah is al-Ṭaʿmiyyah,[62] a small area of farms with ten inhabitants.

I spent the following two days at Buraydah and on 17 August set off once more for a visit to ʿUnayzah.

So as to accept an invitation from a wealthy local, Shaykh Naṣr, who was living in the village of al-Khabb,[63] I made my way there. It is two miles away to the south by 67° west.

To the west of Buraydah the sands form long ridges running north–south. Al-Khabb extends in the same direction in the second valley over from Buraydah. It is four kilometres long and boasts magnificent estates. Shaykh Naṣr's is one of the loveliest and contains 700 sixty-year-old palms, which means that they are in the full vigour of their prime. Because its water has dwindled in the thirty years that it has been in his possession, he has decided to sell it, and an admirer is at this very moment offering 5,000 riyals for it, i.e. about [492] 20,000 francs, which makes each palm tree worth about seven riyals. In Ḥāʾil, one palm tree is generally worth ten riyals. This property brings Shaykh Naṣr an annual revenue of about 2,000 francs, a sum that makes him a wealthy man in al-Qaṣīm.

I only left al-Khabb at the afternoon (*ʿaṣr*) prayer, towards three o'clock, and then made my way to the south-east. After two kilometres I came across the gardens of Ḥuwaylān, which I went along for three kilometres, when

[62] [Al-Ṭaʿmiyyah, Huber's Althamïah: probably al-Ṭuʿmiyyah or al-Ṭuʿmiyyāt is meant, about 20 km west of al-Shamāsiyyah. See Translation Part III note 223.]

[63] [Al-Khabb has the meaning of a long, narrow strip of ground between sand dunes (Groom 1983: 138). As a result there were several villages in this area with that name.]

almost immediately there began al-Quṣayʿah, which also extends north–south for two to three kilometres.

These three villages of al-Khabb, Ḥuwaylān and al-Quṣayʿah, although in full dune country, are nevertheless situated in a fold in the ground which is clear of sand, and in this respect they resemble Ğubbah to the north of Ğabal Ağā, and the wells of Shaqīq and Zuhayrī to the south of al-Ğawf.

Two hours after my departure from al-Khabb, I left the valley along which these three places stretch and marched once more over the sands, going south by 10° east. It is from this point on as far as the town of ʿUnayzah that the way becomes very dangerous by reason of the continual passing and repassing of the nomads encamped to east and west of this locality.

Having traversed the sands from five to eight o'clock in the evening, I reached Wadi Rimah and the first of its palms. It took me half an hour to cross the wadi and reach the sands again on the other side, the right [south] bank. It was too late to enter ʿUnayzah, so I made camp on the edge of the wadi near the hut of a *fallāḥ*,[64] one of the guardians of the palms.

The stretch of the Wadi Rimah passing close to ʿUnayzah is completely planted with palms belonging to the people of that town. From the setting of the fruit till the date harvest, their cultivators live there and form the village known as al-Wādī. During winter a part of this population lives in the town. The water in this stretch of the wadi [493] is only one or two metres down, so that the palms have no need of irrigation as they do elsewhere. They grow under the same conditions as those of ʿUqdah, Ḥaql, Ğaww and other places in Ğabal Shammar.

The palm plantations in Wadi Rimah are of very ancient origin. Formerly there were even two towns there, or probably two large, very thriving villages. One, to the north-east of ʿUnayzah, was called al-Wahlān; the other, to the north-north-west, went by the name al-ʿAyāriyyah. Today they have completely disappeared, as they were evidently built of sun-dried mud. However, Shaykh Ghānim, whose acquaintance I made in ʿUnayzah, assured me that dressed masonry with inscriptions had still been visible some twenty years before in the second of these two places. Since then they must have disappeared, but it is more likely, if they truly

[64] [*Fallāḥ* is a term usually used to denote Egyptian peasant farmers, *fallāḥīn*. Here it is used to refer to the non-tribal cultivators, or *khaḍīriyyūn*, found in all the large Nağdī oasis settlements, who were tenants, share-croppers and guardians in the plantations, and also worked as artisans and petty merchants in the towns. (Facey 1992: 69–70).]

existed, that their weight would have made them sink into the soft ground of the wadi.

The following morning saw me on the move with the rising sun, and an hour brought me up to ʿUnayzah, the northern aspect of which is rather grand. It took me a good half hour to pass through the gardens and the first houses to reach the fortress of the Emir Zāmil.

Emir Zāmil, who has played an important role in the history of his country, was fifty-two years old in 1880. He is a small man who walks with a limp, having sustained a bullet wound in combat. With his wide forehead and lively and highly intelligent eyes, his whole appearance is that of a wily old fox.[65]

After reading the letter that Muḥammad Ibn Rashīd had given me for him, he was still obviously very puzzled and anxious. So I tried to calm him down by saying that I had only come to spend two or three days visiting the town. At first he was against me going outside the fortress, but without letting him finish I assured him firmly that I had not made my journey just to stay locked up in his reception hall.

[494] However, we ended by getting along well, and agreed that I would only go out accompanied by my Shammari and two of his own men; as for everything else, complete freedom. Like Emir Ḥasan of Buraydah, he urged me to wear my grand Shammar shaykh's robes at all times and to keep my sword in my hand. 'Ah,' he went on, 'Why have you come here during Ramaḍān?' I assuaged his anxiety as best I could, reassuring him that all would be well. '*Inshāʾ Allāh*,' he added.

To be able to appreciate how full of danger my presence was for Zāmil, one has to realize that the people of ʿUnayzah are some of the most fanatical zealots anywhere to be found, and that Zāmil is not an all-powerful emir like Ibn Rashīd of Ḥāʾil. ʿUnayzah today is a virtually independent town, a republic of which he is only president by consent.

In the event, everything passed off well. I was able to make all my excursions and even found two friends. One, ʿAbd al-ʿAzīz ibn Muḥammad

---

[65] [Zāmil ibn ʿAbdallāh ibn Sulaymān Āl Zāmil was an important figure in the history of al-Qaṣīm. He became governor of ʿUnayzah in 1869, and befriended and protected Doughty during the latter's visits in 1878, when he was at his most vulnerable. He was a staunch supporter of the Imām ʿAbdullah ibn Fayṣal Āl Saʿūd and lost his life while commanding the anti-Shammar coalition in its final defeat at the Battle of Mulaydah in January 1891. See note 45 above. (Doughty 1936 ii: 357–77, 404, 424, 442–3, 460–73; Winder 1965: 244–5, 276–7.)]

al-Bassām, was a wealthy merchant who had visited India and Persia.[66] The other, Shaykh Ghānim, had spent two years in Constantinople.

The chief of the kind of urban guard that Zāmil maintains, a man named Ṭakīl, was one of the two soldiers that Zāmil assigned to me for my protection. He was a man of forty-five who had travelled, I believe as a dervish, through Mesopotamia, Kurdistan, Syria and Egypt, and who as a result had somewhat broader horizons than his compatriots. He was very useful to me during my brief stay in ʿUnayzah and fended off numerous importunities. Several times I even had to quell his zeal when, wielding his baton or sword with an excess of vigour, he charged the crowd that followed me around constantly and pressed in upon me a little too closely from time to time.

According to what I was told by Zāmil and others, ʿUnayzah would have been founded 1,050 years ago, some say 1,150. This first town did not occupy the current location, but lay a mile farther west. Abandoned or destroyed [495] after 320 years of existence, it was rebuilt where it stands today.

These days the territory of ʿUnayzah is very small. Outside the town it comprises only al-Shibībiyyah[67] nine miles to the south, a ruined village of which there remains only the fortress which is itself in ruins. In winter they sometimes sow cereal crops there.

Seven miles to the east lies Rawḍat al-ʿAwshaziyyah[68] with 100 inhabitants. Lastly there is al-Wādī, to the north, with its 500 inhabitants.

In my opinion ʿUnayzah itself must have a population of 18,000 or at most 20,000. It possesses fifteen mosques including the congregational Friday mosque,[69] and four schools, one of which is for girls.

Having formed an integral part of the Wahhābī empire almost from the start, it remained in this state of dependence until the death of Fayṣal in

[66] [This may be the al-Bassām that Doughty met two years before, 'the most travelled of the foreign merchants' with an interest in medicine (Doughty 1936 ii: 402–3). In his 65-page handwritten report dated 27 March 1882, Huber adds: 'At this point, on the edge of Naǧd proper, I would have had the strong desire to push on as far as Zulfī, Shaqrā and even al-Dirʿiyyah and al-Riyāḍ, but I lacked the means to do so, and to my great regret had to turn back.' (French national archives, Pierrefitte-sur-Seine, Dossier F/17/2976/1:1, 'Mission au Thibet et dans l'Asie centrale', 1878–82, item 79, p. 44.)]

[67] [Al-Shibībiyyah is in fact about 25 km west by south of ʿUnayzah.]

[68] [Al-ʿAwshaziyyah is sometimes also known as al-ʿAwsağiyyah.]

[69] The *ǧāmiʿ*, as we saw above, is the main mosque which everybody must attend to perform the Friday midday prayer. (CH) [See Translation Part I, pp. 107–8 for Huber's comments on the Friday mosque as a useful means of calculating the population of Naǧdī towns.]

1865.[70] Following that, it profited from the civil war that broke out almost immediately among the four sons of the defunct emir:[71] Saʿūd, ʿAbdullah, ʿAbd al-Raḥmān and Muḥammad. Saʿūd on his death left two sons, Muḥammad and ʿAbd al-ʿAzīz, to whom ʿAbdullah, who had succeeded his father as emir of Naǧd, ceded the district of Khark or Kharǧ.[72]

Almost immediately on the death of Saʿūd, a long war of succession broke out between his brothers ʿAbdullah and Muḥammad. After various vicissitudes they made peace and ʿAbdullah retained power. But during the civil war the Wahhābī empire had disintegrated. Part of it had been taken by the Turks in the Persian Gulf, and in the interior several large towns reasserted their independence. Among them were ʿUnayzah and al-Rass.[73] The former of these two towns has paid no tax to the ruler of Riyadh since 1867. Such is the situation in Naǧd today. I can only touch upon it here, as I am reserving [496] the part dealing with the history of central Arabia for another work.[74]

I set off again from ʿUnayzah on the evening of 20 August after the sunset prayer. Emir Zāmil had taken extraordinary precautions against anything untoward befalling me on his territory. The great square in front of the main mosque, onto which opens the *cul de sac* where Zāmil resides, had been emptied of people, and armed men positioned in the five streets leading onto the square were barring all comings and goings. I took the same route by which I had arrived. Far ahead I could hear other men busily pushing back people wanting to reach the square, and the shouts and clamour of those being bottled up reached my ears. On drawing closer I could see that the emir's men were all brandishing drawn swords. As I went forward with my Shammari, the men who were blocking the streets withdrew behind me.

---

[70] [The Imām Fayṣal ibn Turkī Āl Saʿūd was the most prominent ruler of the Second Saudi State, governing from Riyadh from 1843 to 1865. He was succeeded by his son ʿAbdullah, whose rule was challenged by his brothers, particularly Saʿūd, plunging the Saudi domain into a civil war that ultimately led to the dominance in Naǧd of its one-time dependant, Ḥāʾil.]

[71] [The Saʿūdī rulers never referred to themselves as emirs. They adopted the style Imām, a religio-political title that emphasized their role not just as heads of state but as leaders of the Wahhābī reform movement.]

[72] [Saʿūd died in 1875. Al-Kharǧ is the fertile, historic and well-watered district 75 km south-east of Riyadh.]

[73] [Al-Rass was the third most important town in al-Qaṣīm, lying 50 km south-west of ʿUnayzah.]

[74] [Huber of course never produced such a work, as he was murdered in the Ḥiǧāz in July 1884 towards the end of his second great Arabian journey. See Introduction pp. 61–3]

What I found most astonishing was not so much the emir's care for my welfare as manifested by this show of force – of which he had given me no warning – as the brutality with which I witnessed his soldiers carrying out their duty. A townsman who did not immediately back away and merely wanted to ask for an explanation, was surrounded in the blink of an eye by five men of my escort and, before I was able to intervene, laid out cold on the ground, concussed by the blows to his head from their sword hilts. He was left lying in the middle of the road, with no one to tend to him.

Once I had reached the outskirts of town I was able to make a count of my protectors, who numbered seventeen. I wanted to send them back, but they told me they were under orders to escort me to within sight of Buraydah. We halted for a moment, they all lit their matchlock fuses, and then we moved on. They then split up into three groups that marched twenty metres on either side of me and to my rear.

After an hour we came within sight of Rawḍān, [497] a village of 120 people that we passed by, and a few minutes later were making camp in the Wadi.

Setting forth once again shortly before three o'clock, at five we passed in front of Khaḍar,[75] where Zāmil's escort left to go back to ʿUnayzah. Five kilometres farther on we came within sight of Ṣubayḥ and soon afterwards we were back in Buraydah.[76]

Besides the places mentioned in the course of my journeys in al-Qaṣīm, I should add some others, even though I was unable to obtain sufficiently precise information as to their positions to enable them to be plotted on the map.[77] In Arab countries there is no action so indiscreet, and in central Arabia I might add, so dangerous, as that of making geographical enquiries. Orientalists are well aware of this, and geographers will I hope forgive me for the shortcomings that I have just identified.

The places omitted from the map are located in the triangle formed by

[75] [Khaḍar: a settlement 8 km south of Buraydah, near the left bank of Wādī Rimah, at 26° 14' 59" N 043° 59' 57" E (GeoNames).]

[76] [In his 65-page handwritten report dated 27 March 1882, Huber adds: 'My Shammari possessed no greater delight than in being able to recount how he had been with me in ʿUnayzah and had returned alive.' (French national archives, Pierrefitte-sur-Seine, Dossier F/17/2976/1:1, entitled 'Mission au Thibet et dans l'Asie centrale', 1878–82, item 79, p. 45.)]

[77] [For Huber's full list of settlements in al-Qaṣīm, see the end of Translation Part III, pp. 271–3.]

ʿUnayzah, Buraydah and Rawḍah. They include al-Shīḥiyyah (twelve miles west of Buraydah),[78] al-Bukayriyyah, al-Hilāliyyah, al-Khabrāʾ, al-Riyāḍ,[79] and Binhāniyyah.[80]

To the east of Buraydah, between that town and Wadi Rimah, are also to be found two small villages named Ḥanayẓil[81] and Abā ʾl-Dūd.

Lastly, there is a final village called Duwayrah, situated a little distance to the west or south-west.

A few kilometres west of Ḥuwaylān lies an abandoned village called Ruwayḍiyyah.

I stayed two more days at Buraydah, departing from there to return to the Ǧabal on 23 August.

Leaving towards nine o'clock in the morning, I reached al-Shuqqah two hours later and this time halted there for two hours. On leaving, I took a route farther to the east than the one I had followed to come to al-Qaṣīm, which enabled me to visit two places that I had not yet seen.

Having left al-Shuqqah an hour after noon and ridden north by 65° west for a full three hours, [498] I reached Ūthāl, a village of 250 souls with a good situation in a sandstone basin two miles long by one mile wide.[82] To find water at the same depth all year round, one has only to bore through the sandstone layer forming the bedrock of the basin, which varies from two to five metres in thickness. The village of Ūthāl does not form a compact whole, but comprises six groups of properties. The water is not drinkable everywhere. Between al-Shuqqah and Ūthāl a stony desert predominates, with the sandstone continually showing through.

Next morning I left Ūthāl and, after a ride of fully seven hours across the stony desert of al-Buṭayn, reached Quṣaybāʾ.[83]

---

[78] [Huber's distances are very inaccurate as they were based on hearsay. Al-Shīḥiyyah is 5 km west by north of al-Rass, which is itself some 75 km south-west of Buraydah.]

[79] [Al-Khabrāʾ and Riyāḍ al-Khabrāʾ are about 8 km apart and lie about 35 km due west of ʿUnayzah.]

[80] [Binhāniyyah: possibly a misspelling of al-Nabhāniyyah, about 45 km west of al-Rass.]

[81] [Ḥanayẓil: spelt thus in Arabic in the margin of Huber's handwritten manuscript, and in Huber 2003: 85.]

[82] [Ūthāl: situated 7 km east of ʿUyūn al-Ǧawāʾ, at 26° 30' 48" N 043° 40' 31" E (GeoNames).]

[83] M. Huber wrote Q'eçeïbà, and the name as written in Arabic in the margin of his manuscript would prove his spelling correct. We would nonetheless correct an indisputable error. Q'eçeïbà is no more than the diminutive of *qaṣbah*, castle. (The

The desert of al-Buṭayn is one of the most terrible I have ever experienced. On leaving Ūthāl one goes for about an hour across a barren tract of sandstone debris, which is immediately succeeded by one of rounded pebbles as far as Quṣaybāʾ. During the whole of this long line of march there is not a single sprig of greenery. It is a desolation that defies description.

Quṣaybāʾ too occupies a natural basin similar to those previously described, but deeper: its rim is thirty metres high. Also, the palms of the village cannot be seen until one reaches the very edge of the basin. But two miles before arriving one can see the towers commanding the heights to keep a watch on the surroundings.

Quṣaybāʾ, once very powerful, is still today one of the most important places in northern[84] al-Qaṣīm. The shaykh of the place assured me that there were 2,000 rifles there, but this figure is a manifest exaggeration and I estimate the population at no more than 3,000 souls at most. At first sight one might actually be tempted to accord it a larger one [499], because the whole place stretches for more than four kilometres along the western cliff of the basin in which it nestles; but close observation reveals a large number of properties to be abandoned and falling into ruin. Here more frequently than elsewhere it happens that a well suddenly collapses or the water gives out. So then the farmer has no other recourse than to go a little farther off to dig a new well and start plantations afresh.

There is another curious phenomenon that also sometimes afflicts Quṣaybāʾ. From one day to the next a well that has been sweet for generations will suddenly produce nothing but salty or bitter water. The water is also abundant and stays at a constant level throughout the year.

One of its water sources represents so rare a phenomenon in Arabia that it is famed far and wide. Thus I had already learnt in the Ǧabal that there was a spring at Quṣaybāʾ, and now its existence was confirmed. The shaykh himself led me there and so I was able to note that it was a natural artesian spring flowing consistently at about one litre per second. As the well has probably never been cleared out, the water is blackish, putrid and undrinkable. Because of the mud I was unable to measure its depth, which I was told was twenty metres – in my

Editors.) [The official spelling in Saudi Arabia confirms Huber's spelling, Quṣaybāʾ, which is retained in this translation, as against the Quṣaybah recommended by his editors.]

[84] [*Sic*; Huber wrote *méridional*, 'southern', but presumably meant *septentrional*, 'northern'.]

view too high a figure. The temperature of the water taken at a depth of five metres is very high: I found it to be 29.1°. Nevertheless it is possible that that is not so far from the average annual temperature of the region, as it seems that Quṣaybā' is subject to its own peculiar climatic conditions. All the inhabitants assured me that it never gets cold and that they felt no difference in temperature between summer and winter. Besides, the preceding winter, which had proved so hard for the palms of al-Ǧawf, Shammar and the rest of Naǧd, had not made itself felt here. From all this, one may conclude that Quṣaybā' must be situated at the centre of a vast [500] depression and probably at a level several hundred metres lower than the rest of al-Qaṣīm.

The abundance of water and the high temperature in this place ensure the persistence of two perennial scourges: mosquitoes and fevers.

Quṣaybā' has had a reputation since earliest antiquity of producing the best dates in al-Qaṣīm.

But here in this oasis, which could be a paradise, there languishes a thoroughly wretched-looking populace. The sight of the numerous abandoned properties leads one to wonder about the cause of its depopulation. Is it the air, the water, or the food? Without dismissing the influence of the latter two factors, I believe the most active cause to be the air, full as it is of miasmas rising from the plentiful stagnant pools that the prevailing westerly winds fail to refresh because, on this side, the oasis is completely sheltered by the cliff of the basin in which it lies. Whatever the reason may be, it will be a long time before I forget the thin, drawn features and the emaciated, weak and undeveloped physiques of the local people.

At the east-north-eastern end of the basin of Quṣaybā' stands a great property called Mashkūk.[85]

Right at the northern end of the village, on a spur of the cliff of the basin, are the ruins of an antique edifice built of dressed stones known by everyone in Naǧd as the Qaṣr ʿAntar Akhū Mārid.[86] In the minds of the local people, the word *akhū* relates to the word *qaṣr*, signifying that this castle is the brother of the castle of Mārid at ʿAyn Ibn Fuhayd.

[85] [Possibly Mashqūq is meant, actually at the north-western end of the Quṣaybā' basin, at approx. 26° 55' N 043° 31' E (GeoNames).]

[86] [The name ʿAntar is doubtless a reference to the pre-Islamic Naǧdī knight and poet ʿAntarah ibn Shaddād al-ʿAbsī, also known as ʿAntar (AD 525–608), celebrated for his feats of valour in war and his adventurous life.]

There remains very little of this ruin: only the line of the walls at ground level and a few scattered stones. I could find no trace of inscriptions, and the locals assured me that they had never noticed any.

The next day before dawn, I set off again from Quṣaybāʾ for al-Kahfah. After a two-hour ride [501] north by 15° west, we reached another basin called al-Ḥamūdiyyah enclosing six abandoned properties. It has no palm trees, and the nomadic Arabs come there sometimes to sow the fields with barley and wheat. These fields have been lying fallow for more than ten years but, under the kindly sky, the buildings and wells are perfectly preserved and the latter have water in abundance. I stopped there for half an hour to eat a few dates.

We soon resumed our journey, and towards nine o'clock set out across another desert tract of unparalleled desolation, composed entirely of sandstone debris and with no sign at all of vegetation. I was suffering greatly from the heat and most of all from that radiating from the ground. This stony desert lying between Quṣaybāʾ, al-Quwārah and al-Kahfah goes by the name of Tirmuṣ.[87] At last, at four o'clock in the afternoon, we were able to make out al-Kahfah, which we reached two hours later.

On the matter of plotting my route between Quṣaybāʾ and al-Kahfah on the map, I must point out that the detours so noticeable on it were not necessitated by the nature of the terrain, which is perfectly negotiable, but by our own uncertainty as to which direction to follow. Along this route, which is in any case very seldom used, there was neither path nor track. The stony ground retained no footprints at all and my companion Ṭrād was only familiar with the usual route to al-Qaṣīm via al-Quwārah. What put us in this predicament was that the shaykh of Quṣaybāʾ, in pointing out the direction we should take that morning for al-Kahfah in the usual manner of the desert, that is by raising his open hand vertically and slicing the horizon, had indicated it a little too far to the north.

Shaikh ʿAmr showed how pleased he was at to see me return safe and sound, and gave me another very warm welcome, but I did not darken his door and stayed in camp in the sand outside to facilitate an early departure. [502] He was keen even so to treat me as his guest, and after supper sent out two men to watch over my camels and possessions the whole night through, even though six of the emir's horsemen, whom I had come across there, had immediately been placed at my disposal.

[87] [For this Arabic spelling of Tirmuṣ, see the margin of Huber's handwritten manuscript, and Huber 1891: 691. For the spelling Turmus, see Musil 1928a: 65.]

Next day we had left in good time when, two leagues from al-Kahfah, we were alerted to brigands. We gave them chase but they got away under cover of darkness, making us lose almost three hours, so that we only reached Fayd towards sunset.

Leaving the next morning, I crossed Ǧabal Salmā by the valley of al-Withr, and passing in front of Qaṣr al-ʿAdwah,[88] a property abandoned at the present time, I went and camped for a few hours close to Ǧabal Fataq before returning to Ḥāʾil on 28 August, after an absence of twenty-eight days.

ǦABAL ǦILDIYYAH

On 22 September [1880], while the emir was mounting a raid to the south of Wadi Rimah,[89] I made a trip to Ǧabal Ǧildiyyah, a full day's journey to the east of Ḥāʾil, where I had been told there were inscriptions.[90]

Leaving Ḥāʾil at four o'clock in the afternoon, my guide and I went north by 77° east for an hour.

Next morning, having set out before dawn, it took us an hour to reach the limit of the granite terrain, which gives way immediately to sandstone. A little later we made camp close to a great sandstone block known as Umm al-Ruǧūm, which had been totally covered with Himyaritic inscriptions, but which time had almost completely obliterated. I was however able to copy four very legible ones.[91]

Fifteen kilometres farther on, to the north by 80° east, are the [503] rocks of Bāʿūr, where there is also a *ghadīr*[92] of the same name, and where I found three more inscriptions and some fairly accurate drawings of animals.[93]

[88] [Al-Withr, spelt thus in Arabic in the margin of Huber's handwritten manuscript. Al-ʿAdwah or al-ʿIdwah is at 27° 17' 51" N 042° 16' 25" E (GeoNames).]

[89] [In his 65-page handwritten report dated 27 March 1882, Huber says that this raid was directed against the Muṭayr and lasted from 23 September until the emir's return to Ḥāʾil on 12 October. (French national archives, Pierrefitte-sur-Seine, Dossier F/17/2976/1:1, entitled 'Mission au Thibet et dans l'Asie centrale', 1878–82, item 79, p. 47.)]

[90] [Huber went to Ǧabal Ǧildiyyah again during 9–12 November 1883 with Julius Euting (Huber 1891: 78–92; Euting 1896: 227–33).]

[91] [These are nos. 25–28 in Appendices 1 and 2. (MCAM)]

[92] A natural basin in the rock retaining rainwater and used by nomads when pasturing their flocks and herds in this area. *Ghadīr*s are numerous in the Ḥamād and the Arabia Petraea of antiquity, that is to say in the stony sandstone and limestone deserts. (It is the *ghedîr* or *rhedîr* of the Sahara.) (CH) [*Ghadīr*: a pool of water left by a flood, a waterhole in the rocks (Groom 1983: 91).]

[93] [These are nos. 29–31 in Appendices 1 and 2. (MCAM)]

Farther on still in the same direction stands the rock outcrop of al-Buwayb, where I made camp having copied six inscriptions.[94]

Two hours after sunrise next morning, I arrived in front of an isolated peak that had once been joined to Ǧabal Ǧildiyyah and on which inscriptions were to be found, most of them fortunately well-preserved. This fragment of mountain also bears the name al-Buwayb. I copied twenty-eight inscriptions there, all of them Himyaritic.[95]

At the base of al-Buwayb there forms the wadi of the same name that flows towards Baqʿāʾ to the north-east.

Ǧabal Ǧahannah stands five miles south-south-east of Ǧabal Ǧildiyyah.

Four miles north by 80° west of al-Buwayb, I found three more inscriptions on a rock,[96] and six more[97] three miles farther on in a little tributary of Wādī Shaqīq, on a rock about twenty metres high called al-Ṣaʿlikah.[98]

Wādī Shaqīq, which forms in this area, runs for about twelve miles north-east and loses itself in the basin containing the wells of al-Khāṣirah.[99]

On the following day, 25 September, I returned to Ḥāʾil. My excursion had yielded the following results: [504]

1. Fifty Himyaritic inscriptions;[100]

2. Proof that the granitic region extends only a very little to the east of Ḥāʾil, something that I had not believed, as after my journey to al-Qaṣīm I had supposed that directly to the east of Ḥāʾil the granite stretched at least to the longitude of Fayd;

3. The new observation, established by the courses of the wadis, of the trending of Ǧabal Shammar to the north-north-east from a point which I place for the time being between south and west beyond Ǧabal Aǧā from the viewpoint of Ḥāʾil. This

[94] [These are presumably nos. 32–37 in Appendices 1 and 2. (MCAM).]

[95] [These are nos. 38–65 in Appendices 1 and 2. As usual, for Huber's use of the term Himyaritic, see Translation Part I note 158. (MCAM)]

[96] [These must be nos. 75–77 in Appendices 1 and 2. (MCAM)]

[97] [These are nos. 69–74 in Appendices 1 and 2. (MCAM)]

[98] Lady Anne Blunt too saw this rock, which she calls Saylyeh, and the inscriptions, which M. Rassam told her were in ancient Phoenician characters, which she doubted and with reason, as these inscriptions are all Himyaritic. See Blunt 1882: 324–5. (CH) [For the spelling of al-Ṣaʿlikah, see Huber 1891: 101, where he gives it in Arabic.]

[99] [Huber gives the Arabic spelling for this in the margin of his handwritten manuscript, and also in Huber 1891: 95.]

[100] [These are nos. 25–74 in Appendices 1 and 2. (MCAM)]

fact had already been partially revealed to me by the course of the Wādī Ḥā'il.

I also ascertained that this region, though being just a stony desert, nevertheless contains better grazing than the granite terrain situated to the south. Sandstone, being soft by nature, is easily penetrated and eroded into hollows by water. Also, the whole area that I crossed between Bā'ūr and Ǧabal Ǧildiyyah is ravined and contains a little sand, which encourages the growth of plants. Finally, it contains numerous *ghadīr*s or rainpools which, during rainy winters, can retain their water right up until the month of May.

THE ḤIǦĀZ

It was not until 30 October that I was able to visit the oases to the west.[101] The emir had assigned me a guide with a very good knowledge of the country between Ḥā'il and Taymā'. At Taymā' or al-'Ulā the emir's governors would have to procure another guide for me to go on to Khaybar and, from there, to return to Ḥā'il.

The name of my guide, a Shammari from the tribe of Suwayd, was 'Aǧlān ibn Ǧa'ārī.[102]

The usual route from Ḥā'il to Taymā' passes through the Rī'at al-Salf,[103] but as I wanted to determine as [505] precisely as possible the extent of Ǧabal Aǧa, I took a route to the north so as to go around it.

[101] [In his 65-page handwritten report dated 27 March 1882, Huber describes the emir's unwillingness to let him go to Taymā' and farther west into the Ḥiǧāz, a disappointment that made him ill. Eventually, having visited Huber three times, the emir relented and told him to be patient until the raid against the Muṭayr was over. (French national archives, Pierrefitte-sur-Seine, Dossier F/17/2976/1:1, entitled 'Mission au Thibet et dans l'Asie centrale', 1878–82, item 79, pp. 46–8.)]

[102] [Suwayd: one of the four main tribes of the Sinǧārah division of the Shammar confederacy (Musil 1928a: 31–2). Ǧa'ārī: for Huber's G'aâry, based on the place called al-Ǧa'āra in the Iraq borderlands south of Naǧaf (Musil 1928a: 188). Huber confirms this Arabic spelling in the margin of his handwritten manuscript.]

[103] *Rī'ah*: a defile or pass. The Rī'at al-Salf crosses Ǧabal Aǧā from side to side, beginning to the south of Qufār and emerging near Mawqaq. (CH) [*Rī'ah* means 'a road or passage through a cleft in the mountains' (Groom 1983: 245). The location of Rī'at al-Salf in relation to Qefār/Qufār is shown in Huber 1891: Atlas flles 6 and 11, inset entitled Vallée de Aqdah. Huber and Euting passed up it in 1884 (Huber 1891: 209–12; Euting 1914: 109), and Doughty gives a good description of it (1936 i: 632–3). (MCAM/WF)]

Having only left Ḥāʾil at midday, we made camp on the evening of our first stage to the north of Ǧabal Aǧā.

The next day, after a three-hour ride, we entered the Nafūd and at three o'clock in the afternoon we made camp a kilometre north of Ǧabal Ḥashab[104] to await my guide.

Towards midday we had passed the wells of al-Ḥufayrah, eleven in number.[105] Their sides are lined with dressed masonry and they are of great antiquity. The upper granite blocks are polished totally smooth and are deeply grooved as a result of wear from the well-ropes. They are about twenty metres deep and three metres wide.

They are situated in a basin of the same kind as that of Ǧubbah, but which is only about four square leagues in area.[106] To the east of the basin stands a large dwelling and to the west some palms about forty years old. Everything was abandoned only about five years ago by the owners, who reverted to their nomadic way of life.

Next day, the 1st of November, we rode for a mere nine hours and encamped that evening near the tent of a nomad of the Sinǧārah.[107]

Shortly after we had started off again in the morning, Ǧabal al-Mismāʾ momentarily came into view and I took a bearing on it. The same went for the headland known as Sumayr Ṭuwayl, at the base of which nestles the little village of Ṭuwayl, more commonly known as al-Ṭuwayyah,[108] with its ten plantations and eighty inhabitants.

At midday on 2 November, having moved off again at sunrise and marched for six hours, we reached the wells of al-ʿUbaysah[109] at the foot of some granite hills of the same name. These wells belong to the ʿAbrayt[110] Arabs, whose rangelands are in the Nafūd between those of the Sinǧārah to

---

[104] [Ḥashab: spelt thus in Arabic in the margin of Huber's handwritten manuscript, and also in Huber 2003: 92, for Huber's Hašab.]

[105] [Spelt thus in Arabic in the margin of Huber's handwritten manuscript. These wells were located in the basin in the sands known as al-Ḥafār, aka al-Ḥufayr, a village at 27° 38' 59" N 041° 16' 45" E (GeoNames).]

[106] [Four square leagues would equal 64,000 square metres or 6.4 hectares.]

[107] [See note 102 above, showing that Huber's guide was himself of the Sinǧārah division of Shammar.]

[108] [Ṭuwayyah, at 27° 39' 56" N 040° 57' 57" E (GeoNames).]

[109] [Biʾr ʿUbaysah: at 27° 25' 03" N 040° 42' 38" E (GeoNames). Musil's al-ʿObejse (Musil 1928a: 97–8).]

[110] [ʿAbrayt (Huber's 'Abreït): These are possibly the Āl Brayk, a family of Āl Mufaẓẓal of the ʿAbdah tribe of Shammar (Musil 1928a: 33).]

the east and the Banī Wahhāb [506] to the west. They are very ancient and they too are lined with blocks of black granite veined with white. The water, which is excellent, lies twelve metres down. The diameter of the wells is just 1.2 metres.

Ten kilometres north of the wells of al-ʿUbaysah lies the well of Ramādah, and fifteen kilometres farther on, to the north-north-west, the well of Sālimī.[111] The water in both of them is very bitter and can only be used for watering animals.

Beyond both of these wells, thirty-five kilometres north-west of the wells of al-ʿUbaysah, lies Ǧabal Ḥibrān,[112] which is eight miles long from north-east to south-west. Thirty kilometres farther on still in the same direction lies Ǧabal Fardād, likewise oriented north-east to south-west, but with a length of about forty kilometres.[113]

These two mountains are of interest in that they are composed of sandstone, so enabling us to determine approximately the line of demarcation between the sandstone and granite geology, even beneath the sands of the Nafūd. This line, to my mind, must be located a little distance from the route that I had been following from the wells of al-Ḥafrah to those of al-ʿUbaysah, but passing to the north of Ǧabal Ḥashab and the wells of al-Ḥafrah.

Forty-five kilometres to the south by 70° east of al-ʿUbaysah, beyond the Nafūd and not far from Ǧabal Aǧā, lies Mawqaq.[114] This very ancient place was once highly important and, after Qufār and Mustaǧiddah, the largest in the Ǧabal. Nowadays in deep decline, it possesses just ten plantations, as follows:[115]

Al-Drūb	100 inhabitants
Lazzām	50
Mashrifah	60
Al-Sirḥānī	50

[111] [Biʾr al-Sālimī, at 27° 28' 13" N 040° 34' 23" E (GeoNames).]

[112] [Ǧabal Ḥibrān is at 27° 40' 22" N 040° 28' 36" (GeoNames).]

[113] [Fardād: Huber's Fredâd, most probably Musil's two table mountains of Fardet an-Naẓīm and Fardet aš-Šemūs (Musil 1928a: 100). These are actually about 20 km WSW of Ḥibrān, at 27° 34' 25" N 040° 19' 00" E, and 27° 31' 35" N 040° 17' 10" E (GeoNames).]

[114] [Huber visited Mawqaq with Euting on 25–26 January 1884 (Huber 1891: 215–16; Euting 1914: 111–13). See also Musil 1928a: 93–4, 97–8.]

[115] [Huber (1891: 216) recorded the names in Arabic of all but three (Salāmī, al-Matnah and Sanūd) of these plantations or *sūqs* in January 1884.]

	Al-Kharābah	90
	Salāmī	30
[507]	Al-Matnah	20
	Shilīl	50
	Sanūd	20
	Shuwaymah	30

Mawqaq is sorely tested by the regular fevers that afflict it every year, from autumn right up to summer. In 1870, cholera brought by the caravan returning from Mecca carried off a quarter of its population.

Six miles south of Mawqaq lies Bidaʿ Ğufayfā, commonly known as Ğufayfā, with about a hundred inhabitants.[116]

After an hour's halt at the wells of al-ʿUbaysah we resumed our westward march and made camp towards five o'clock in the evening under the tent of Shaykh Farḥān ibn ʿĪsā, of the *Drelha tribe.[117] I had already made the acquaintance of this shaykh in Ḥāʾil, and he accorded me a very warm welcome.

The following day, a four-hour march brought me to the edge of the Nafūd, and four kilometres farther on I was at the walled well of al-Murayr,[118] which is fifteen metres deep by 1.2 metres in diameter. The water is very bitter and salty, usable only for watering animals.

The little mountain of al-Ḥaʿb is ten kilometres to the south-south-east, and that of al-Wurayk[119] the same distance to the south-south-west. Both are of dark red granite.

Having left al-Murayr after a one-hour halt, we rode on for another four hours across the desert separating that well from the two mountain ranges of al-Mismāʾ and al-ʿAwğā, and then made camp at sunset. This desert, where the bare rock is constantly visible, is nothing but a monotonous, flat plain with very little vegetation.

[116] [This Ğufayfā (spelt thus in Arabic in the margin of Huber's handwritten manuscript) is in fact about 25 km south-west of Mawqaq. See Guarmani 1938: 90. Not to be confused with al-Ğufayfah on the other side of Ğabal Ağā, approximately 75 km west-south-west of Ḥāʾil.]

[117] [Drelha: I have not been able to identify this tribe.]

[118] [Huber writes El Mereïd, but this is certainly meant to be the well of al-Murayr, at 27° 21' 06" N 040° 27' 04" E (GeoNames).]

[119] [Al-Ḥaʿb (spelt thus in Arabic in the margin of Huber's handwritten manuscript), for Huber's El H'ab. Ğabal al-Wurayk is at 27° 18' 00" N 040° 24' 00" E (GeoNames).]

On 4 November, having set off before dawn, it took me five hours to reach the southern tip of Ǧabal al-ʿAwǧā, which is joined seamlessly to the northern part of Ǧabal Mismāʾ. Both mountains are sandstone formations situated outside the Nafūd. It is noteworthy that they both trend in the same direction [508] as Ǧabal Aǧā, that is, from north-north-east to south-south-west.

From the point at which I approached Ǧabal Mismāʾ I found a small Kufic inscription, and in the southern part where there is a *ghadīr* or rainpool, I saw and copied eleven Himyaritic inscriptions.[120]

For a moment I had a view of Ǧabal Ḥibrān from the base of Ǧabal Mismāʾ and I was able to take a bearing on it.

We resumed our way after a three-hour halt at the Ǧabal Mismāʾ rainpool and crossed the mountain, which was facilitated by a high dune of Nafūd sand which the westerly winds had blown over it. After three and a half hours on the march we encamped in the stony desert that stretches between the mountains of al-Khanẓuwah[121] and Mismāʾ, and which is no different from that between Mismāʾ and al-Murayr.

Next day, a five-hour march brought us to the northern tip of Ǧabal al-Khanẓuwah, which is composed entirely of sandstone and is in the process of being eroded away. It gives me the impression of having supplied a considerable portion of the sands forming the Nafūd. We stopped there for about an hour to take notes and eat some dates. We then crossed the mountain and three hours later rounded Ǧabal ʿIrnān[122] too. Shortly after, we entered the Nafūd again, keeping to a course north by 80° west, and by four o'clock in the evening we were making camp close to the

[120] [These are nos. 75–84 in Appendices 1 and 2. (MCAM)]

[121] [For Huber's Kheñloûah. Ǧabal al-Khanẓuwah, aka al-Khandhuwah, is at 27° 07' 44" N 039° 51' 15" E (GeoNames).]

[122] I am compelled to express my reservations about the dimensions of this famous mountain. Almost all the information available to me gives it a length of 40 km, whereas my own estimate and triangulations give it a length of no more than 17 or 20 km at most. However, perhaps the Arabs are not completely wrong and the mountain, which is composed of very friable sandstone, does continue southwards for another 20 km; but its summits, eroded by meteorological forces in the same way as its neighbour Ǧabal al-Khanẓuwah, have been reduced to sand and have gone to swell the dunes of the Nafūd. So this part of the range, naturally lower than the northern part, would be lying below the horizon at the point where I was taking my bearings. (CH) [Huber was more or less correct about the dimensions of Ǧabal ʿIrnān. He seems to have turned sharp north at this point and gone up the eastern side of ʿIrnān, so as to end the day south of the wells of Qulbān in the Nafūd.]

tent of an Arab named Khalaf, of the Awlād ʿAlī tribe, who despite his obvious poverty [509] absolutely insisted on treating me as his guest, and slaughtered a sheep.

We were encamped only a few kilometres from the wells of al-Qulbān[123] to the north, to which a ride of barely a couple of hours took us on the next day.

The siting of these wells is picturesque in the extreme. There are three of them, and they occupy the base of an immense *fulǧ* or horse-shoe-shaped dune which is at least eighty metres deep and which maintains all the perfect regularity of its form.[124] The wells are seventeen metres deep and lined with masonry. The water is cloudy and has a slightly saline taste, but is good to drink even so. I found its temperature to be 22.5°. When we arrived, the bedouin had already been encamped there for three hours and were depleting the supply by watering their animals.

About twenty-seven kilometres west of these wells and likewise in the Nafūd are the wells of Ḥayzā,[125] the water of which is the same as that of the wells of al-Qulbān. I was told their depth was forty-five metres.

Within a radius of about five miles around the wells of al-Qulbān, the Nafūd is very rugged and painful to cross.

I left the wells towards eight o'clock next morning, and five and a half hours later, going almost exclusively south-west, reached the edge of the Nafūd and the tent of Shaykh Mishʿal, where I spent the rest of the day, and the night too.

Taking my leave of Shaykh Mishʿal on the morning of 7 November, I rode straight towards the northern tip of Ǧabal Ḥalwān, the bearing of which I took as north by 74° west. The first four kilometres led me to the farthest extremity of the Nafūd, which we quitted at that point never to return. But it was never lost from view, and its outline was constantly visible to the north of my route and all the way to Taymāʾ, at distances varying from six to eighteen kilometres.

---

[123] [Al-Qulbān, at 27° 29' 48" N 039° 44' 38" E (GeoNames).]

[124] [For *fulǧ*, the horseshoe-shaped dune, and *qaʿr*, the depression that it encloses, see Translation Part I, notes 82 and 83. Gertrude Bell photographed al-Qulbān on her 1913–14 journey through northern Arabia.]

[125] [Ḥayzā, aka Ḥayzān, at 27° 29' 25" N 039° 12' 18" E (GeoNames), is actually more like 50 km due west of al-Qulbān. Gertrude Bell went through Biʾr Ḥayzān too on her 1913–14 journey and photographed it.]

From the point where we left the Nafūd, a six-hour ride brought me [510] to some tents of the ʿAnizah Arabs encamped about five miles before Ğabal Ḥalwān. I stopped with them, in the tent of Shaykh Mirbaṭ.

In appearance, the stony desert looked the same as the one we had encountered on leaving the well of al-Murayr, but limestone had taken over from sandstone, and close to my camp that evening evidences of volcanic origin once again made their appearance.

Next morning, after we had rounded the mountain of Ḥalwān,[126] a march of about six hours brought us to the rock outcrops of Khālah,[127] where we made camp.

Shortly after leaving camp the next morning, I came upon a large volcanic plateau which gives a plausible impression of a Roman road having existed there. The entire plateau appeared to be paved with large, carefully dressed square blocks.

The rocks of Khālah are a collection of sandstone teats, whitish and isolated from each other, circular at the base, and with ovoid summits. Their base diameters vary from thirty to thirty-five metres, and they are ten to fifteen metres high. Like the Ḥalwān, ʿIrnān and al-Khanẓuwah ranges, this ensemble of elevations is oriented from north-north-east to south-south-west. The intervals between the teats are filled with sand and contain a little vegetation.

On the following day, 9 November, I went for about ten kilometres through this Khālah district of teat-like outcrops and soon after reached a stony desert of black sandstone that looked as if it had been scorched. As I completed my first twenty kilometres, that is to say at about 37° of longitude,[128] I came across a very curious formation that I shall call laminated sandstone. It is as if layers of sandstone from one to two centimetres thick had been superimposed on each other and then, having been subjected to fierce heat, had curled up and lifted around their edges just as would layers of parchment. There too I saw pieces of bedrock, circular and square in section, rising up [511] from the ground like portions of columns, all of volcanic origin. I had previously noted the same phenomenon between al-Kahfah and al-Quwārah, and north of Quṣaybāʾ.

[126] [Here Huber writes Kheňloûah (i.e. al-Khanẓuwah), not Ḥalwān, but he had left the former behind three days before and was now in the vicinity of Ğabal Ḥalwān, so the latter must be meant. Ğabal Ḥalwān is at 27° 18' 19" N 039° 09' 02" E (GeoNames).]

[127] [Possibly this should be Khawlah.]

[128] [In fact Huber was at approx. 38° 55' E at this point. He realized on his return to Paris that his longitude calculations were incorrect because his chronometer had been defective: see Appendix 4, Letter no. 3 dated 18 May 1882.]

Those very same sandstone 'sausages' had been taken by Palgrave to be the remains of monuments, calling to mind some ancient cult of the planets.[129]

A little later, when I spotted one of the peaks of Ǧabal Ghunaym, I was able to take a bearing on the direction of Taymāʾ, which lies to the north of that mountain. At about the same time I was able to take a bearing on Ǧabal Burd[130] to the south of my route. After a full eight hours' ride, I made camp in this stony desert.

Next morning, 10 November, having got going at five o'clock, I halted at ten close to Ǧabal Ghunaym, and two hours later reached Taymāʾ.

Ibn Rashīd has a governor at Taymāʾ, ʿAbd al-ʿAzīz al-ʿAnqarī, for whom he had entrusted me with a letter. So I was given a most respectful and indeed a most cordial welcome.

This oasis is certainly a site of the greatest antiquity. The Bible already refers to it under the name 'Thêmâ', and the oriental writers[131] all mention it as an important ancient city. Ptolemy lists it under the name Thaima (Θαιμα) and gives its position more or less exactly as 71° 0' of longitude and 27° 0' of latitude.[132] The inhabitants, who are vaguely aware of its great antiquity, told me that their city had already been destroyed three times, and that it had been abandoned for several centuries before being repopulated. Also, at one kilometre to the south-west of Taymāʾ, there lies a heap of ruins with dressed masonry and fragments of columns half covered by the sands, which the local people call Tūmā and regard as the most recent of their ancient towns.

---

[129] [For Palgrave's 'Arabian Stonehenge', see Palgrave 1865 i: 251–2. Palgrave claimed to have seen the remains of standing stones a few miles north of ʿUyūn al-Ǧawāʾ in al-Qaṣīm, which he argued were evidence of ancient Arabian star and planet worship.]

[130] [Ǧabal Burd or Bird is a very prominent landmark, visible from miles around, at 27° 04' 07" N 038° 58' 31" E (GeoNames).]

[131] [Huber does not give sources, but is presumably referring to the mediaeval Arab geographers. Taymāʾ is mentioned by many of these, including Ibn al-Faqīh, al-Iṣṭakhrī, al-Hamdānī, al-Muqaddasī, al-Bakrī and Yāqūt: see Musil 1928a, Appendix VI, pp. 227–9.]

[132] [Ptolemy's latitude figure is surprisingly accurate, as Taymāʾ is at 27° 35'. Ptolemy's longitude system began with 0° longitude at the Fortunate Isles in the Atlantic (either the Cape Verde Islands or the Canaries), and his 70° 27' of longitude would place Taymāʾ much too far to the east. This was exacerbated by his overestimate of the circumference of the Earth by about 40 percent, making his degree of longitude correspondingly too wide to be plotted accurately onto the Earth's actual surface. The modern longitude of Taymāʾ from the Greenwich meridian is approx. 038° 30' E.]

The inscriptions that I collected there are not numerous but they are of enormous interest, as much for [512] their antiquity as for the archaic form of their characters. One of them is Nabataean, a second is Aramaic, and a third remains to be determined.[133] I draw Taymāʾ to the attention of the next explorer to go there so that excavations can be carried out, as I am quite certain that he will unearth archaeological treasures.

Tūmā was built of black basalt stone similar to that of the ruined towns of the Ḥawrān and Ǧabal Druze. One curious detail is that in an old ruined building adjoining the house of ʿAbd al-ʿAzīz al-ʿAnqarī and belonging to him, I spotted once again a portion of the ceiling made out of long beams of this same stone, just like the ones in the Ḥawrān.

The wonder of Taymāʾ today is its well, which is celebrated throughout Arabia. As I was frequently told, 'a hundred camels ceaselessly draw water from it'. Having checked, I found no more than seventy-five well wheels in place, but I owe it to the truth to confirm that a hundred could be mounted should the need arise.

The shape of this well, which is a little irregular, more or less resembles a square with rounded corners and has sides measuring about 20 metres. The height of the walls varies considerably: two sides are 10.5 metres from ground level to the bottom of the well, another is 12.5 metres, and the fourth is 15.5 metres. The water is about three metres deep, and never rises nor falls whatever the season.[134] It is limpid and pleasant to drink once it has been

---

[133] [These are nos. 85, 86 and 87 in Appendices 1 and 2. Of these, no. 85 is such a bad copy that it has not been possible to identify it. This is the text the script of which Huber says 'remains to be determined'. No. 86 (printed upside-down) is also a very bad copy of a Taymāʾ Aramaic (not 'Nabataean') inscription, *CIS* ii 336, which was published from Euting's copy, and no. 87 is a copy of an Imperial Aramaic inscription, published as *CIS* ii 114 from a copy by Euting. It is striking that Huber, though generally credited with the discovery of the Taymāʾ Stele which is now in the Musée du Louvre in Paris, does not mention it here, and in fact mentions it nowhere in his reports or letters until Euting brought the Stele to his attention on 17 February 1884 (Huber 1891: 317–19; Euting 1914: 156–61). If he had indeed seen it on this 1880 visit, it is inconceivable that he would not have mentioned it. (MCAM/WF)]

[134] [Doughty in March 1877 (1936 i: 335–6) estimated the water level to be 7 fathoms down, that is about 15 m, which tallies with Huber's figures. Carruthers in late February 1909 (1935: 90–2) estimated the surface to be about 30 feet (less than 10 m) down. He also records the local opinion that the level remained constant regardless of the season or the amount of water extracted, which however seems unlikely. In February 1884, Euting reckoned the water was 15 m below ground level but estimated the length of the camel-draw track at 30 m, so he must have seen the water

cooled in water-skins. All the local people assured me that drinking it at the well itself, that is to say tepid, would make one very ill.

In the eastern wall of the well, at about a metre above the level of the water, are three openings in the rock about fifty centimetres wide by seventy in height. Their origin or purpose are not known, nor had anybody ever dared go into them.

The walled farmsteads[135] at Taymāʾ amount to sixty in number, each with five or six families, which would give a population of about 1,500 souls.

[513] The dates of Taymāʾ are the best in all northern Arabia, excepting only two or three varieties that grow in small quantities in al-Ǧawf and at Ḥāʾil.

The water of the well in this oasis never diminishes even after several years of drought, so that harvests can be relied upon. Also, real estate at Taymāʾ has a value that I have encountered nowhere else. A property sells for 15 to 20 *riyāl*s[136] per palm tree, whereas at Ḥāʾil even the handsomest palms never fetch more than 10 *riyāl*s.

Taymāʾ being situated at a higher altitude than Ḥāʾil, its plantations suffered more damage than those of the Ǧabal during the harsh winter of 1879–80. Though the palms proved resilient, the vines, pomegranates, peaches and figs have hardly borne fruit this season.

Taymāʾ sells its dates almost exclusively to the Sharārāt Arabs. The Ruwalah too sometimes venture this far, but not every year. It is the Sharārāt who supply Taymāʾ with butter and sheep.

The two great ʿAnizah tribes that make up the Banī Wahhāb, that is the Fuqarāʾ and the Awlād ʿAlī, whose grazing lands also extend as far as Taymāʾ, do not obtain their supply of dates from there but from Khaybar. As proprietors of palm groves at Khaybar, the Fuqarāʾ have scarcely any need at all to buy dates.

While awaiting the complete publication of the lists of the tribes and their numerous subdivisions which I plan to make available at a later date, I

at a high level, perhaps because of the winter season and recent heavy rainfall during the winter of 1883–84. The logic of the well mechanism demands that if the water surface is 15 m below ground, then the track required need not be much longer than that: add a metre for submerging the bucket, and a few metres for a turning space at the end of the track. So a 30-metre track suggests that the water level in Euting's day could sometimes be 25 m or more below ground.]

135 [Huber uses the term *qulbān*, in the sense of enclosed plantations and gardens with houses and a well.]

136 The *riyāl* is worth from 4 francs 50 cents to 4 francs 80 cents. (CH)

set forth here the composition of the Banī Wahhāb, which is of such interest in every way, and which is divided into the two great branches of the Awlād ʿAlī and the Fuqarāʾ.

The tribes of the Awlād ʿAlī branch are as follows:[137]

> Līdiān – *El Mes'ad – al-Sanad – al-Muraykhān – al-Rikāb – al-ʿAṭayfāt – al-Mashṭaʾ – al-Ṭulūḥ – [514] al-Khālid – al-Rubaylāt – al-Dumǧān – al-Tuwāliʿah – al-Mushrif – al-Khayl – al-Dhuwaybah – *El Šer'abah.

That is sixteen tribes in total, with about 600 tents. The paramount shaykh at the present time is called Muṭlaq ibn Raǧāʾ Alayd.[138]

The tribes of the Fuqarāʾ are nine in number:[139]

> Al-Mubārak – al-Shafaqah – al-Huǧūr – al-Khamʿalī – al-Ṣuhbān – al-Mughāṣīb – al-Firaʿīn – al-Ḥuwaykim – al-Ǧamʿāt.

These nine tribes together possess about 400 tents. Their paramount shaykh, who pitches his tent with the al-Mubārak, is called Muṭlaq ibn Ḥumayd.

As I have indicated on the map, the Banī Wahhāb range over the desert of al-Shifah,[140] with Taymāʾ marking their northern limit and the Ḥarrah[141] their southern. The Awlād ʿAlī have the better share, because

---

[137] [Between 1908 and 1914, Musil (1927: 84) recorded six of these names in proper transliterated form: al-ʿAṭayfāt, al-Ṭulūḥ, al-Rubaylāt, al-Dumǧān, al-Tuwāliʿah, al-Mashṭaʾ. Jaussen and Savignac (1914: 4 n. 3) listed six of the names recorded by Huber in their list of nine Awlād ʿAlī clans, as follows: al-Ḥamamdah, al-Sanad, al-Murayghān, al-Rikāb, al-ʿUṭayfāt, al-Dumǧān, al-Khālid, al-Mushaytah, and al-Ṭuwalḥah. Huber's El Sened, El Mereîkhâñ, El Rekâb and Dzoueïbah are recorded in Oppenheim ii: 348–9 as El-Sened, El-Meraykhān, El-Rekāb and El-Dhuwaybah. The proper spellings of Huber's Lîdiâñ, El Mes'ad and El Šer'abah clans remain uncertain.]

[138] [Huber writes Aleïd (Alayd), but on 23 March 1884 refers to this individual as Muṭlaq al-Alaydah, writing it in Arabic as al-Alādah (1891: 438).]

[139] [Four of these correspond to names on Jaussen and Savignac's (1914: 3) list of nine Fuqarāʾ clans (*ḥamāʾil* (sing. *ḥamūlah*) as follows: al-Shufayqah, al-Ḥamdān, al-Ǧanāʿāt, al-Mughāsib, al-Zuwārḥah, al-Rashaydah, al-Ḥuǧūr, al-Saqārah, and al-Ghamāḥlah. By the time Oppenheim was writing (1943), only five of those listed by Huber were still in the Fuqarā, viz: al-Shafaqah, al-Huǧūr, al-Khamʿalī, al-Mughāṣīb and al-Ǧamʿāt. Oppenheim gives the other tribes as al-Zuwārʿa, al-Ḥamdān and al-Ṣaqara (ii: 348). (MCAM/WF)]

[140] [Al-Shifah: I have been unable precisely to identify this tract of desert, which Huber names Ašefah.]

[141] [i.e. Ḥarrat Khaybar, the great *ḥarrah* or volcanic lava field in which Khaybar is situated.]

their territory includes part of the Nafūd. On the other hand, the Fuqarā᾽ have part of their territory crossed by the Darb al-Ḥağğ, which is a perennial source of profit for the Arabs. Besides, as mentioned above, they own the palm groves of Khaybar which supply them with their annual provision of dates.

The desert immediately surrounding Taymā᾽ is called al-Ğuraydah.[142]

On 13 November [1880] I left Taymā᾽ to go to Madā᾽in Ṣāliḥ. On this first day I made only thirty or so kilometres, and those not in a straight line, because at the last moment my guide ʿAğlān took it into his head to ask the nomads for two men to come with us as reinforcements in view of the insecurity of the route. I camped that evening in the tent of Shaykh Muḥsin, who was just then in Mecca with the camels he had rented out to the *ḥağğ*.

The next day we managed just ten or so kilometres, in a south-westerly direction.

We resumed our south-westerly course on 16 November. After a ride of five hours we reached Ğabal [515] Sharqī, which is some ten kilometres long and aligned more or less north–south, parallel to Ğabal Gharbī, from which it is separated by a valley five or six kilometres in width. These two *ğabal*s, with hills from forty to fifty metres high, are composed of very friable sandstone, and though surrounded by a great deal of sand are completely barren. They are a prolongation of the terrain that begins immediately south-west of Taymā᾽, where the ground loses the volcanic aspect that it has to the south-east and turns into a desert of tumbled rocks. In some places one can liken it to a raging sea suddenly turned to stone.

Situated at the end of the valley separating the ranges of Sharqī and Gharbī are the wells of al-Ghawāṭ.[143] There are about thirty of these and their water lies from four to six metres down, immediately beneath the sand layer. The quality is good. The wells are not masonry-lined.

On leaving the wells we went about twenty kilometres more before making camp.

On the following day, 17 November, a three-hour ride brought us close to an immense rock hollowed out in the form of a pointed arch with a vault

[142] [Huber 1891: 331 gives the Arabic of this.]

[143] [cf. *ghawṭah*, a depression, a place with water and pasture (Groom 1983: 94–5). In the margin of his handwritten manuscript Huber gives the Arabic spelling Raḥiyāt for this place, but he must have changed his mind.]

about twenty-five metres high. The two interior walls were completely covered with inscriptions and sculpted animals but, alas, time had effaced them all, and I was able to make no more than a single copy. This rock bears the name al-Ruqqab.[144]

Five kilometres farther on, I halted near an even more remarkable rock. In total isolation, it is all of a piece. In form it is a wall about 300 metres long, fifty metres high and ten metres thick. The rock surfaces are so flat they might have been dressed with a chisel. The lower parts were also covered in inscriptions, but they had been washed by the rains and sand-blasted by the winds. Nonetheless I was happy to be able to find one that I could copy with certainty, and curiously [516] enough, it was a Nabataean inscription,[145] whereas the one I had copied at al-Ruqqab was Himyaritic.[146] This cyclopean wall is called Miqraṭ al-Dabūs.[147]

Two hours later I reached the *qalʿah*[148] of al-Ḥiğr on the Darb al-Ḥağğ, called Madāʾin Ṣāliḥ by the Muslim authors. This station is exactly half way between Damascus and Mecca.

This is the location of the famous stone houses hewn into the mountain, as related by numerous Arab writers. With the exception of Mr Doughty, no infidel before me has ever set eyes on them.[149] To be absolutely precise, they are not houses but rather funerary chambers cut into the sandstone with a great deal of care. Almost all of them have monumental doorways with Nabataean and Aramaic inscriptions above them.[150]

---

[144] [Al-Ruqqab: Huber 1891: 400 gives the Arabic of this. Here and in his handwritten manuscript he spells it El Rekob. The inscription is no. 88 in Appendices 1 and 2. (MCAM/WF)]

[145] [This is no. 89 in Appendices 1 and 2. Huber recopied it in 1884 (1891: 452 no. 96) and it was later published as *CIS* ii 291. (MCAM)]

[146] [That is, 'Thamudic'. (MCAM)]

[147] [For Huber's Miqrath el Deboûs; Huber gives the Arabic spelling in the margin of his handwritten manuscript. A name possibly related to *magharah*, meaning a precipice or canyon (Groom 1983: 92), and *dabbūs*, a pin.]

[148] *Qalʿah*: a fortified place, citadel. (The Editors)

[149] [Doughty visited Al-Ḥiğr/Madāʾin Ṣāliḥ in 1876–77, just three years before Huber, and made drawings of several of the façades of the tombs and squeezes of most of the tomb inscriptions (1923 i, 104–36). The latter were published in Doughty 1884. (MCAM)]

[150] [Although most of the Nabataeans in al-Ḥiğr probably *spoke* Arabic, they wrote in a dialect of Aramaic and a particular form of the Aramaic script. The inscriptions over the monumental tombs at al-Ḥiğr are all in Nabataean and date from the 1st century AD and none are in the earlier 'Imperial' or 'Official' Aramaic which had been the language of the administrations of the Neo-Babylonian (626–539 BC) and

Al-Ḥiǧr is situated in the lowest part of the valley between the mountain range known as al-ʿUwayriḍ,[151] a sandstone massif though of volcanic origin, and the mountain of ʿAǧayb,[152] where the granite reappears.

The rock outcrops of al-Ḥiǧr containing the funerary chambers are identical to those of al-Khālah, to the west of Ǧabal Ḥalwān. They are isolated outcrops shaped like beehives, in each of which a tomb has been carved. The doorways, almost always monumental in scale, are usually located several metres above ground. The interior walls of the chambers are inset with carved cavities or loculi suitable for receiving a body. Frequently too a grave has been hewn into the floor of the chamber. The funerary chambers seem never to have been provided with doors – at least the stone bears no trace of any closing apparatus.[153]

Along with al-Ǧawf in the Yemen,[154] this area is of the greatest interest in Arabia and I propose to pay it a more detailed visit on a later occasion.

[517] The inscriptions at al-Ḥiǧr are almost all Nabataean.

Other than the *qalʿah* or fort, there is no longer a single standing structure at al-Ḥiǧr. This fort is one of the caravan stations for the pilgrims travelling each year from Constantinople to Mecca. The fort's commandant is Muḥammad Ibrāhīm, an Algerian in the retinue of the Emir ʿAbd al-Qādir.[155]

Achaemenid Persian (*ca.* 539–330 BC) empires. Huber was not an epigraphist and so was not able to distinguish clearly between the two. (MCAM)]

151 [Huber writes 'Aouarah for this, but his positioning of it on the map at the end of Huber 1884b (see fold-out in this volume) makes it clear that he means Ḥarrat ʿUwayriḍ, the great massif running north–south to the west of al-ʿUlā and Madāʾin Ṣāliḥ.]

152 [Ǧabal ʿAǧayb, to the east of al-ʿUlā and Madāʾin Ṣāliḥ.]

153 [In fact, a careful study shows that this is untrue and, as might be expected, the closing of individual tombs varied considerably. The majority of monumental tombs seem to have been closed with a wooden door while any of those permitted to be buried in it were still alive, after which the doorway was finally sealed with a wall of dressed stones and mortar. For a detailed description, see Nehmé 2015 i: 80–8. (MCAM)]

154 [The Yemeni Ǧawf lies north-east of Ṣanʿāʾ, the modern capital of Yemen, and is an area of many ancient cities. In antiquity, it was first occupied by a number of small 'city-states' under strong Sabaean influence and then became the seat of the kingdom of Maʿīn. Huber had presumably heard about its archaeological and epigraphic riches through the work of his compatriot Joseph Halévy, who in 1869–70 was the first European to visit the Ǧawf. (MCAM)]

155 [ʿAbd al-Qādir (1808–83), emir of Mascara, was the military and religious leader who founded the first Algerian state by wresting large parts of it from the French – who had begun their conquest in 1830 – by both fighting and making treaties with them. He organized a well-run and well-armed polity. When, in 1840, the French

He only stays there during the Ḥaǧǧ season; the caravan, which is still at Mecca, will collect him on its return journey to Damascus. With the four irregular soldiers under his command and a mule, he is charged with drawing water from the well inside the fort and pouring it into the masonry cistern situated behind it so that the pilgrims can make convenient use of it as they pass through.

At noon on 17 November I took my departure from al-Ḥiǧr, and at four o'clock in the afternoon arrived in al-ʿUlā.[156]

From the outside, the appearance of this little town is extremely picturesque. The very narrow streets are winding and more than a little filthy, calling to mind the Jewish quarter in Damascus. The physiognomy of the people, who have very much the appearance of sons of Heber,[157] completed the illusion.

I went down to the house of Muḥammad Saʿīd ibn Saʿīd,[158] a slave of the Emir Muḥammad Ibn Rashīd, who is his governor here. As the emir had entrusted me with a letter for him, I was given the warmest of welcomes.

Al-ʿUlā, which is completely constructed of mud,[159] is divided into two more or less equal parts by an isolated rock outcrop about forty metres high, which is almost sheer on every side and surmounted by the ruins of a fort. These two halves of the town each have a shaykh or emir; the southern portion is the more considerable of the two.

---

government decided to conquer the whole of Algeria, ʿAbd al-Qādir mounted a strong resistance to the army of General Bugeaud, but by July 1846 had to flee to Morocco. However, finding himself unwelcome there, he returned to Algeria in 1847 and made a dignified surrender. He was imprisoned in France where he studied both Christianity and Freemasonry, but in 1852 he was allowed to go to Damascus, where he lived for the rest of his life with a large pension provided by the French government and a guard from the Kabyle people of Algeria. There, he wrote his famous book on syncretism, which was quickly translated into French as *Rappel à l'intelligent, avis à l'indifférent* and published in 1858. He died in 1883, the year Euting and Huber were in Arabia. (MCAM)]

156 [Huber had halted in Madāʾin Ṣāliḥ for hardly more than a couple of hours, and does not explain why he spent so little time there. Possibly he was anxious to present himself to Ibn Rashīd's governor in al-ʿUlā and receive official protection before exploring further.]

157 [Heber: in the Bible (Genesis 10–11), a great-grandson of Noah's son Shem, and the ancestor of the Israelites and Ishmaelites.]

158 [This is the same governor with whom Huber and Euting were to have dealings in March 1884 (Huber 1891: 404; Euting 1914: 220, 222 *et seq.*).]

159 [It is puzzling that Huber should say this. Much of the old town of al-ʿUlā is built of stone.]

Without being able to tell me why, the emir had already warned me in Ḥāʾil that if I persisted in my desire to go to al-ʿUlā and Khaybar, I would fall very ill. As things turned out, from the day after my arrival at al-ʿUlā I fell victim to an extraordinary malaise [518] characterized by loss of strength, listlessness, nausea, vomiting, headaches and profuse sweating. I had been poisoned by the fever-laden vapours rising from the swampy grounds in the gardens. The inhabitants, all negroid to varying degrees, do not feel the effects or, if they do, are less affected by them.[160]

The population of about 1,500 souls looked to me like a blend of negroes and Jews. Their skin colour is more or less what would result from a mixture of shades nos. 36 and 51 in the classification 'Colours of the Skin' in the *Instructions générales de la Société d'anthropologie de Paris*, 2nd edition. Shade no. 50 would be too dark, which is to say that there are no pure negroes properly so-called. But, if the colour is sometimes absent, the prognathous character of the face is a constant feature. The less prognathous individuals are also those of a lighter colour, and these form the élite of the place. These more favoured traits arise through marriage with their nomadic bedouin neighbours, the ʿAnizah tribespeople, and of course the Jews.[161]

---

160 [Anecdotal evidence such as this that black populations originating in sub-Saharan Africa appear to benefit from some hereditable immunity to malaria is plausible though not yet fully understood. According to current scientific research, the malaria inhibitor in Arabian populations is thalassaemia, whereas in Sudan and West Africa, where the agricultural slaves in Arabia are thought to have originated, the inhibitor is Dufy negativity, which is not found in Arabia. Nonetheless, malarial resistance taken together with the centuries-old slave trade of the region would explain the prevalence of people of African genetic heritage in the Ḥiǧāz oases: they were resistant to the fever and so better able to survive (Reilly 2015: 102–22; but see also Kloss 2016).]

161 This statement would require some proof that M. Huber has perhaps discovered. (The Editors). [Huber's editors are clearly seeking to dissociate themselves from this statement, even though it is not clear what Huber is driving at here. His use of the term *nègre*/'negro', to mean 'black African', is conventional for his time and need not be understood as pejorative. In general he shows an interest in the biology of race typical of 19th-century Europeans, at a time when many scientists and explorers were obsessed with comparing racial characteristics and measuring physiological differences between races. This pursuit only became dubious when objective observation evolved into efforts to draw up league tables of supposed biological superiority, with Europeans of course at the top. Huber seems to have been free of such value-ridden racism, but his implied view that Jews exhibited distinct racial characteristics is odd to modern eyes, given that Jews around the world are as widely varied as the human race at large. He does not explain what he means by distinctly Jewish racial traits.]

Al-ʿUlā has always had to suffer the depredations of the Arab nomads, whether ʿAnizah or Balī, against which the Ottoman government, to which it used to pay tax, has given them no protection whatever. Since Ibn Rashīd has absorbed the little town into his territory, it no longer has anything to fear from the ʿAnizah. Nor do the Balī dare take any open action against it for fear of reprisals or an invasion of their territory by the Shammar emir. But they continually scour the countryside between Taymāʾ and al-ʿUlā, especially the surroundings of the latter town, pillaging every lone victim they come across. So everybody goes armed all the time, even just to go to the gardens.

Al-ʿUlā enjoys an extraordinarily thriving situation. Its palms are irrigated by six springs, two of them flowing with great force, producing a total volume of water that [519] is surplus to requirements. I was assured that one or even several years of drought had had no impact on the output of these springs. Also, the people here cultivate not just date palms but all the wheat, barley and *houra'*[162] that they need. Their gardens also contain a multitude of peach, orange, lemon, fig and pomegranate trees and vines, not to mention melons, watermelons and tobacco too.

The availability of these springs has freed the people of so irksome a task as the drawing up of water, along with the maintenance of the beasts of burden necessary for lifting it.

At al-ʿUlā the value of a palm tree varies from eight to twenty riyals according to circumstance. As each palm produces an average annual revenue of four riyals, there are some wealthy people there. Thus the shaykh of the northern quarter, ʿAmr ibn ʿAbd al-Ghānī ibn Budayr, possesses four hundred palms.

I have already mentioned the Balī, those turbulent neighbours of al-ʿUlā. Their territory, which begins at the same latitude as the ʿUwayriḍ[163] massif, stretches all the way north to the Sinai peninsula, between the Red Sea to the west and the Sharārāt Arabs to the east. They were once wealthy and powerful but, following a raid on them in 1853 by the Ǧāzī[164] Arabs, they lost all their

---

[162] [This is almost certainly a misprint for *dhoura'*, i.e. *dhura* (sorghum or millet), a staple crop in the Hiǧāz and south-west Arabia. Doughty (1936 i: 337; ii: 119) noted the cultivation of this crop at Taymāʾ and Khaybar, where Huber himself mentions it (see note 202 below).]

[163] [ʿUwayriḍ: see note 151 above.]

[164] [By 'Gazy' Arabs, Huber must be referring to the Ḥuwayṭāt, the dominant tribe of the far northern Ḥiǧāz and southern Jordan, whose chiefs were known by the patronymic Ibn Ǧāzī (Musil 1926: 7).]

horses. Since then they have not been able to mount military campaigns and have fallen on very hard times. As they just inhabit mountainous areas, they possess only the few camels necessary to transport their tents. All their wealth consists of goats, the meat of which they dislike because of its unpleasant smell. All their grazing grounds are located in the mountains. They do have plenty of water.

The names of their tribes are as follows:[165]

> Al-Muwāhīb – al-Fuwāḍlah – al-Harūfā – al-Saḥamah – al-Fray'āt – al-Ḥamrān – al-Ramūṭ – [520] al-Hamūr – al-Ma'āqlah – al-Waḥshah – al-Wābṣah – al-Zabālah – al-'Arādāt

The patronymic of their shaykh is Ibn Rifādah.[166]

I was only able to obtain very contradictory information about the strength of the Balī, as nobody ever penetrates into their mountain fastnesses. But I believe the most accurate estimate to be that they number between 400 and 600 tents.

The mountains of the Balī contain numerous rainpools or reservoirs of water and, despite being unable to obtain any firm information in this regard, I nevertheless believe that they must also harbour a multitude of inscriptions and also perhaps even the remains of monuments contemporary with those of al-Ḥiğr and al-'Ulā, and produced by the same civilization. An expedition there would surely uncover materials of great interest.

It was not until ten days after my arrival that I was able to visit the ruins of ancient al-'Ulā,[167] and on this occasion I experienced another demonstration of the insecurity of the country. Although the two settlements are separated by just a couple of kilometres, Muḥammad Sa'īd only let me go there escorted by nine locals, all armed with guns, with himself as one of the party.

---

165 [In the list that follows, Huber (1891: 485) gives the Arabic for al-Muwāhīb, al-Saḥamah, al-Fray'āt and al-Fuwāḍlah. Musil (1926: 211) also lists all of these tribes in transliterated form with the exception of al-Fray'āt, al-Ḥamrān, and al-Hamūr. For the latter two, I have followed Huber 2003: 104.]

166 [The Ibn Rifadah shaykhs were of al-Ma'āqlah and were based at al-Wağh on the Red Sea coast.]

167 [These ruins are today known as al-Khuraybah, 'the little ruins', and are the remains of the ancient city of Dadan.]

These ruins today go by the name of Nâqat Ṣāliḥ or 'Ṣāliḥ's Camel',[168] or again of Ḥalwiyyat al-ʿAliyyah,[169] both of them modern names. They are situated on a knoll to the north of al-ʿUlā, and are no more than a shapeless jumble of dressed masonry and sculptures. Not a single wall remains standing, but one can still discern the outlines of some buildings, the foundations of which are level with the ground. There are also remains of columns and decorative bricks.

The centre of this ruin field is dominated by a small square, in the centre of which stands a huge circular tank carved out of a single block of sandstone, two and a half metres tall and two metres in diameter. Apart from two cracks, this enormous basin is in a very good state of preservation. Its internal and external surfaces are covered in Himyaritic and Arabic characters that are almost completely erased. [521] It is difficult today to fathom the purpose of this monument.

Colossal sheer cliffs rear up to more than 200 metres in height on the eastern side of the al-ʿUlā valley. At their base have been dug about 200 funerary chambers, identical to those at al-Ḥiğr except for the lack of monumental doorways. Often instead of a chamber their makers were content just to excavate an opening into which they could insert a body. These openings are thus of the same form as the compartments for the dead to be found in the mortuary towers of Palmyra.

Several of these chambers are unfinished, and the site as a whole shows signs of the work having been suddenly interrupted. There are also some inscriptions carved above ground level, though it is impossible to deduce how the artist was able to reach their position, whether from above or below.

[168] [The *Qur'ān* (Sūrat al-Naml, verses 73–77) tells how the Nāqah or 'She-camel of Allāh' was brought forth by divine intervention as a means of sustenance for the Thamūd and as a test of their allegiance to the One God. Those cleaving to their old gods hamstrung the camel and divine retribution followed in the form of the destruction of the 'Cities of Ṣāliḥ', i.e. Madā'in Ṣāliḥ. In Muslim tradition more generally, for example as recorded in al-Ṭabarī (Brinner 1987: 41–4), the She-camel emerged miraculously from the rock and gave birth to a calf. Ṣāliḥ told the Thamūd that the She-camel and the people were to drink from their water source on alternate days. On days when they were not allowed to drink water, the She-camel provided the people with milk.]

[169] [Euting (1914: 239–40) records the local name Ḥalāwiyyat al-Nebī Ṣāliḥ (حلاوية النبي صالح), which denotes the circular stone tank in the centre of the site, described in the next paragraph, rather than the site itself.]

These mortuary chambers are known as al-Khuraybah[170] and also as Dār Thamūd.[171] I collected thirty-three inscriptions there.[172]

Al-ʿUlā has a hot climate, and it seems that it never has a cold winter, for that of 1879–80 did not even make itself felt here. Having recorded the temperature of the springs on four different occasions and at different times of day, I found a variation of only a few tenths of a degree between them, and all the figures taken together gave me an average of 28.9°, which indeed indicates a hot climate. The lowest temperature observed during my stay at al-ʿUlā was the minimum on 28 November, which I recorded as 13.1°.

I left al-ʿUlā on 29 November after a twelve-day stay. Ibn Saʿīd escorted me with seventeen armed men for a distance of five miles. The journey from al-ʿUlā to Khaybar is even more dangerous than that from Taymāʾ; one is conscious of the proximity of Turkish-controlled territory.

[522] A three-hour ride brought us to a little ruined town, or rather one where there were no longer even any ruins, because it had probably been built of mud. Nonetheless there still existed two sections of wall built of baked brick. The ground was covered with fragments of brick, glazed pottery and coloured glass. The name of this town has not been preserved. At al-ʿUlā, where the people are very devout, they know it as Dār al-Naṣāra.[173] The bedouin name for it, together with the territory enclosed between the two mountains of ʿAǧayb and Mughayrāʾ, is Mabī.[174]

On top of a small hill are the remains of a tower built of stone and mud where I had been told there was an inscription, but I was unable to find it.

We halted for an hour at Mabī and then continued our route south-eastwards. At three o'clock in the afternoon we crossed the Darb al-Ḥaǧǧ, leaving it on our right, and at five o'clock we were making camp behind the last spurs of Ǧabal Mughayrāʾ [i.e Muraykhah], a granite mountain like Ǧabal ʿAǧayb which we had already passed, as the granite terrain had already become predominant once more two kilometres south of al-ʿUlā. With it we

[170] In French, 'the little ruin'. (The Editors.) [The name al-Khuraybah properly denotes the ruin field as a whole, not just the tombs in the cliff; see note 167 above.]

[171] [The dwelling-place of (the tribe of) Thamūd. (MCAM)]

[172] [These are nos. 91–123 in Appendices 1 and 2 (MCAM)]

[173] Dār al-Naṣāra: 'abode of Christians'. (The Editors.)

[174] [From this it is clear that Huber was at the site known today as Mabiyāt, 20 km south of al-ʿUlā, and dating to *ca.* AD 650–1230. There is a village nearby called Mughayrāʾ, which Huber, rendering it as Mereîrah, may have understood as the name of the neighbouring Ǧabal Muraykhah.]

were entering the territory of the ʿAnizah Arabs, who are independent but allied with the Shammar.

It is the great ʿAnizah branch of Awlād Sulaymān who inhabit this region. Their tents are scattered from Ǧabal Mughayrāʾ [i.e. Muraykhah] all the way west to the southern environs of Yanbuʿ.

Its principal tribes are as follows:[175]

> Al-Ǧaʿāfrah – Āl Fuẓayl – al-Murtʿad – Āl ʿAwāǧī – al-Bikār – al-Ghaẓawrah – Āl Murayḥim – al-Nihāt – al-Maṭradah – al-Suhūl – al-Khamashah – al-Saʿīd – al-Nuwāmasah – al-Shamlān

The Awlād Sulaymān are more numerous than the Banī [523] Wahhāb, who also are of ʿAnizah, as we saw above. They are also poorer, but to compensate they possess the inestimable benefit of freedom, which is nowhere more vital than in semi-civilized societies. They are totally independent both of the Turkish government, with which they are at enmity, and of the Shammar emir, with whom they are friends.

They possess some good grazing lands in their mountains, better than those of the Balī, and like the latter they have plenty of water. They also possess relatively more firearms than the Balī.

All the very mountainous country between al-ʿUlā and Khaybar bears the name al-Ḥiǧr. It is a granite desert of terrifying barrenness: nothing but *baṭḥāʾ* and still more *baṭḥāʾ*, and scarcely a blade of vegetation.[176]

The day after our departure from al-ʿUlā we made fifteen miles through this desert. That morning, at a distance of eight miles, we had passed Ǧabal Nakhr, which is twelve miles long from east to west. In the evening we reached the fort of Zumurrud,[177] a station on the Darb al-Ḥaǧǧ, near which we spent the night.

---

[175] [The list of fourteen tribes that follows has been checked and corrected against the list of Awlād Sulaymān tribes given by Musil and collected by him in 1915 (1928a: 95–6), in which he gives properly transliterated versions of nine of those mentioned by Huber. It seems that Huber was in error in listing the al-Ghaẓawrah as El Fadhâouarah, and al-Khamashah as El Rhemešah; alternatively, the erroneous first letters of each of these may have been misprints. The remaining five are conjectural: al-Murtʿad (for Huber's El Mert'ad); al-Bikār (for El Bekâr); al-Nihāt (for El Nehât); al-Maṭradah (for El Methredah, see Oppenheim ii: 349); al-Nuwāmasah (for El Noumesah, see Oppenheim ii: 349). Huber 2003: 106 gives an Arabic version of this list.]

[176] [On *baṭḥāʾ*, see Translation Part I, note 155.]

[177] [Qalʿat Zumurrud: at 26° 10' N 038° 25' E (GeoNames).]

On 1 December we managed only fourteen miles going along parallel with the Darb al-Ḥaǧǧ, and made camp that evening at Qalʿat al-Ṣawrah,[178] another station on the pilgrim road, at the foot of the mountain of Sinn.[179]

Behind the fort is one of the most beautiful wells that I have ever seen in Arabia.[180] Circular in shape, it is about fifteen metres in diameter and thirty or so metres deep. It is completely lined with dressed masonry.

The distance as the crow flies between this fort and Zumurrud is short on the map; it is the terrain separating them that is very rugged and difficult.

On the day following we made just fifteen miles to the east-south-east, and that evening we stopped with Khālid tribespeople of the Banī Wahhāb, who were encamped there with [524] about sixty tents. These were the first nomads that we had encountered since leaving al-ʿUlā. The country we had traversed had been even more mountainous than that of the day before.

The Khālid encampment was at the foot of Ǧabal ʿAnāmah,[181] a granite massif extending for about forty kilometres north-north-east to south-south-west.

On 3 December we managed only twelve miles due to the poor progress of my guide Marzī's camel.

Having rounded Ǧabal ʿAnāmah in the morning by a short but very narrow and rugged valley, we suddenly found ourselves before a vast and deeply gullied plain, from which rose a disorderly assortment of blackish, reddish and greenish granite peaks. I took the bearings of the mountains of al-Dahām and those of Khaybar in the distance in front of us; the oasis of Khaybar is situated between them. The entire horizon from east to west was filled by a plateau outlined with extraordinary sharpness and seeming to sparkle in the sun. This was the Ḥarrah,[182] an immense lava field that stretches almost all the way to al-Madīnah.

---

178 [Qalʿat al-Ṣawrah, also known as al-Biʾr al-Ǧadīd, at 26° 01' 14" N 038° 34' 59" E (GeoNames). This is where Huber turned off the Ḥaǧǧ route to head in a more easterly direction towards the *ḥarrah*.]

179 [Ǧabal Sinn, at 26° 00' N 038° 37' E (GeoNames).]

180 [Known as al-Biʾr al-Ǧadīd, 'the new well' (see map entitled *Arabian Peninsula* (1973). Scale 1:2,000,000).]

181 [Ǧabal ʿAnāmah: Huber spells this Ânemâř, but the massif of ʿAnāmah must be meant, at 26° 00' N 038° 48' E (GeoNames). It is marked east of al-Ṣawrah on the 1:1,000,000 map entitled *Medina* (1960). It extends NNW–SSE rather than, as Huber states, NNE–SSW. Huber would have followed its western side before rounding its southern end and heading east into the *ḥarrah*.]

182 [Ḥarrah: i.e. Ḥarrat Khaybar, the basalt wilderness extending 200 km from the north-west to al-Ḥanākiyyah in the south-east, and merging with Ḥarrat Hutaym to the east.]

Before we left the last rocks of Ǧabal ʿAnāmah behind us, which still afforded us some cover, and ventured forth over this bare open plain where brigands would have no trouble spotting us, Marzī, who was very devout, performed a short prayer. He invited me to do the same, so that Allāh would protect us and fend off all danger from our path. We made camp that evening in a ravine that provided us with excellent shelter.

The next day a ride of two miles east, followed by twelve miles south by 65° east, brought us to Khaybar.[183]

We had had to abandon Marzī's camel that morning because it was unable to go any farther over this rough terrain, even though we were only going slowly. So my mount had to take on a double load and my poor guide had to go on foot.

At the precise point where our route turned south by 65° east, the terrain was strewn with black basalt boulders, and the Ḥarrah began.

[525] After the first five kilometres over the Ḥarrah, we came across a ravine which according to Marzī would be a little tributary of Wādī al-Ṭibiq. At this point the ravine becomes a true paradise, in sharp contrast to the surrounding terrain. It is full of wild palms and very vigorous vegetation. Birds were twittering and a gentle breeze was blowing, setting up a delightful rustling in the long fronds of the palms. Water is no more than a metre down. This garden of delights amidst the horrors of the Ḥarrah goes by the name of Khaḍrān.

Since 1874, Khaybar has belonged to the Turks, who took it from Ibn Rashīd.[184] They have a *mudīr* stationed there with twelve regular soldiers. This *mudīr*, ʿAbd Allāh al-Ṣirāwān by name, is the very same man who maltreated Mr Doughty and imprisoned him for two and a half months.[185]

[183] [On 4 December 1880, according to Huber's 65-page handwritten report dated 27 March 1882. (French national archives, Pierrefitte-sur-Seine, Dossier F/17/2976/1:1, entitled 'Mission au Thibet et dans l'Asie centrale', 1878–82, item 79, p. 51.)]

[184] [Doughty records that when he arrived in November 1877 the Ottomans had been in charge at Khaybar 'for five years', which would put their takeover from Ibn Rashīd in 1872 rather than 1874 (Doughty 1936 ii: 140–1). Khaybar had been taken over by Ḥāʾil during the reign of Ṭalāl ibn ʿAbd Allāh al-Rashīd (r. 1847–68) (Winder 1965: 156, 240). Guarmani was in Khaybar from 29 February to March 1864 while it was under the rule of Ḥāʾil (Guarmani 1938: 26–8, 82–3). Huber later offered to intercede with the French government to negotiate with the Ottomans to have it returned to Ibn Rashīd's control (see Appendix 5, Letter no. 2 dated *ca.* 10 April 1883, from Huber to the Emir Muḥammad Ibn Rashīd).]

[185] [Doughty spent three and half months in Khaybar, from the end of November 1877 to mid-March 1878, and devotes a large part of the second volume of *Arabia Deserta* to it (Doughty 1936 ii: 97–236). He was detained under house arrest in the oasis

Thanks to the imperial *firmān* that I had taken care to provide myself with, he accorded me a very handsome welcome and I stayed for twelve days as his guest.

The oasis of Khaybar, with its springs and abundant water, must certainly have been a centre of settlement for as long as Arabia has been peopled. The earliest documentary evidence shows us that it was inhabited by Israelites. Whether they arrived following their last Babylonian captivity (537 BC),[186] or the one that brought Sennacherib's campaign down upon them (700 BC), or some other still earlier cataclysm of the kind so frequent in Judea, they must have found Khaybar already inhabited by people whom they would have been forced to expel and dispossess. Who were these indigenous people? We still do not know, but it is likely they were Yemenites.[187]

Khaybar played a leading role at the dawn of Islam, and the destiny of the future religion depended [526] for a brief historical moment on its struggle with this oasis. But ʿAlī, who had been sent against it by the Prophet, reduced it and killed all its inhabitants, according to the Arab authors.[188]

---

rather than 'imprisoned' as Huber says, while the Ottoman authorities in al-Madīnah decided what was to be done with him; eventually he was sent back to Ḥāʾil, from which he had only just been expelled (Doughty 1936 ii: 146, 180–1). Philby (1957: 32–47) gives a detailed account of Khaybar in 1950.]

186 If it was indeed Israelites returned from their last captivity in Babylonia who were settled in Khaybar, Aramaic inscriptions must certainly be found there. It is the case that on their return from captivity, the Jews no longer understood ancient Hebrew, and Aramaic had become their normal usage; they had even adopted its alphabet. (CH) [It is not correct to say that they had all forgotten Hebrew, but Aramaic seems to have become the normal language of conversation for a great many of them. It is also true that they started to write Hebrew in the Aramaic alphabet, and indeed what is nowadays thought of as the 'Hebrew square script' is actually a descendant of the Aramaic script which the Jews learnt in Babylon. (MCAM)]

187 [We have no evidence of how or when the Jews came to Khaybar or whether they drove out those they found there or integrated with them, though the latter is the more likely if they were refugees from a 'cataclysm'. There seems no reason to suppose that the indigenous population was from what is now Yemen. However, Khaybar (in the Babylonian form *Ḫibrā*) is mentioned as one of the western Arabian oases on the south-to-north trade route which the last king of Babylon, Nabonidus (r. 556–539 BC) conquered before settling in Taymāʾ for ten years of his 17-year reign (Beaulieu 1989: 149–85). It is possible that some Jews came with him and stayed on after he left. However, until systematic surveys and excavations take place in Khaybar we shall have no firm evidence for its pre-Islamic history. See also Translation Part III note 1. (MCAM)]

188 [ʿAlī ibn Abī Ṭālib, the Prophet Muḥammad's cousin and son-in-law and celebrated warrior, is said to have played a decisive part in the prolonged siege of Khaybar in

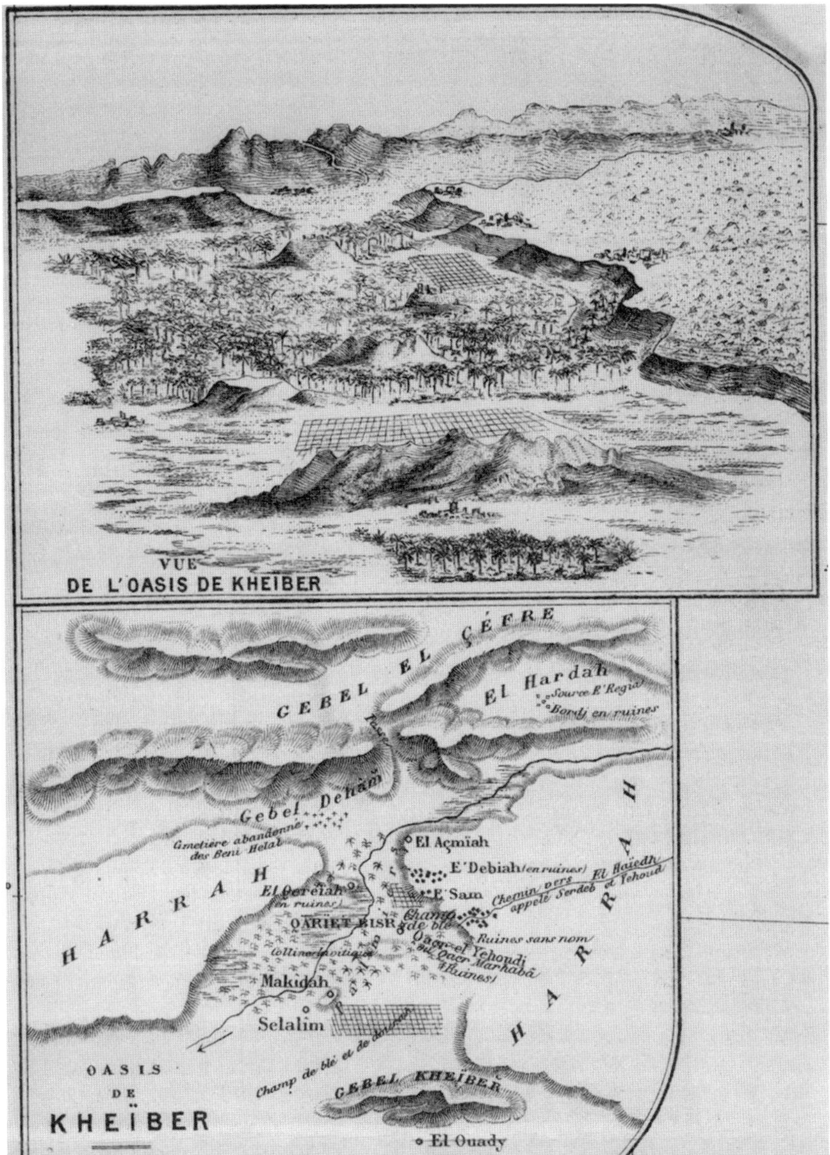

The two bird's-eye views of Khaybar from Huber's fold-out map attached to Huber 1884b. These were drawn by Julius Euting to Huber's instructions (see Appendix 10, Letter no. 5 dated 2 November 1885 from Euting to Philippe Berger).

The same authors report that there were once seven villages in the oasis. Today there are just three inhabited ones, and I was hard put to discover any trace of the others.

The centre of Khaybar is the completely isolated basalt outcrop called Marḥabā, which was once crowned by the castle of the same name. The name Marḥabā is the sole ancient name from this oasis that the pre-Islamic authors have passed down to us. Today, it is commonly known as Qaṣr al-Yahūdī, 'the Jew's castle'. The outcrop is an elliptical massif aligned north-north-west–south-south-east. Its table-top summit measures 200 metres long by ten to fifteen metres wide,[189] and is on the same level as the Ḥarrah.

Along the base of this rock and a little way up it, on its southern side, stretches the main village of Khaybar, Qaryat Bishr. The palm plantations begin immediately and completely surround Marḥabā and the village. The palms of Qaryat Bishr are watered by springs that rise in the village itself, and by others outside it. Those rising in the village are six in number, and named as follows:

Ṣafṣāfah – Ibrāhīm – ʿAlī[190] – al-Rayyā – al-Shalālah –
al-Buwayrah

The last has the coolest water of all the springs in Khaybar. The spring of ʿAlī is the largest.

Here finally are the average temperatures taken at these springs during my stay in Khaybar:

AD 628 and to have killed the Jewish leader Marḥab ibn Abī Zaynab, but there is no evidence that he had all the inhabitants killed. After their defeat, the Jews are recorded as having reached an agreement with the Muslims allowing them to continue to tend their plantations on condition that they gave half the produce to the victors. They were expelled soon after from Arabia by the Caliph ʿUmar ibn al-Khaṭṭāb (r. AD 634–44), but a Jewish community in Khaybar is recorded by Benjamin of Tudela in the 12th century AD. There were still many Jews there in AD 1503, when Ludovico di Varthema visited it, but Burckhardt and Burton in the 19th century reported that they were no longer there. A folk memory of them survived and Doughty records some of the various fables that had accumulated around them. (Carruthers's note 1 in Guarmani 1938: 83; Doughty 1936 i: 170, 362, 435, 550, 641; ii: 146).]

[189] [*Sic*. Huber's measurements of the hilltop, which is entirely covered by Ḥuṣn Marḥab, as 200 m long by 10–15 m wide are inaccurate. It is in fact about 100 m long by 20 m wide (see Gilmore et al. 1982: 20–1; plates 12A and 20A. Doughty (1936 ii: 122), also inaccurately, tells us that it was 200 paces long by 90 paces wide.]

[190] [Named thus as it was traditionally held that on this spot ʿAlī killed Marḥab, according to Philby (1957: 35–6).]

Ṣafṣāfah	29.9°
Ibrāhīm	31.0°
ʿAlī	29.1°
al-Rayyā	31.8°
al-Shalālah	29.4°
al-Buwayrah	26.6°

[527]

The second village is called Umm Kīdah[191] and is situated about three kilometres south-south-west of Marḥabā. Instead of being built like Qaryat Bishr in the bottom of the oasis where the palms are, Umm Kīdah is sited up on the *ḥarrah*.

This village contains the following five springs:

Al-Baḥr – al-Buraykah – al-Sulaymah – Salālīm – Umm al-Misk

The third village, al-ʿAṣmiyyah,[192] situated about two miles north of Marḥabā, is likewise built up on the *ḥarrah*. Al-ʿAṣmiyyah possesses four springs, to wit:

Al-Ḥāmiyyah or al-Ḥāmī[193] – al-Ǧumāmah – ʿAlī – Ṣanbūrah

The spring of al-Ḥāmiyyah is the largest.

The population of Khaybar, which can count 300 rifles, is about 1,200 souls distributed as follows:

Qaryat Bishr possesses	120 houses
Umm Kīdah	100 houses
al-ʿAṣmiyyah	20 houses

There is just a single school at Khaybar, located in Qaryat Bishr, but it is very little attended and indeed hardly ever open. It is run by the religious leader, who in Khaybar is not called the *khaṭīb* as in the Ǧabal, but the *raʾīs al-masǧid*.[194]

There are five mosques, of which two are in Qaryat Bishr, two at Umm Kīdah, and one at al-ʿAṣmiyyah.

---

191 [Huber writes Makîdah but I have followed Doughty (1936 ii: 109) and Philby (1957: 36) in calling it Umm Kīdah.]

192 [Al-ʿAṣmiyyah: spelt thus after Doughty 1936 ii, index. Also according to Doughty (1936 ii: 116–18, 587) known as Qaryat al-Faqīr.]

193 [Al-Ḥāmiyyah or al-Ḥāmī: spelt thus following Huber 2003: 110.]

194 [*Raʾīs al-masǧid*: i.e. head of the mosque.]

Yet another significant palm plantation is situated eight kilometres to the south of Marḥabā, beyond Ǧabal Khaybar. Its twenty or so inhabitants are accommodated in a single fort. This place is known as al-Wādī.[195]

Thirty kilometres farther south there are [528] a large number of copious springs that have created a small lake called Quṣaybah.[196] The water from this lake flows along a natural channel six to seven kilometres in length, into a basin to the north where it forms another lake, called Thamad.[197] Between the two lakes, two great construction works rise on the sides of the channel, two kilometres apart. The southernmost one is called Qaṣr al-ʿAdam, and the one to the north, Qaṣr al-Bint.[198]

To the north of the Thamad lake, the water continues to flow across the Ḥarrah, but in a north-westerly direction, to join the Wadi al-Ṭibiq after it has irrigated the palms of two uninhabited places, Hadanah and Ǧarāyah.[199]

---

[195] [This is Wādī al-Gharas, described in Philby 1957: 20–5, 29.]

[196] [Quṣaybah would seem to be the diminutive of *qaṣābah*, 'a dam constructed at a place eroded by water' (Groom 1983: 227). It is the location of the great ancient dam on Wādī al-Gharas, Sadd al-Quṣaybah, also known as Sadd al-Bint or Qaṣr al-Bint. See note 198 below. (MCAM/WF)]

[197] Tsemed, or Themed, is not a proper name, but rather the Arabic word for a sump or a waterhole more or less flush with the ground surface; it is generally dug in the bed of a valley. (The Editors.) [See also Groom 1983: 290, where *thamad* is defined as a hollow where water collects.]

[198] [These two ancient dams are marked as Huber describes them, as Qaṣr al-ʿAdm and Qaṣr al-Bint between the 'lakes' of Quṣaybah and Thamad, on the 1:1,000,000 map entitled *Medina* (1960), but this map merely reproduces Huber's own map. The USGS 1:500,000 map of 1959 entitled *Geographic Map of the Northeastern Hijaz Quadrangle* gives more accurate locations. The great dam now known as Sadd al-Bint, in Wādī Thamad some 30 km south of Khaybar, which in its original state was some 135 m long by 20 m high before it was breached by floodwaters, is probably of pre-Islamic origin like other dams in the Khaybar area. There are at least five other such *sayl* or flood-control dams in the vicinity, including Sadd Ḥaṣīd (located in Shaʿīb Ḥaṣīd, which joins Wādī al-Gharas from the east a few km north of Quṣaybah), Sadd Mashqūq (just east of Khaybar itself) and Sadd Zaydiyyah (Twitchell 1953: 40–1; Philby 1957: 26–31, 37, 39; Gilmore et al. 1982: 20). Kay (1978: 72) states that Sadd Quṣaybah, also known as Qaṣr al-Bint, 'in Wādī al-Silsilah', is 'the most impressive of all the Hejaz dams', and also that Sadd Quṣaybah and Sadd Ḥaṣīd are the two major dams of the Khaybar region. (MCAM/WF)]

[199] [Wadi al-Ṭibiq: this must be the wadi named Ṭubǧah marked as flowing southwards into the Wadi al-Ḥamḍ just south of Hadiyyah at 25° 35' N 038° 40' E, on the USGS 1:500,000 map of 1959 entitled *Geographic Map of the Northwestern Hijaz Quadrangle*. It drains the Ḥarrah from NNE to SSW, from the heights west of Khaybar. From Huber's description it is probable that he applied the name 'Wadi al-Ṭibiq' to the whole Wadi Ṭubǧah–Wadi Ghamrah system. Wadi Ghamrah is marked

The palms of Ğarāyah belong to the Khālid section of the Wuld ʿAlī.

The watercourse from the lake of Quṣaybah as far as Ğarāyah has a perennial flow. There are fish, frogs and shells[200] in it, just as one finds in the channels of Khaybar oasis.

From the Thamad lake to where it debouches into the Wadi al-Ṭibiq, this watercourse is known as the Wadi Thamad. At Khaybar I was assured that before joining the Wadi al-Ṭibiq, the Thamad was joined by the Wadi Saghīr. Later I was told a different story by some ʿAnizah Arabs, who said that the Saghīr, originating outside the Ḥarrah immediately to the south of Quṣaybah, joined Wadi Ṭibiq directly at a point about fifteen kilometres farther east than the Thamad. I have adopted this latter version as I have reason to believe that it is more accurate than the former.

Wadi Saghīr contains a large number of palms belonging to the ʿAnizah tribe of Shamlān.

[529] There are a multitude of palms between Quṣaybah and Thamad but, as a result of a curse laid upon them by the Prophet Muḥammad, they have gone wild. However, not all the palms can have fallen under the curse because some of them produce good dates.

The ancient saying, 'Carrying dates to Khaybar', the equivalent of our 'Taking water to the sea', still holds good. The palms of Khaybar are almost beyond number, and it is easy to understand why they are so widely propagated, or are allowed to propagate themselves, because they need no care and the water is so superabundant. But, as often happens when nature vouchsafes such largesse, the Khaybar people abuse it. Having very little to do, they prefer to do nothing at all, and through their negligence their palms have fallen into such decay that they only produce what are probably the smallest and poorest-quality dates in the whole of Arabia.[201]

---

as running SSW–NNE to the north of Khaybar on the USGS 1:500,000 map of 1959 entitled *Geographic Map of the Northeastern Hijaz Quadrangle*, draining the Ḥarrah towards the north. Hadanah and Ğarāyah: I have been unable to find these two places, and have adopted the spelling given in Huber 2003: 110. They are not marked on the USGS 1:500,000 map of 1959.]

200 These shells are of the genus Melania. (CH) [Probably *Melanoides tuberculata*, a species of freshwater snail.]

201 [For a very useful account of the population and agriculture of Khaybar, including the impact of malaria, see Reilly 2015: 82–101, though there is no mention of the historic dams of the area.]

The palms of Khaybar belong to the Fuqarāʾ Arabs, one of the two branches of the Banī Wahhāb, whose range covers the region between Khaybar and Taymāʾ. Their trees are cultivated by the people of Khaybar on a share-cropping basis, in other words for a half of the harvest. When the time approaches, all the Fuqarāʾ turn up and take up position around the oasis to check the harvest and take delivery of their due.

As with all palm cultivation, there is in Khaybar too a constant cycle of a good harvest being followed by a poor one, then a good one, and so on. 1880, when I was passing through, was a year of plenty.

A fact that conveys an idea of the inferiority of their produce is that the value of a palm tree at Khaybar is only one to one and a half *riyāl*s. It will be recalled that the value at Ḥāʾil is ten *riyāl*s, while at Taymāʾ and al-ʿUlā it can even reach as much as 20 *riyāl*s.

In addition, a little wheat, *dhura*,[202] and a very small amount [530] of barley are grown. But nobody grows vines, peaches, figs or pomegranates.

In terms of physical appearance, the people of Khaybar resemble those of al-ʿUlāʾ but are of a much darker hue.[203] They are much less religious too, and are also reputed to be exponents of the heinous practices of witchcraft and sorcery. They concoct potions from corpses or body parts that they go to disinter by night in the cemetery. To all these alluring characteristics they add that of being dextrous thieves, with the people of al-ʿAṣmiyyah taking top prize in that category. They are also mean, spiteful and dirty; in short, there is very little to recommend them.

About four miles north of Marḥabā, in the mountain of al-Dahām, there is a series of valleys together measuring eight to ten miles in length from east to west, by two miles wide. Five ruined towers (*burūǧ*) can be seen there. The whole area is called al-Ḥarḍah.[204] There is also a spring there called ʿAyn Raǧīʿa, and a hundred or so wells.

---

[202] [Called 'dourra' here by Huber, and elsewhere *dhoura*'. See note 162 above.]

[203] [In his 65-page handwritten report dated 27 March 1882, Huber says that all the inhabitants of Khaybar were black and that the white people there would have been killed by fever. 'In fact,' he says, 'during the eleven days of my stay there I rarely had a day without illness', an unhealthiness he ascribes to the stagnant water lying everywhere. (French national archives, Pierrefitte-sur-Seine, Dossier F/17/2976/1:1, entitled 'Mission au Thibet et dans l'Asie centrale', 1878–82, item 79, pp. 51–2.)]

[204] [Al-Ḥarḍah: I have been unable to find this place on a map, and have adopted the spelling given by Huber in Arabic in the margin of his handwritten manuscript. It is not marked on the USGS 1:500,000 map of 1959 entitled *Geographic Map of the Northeastern Hijaz Quadrangle*.]

Al-Ḥarḍah was once a settled place, but nowadays the people of Khaybar go there from time to time, though not every year, to sow wheat, which grows very well there.

I found no more than eight inscriptions at Khaybar that I could be sure of reading clearly.[205] Some rock faces, often hundreds of metres long, were covered in them, but all had been washed away by the rains or crumbled under the heat of the sun, and no longer present any characters capable of being identified with certainty. In an old cemetery to the north-west of Marḥabā I also found a Kufic inscription.[206]

[To be continued]

205 [These are nos. 124–131 in Appendices 1 and 2. (MCAM)]
206 [Huber does not seem to have published this. (MCAM)]

PART III

A JOURNEY IN CENTRAL ARABIA: AL-ḤAMĀD, SHAMMAR, AL-QAṢĪM AND AL-ḤIĞĀZ (concluded)

Bulletin de la Société de Géographie 7th series, no. 6, 1885, 1st trimester, pp. 92–148

By Charles Huber

Commissioned by the Minister of Public Education 1878–1882

I LEFT KHAYBAR on 15 December [1880]. My plan was to ride across the whole breadth of the Ḥarrah as far as al-Ḥā'iṭ.[1] The territory along this route belongs to the Hutaym Arabs, from whom I had to procure a guide. But Marzī, who was accompanying me from al-ʿUlā, continued in my service even so, and would only have to leave me when we reached Ḥā'il.

It is inadvisable to travel alone with a Hutaymī if one wishes to command respect, and in my opinion it was a mistake for Doughty to go to Ḥā'il with two Hutaymi guides, a *faux pas* which, as it turned out, triggered his immediate expulsion.[2]

---

[1] [The name al-Ḥā'iṭ (alternatively al-Ḥāyiṭ) is related to *ḥawṭah* and means a walled plantation (Groom 1983: 100, 109). Like Khaybar (Babylonian *Ḫibrā*), al-Ḥā'iṭ, also known as Fadak (Babylonian *Padakku*), was one of the oases conquered by Nabonidus (r. 556–539 BC), the last king of Babylon, on his campaign in western Arabia (see Translation Part II n. 187, and note 23 below). This was confirmed recently by the discovery at al-Ḥa'iṭ of a large relief showing an image of Nabonidus with a much-damaged cuneiform inscription, on which see Hausleiter and Schaudig 2016. (MCAM/WF)]

[2] [On the necessity of travelling in style in Arabia, and with powerful protection, see Philby 1928: 293.]

The Shammar regard themselves as the noblest of the Arabs, and so they are. To their way of thinking, the tribespeople next in rank are the ʿAnizah, who are accorded this status not because of their nobility or the purity of their blood, but rather because of their numbers and power. After them come the Sharārāt, and it is only at the very bottom, as pariah tribes, that the Ṣulubah and Hutaym find themselves.[3] The principal Hutaym tribes are as follows:[4]

> [93] Ibn Samrah – Ibn Bālarak [or possibly Barrāk] –
> al-Muhaymizāt – al-Farādasah – al-ʿAwāmarah – al-Maḍābarah

The Ibn Samrah [tribe] are generally to be found around Khaybar.

The Muhaymizāt encamp around al-Madīnah and are at war with the Shammar.

The Maḍābarah range over al-Qaṣīm and pay tribute to the Emir Ḥasan [of Buraydah].

The Ibn Samrah count among their number eight tribes that are dubbed by the Turkish government 'Birindği', that is to say, the paramount ones. These same tribes refer to themselves by the name al-Dhība.[5]

My guide across the Ḥarrah was Ibn Samrah's own son, a big, handsome lad of about twenty-eight, very helpful and obliging. He bore the taunts and insults that Marzī heaped upon him all day with the patience of an angel.

We set off from Qaryat Bishr at ten o'clock in the morning and forty-five minutes later emerged from the low ground, where the palms of Khaybar grow, to climb onto the plateau of the Ḥarrah. The track took us straight away through the ruins of an ancient stone-built village. The path is terrible and goes across ground strewn with boulders, some of them a cubic metre and a half in size. The direction is indicated by no more than a slight reflective sheen on the surface of the stones. So hard is the basalt rock that the comings and

---

3 [On the Ṣulubah, see Translation Part II note 56, and note 159 below. On the pariah tribes of Arabia, see Oppenheim 1939–68 iv/1: 101–54. (MCAM/WF)]

4 [These spellings of Hutaym tribes are based on Oppenheim iv/1: 123–4, as follows: Ibn Samra (Huber: Ebn Semerah) is given as the shaykh of the al-Dhība tribe of the Hutaym (see note 5 below); Ibn Barrāk (Huber: Ebn Bâlerak) is given as the shaykh of the Hutaym (Banī Rashīd); Al-Muhaymizāt is Huber's El Mehîmezat; al-Farādasa (Huber: El Feredesah) is listed as a subtribe of the Muhaymizāt; al-ʿAwāmara is Huber's El 'Aouâm̃erah; Al-Maḍābara is Huber's El Medhaberah. Musil (1928a: 108) lists clans of the Hutaym but none of these appear on it. Dickson (1949: 606) provides a useful appendix. (MCAM/WF)]

5 [Al-Dhība: Huber's Âdzeïbah, which in the margin of his handwritten manuscript he writes in Arabic as Adhaybah. See Dickson 1949: 606.]

goings of perhaps fifty centuries have been unable to make any impression upon it.

The path from Khaybar to al-Ḥā'iṭ goes by the name of Sirdab al-Yahūd or Sirdab al-Kuffār (the Jews' or Unbelievers' Way).[6]

After the first five kilometres, a score of stone cairns appear along the path, spaced about twenty to thirty metres apart, called Ruǧūm al-Yahūd.[7] Lying beneath them are the Jews slaughtered by ʿAlī, Ibn Samrah's son told me, and every passerby adds a stone to the pile.

[94] Towards four o'clock in the afternoon we were close to the little hill of Fikal,[8] two miles to the south of my route, and an hour later we were making camp in the Wādī Suways.[9] I took a bearing on Ǧabal Karsh to the north of our camp, and on Ǧabal Ghamr to the north-north-west, which is sixteen miles long.[10] Both are composed of granite and stand out from the Ḥarrah which, in this direction, stretched another twenty kilometres away to my left.

The next day we went about sixteen miles, two of them in a south-easterly direction.

By nine o'clock in the morning we had crossed the Wādī Suways again, and at midday we were halting near the rainpool of al-Maqnaʿ,[11] in which a little water was still standing.

---

[6] [*Sirdāb* means vault or cellar, so it is curious that it is used here to mean a path or way. According to Hava it can also mean 'underground passage'. Huber was going north-east out of Khaybar before bending eastwards to make his way through the northern part of the Ḥarrah to al-Ḥā'iṭ. (MCAM/WF)]

[7] ['The Jews' Tombs', Arǧūm al-Yahūd as Huber writes in Arabic in the margin of his handwritten manuscript.]

[8] [Huber writes Fekah, but this is most probably Ǧabal Fikal, about 15 km north-north-east of Khaybar at 25° 48' 00" N 039° 35' 00" E (GeoNames). It is not marked on the USGS 1:500,000 map of 1959 entitled *Geographic Map of the Northeastern Hijaz Quadrangle*.]

[9] [Wādī Suways: I have been unable to identify this (it is not marked on the USGS 1:500,000 map of 1959 entitled *Geographic Map of the Northeastern Hijaz Quadrangle*), but it must run roughly east to west into Wādī Ṭibiq/Wadi al-Ghamrah.]

[10] [Ǧabal Karsh: Huber writes Qers, but this is probably Ǧabal Karsh on the northern edge of the Ḥarrah, at 26° 06' 00" N 039° 39' 00" E (GeoNames). Ǧabal Ghamr: probably Ǧabal al-Ghamrah on the east bank of the Wadi al-Ghamrah, 25 km north of Khaybar.]

[11] [Al-Maqnaʿ (Huber's El Meqen'a): written thus in Arabic by Huber in the margin of his handwritten manuscript. The mention of craters in the next paragraph suggests that Huber had reached the northernmost of the volcanoes forming the N–S range of Ǧibāl al-Abyaḍ, about 60 km east by north of Khaybar (see the USGS 1:500,000 map of 1959 entitled *Geographic Map of the Northeastern Hijaz Quadrangle*). The highest point is Rā's al-Abyaḍ (see note 14 below).]

Since morning we had crossed five craters with slightly elevated rims and of very disparate diameters. These craters are devoid of stones and are filled instead with a clayey yellow soil, which at the time of my visit rendered the crossing difficult and in places impossible, so slippery had the ground become as a result of the last rains.

Our deviation to the south-east had been necessitated by a fine rain that had begun to fall. We would have to spend the night under a tent and our guide had assured us that we would find some in that direction. We did indeed soon come across five miserable little Hutaym booths, and installed ourselves in the largest. Despite that, we were not spared the rain. The storm broke towards ten o'clock in the evening, the tent was inundated with water, and I decided to put my instruments on my knees to protect them and go outside to sit on a rock, where I could cover myself with my cloaks and rugs. It was a wretched night, followed by a depressing morning.

That day we went just a mile to the north to pick up our path again, and another eight miles in our east-north-easterly direction.

Almost immediately after we had resumed our journey towards [95] al-Ḥāʾiṭ, the path took us across some truly awful terrain. It was like an enormous boiling soup of molten iron suddenly frozen solid, with some of its bubbles bursting to reveal deep holes and edges of slag as sharp as glass. From time to time deep crevasses appeared, resulting from shrinkage caused by cooling, adding to the chaos and horror of this extraordinary phenomenon. This area is two miles wide and is called al-ʿAbr.[12]

The lava slag is so hard that, though it has been crossed and re-crossed over long centuries past, it has not even developed the slight reflective sheen that shows the way on the basalt of the Ḥarrah. Just as in the Great Nafūd, the path across al-ʿAbr is recognizable only from the camel droppings that every bedouin makes it his business to squash onto the slag as they fall from his beast. These droppings, flattened in this way, stick to the rock for several years, thus indicating the direction to follow.

We camped that evening between the two mountains of Ghaynāt and Ghunaym, the former to the north and the latter to the south.[13] Still farther

[12] Probably better spelt El-'Abir. (The Editors.) [Huber gives El H'abr, which he writes in Arabic as al-Haʿbīr in the margin of his handwritten manuscript. But his editors are correct: the area is al-ʿAbr, at 25° 58' 00" N 040° 04' 00" E (GeoNames).]

[13] [Ǧabal Ghaynāt: 26° 02' 00" N 040° 07' 00" E. Ǧabal Ghunaym: about 8 km south by east of Ghaynāt at 25° 58' 00" N 040° 09' 00" E. (GeoNames).]

to the south, more or less equidistant from each other, were the following mountains:[14]

Rāʾs al-Abyaḍ – Lā Kalīl – Ramāḥah – al-ʿĀqr

These six mountains are themselves located along a rise in the ground in the form of a donkey's back. Rāʾs al-Abyaḍ is the highest of them.

This chain of summits is worthy of note because it forms the watershed of northern Arabia. Run-off from the rains flows westwards to the Red Sea and eastwards to the Persian Gulf. It is in the vicinity of Ǧabal Abyaḍ that the source of the great Wādī Ermek [*viz.* Rimah] is to be found, which has its outlet to the sea close to Baṣrah.[15] By determining this point, which ordinary maps either do not show or which they represent as [96] lying beyond Taymāʾ and as far north as Tabūk, I believe that I have advanced our knowledge of the hydrography of northern Arabia.

At the end of the present work I shall include a short notice explaining the layout of the route I have adopted for the course of Wādī Ermek, which differs greatly from that shown on previous maps.[16]

As for the name Ermek which I have been giving to the same wadi, instead of the name Roummah which is currently used for it and under which it already appears in the early Arab writers, I can affirm that I have never heard any other name for it, and that the latter is totally unknown in the region of the wadi itself as well as in the Ǧabal.[17]

The rains that fall on the western slope of the Rāʾs al-Abyaḍ massif flow down to form the Wādī al-Ṭibiq, which traverses the entire Ḥarrah on its westward course, passing a few kilometres south of Ǧabal Khaybar before emerging from the Ḥarrah and going on to join the Wādī al-Ḥamḍ in the vicinity of Ǧabal Hadiyyah, a station on the Darb al-Ḥaǧǧ about sixty kilometres west of Khaybar.[18] Wādī al-Ṭibiq is joined by several small

---

[14] [These mountains, actually south-south-west of Huber's location, are the north–south range of extinct volcanoes named Ǧibāl al-Abyaḍ that forms the watershed of northern Arabia, as Huber was about to realize. He was the first explorer to demonstrate this.]

[15] [On Wādī Rimah and Huber's use of the name Ermek, see Translation Part II, note 58.]

[16] The author, busy with the preparations for his last [1883–84] journey, was unable to write the notice of which he speaks in this paragraph. (The Editors.)

[17] [It is noteworthy that despite this assertion Huber refers to it as 'ouâdy Roumah', not Ermek, in the diary of his 1883–84 journey (Huber 1891: 616). See note 15 above.]

[18] [Wādī al-Ṭibiq: spelt thus in Arabic in the margin of Huber's handwritten manuscript. See Translation Part II note 199. The Wādī al-Ṭibiq/Ṭubǧah–Wādī Ghamrah system

tributaries on its way across the Ḥarrah, but on my map I have shown only those whose courses I can be fairly certain about. These are the Suways and the Thamad and, outside the Ḥarrah, the Saghīr.

Here I must note a particular fact that seemed odd to me, and which I learned from a Ḥarbī Arab and from a Hutaymī whom I met beyond al-Ḥā'iṭ. They assured me that the highest tributaries of Wādī al-Ṭibiq rise as far up as Ǧabal Makhīd, to the north-north-east of Rā's al-Abyaḍ and thus outside the Ḥarrah. I was at the time already several leagues north of al-Ḥā'iṭ, a long way from well-informed people up there, and later I was only able to obtain contradictory reports on this question.

Wādī al-Ḥamḍ rises to the north of al-Madīnah, and [97] then runs parallel to the Ḥarrah, that is to say north-westwards, up to Hadiyyah where it is joined by Wādī al-Ṭibiq. It then turns westwards,[19] is joined by the Wādī al-ʿUlā, and finally debouches into the Red Sea south of the little village of al-Wağh.

Wādī al-Ḥamḍ does not contain palm plantations like its other tributary wadis, but it does contain numerous wells.

Wādī al-ʿUlā, which I have just mentioned, rises in the basin of al-Ḥiğr and flows southwards from there for a distance of three days' march before debouching into the Wādī al-Ḥamḍ in the territory of the Banī Ǧuhaynah, who are a section of the Banī Kalb.

The little natural cave called Maghniyyat al-Āsūdah[20] is situated between the two mountains of Ghaynāt and Ghunaym and is formed of blocks of basalt. It is 1.2 metres high by two metres deep and about three metres long, and was just big enough to shelter all three of us from the rain that fell for the whole of that night.

The next day, 18 December, we made twenty miles going north by 72° east, straight towards al-Ḥā'iṭ.

After the first five miles we were able to make out Ǧabal Ḥamādah,[21] at the south-eastern foot of which the village is situated. For some time towards midday we went along Wādī Ghunaym, which rises by the mountain of the

is in fact aligned NNE–SSW, with a watershed to the west of Khaybar. Hadiyyah is a station on the pilgrimage route a few kilometres south of al-Mudarrağ.]

[19] [Wādī al-Ḥamḍ turns west-north-west here rather than due west.]

[20] [Maghniyyat al-Āsūdah: Huber calls this cave Meghrenïah el Âsoûdah, but spells it thus in Arabic in the margin of his handwritten manuscript.]

[21] [There is a Ǧabal Ḥamādah at 26° 09' N 040° 34' E (GeoNames) about 18 km north-east of al-Ḥā'iṭ, though Huber seems to be referring to another mountain of the same name closer to the oasis.]

same name, passes to the north of Ǧabal al-Baṣr[22] and then leaves it to join Wādī Ermek [*viz.* Rimah] a little distance farther on.

To the south of Ǧabal al-Baṣr stands Ǧabal Kanāt or Abū Zayd.

After Maghniyyah the path becomes terribly arduous and difficult to follow.

On the following day, three full hours of marching brought us to al-Ḥāʾiṭ. The tops of its trees are only discernible half an hour before getting there, because this place and its encircling palms are situated like Khaybar in a hollow of the Ḥarrah.

[98] Before descending the slope of the Ḥarrah, the path runs for fifteen minutes or so across the ruins of a very ancient place built of dressed masonry. In former times there were several circular towers, but today almost everything is level with the ground. This was al-Ḥāʾiṭ of yore which, like the old villages of Khaybar, was built above the Ḥarrah and not, as today, down in the hollows where the people are decimated by fevers.[23] In addition, al-Ḥāʾiṭ has a fresh and pristine aspect that is shared by neither Khaybar nor al-ʿUlā, with which in other ways it has plenty in common, such as its negro population, its agues, and the inestimable good fortune of having its palms irrigated by its springs.

The negro population of al-Ḥāʾiṭ, while not as light-skinned as the people of al-ʿUlā, is lighter-skinned than that of Khaybar.

In view of its proximity to the Shammar capital, al-Ḥāʾiṭ lacks its own special governor, unlike al-Ǧawf, Taymāʾ and al-ʿUlā, and comes under the direct administration of the emir's government. It is a man named Ǧābir, the wealthiest property-owner, who receives guests and who is accorded the title of shaykh.

This very thriving oasis possesses twice as many palm trees as al-ʿUlā but, as they are not in such fine condition, the harvest is smaller and of inferior quality. Nevertheless the yield and the fruit are far superior to those of Khaybar. Al-Ḥāʾiṭ does not have the *ḥilwah* dates as al-ʿUlā does, but the

---

[22] [Ǧabal al-Baṣr: about 30 km south-west of al-Ḥāʾiṭ, at 25° 51' 02" N 040° 15' 18" E (GeoNames).]

[23] [Huber is the first traveller to record these ancient remains. Al-Ḥāʾiṭ has a very long history of settlement and has been shown to be 'Padakku' (Fadak), one of the places in the northern Ḥiǧāz conquered by the Babylonian king Nabonidus in the 550s BC, along with Temaʾ (Taymāʾ), Dadanu (Dadan), Iadikhu' (today Yadīʿ/al-Ḥuwayyiṭ, 50 km south of al-Ḥāʾiṭ), Khibra (Khaybar), and Iatribu (Yathrib, today al-Madīnah). See Winnett and Reed 1970: 91; Eph'al 1982: 180; Hausleiter and Schaudig 2016.]

soil produces other highly valued varieties, the best of which are the *qasb*, *birnī*, *furaysī* and *kālib*.[24]

The dates of al-Ḥāʾiṭ are purchased by the Hutaym, Ḥarb and Shammar Arabs.

The palms of al-Ḥāʾiṭ once belonged to the ʿAlī, a tribe of about 200 tents who are part of the great ʿAnizah confederation. When the oasis was annexed by the Shammar emirate through the efforts of ʿUbayd,[25] the Emir Ṭalāl, who was in power at the time,[26] [99] exacted the usual tribute of five percent to be paid by the ʿAlī. The latter obliged for four years, but then refused to pay the tribute any longer. Ṭalāl then mounted a raid against them, as a result of which the ʿAlī withdrew to be near the other great tribes of the northern ʿAnizah along the banks of the Euphrates. The emir then took their place as owner of the palms. The people pay the emir half of the harvest, in addition to a tax of ten percent on their own half share of it.

The inhabitants also cultivate wheat, barley and *dhura*.[27] They possess neither livestock nor beasts of burden.

The plantations of al-Ḥāʾiṭ are irrigated by three springs, which start from al-Shalālah, al-Ṣufayrī and Abū Sulaymān.

The first two of these flow at a rate of about three litres per second between them, and rise at the same hill, al-Ṣufayrī, which forms part of the Ḥarrah just below a ruined tower called Qaṣr al-Ṣufayrī, to the north-north-west of the village. The spring of Abū Sulaymān, also known as ʿAlī, flows from the west and, with an output of about eight litres per second, has the strongest flow of the three.

The output of the springs seems not to depend on whether the season has been good or bad. It had rained during the winter of my visit, that is

---

[24] [With thanks to Yousef al-Bassām of ʿUnayzah and to James Budd for identifying these varieties.]

[25] [ʿUbayd ibn ʿAlī ibn Rashīd was the brother of the first politically significant Rashīdī emir of Ḥāʾil, ʿAbd Allāh ibn ʿAlī al-Rashīd (d. 1847). Though often seen as the power behind the throne, ʿUbayd acquiesced in the succession of ʿAbd Allāh's son Ṭalāl, but continued to exert great influence over the affairs of the emirate until his death in 1869 (Winder 1965: 156, 239–40). He was the father of Ḥamūd ibn ʿUbayd, who was himself the second power in the land after the Emir Muḥammad, and who was so well known to the Blunts, Huber and Euting.]

[26] [Ṭalāl ibn ʿAbd Allāh al-Rashīd ruled in Ḥāʾil from 1847 till his death in 1868, reputedly by his own hand. (Winder 1965: 156, 240).]

[27] [For *dhura*, millet, see Translation Part II, notes 162 and 202.]

to say 1879–80,[28] but before that there had been four dry winters with no perceptible variation in their flow.

The temperatures of these springs are not quite as high as those of Khaybar. Here are the averages I took:

al-Shalālah	+ 28.5°
al-Ṣufayrī	+ 28.2°
Abū Sulaymān	+ 26.8°

I was assured that the last of these was invariably cooler than the first two. The water from all three is potable.

[100] The inhabitants told me that other springs had dried up, but that water emerges from the ground at various places in winter to form marshes that disappear later in springtime.

A highly valued variety of tobacco is grown at al-Ḥāʾiṭ that fetches half a riyal per measure (about half a kilogram). The tobacco grown at Khaybar, al-ʿUlā and Taymāʾ is much inferior to that of al-Ḥāʾiṭ. Also, this same quantity sells at al-ʿUlā for a quarter of a riyal, and at Khaybar for one piastre.[29] In Taymāʾ they smoke a kind of hay that everyone collects.

The numerous ruins still extant at al-Ḥāʾiṭ are testament to this city once having been at least as important as Khaybar, if not more so. It comprised two large quarters, one to the south-east and the other to the north-west of the present-day village. The names of these are lost to memory. The people today refer to the first group of ruins by the name Kharāb al-Naṣārā ('the ruins of the Christians'), and the second by the name Kharāb al-Yahūdī ('the ruins of the Jew'[30]). Present-day al-Ḥāʾiṭ is itself built on ancient foundations of dressed masonry, and there are still remains of some very curious old edifices, among them a square building accessed by an external stairway leading to the first floor. Inside the building is a well.

The structure known as Qaṣr al-Zaḥlānī[31] is a square building of dressed masonry in the same style, also with an external stairway. What would be the ground floor has neither door nor window, nor any other form of opening.

[28] [*Sic*. Huber means the winter of 1880–81. He had arrived in al-Ḥāʾiṭ on 19 December 1880.]

[29] 1 piastre = 0 francs 20 cents. (CH)

[30] Probably better, for consistency, as Kharāb al-Yahūd, 'ruins of the Jews'. (The Editors.)

[31] Huber's Qaçr Āzehelâny, written in Arabic as Qaṣr al-Zaḥlānī in the margin of Huber's handwritten manuscript.

The present-day town of al-Ḥāʾiṭ, which is two miles long from east to west along a fissure in the Ḥarrah, comprises three quarters. The first and largest is called Wādī Saʿfan; the second and smallest, situated 100 metres to the south-west, is [101] al-Shurayf; and the third, in the same direction but 500 metres farther on still and on a small hill, is called al-Quṣayr.[32]

At the base of this latter hill are some ancient tombs built of coarse stones, with walls, some of them crumbled. The tombs are oriented from east to west.

From the top of the Ḥarrah at al-Ḥāʾiṭ I was able to obtain bearings on the mountains of Kanāt, Qarn, Ḥulayfah and Tīn to the south and south-west [*sic*; south-east].

These bearings will enable me to trace the limits of the Ḥarrah on this side.

I left al-Ḥāʾiṭ at half past nine on the morning of 24 December, and at eleven o'clock reached the outer edge of the Ḥarrah. It does still continue, but in a more or less sporadic fashion, for about twelve kilometres to a point beyond Ǧabal al-Athqab, sixteen kilometres from al-Ḥāʾiṭ.[33]

There are remains of thirty or so ruined dwellings at the foot of the latter mountain, in a break in the Ḥarrah.

A few minutes after leaving the Ḥarrah completely behind, I at last crossed the Wādī Makhīd, which comes down from the mountain of the same name about forty kilometres to the north-west of my route. During my journey I made camp nine kilometres beyond this wadi, which contained some water.

A terrain of compact, clayey soil covered in gravel begins not far from Wādī Makhīd. It has a desolate uniformity and is almost completely barren. Nor does one see any bedouin encampments, any more than between Rāʾs al-Abyaḍ and al-Ḥāʾiṭ. This desert bears the name of al-Zarb.

From our camp, we had Ǧabal al-Bān a few kilometres to the north-west. It is a slightly elevated massif. In front of us stood the little Ǧabal al-Zalf,[34] a mountain of the same kind six miles in length.

---

[32] 'Little Castle'. (The Editors.)

[33] [Ǧabal al-Athqab, which Huber recorded as Āçeqâber and writes in Arabic in the margin of his handwritten manuscript as Āṣqābir, is indeed about 16 km north-east of al-Ḥāʾiṭ at 26° 06' 07" N 040° 34' 26" E (GeoNames). Huber was now following an approximately north-easterly course from al-Ḥāʾiṭ to Mustaǧiddah.]

[34] [Possibly Ǧabal Dhilf, at 26° 18' N 040° 44' E (GeoNames). Huber writes it in Arabic as al-Zalf in the margin of his handwritten manuscript.]

[102] We set off next day a little before eight o'clock, and two hours later I was on Ǧabal al-Zalf. Shortly before that I had been able to obtain a bearing on Ǧabal Rakhah[35] sixteen miles away, which is itself just seven miles from Wādī Rimah.

Leaving Ǧabal el-Zalf, we marched north by 65° east, and immediately found ourselves once more on purely granite terrain.

Three miles farther on I obtained a bearing on Ǧabal Ḍibīy, twenty-five miles to the south-west [*sic*; south-east] and close to where Wādī al-Qahd flows into Wādī Rimah. A little farther on still I crossed Wādī al-Qahd close to the peak of the same name.

Wādī al-Qahd originates twenty-two kilometres north-north-west of its namesake mountain, near the village of Zarghaṭ.[36]

Four kilometres north-north-west of the little Ǧabal al-Qahd stands another small mountain named al-Furs.[37] Five miles south-west of that is Ǧabal Wasmah.[38]

At sunset we made camp in the desert of Qalanqūwah, which follows that of al-Zarb.

The next day, 26 December, we made fourteen miles. By eight o'clock in the morning we were crossing Wādī Mubaḥil,[39] which forms near Ǧabal Ruwaysah and flows into Wādī Ermek [*viz.* Rimah]. Towards midday we reached Ǧabal Daqaya[40] al-Asmar, a granite hill about fifty metres high, which is forty miles[41] south of a similar hill by the name of Ǧabal Daqaya al-Aḥmar.[42]

---

[35] [Written Rakkah in the published article, but this is a misprint: Huber spells it Rakhah in his handwritten manuscript, both in the French text and in Arabic in the margin. It is marked as Ǧabal al-Rakhā at 26° 13' N 040° 53' E on the USGS 1:500,000 map of 1959 entitled *Geographic Map of the Northeastern Hijaz Quadrangle*]

[36] [Wādī al-Qahd rises near al-Shimlī at the northern tip of the Ḥarrat Hutaym, and flows south-east past Zarghaṭ and Zurayghiṭ (aka Ẓarghaṭ and Ẓurayghiṭ) towards Ǧabal Ḍibīy, before joining Wādī Rimah (1973 map entitled *Arabian Peninsula*, 1:2,000,000).]

[37] [Ǧabal al-Furs: 26° 30' 44" N 040° 47' 45" E (GeoNames).]

[38] [Ǧabal Wasmah: 26° 18' 30" N 040° 49' 51" E (GeoNames).]

[39] [Mubaḥil: spelt thus in Arabic in the margin of Huber's handwritten manuscript.]

[40] [There is a hill named Daqaya at 26° 33' 00" N 041° 25' 00" E on GeoNames, but it is not clear whether this is Daqaya al-Asmar or Daqaya al-Aḥmar. This Daqaya is about 20 km south-west-south of Mustaǧiddah.]

[41] [Forty miles: this is much too far away from the other Daqaya for Huber to have been in both places on the same day, so this distance of '40 milles' is an error. The two mountains named Daqaya were close to each other, so Huber may have intended to write '4 milles'.]

[42] Al-Asmar: 'the Brown'; al-Aḥmar: 'the Red'. (CH)

From the summit of Daqaya al-Aḥmar I was able to obtain a bearing on Ğabal Rummān, at the foot of which lies Mustağiddah.

These two peaks of Daqaya mark the limit of the grazing lands of the Hutaym.

We left at seven o'clock in the morning on 27 December, [103] and three hours later I could see from afar the palms of Mustağiddah, which I reached in another two hours.

Already during my passage through Khaybar it was being noised abroad there that the emir had set out to conduct a raid in the south. This news was confirmed to me at al-Ḥāʾiṭ, and on arrival at Mustağiddah I learned that the campaign had been directed against the ʿUtaybah Arabs, who range between Mecca and al-Riyāḍ.[43] The shaykh of Mustağiddah, who gave me this information, added that the campaign force had camped just the day before in Wādī Rimah, and that as a result he was expecting to see them at any moment as they made their return to Ḥāʾil. So I decided to wait at Mustağiddah to see them on their way back. But in the middle of the night a messenger arrived from the emir tasked with making enquiries about me and reporting back with my news. The whole campaign force was encamped some ten leagues to the south of Mustağiddah. I immediately made Marzī jump onto my own *dhalūl* with instructions to go and greet the emir on my behalf and thank him for his attention.

The messenger told me that the raid had been very successful and had produced excellent results, with no spilling of blood. About 800 camels, 5,000 sheep and goats, six slaves and seven horses had been captured. The ʿUtaybah had fled with their lives, and the emir had not wished them to be pursued.

The next day Marzī returned at three o'clock in the afternoon, having made fast time. The emir gave me to understand that he would be spending the following morning before Mustağiddah, and that he would send an escort to seek me out so that I might return to Ḥāʾil with him, and that I should hold myself in readiness.

And indeed early in the morning on 29 December the plain was covered with flocks and herds, bands of bedouin and the emir's men, all hastening their steps as they made their way northwards. Even so, the bulk of the campaign force was passing with the emir at about two leagues to the west of Mustağiddah. Towards noon four horsemen arrived who had been sent by

---

[43] [Huber writes El Râïd, but al-Riyāḍ must be meant.]

the emir to collect me. But I had no intention at all of returning to Ḥāʾil [104] at breakneck speed, as I knew the emir would be doing.

I therefore entrusted the escort with my thanks to the emir as well as my excuses for turning down his invitation, as I was intent on returning by way of a small detour.

We set off straight away and a ride of a full four hours brought us to Quṣayr,[44] a small village of forty or so inhabitants, where we spent the night.

On 30 December, three more kilometres brought us above the little Ǧabal al-Ṣafrāʾ to the village of Ghazzālah,[45] which I only passed by. I halted eight kilometres farther on at the hamlet of al-Maḥāsh with its ten inhabitants, where I spent the night.

The next day I set off towards Ǧabal Shubaykah, a mountain of red granite, where there are some palm plantations like those at ʿUqdah. Shortly after, I passed in front of Ǧabal Sarrāʾ[46] and made camp a little farther north, in the bed of a *shaʿīb*.[47]

The following day was 1 January 1881. I was only able to get going towards ten o'clock due to the negligence of my men, who had let my *dhalūl* wander off. It was not found until two days later. As there was nothing to keep me in this area, with which I was already familiar, I forced the pace of my mount and reached Ḥāʾil at seven o'clock in the evening.

My exploration of the west had taken seventy-four days.

FROM ḤĀʾIL TO BAGHDAD

On 10 January [1881], the Persian pilgrims coming back from Mecca and al-Madīnah had arrived in Ḥāʾil, and were going to leave again on the 17th to return to their homeland via Baghdad. I resolved to accompany them.[48]

---

44 [i.e. Quṣayr al-Turkī, also known as Ghaẓwar, beneath the south-west corner of Ǧabal Rummān.]

45 [Ghazzālah lies at 26° 47' 18" N 041° 19' 16" E, about 30 km west-north-west of Mustaǧiddah, on the western side of Ǧabal al-Rummān.]

46 [Ǧabal Sarrāʾ, the inscription site visited before by Huber (see Translation Part I pp. 140–3), is at 27° 03' 35" N 041° 32' 52" E.]

47 *Shaʿīb*: ravine. (The Editors.) [Also with the meaning of a rugged tributary wadi.]

48 [Huber made this decision because the emir Muḥammad al-Rashīd refused to grant permission for him to go to Ǧiddah due to the dangers en route (see Huber's 65-page handwritten report dated 27 March 1882, French national archives, Pierrefitte-sur-Seine, Dossier F/17/2976/1, entitled 'Mission au Thibet et dans l'Asie centrale', 1878–82, item 79, p. 54). In a letter from al-Ǧawf to Maunoir at the Société de

I took my departure from Ḥāʾil at midday, heading north-east. Three hours later the granite terrain came to an end and the sandstone re-appeared. [105] Half an hour later I made camp with the Ḥağğ in the Umm Ādhan[49] area.

On the following day we managed a mere seven miles, all the time in a north-easterly direction, and pitched camp close to Wādī Shaqīq. Some rocky gullies still contained water from a month earlier. There was also plenty of scrub in this valley to provide the firewood we needed. Water and wood are the only things that the *ḥağğī* needs; as for sustenance, he brings his own food with him.

On 19 January, we only marched from seven until eleven o'clock, covering eleven and a half miles. Our camp was set up at the wells of al-Khāṣirah.[50] These wells, about thirty in number, are situated in a scarcely discernible depression and are dug directly into the clayey ground. The water is six or seven metres down and not very good. The water itself is not deep, as all of these wells are somewhat silted up. They are located just where the Wādī Ḥāʾil comes to an end. It does not continue any farther eastwards to flow into the Wādī Ermek [*viz*. Rimah], as has been believed up until now.

Generally, the surroundings of wells are stripped of all vegetation and hence of fodder and wood. At al-Khāṣirah we had the added inconvenience that after twenty-four hours the wells ran dry. Even so, we halted there for four days.

On its departure from Baghdad for the holy cities, the Ḥağğ caravan comprised some 800 people. On its return there were about 4,000 of them, so they of course lacked sufficient camels to take them to Mesopotamia. The

Géographie, read out at a meeting on 15 October 1880, Huber had stated his intention of going from Ḥāʾil to Ğiddah (*Bulletin de la Société de Géographie*, 6th series, Vol. XX, 1880, p. 471). On 6 December 1880, he had written to de Quatrefages from Khaybar confirming that he planned to complete his exploration of northern Arabia by going from Ḥāʾil to Mawqaq and then Ğiddah, not to Iraq (Huber 1881: 270). Maunoir (1883: 56) later recorded that Huber had been prevented from going from Ḥāʾil to the Red Sea by both shortage of funds and tribal unrest along the route. See Appendix 3, Letter dated 2 January 1882 from Huber in Ḥāʾil to Maunoir, explaining that tribal unrest was blocking the route to Ğiddah.]

49 [Huber puzzlingly spells this Āmâdzeň, but on his November 1883 visit he recorded the Arabic version of this name (Huber 1891: 78).]

50 [Huber (1891: 95) gives the Arabic for al-Khāṣirah. See also Euting 1896: 239. Al-Khāṣirah is at 27° 47' 43" N 042° 02' 15" E (GeoNames).]

Ḥarb[51] tribesmen who had conducted the caravan from the holy cities as far as Ḥāʾil wanted to go home as usual. But the emir, faced with the shortage of camels, had to ask them to stay on with the caravan as far as Mashhad ʿAlī.[52] Most of them agreed to do so, but there was still a shortfall in camel numbers. The emir [106] then sent messenger after messenger out into the desert to make the nomads come in with their beasts. But the Arabs were unhappy about the rate of hire, which they considered the emir to have fixed too much in the Persians' favour, and were in no hurry to co-operate.

During all this time the poor pilgrims, as well as the Ḥarb and the Shammar, were the guests of the emir, according to bedouin custom. By my estimation, that added up every day to 2,500 to 3,000 more mouths than usual to feed, and they were devouring a colossal amount of provisions.

So as to rid himself of all these superfluous consumers, the emir made the Ḥağğ leave Ḥāʾil, though he did make a gift to the needy of a fortnight's worth of dates. But as some of the pilgrims were still without camels, we had to stay encamped where we were.

On 24 January, faced with the crescendo of pilgrims' complaints, the *amīr al-ḥağğ*[53] led the mounted portion of the caravan as far as Baqʿāʾ,[54] thirty or so kilometres to the north-east of al-Khāṣirah. During the night the camels returned to the latter place and brought along the rest of the pilgrims the next day. This was done repeatedly over the course of several days, until the threats issued by the emir against the bedouin by means of his emissaries had prevailed upon the former to turn up with their camels.

---

[51] M. Huber writes Ḥarby, which is the singular of Ḥarb. (The Editors.) [The Ḥarb were the main bedouin tribe in the region between Mecca and al-Madīnah and made good business out of conducting pilgrims and occasionally preying on them. It would be a Ḥarbī tribesman who murdered Huber near Rābigh on 29 July 1884.]

[52] [Mashhad ʿAlī: the Martyrium or Tomb of ʿAlī, son-in-law of the Prophet Muḥammad, located in the city of al-Nağaf near al-Kūfah in Iraq, the terminus of the Darb Zubaydah. ʿAlī is venerated by Shīʿah Muslims, for whom Nağaf is the third holiest site after Mecca and al-Madīnah, and a place of pilgrimage in its own right.]

[53] The *amīr al-ḥağğ* is the commander-in-chief of the pilgrim caravan. From the point of departure to the point of arrival he has complete authority, like a captain on board his ship. The man filling this role was one of Ibn Rashīd's slaves named ʿAbd al-Raḥmān. (CH)

[54] [For Baqʿāʾ in November 1883, see Huber 1891: 92–4; Euting 1896: 235–6. The Blunts visited Baqʿāʾ in February 1879: Lady Anne calls it 'Taybetism', i.e. Ṭayyib al-Ism, and gives a lengthy description of it (Blunt 1881 ii: 49–52). It is at 27° 54' 23" N 042° 23' 20" (GeoNames).]

Here are the rates of hire fixed by the emir for camels from Ḥāʾil to Mashhad ʿAlī:

For a rider with his *khurǧ*:[55]	7 riyals
For a loaded camel:	10 riyals
For a camel loaded with a *shuqdūf*[56]	13 riyals

[107] The bedouin had been asking for these prices to be raised to 10, 15 and 18 riyals respectively.

Baqʿāʾ enjoys a very picturesque situation in a huge basin of whitish sandstone stretching from east to west. The village comprises two groups of dwellings, the eastern one called Ṣaḥbī,[57] the other to the west called al-Luwaymī.[58] Between these two stands a small group of four houses called Sharqī, which is regarded as very ancient and which was once called al-Ḥammām, or again Murayqib. Beside it stands an isolated property with no palms and surrounded by fields, named al-Quṣayfah, and a little farther off is a final group of homesteads named Quwayʿān.[59]

The middle of the basin is covered in a thick bed of extremely bitter salt.

The water, which is generally of poor quality and salty, is found at a depth of eight to ten metres. The wells have very large mouths as the sandstone into which they are dug is very soft. The water is abundant and its level never changes. One single well, the one at the *qaṣr* of al-Luwaymī, produces

[55] *Khurǧ*: double travel bag that hangs on each side of the camel. (The Editors.) [See Translation Part I, note 164.]

[56] [Huber writes 'avec deux baldanquins pour deux personnes', 'with two canopies for two people'. What he means is a *shuqdūf*, best described by Eldon Rutter in 1925: 'The shugduf, or camel litter, consists of a pair of stretchers, each of which is over five feet in length and two and a half feet broad. These are constructed … of a wooden framework strung with plaited fibre cords. A dome-shaped hood of bent sticks, over which the occupant ties his carpet, acts as a protection from the sun. The two stretchers are fastened together, side by side, with ropes; and they rest one on either side of the camel's saddle.' (Rutter 2015: 172).]

[57] [On his visit in November 1883, Huber calls the eastern village Sharqiyyah (Huber 1891: 93n), and adds a third one, 'Gulfy' (Huber 1891: 93). I have followed Huber 2003: 130 in calling the eastern village Ṣaḥbī, for Huber's Çeheby.]

[58] [Huber writes 'El Oueîmy', i.e. al-Uwaymī, for al-Luwaymī – a mistake frequently made by European travellers when hearing names beginning with 'L' prefixed by the definite article *al-*.]

[59] [In November 1883 Huber calls the fields of wheat at Baqʿā al-Quṣayfah and al-Quṣayfān, giving them in Arabic script, and does not mention Quwayʿān (Huber 1891: 93).]

passable water, which is both milky and bluish, calling to mind the water of the Rhine. This well is called al-Samḥah.

The two quarters of Ṣaḥbī and al-Luwaymī each possess a large square *qaṣr* built of rubble and mortar without lime,[60] with turrets at each corner. The interiors are full of the hovels of the inhabitants, which reminded me of the filthy village at Palmyra enclosed within the Temple of the Sun. The *qaṣr* at Ṣaḥbī is the bigger of the two.

The palms at Baqʿāʾ are handsome specimens and produce a good variety of date. Wheat and barley too are planted there every year.

Not far from Baqʿāʾ I noticed sandstone objects of a very curious form. These were little, perfectly spherical balls, from the size of a pea to that of the marbles [108] that children play with. The balls, embedded in the sandstone, are themselves of an extremely hard sandstone with lime cement. Others contain hydrated manganese oxide cement and exhibit botryoid forms[61] reminiscent of the sandstone of Fontainebleau. On one of the sandstone sites that I have described there was a bivalve shell that appeared to be a cardite.[62] This ball-shaped sandstone is called *rashrash*[63] by the local people.

The Ḥağğ had encamped about a kilometre to the north-east of Baqʿāʾ on a plateau of bare rock called Quṭayān.[64]

We left Baqʿāʾ on 26 January and went for about twenty kilometres, keeping a constant direction of north by 65° east. Our campsite that day was called Lughuf[65] al-Nafūd and also al-Ghabiyyah.

A short distance away to the north, the Nafūd rose like a wall forty metres high. From the top of it I was able to take a bearing on Ǧabal Ǧildiyyah, which I had also managed to do at Baqʿāʾ.

We resumed our journey two days later and followed the edge of the Nafūd, which at that point curved slightly towards the south, while our direction was south by 80° east. A ride of thirty kilometres brought us up to the wells of

[60] [i.e. mud mortar.]

[61] [Botryoid: formed like a bunch of grapes.]

[62] [Cardite: a bivalve mollusc of the genus *Cardita*. (MCAM)]

[63] [Huber calls this '*restres*'. Euting (1896: 234 and n. 3) called it pea-ore or 'ráschrasch' when he visited Baqʿā with Huber in November 1883: 'The bedouin collect the balls of pea-ore and sort the regular ones by size. They then swap them amongst themselves according to the calibre of their guns, thereby saving the precious lead.']

[64] [Quṭayān: spelt thus in Arabic in the margin of Huber's handwritten manuscript.]

[65] 'The pellet of the dunes'. (The Editors.) [*Lughuf* actually means 'the eroded border of a sand desert', according to Groom 1983: 154, which would be a more plausible rendering.]

al-Shuʿaybah,[66] where we rested up for that day as well as the next. During these two days, the country was shrouded in mist, a pale sun shone, and the temperature was low. The compass needle was constantly waving around.

There are about thirty wells at al-Shuʿaybah and their water, which is very saline and bitter, is five or six metres down.

On 30 January we went a few more kilometres, first to the south-south-east and then eastwards. Having at that point reached the track of the route to Baghdad,[67] we began to march northwards and entered the Nafūd, which in this region is not at all terrifying and cannot be compared to the Nafūd in the centre of Arabia. [109] By and large it only consists of sand hills separated by stony valleys. After a march of thirteen miles we reached a place called al-Shāmah.[68]

On 31 January, we went another thirteen miles in a northerly direction to go and make camp at the wells of Turabah,[69] where we rested for four days.

There are two wells here. They are masonry-lined and have water at a depth of about ten metres. This water was foul, stinking and bitter when we arrived, but once the *ḥağğī*s had quickly exhausted it, it was replaced by water of better quality.

Mitʿab, one of the last Shammar emirs,[70] had a mud fortress built in this

---

[66] [The wells of Shuʿaybah are at approx. 27° 52' N 042° 45' E, a few kilometres west of the nearest point on the Darb Zubaydah. The Blunts visited them in February 1879 ('Shaybeh') and estimated their number at forty (Blunt 1881 ii: 54–5).]

[67] [Huber only touched upon the Darb Zubaydah at this point and immediately turned north away from it, towards the wells of Turabah. He would rejoin the Darb Zubaydah at Birkat al-ʿAshshār (see below).]

[68] [Al-Shāmah: 'hills of different colours; dark, undulating country with hills of rose-tinged sand' (Groom 1983: 266). They were crossing the Shāmat Zarūd at this point (al-Rashid 1980: Map III section 1).]

[69] [Turabah is situated in a sandy area on the alternative Ḥağğ route to the west of the Darb Zubaydah (see next note). The fort there ('Kasr Torba') was visited by the Blunts in February 1879 and they were prevented from watering there (Blunt ii: 61).]

[70] [Mitʿab succeeded his brother Ṭalāl as emir in 1868 but ruled for only ten months before he was assassinated by Ṭalāl's eldest son, Bandar (Winder 1965: 242–3). Musil, visiting Turabah in March 1915, ascribes the fort's construction not to Mitʿab but to Bandar in 1869 (Musil 1928c: 157). The fort would have been built as part of the Rashīdī dynasty's effort to develop infrastructure for the Ḥağğ route via Ḥāʾil. This route took a westward turn off the Darb Zubaydah somewhere in the region of Birkat al-ʿAshshār, to go via Turabah and Baqʿāʾ to Ḥāʾil. The Darb Zubaydah could be rejoined south of Ḥāʾil at Samīrā, 'which lies in the path between J. Shammar and the Hejâz' (Doughty 1936 ii: 325–6). Fayd, the old half-way station on the Darb Zubaydah on the eastern side of Ğabal Salmā, was thus bypassed and lost its

place and installed a garrison to prevent Arabs other than the Shammar and their allies from drawing water here. Muḥammad, the current emir, maintains a permanent presence of three men in it for the same purpose.

It is the Shammar tribes of ʿAbdah and Tūmān[71] who have their encampments in these areas and use the water of Turabah.

The environs of Turabah are extraordinarily arid. It is set in a stony desert with scattered islets of sand two to three centimetres thick. The subsoil is a conglomerate of pebbles, quartz, flint and very compacted limestone that seems to be cemented together by a white mortar. This desert, which extends a long way to the east, bears the name al-Ḍubayb[72] al-Kabīr.

The wells of al-Khaḍrāʾ, fourteen in all, lie twelve miles north-east of Turabah.[73] Simply cut down through the rock, they are not furnished with masonry lining and are fifteen to sixteen metres deep by two in diameter. The water is slightly bitter. In former times these wells belonged to the ʿAbdah, but these days all the Shammar tribes can make use of them.

Fifteen miles to the east of al-Khaḍrāʾ lie the two wells of al-Hāshimah.[74] Less deep than those of Turabah, they are masonry-lined and contain good water.

[110] Approximately ten kilometres to the east of the wells of al-Hāshimah are two other wells called Zarūd,[75] of the same depth as the ones at Turabah, and masonry-lined. Their water is of inferior quality to that of the wells mentioned previously.

---

prominence, even though that section of the Darb via Zarūd, al-Ağfar and Fayd offered a much more direct connection between Iraq and the holy cities.]

[71] [The ʿAbdah and Tūmān were two of the four main divisions of the Shammar group of tribes, along with the Sinğārah and Aslam. The Rashīdī dynasty in Ḥāʾil belonged to the ʿAbdah (Musil 1928a: 31–3; Al-Rasheed 1991: 22–3).]

[72] [Al-Ḍubayb: see the map entitled *Arabian Peninsula* (1973), scale 1:2,000,000; also al-Rashid 1980, Map III, Section 1, for the location of Ğāl al-Ḍubayb extending east and south of Khaḍrāʾ. Huber spells it in Arabic al-Ẓubayb in the margin of his handwritten manuscript.]

[73] [The wells of al-Khaḍrāʾ: just to the west of the important station of al-Thaʿlabiyyah/al-Bidʿ on the Darb Zubaydah (al-Rashid 1980: 114–15). Huber did not visit al-Khaḍrāʾ and was relying on informants. The Blunts joined the Darb Zubaydah at al-Khaḍrāʾ ('Khuddra') on 12 February 1879 (Blunt 1881 ii: 61–2).]

[74] [Al-Hāshimah is actually located some 30 km or more south of al-Khaḍrāʾ (see the map entitled *Arabian Peninsula* (1973), scale 1:2,000,000; also al-Rashid 1980: 117–18). Huber of course did not visit it and was relying on informants.]

[75] [Zarūd is actually south-east of al-Hāshimah and was an important station on the Darb Zubaydah (Musil 1928a: 212–14; al-Rashid 1980: 116–17). Again, Huber had not visited it and was relying on informants.]

These wells, which are all situated in the Nafūd known as Maẓhūr,[76] were once the exclusive property of the ʿAbdah. The Nafūd in this part is a narrow band of sand ten or so kilometres in width which branches off from the Great Nafūd and takes an easterly direction.[77]

We left Turabah on 4 February, crossed the sand strip of the Nafūd al-Maẓhūr, and went on to make camp at midday a few kilometres beyond the place known as al-Matāyīh,[78] in the stony and sandy desert of ʿIrq al-Ẓuhūr.[79]

A day's march, that is about forty kilometres to the west of al-Matāyīh and in the Nafūd, lie the three wells of al-Ḥayāniyyah,[80] the depth of which I was informed had to be sixty metres (?). Half of the shaft would go down through the sand and be lined with masonry, while the rest would be dug down through the rock. Their water is very good.

A few kilometres to the east of al-Matāyīh in the desert of ʿIrq al-Ẓuhūr are the heads of two small watercourses, the Wādī Khathāl and the Wādī Khawr Wuqayyān,[81] which flow for a distance of about thirty miles towards the north-east in the valley of Abā al-Ṣīrān,[82] between the Nafūd Zarūd to the south and

[76] [The ʿIrq al-Maẓhūr (which Huber here spells Matsoûr) is an area of longitudinal sand dunes that contributes to the beginning of the Dahnāʾ dune system running down eastern Arabia. See the map entitled *Arabian Peninsula* (1973), scale 1:2,000,000.]

[77] [Actually a south-easterly direction.]

[78] [Al-Matāyīh: Huber spells this El-Metseîâha (and in Arabic al-Mathiyāhah in the margin of his handwritten manuscript), but it seems to be the place that Musil names as al-Matāyīh, an area of small gullies running down towards the northern sand strips of the Dahnāʾ, located to the north of Khaḍrāʾ (Musil 1928a: 158). Al-Rashid (1980, Map III, Section 1) locates al-Matāyīh just north-west of Khaḍrāʾ.]

[79] [ʿIrq al-Ẓuhūr appears to correspond to the ʿIrq al-Lubayyid on the map entitled *Arabian Peninsula* (1973), scale 1:2,000,000, also marked on Map III, Section 1 in Al-Rashid 1980.]

[80] [Al-Ḥayāniyyah, at approx. 28° 42' N 042° 15' E was a famous watering place in the eastern Nafūd, with an imposing fort that was photographed by both Gertrude Bell and Capt. Shakespear in 1914.]

[81] [Wādī Khathāl and Wādī Khawr Wuqayyān seem to be two of the small wadis situated in the al-Taysiyyah region east of the Darb Zubaydah, just north of the latitude of the station of Birkat al-ʿArāʾish, marked on the map entitled *Arabian Peninsula* (1973), scale 1:2,000,000, at approximately 28° 30' N 043° 20' E. GeoNames places Shaʿīb Khathāl at 28° 36' 00" N 043° 33' 00" E; and Shaʿīb Wuqayyān at 28° 35' 18" N 043° 33' 08" E. See also Al-Rashid 1980: 114, and Map III, Section 1. Birkat al-ʿArāʾish was also known as al-Muhallabiyyah.]

[82] [Abā al-Ṣīrān: I have been unable to identify this valley, which Huber spells Âbâleçrâñ (and in Arabic Abālaṣrān in the margin of his handwritten manuscript), and have followed the suggested Arabic rendering in Huber 2003: 133.]

a mountainous area to the north, the name of which I was unable to ascertain.[83]

Before reaching al-Matāyīh, the route goes along for several kilometres between the remains of two walls spaced twenty to thirty metres apart.[84] These are testament to the walls built from Baghdad to Mecca by Zubaydah, wife of Hārūn al-Rashīd, both of whom, according to the Arab authors, were under an obligation to enable even the blind to perform the pilgrimage to the holy cities. The route is still called the Darb Zubaydah today in memory of this princess.

[111] We resumed our march at six o'clock in the morning on 5 February. At nine o'clock the Nafūd began again, and two full hours later we made camp outside the sands at a place named Bilağbiyyah.[85]

We had come across no water at all ever since our departure from Turabah, and the *ḥağğīs* were beginning to run out of it. On this day water was selling for one rupee[86] per water-skin. Luckily at seven o'clock that evening there was a heavy fall of rain, which sent a little water into the hollows.

The next day, 6 February, a northward march of twenty-two kilometres followed by six kilometres to the north-north-west, all the way over the same stony desert, brought us to al-ʿAshshār.[87]

---

[83] [Again Huber is relying on informants for this information and it is not easy to check his information against modern maps. This 'mountainous area' was perhaps the extensive rugged region marked as al-Ḥajarah on the map entitled *Arabian Peninsula* (1973), scale 1:2,000,000. It runs NW–SE, and the Darb Zubaydah crosses it at al-Ğumaymah.]

[84] [Such pairs of walls sometimes more than 100 m in length were typical of parts of the route of the Darb Zubaydah. See e.g. Musil 1928a: 189; al-Ḥilwah et al. 1982: 41. It is not clear from Huber's account that he actually saw these walls himself, or that he had himself yet reached the track of the Darb Zubaydah.]

[85] [There are indeed small Nafūd sand strips crossing the Darb Zubaydah just north of Birkat al-ʿArāʾish: see the map entitled *Arabian Peninsula* (1973), scale 1:2,000,000. I have been unable to identify Huber's Belegbïah, which he spells in Arabic Bilağbiyyah in the margin of his handwritten manuscript.]

[86] The rupee is worth 2 francs 15 cents. (CH)

[87] [This seems to be the point at which the Ḥağğ caravan first joined the Darb Zubaydah. Huber spells this place El 'Ašak, but his distance of march would put him at Birkat al-ʿAshshār (28° 42' N 043° 22' E), also known as al-Biṭān, one of the largest stations on the Darb Zubaydah, with at least two stone-built cisterns or *birkah*s. Thus I suspect an error here, even though Huber clearly writes al-ʿAshak in Arabic in the margin of his handwritten manuscript. See Musil 1928a: 178, 206; Al-Rashid 1980: 113–14. Ḥilwah et al. (1982: 41–4 and Plate 58) gives a detailed description of the remains on the site, including a large *birkah* with inner dimensions of 64.5 by 51.5 m. This seems not to tally with Huber's description, unless his measurement can be understood as being of outer rather than inner dimensions, the discrepancy being accounted for by

It is here that I saw the first of the famous basins (*birkāt*) constructed by Zubaydah all along the route to collect the run-off from rain for the water needs of the pilgrims.

Birkat al-ʿAshshār was situated about a mile west-south-west of our encampment.

This beautiful construction, in dressed masonry lined with cement, is in a perfect state of preservation. It measures ninety metres by sixty-one, and is about ten metres deep. The cistern is half-way along a large plateau and straddles the stream that flows down from it, thus intercepting all its water. The internal north and south walls of the cistern descend to the bottom in a series of high, wide steps. Probably only a little rain had fallen in the region because the cistern had nothing but a little liquid mud in the bottom, with which the *ḥağğī*s nonetheless filled their water-skins. Next to the cistern, on the plateau, were the remnants of buildings that had once served as dwellings.

Close to the pilgrim encampment was a second cistern, smaller than the one I have just described, as well as being less well preserved and entirely silted up with sand.

On 7 February, after a twelve-mile stage going north by 10° west, we reached Birkat Ashabah.[88]

This station comprises three cisterns, a large building and about a hundred small houses, all of them of dressed masonry. Hence it was once an important place.

Immediately to the north of Ashabah there is another section of the Darb Zubaydah, about five miles in length. Along that stretch, the walls lining the route are constructed with a great deal of care.[89] They are sixty to seventy centimetres thick and about one metre high. Occasionally one comes across the remains of a small square building in cut stonework, measuring about

---

the steps down. However, none of the other sites described by al-Ḥilwah et al. along this section of the Darb Zubaydah contain a *birkah* of the dimensions given by Huber. And Huber's description of the *birkah* as straddling the wadi tallies closely with the site description and plan given in al-Ḥilwah et al. 1982: 42 and plate 63.]

88 [Or al-Shabah. I have been unable to identify this site, spelt Ašabah by Huber, which seems to be situated in the vicinity of Birkat al-Ḥamrāʾ, about 20 km south of al-Shīḥiyyāt. No site of this name is mentioned in Musil 1928a, Al-Rashid 1980 or al-Ḥilwah et al. 1982.]

89 [These are perhaps the walls remarked upon by the Blunts on 14 February 1879, south of al-Shīḥiyyāt (Blunt 1881 ii: 68; al-Rashid 1980: 142–3). If so, this would locate Ashabah, which Huber states lay immediately to the south of this stretch of the Darb.]

eight metres a side. It is built on the outside of the wall forming the edge of the road, with a door giving access to the roadway, the width of which is a consistent twenty-five metres.

At six o'clock next morning we resumed our northward march, and an hour later we passed between a circular cistern to our left and a ruined fort on our right. This place bears the name Ğisr[90] Ibn ʿAṭiyyah.

A second hour on the march brought us up to a ruined fort called Falayt ibn Qanat.[91]

Four and a half hours after our departure we were pitching camp at al-Shīḥiyyāt.[92]

This station, which is situated in a slight depression, possesses two cisterns, one circular and the other square, as well as the remains of buildings of considerable size, among them a fort the walls of which still rise to several metres above ground. All the others are more or less level with the surface.

Both cisterns have been constructed with extreme care and with a solidity that has ensured their survival intact to the present day. The walls of the square cistern are of dressed masonry, while those of the circular one are of rubble rendered in cement. The north and south walls of the square cistern had undergone a later repair with the construction in front of them of a second wall of mortar and [113] broken stones. This precaution proved

---

[90] Probably better as *Djasr*, pavement or causeway. (CH)

[91] [Falayt ibn Qanat: spelt thus in Arabic in the margin of Huber's handwritten manuscript. I have been unable to identify this site, which is not mentioned in Musil 1928a, al-Rashid 1980 or al-Ḥilwah et al. 1982. Below, p. 238, Huber mentions that this fort lay on the edge of the last vestige of Nafūd sands, which could help to locate it somewhere just south of al-Shīḥiyyāt.]

[92] [Huber spells this Âšeîhebat, but I agree with al-Rashid in identifying it as al-Shīḥiyyāt (al-Shuqūq), at 29° 06' N 043° 29' E. (al-Rashid 1980: 83–4, 112; al-Ḥilwah et al. 1982: 46–50). Possibly Huber recorded the spelling as he heard it in Arabic, and when transcribing it in roman letters inadvertently confused *yāʾ* with *bāʾ*; this seems to be confirmed by his Arabic rendering of the name in the margin of his handwritten manuscript. Musil also visited the site (1928a: 187). To reach al-Shīḥiyyāt from Birkat al-ʿAshshār, Huber would have passed by, in addition to the Birkat Ashabah that he mentions, the four small stations of Ḥamad (Birkat al-Shaykhah), al-Ḥamrāʾ (al-Rustumiyyah), Khunayfis al-Ğunūbī, and Khunayfis al-Shamālī (Qaṣr Umm Ğaʿfar) (al-Rashid 1980: 84–5, 112–13; al-Ḥilwah 1982: 44–6). The unnamed cisterns and fort described by the Blunts on 15 February 1879 'in a valley called the Wadi Roseh' closely match Huber's description of al-Shīḥiyyāt (Blunt 1881 ii: 70–1; 'Birket Shiehayad' on the Blunts' folding map). Huber's reference to both a rectangular and circular *birkah*, as well as a fort and many other buildings, makes his Âšeîhebat tally closely with the remains recorded on the site by al-Ḥilwah et al. (1982: 48–50).]

useless, as the supplementary walls have crumbled away while the original ones have remained standing.

The walls of the fort too are of dressed masonry, but they are very rough. Close by the fort there is a beautiful though waterless well, forty metres deep by three in diameter.

The two cisterns were half filled with water that was a little yellowish, but of good quality and sufficient for the water needs of ten pilgrim caravans like ours.

The position of the famous wells of Līnah[93] was pointed out to me from our camp at al-Shīḥiyyāt. The wells must be just to the east, thirty or more miles away. There are about 300 wells there, twenty-five metres deep and all hewn down through the rock. The water is good, but without being what the Arabs call 'sweet'. They belong at all times to the ʿAbdah Arabs, already mentioned, whose range lands extend up to there.

ʿAbdullah, one of the emir's men who was part of the Ḥaǧǧ escort, explained to me that the wells of Līnah were not the work of man, because no human would have been able to dig down through the white rock, which was as hard as metal. It was Solomon son of David[94] who, passing by there one day thirsty and waterless, commanded the *ʿifrīt* (demons) to dig him these wells in a single hour. The dutiful demons set to work straight away but, the rock being so hard, they were only able to finish the job in two hours despite their zeal.

On 7 February, the Ḥaǧǧ set off again at seven o'clock. Two hours later we were passing by the remains of a fort named Bātil Aṭūl. A few kilometres farther on came the ruins of a small isolated stone building named Qaṣr ʿAqlat al-Ghunaymī. A short while later we reached Zubālah.[95]

---

[93] [The area of the Līnah wells, about 50 km south-east by south of al-Shīḥiyyāt (at approx. 28° 48' N 043° 42' E), served as Musil's base for his 1915 journey across northern Naǧd to al-ʿUlā and back, though he gives little information about them. See Musil 1928a: 157, 183.]

[94] [Sulaymān ibn Daʾūd, the mythical figure often credited in Arab folklore with marvellous feats that defied credible explanation. He was served by an ever-obedient corps of *ʿifrīt* or demons.]

[95] [Zubālah (29° 24' N 043° 33' E): one of the important Darb Zubaydah stations (see Musil 1928a: 188–9; al-Rashid 1980: 81–2, 110–11; al-Ḥilwah et al. 1982: 52–5). From al-Shīḥiyyāt, Huber would have passed by the pilgrim stations of Birkat Umm al-ʿAṣāfir (Dhāt al-Tanānīr, at 29° 12' 33" N 043° 34' 16" E, and about 15 km north-east of al-Shīḥiyyāt and two-fifths of the way from there to Zubālah) and al-Shaḥūf (al-Ruḍam), though he does not mention either of them (al-Rashid 1980: 82–3, 111–

This is the most important of the stations we had passed through since al-ʿAshshār. It occupies an oval basin measuring four kilometres by two. The ground is of solid rock, [114] such that rainwater, having nowhere to go outside the basin and being unable to soak into the ground, collects in the hollow and only disappears through evaporation. Even so, four large cisterns were built which just now were full of water.

The dwellings, of considerable size, were constructed to the south of the cisterns and above the depression occupied by them. They were thus visible from very far away and useful as landmarks in this desert of such emptiness and uniformity.

Between the cisterns and the buildings there are five great wells two and a half to three metres in diameter and from forty to fifty metres deep. When I was passing through they had water in them, but this was probably rainwater. The upper parts of these wells are masonry-lined, the remainder being cut down through the rock.

The buildings are no longer anything more than shapeless heaps. Because the stone used in their construction is by nature friable, weather conditions have caused it to crumble away. The cisterns too have partly crumbled away.

From al-Shīḥiyyāt onwards the terrain had once again become volcanic, but at Zubālah this became even more of a feature.

We set off again at seven o'clock on 10 February. A few minutes later we were crossing the *shaʿīb* Abā al-Ruwāth[96] which, thanks to the rain that had fallen all night, at that moment had two feet of water in it to a width of 100 metres. This *shaʿīb* must run for fifty or sixty kilometres from west to east.

By eleven o'clock we were making camp at al-Ǧumaymah,[97] a depression in the lowest part of which a beautiful square cistern had been built, in an excellent state of preservation. It was about thirty metres square by four deep. Its construction is very ingenious. The water flows into the reservoir, which

---

12; al-Ḥilwah et al. 1982: 50–2). I have been unable to identify Bātil Aṭūl (Huber's Bâtel Athoul) and ʿAqlat al-Ghunaymī (Huber's 'Aqelâ El-Renemy), but both must have been in the vicinity of Birkat al-ʿAṣāfīr.]

96 [For the *shaʿīb* or tributary wadi of Abā al-Ruwāth, see Musil 1928a: 188.]

97 [For al-Ǧumaymah (also known as Birkat al-Ǧurays), which is located just east of Rafḥāʾ on the Saudi–Iraqi border, see Blunt 1881 ii: 84; Leachman 1911: 267–8; Musil 1928a 189, 207; al-Rashid 1980: 79–80, 110; al-Ḥilwah et al. 1982: 55–7. Huber would have passed by the small station of al-Ǧilbābī (al-Qubaybāt) en route to al-Ǧumaymah, though he does not mention it.]

was [115] full to the brim, through a side channel most probably devised to allow the sand and earth suspended in the water to settle.

The walls of the cistern were 1.3 metres thick, and its interior was faced with dressed stones, not covered with cement. This one had steps leading to the bottom just like the cisterns I had seen before.

On 11 February, we marched north by 5° west for sixteen miles and made camp at al-Ẓafīrī, where there is a beautiful and perfectly preserved cistern.[98]

Towards nine o'clock in the morning we had seen the summit of a hill just pointing a little above the horizon. Its name is al-Qawr ʿAṭiyyah.[99]

About ten kilometres before reaching our camp, we had already come across a cistern with the same name, al-Ẓafīrī, as the one we were now camping by.[100] They are both very well preserved, but neither one contained any water. Nor were there any buildings nearby.

Some kilometres to the north of our encampment there is a third cistern likewise bearing the name al-Ẓafīrī. This one is about twelve metres in diameter, and was full of sand right up to the brim.

So as to differentiate between these three identically named cisterns, the Arabs qualify them by 'southern', 'northern' and 'middle'.

Thus we were encamped near Middle Birkat al-Ẓafīrī, and from this point I could see, in a perfectly horizontal long line, a ridge designated Ǧāl al-Baṭn.[101] Next day as we were crossing it, I realized that this was not a hill, but a scarp up onto a plateau.

It is at this point, at the Ǧāl al-Baṭn, that the stony desert terminates. It had begun where the Darb Zubaydah finally leaves the Nafūd, that is to say at Birkat Falayt ibn [116] Qanat. This stony limestone desert, which is

---

98 [Probably so-called because it is in the territory of the Ẓafīr tribe. This station is at 29° 59' N 043° 37' E. To reach this al-Ẓafīrī, Huber would have had to pass by several stations on the Darb Zubaydah, namely al-Thulaymah (al-Haytham), Qibāb Khāliṣah, al-Qāʿ, and Birkat al-ʿAmyā (Musil 1928a: 190; al-Rashid 1980: 77–9, 109–10; al-Ḥilwah et al. 1982: 57–61). However, he makes no mention of them, with the possible exception of Birkat al-ʿAmyā (see note 100 below).]

99 [Al-Qawr ʿAṭiyyah (Huber's El Qoûr 'Athïah): I have been unable to identify this hill.]

100 [It is probable that this southern Birkat al-Ẓafīrī is in fact Birkat al-ʿAmyā (29° 53' N 043 37' E), which is located just 11 km south of the al-Ẓafīrī where Huber was encamped (al-Rashid 1980: 109; al-Ḥilwah et al. 1982: 60–2).]

101 [Ǧāl al-Baṭn: see Musil 1928a: 190. *Ǧāl* means 'escarpment'.]

uniformly consistent, is called al-Ḥağarah.[102] To the north-west it extends as far as Widyān, four days' march away; to the south-east it stretches to al-Ḥasā', three days' march from the Darb Zubaydah. This immense tract is characterized everywhere by extreme aridity and barrenness.

I have just mentioned Widyān.[103] This name designates neither a *shaʿīb* nor a wadi, but a region of low ground in the Ḥamād, north of the Nafūd and east of al-Ğawf, which slopes towards the north-east for more than 120 miles. It affords good grazing. I must observe here that I heard no one speak of Widyān either in al-Ğawf or in the Ğabal. A shaykh of the ʿAnizah, who accompanied the Ḥağğ for two days from Washrāf,[104] told me what little I know about it, and it is according to this information that I have included it on my map.

On 12 February, we set off for the north at seven o'clock and, an hour later, passed by the northern Birkat al-Ẓafīrī just mentioned. A little farther on, we came up before the Ğāl al-Baṭn, and climbed its extremely steep slope.[105]

The ascent, which is via a torrent bed, is very difficult and plenty of camels tumble down it. The Arabs assured me that everywhere except at this particular spot the Ğāl al-Baṭn is insurmountable, even by a man.

The torrent has been diverted in part into a basin constructed at the base of the slope, which is completely silted up.

On reaching the top of the Ğāl al-Baṭn one can in fact see, as I said before, that it is not a hill, because the land continues northwards without a break as an immense plateau.[106] Hence to someone coming from the south it presents a step forty or fifty metres high to climb.

The ground at the base of the Ğāl al-Baṭn is undulating and gullied by water, and there is some grazing to be had.

---

[102] [Al-Ḥağarah is an extensive tract marked on the map entitled *Arabian Peninsula* (1973), scale 1:2,000,000, running from NW to SE between the northern Dahnā' sands and the Iraq borderlands. It is cut by many parallel watercourses flowing towards the north-east. It forms part of the south-western limit of the territory of the Ẓafīr tribe (Ingham 1986: 21–5).]

[103] [Al-Widyān (a plural of *wādī*): a desert region east of Wādī al-Sirḥān and the Ḥamād characterized by wadis and *shaʿīb*s flowing towards the north-east and Mesopotamia.]

[104] [Washrāf: near Wāqiṣah, see pp. 242–3 below.]

[105] [This difficult ascent and the problems it posed for camels are vividly described by Lady Anne Blunt on 21 February 1879 (Blunt 1881 ii: 89–91).]

[106] [According to Lady Anne Blunt this flinty plain is called 'Mahamiyeh' (Blunt 1881 ii: 91) and marks the line at which the Shammar and ʿAnizah spheres of influence meet.]

[117] This uplift, the orientation of which is from north-west to south-east, stretches for a distance of about 160 kilometres, of which approximately one-third extends to the west of the Darb Zubaydah, and the remainder to the east.

We made camp two leagues beyond the Ǧāl al-Baṭn near Birkat al-ʿAqabah.[107]

This is one of the most important stations along the route. It possesses a magnificent cistern 110 metres long by 60 wide, in part ruined and full of sand. It contained some water.

A second, ruined cistern contains no water.

But its most remarkable feature is its four great wells, which are some of the most beautiful I have ever seen. The first, situated to the north of the great cistern, is a square one of 4.5 metres a side. It is lined with stone from its mouth to about eight metres down; the remainder is hewn through the rock.

A second well, sited in the middle of a large ruined building, is also square, measuring four metres a side.

A third one is just two metres in diameter, and a fourth, situated fifty metres to the north of the great cistern, measures four metres a side.

All these wells, which are veritable works of art created with the utmost attention to detail, are sixty metres deep. Alas they contain no water and all that immense labour has totally gone to waste.

The ruined buildings are of considerable extent and testify to the importance of this station.

The next day, resuming our northward course, we made eleven miles and pitched camp in ʿAthāmīn.[108]

Immediately on leaving al-ʿAqabah the route once again begins to be edged by walls, relics of the works of Zubaydah. But here they are better preserved than the preceding ones, and in some places rise to a height of two metres. When new, they must have been even higher, because the walls have lost their cappings and are damaged. However, I [118] do not think that this height of two metres can have existed everywhere, nor their thickness, which varies from half a metre to 2.7 metres. These walls to the north of al-ʿAqabah

[107] [Birkat al-ʿAqabah, approx. 30° 08' N 043° 37' E (al-Rashid 1980: 75–7, 108–9).]

[108] [Birkat ʿAthāmīn, at 30° 20' 05" N 043° 38' 31" E (GeoNames), is close to the Saudi–Iraqi border and is the last station on the Darb Zubaydah to lie within the present-day Kingdom of Saudi Arabia. However, it does not appear to have been included in the surveys conducted by Dr Saʿd al-Rashid and the Department of Antiquities and Museums in the 1970s and 1980–81.]

are more crudely constructed than those that survive south of al-Matāyīh.[109] The stones in the vicinity of al-ʿAqabah are all rough, very large, and simply laid one on top of another, with no mortar at all as bonding.

Six kilometres north of al-ʿAqabah there is a ruined fort. In a slight dip in the ground eight kilometres farther on, there is a square cistern measuring fifteen metres a side. It is visible from some distance away because the soil extracted during its construction had been thrown out onto its northern and southern sides to form two little brownish mounds which, thanks to the featurelessness of this desert, are visible from afar. The cistern was full of water. Fort and cistern bear the name of the district, ʿAthāmīn.[110]

Before one reaches this cistern, a long horizontal band running east–west comes into view that calls to mind an uplift like that of Ğāl al-Baṭn. But on reaching it towards eleven o'clock, I could see that it was in fact a long line of small, isolated flat-topped hills, running from north-east to south-west. These hills are typically elliptical in shape, with a height of only about fifteen metres. The length of the elevated feature, which bears the name ʿAthāmīn, is fifty kilometres.

A small group of hills situated eight miles away to the north by 50° west of our encampment, is called ʿAthmān.

On 14 February we set off towards seven o'clock, and half an hour later we could see in front of us a small peak that we quickly reached, by the name of Ğabal al-Fahdah.

At the same time as this miniature mountain came into view I discerned, likewise to the north, an uplift calling to mind [119] those of Ğāl al-Baṭn and ʿAthāmīn. It did not take us long to get there and I could see then that it was more like the former than the latter. First we had to climb up one step and then, a hundred metres beyond, a second one. The two steps together scarcely amounted to a half of the height of Ğāl al-Baṭn. On reaching the top we found ourselves on a totally bare plateau.

This elevated feature, which is also oriented from north-west to south-east, is about sixty kilometres in length and bears the name Ğāl Wāqiṣah.[111]

We went another two kilometres beyond Ğāl Wāqiṣah and made camp

---

[109] [This is a puzzling statement as Huber did not join the Darb Zubaydah until Birkat al-ʿAshshār, north of the Matāyīh area (see pp. 233–4 above). He must have been relying on informants.]

[110] ʿAthāmīn is the plural of ʿAthmān, more usually pronounced ʿUthmān, a man's name. (The Editors.)

[111] [See note 113 below.]

near a depression in the ground that the last rains had transformed into a small lake, and which is called Washrāf.

Our encampment here occupied a plateau having the form of a very flattened bowl, five miles long by two miles wide. Into the bottom of this bowl had been sunk sixty or so wells, each a metre in diameter. The majority of these wells were now submerged by the lake resulting from the winter rains. I saw just a single one measuring eight metres a side, but all of them were dug down into the rock. The water is disgusting.

The Arabs told me that there had once been a great city there. Is that a legend based on the number of wells, or on the quantities of rubble scattered all over the place? I certainly did see remains of foundations of old buildings, but they were no more considerable than at previous stations. Whatever the truth, apart from the wells there is nothing there any longer, not even *ḥaṭab*,[112] and many of the pilgrims were unable to prepare their food for the lack of anything to cook with.

Situated to west of the route, and shortly before reaching Ǧāl Wāqiṣah, is the well of Wāqiṣah,[113] which is eighteen metres deep and has sweet water.

[120] Three very ancient wells still survive in the Wāqiṣah and ʿAthāmīn area. They are in a line running north-east from ʿAthāmīn to the end of Ǧāl Wāqiṣah.

The first, located twelve kilometres from the *birkah* [sc. ʿAthāmīn], is al-Ǧill,[114] with a depth of seventy metres.

The second, twenty-two kilometres away, is called al-Shubrum,[115] at eighty metres' depth.

The third, al-ʿĀʿah,[116] at twenty-six kilometres from the *birkah*, is eighty-seven metres deep.

The water of al-Ǧill may be bad, while that of the other wells may be good. As for their depths, I naturally have every hesitation in giving these

---

[112] *Ḥaṭab*, firewood. (CH)

[113] [A well named Wāqiṣah is situated on the Darb Zubaydah at approximately 30° 39' N 043° 46' E (map entitled *Arabian Peninsula* (1973), scale 1:2,000,000). It is Lady Anne Blunt's 'well of Wakisa' (Blunt 1881 ii: 87). See also Musil 1928a: 193, 232–6.]

[114] [Al-Ǧīll: at 30° 22' 53" N 043° 57' 39" E (GeoNames).]

[115] [Al-Shubrum is marked on the map entitled *Arabian Peninsula* (1973), scale 1:2,000,000, at approx. 30° 15' N 043° 56' E. This is about 30 km south-east of ʿAthāmīn, and the three wells run more or less north–south, so Huber's information was far from accurate. See Musil 1928a: 193.]

[116] [Al-ʿĀʿa, at approx. 30° 12' N 044° 02' E, is mentioned in Musil 1928a: 186.]

according to what I was told by the Arabs, to whom lengths in metres are meaningless, especially when it comes to the depth of a well.

The desert to the east of these wells is known as Ǧāl al-Bisāsah. I do not know what exactly this designation relates to, as I was assured that there is no *ǧāl* or escarpment properly so called.

The whole ʿAthāmīn area between the two *ǧāl*s of al-Baṭn and Wāqiṣah is a totally barren flint desert. However, the flint disappears between Ǧabal al-Fahdah and Ǧāl Wāqiṣah. The bedouin call these flints by the name *ṣalābīkh*,[117] and more specifically the name *ṣalābīkh Wāqiṣah*. But I think this term is only in common usage among the ʿAnizah.

Five miles to the north of our encampment at Washrāf lies the line of demarcation between the territories of the two most powerful tribes in Arabia, the Shammar and the ʿAnizah.[118] This line passes more or less along the latitude of the wells of al-Shubaykah,[119] which lie five miles north-west of Washrāf.

These famous wells, numbering some three hundred in all, are not ancient and were dug by the Arabs of today, that is to say since the start of the Hiǧrī era. They are [121] just two, three and four metres deep. I was assured that they only contain water when it rains. So this would make them cisterns rather than wells, a belief supported by the fact that the water in them is putrid, bitter and salty.

On 15 February, an argument between two hameladars[120] and their bedouin camel-owners caused the Ḥaǧǧ to remain encamped at Washrāf.

I have already remarked that the terrain between Ǧabal al-Fahdah and Ǧāl Wāqiṣah differs from that of ʿAthāmīn to the south, which was flinty ground. At Wāqiṣah limestone too is present, but of very varied types, as can be judged from the samples brought back, which are as follows:

---

[117] [*Ṣalbūkh*, pl. *ṣalābīkh*, the normal term for flint in central Arabia (Groom 1983: 255).]

[118] [Compare this with Lady Anne Blunt's observation in note 106 above.]

[119] [The wells of al-Shabakah, also known by their diminutive name al-Shubaykah, are at approx. 30° 50' N 043 42' E. At this point the Darb Zubaydah follows the Wādī Shabakah, Lady Anne Blunt's 'Wadi Shebekkah' (Blunt 1881 ii: 91–2).]

[120] Hameladar: the name given to those who undertake, for a fixed price, the transport of the Persian pilgrims from Mesopotamia to the holy cities. (CH) [These were camel contractors or middlemen, usually Arabs of Naǧaf, who rented camels from the bedouin and leased them out to groups of pilgrims. As part of the deal they undertook to accompany the Ḥaǧǧ caravan personally and ensure that their clients were safely transported. Lady Anne Blunt has much to say about these 'hemeldaria, or contractors for the Haj' (Blunt 1881 ii: 83–4).]

1. Limestone sprinkled with grains of quartz;
2. Grey crystalline limestone;
3. Concretized limestone;
4. Very compact limestone, polished as if varnished on the surface, probably by sand-blasting.

At Washrāf the prevalent limestone is of an extremely flinty type that scratches glass, and which is full of cavities and veins of limestone like travertine.

Progress was resumed on the 16th, and a thirty-kilometre march brought us to al-Ṭalḥāt,[121] one of the most important stations on the Darb Zubaydah.

There are ruins there of a hundred or so small houses and a large *khān* or caravanserai, the walls of which still stand four or five metres high.

In addition there are three cisterns, one circular and two square. Both of the two latter are double ones.[122] But most astonishing of all are two square wells, which are hewn into the rock all the way down. About seventy metres deep and measuring five metres a side, they had been made with perfect precision and attention to detail. I had so far seen nothing so [122] elaborate, for these wells are lovelier and deeper even than the ones at al-ʿAqabah. When I passed that way they were dry, just as they have probably always been.

The cisterns themselves were also dry, which was not so surprising as they were silted right up to their feeder channels. It had rained here as it had throughout the area, as was attested by the vigorous vegetation growing in all the hollows in the ground.

One hour before reaching al-Ṭalḥāt, we came across the ruins of an isolated building which had no particular name.

From a point ten kilometres north of Washrāf the ground once again changes character. Limestone, both concretized and compacted, and flint resembling jasper, become the dominant rock types as far as al-Ṭalḥāt.

This station still bears the name Mafraq al-Darb,[123] because the road

[121] [Al-Ṭalḥāt, which Huber spells Âthelahât, is the plural of *ṭalḥ*, a large-trunked acacia tree, *Acacia gerrardii*, prevalent in central and northern Arabia (Mandaville 1990: 170). Birkat al-Ṭalḥāt is at approx. 30° 56' N 043° 54' E, about 15 km north-east of Birkat al-Samīʿah, which Huber does not mention.]

[122] [By 'double', Huber is probably referring to a settling tank adjacent to each *birkah*, built to allow sediment to be trapped before the water flowed into the main cistern. Settling tanks were a common feature of the Darb Zubaydah cisterns.]

[123] [*Mafraq*: a crossroads or junction of routes.]

divides here, with one branch going direct to Nağaf, the other to Qaṣr al-Sayyid.[124]

On 17 February, we changed direction and marched north by 20° east.

At eleven o'clock we passed by the station of al-Ḥammām[125] without stopping there. It comprises a fort, a well and a cistern. The fort is one of the best-preserved on the route and contains a completely vaulted room which is still intact. The cistern too is well-preserved and contains water.

One hour later, having covered thirty-five kilometres from al-Ṭalḥāt, we made camp at the station of Ḥamad,[126] consisting of just a square cistern.

On the following day, two hours after having set off at six o'clock in the morning, we passed by the station of Mughīthah,[127] where there is a fort and two cisterns. Twenty kilometres farther on we made camp on the banks of Shaʿīb al-Khathʿamī, not far from the fort and cistern of Umm Qurūn.[128]

From al-Ṭalḥāt all the way to the streambed of al-Khathʿamī, the [123] country has the appearance of a stony desert devoid of vegetation. The latter streambed is dry, but as it has already had some water this winter it is full of greenery. We found both grass and firewood.

On 19 February, we set off at six o'clock and marched more or less north by 10° west.

After three hours on the move we crossed Shaʿīb Aṣb, which must have its source in the wells of Shubaykah and flow into the Shaṭṭ al-ʿArab in the vicinity of Baṣrah.

An hour after crossing Shaʿīb Aṣb, we came to Shaʿīb Abū Khamsāt, where there was plenty of greenery. We moved on and made camp another hour farther on.

---

[124] [From Huber's spelling, e'Seïd, it is not clear whether Qaṣr al-Sayyid or al-Saʿīd is meant. I have opted for the former, as elsewhere he renders Saʿīd as S'aïd. The reference is probably to a well to the east of Huber's route and south of Nağaf because he mentions it again nine paragraphs below (p. 246), implying its proximity, and not to Qaṣr al-Sayyid Qāsim near Karbalāʾ which is north of Nağaf and 72 km south of Baghdad.]

[125] [Al-Ḥammām ('the Bathhouse'): about 20 km north-east of al-Ṭalḥāt, at 31° 04' N 044° 04' E (GeoNames).]

[126] [Birkat Ḥamad: about 16 km north by east of al-Ḥammām, at 31° 15' N 044° 05' E (GeoNames).]

[127] [Biʾr Mughīthah, or Umm Ghīthah: about 12 km NNE of Birkat Ḥamad, at 31° 21' 20" N 044° 08' 05" E (GeoNames).]

[128] [Umm Qurūn, aka Umm Karūn: Huber spells this Ouâmeqroûn (i.e. Umm Qurūn). Umm Qurūn/Karūn is about 25 km north-east by north of Mughīthah, at 31° 32' 16" N 044° 13' 48" E (GeoNames).]

We had Qaṣr al-Sayyid a few kilometres to the east of our encampment, with its single spring. A few kilometres to the south-east of us was Qaṣr Ruhaym,[129] with a spring of bitter water.

Since eight o'clock in the morning we had been able to see before us the gilded cupola of the Mosque of ʿAlī at Nağaf, shimmering like the sun. It was a view that heartened everybody and consigned their past sufferings to welcome oblivion.

Everyone was ready long before dawn on the next day, 20 February. We moved off at six o'clock, and an hour and a half brought us to the 'Sea of Nağaf',[130] which we left on our right so as to go around it. Marching first north-east, then east and finally south-east, I arrived at Holy Nağaf a few minutes before midday.

The bedouin had wanted to get the better of Ibn Rashīd by refusing to transport the pilgrims on the terms set by him. But finally, under the pressure of his threats, they had opted to supply their worst camels, which had forced the Ḥağğ to restrict its marches to only six or seven hours a day. It had thus taken us thirty-five days to go from Ḥāʾil to Nağaf, a journey that can normally be done easily in twelve.

I stayed several days at Nağaf and Karbalāʾ,[131] happy [124] to indulge once more in the pleasures of a civilization more advanced than that of the desert-dwellers. The plague had broken out at Nağaf and I had to go into fifteen days' quarantine at al-Musayyib[132] before being able to enter Baghdad, which I did not reach until 18 March. I was given the most cordial, frank and friendly welcome by our consul, M. Péretié, combined with comprehensively Oriental hospitality.[133] I shall be eternally grateful to him.

---

[129] [For Qaṣr Ruhaym in 1879, see Blunt 1881 ii: 95–7. Wallin went through it 1848 and calls it Qaṣr al-Ruheímí (Wallin 1850: 339).]

[130] [The 'Sea of Nağaf', Baḥr al-Nağaf, is a large shallow lake and wetland lying immediately south and south-east of the city of al-Nağaf. It occupies a depression between the desert edge and the alluvial plain of the Middle Euphrates.]

[131] [Karbalāʾ, site of the Battle of Karbalāʾ in AD 680 and of the tomb of the martyred Imām Ḥusayn ibn ʿAlī, is like Nağaf a city of pilgrimage for Shīʿah Muslims. It is about 70 km north by west of Nağaf and 90 km south-south-west of Baghdad. Huber spent several days in both towns, falling ill in Karbalāʾ, and did not reach Baghdad until 18 March 1881 (Huber's 65-page handwritten report dated 27 March 1882, French national archives, Pierrefitte-sur-Seine, Dossier F/17/2976/1:1, entitled 'Mission au Thibet et dans l'Asie centrale', 1878–82, item 79, p. 54).]

[132] [Al-Musayyib: a town occupying both banks of the Euphrates south of Baghdad.]

[133] [In his 65-page handwritten report dated 27 March 1882, Huber states: 'I lacked the means to return to Europe and the French consul had no orders to provide me with

One word more before closing this account of the itinerary from Ḥā'il towards Iraq. There are three routes commonly used, which the Arabs designate as follows:

- The Darb al-Samāwah: this leaves the latter place on the banks of the Euphrates and goes to the Ǧabal via Līnah.
- The Darb Ghazāl, which can leave from any point in Mesopotamia, and veers a little westwards before going south, passing to the west of the wells of Shubaykah and striking boldly into the Nafūd. This journey can only be undertaken by men with good mounts. It is probably the route followed by Wallin in 1848.[134]
- The Darb Zubaydah or Darb Sulṭānī, which runs between the two previous routes. That is the one followed by me and which I have just described.

But one should understand that this latter route, despite the luxury of its cisterns, is not practicable at all times, because the winter rains are not regular. All the Arabs told me that before the winter of 1880–81 there had been three winters without rain, during which not a single cistern had contained any water, and that before these three winters there had been nine others of drought. Hence out of thirteen years this route had been practicable only for three. The pilgrim caravans for which it was constructed can make use of it even less often, given that the pilgrimage usually coincides with a hot month rather than a cool one.

The builders of the Darb Zubaydah well understood [125] this inconvenient fact and tried to counteract it by sinking wells next to their enormous cisterns. We have seen how pertinacious they were from the beautiful works they carried out at the stations of al-Ṭalḥāt and al-ʿAqabah. But Allah was decidedly not on their side, because they failed to find water.

Here now are some notes on the most frequented route, the Darb al-Samāwah going via Līnah which, for lack of more precise details, I have not been able to mark on my map.

---

them' (French national archives, Pierrefitte-sur-Seine, Dossier F/17/2976/1:1 entitled 'Mission au Thibet et dans l'Asie centrale', 1878–82, item 79, pp. 54–5).]

[134] [Huber is probably correct about this. Wallin describes his 1848 journey from near Ḥā'il to Naǧaf (Mashhad ʿAlī) in Wallin 1850: 336–9.]

On leaving al-Samāwah, a full day's march leads to al-Ǧafrah,[135] a station provided with wells. This place is made dangerous by the al-Zayyād[136] Arabs, who make robbery their business. They all have horses and are constantly marauding.

The second day leads already into the desert of al-Ḥağarah and camp is pitched in a place known as Abū Khuwaymah, where there is only water in winter, in a rainpool.

The third day's stop is made at al-Salmān,[137] where there are numerous wells with bad water.

The fourth day leads to Ḥaqiy al-Firdaws,[138] a slight, elongated depression in the ground about 500 metres in length which retains green vegetation all year round. It has no wells but, after the rains, water remains there for a long time.

The fifth day's camp is made at al-Khādīd, where only rainwater is available.

On the day six, camp is made at Ǧāl al-Baṭn, where either rainwater is available or else water from the wells at Līnah.[139]

My information on this route goes no farther than this point.

---

[135] The name written in the margin of the manuscript by M. Huber would authorize us to correct his transcription thus: al-Ǧufrah. (The Editors.) [Wallin corroborates this, calling it Jufratu al-ʿIraq (Wallin 1850: 339).]

[136] [Al-Zayyād: perhaps a clan of the Hushaym division of the Muntafiq tribe of southern Iraq.]

[137] [Al-Salmān wells are marked on the map entitled *Arabian Peninsula* (1973), scale 1:2,000,000 at approx. 30° 31' N 044° 32' E.]

[138] [Ḥaqiy: according to Musil (1928a: 193 n. 108) this is a diminutive form of Ḥaquw, escarpment. Groom (1983: 104) defines Ḥaquw as 'a rugged place elevated above a torrent', or 'any place reached by a watercourse'. I have been unable to locate either this place or al-Khādīd in the next paragraph.]

[139] [Huber's information seems to be at fault here, as the escarpment of Ǧāl al-Baṭn and the wells of Līnah would be too far apart to be easily accessible from each other. See pp. 238–41 and 236 above for these two locations.]

[126] From Baghdad to Damascus via the Ḥamād

From Baghdad one only has to make a choice of route by which to make the return journey to France.[140] The most usual way is the sea voyage via Baṣrah and Suez. This is the least tiring method though also the longest.

One of the land routes involves going from Baghdad to Mosul[141] and from there to Alexandretta, via either Urfa or Ḥalab [Aleppo]. This is done on horseback.

Finally there is another, much shorter way, using the desert route. It involves going from Baghdad to the Euphrates, and crossing it at Ṣaqlāwiyyah.[142] Then one carries on upriver along the right bank as far as Dayr,[143] where one turns south-west to go to al-Sukhnah,[144] Palmyra and finally Damascus. Water is available every day or two and the journey is made on a *dhalūl*. Unfortunately it lays the traveller open to the depredations of the great ʿAnizah tribes who inhabit these very parts of the Syrian Desert.

This is the route usually followed by the small caravans going between Baghdad and Damascus.

However, the direct route across the Ḥamād between Baghdad and Damascus ought to be be of greater scientific interest than these. This journey

140 [Huber here tells us nothing about how he spent his time in Baghdad between the end of February and the end of November 1881. But in his 65-page handwritten report dated 27 March 1882, he tells us more: 'Not wishing to abuse the hospitality offered me [by the French consul], I left Baghdad on 3 April to go and stay in Ḥillah, near the ruins of Babylon, where I spent the summer, mostly suffering from stomach pains. My stay in Ḥillah was not entirely fruitless and in the excavations of the ruins I was lucky enough to acquire some skulls of Arabs of the Ğazīrah and, more precious still, five Assyrian skulls. I also collected some bricks there, as well as some marble and alabaster stamp seals, a marble plaque, and some terracotta cylinders all covered in cuneiform inscriptions' (see French national archives, Pierrefitte-sur-Seine, Dossier F/17/2976/1:1 entitled 'Mission au Thibet et dans l'Asie centrale', 1878–82, item 79, pp. 54–5). We know too that he was assigned by the French government to investigate the plague then prevalent in Iraq (see Appendix 5, Letter No. 3 dated April 1883 to Ḥamūd ibn ʿUbayd al-Rashīd in Ḥāʾil). He is also known to have taken part in British Museum archaeological investigations at Sippar in Babylonia. These were under the direction of the archaeologist Hormuzd Rassam, an Assyrian Christian born in Mosul who became a protégé of Austen Layard's, was eventually naturalized British, and served as a British diplomat (see Introduction note 64). (MCAM/WF)]

141 The Arabic name is al-Mawṣil. (The Editors.)

142 [Ṣaqlāwiyyah: five miles north-west of Fallūğah, on the Euphrates.]

143 [i.e. Dayr al-Zawr.]

144 [Al-Sukhnah: in the Syrian Desert about two-thirds of the way from Dayr al-Zawr to Palmyra.]

has been made for several years by lone Arab riders operating the postal service between these two cities on behalf of the English consul in Baghdad.[145]

I therefore made preparations to follow this route and, having obtained the necessary guide, left Baghdad on 1 December 1881.

Leaving the city at five o'clock in the evening, I made just four miles before nightfall, and went and made camp not far from ʿAqar-Qūf,[146] close to some Banī Tamīm tents.

[127] Next day, the 2nd of the month, we started off at three o'clock in the morning, and twelve hours later reached Ṣaqlāwiyyah on the banks of the Euphrates.

The alluvial plain of the Tigris extends up to half way along the route, as far as Qaṣr al-Nuqṭah. Farther on, the ground becomes pebbly and stony. The soil composition is very complex. I have in fact picked up lamellar gypsum, flint in the form of light grey or yellowish pebbles, jasper with a craquelure of quartz veins, glassy white quartz pebbles, grey sandstone, and earthy limestone.

An hour before we reached Ṣaqlāwiyyah, the ground surface consisted of marble and mica.

After Qaṣr al-Nuqṭah the vegetation begins to resemble that of the Ḥamād, and the terebinth trees[147] typical of the Ǧazīrah[148] disappear, with one or two exceptions.

---

[145] The Ottoman government has initiated a similar service along the same route about a year ago. (CH) [This crossing of the Syrian Desert from Damascus to Hīt or al-Ramādī on the Euphrates dates back at least to the early Islamic era and came into regular use as a fast dromedary mail route from 1837 (Grant 1937: 170–1, 255–9). It was known as the Darb al-Sāʿī (the 'Courier Road'). It was still being used as a rapid mail route in 1908 when Musil described it (Musil 1927: 30, 69–70, 76–7, 527). Musil's maps at 1:1,000,000 scale (*Northern Arabia*, 1928c) mark the Darb al-Saʿī along its whole route, which was about 600 km in a very direct line. Gertrude Bell travelled along it from Damascus to Hīt during 9–23 February 1911, going through the same places as Huber and photographing some of them (Gertrude Bell Archive website). Leachman (1914: 505) states: 'The camel rider whose duty it was to carry the post from Damascus to Baghdad generally covered an average of 60 miles a day for nine days.']

[146] [ʿAqar-Qūf: the ancient Dur Kurigalzu, dating back to the Kassite era of Babylonian history in the late 15th and early 14th centuries BC. Its famous ziggurat, well-preserved and 30 km west of the centre of Baghdad, was a landmark for travellers.]

[147] [Terebinth trees: the terebinth or turpentine tree is a species of *Pistacia* native to Iran and the Mediterranean.]

[148] [Al-Ǧazīrah ('the Island') was a term used to denote the northern reaches of Mesopotamia between the Euphrates and the Tigris, south to a line running between al-Tikrīt and Anbar – a region that comprises part of northern Iraq and extends into Turkey and north-eastern Syria.]

Next day we crossed the Euphrates in a ferry fifteen minutes from the village, an exercise that took no more than a quarter of an hour. We straight away set our course to the north by 70° west for al-Ramādī, where we arrived at four o'clock to go and make camp in the open fields an hour's march farther on.

The entire right bank of the Euphrates from Ṣaqlāwiyyah to al-Ramādī for a width of 500 to 1,000 metres is under cultivation by the sedentary Arabs of the *Abū Fahat, *Ourdemy and *Mehamtah tribes.

The countryside is totally different. It is no longer the immense alluvial plain of the Ǧazīrah: the alluvium stops at one to five kilometres away from the Euphrates. The ground rises imperceptibly, forming an uplift of fifteen to twenty metres, composed of friable sandstone in a crumbling state.

We set off at four o'clock in the morning on 4 December and reached Hīt[149] nine hours later. Since eight o'clock its direction had been indicated by a column [128] of black smoke produced by the distillation of its mineral essences.[150]

This little town, one of the oldest in the world and surely pre-dating Babylon, is today situated 150 metres to the west of its ancient location. Present-day Hīt occupies the site of the citadel of the ancient town, on a rock overlooking the river that forms a precipice on this side. On the left bank opposite lies a single plantation of 200 twenty-year-old palms. They are irrigated by means of two of those enormous wheels driven by the current which bring up the water with a deafening groan and which are peculiar to the Euphrates region. At its base, to the east of Hīt, is one more garden with 100 palms. That is all the greenery there is.

It is generally known that beyond Hīt the range of the date palm extends up to ʿĀnah, but that point marks the northern limit of this tree's productivity and beyond that it no longer bears fruit.

---

149 Hît, the ancient His of Herodotus. (CH) [The place identified by Huber is actually called Is in Herodotus (*Histories*, Bk 1: 179) which, from its abundance of naturally occurring bitumen, is generally accepted to be located at present-day Hīt: 'Now there is another city distant from Babylon a space of eight days' journey, of which the name is Is; and there is a river there of no great size, and the name of the river is also Is, and it sends its stream into the river Euphrates. This river Is throws up together with its water lumps of asphalt in great abundance, and thence was brought the asphalt for the wall of Babylon.']

150 [Distillation and cracking of bitumen by heating was used to produce naphtha and kerosene, and the techniques had been known from at least early Islamic times (Bilkadi 1984).]

The territory of Hīt is in the form of a depression comparable to the basins I saw in al-Qaṣīm. One end of this basin is adjacent to the Euphrates, and it is at this precise point that Hīt is located.

The countryside has a bare and desolate appearance. For several kilometres around there rise small springs saturated with hydrogen sulphide, which exacerbates the foul-smelling atmosphere already heavily polluted by the black smoke from the carbides [*sic*; 'carbures', though hydrocarbons must be meant] used as fuel to distil those very same carbides.

The village gives the impression of a ruin. A minaret located at its southern angle is visible from a great distance when coming from al-Ramādī.

Hīt's existence is entirely dependent on its bitumen springs, which are apparently inexhaustible.

According to the mineralogical samples that I have brought back, the soil of the locality is composed chiefly of gypsum, quartz and phthanite pebbles; zoned, banded and occasionally manganese-bearing flint; hyaline quartz; black limestone pebbles, very [129] compact and sometimes tubular; and quartzy sandstone with limestone cement.

Between al-Ramādī and Hīt, the Euphrates flows in an arc to the north such that it is lost to view, and as the alluvium does not extend as far into the inside of the curve, almost all the route has to go over a gravel desert that bears the name Abū al-Rāyāt.[151]

Hīt is where water-skins are filled from the Euphrates for the desert crossing. We moved off again towards five o'clock in the evening, going north by 75° west, to arrive at eight o'clock at Kubaysah, a village of 500 souls surrounded by well-maintained walls, outside which we spent the night.[152]

The gardens of Kubaysah are in a separate enclosure to the north of the village. A copious spring flows along the edge of them, but the water is bitter and salty. Potable water for consumption by the whole village is only available from a single well 500 metres outside the walls.

This little town, at the gateway to the desert, is the seat of a *mudīr* responsible for collecting tax on behalf of the Ottoman government. But that is the sole benefit to the inhabitants of their nationality[153] because, even though they are victims of continual raiding by the ʿAnizah Arabs,

---

[151] [Khān Abū al-Rāyāt is located about two-fifths of the way from al-Ramādī to Hīt at the southern point of a bend in the Euphrates, at approx. 33° 29' N 043° 2' E.]

[152] [Kubaysah is about 22 km west by south of Hīt.]

[153] [i.e. as citizens of the Ottoman Empire.]

they have never witnessed a single intervention by the authorities to protect them.

We left Kubaysah at six o'clock in the morning on Monday 5 December; from now on we would encounter no habitation until we reached Syria. A tempestuous icy blast blew from the north all day, sometimes preventing our camels from moving forwards.

After six hours on the march our route, southwards by 60° west, brought us to Qaṣr al-Khubbāz.[154] Here we made a halt in the bed of a *shaʿīb* of the same name which, having formed on the plateau surrounding the *qaṣr*, takes a north-easterly direction, passes by Kubaysah, and from there flows into the Euphrates.

[130] Qaṣr al-Khubbāz is the first station on a route from Baghdad to Damascus that is also known as the Darb Zubaydah, like the one leading from Iraq to the holy cities of the Ḥiǧāz. That is to say, the installations along the route are attributed to the same princess.

In front of Qaṣr al-Khubbāz the ground drops abruptly for about forty metres, and by the side of the fort there descends a torrent in the bed of which a large, generously proportioned cistern has been built of dressed masonry. Everything is in ruins but even so it is easy to see that its construction is of the same type as on the southern Darb Zubaydah. The walls of the fort still stand up to three metres high and the arch of the gateway is still intact.

On leaving al-Khubbāz we kept on for twenty-five kilometres in the same direction, north by 65° west, and made camp at Riǧm al-Ṣābūn,[155] the name of a small hillock on which there is a lone structure of large blocks, now completely ruined.

---

[154] [Qaṣr al-Khubbāz is about 36 km west by south of Kubaysah. Maj. A.L. Holt describes this as a fort and cistern on this 'Darb Zobeidah' between Baghdad and Damascus (see next paragraph), and provides a photograph (Holt 1923: 261 and facing p. 264). He also lists Qaṣr ʿĀmiǧ and Qaṣr Muḥaywir as part of the Darb, both of which Huber was about to pass through.]

[155] [Riǧm al-Ṣābūn (lit. 'cairn of soap') is in fact 80 km not 25 km west of Qaṣr al-Khubbāz, and it is hard to see how Huber could have reached it in half a day. See map entitled *Baghdad*, scale 1:1,000,000, 33° 32' N 041° 20' E; Holt 1923, folding map. The explanation may be that he has inadvertently switched Riǧm al-Ṣābūn (which he would have reached on 6 December), with Qara ʿĀmiǧ and Qaṣr ʿĀmiǧ, which came before Riǧm al-Ṣābūn, and not after it as he has sequenced them here. Interestingly, Musil too places Riǧm al-Ṣābūn much too far east on his 1:1,000,000 map (1928c): see f16. An alternative explanation for this apparent error could be that there were two places named Riǧm al-Ṣābūn.]

On 6 December, just as we were setting off in the morning, the thermometer stood at minus 5.9°, and there was still a strong north-westerly wind blowing. No one had been able to sleep because of the cold.

A few kilometres beyond Riğm al-Ṣābūn brought us to the settlement of Qaʿrah ʿĀmiğ, and after a march of five hours we reached Qaṣr ʿĀmiğ.[156]

Qaṣr ʿĀmiğ is built on the most sloping part of a plateau. All that remain are foundations at ground level and the gateway with its arch. A little way to the west of the fort is a square cistern measuring twelve metres a side, but it is silted up with sand to ground level.

All the way from Hīt the desert maintains the same uniformity. It is nothing but vast plains with occasional slight undulations.

We went another forty or so kilometres from Qaṣr ʿĀmiğ and then made camp.

The night of 6–7 December was even colder than [131] the one before. The thermometer plunged to minus 10.1°. Fortunately the wind had abated somewhat compared with previous days.

Moving on at seven o'clock in the morning, a ride of three hours brought us to Wādī al-Muʿayshir,[157] which traces its source to about five miles to the south-east of my route. It flows to the north-west for about twenty kilometres, where it joins the Wādī Ḥawrān.

An hour before reaching Wādī al-Muʿayshir, I happened upon a curious thing. On both sides of the track there were the remains of enclosure walls identical to the ones I had seen on the southern Darb Zubaydah. I was able to follow these walls for a distance of about two kilometres.

Two and a half hours after leaving Wādī al-Muʿayshir, we halted in the Wādī Ḥawrān near the wells of Muḥaywir.[158] The ruins of Qaṣr Muḥaywir, its walls no more than a metre high, stand on the right bank of the wadi. The arched gateway is also still standing.

---

[156] [Qaṣr ʿĀmiğ is situated by Shaʿīb ʿĀmiğ. Captains Butler and Aylmer went through this area in 1908 on their way from Hīt to al-Ğawf (Butler 1909: 522). The *qaṣr* was photographed by Gertrude Bell in February 1911.]

[157] [Wādī al-Muʿayshir is about 18 km west of Riğm al-Ṣābūn.]

[158] [Muḥaywir: at 33° 32' N 041° 05' E (GeoNames). Huber calls this place ʿAywir, but he must have misheard the name of this important stopping place with its fort, which was photographed by Gertrude Bell in February 1911 (see also Musil 1927: 69, 527, 531). Wādī Ḥawrān is Iraq's longest wadi, rising just east of Ğabal ʿUnāzah at approx. 32° 15' N 039 13' E, close to where the modern borders of Saudi Arabia, Jordan and Iraq meet. It then flows more or less northwards to Ruṭbah, and thence east-north-east to the Euphrates about 50 km north of Hīt.]

The twelve wells of Muḥaywir are sunk into the actual bed of the wadi close to the right bank. Seven of them are filled in. They have been dug down through the gravel and their sides are retained by large rounded boulders taken from the wadi itself. The water is very good and is four metres down.

On the opposite bank facing Qaṣr Muḥaywir stands a ruined tomb, and all around it is a wide space with more tombs. This is the cemetery of the Ṣulubah, who also own the wells.[159]

According to my men, the Wādī Ḥawrān rises four or five days' march to the south-west of Muḥaywir, which would be about 200 kilometres, and its mouth on the Euphrates is three or four days' march away in the opposite direction. Other intelligence offers less reliable figures. The Ṣulubah north-east of the Nafūd had all told me that the total length of Wādī Ḥawrān did not exceed six or seven days' [132] march. The ʿAmārāt Arabs to the east of Karbalāʾ had given me more or less comparable figures. I confess that this latter information has influenced my tracing of the route and that I have not ventured to follow the compiler of the map attached to the journey of Lady Anne Blunt, who reports the head of the wadi at 036° 07' of longitude east, that is to say a whole degree more to the west than my calculations.[160]

According to sheet V of the course of the Euphrates by Col. Chesney, the Wādī Ḥawrān debouches into it twenty-five English miles to the north by 37° west of ʿĀnah.[161]

At Muḥaywir the banks of the wadi disappear and its bed is filled with coarse gravel, stones and rounded pebbles, all signs of an intermittently torrential weather regime.

The environs of Muḥaywir are rugged and the mountains are mostly composed of a dense limestone. My guides designated them all by the generic name of the mountains of Muḥaywir, but the various summits probably have specific names known only to the Ṣulubah who frequent this area in spring.

---

159 [On the Ṣulubah of this region, see Butler 1909: 523; Leachman 1914: 502–3; Holt 1923: 264. See also Translation Part II note 56.]

160 [Huber is unfair on Lady Anne Blunt's cartographer who, though still far from accurately, marks the sources of Wādī Ḥawrān at roughly 038° 40' E, not 036° 07' E as Huber claims. His longitude was thus more accurate than Huber's, though neither was close.]

161 [Col. Chesney's map was in error on this point (Chesney 1850). The Wādī Ḥawrān joins the Euphrates about 75 km downriver from ʿĀnah as the crow flies.]

Once the camels had been watered and our water-skins replenished, we set forth again and made about thirty more kilometres westwards. We were thus reaching the end of this desert, which offered nothing to see other than vast plains with long, low undulations of ground barren of all vegetation. It had begun west of Riǧm al-Ṣābūn, and it goes by the name of al-Ḍāyʿa as well as al-Ḍuwiyʿa (employing the emphatic *ḍād* in these two names).

Having left this area, on 8 December we came to the hillier country of al-Qaʿrāʾ, which is also less barren. The soil is good and produces rich pasture. At about ten o'clock in the morning I even saw some *nuṣī*[162] in a little valley where we had halted to eat, and let our camels out to graze.

I was able to take bearings on various summits visible from this stopping-place, all of them situated within the al-Qaʿrāʾ area:[163]

[133]	North by 22° west:	al-Ḥadar
	North by 60° west	Marbuṭ al-Ḥisān
	North by 70° west:	al-Naʿqah[164]
	South by 50° west:	al-ʿAfāyif

The last is the biggest of them.

In the distance in front of us, and just to our west, stretches a long mountain range called al-Malūṣah,[165] which we reached after eight o'clock in the evening and where there are wells.

Two hours before that we had had an alarm. We had just ascended the steep slope of a small hill, and when we reached the top we suddenly spotted the glow of a camp fire at a distance that I estimated to be five or six kilometres to the south. Men who could allow themselves to behave so blatantly, at

---

[162] [*Nuṣī*: *Stipagrostis plumosa*, a perennial grass; see Translation Part I note 88.]

[163] [The mountainous Qaʿrah area was crossed by Musil in 1908 and he mentions the same topographical features as Huber (Musil 1927: 62–4). Marbūṭ al-Ḥisān is at 33° 40' 15" N 040° 21' 43" E (GeoNames).]

[164] Perhaps better as El-Nâqah, because of the meaning. El-N'aqah [Huber's rendering] denotes a particular shepherd's cry when he wants to guide his flock; El-Nâqah means the camel. (The Editors.) [I have preferred to retain Huber's rendering in a corrected form, following Musil's use of this name (Musil 1927: 62).]

[165] [Ǧabal al-Malūṣah: at 33° 32' N 040° 12' E (GeoNames). According to Musil (1927: 59, 63–4) this name is Mloṣi. I have followed the Arabic version given in the margin of Huber's handwritten manuscript. The wells are about 50 km north by west of Ruṭbah. Coming from Damascus in 1912 on his way into central Arabia, Leachman turned south from the Damascus–Baghdad route at this point, 'close to the wells of Ghara or, as they are sometimes called, Meluse, or Bir Meluse on most maps' (Leachman 1914: 502).]

such an hour and in the desert, would have to have strength in numbers, and their presence here did not bode well. It was obviously the raiding party that the bedouin coming in from the desert, whom we had encountered a few kilometres from Kubaysah, told us that they had had to circumvent in these parts.

So, veering off abruptly to the right, we forced our march a little.

The wells of al-Malūṣah are also called al-Rāḥ, or again al-Agharī.[166]

The business of drawing up water from wells and watering the camels is always quite time-consuming, especially if the wells are deep. The difficulty is all the greater if the operation has to be performed at night, given how hard it is to identify the good wells, a process that involves having to investigate each one and take soundings one after the other. Also, when there is danger about and one is aware, as we now were, of being in the vicinity of a raiding party, it is vital [134] to do everything softly and quietly. One communicates strictly *sotto voce*, and the camels, which must be given no cause to bellow, have to be treated with particular respect.

Nevertheless an hour was sufficient for all to be completed to our liking, and at one o'clock in the morning we moved on to make camp eight kilometres beyond, among some great limestone boulders near Shaʿīb Samḥān.[167]

This *shaʿīb*, which originates not far to the south of our encampment, flows north-east and after about fifty kilometres joins Wādī al-Ratqah, which itself flows towards the Euphrates. I have reason to believe that it does not do so direct, but that it must be one of the tributaries of Wādī Ḥawrān.[168]

The sand of Shaʿīb Samḥān is a loamy silt with a large admixture of limestone, together with flint and carbonate of lime.

On 9 December, we left at seven o'clock in the morning and halted at ten in the al-Ḥarrī[169] area, which is a stony desert tract (with big shards of flint and limestone) but which needs no more than three full hours to cross.

Straight afterwards we marched on into the Ṣuwāb district.

---

166 [Shaʿīb al-Agharī, at 33° 26' N 040° 15' E (GeoNames), joins Wādī al-Malūṣiyyah from the south near the wells of Malūṣī/Ābār al-Malūṣī at approx. 33° 30' N 040° 06' E (GeoNames). Biʾr al-Rāḥ is in Wādī al-Malūṣiyyah some way east of the wells of Malūṣī.]

167 [Shaʿīb Samḥān: a wadi running south–north to the west of the wells of Malūṣī (Musil 1927: 74), and shown at e11 on Musil's 1:1,000,000 map *Northern Arabia* (1928c).]

168 [According to Musil's map, Shaʿīb Samḥān joins neither Wādī al-Ratqah nor Wādī Ḥawrān, nor is Wādī al-Ratqah a tributary of Wādī Ḥawrān.]

169 [Ğabal al-Ḥarrī is at approx. 33° 32' N 039° 54' E (GeoNames).]

At 3.30 p.m., 4.20 p.m. and 4.35 p.m., I crossed three small tributaries of Shaʿīb Ṣuwayb one after another; they start in that area and flow north to join Wādī Ṣuwāb.[170]

The three Ṣuwayb *shaʿīb*s are streams of no more than six to eight metres in width, with banks thirty centimetres high.

According to my men, Wādī Ṣuwāb joins the Euphrates between Dayr [al-Zawr] and Wādī Ḥawrān, but no one was able to pinpoint the junction precisely, nor even to say whether it is above or below ʿĀnah. In any case, on examining Col. Chesney's beautiful map of the Euphrates, I saw on Sheet IV, which shows the course of the river between Abū *Saïde [135] and *Werdi, that on its return through the desert the expedition came across Wādī Ṣuwāb, at 36 miles[171] north and 78° west of *Werdi (34° 29' 4" Latitude N.). With this fixed point and bearing in mind the configuration of the terrain near this part of the Euphrates, I believe that I can locate with confidence the junction of this wadi with the great river between 34° 45' N and 34° 55' N of latitude, that is to the south of Dayr, which is at 35° 20' 7" N.[172] One is naturally entitled to some surprise that Col. Chesney's expedition failed to notice this junction, when its record of the course of the Euphrates was otherwise so meticulous.

The dominant types of rock in the Ṣuwāb area are flint and a red limestone. The sample I took from the bed of the actual wadi is a silt with a heavy admixture of reddish limestone perhaps derived from the erosion of the red limestone.

On 10 December, we kept going in our direction of north by 80° west. After two miles we found ourselves leaving the Ṣuwāb area and entering that of al-Wāliğ, and almost immediately after that we were riding north by 25° west. We took this more northerly course so as to circumvent a volcanic area to the south of our route which is very difficult to cross.[173]

---

[170] [For Wādī Ṣuwāb, see Musil 1927: 60–1, and map d12 and e11–12.]

[171] The English statute mile of 1,609 metres. (CH)

[172] [Wādī Ṣuwāb joins the Euphrates near al-Ṣāliḥiyyah at approx. 34° 45' N, so Huber was correct.]

[173] [Al-Wāliğ and Shaʿīb al-Wāliğ (at 33° 38' 19" N 039° 18' 41" E): see Musil 1927: 75. On the volcanic nature of this area, see e.g. Holt 1923: 262–3, in particular the great crater that he calls 'Mukhaimum al Walaj (the hiding-place of the Wādī Wālaj)'. Holt's 'Mukhaimum' is possibly a diminutive of *makman* 'a hiding place' or *mukmān* 'elliptical volcanic basins surrounded by lava and cliffs' (Groom 1983: 204). Thus Mukaymun al-Wāliğ would be a correct rendering. (MCAM/WF)]

It took us almost six hours to cross the Wāliğ area and reach that of Khuwaymāt,[174] which is not in any way distinct from what came before it – always the same naked appearance, the same complete absence of vegetation of any kind. The ground is covered in flint debris which looks lacquered, so much does it glisten in the sun. This desert resembles the one stretching to the east of al-Ğawf, between there and the desert of Walmā, except that the stones of al-Wāliğ and Khuwaymāt are coarser.

In al-Wāliğ we had resumed our westward course.

A night march brought us to the end of the Khuwaymāt district and the beginning of that of Shaʿlān.

[136] At 7.30 we witnessed a curious celestial phenomenon. A magnificent meteor, a veritable globe of fire with the apparent diameter of a large orange, appeared in the vicinity of Alpha Aquilae,[175] shot across the sky to the south, passed through Orion and disappeared behind us to our left, all the time illuminating us with a bright light as if from an electric fire. Fifty-five seconds later the noise of an explosion as loud as several cannon blasts reached our ears.

For the entire duration of this event Zayd, one of my men, cried out in the utmost terror 'Allāhu Akbar! Allāhu Akbar! Al-salām ʿala Sayyidna Muḥammad!' ('God is Most Great! God is Most Great! Peace be upon our Lord Muḥammad!') He kept repeating this phrase ten or so times, and then announced to us that this was an omen that our journey would come to a bad end.

'Is that not so, sir?' he said, addressing me.

'Yes, if it had occurred at the start of our journey,' was my reply. 'But now it has come too late to apply to us. So much the worse for anyone who has seen that sign and decides to go ahead even so, and sets off on a journey tomorrow.'

My explanation only half-reassured him.

Next morning, I took bearings on the following small mountains:

- Al-Ghrāb, at about ten miles north by 45° west
- Shaʿlān,[176] at about three miles north by 80° west

[174] [Khuwaymāt: an area of hills and valleys at approx. 33° 38' N 039° 14' E (GeoNames; see also Musil 1927: 75). Huber had here just crossed the modern Iraq–Syria border.]

[175] [Otherwise known as Altair, the brightest star in the constellation Aquila.]

[176] [Shaʿlān: an area of *shaʿīb*s trending north by east. Musil marks Khabrāʾ Shaʿlān at e10 on his 1:1,000,000 map *Northern Arabia* (1928c).]

- Al-Tinf and al-Tunayf,[177] at about sixteen to eighteen miles to the south by 45° west

In the vicinity of Ǧabal Shaʿlān, al-Tinf and al-Tunayf, there are rain-pools that retain water when the winter rains have been plentiful, and then the Fadʿān and Sbāʿ[178] gather there in the springtime.

We spent two and a half hours crossing the Shaʿlān tract, and immediately after that reached the Khawr al-Tinifāt area, where we made camp after three o'clock in the afternoon in a [137] delightful valley full of *ḥaṭab* and forage, including plenty of *nuṣī*. The terrain had in fact changed along with the landscape. The vast, monotonous and naked plains of al-Ḥarrī, al-Wāliğ and Khuwaymāt had given way to a rugged countryside of hills and valleys. Nor was the ground any longer littered with small stones like musket balls, but with fragments of rock more in the form of pebbles, which often seemed to have been crushed like the stones destined for embedding on the tarmac roads at home. Sometimes too, though less often, these stones were the size of our rubble hardcore, and their composition of quartz and crystalline limestone hinted at the proximity of volcanic terrain.[179]

We moved off again at five o'clock and went to make camp at ten o'clock in the desert tract of Zarqa Kabūd.[180]

Up until today, and ever since our departure from Kubaysah, we had been suffering greatly from the cold. Almost every morning the thermometer stood at minus 10°, and during the day the mercury hardly rose above 10° or 12°. Our water-skins stayed frozen even though I had taken the precaution of wrapping them in blankets, and despite remaining slung day and night on our camels' flanks. Twice we had to make morning starts on empty stomachs because we had been unable to melt enough water to make tea or coffee. Our

---

177 [Al-Tinf and al-Tunayf: mountains at approx. 33° 31' N 038° 43' E, and 33° 35' N 038° 47' E respectively (GeoNames). Musil marks them at e9 on his 1:1,000,000 map *Northern Arabia* (1928c).]

178 [Fadʿān and Sbāʿ: two of the main ʿAnizah tribes of the Syrian Desert. For the Fadʿān and its clans, see Musil 1927: 55–6.]

179 Quartzite and crystalline limestone are metamorphic rocks, that is to say rocks the substance of which has been altered or modified by the effects of heat, but under conditions of high pressure that do not exist on the Earth's surface. It would seem preferable therefore to use the expression 'plutonian terrain'. (The Editors.)

180 [Huber spells this Kaboût, but Musil mentions a Khashm Kabūd in this vicinity (Musil 1927: 37, 45, 61) and shows it at e–f8 on his 1,000,000 map *Northern Arabia* (1928c).]

melted butter[181] looked like marble, and we had to resort to a sword to cut the skin containing it.

Our greatest fears were for our camels. These poor beasts, who served us during the night as windbreaks, were frozen completely stiff by morning. To get into the saddle we had to let them stand up first and [138] then clamber onto their backs. It was not until afternoon that they were defrosted enough for us to be able to urge them on faster.

On 12 December, it took us two hours to cross the desert tract of Zarqa Kabūd, which owes its name to the black basalt stones all over its surface.[182]

Next we found ourselves in the desert tract of Laqṭah, which is just ten kilometres wide and which we quickly traversed. It was immediately followed by that of al-Shaḥamī.[183]

Towards midday we had the pleasure of sighting the peak of Ǧabal ʿĀda, which is situated to the south of Qaryatayn and on which I took a bearing of north by 70° west.[184] It was an old acquaintance that I had made during my wanderings with the Ruwalah in the Syrian Desert,[185] and that showed us that we were nearing the end of our journey.

We made our way across the al-Shaḥamī desert tract to that of al-Murrah.[186]

Three miles to the south of my route, and about four kilometres from the end of Shaḥamī country, are to be found three rainpools located where the little Shaʿīb al-Shaḥamī comes to an end, having risen farther to the south. Along with the territory around them, they belong to the Ṣulubah Arabs, who go there in springtime when there is water in the pools.

The stony desert comes to an end at al-Murrah, and we began to tread upon good productive soil covered with rich pasture. Despite that, our *dhalūl*s would not eat with any enthusiasm. They stood staring at the horizon and yawning, and letting the strands of vegetation they were chewing fall to the ground. It was because the poor creatures were thirsty. They had had nothing

181 [*Beurre fondue*, 'melted butter': a reference to the clarified butter or ghee that was a major product of the desert tribes and a staple article of diet.]

182 [Huber does not explain this and it is not clear what he means.]

183 [Laqṭah is north-west of Ǧibāl Tinf and Tunayf. It is the name of a *shaʿīb* and a rainpool (Musil 1927: 75). Al-Shaḥamī: see Musil 1927: 77–9, and e8 on his 1,000,000 map *Northern Arabia* (1928c).]

184 [Ǧabal ʿĀda: Musil (1927: 11, 34, 36, 80) describes this prominent mountain.]

185 [For Huber's time with the Ruwalah before this journey, see Introduction p. 16.]

186 [Al-Murrah: Musil's Sowḥ Murra, a shallow valley (Musil 1927: 39, 77–81).]

to drink since the wells of al-Malūṣah – that is, on 8 December, at eleven o'clock in the evening.

As our own supply of water had also run out (there was only enough left for a single meal), we had absolutely no option but to hasten on our way.

At half past three we made a halt in the desert of [139] al-Murrah, and an hour and a half later we resumed our march until one o'clock in the morning on 13 December.

Having rested for two hours, we started off again at three o'clock in the morning. Ten miles brought us to the end of the Murrah tract and to the beginning of al-Hayl,[187] with a small wadi of the same name.

Al-ʿAyẓar[188] comes after al-Hayl, with the wadi of Sabaʿ Biyār.[189]

Al-ʿAyẓar is bounded on the west by a great square building of dressed masonry called Qaṣr Ṣayqal,[190] which marks the start of the area of the same name.

The Ṣayqal tract extends as far as Qaṣr al-Shāmī, a march of three hours and forty minutes from Qaṣr Ṣayqal.

Leaving Qaṣr al-Shāmī, we went another thirty kilometres to Birkat Sanabayn,[191] which is only six kilometres from the village of Ḍumayr,[192] where we were happy to arrive at five o'clock in the evening.

The terrain had become stony again just a few kilometres before we reached Ḍumayr.

On the following day, 14 December, having left Ḍumayr at eleven o'clock in the morning, I reached Damascus before five o'clock in the evening.

Ḍumayr is well known, as is the route from there to Damascus.

---

187 [Al-Hayl: a wadi bed and its surrounding area (Musil 1927: 39–41). At 33° 40' 00" N 037° 54' 00" E (GeoNames).]

188 [Musil's Umm ʿAjẓer (1927: 39). Huber spells it in Arabic al-ʿAythar in the margin of his handwritten manuscript.]

189 [Sabaʿ Biyār, or 'Seven Wells', about 70 km east by north of Ḍumayr. Huber was crossing the wadi to the south of the wells.]

190 [Qaṣr Ṣayqal: at 33° 41' 00" N 037° 08' 00" (GeoNames). See also Musil 1927: 34, 77–8, 82. Huber spells it Sayqal.]

191 [Sanabayn: east-south-east of Ḍumayr, at 33° 37' 16" N 036° 44' 42" E (GeoNames).]

192 [Ḍumayr, at 33° 38' 38" N 036° 41' 38" E, is 40 km east by north of Damascus and an important junction of the Darb al-Sāʿī with the Damascus–Palmyra route. From there, Huber would have reached Damascus by the usual route through ʿAdrā and Dūmā.]

THE GEOGRAPHY OF THE SHAMMAR EMIRATE

The region north of Ḥā'il

Ḥā'il, the capital of the emirate, is situated at the foot of Ǧabal Samrā.

The centre of Ḥā'il at the present day comprises twelve *sūqs* or quarters, as follows:[193]

> Bārzān[194] – Lubdah – al-Ǧabārah – al-Ǧarād[195] – al-Ǧadīdah – Samāḥ – al-ʿAbīd – al-Khanaqah – Warbiyʿah – Suwayflah – al-Khuraymī – Mufayḍah.

Samāḥ and al-ʿAbīd are the last to have been developed. Al-ʿAbīd, as it name implies, is entirely inhabited by [140] black slaves belonging to the emir. The water from the well of Samāḥ is the best in Ḥā'il. The town is about four kilometres in length, from Sūq Warbiyʿah in the east to Sūq Samāḥ in the west.

Water is close to hand in all the eastern *sūqs*, but it is bitter and undrinkable.

The population of Ḥā'il is 15,000 at most.

- Al-Waṣīd or al-Waqīd,[196] fourteen kilometres to the north by 31° east of Ḥā'il. Founded towards 1835. 150 inhabitants.
- Al-Ǧithāmiyyah, twenty kilometres north by 35° east of Ḥā'il. 100 inhabitants. This place has been in existence since 1830.
- Al-Laqīṭah, twenty-two kilometres north by 10° east of Ḥā'il. 500 inhabitants. It was founded at the same time as al-Ǧithāmiyyah.
- Umm al-Qulbān, sixty-two kilometres north by 32° west of Ḥā'il, in the Nafūd. 30 inhabitants.
- Qanā', fifty-seven kilometres north by 47° west of Ḥā'il, in the Nafūd. 100 inhabitants.
- Al-Ṭuwayyah or Ṭuwayl, ninety kilometres north by 74° west of Ḥā'il, in the Nafūd. 120 inhabitants.

---

[193] [See Euting 1896: 173 for a sketch plan of Ḥā'il in 1883–84 that locates some though by no means all of these *sūqs*.]

[194] [Huber (1891: 157) describes how this central quarter of the town was previously known as Amghīdah.]

[195] [Al-Ǧarād: for the Arabic, see Huber 1891: 186.]

[196] [Properly perhaps al-Waqīd (GeoNames). See Translation Part II, note 2.]

- Ğubbah, 130 kilometres north by 62° west of Ḥāʾil, in the Nafūd. 400 inhabitants.
- Al-Ğawf, once known as Dūmat al-Ğandal. A town situated to the north of the Nafūd, 320 kilometres north by 25° west of Ğubbah. It comprises fifteen quarters grouped together but separated by walls. It has around 12,000 inhabitants. An oasis of great antiquity, going back to before the 7th century BC.
- Qārā, thirty-two kilometres north by 70° east of al-Ğawf. 1,000 inhabitants.
- Saḥārā, five miles north-west of al-Ğawf. 50 inhabitants.
- Ḥasiyyah, seven kilometres north by 35° west of al-Ğawf. 50 inhabitants.
- Ğāwā, twenty-one kilometres north-east of al-Ğawf, on the route to Sakākā, with wells and springs. Today abandoned.

[141] • Muwaysin, at exactly half way between al-Ğawf and Sakākā, with wells and springs.[197] Currently uninhabited.

These five latter places are generally thought to be as ancient as al-Ğawf itself.

- Sakākā, thirty-five kilometres north-east of al-Ğawf, with 8,000 inhabitants, has existed for only a century.
- Kāf, in Wādī al-Sirḥān, 250 kilometres south by 25° east of Damascus. Populated for half a century, it has 90 inhabitants. Palm trees and salt production.
- Ithrah, six miles east-south-east of Kāf. A small and very ancient oasis which, having been abandoned, was repopulated only half a century ago. Water from springs, as at Kāf. 100 inhabitants.
- Baqʿāʾ, ninety-five kilometres north by 66° east of Ḥāʾil. 400 inhabitants. An ancient town and station on the Persian pilgrim route.
- Turabah, a fort built on the road from Ḥāʾil to Baghdad, close to wells of the same name, with a garrison of a few men. No

[197] [Muwaysin, at 29° 50' 50" N 039° 59' 36" E, is actually situated 12 km north-east of Dūmat al-Ğandal and 30 km south-west of Sakākā (al-Sudairī 1995: 88), thus much closer to al-Ğawf than to Sakākā.]

plantations. It is situated at two days' march north by 55° east of Ḥāʾil.

- Al-Ḥayāniyyah, three or four days' march north of Ḥāʾil, in the Nafūd. It is a fort with five wells, inhabited by two Ṣulubah families. 10 inhabitants.
- Tarbiyyah,[198] half a day's march east of al-Ḥayāniyyah. A fort with two wells. 10 inhabitants.

The region south of Ḥāʾil

The catchment of Wādī Ḥāʾil – the catchment of Wādī Ermek [Rimah] – the Ağā mountain range

- Al-Wusayṭah, 3 kilometres south-west of Ḥāʾil. 50 inhabitants.
- ʿUqdah, a series of little valleys in Ğabal Ağā containing ten small villages, the sole access to which is located twelve kilometres south by 70° west of Ḥāʾil. These villages are: Al-Qanī – al-Waybār – al-Nabaytah – al-Sāqah – [142] Huṣnā – al-Maʿā – al-Ghaḍyān[199] – al-Ḥāʾiṭ[200] – Ramīḍ[201] – al-ʿAliyyā.

Altogether, these villages have a population of about 800 people, of whom part are nomadic and only reside in ʿUqdah during the harvesting of the dates belonging to them.

- Qufār, once the Shammar capital, is still very important today. Situated nineteen kilometres south by 30° west of Ḥāʾil at the foot of the Ğabal, it extends for four kilometres between the mountain range and Wādī Ḥāʾil, but within that area are many abandoned properties. It comprises four small discrete towns: Al-Ḍabaṭ[202] – Al-Khishmāyah – al-Ḥimād – Warkdiyyah.

---

198 [I can find no record of this place. Possibly Huber was misinformed.]

199 [al-Ghaḍyān: an area where *ghaḍā* trees (*Haloxylon persicum*) grow; rough ground (Groom 1983: 90–1; Mandaville 2011: 249).]

200 [Not to be confused with al-Ḥāʾiṭ in the Ḥarrat Hutaym, to the east-north-east of Khaybar.]

201 [Ramīḍ, perhaps Rumayḍ: from *ramḍ*, meaning ground that is very hot from the sun (Groom 1983: 238).]

202 [The term *ḍabaṭ* seems to have been used in Qufār like *sūq* to denote a quarter of the town, and requires a name to follow it. Huber seems to have misunderstood this here.

The first three of these each possess a principal mosque. The people of Warkdiyyah, who do not have one, go to the Ḥimād quarter to perform the midday prayer on Fridays.
The population, who trace their descent from the Banī Tamīm, stands at 8,000 at most.

- Al-Qaṣr, situated forty-eight kilometres south by 22° west of Ḥā'il. It comprises three *suqs* or quarters, as follows:

  Al-Qabal, with 40 houses
  Al-Rashd, with 60 houses
  Al-Nafīd, with 35 houses

  Perhaps 135 houses in total with 600 inhabitants.

- Mawqaq, as the crow flies about seventy kilometres south by 60° west of Ḥā'il, situated on the western slope of Ǧabal Aǧā. It can be reached in a day from Ḥā'il on a good *dhalūl*. Mawqaq, comprising ten plantations, has about 520 inhabitants.
- Bidᶜ Ǧufayfā, six miles south of Mawqaq, with 100 inhabitants.
- Al-Ṣafrā', two days' march south-south-east of Ḥā'il, with 25 inhabitants. No palm trees, but grain cultivation. The wells are saline and bitter.
- [143] Al-Rawḍah, eighty kilometres south of Ḥā'il. 1,000 inhabitants. (?)[203]
- Al-Ḥufnah,[204] fifteen kilometres north by 55° east of al-Rawḍah. 50 inhabitants.

When he described Qufār again, during his 1883 visit, he listed two quarters of the town as Ḍabaṭ al-ᶜAyādah and Ḍabaṭ al-Khishmāt (Huber 1891: 155).]

203 [Huber here signals uncertainty about this place. He may be referring to al-Rawḍah in Ǧabal Rummān, about 22 km north-east of Mustaǧiddah. This Rawḍah is located next to, and may occasionally have lent its name to, the important settlement of al-ᶜAwsaǧiyyah (aka al-ᶜAwshaziyyah), itself at 26° 49' N 041° 41' E (GeoNames), which otherwise he does not mention.]

204 [Al-Ḥufnah and al-Ḥufaynah: the Arabic spelling for these is confirmed in Huber 1891: 181, 189. Modern-day al-Ḥufnah is actually located about 12 km south-south-east of Mustaǧiddah at 26° 35' N 041° 36' E (GeoNames), and not where Huber has placed it.]

1. Charles Huber's *carte de visite* featured this portrait photograph taken in Strasbourg in the studio of Gerschel Frères (4th floor, 3 rue de la Meisengasse) in 1882 or early 1883. This is one of only two known images of Huber, the other being the photograph of him in Arab dress shown over the page (Illustration no. 2).

2. Charles Huber in Arab dress, in a studio photograph taken in Strasbourg by Gerschel Frères in 1882 or early 1883. Personifying the quintessential Arabian traveller of the time, he appears to be wearing the clothes he wore in Arabia on his first journey. It is easy to dismiss his pose and the *mise en scène* as laughably Orientalist, reflecting the contemporary European public's taste for photographs of the people of the Bible lands and their supposedly languorous lifestyle. But, in Huber's defence, this was no masquerade. He had travelled more than 5,000 kilometres on camelback under gruelling conditions, symbolized by his trusty camel-stick, and was perfectly at ease reclining on an elbow-rest in camp. His attempt at authenticity has been undermined only by the completely inappropriate backdrop, typical of the visual clichés peddled by contemporary photographers.

3. Maḥmūd, Huber's servant and travelling companion, poses for the camera in October 1884 in the courtyard of the Dutch consulate in Ǧiddah for this photograph by Snouck Hurgronje. He was awaiting instructions to proceed to the French vice-consulate.

4. Huber carved his name in Arabic at al-Āyy, at the southern tip of Ğabal Mismāʾ, where he and Euting camped on 6 February 1884: 'Charles Huber *fransāwī*', 'Charles Huber the Frenchman'. (See Huber 1891: 252–9.)

5. Huber and Euting's graffiti signatures were carved together on this rock at Ğabal Mismāʾ, south of the Great Nafūd, as they made their way between Ḥāʾil and Taymā in early February 1884. This is the only known occurrence of Euting's signature on a rock in Arabia.

6. Huber carved his name at the great sandstone formation of al-Maḥaǧǧah, where he and Euting camped on 10–12 February 1884 (see Huber 1891: 279–90). This was discovered by Florent Égal in 2015. Qurūb al-Sharq, carved in Arabic, appears to be a place name but Huber does not record it. The Arabic to the right of the date appears to be the signature of Huber and Euting's servant, Maḥmūd.

7. On the trail of Charles Huber, from left to right: Abdulrahman al-Shaya, founder of Horizons Tours, Riyadh; Mohammed al-Ma'rek, specialist on Huber and Euting who continues to track their footsteps in Arabia; Florent Égal, photographer and author of the website https://www.saudiarabiatourismguide.com.

8. The Taymāʾ Stele, front and side. The inscription is in Imperial Aramaic and dates probably to 500 BC (Stein, in press). It has been in Paris, in the Musée du Louvre (AO 1505), since Félix de Lostalot brought it from Ǧiddah in June 1885. The inscription deals with the introduction of the cult of Ṣalm of Hgm, a particular manifestation of Ṣalm (the chief deity of Taymāʾ), into an existing temple dedicated to another manifestation, Ṣalm of Mḥrm, and two other deities, Šnglʾ and ʾAšīmaʾ. Most of it consists of the conditions for the support of Ṣalmšēzeb son of Peṭosiris, the priest of Ṣalm of Hgm, and his family. On the side of the slab is the picture of this priest and the inscription 'Ṣalmšēzeb the priest'. (With thanks to M.C.A. Macdonald.)

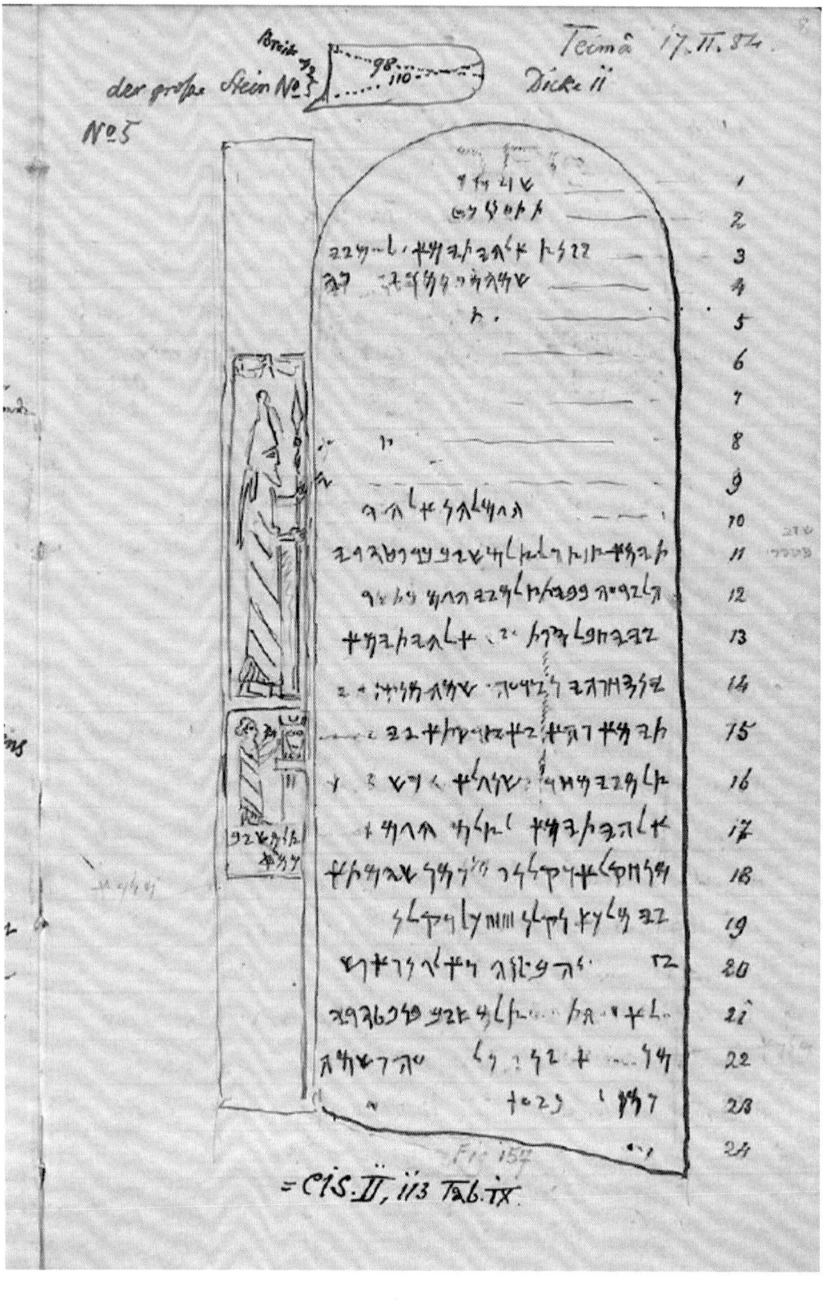

9. Euting's first drawing of the Taymāʾ Stele, from his Notebook V, 17 February 1884 (Tagbuch 15.2.84 to 20.4.84. Md676-22). Euting made two further copies of the Stele based on this one (see Illustrations 10 and 11).

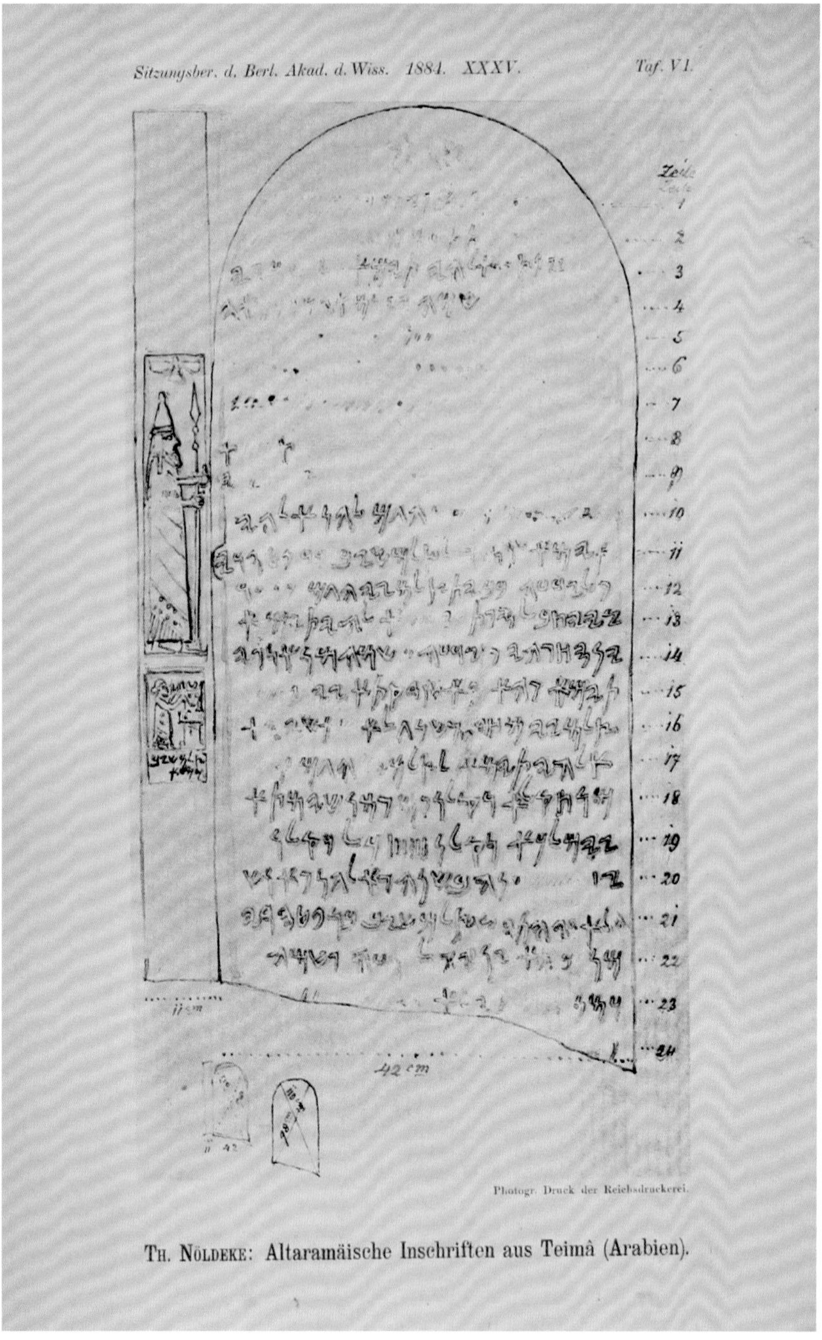

10. Euting's drawing of the Taymāʾ Stele published in Nöldeke 1884.

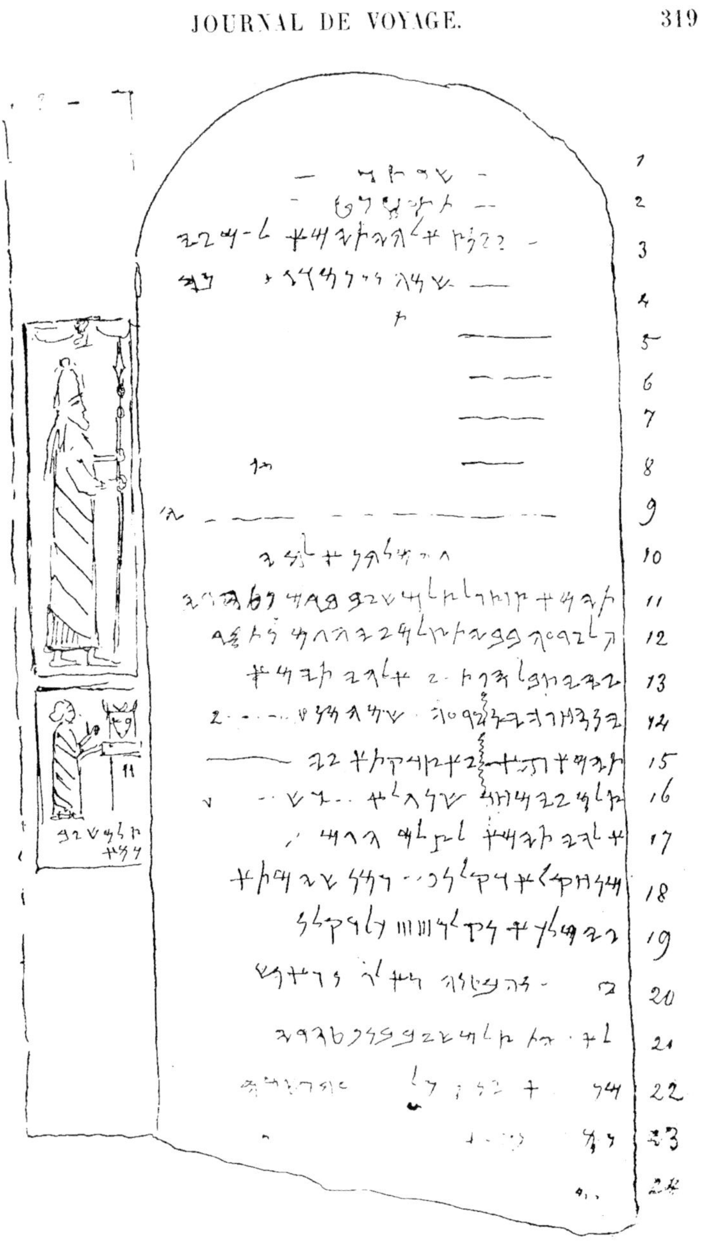

11. Euting's drawing of the Taymāʾ Stele from Huber 1891: 319. He had drawn this into Huber's notebook in February 1884, at the same time as he drew Illustration no. 9 into his own notebook.

12. This portrait of Julius Euting in Arab dress is dated 25 February 1885. It was done by Adolf Meckel von Hemsbach (1856–93), a German landscape artist who travelled in the Near East and produced a number of fine Orientalist paintings. He had been to school in Stuttgart, where it is possible he knew the Euting family. It was reproduced as the frontispiece to Euting's *Tagbuch einer Reise in Inner-Arabien*, vol. 2 (1914). The seal at the bottom shows the name by which Euting was known in Arabia, ʿAbd al-Wahhāb.

13. Sī ʿAzīz bin Shaykh al-Ḥaddād, who retrieved Huber's body from near Rābigh, and fetched Huber and Euting's belongings from Ḥāʾil, photographed in 1884 by Snouck Hurgronje in the courtyard of the Dutch consulate in Ǧiddah.

14. Charles Huber's tomb in the non-Muslim cemetery at Ğiddah, photographed by Fr Raphaël Savignac in 1917. The rear side reads: 'Juillet 1884. Mort pour la science'. The inscription at the foot reads: 'Monument élevé à sa mémoire per les soins du Ministère de l'Instruction Publique. – France'. (See Jolly 1893: 362–3).

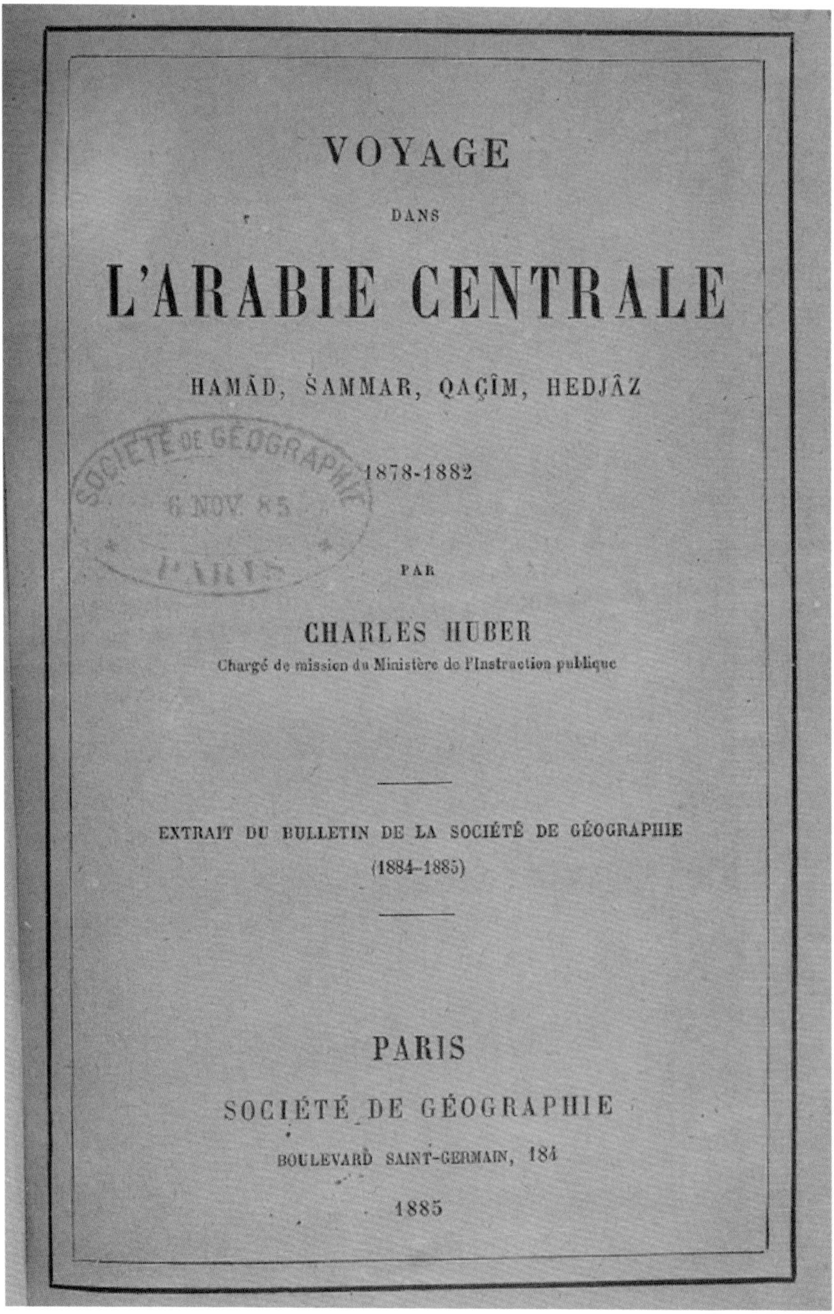
VOYAGE

DANS

L'ARABIE CENTRALE

HAMÂD, ŠAMMAR, QAÇÎM, HEDJÂZ

1878-1882

SOCIÉTÉ DE GÉOGRAPHIE 6 NOV. 85 PARIS

PAR

CHARLES HUBER

Chargé de mission du Ministère de l'Instruction publique

EXTRAIT DU BULLETIN DE LA SOCIÉTÉ DE GÉOGRAPHIE

(1884-1885)

PARIS

SOCIÉTÉ DE GÉOGRAPHIE

BOULEVARD SAINT-GERMAIN, 184

1885

15. The cover of Huber 1885, the one-volume reprint issued by the Société de Géographie de Paris of Huber's three articles on his first Arabian journey in its *Bulletin*.

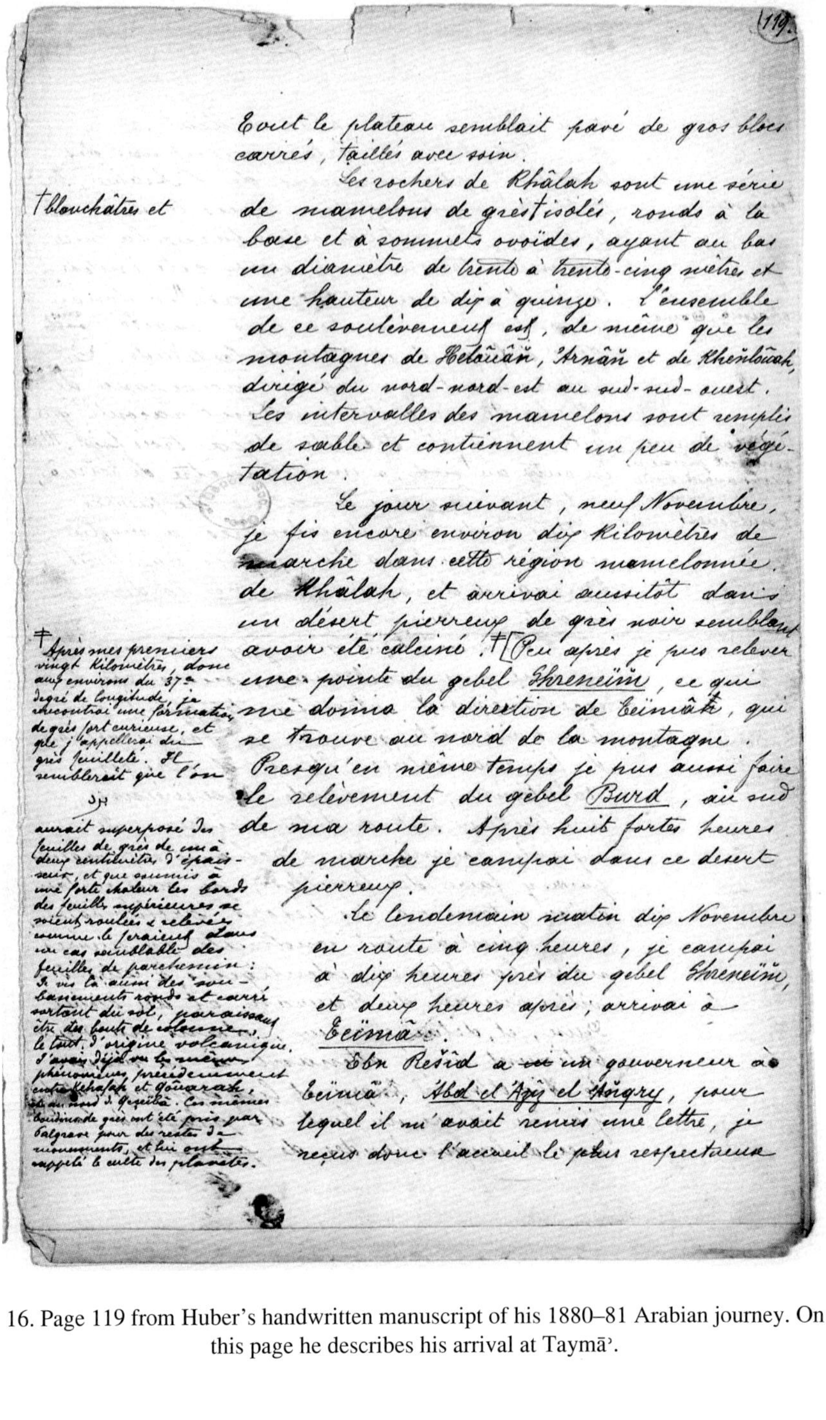

119

Tout le plateau semblait pavé de gros blocs carrés, taillés avec soin.

Les rochers de Khâlah sont une série de mamelons de grès †isolés, ronds à la base et à sommets ovoïdes, ayant au bas un diamètre de trente à trente-cinq mètres et une hauteur de dix à quinze. L'ensemble de ce soulèvement est, de même que les montagnes de Helâuân, 'Arnân et de Khenbouah, dirigé du nord-nord-est au sud-sud-ouest. Les intervalles des mamelons sont remplis de sable et contiennent un peu de végétation.

Le jour suivant, neuf Novembre, je fis encore environ dix kilomètres de marche dans cette région mamelonnée de Khâlah, et arrivai aussitôt dans un désert pierreux de grès noir semblant avoir été calciné. †[Peu après je pus relever une pointe du gebel Ghreneïm, ce qui me donna la direction de Teimâ, qui se trouve au nord de la montagne. Presqu'en même temps je pus aussi faire le relèvement du gebel Burd, au sud de ma route. Après huit fortes heures de marche je campai dans ce désert pierreux.

Le lendemain matin dix Novembre en route à cinq heures, je campai à dix heures près du gebel Ghreneïm, et deux heures après, j'arrivai à Teïmâ.

Ebn Reŝîd a ~~eu~~ un gouverneur à Teïmâ, 'Abd el 'Azîz el Hâgry, pour lequel il m'avait remis une lettre, je reçus donc l'accueil le plus respectueux

†blanchâtres et

† Après mes premiers vingt kilomètres, donc aux environs du 37e degré de longitude, je rencontrai une formation de grès fort curieuse, et que j'appellerai du grès feuilleté. Il semblerait que l'on

34

aurait superposé des feuilles de grès de un à deux centimètres d'épaisseur, et que soumis à une forte chaleur les bords des feuilles supérieures se soient roulées & relevées comme le feraient dans un cas semblable des feuilles de parchemin: Je vis là aussi des soubassements ronds et carrés sortant du sol, paraissant être des fûts de colonnes. Le tout, d'origine volcanique. J'avais déjà vu les mêmes phénomènes précédemment entre Kehafah et Qouarah, [illegible] au nord de Gezeïla. Ces mêmes [illegible] de grès ont été pris par Palgrave pour des restes de monuments, et lui ont rappelé le culte des planètes.

16. Page 119 from Huber's handwritten manuscript of his 1880–81 Arabian journey. On this page he describes his arrival at Taymāʾ.

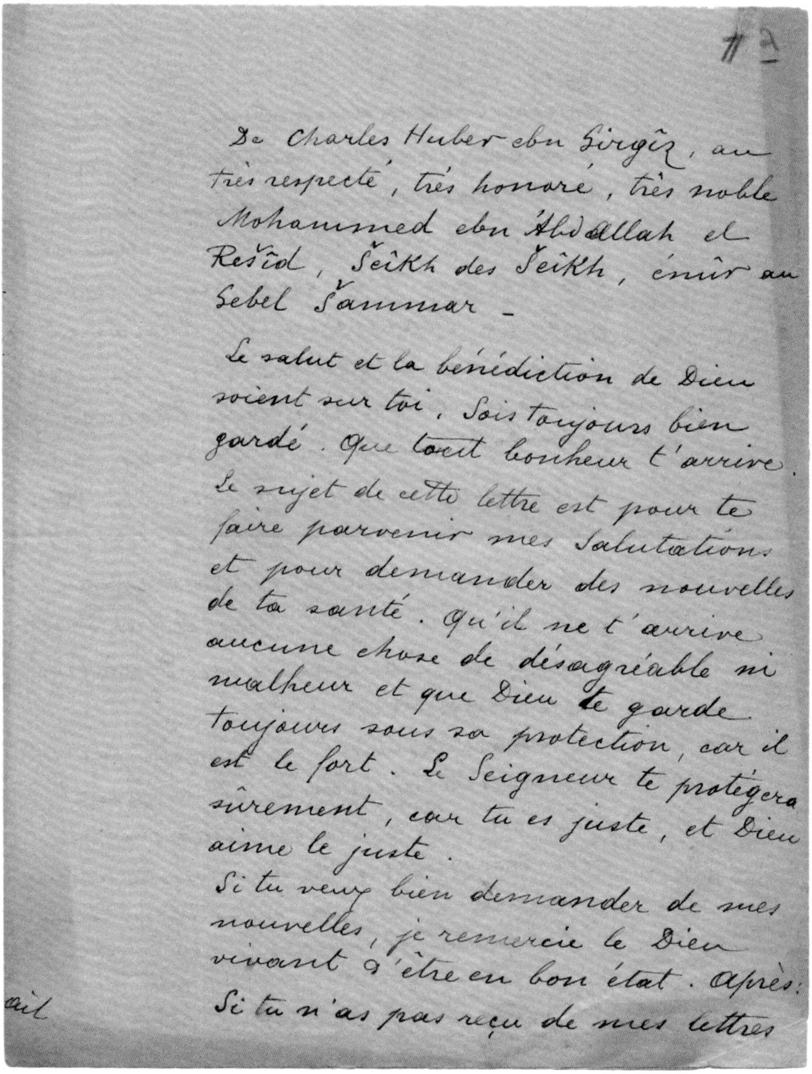

#2

De Charles Huber ebn Sirgîz, au
très respecté, très honoré, très noble
Mohammed ebn Abdallah el
Rešîd, Šeîkh des Šeîkh, émir au
Sebel Šammar —

Le salut et la bénédiction de Dieu
soient sur toi. Sois toujours bien
gardé. Que tout bonheur t'arrive.
Le sujet de cette lettre est pour te
faire parvenir mes salutations
et pour demander des nouvelles
de ta santé. Qu'il ne t'arrive
aucune chose de désagréable ni
malheur et que Dieu te garde
toujours sous sa protection, car il
est le fort. Le Seigneur te protégera
sûrement, car tu es juste, et Dieu
aime le juste.
Si tu veux bien demander de mes
nouvelles, je remercie le Dieu
vivant d'être en bon état. Après:
ail Si tu n'as pas reçu de mes lettres

17. Huber's letter from Paris to the Emir Muḥammad Ibn Rashīd in Ḥā'il, dated *ca.* 10 April 1883, informing him of his plan to return to Arabia with Julius Euting. This was translated into Arabic by Euting before being sent to Damascus to await a courier for Ḥā'il.

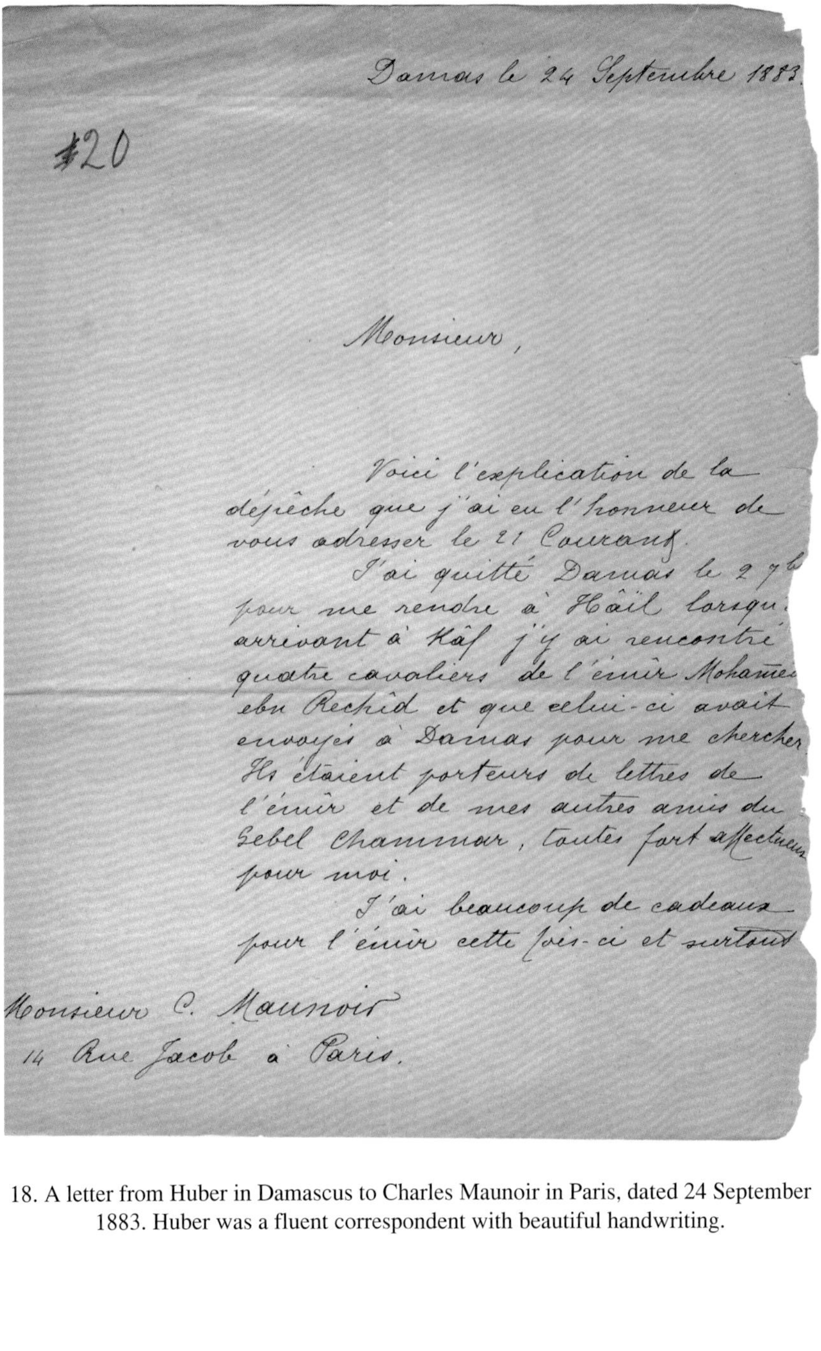

Damas le 24 Septembre 1883.

#20

Monsieur,

Voici l'explication de la dépêche que j'ai eu l'honneur de vous adresser le 21 Courant.

J'ai quitté Damas le 2 7b pour me rendre à Haïl lorsqu arrivant à Kâf j'y ai rencontré quatre cavaliers de l'émir Mohame ebn Rechîd et que celui-ci avait envoyés à Damas pour me chercher. Ils étaient porteurs de lettres de l'émir et de mes autres amis du Gebel Chammar, toutes fort affectueu pour moi.

J'ai beaucoup de cadeaux pour l'émir cette fois-ci et surtout

Monsieur C. Maunoir
14 Rue Jacob à Paris.

18. A letter from Huber in Damascus to Charles Maunoir in Paris, dated 24 September 1883. Huber was a fluent correspondent with beautiful handwriting.

- Al-Ḥufaynah, one kilometre north-east of al-Ḥufnah. 20 inhabitants.
- Samīrā, about 100 kilometres south by 10° east of Ḥāʾil. Samīrā possesses no palm trees and has only fields of wheat. Water is very plentiful and only two metres down. This place is very ancient and counts about 400 inhabitants.[205]
- Al-Mustağiddah, about 100 km south by 10° west of Ḥāʾil. A very ancient town and once as populous as Qufār. Nowadays it is one of the stations of the Persian pilgrim caravan, and its population amounts to 700–800 at most.
- Al-Sulaymī, twenty-two kilometres south of al-Mustağiddah. A small village with three plantations and 30 inhabitants.
- Shatawī, twelve kilometres north-north-west of al-Mustağiddah, and four miles east of al-Maḥāsh. It possesses 600 palm trees, which water themselves from the subsoil like those of ʿUqdah.[206] They belong to the *El Eslé[207] Arabs who come to Shatawī from time to time in winter to sow wheat there. In summer they are there only during the ripening season of their palms. Shatawī is situated near a small *ğabal* of the same name.[208]
- Al-Maḥāsh, a property with a well, the water of which is eighteen metres down. 50 palm trees, 6 inhabitants.
- Al-Ghazzālah, eight kilometres south-south-west of al-Maḥāsh, comprises two large plantations. 80 inhabitants.

[144] • Al-Quṣayr.[209] Three large plantations 600–700 metres apart, with palm trees and fields of barley. One of these plantations, the one to the west, has water that is not potable. Sweet water

---

[205] [Samīrā was an important station on the Darb Zubaydah (Al-Rashid 1980: 95–7).]

[206] This is what the Arabs of the Souf call a *ghirs ṭuluwʿ*, a 'rising plantation'. The water in a substrate of the soil, into which the roots of the plant penetrate, rises into the tree through hollow fibres, thus irrigating it. (The Editors.) [The area around Ğarash north of ʿAmmān in Jordan is known as the Souf, but it is not clear whether that is what is meant here by Huber's editors.]

[207] [I have been unable to identify this Shammar clan in Oppenheim or elsewhere.]

[208] [I have been unable to locate Shatawī.]

[209] [Huber does not specify the location of this al-Quṣayr. A possible candidate is Quṣayr al-Turkī near al-Mustağiddah.]

is at twenty-four metres' depth, the same as at al-Mustağiddah and al-Ghazzālah. 30 inhabitants.

- Ghamr, 8 km north-west of al-Maḥāsh, at the foot of a small *ğabal* of the same name. No wells. Water is in the cisterns or rainpools. The palm trees of Ghamr are in the mountains and are self-watered from the subsoil like those of ʿUqdah.
- Ghaẓwar, fourteen kilometres south by 55° west of al-Mustağiddah.[210] 25 inhabitants.
- Zarghaṭ,[211] fifty kilometres north of al-Ḥāʾiṭ. A single plantation, with fifty palms and fields of wheat and barley, inhabited by a Hutaym family. 8 inhabitants. One well with water at a depth of two metres. This location is incorrectly positioned on the map; it should, I think, be farther to the south-east.
- Al-Ḥāʾiṭ is located to the north [*sic*; south is meant], on the eastern edge of the Ḥarrah [Ḥarrat Hutaym]. An oasis of great antiquity, today comprising the three following *sūq*s: Wādī Saʿfān – al-Shurayf – al-Quṣayr.
- Al-Ḥuwayyiṭ,[212] about twenty kilometres south of al-Ḥāʾiṭ, in the Ḥarrah near Ğabal Kanāt.[213] 70 inhabitants.

The region to the west of Ḥāʾil
The Ḥiğāz

- Taymāʾ, an oasis of great antiquity north of Ğabal Ghunaym, six days' journey to the west of Ḥāʾil. Sixty plantations with a population of about 1,500.
- Al-ʿUlā, an oasis of great antiquity, and situated two full days'

[210] In the margin of M. Huber's manuscript this name is written in Arabic. The Arabic spelling must be rendered as Ghaẓwar, the meaning of which is 'greenish, sticky clay'. (The Editors.) [This place is probably Quṣayr al-Turkī, aka Ghaẓwar, a few kilometres south-east of al-Ghazzālah and not south-west of al-Mustağiddah.]

[211] [Huber confusingly spells this Dheraghrath, but he means either Zarghaṭ (or Ẓarghaṭ, at 26° 32' 00" N 040° 29' 00" E) or, less probably, Zurayghiṭ (or Ẓurayghiṭ) a few kilometres to the south-east. Both of these settlements are on the eastern side of the northern section of the Ḥarrat Hutaym.]

[212] [Al-Ḥuwayyiṭ is in fact about 50 km south of al-Ḥāʾiṭ, at 25° 38' 18" N 040° 23' 45" E.]

[213] [I have been unable to identify this mountain.]

[145] journey to the south-south-west of Taymāʾ. Al-ʿUlā has been under the rule of the emir of Ǧabal Shammar since 1878. Beautiful palm plantations irrigated by abundant springs. Possesses very interesting ancient ruins. Approximately 1,500 inhabitants.

The region to the east of Ḥāʾil

- Ṭābah, in Ǧabal Salmā, two days' journey south-east of Ḥāʾil. 250 inhabitants.
- Al-Sabʿān, at the southern extremity of Ǧabal Salmā and two days' journey from Ḥāʾil.[214] 500 inhabitants.
- Fayd, a village of great antiquity which was once a station on the Persian pilgrim road, the Darb Zubaydah.[215] Population much reduced today, to 250 inhabitants. Everyone travelling between Ḥāʾil and al-Qaṣīm goes through Fayd.
- Al-Kahfah, situated to the north by 65° east of Fayd.[216] It is the last settlement in the Shammar emirate on the route to al-Qaṣīm. 200 inhabitants.
- Al-Ghumaysah,[217] six kilometres south-east of al-Kahfah. 25 inhabitants.
- Umm al-Khashabah, ten kilometres south-east of al-Kahfah. In ruins.

Summary of places and sedentary populations in the Shammar Emirate

1. Ḥāʾil	15,000
2. Al-Waṣīd	150
3. Al-Ǧithāmiyyah	100

[214] [Al-Sabʿān is not in Ǧabal Salmā. It is actually about 60 km south-south-east of Ḥāʾil, at 27° 02' 43" N 041° 58' 39" E, and about 20 km west of Ṭābah, which is on the western edge of Ǧabal Salmā. It is possible that Huber was confusing al-Sabʿān with al-Ṣafrāʾ, which is off the south-western extremity of Ǧabal Salmā.]

[215] [For the importance of Fayd, see note 70 above, and Translation Part II note 23.]

[216] [Al-Kahfah is actually about 50 km east by south of Fayd. Huber has much to say about this oasis, which he calls Etzhafeh, in his later work (Huber 1891: 688–90) See also Translation Part II note 29, and pp. 156–8).]

[217] [Perhaps properly al-Quraymiṣah (Geonames).]

4. Al-Laqīṭah	500
5. Umm al-Qulbān	30
6. Qanāʾ	100
7. Al-Ṭuwayyah	120
8. Ǧubbah	400
[146] 9. Al-Ǧawf	12,000
10. Qārā	1,000
11. Ṣaḥārā	50
12. Ḥasiyyah	50
13. Ǧāwā (uninhabited)	0
14. Muwaysin (uninhabited)	0
15. Sakākā	8,000
16. Kāf	90
17. Ithrah	100
18. Baqʿāʾ	400
19. Turabah	3
20. Al-Ḥayāniyyah	10
21. Tarbiyyah	10
22. Al-Wusayṭah	50
23. Al-ʿUqdah	800
24. Qufār	8,000
25. Al-Qaṣr	600
26. Mawqaq	520
27. Bidʿ Ǧufayfāʾ	100
28. Al-Ṣafrāʾ	25
29. Rawḍah	1,000 (?)
30. Al-Ḥufnah	50
31. Al-Ḥufaynah	20
32. Samīrā	400
33. Al-Mustaǧiddah	800
34. Al-Sulaymī	30

35.	Shatawī (nomadic population)	0
36.	Al-Maḥāsh	6
37.	Al-Ghazzālah	80
38.	Al-Quṣayr	30
39.	Ghamr	18
40.	Ghaẓwar	25
41.	Zarghaṭ	8
42.	Al-Ḥā'iṭ	500
43.	Al-Ḥuwayyiṭ	70
44.	Taymā'	1,500
45.	Al-ʿUlā	1,500
46.	Ṭābah	250
47.	Al-Sabʿān	500
48.	Fayd	250
49.	Al-Kahfah	200
50.	Al-Ghumaysah	25
51.	Umm al-Khashabah (in ruins)	0
	Total	55,470

[147]

Summary of places and sedentary populations of al-Qaṣīm[218]

1.	Al-Quwārah	120
2.	Quṣaybā'	3,000
3.	Al-Mashkūk	10
4.	Al-Ḥamūdiyyah (uninhabited)	0
5.	Al-Raf[219]	100
6.	ʿUyūn[220]	2,500
7.	Rawḍah	1,500

[218] I include here only those places that are under the control of Emir Ḥasan of Buraydah. (CH)

[219] [I have been unable to identify this place. Possibly it is a typographic error for al-Rafīʿah, 20 km south-east of ʿUyūn al-Ğawā'.]

[220] [i.e ʿUyūn al-Ğawā', see Translation Part II note 35.]

8. Ūthāl	250
9. Al-Qarʿāʾ	800
10. Al-Shuqqah	1,000
11. al-Ṭarfiyyah	60
12. ʿAyn Ibn Fuhayd	600
13. Al-Ṣarīf (nomadic population)	0
14. Al-Nabqiyyah	35
15. Al-Rakiyyah	5
16. Rawḍah	150
17. Buraydah	10,000
18. Al-Khabb	500 (?)
19. Ḥuwaylān	350 (?)
20. Al-Quṣayʿah	200 (?)
21. Ruwayḍah (uninhabited)	0
22. Ṣubayḥ	500 (?)
23. Al-Muraydīsiyyah[221]	100
24. Khaḍar[222]	400
25. Al-Ṭaʿmiyyah[223]	10
26. Al-Shamāsiyyah[224]	250
Total	22,440

The following places in the province of al-Qaṣīm are at this time (1880) dependent on the town of ʿUnayzah, or else are independent:

Al-ʿAyāriyyah (in ruins)	0
Al-Wahlān (in ruins)	0

221 [Huber writes this place as Al-Buraydisiyyah, but that is certainly a misprint for al-Muraydīsiyyah, a small settlement 5 km south-west of Buraydah.]

222 [Khaḍar: a settlement 8 km south of Buraydah, near the left bank of Wādī Rimah, at 26° 14' 59" N 043° 59' 57" E (GeoNames).]

223 [Al-Ṭaʿmiyyah: a settlement about 15 km south-east of Buraydah, on the right bank of Wādī Rimah, at 26° 15' 38" N 044° 05' 41" E (GeoNames). See Translation Part II note 62.]

224 [Al-Shamāsiyyah: about 30 km east of Buraydah, at 26° 19' 34" N 044° 15' 31" E (GeoNames).]

	Rawḍat al-ʿAwshaziyyah	100
[148]	ʿUnayzah	20,000
	Al-Wādī	500
	Rawḍān	120
	Al-Shibībiyyah (in ruins)	0
	Al-Shinānah	200 (?)
	Al-Rass	3,000

APPENDICES

APPENDIX 1

Inscriptions collected in Central Arabia (1878–1882[1])

Bulletin de la Société de Géographie 7th series, no. 5, 1884, 3rd trimester, pp. 289–303

By Charles Huber

Commissioned by the Minister of Public Education

Ǧabal Sarrā' is an isolated granite outcrop situated about forty miles south by 15° west of Ḥā'il, the Shammar capital. A narrow valley affords passage for the route between Mustaǧiddah and Mecca. Inscriptions 1–6 are to be found on the southern rock face of the pass, at five or six metres above ground, and they appear to have been coarsely inscribed with the point of a pick.

Inscription no. 1[2] is 75 cm high by 60 cm wide.

Inscriptions nos. 2, 3, 4, 5 and 6[3] are cut into blocks spread around the rock face into which Inscription no. 1 is cut.

All the letters are about 3 cm high.

There are wells situated close to the pass.

Inscriptions 7–15 were found on the mountain that gives its name to this whole region, Ǧabal Shammar, also known as Ǧabal Ramīḍ as well as Ǧabal

---

[1] [Huber 1884a. In the original *Bulletin de la Société de Géographie* this is a separate article rather than an appendix. The account of the journey in the course of which Huber collected these inscriptions is to be found in Huber 1884b and 1885a, as translated above. The time period specified, 1878–1882, is inaccurate. Huber recorded all these inscriptions during 1880. See Introduction pp. 16–17.]

[2] [For this and all the inscriptions in this Appendix see the Concordance in Appendix 2. (MCAM)]

[3] [See Translation Part 1 note 162. (MCAM)]

Ağā. They are to be found close to a spot called 'The Mosque',[4] in the valley of Tuwārin.

They are carved into the granite just as they are [290] shown in the plates, that is to say horizontally or vertically.

There are remains of ancient habitation.

Al-ʿUyūn,[5] in al-Qaṣīm, a place of about 1,500 people, is situated twenty-two miles north-west of Buraydah. Al-Rawḍah, with 800 people, lies six miles to the west of al-ʿUyūn. These two centres of population are situated in a depression in the ground bounded by sharply defined cliffs, like an immense basin. They are both of very ancient origin.

Not far from al-Rawḍah there stand some huge, isolated sandstone outcrops, all covered with names, but wholly or in part illegible; I was able to copy only three inscriptions: nos. 16, 17, 18, and a tribal mark or *wasm* (no. 19).[6]

ʿAyn ibn Fayd,[7] a village of 600 people situated 28 miles north of Buraydah at 22°, is very ancient and possesses wells of undrinkable water. Three kilometres to the north of the village at 70° east, are to be found the ruins of a stronghold called Qaṣr Mārid. On its northern side the rock rises three metres above ground level; this rock is completely covered with names and inscriptions, but they have been effaced by time. I was able to decipher only nos. 20, 21, 22 and 23.[8]

Two kilometres north-west of ʿAyn ibn Fayd [*sic*; Fuhayd] is an ancient crater just above the ground, of about 500 square metres. Over all this area are scattered blocks of sandstone, the biggest of which are covered with inscriptions and names, most of them in Arabic. I was able to decipher only no. 24.[9]

Ğabal Ğildiyyah, located roughly thirty miles west[10] of Ḥāʾil, is of sandstone formation. Its surroundings are cut by gullies, and numerous hollows in the rock serve as catchments for the rains in winter. Inscriptions 25–74 are located close to each of these natural watering places.

---

4 [That is, al-Masğid, see Translation Part II p. 149. (MCAM)]
5 [i.e. ʿUyūn al-Ğawāʾ, see Translation Part II note 35.]
6 [See Translation Part II, pp. 11–12. (MCAM)]
7 [*Sic*; properly ʿAyn Ibn Fuhayd.]
8 [See Translation Part II p. 165. (MCAM)]
9 [See Translation Part II p. 165. (MCAM)]
10 [*Sic*; actually east of Ḥāʾil.]

Inscriptions 25, 26, 27 and 28 were copied on the great block of Umm al-Ruğūm; 29, 30 and 31 in Wādī Bāʿūr. Nos. 38–65[11] were all [291] copied on the rock of al-Buwayb. Finally, nos. 69–74 are located on a rock called al-Ṣaʿlikah[12] in the Wādī Shaqīq.

Ğabal Mismāʾ is about 70 miles to the south by 70° west of Ḥāʾil. It is a sandstone formation and at its base is a hollow where rainwater collects. Here inscriptions 78–84 are to be found. Nos. 75, 76 and 77 were discovered in another place on the mountain.

The three fragmentary inscriptions marked 85, 86 and 87 were copied at Taymāʾ on stones that were brought in as rubble in the construction of the present village. They evidently come from the ruins of an early Taymāʾ, located to the south of the modern-day village, and which are known as Tūmā.

Inscription no. 88 is located on a sandstone rock called 'é' rekeb' [al-Ruqqab] between Taymāʾ and Madāʾin Ṣāliḥ.

Six miles north of Madāʾin Ṣāliḥ, one encounters sand dunes and very singular sandstone formations called Miqraṭ al-Dabūs.[13] Large numbers of inscriptions are to be found there, but they have all been washed by the rains or eroded by the winds. I was able to copy only no. 89.

No. 90 is the only one I have recorded from Madāʾin Ṣāliḥ, where there are very many extensive and very well-preserved inscriptions above the monumental entrances of the tombs carved into the rock. They are too high to be readable from the ground and I lacked the means to help me lift myself up to their level.

Al-ʿUlā, ten miles [*sic*; actually about fourteen miles] south of Madāʾin Ṣāliḥ, has around 1,500 inhabitants. There I counted almost two hundred burial chambers carved into the rock, but with far fewer inscriptions and those less well fashioned. I copied those numbered 91–123.

No. 91 has letters carved in relief. No. 96 is located above the doorway of a burial chamber.

[292] The third line of no. 101 is in a differently carved style from the first two lines.[14]

---

[11] [Huber does not give the provenance of nos 32–37, beyond Ğabal Ğildiyyah. (MCAM)]

[12] [For this name, spelt variously Ṣaʿlikah and Ṣaʿlīkah, see Huber 1891: 101; Euting 1896: 240 n.1]

[13] [See Translation Part II note 147.]

[14] [They are of course two different inscriptions, see Appendix 2. (MCAM)]

All the rocks in the environs of Khaybar are covered with drawings of men, animals and inscriptions, but the only ones I found to be legible were the ninety-nine words of inscriptions 124–131.[15]

Khaybar is situated about eighty miles north of al-Madīnah.

Al-Ḥāʾiṭ is located about sixty-five [actually seventy-five miles in a straight line] miles north by 25° east of Khaybar and, like the latter, occupies a rift in the stony desert of the Ḥarrah.[16]

All the rocks around it are covered with inscriptions of which only a few are still legible; these are represented here by nos. 132–146.

[15] [This statement is bizarre. There are only 52 letters in these inscriptions and in any case Huber would not have known how to divide the inscriptions into words since he was unable to read them. (MCAM)]

[16] [*ḥarrah*: the black basalt broken-up lava-flows of ancient volcanic origin.]

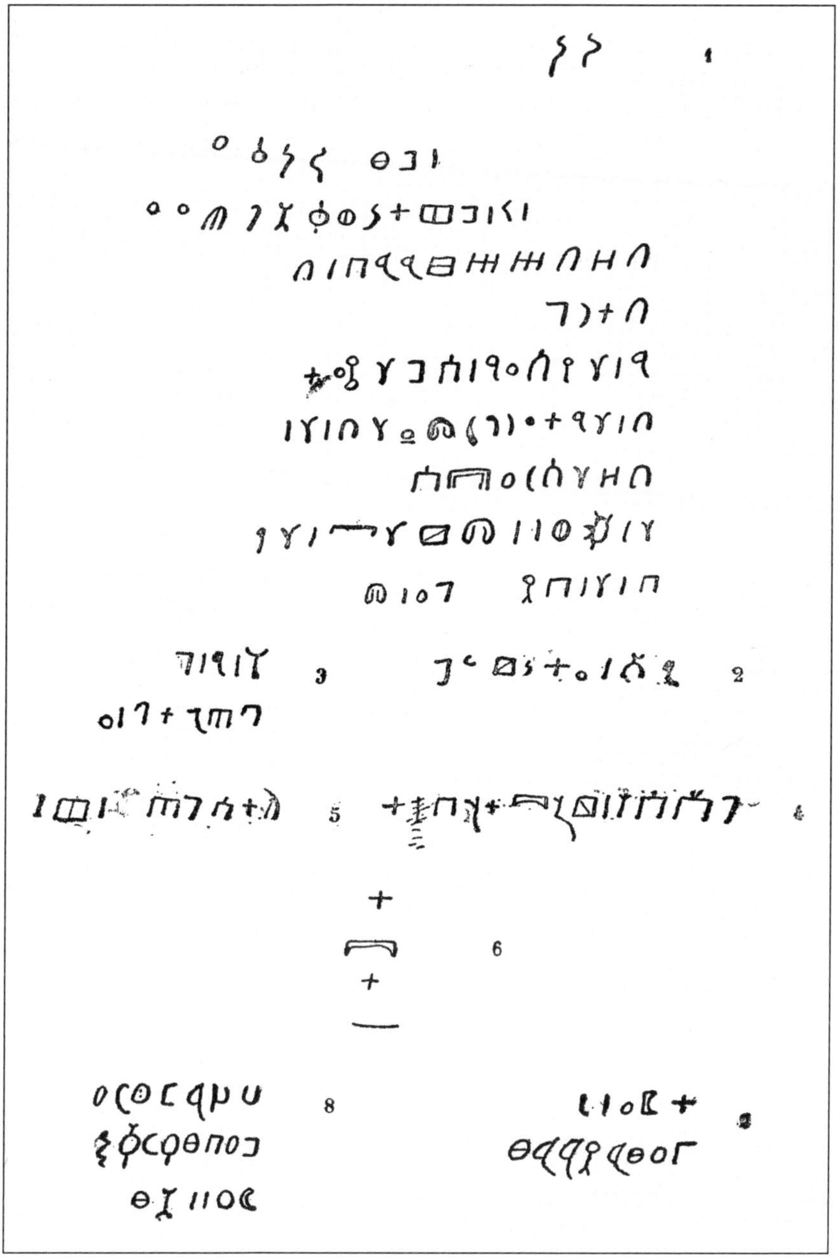

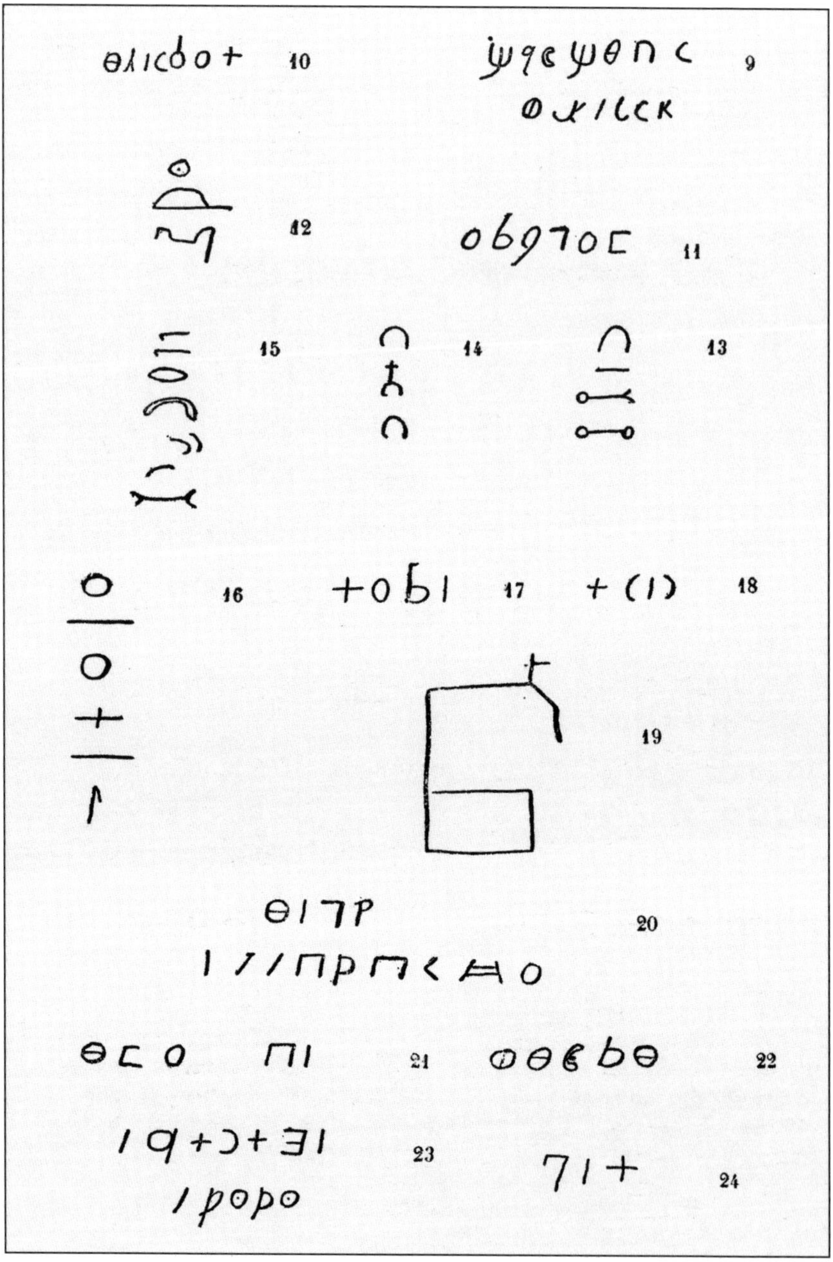
10
9
12
11
15
14
13
16
17
18
19
20
21
22
23
24

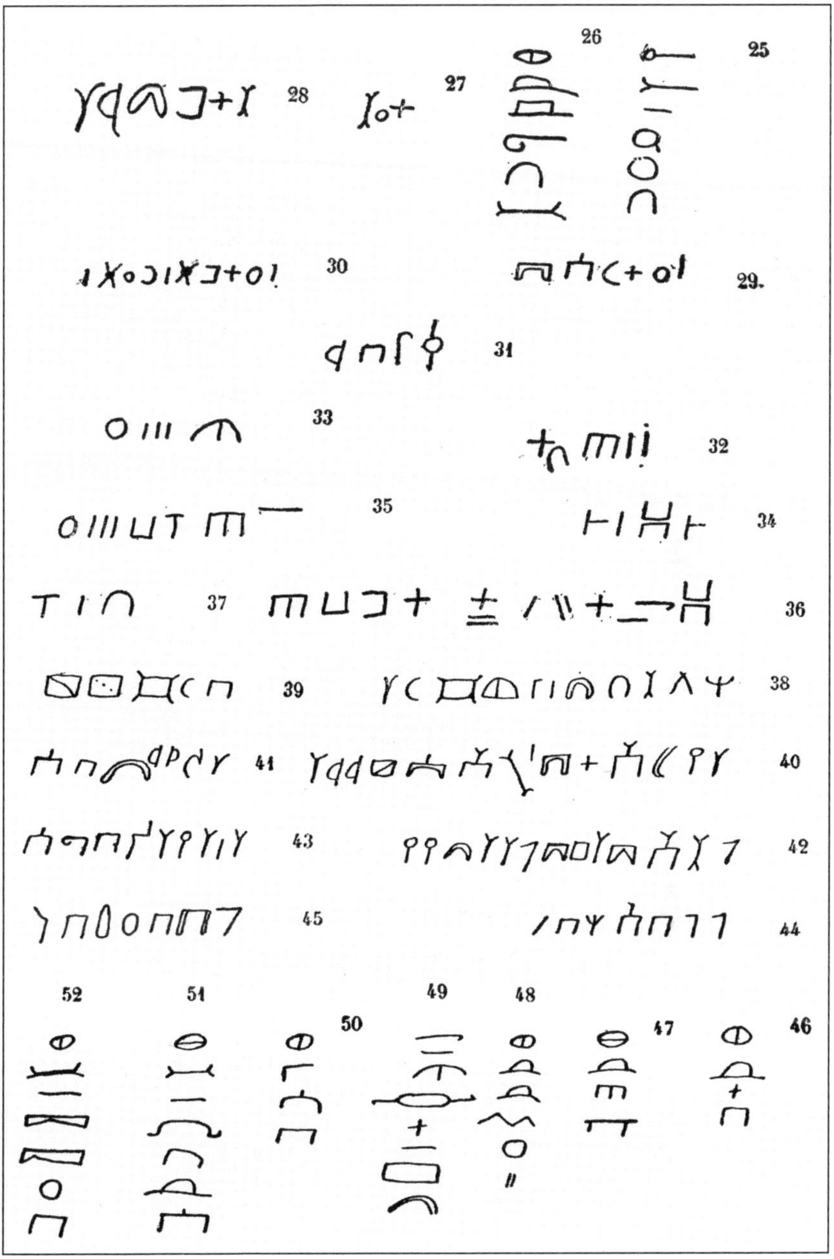
25
26
27
28
29.
30
31
32
33
34
35
36
37
38
39
40
41
42
43
44
45
46
47
48
49
50
51
52

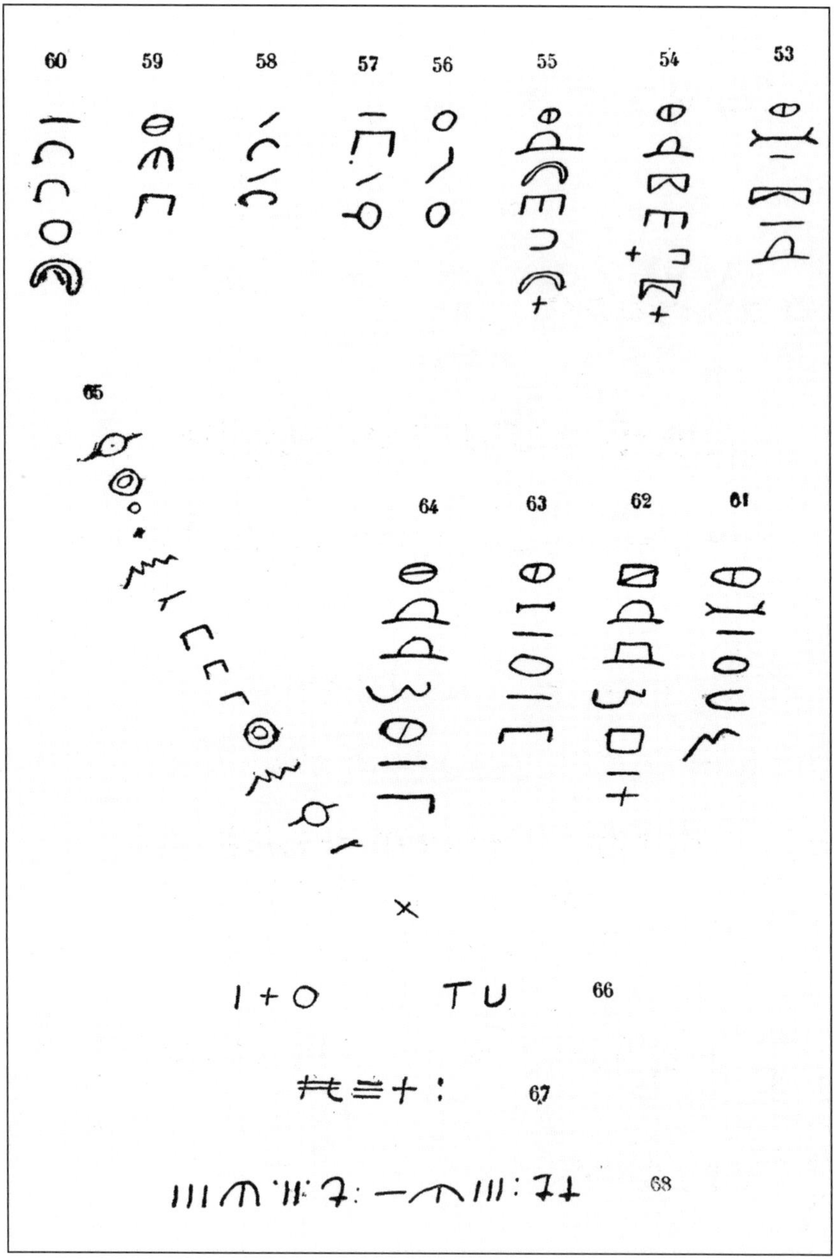
60
59
58
57
56
55
54
53
65
64
63
62
61
66
67
68

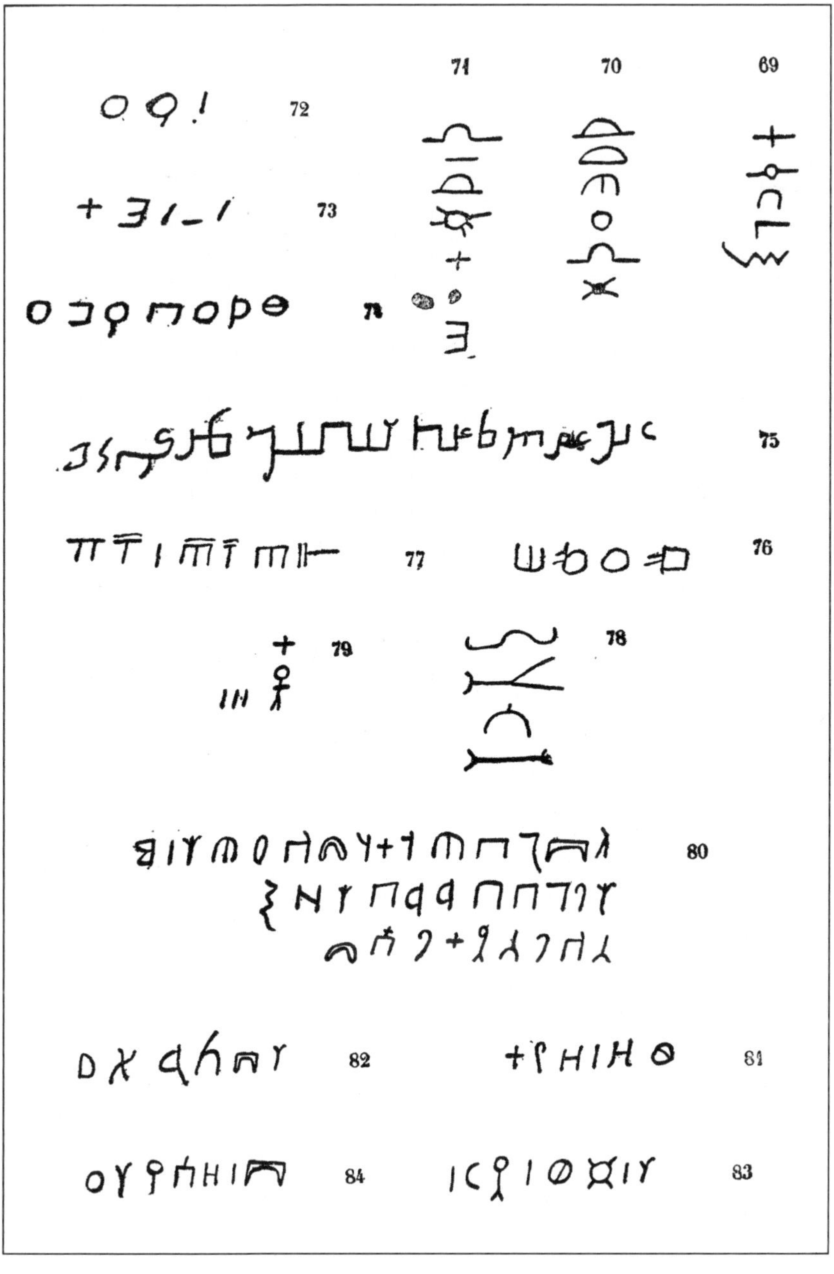
71
70
69
72
73
74
75
77
76
79
78
80
82
81
84
83

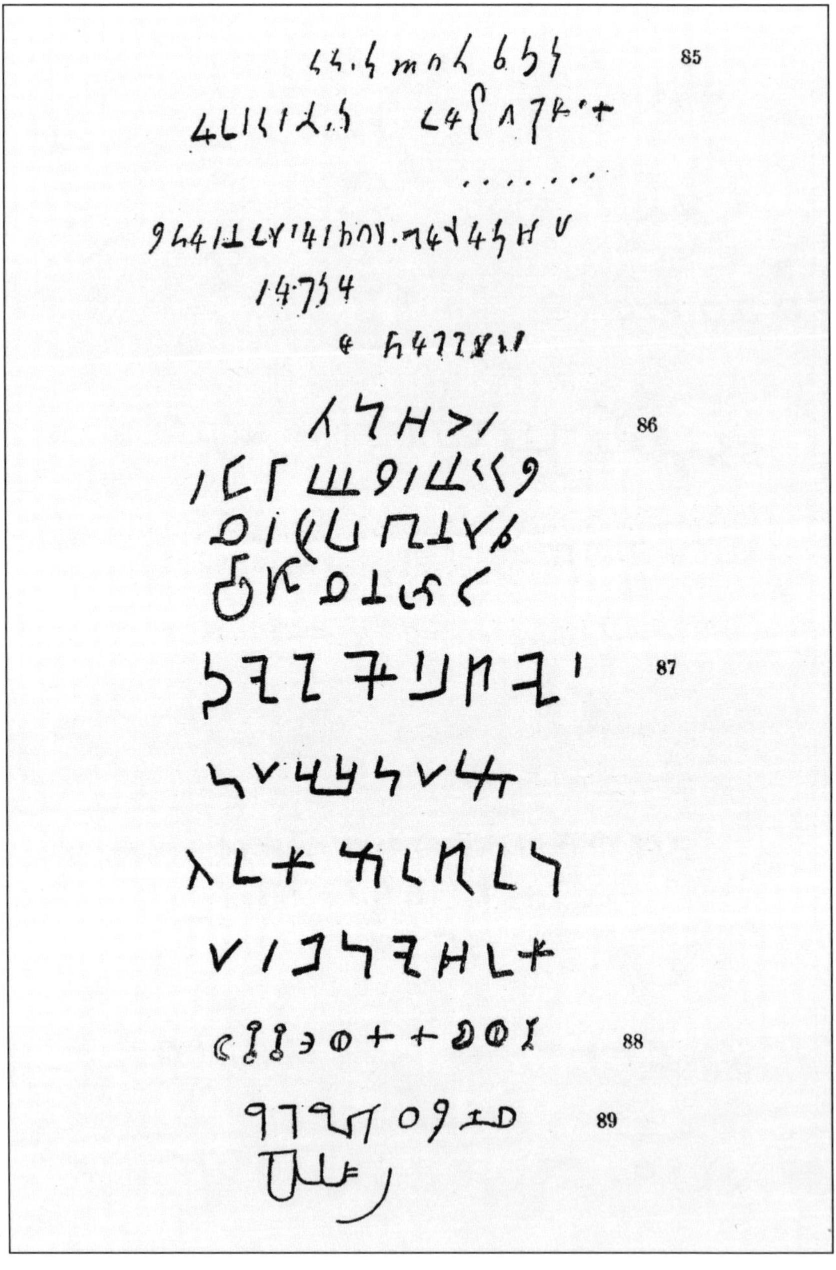
85
86
87
88
89

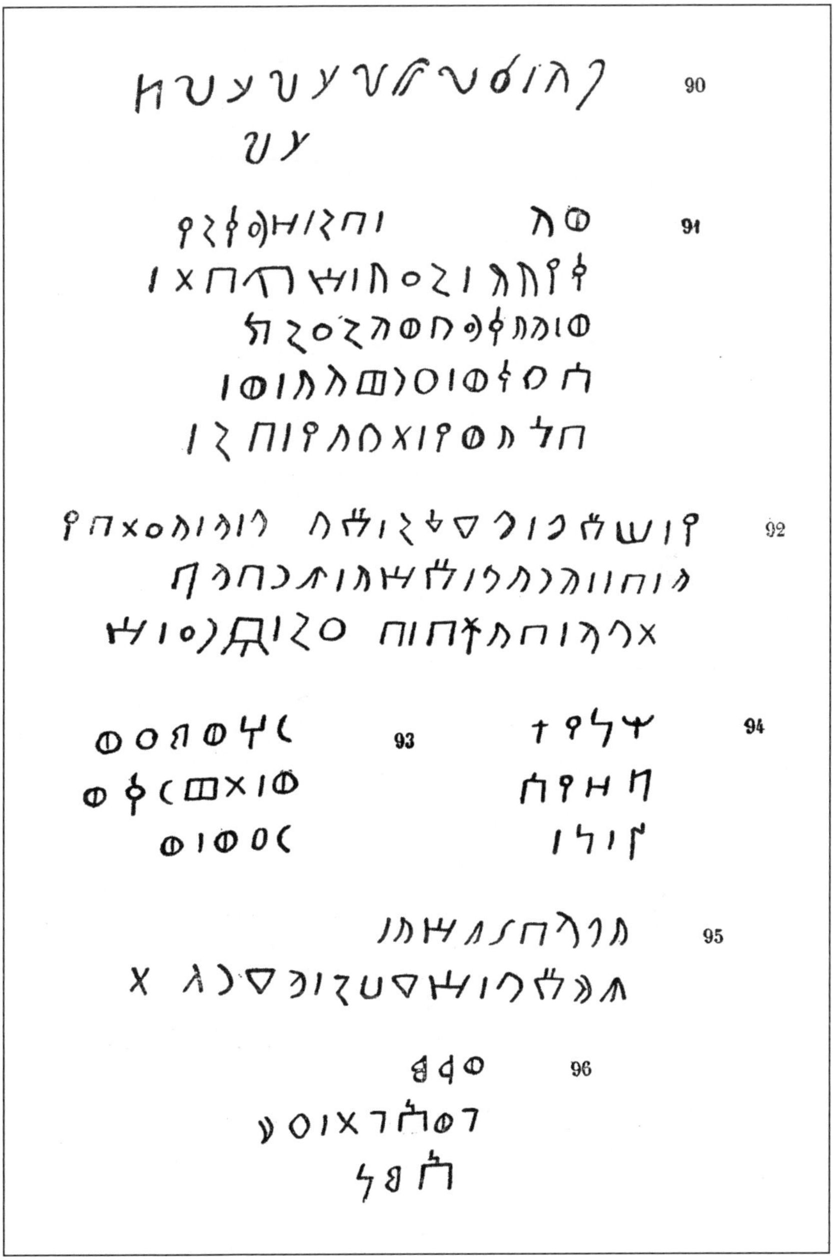
90
91
92
93
94
95
96

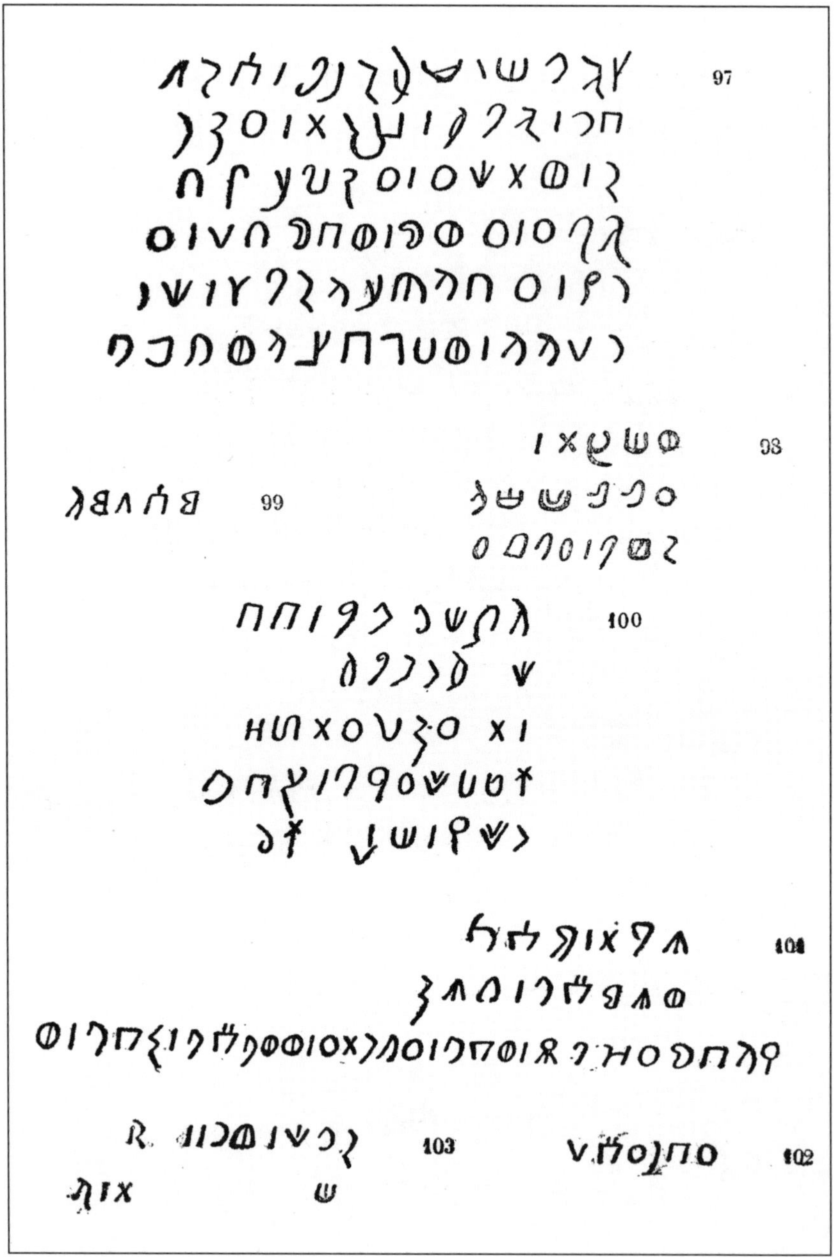
97
98
99
100
101
102
103
R.

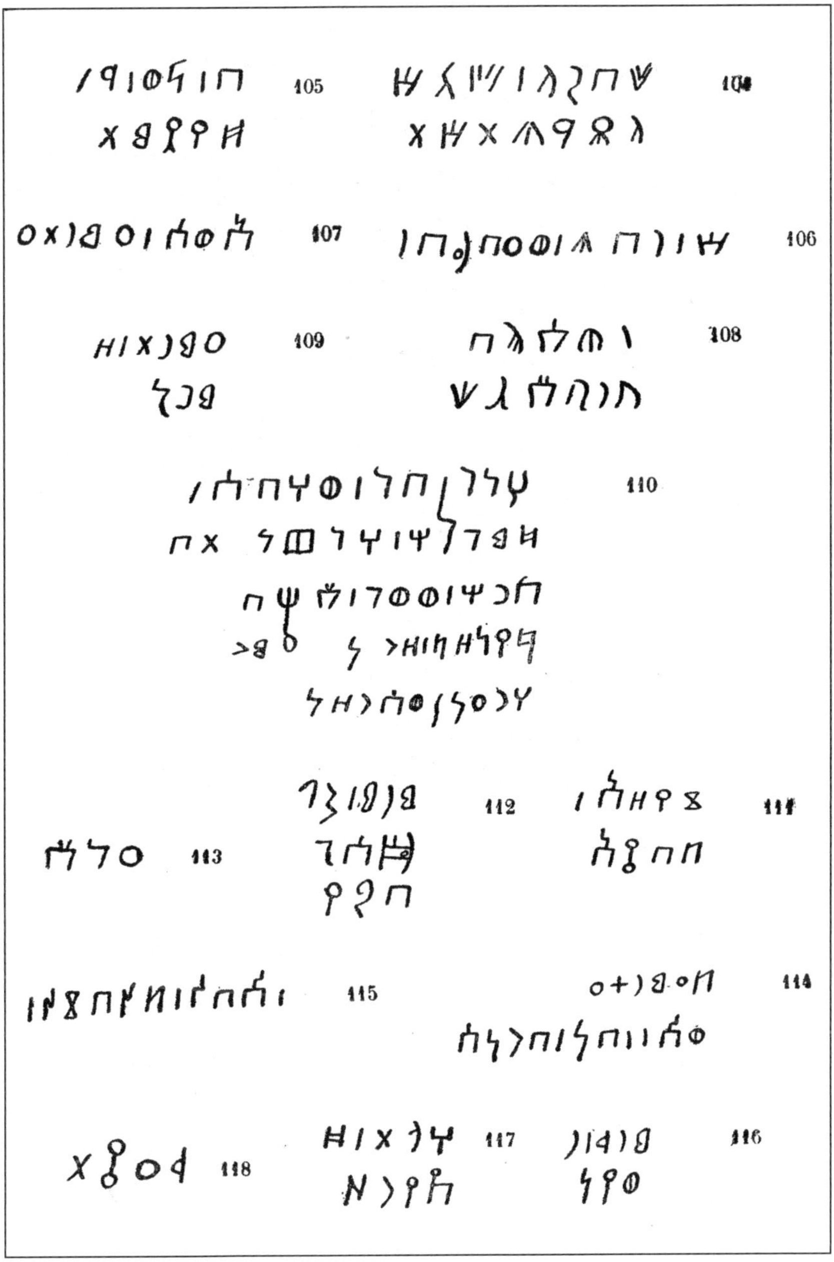
105
104
107
106
109
108
110
112
111
113
115
114
117
116
118

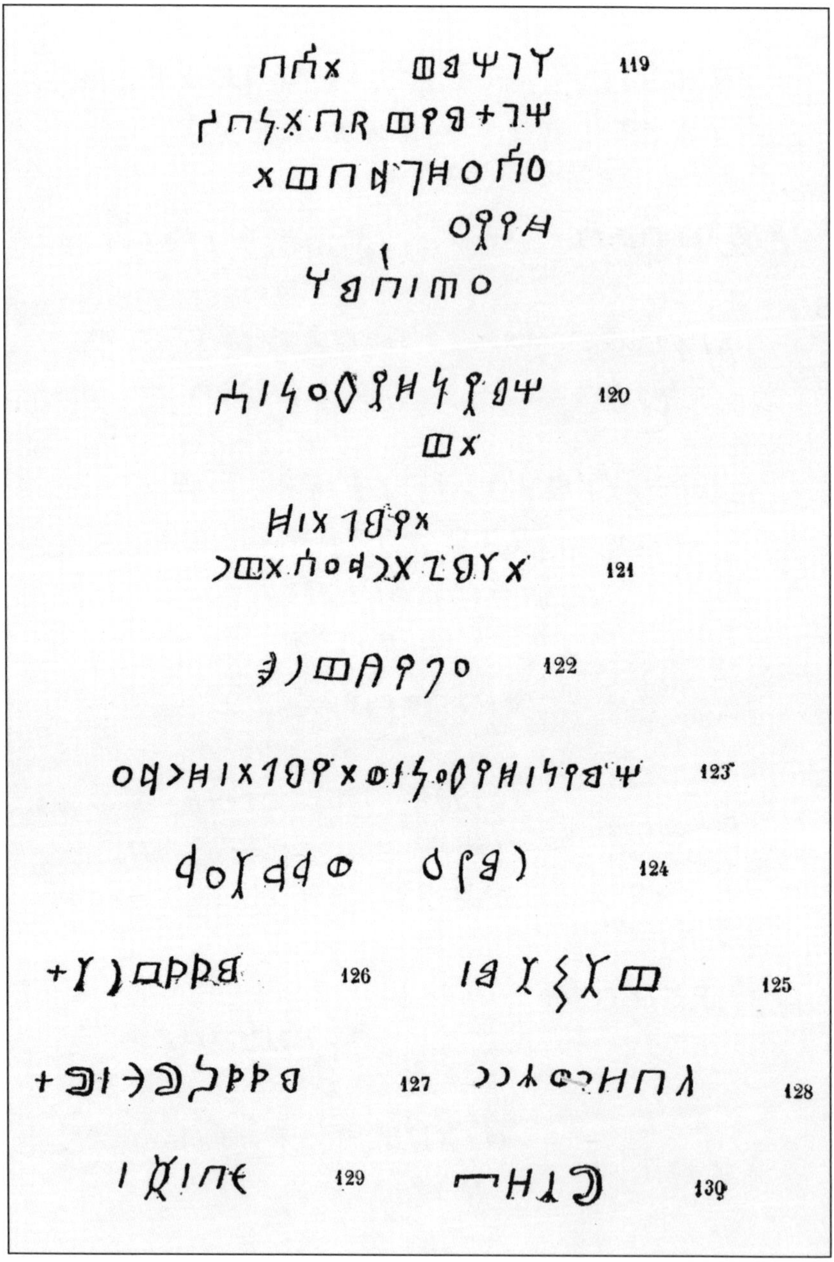
119
120
121
122
123
124
126
125
127
128
129
130

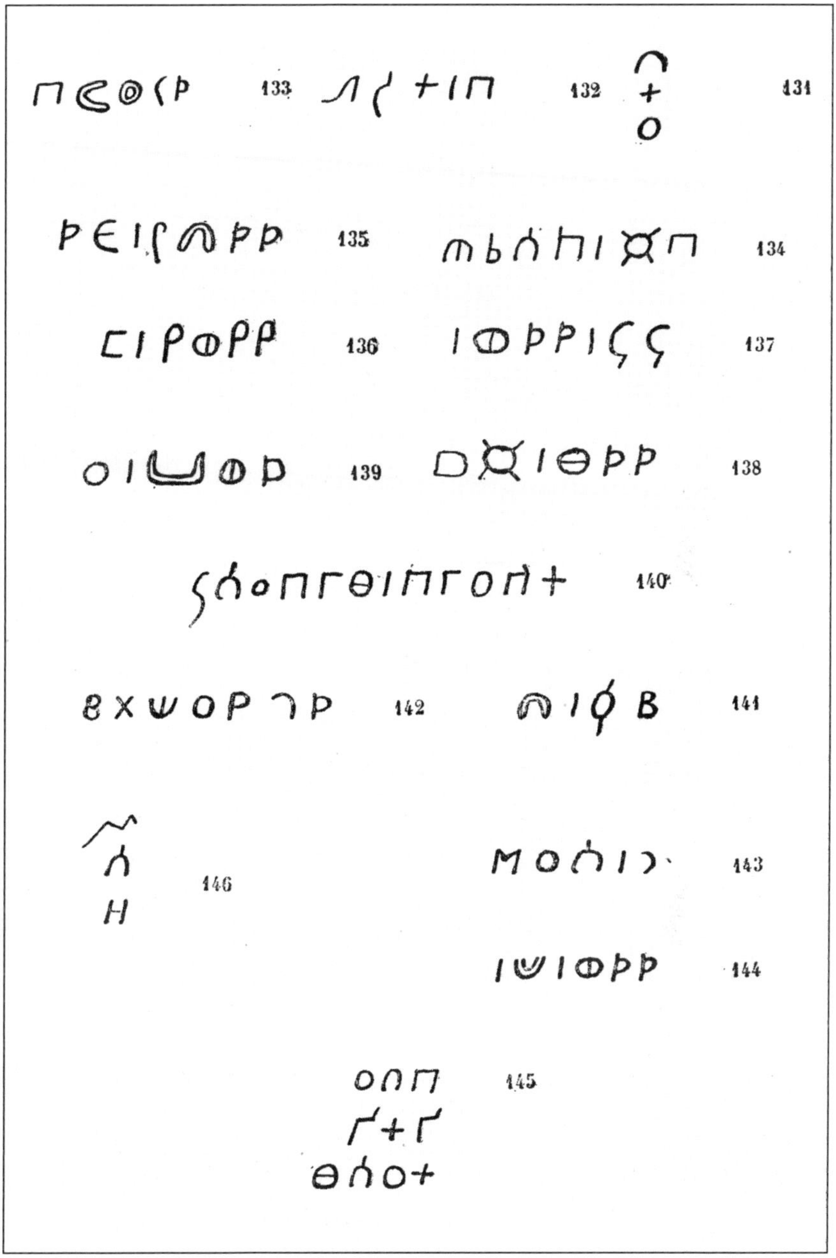
133
132
131
135
134
136
137
139
138
140
142
141
146
143
144
145

APPENDIX 2

Concordance of the inscriptions recorded by Huber on his first Arabian journey

By Michael C.A. Macdonald

SOME OF THE 146 inscriptions recorded by Huber in 1880, and shown in Appendix 1, had already been copied by Doughty in 1878 (published in Doughty 1884), and these and others were recopied by Huber and Euting on their journey through Arabia in 1883–84, and subsequently by Jaussen and Savignac in 1907, 1909, and 1910 (Jaussen and Savignac 1909–22, vols. I and II). However, 71 of the 146 copies here remain our only records of these inscriptions, namely nos. 7–37, 66–68, 72–74, 76–77, 79, 85, 88, 94, 109–110, 113, 116–117, 121, and 124–146.

In this concordance, the sigla are as follows:

HuIR: inscriptions published in Huber 1884a.

Hub: the inscriptions in Huber 1891 with page number followed by inscription number.

HU: van den Branden's (1950) renumbering of all the inscriptions copied by Huber on the 1883–84 expedition.

Eut: the inscriptions copied by Euting on the 1883–84 expedition.

WHI: the inscriptions from the Ḥāʾil area published with many photographs in Winnett and Reed 1973.

JSLih, **JSNab** and **JSMin**: the Dadanitic (formerly 'Lihyanite'), Nabataean and Minaic inscriptions published by Jaussen and Savignac 1909–22, vols. I and II.

Müller, D.H: refers to Müller, D.H. 1889.

vdB: refers to the page number in van den Branden 1950, in which all the so called 'Thamudic' inscriptions[1] known at that time were collected and republished by provenance.

[1] For an explanation of the term 'Thamudic' see Macdonald 2000: 42–5 and Macdonald and King 2000.

Ğabal Sarrā'

HuIR	Hub	HU	Eut	WHI	vdB
1	221–2, 1–2	187, 188, 789	226 (2 copies)	202a–f	pp. 113–16
2	223, 5	192	229	201	p. 110
3 a	—	—	227 a	—	—
3 b	223, 4	191	227	195	p. 109
4	224, 10	197	232	193	p. 111
5	223, 6	193	230	194	p. 110
6	223, 3	190	228	200	p. 109

'The Mosque' in the valley of Tuwārin, Ğabal Shammar

HuIR	Hub	HU	Eut	vdB
7	—	—	—	p. 111
8	—	—	—	p. 112
9	—	—	—	p. 112
10	—	—	—	p. 112
11	—	—	—	pp. 112–13
12	—	—	—	p. 113
13	—	—	—	p. 113
14	—	—	—	p. 113
15	—	—	—	p. 113

Near al-Rawḍah

HuIR	Hub	HU	Eut	vdB
16	—	—	—	p. 116
17	—	—	—	p. 116
18	—	—	—	p. 116
19	—	—	—	p. 116 [*wasm*]

Near ʿAyn ibn Fuhayd

HuIR	Hub	HU	Eut	vdB
20	—	—	—	pp. 116–17
21	—	—	—	p. 117
22	—	—	—	p. 117
23	—	—	—	p. 117

2 km north-west of ʿAyn ibn Fuhayd

HuIR	Hub	HU	Eut	vdB
24	—	—	—	p. 117–18

Ǧabal Ǧildiyyah: Umm al-Ruǧūm

HuIR	Hub	HU	Eut	vdB
25	—	—	—	p. 84
26	—	—	—	p. 84

27	—	—	—	p. 84
28	—	—	—	p. 85

Ǧabal Ǧildiyyah: Wādī Bāʿūr

HuIR	Hub	HU	Eut	vdB
29	—	—	—	p. 85
30	—	—	—	p. 85
31	—	—	—	p. 85

Ǧabal Ǧildiyyah: place unspecified

HuIR	Hub	HU	Eut	vdB
32	—	—	—	p. 85–6
33	—	—	—	p. 86
34	—	—	—	p. 86
35	—	—	—	p. 86
36	—	—	—	p. 86
37	—	—	—	p. 87

Ǧabal Ǧildiyyah: al-Buwayb

HuIR	Hub	HU	Eut	vdB
38	81, 24	106	131	pp. 78–9

39	81, 20	102	107 a	p. 77
40	81, 22	104	108	p. 78
41	81, 23	105	107 b	p. 78
42	81, 21	103	109	pp. 77–8
43+44	80, 17	99	113+112	pp. 76–7
45	81, 27	109	106	p. 79
46+52	80, 10+9	92+91	114+116[2]	p. 75
47+51	80, 16+15	98+97	117+118	p. 76
48	81, 18	100	111	p. 77
49	81, 19	101	110	p. 77
50	80, 12	94	115	p. 75
51 [see 47]				
52 [see 46]				
54+53[3]	80, 8	90	122+123+121	pp. 74–5
55	80, 7	89	125	p. 74

[2] This is clearly an incorrect combination by van den Branden (1950: 75) of two separate inscriptions into one, a combination for which he gives no justification. As can be seen in Huber 1884a: 295; 1891: 80 and Euting Notebook III (Md676-20_145) = Jamme 1974: pl. 6 B, the two lines are separated by other inscriptions.

[3] While van den Branden's combination HuIR 54 + 53 is feasible, the publication of all Euting's copies (Jamme 1974: pl. 6B and Euting's Notebook III, 71r = Md676-20_145) shows that Eut 121 is on a completely different rock, something which was not clear on either of Huber's copies.

56	—	—	124[4]	p. 81
57	80, 14	96	120	p. 76
58	80, 13	95	119	p. 76
59+60	81, 25+26	107+108	104+103[5]	p. 79
61+62	80, 3+4	85+86	129+130	p. 73
63+64	80, 1+2	83+84	127+128	p. 73
65	81, 28	110	105	p. 79
66	—	—	—	p. 87
67–68 [probably *wusūm*]				p. 87

Ǧabal Ǧildiyyah: al-Ṣaʿlikah in Wādī Shaqīq

HuIR	**Hub**	**HU**	**Eut**	**vdB**
69	101, 6	181	220	p. 106
70	101, 2	177	216	pp. 105–6
71	101, 3 [?]	178	217	p. 106 [?]
72 [probably a *wasm*]		—	—	p. 108
73	—	—	—	p. 108
74	—	—	—	p. 108

[4] A *wasm* (tribal mark).

[5] Again, Euting's copies show that these are two inscriptions which are not side by side (Jamme 1974: pl. 5B ; Euting's Notebook III, 70r = Md676-20_143) and so it is unlikely that they form a single text.

Ǧabal Mismā: one part of the mountain

HuIR	Hub	HU	Eut	vdB	*CIS* ii
75 [Nabataean][6]	254, 1		1885: 6, nab. 34		340
76 [?]	—	—	—		
77 [?][7]	—	—	—		

Ǧabal Mismā: a hollow where rainwater collects

HuIR	Hub	HU	Eut	vdB
78	253, 8	202	239	p. 120
79 [*wasm*?]	—	—	—	
80, a	265, 62	258	300 a	p. 136[8]
80, b–c	265, 63	259	259 b, c	p. 136[9]
81	265, 61 b	257, b	299, b	pp. 135–36[10]

[6] HuIR 75 is a Nabataean graffito which Huber copied three times on 6 February 1884 as well as taking a squeeze (1891: 254). Euting also copied it twice (Euting Notebook IV, 63b–64r (d676-21_194)) and it was published in Euting 1885: 7, Fig. 3, nab 34, and again in 1893 as *CIS* ii, no. 340. No satisfactory reading of it has yet been published.

[7] HuIR 76–77 are probably not inscriptions and were not recopied.

[8] Note that there is a misprint in van den Branden 1950: 136 where this inscription is labelled as 'HuIR 81', instead of 80, 1.

[9] Note that there is a misprint in van den Branden 1950: 136 where this inscription is labelled as 'HuIR 80 1.2 et 3', instead of 80, 2–3.

[10] Note that van den Branden (1950: 135) reads HuIR 81 (= Hub 265, 61b) as the second line of HU 257 without mentioning this.

82+84	265, 59	255	297	p. 135[11]	
83	265, 60	256	298	p. 135	
84 [see 82]					

Taymā᾽: on rubble brought from Tūmā

HuIR	**Hub**	**Eut**	**Doughty 1884**	**vdB**	***CIS* ii**
85[12]	—	—	—		—
86	322, 3	1885: nab 40	Pl. XXVII, f. 51		336
87	320, 2	Nöldeke 1884: 819–20	—		114

On a sandstone rock called ‘É’ rekeb [= al-Ruqqab] between Taymā᾽ and Madā᾽in Ṣāliḥ

HuIR	**Hub**	**Eut**	**Doughty 1884**	**vdB**
88[13]	—	—	—	p. 136

Miqraṭ al-Dabūs, six miles north of Madā᾽in Ṣāliḥ

HuIR	**Hub**	**Eut**	**Doughty 1884**	**JS**	***CIS* ii**
89	452, 96	—	—		291

[11] Note that there is a misprint in van den Branden 1950: 135 where HuIR 82–84 should read HuIR 82+84

[12] HuIR 85 is such a bad copy that it has proved impossible to identify it with any of the inscriptions recorded by Huber and Euting on their visits to Taymā᾽ in 1884.

[13] This was a chance find on a rock between Taymā᾽ and Madā᾽in Ṣāliḥ and was not rediscovered and copied on the 1884 journey.

Madā'in Ṣāliḥ

HuIR	**Hub**	**Eut**	**Doughty 1884**	**JS**	***CIS* ii**
90	—	1885, Nab 3	Pl. VIII, f. 12	Nab 16 lines 11–12	198 lines 11–12

Al-ʿUlā

HuIR	**Hub**	**Eut**	**Doughty 1884**	**JS**	**Müller, D.H.**	**vdB**
91	396, 7	—	Pl. XII, f. 20	Lih 54	1889: 60–62, no. 4	
92	393, 1	—	Pl. XVI, f. 30/1	Lih 55	1889: 58–59, no. 1	
93[14]	—[15]	squeeze 28	Pl. XII, f. 21	Lih 38	1889: 66, no. 12	
94	—	—	—	—	—	
95	—	798+800	—	Lih 260,b+262	1889: 81, no. 39	
96	—	873	Pl. XIV, f.25 [?]	Min 159+164	1889: 53, nos XLVII+XLVIII	
97	—	826	—	Lih 70	1889: 82, no. 52	
98	—	825	—	Lih 69	1889: Pl. VII	

[14] Huber's copy is upside-down.

[15] It should be noted that on the 1883–84 journey, Huber spent only the day of 17 March and the morning of the 18th in al-ʿUlā (1891: 404–5) before returning alone to Madāʾin Ṣāliḥ while Euting continued to record inscriptions in al-ʿUlā (see Euting 1914: chapter 14). Thus there are copies of only 14 inscriptions from al-ʿUlā in Huber 1891 where they have been collected together on pp. 393–8, and of these only HuIR 91 and 92 had been copied by him on his previous journey.

99	—	826a	—	Lih 244	1889: 83, no. 53	
100	—	827	Pl. XIII, f. 23	Lih 68	1889: 83, no. 55	
101, a+b	—	841	Pl. XIII, f. 23	—	1889: Pl. VII	
101, c	—	839+840[16]	Pl. XIII, f. 23	—	1889: Pl. VII	
102		826 b	Pl. XIII, f. 22	Lih 243	1889: 83, no. 54	
103	—	—	—	Lih 67 [?]	—	
104	—	844	Pl. XIII, f. 22	Lih 66	1889: 84, no. 58	
105	—	868	—	—	—	
106	—	846	—	—	1889: 84–85, no. 60	
107	—	869	—	—	—	
108	—	848+849	Pl. XIII, f. 23	Lih 230	1889: 85, no. 62	
109–110	—	—	—	—	—	
111	—	865	—	Min 175	1889: Pl. VIII	
112	—	852–854	Pl. XIV, f. 24	Lih 226	1889: 85, no. 64	
113	—	—	—	—	—	p. 426
114		860+861			1889: 51, nos. XXVII+XXVIII	
115		863		Min 177	1889: 52, no. XXXIX	
116–117	—	—	—	—	—	
118	—	856	Pl. XIV, f. 24	—	1889: 51, no. XXXV	p. 426

[16] Eut 840 is a second copy of the first thirteen characters in Eut 839.

119	—	—	—	Min 148		
120		882		Min 162		
121	—	—	—	—	—	
122	—	—	—	Lih 219	—	p. 427
123	—	881	—		1889: 55, no. LVI	

The environs of Khaybar

HuIR	Hub	vdB
124	—	p. 478
125	—	p. 478
126	—	p. 478
127	—	pp. 478–9
128	—	—
129	—	p. 479
130	—	p. 479
131	—	p. 479
132	—	p. 479
133	—	pp. 479–80
134	—	p. 480
135	—	p. 480
136	—	p. 480

137	—	p. 480
138	—	pp. 480–1
139	—	p. 481
140	—	p. 481
141	—	p. 481
142	—	p. 481
143	—	p. 481
144	—	pp. 481–2
145	—	p. 482
146	—	p. 482

APPENDIX 3

Correspondence with the Ministry of Public Education and Société de Géographie, 1878–83

THE DOCUMENTS presented here are held in the archives of the Ministère de l'Instruction publique et des Beaux-Arts, housed at the Archives nationales at Pierrefitte-sur-Seine, Paris. They are a selection from those comprising Dossier F/17/2976/1:1, entitled 'M. Huber (Charles), Mission au Thibet et dans l'Asie centrale (recherches scientifiques, anthropologique et géographiques)'. This comprises 107 items between 3 December 1878 and early 1883. The title of this folder is a misnomer, arising from Huber's over-ambitious expedition proposal set out in Letter no. 1 below. The entire correspondence in fact relates solely to his first Middle Eastern journey, in Syria, northern Arabia and Iraq.

Thanks go to Prof. Maria Gorea for making these documents available, and to Barbara Newton for translating Letters 4 and 8 from G.A. Le Bel. Editorial interpolations are shown in square brackets.

LETTER NO. 1, WITH HUBER'S PROPOSED ITINERARY

This letter comprises items nos. 1 and 1 bis in Dossier F/17/2976/1:1.

Date: 3 December 1878
From: Charles Huber
To: the Minister of Public Education

Monsieur le Ministre,

I am taking the respectful liberty of informing you that I am on the point of departing on a scientific journey in Central Asia. This journey, which has for long been gestating and under consideration, will last for several years and will be carried out for the purpose of advancing philological and ethnographic knowledge. Besides that, my plan is to map the course of my entire itinerary and to compile geographical data, the precision of which will be assured by the employment of thermometer, barometer and sextant.

Nor will natural history be neglected and I shall bring for this purpose a small selection of instruments which have been entrusted to me by the Museum.[1]

My project has been submitted to linguists, anthropologists and geographers of our learned societies in Paris, and has received their approval.

As this journey is to be made for purely scientific purposes, and as the costs necessitated by the preparations have already far exceeded my forecasts, I am taking the extreme liberty, M. le Ministre, of addressing to you my petition that you may be good enough to grant me a subvention of 8,000 francs.[2]

In return, I will undertake to send you either my travel journal or a report on results each time that they are obtained. In addition, the scientific societies would receive the data and documents that would seem to me naturally aligned with their interests.

In the hope that you will deign to give my request a favourable reception, I respectfully beg you, M. le Ministre, to accept the assurance of my deep gratitude and high esteem.

Charles Huber
12, rue de l'Odéon [Paris]

Note of recommendation added to letter

3 December 1878

The undersigned takes the liberty of recommending to M. le Ministre de l'Instruction publique the request of M. Ch. Huber, his compatriot, who

[1] The Musée d'histoire naturelle, Paris, with whose chairman, Jean Louis Armand de Quatrefages de Bréau (1810–92), Huber would correspond during his Arabian journey. De Quatrefages, a prominent French biologist, had been educated at Strasbourg University. See Huber 1881 for an example of their correspondence.

[2] 8,000 francs in was equivalent to approximately £19,400 in the year 2000 (www.historicalstatistics.org).

seems very well prepared to profitably undertake the perilous journey for which he is requesting a subvention.

Ad. Wurtz[3]
Member of the Institut

3 December 1878

Itinerary of my projected journey in Central Asia

A caravan route leaving Gaza towards the south passes through Bir Abu *Areibe [*sic*] and *Berein el Themmed [*sic*] to reach ʿAqabah at the top of the gulf of the same name (32.5° [*sic*] longitude by 29.5° latitude) on the Red Sea.[4] Heading eastwards from ʿAqabah I shall reach Mudawwarah, which belongs to the Sharārāt tribe, and then continue on my way southwards through the little town of Tabūk, *Dhahr el Megir [*sic*], Akhḍar, etc.; and then entering [the territory of the] Thamūd from the east I shall pass through Madāʾin Ṣāliḥ, al-ʿUlā, *Biar Ganesse [*sic*] and the town of Hedie [*sic*; Hadiyyah] to reach al-Madīnah.[5] From there I shall go by the route of *El Khona [*sic*] and *El Kobab [*sic*] to Mecca.[6]

I shall leave the Ḥiğāz for the Yemen, going via Ğabal *Kora [*sic*],[7] and then through the territory of the ʿUtaybah, Wadi Subayh and Wadi Shahrān (the routes through which are little if not at all known) so as to reach the

[3] Charles Adolphe Wurtz (1817–84) was a Protestant French-Alsatian chemist born in Strasbourg who became an influential scientist, writer and educator.

[4] The route envisaged by Huber was probably that from Gaza to Beersheba and thence to Wadi al-ʿArabah and ʿAqabah.

[5] Huber's planned route southwards from Mudawwarah clearly follows that of the Syrian Ḥajj from Damascus. I have been unable to identify his Biar Ganesse.

[6] I have been unable to identify Huber's proposed route from al-Madīnah to Mecca. It is possible that El Khona denotes Badr Ḥunayn; if so, he was opting for the westerly route running towards the coast and on to Rābigh, and then slightly inland through Khulayṣ and ʿUsfān. On the other hand, El Khona possibly denotes a wadi named al-Khunak mentioned by Burton, in which case Huber was planning to take the inland route between al-Madīnah and Mecca (Burton 1893 ii: 70). I have been unable to identify Huber's El Kobab.

[7] From this we can deduce that Huber planned to go from Mecca to al-Ṭāʾif, since by Kora he seems to refer to Ğabal Kurā/Karā, the great escarpment overlooking the Tihāmah plain that is part of the rugged mountain chain of western Arabia. Ğabal Kurā is located on the southern, precipitous route between Mecca and al-Ṭāʾif, best described in early 1926 by the Englishman Eldon Rutter (Rutter 2015: 284, 309–18).

Yemen from the north-east.[8] I shall cross the latter country as far as the south towards the 14° parallel, staying amongst the *Abybda [*sic*], the [people of] Wadi Nağrān, and wherever else the opportunity and possibility present themselves.[9]

Due to the impossibility of crossing the deserts of al-Akhaf (sand dunes)[10] and the Rubʿ al-Khālī, I shall probably go back up through Yemen and the Ḥiğāz on their extreme eastern side as far as Djebel A'ared [*sic*],[11] along the western face of which passes the caravan route from Mecca to al-Qaṭīf on the Persian Gulf. In taking advantage of this route my plan is not to follow its entire length, but to stop among the oases that are to be met with along it after two-thirds of the way towards 43° to 44° of longitude and 25° of latitude, of which the chief town is al-Dirʿiyyah.[12] This line of oases, of which the main ones are al-ʿĀriḍ, al-Washm, al-Qaṣīm[13] and al-Shammar [*sic*] goes from south to north. I shall follow it as far as the latter and then head from there to the Euphrates.

I shall go up the Euphrates as far as the mouth of the Tigris and then on to Baghdad. There I shall enter Persia by crossing the mountains of Pushti-Kuh and the Karkheh river on their eastern slope, directing my steps from there to Tehran. On leaving that city, my route passes to the south of the great salty steppe, through the provinces of ʿAjamī Iraq and Khurasān, to reach 35° of latitude at the altitude of Herat.

---

8 Huber seems to have obtained these names from the map of Nağd that appeared in Mengin 1823. On this, 'Ouâdy-Soubey' is placed roughly in the area east of Ḥarrat al-Buqūm/Nawāṣif drained by Wadi Ranyah, leading to Subayʿ territory; while 'Ouâdy Chahran' denotes the Bīshah area (Mengin 1823: Atlas). Shahrān also appears as a district on Palgrave's map of Arabia (Palgrave 1865 i: folding map facing p. 1).

9 Huber's sketchy presentation of the enormous region between al-Ṭāʾif and Nağrān could have been greatly expanded if he had consulted Tamisier 1840, which he does not seem to have done. His knowledge of Nağrān was probably derived from Joseph Halévy, who spent time there in 1870 (Halévy 1873 and 1877; see note 43 below).

10 Huber's al-Akhaf appears to be a corruption of al-Aḥqāf, the 'sand dunes' or 'winding tracts', a term often used by mediaeval Arab geographers to denote part of the great sand desert of the south. It is also the name of Sūrah 46 of the Qurʾān.

11 Djebel A'ared: Ğabal ʿĀriḍ, i.e. Ğabal Ṭuwayq.

12 This mention of al-Dirʿiyyah, which had ceased to be the chief town of this region in 1818 when it was destroyed by the army of Ibrāhīm Pasha, confirms that Huber was consulting the map of Nağd that appeared in Mengin 1823 when planning his route (Mengin 1823: Atlas). This map was well out of date by Huber's time.

13 These are of course not oases but districts of eastern (Lower) Nağd with settled populations.

I plan to take three years to complete this itinerary, which is to say that I shall not cut short the duration of my stops anywhere, but shall take whatever time is necessary to make all my observations. As stated in my request for this expedition, these observations will all be scientific and will cover, in addition to the general instructions, all the particular points to which the various learned societies will wish to draw my attention.

Should my health hold up as far as the eastern frontier of Persia, I shall continue straight on with my journey by crossing Kafiristan and Dardistan so as to reach Tibet via the high plateaux of these regions.

Huber

Letter no. 2

This letter formally accepting Huber's proposal is item no. 7 in Dossier F/17/2976/1:1.

Date: 17 December 1878
From: the Ministry of Public Education, Paris
To: M. Charles Huber, 12 rue de l'Odéon

Monsieur,

I have the honour to inform you that at its meeting on the 11th of this month (December), the view of the Expeditions Committee was that the expedition requested by your letter of the 3rd of this month should be granted to you.

The order, due to budgetary considerations, will not be able to be made until after 1 January 1879.

Please receive etc.
The Minister

Letter no. 3

This letter is item no. 25 in Dossier F/17/2976/1:1.

Date: 12 April 1879
From: First Office, Division of the Interior, Government of Algeria
To: the Minister of Public Education, Paris

Monsieur le Ministre,

On the subject of M. Huber, bearer of a diplomatic passport.

On the 5th of this April, M. Huber (Charles Auguste), bearer of a diplomatic passport, presented himself to me.

In accordance with the general recommendations contained in this document, I issued him at his request with a free first-class passage to Tunis, and authorized him to obtain from the various government offices any administrative publications relevant to Algeria that could be of use to him. I believe that I should now provide you with some confidential information about the person in question which my administration has come by, as M. Huber had been attached for several months during 1874 as an auxiliary to the Directorate-General of Civil Affairs.

This information, contained in the note quoted below, the original of which is filed in M. Huber's administrative dossier, will perhaps be of some use to you:

> The result of the information, collected at Strasbourg by the German consul, is that M. Charles Auguste Huber was born in Strasbourg on 19 December 1847, that he is the legitimate son of Georges Huber, shoemaker, and Elisabeth Stapfer. The police commissioner of Strasbourg has gathered the following from the information office in the city hall:
>
> 'M. Huber was a student of chemistry in the said city during 1866, 1867 and 1868. In 1869 he was a clerk in a recruitment agency. On 27 March 1868, he would have been punished/sentenced [il aurait été puni/condamné] to six months in prison for theft. At the beginning of 1871 he went to Nancy, from where he returned to Strasbourg towards the end of 1873, so as to go, in the month of January 1874, to Africa. M. Huber's parents live in Strasbourg, at Leimengasse 4.'
>
> Please accept, etc.

LETTER NO. 4

This letter is item no. 31 in Dossier F/17/2976/1:1. It is a defence of Huber against supposedly false rumours by a friend and prominent Alsatian businessman, G.A. Le Bel, who had interests in the oil-sands mines at Pechelbronn, north of Strasbourg. M. Le Bel seems to be unaware of the allegation that Huber had been imprisoned for theft in 1868, and focuses instead on Huber's difficulties with his nationality.

Date: 8 August 1879
From: G.A. le Bel, 12 rue de l'Odéon, Paris
To: the Minister of Public Education, Paris

Monsieur,

Yesterday I saw the letter of which I spoke to you, the contents of which had been transmitted to me rather inaccurately. It is written in a far from hostile tone by someone who had received M. Huber in Algiers and who states that people are mistaken about him. I have made a copy of the passage that is of interest to us, as follows:

> An unfavourable rumour is circulating that M. Huber, who had already been employed at the governor-general's office (of Algeria), was dismissed in 1874 as a consequence of information from Alsace gathered on his account in Strasbourg itself. A Frenchman in France, he is said to have opted in Strasbourg for German nationality, which would not have prevented him from being condemned to three months' imprisonment, as I have been told. You must understand that this information was given to me in confidence; moreover, I think I know that the governor-general wrote to the foreign ministry. Your good faith has undoubtedly been taken by surprise ... etc.

All this is of course only a rumour and it would be more than ever necessary to know the contents of the letter which has clearly been sent to the foreign ministry. There are, furthermore, several facts reported in it which have widely varying implications. I do not think that M. Huber was employed by the governor-general's office but he did travel for a long time with all sorts of official recommendations, which could be regarded as tantamount to being employed. It is not impossible that, without his knowledge, information was given about him in Strasbourg, and that his return to that city, as it coincided with this investigation, was construed as a 'dismissal'.

I need only remind you of the marked and frequent tendency among the general public to regard as an agent any traveller who takes the trouble to visit unexplored regions under the pretext of anthropological research!

This then raises another question: 'Frenchman in France' etc .... Everyone is more or less familiar with the dilemma. Unfortunately one cannot feed oneself on the title of French citizen. As a consequence many Alsatians, after opting for France, have been obliged to return home to earn their bread, and in France there are people, whom I shall not mention but who are only too numerous, who make it a crime for them to do so. Moreover, it may be that in the same way as it was for Messieurs O. and A. Scheurer and many others, this option has been simply annulled by the German government. Of course, this increases the score that we shall one day have to settle with the above-mentioned government, but it does not prevent the options from being valid, and our servant [Huber], who spends at least six months of the year in Paris, only evaded the annulment of his option by a series of fortunate circumstances.[14] But even had he failed to do so, he would still be an honourable man, neither more nor less.

Thirdly, the 'information' was obtained either privately or officially. I do not think that the latter is likely, but you never know whom you can trust nowadays given the incoherence of French foreign policy. In any case, the Alsatian government would have replied 'The police are after him', which is not surprising in view of what I have told you. If on the other hand the information comes from Monsieur X or Y, we are in the dark and we must try to find our way out of it. The person who provided this information may be either badly informed or bearing a grudge. In any case it is not acceptable to damage a man's reputation because of a simple assertion from a private person, especially when it is provided in a dubious manner.

What is not in doubt, however, is that my friend has given striking proof of his French feelings. I preferred to write this long letter rather than take up more of your time and to trespass on your benevolence, for which I must thank you once again. My business obliges me to be in Alsace on the 20th of this month. I shall have the honour in any case of seeing you as I pass through.

Meanwhile, please receive the assurance of my perfect devotion.

G.A. Le Bel
12 rue del'Odéon
In Alsace, at the mines of Péchelbronn, near Soultz-sous-Forèts, Basse Alsace

---

[14] For more on Huber's nationality problems, see Appendix 4, Letter no. 10 dated 25 November 1882 from Huber to Maunoir.

Letter no. 5

This letter is item no. 32 in Dossier F/17/2976/1:1.

Date: 21 August 1879 (actually sent on 1 September 1879, see item 35, and Letter no. 7 below)
From: the Minister of Public Education, Paris
To: the Consul of France, Strasbourg

Monsieur le Consul,

Towards the end of last year, on the recommendation of deputies and scholars, I commissioned M. Charles Huber, a native of Strasbourg, to carry out a scientific expedition to Tibet and in Central Asia.

Some time after the departure of this scholar, the Governor-General of Algeria wrote to the Ministry of Foreign Affairs that according to information supplied to him, M. Huber (Charles Auguste), bearer of a diplomatic passport, may have been sentenced, on 27 March 1868 in Strasbourg, to six months in prison for theft. As against this, the testimonials I have received from the most eminent and honourable people on the subject of M. Huber have been absolutely satisfactory, and I am wondering whether it is the same individual that is in question, or whether the Governor-General of Algeria might have been misled by a case of mistaken identity.

Hence I would be most obliged, M. le Consul, if you would be good enough to provide me with all the information you are able to obtain on this traveller, to make sure that individuals are not being confused; and, if there does in fact exist a criminal sentence, to specify the circumstances of it.

I would also be most grateful if you would send me the results of your research as promptly as you can.

Accept etc.,
Le Ministre

Letter no. 6

This letter is item no. 33 in Dossier F/17/2976/1:1.

Date: 28 July 1879
From: Charles Huber, ʿAyn Warakat, Lebanon[15]

[15] Huber's Aïn Ouarakat (Liban): I have been unable to identify this place.

To: the Minister of Public Education, Paris

M. le Ministre,

By an order made in December last, you were kind enough to entrust me with a scientific expedition in Arabia and Central Asia.

A succession of various tasks at the Observatory of Montsouris and the Museum of Natural History, as well as the preparation of various scientific instruments, delayed my departure until the month of May just passed. The constantly unfavourable skies over Paris at the beginning of this year also forced me to spend a month in Algiers to test and practise with my astronomical instruments.

I have been in Syria for two months and am at present at the Madrasah of ʿAyn Warakat to study the dialects of Arabia. At the same time I am in negotiation with the two tribes that share the Syrian Desert and whose ranges extend as far as al-Ğawf, with a view to obtaining entry to the region and a treaty of friendship. Crossing the north Arabian desert is impossible without the consent and assistance of these people.

It will be towards the end of September next that I plan to find a place in one of their encampments in the environs of Damascus. I shall organize my little caravan straight away and set off on my journey to the south. Furthermore, just now I am thinking of sending you, M. le Ministre, a detailed report on the route that I shall definitely take as well as all the other interesting information arising from my expedition.

During my journeys here I have collected some flasks of interesting insects which will fill in the gaps and replace spoiled items in the Museum [of Natural History]. I also possess a series of rock samples and of fossils typical of the [tectonic] uplift of the Lebanon. The number of these and various other objects will increase still more until my final departure, after next September, at which time I shall make them the contents of a despatch to your department.

My project to cross Arabia, especially with my instruments, is a risky one, as I am more and more aware, but it is not impossible. For it to succeed, I shall need to collect every piece of useful information, to be well acquainted with the character of the inhabitants, and in a word to have as much luck as possible on my side. I am able to be in such a situation on my departure.

I have the honour, etc.

Ch. Huber
Poste restante, Beirut

LETTER NO. 7

This letter is item no. 36 in Dossier F/17/2976/1:1.

Date: 8 September 1879
From: the Directorate of Criminal Affairs and Pardons, Ministry of Justice, Paris
To: the Minister of Public Education, Paris

M. le Ministre et cher Collègue,

By despatch of the 1st of this month, you were good enough to ask me for information on the subject of M. Charles Huber, a scholar to whom at the end of last year you entrusted a scientific expedition to Tibet and in Central Asia.

In response to your communication, I have the honour to inform you that the criminal records of my department contain no passage relating to the above-mentioned person. However, research carried out in my offices has led to the discovery of two requests that I hasten to communicate to you.

In one of these requests, a M. Charles Huber, aged twenty, a commercial clerk, born in Strasbourg, declared that he had been sentenced by the court in this city on 27 March 1868 to six months' imprisonment for theft, and begged for his release before the expiry of his term.

This information, dear Minister and Colleague, will undoubtedly enable you to shed light on the question of identity which you have been good enough to bring to my attention.

In case this may seem to you insufficient, I would hasten, should you wish me to do so, to intervene with the Minister of Foreign Affairs, to ask him if he would be kind enough to request M. Charles Huber's criminal record from the German authorities. But I fear this may not produce any useful result, part of the police records kept at the Strasbourg courthouse having been destroyed during the bombardment of the city.

I have the honour to ask you to be good enough to send back the items enclosed as soon as you have finished with them.

Accept etc.
Le Garde des Sceaux, Ministre de la Justice
Authorized by: le Conseiller d'État, Directeur des Affaires Criminelles et des Grâces

---

LETTER NO. 8

This letter is item no. 38 in Dossier F/17/2976/1:1. The Alsatian businessman, G.A. Le Bel, comes to Huber's defence once again, ascribing the stories about Huber in Algiers in 1874 to malicious ill-wishers.

Date: 22 September 1879
From: G.A. le Bel, Le Bel et Compagnie, Pechelbronn, Mines d'Asphaltes, Soultz sous Forêts, Alsace
To: the Minister of Public Education, Paris

Sir,

Since my return to Alsace I have been eagerly awaiting news from you, but I am not entirely surprised that I have received no reply to my request for information gathered by the directorate in Algiers. It may be a long while yet before that reaches us.

As a general rule, one cannot state with certainty that a fact does not exist. This is why, faced with the categorical statement that you made to me first of all during my last visit, my first reaction was to think that I had been mistaken. You then went on to say that the way the letter from the directorate was written left doubts. It did not require much reflection to dispel all of these. How could one suppose that a man who in Algiers had conducted a dishonourable affair, but one that had remained unknown in Paris, would go back to Algiers to awaken the sleeping tiger without having been forced to do so in any way. Such behaviour would constitute more than stupidity, it would be sheer insanity. I regret that I do not know the terms of the letter written to the ministry but the gist must be the same as in the one from which I copied: 'Strasbourg where it is said that he served three months in prison etc …' Of course, here we are dealing with Strasbourg and not Algiers, otherwise there would be no ambiguity. As far as the position that M. Huber occupied is concerned, he writes to me that he was for some time attached to the office of the civil and financial services director (M. de Toustain). He left it after handing in a written resignation which is at the directorate, and which was acknowledged as having been received in a letter which can be produced if necessary. M. de Toustain, as well as M. Picard and M. Pilias, both of whom are still today heads of department at the directorate and who know M. Huber, will be able to be consulted on the way things happened. If the reply from the directorate does not arrive, you or I could write to one of these gentlemen. One question arises about this matter: how could all this have happened if it is not based on any exact information? I confess I find it difficult to unravel this aspect of the question. I only know that M. Huber has an enemy who is highly placed at the directorate; what can his motive be? I imagine it is all about a woman. I have written to someone to get information on this point. As far as his position is concerned, he was probably not very well suited to it; his unusual penchant for adventure, and for anthropology and gynaecology, would be more than enough to explain how he came to leave his employment. Add to this the affair of the Arab skulls that he tried to remove from a cemetery near Algiers and which had to be hushed up, and the explanation that I am giving becomes quite probable. As far as I am concerned, a young man only needs to think of undertaking a journey across Arabia for me to consider him hardly suited to office work, but it is a long step from there to a dishonourable sanction.

I do not think that at the ministry they took into consideration the question of the (nationality) option and of the residence in Alsace. I could if necessary send you an option certificate. As for what may have happened in Strasbourg, I can only repeat that the directorate in Algiers is probably no better informed than a dozen young local men who know the underground and official channels of Strasbourg like the back of their hand.

Whatever happens, and even if I have to make the journey to Algiers, I will bring this matter to light. If I am induced to make this journey, I can take with me recommendations such that people will not refuse to tell me the truth about a question which impinges so closely on the honour of a man. In any case I will not be free before December. In expectation of the pleasure of seeing you again, receive my thanks for your friendly kindness and be assured of my devotion.

G.A. Le Bel

LETTER NO. 9 AND ENCLOSURE

This letter and its enclosure comprise item no. 39 in Dossier F/17/2976/1:1. In the enclosure, Huber describes meeting Abbé Pierre Géraygiry, who under the name Barakat had been William Gifford Palgrave's companion during their famous crossing of central and eastern Arabia in 1862–63. Huber would have found Géraigiry a fount of good advice on travelling in Arabia.

Date: 29 October 1879
From: T. Gilbert, French consulate in Damascus, enclosing a letter from Charles Huber
To: Charles Maunoir, Secretary-General, Société de Géographie, Paris

Dear M. Maunoir,

In sending you enclosed herewith the note that Dr [*sic*] Huber left here for you, I am taking advantage of the opportunity to recall myself to your kind memory.

I do not know whether the excellent doctor had told you, but I have done everything that he relied upon me to do for the success of his journey. I have put him in touch with the chief of the Ruwalah tribe, of whom our traveller is currently a guest, and then with the paramount shaykh of the Shammar, who usually spend the winter in the purlieus of Nağd; from where he will be able to continue his journey in peace. Whatever happens between here and Baghdad, I shall not lose sight of him and shall do everything in my power to facilitate his expedition.

Goodbye, dear and excellent Secretary-General, etc.

T. Gilbert
Chargé du Consulat

<u>Enclosure</u>

Damascus, 26 October 1879

M. Maunoir,

Here are all my studies, more or less completed. I left Lebanon about a month ago and since then have been here making preparations for my departure. These too are almost complete and I leave at 5 a.m. tomorrow in the direction of Palmyra, where I shall be in five days' time. I have been a little overworked during these last days because of my preparations, and today I lack the time to write you as long a letter as I would like. This I think I shall be able to do in a few days' time.

Some time ago I had the good fortune to make the acquaintance of Abbé Pierre Géraigiry, who had been Palgrave's travelling companion, and we had a long conversation about their journey.[16] This gave me the satisfaction of

[16] For Abbé Pierre Barakat Géraigiry (1841–1902), see Introduction, note 40.

seeing that my assessment of this work, which is in large part unreliable, is sound. I have been keenly urging Abbé Géraigiry to publish a version giving his side of the story, and a letter I received a few days ago makes me think that he will do it.[17]

I have profited from my stay in Lebanon by collecting a chestful of fossil fish and rock samples characteristic of the uplift of the Lebanon, plus a flask of insects preserved in alcohol. All that will leave in a few days for the ministry, together with a chest of twenty-five Maronite skulls and perhaps as many more from the ancient tombs of Palmyra. I shall not be certain of the latter until a few days' time. I shall then write to M. de Quatrefages.

As you can see, M. Maunoir, I am fulfilling my programme little by little just as I set it out. I shall spend about three or four months travelling in the Syrian Desert to break myself in to bedouin life, accustom myself to their ways, study the routes of my itinerary, and foster some relationships. In spring I shall start out en route for Naǧd. And from there I think I shall have more opportunities to send you my news.

I do not want to close this letter without mentioning a man who has rendered me very great service since my arrival in Damascus. This is M. Gilbert, our French consul, whom you have known from long past. He has put me in touch with a large number of people able to give me useful information, has procured for me letters for some of the tribal chiefs, and in a word has facilitated my task in a truly extraordinary manner. I would be most grateful if, when occasion serves, you could thank him in the name of science.

My friend [G.A.] Le Bel has been entertaining me for some time with funny stories about me. I hope that those in high places will make of them the same as I do.

Please accept, etc.
Charles Huber

Letter no. 10

This letter is item no. 52 in Dossier F/17/2976/1:1. Enclosed with it are two pages transcribing and describing the Ǧabal Sarrāʾ inscriptions.

[17] There is no sign that Géraigiry ever produced such a work, which is a pity. Huber was right to be skeptical of Palgrave's travelogue: see Introduction, note 41.

Date: 11 July 1880
From: Charles Huber, in Ḥā'il
To: the Minister of Public Education, Paris

M. le Ministre,

I have the honour to confirm to you my letter of the 1st of this month, sent via Damascus.[18]

I returned here at 6 o'clock this morning from a trip to Ǧabal Sarrā', a journey of fourteen hours to the south of Ḥā'il, to make a copy of a Himyarite[19] inscription which had been brought to my attention. I am taking advantage of a man who is leaving this evening for Baghdad to send you straight away the result of this excursion. I shall do likewise with all the others that I acquire, because I would like to see them published before this M. Khalīl, about whom I spoke in my above-mentioned letter, is able to publish them.[20]

I am taking the liberty, M. le Ministre, to call your kind attention once again to my letter of the 1st of this month, and pray you to be good enough to follow this matter up as quickly as possible, as any delay would be disastrous for me.

Please accept etc.,
Charles Huber

LETTER NO. 11

This note is item no. 56 in Dossier F/17/2976/1:1. It confirms that Huber served a jail sentence of six months in 1869 [*sic*], and records the ministry's

[18] Huber's letter to the ministry from Ḥā'il, dated 1 July 1880, is no. 53 in Dossier F/17/2976/1:1. Not translated here, it is a 20-page report in which he requests an extension and an additional 15,000 francs, as well as some more instruments. He also records his first awareness of an English traveller known locally as Khalīl. This was in fact Charles Montagu Doughty, though Huber did not know this at the time. Doughty had been in Ḥā'il in October–November 1877 and again briefly in early April 1878 (Doughty 1936 i: 635–72; ii: 15–68, 270–86).

[19] For Huber's use of the term 'Himyarite', see Translation Part I, note 158; Appendix 4, note 20.

[20] Huber refers to his letter of 1 July 1880, no. 53 in Dossier F/17/2976/1:1 (see note 18 above). He was evidently worried that 'Khalīl' would publish these inscriptions before him, but I can find no evidence that Doughty visited Ǧabal Sarrā'. Huber was the first European to record this site, and visited it again with Euting in early 1884. For Huber's 1880 visit to Ǧabal Sarrā', see Translation Part I, pp. 140–3 and notes 161 and 162; Appendix 1, note 3; Appendix 2 p. 294).

dissatisfaction with the results of his expedition so far. Its brevity and abruptness suggests that it is a fragment of a longer note.

Date: 7 October 1880
From: the Office of the Minister of Public Education, Paris
To: not stated

M. Huber had been recommended by the professors at the museum, who were unaware of his past. Later we received the proof, from the Ministry of Justice, that in 1869 [*sic*; 1868] M. Huber had served six months in jail for theft. The Expeditions Committee furthermore has found M. Huber's first report [i.e. the one dated 1 July 1880, see note 18 above] to be pitiful.

[Unsigned]

Letter no. 12

This letter is item no. 61 in Dossier F/17/2976/1:1.

Date: 21 October 1880
From: Charles Huber, in Ḥāʾil
To: the Minister of Public Education, Paris

M. le Ministre,

I have the honour of confirming to you my previous letters.

As part of my itinerary my plan had always been to leave this place with the Persian Ḥağğ caravan coming from Baghdad, which is due to pass by here this very day. But at the last minute various religio-political difficulties arose which, were I to persist in my desire to leave with the Ḥağğ, could create further trouble.

Besides I absolutely do not want to leave here because I still have to go from here to Taymāʾ, Madāʾin Ṣāliḥ, Khaybar etc. etc., and the south-eastern part of Shammar territory – so that I shall be at Ğiddah only towards the end of December next. I hope to find there the funds and the instruments that I requested in a previous letter,[21] and which will be indispensable for me if I am to continue profitably with my exploration of the centre and south of Arabia.

[21] i.e. his letter of 1 July 1880, see note 18 above.

Since my last letter, I have visited al-Qaṣīm and pushed on as far as ʿUnayzah where, despite it being during Ramaḍān, I was able to stay three days and take stock. The emir Zāmil gave me a good reception. I am more or less sure of being able to cross the remainder of Naǧd fully and usefully.

From Ǧiddah I shall have the honour of sending you a resumé of my recent excursions.

Please accept etc.
Charles Huber

LETTER NO. 13

This letter is one of three comprising item no. 66 in Dossier F/17/2976/1:1.

Date: 2 January 1881
From: Charles Huber, in Ḥāʾil
To: not stated, but probably to Charles Maunoir, Paris

Honoured Sir,

I have the honour to confirm to you my letter sent from Khaybar and which must have reached you via al-Madīnah and Ǧiddah.

At this point I have brought to completion the exploration of the whole of northern Arabia. My journey to al-Qaṣīm and ʿUnayzah, Taymāʾ, al-ʿUlā, Khaybar and al-Ḥāʾiṭ has taken me sixty-four days.

The route to Ǧiddah is barred to me just now by the ʿUtaybah and Hutaym, who are harrying the countryside in the wake of a campaign of raiding that Ibn Rashīd, the Shammar emir, has been carrying out against them and from which he returned only yesterday.

I am without news from the ministry, our consul in Ǧiddah not having handed to the messenger that I had sent to him before my departure for the west, a ministerial envelope in his possession, fearing that it would not reach me. But he does write that M. le Ministre has charged him to tell me to return to Paris on my arrival in Ǧiddah. So is my expedition to be terminated? And does the Expeditions Committee no longer wish to continue lending me its support? Yet I was sure of success and of being the first Christian to cross Arabia as such from side to side, and to do so not as an amateur like my predecessors, but as a professional explorer.

Anthropology is still difficult in Arabia. I still have only a single skull, which I have brought back from Khaybar.

If I fail to find anyone to accompany towards Ǧiddah, I shall leave for Baghdad in a few days' time.

Accept etc.,
Ch. Huber

LETTER NO. 14

This letter is the second of three comprising item no. 66 in Dossier F/17/2976/1:1.

Date: 2 January 1881
From: Charles Huber, in Ḥāʾil
To: the Minister of Public Education, Paris

M. le Ministre,

I have the honour to inform you that I returned here this morning having completed my last journey in the Shammar realm. I left Ḥāʾil on 31 October last, and after having reached a peak in the desert that I had been heading towards for five days, I made my way to Taymāʾ, and went from there to Madāʾin Ṣāliḥ on the Darb al-Ḥaǧǧ [from Syria], and thence to al-ʿUlā, still farther to the west. I visited Khaybar and al-Ḥāʾiṭ, and returned here via Mustaǧiddah, Ghazzālah etc., having been away for sixty-four days, much longer than I had planned. But when one gets near to the Darb al-Ḥaǧǧ one enters a very notorious region exposing one to all sorts of dangers and where, in the event, there was no shortage of incidents. I have collected all the data necessary for a perfect understanding of these regions, in which my sole predecessor has been Wallin, who moreover only visited Taymāʾ.[22] I have been able to establish that the watershed of northern Arabia is located on a line joining Taymāʾ and Ǧabal Raʾs al-Abyaḍ, 80–90 miles NNW of al-Madīnah.

[22] This is an odd thing to say about Georg Wallin, who in 1845 and 1848 pioneered European knowledge of the Shammar domain by visiting Ḥāʾil twice and crossing northern Arabia from west to east, covering much of the same ground as Huber (Wallin 1850 and 1854; Kiernan 1937: 231–41). It is interesting however that Huber was familiar with Wallin's travels.

It is from Ra's al-Abyaḍ that the two greatest watercourses of Arabia flow: the Wadi Ermek, which passes between ʿUnayzah and Buraydah in al-Qaṣīm and reaches the sea at Sūq al-Shuyūkh near Baṣra; and the Wadi Debeq [*sic*; Ṭibiq], which after a course of about 150 leagues reaches the Red Sea near al-Wajh.[23]

Helped by the low altitudes of the sun, I was able this time to take bearings everywhere and record astronomical data on all the locations I visited, including the most important places.

Anthropological study, which is so difficult to carry out in Muslim countries, has also been likewise enhanced by the recording of curious and significant findings, among others the existence at al-ʿUlā of a population of light-skinned negroes or, in scientific terms, of prognathous white people.

This last journey of exploration has also allowed me to set precise geological limits to the entire Shammar territory, as a granite uplift.

What the ancient Arabs understood by the Ǧabal is an islet of granite about 150 miles long from north to south and 40–50 wide from east to west. Its slope is from west to east. From the Ǧabal, the terrain slopes down gently to all points of the horizon. The Ǧabal is completely surrounded by sandstone except to the south, or rather the south-south-west, where the terrain is volcanic almost all the way to al-Madīnah. (As there are great differences of opinion among previous travellers about the nature of the terrain in Arabia, I have collected up till now about forty rock samples along my route. These will enable us to establish an accurate geological map of northern Arabia.)

At al-Ḥiǧr [Madā'in Ṣāliḥ] I visited the dwellings dug into the rock and attributed to the Thamūd, as well as those at al-ʿUlā, which have never been mentioned by any previous traveller or geographer. I was able to establish that these were not dwellings but ancient tombs. In the latter place I made copies of all the inscriptions to be found above the entrances to the sepulchral chambers.

Today I shall stop at this point, reserving for another time a more detailed report on this trip.

Before leaving Ḥā'il two months ago, I was able to send by means of the Ḥaǧǧ on its way to Mecca, a messenger to the Consul of France at Ǧiddah to deliver my correspondence, and for him to let me know whether the things requested in my letter of 1 July 1880 were with him.

[23] Wadi Ermek: i.e. Wadi al-Rimah; see Translation Part II, note 58; Part III, notes 15 and 17. Wadi Ṭibiq/Ṭubghah: see Translation Part II note 199.

The reply dated 10 December 1880 which arrived during my absence, and of which I was instantly aware, sent on various letters that had arrived for me, minus 'a letter from the Ministry, dated 19 November, sufficiently important not to be sent to me in a country which in all probability I would have left by the time the messenger arrived'. As a postscript he added: 'The Minister charges me to request you to return to Paris as soon as you reach Ǧiddah.'

My exploration of al-Qaṣīm, including Buraydah and ʿUnayzah, and of Taymāʾ, al-Ḥiǧr, al-ʿUlā and Khaybar, has exhausted all my resources; on the other hand, I have completely finished the exploration of the northern half of Arabia, so I can leave my centre of operations, but I doubt that I shall be able to reach Ǧiddah at this time, and here is the reason why.

On 2 December last, the emir Ibn Rashīd, in order to protect his Ḥaǧǧ caravan, which just then was on its way from Mecca to al-Madīnah and shortly after that was returning to Ḥāʾil, conceived the idea of carrying out a raid on the ʿUtaybah, whose grazing lands lie to the east of the two holy cities. This raid was a complete success and the emir returned from it yesterday, a day before me, with a rich booty. Now, the consequences of this raid are that hardly had the emir arrived back, than the ʿUtaybah, enraged by the loss of 950 camels, almost 5,000 sheep and goats, 12 horses, tents and supplies, etc., set about harrying the countryside in bands of ten to fifteen men, and pillaging and murdering everyone they come across with no regard for their origin.

I doubt that I shall be able to find one or two men courageous enough to accompany me, and the emir has just told me that it is not possible to let me have his men because he is sure that the road is not practicable and that we would all be massacred.

That being my situation, I am forced to attempt the impossible. I am loading up all my things and leaving Ḥāʾil tomorrow evening so as to reach Mustaǧiddah, and from there just five days over the desert would get me to Ḥanākiyyah where there is a Turkish post. If I find a man to accompany me I shall set out on the journey, and if that is the case shall reach Ǧiddah before this letter reaches Paris.

If it is not possible to get to Ǧiddah, I shall come back here and go to Baghdad.

From Ǧiddah I shall have the honour, M. le Ministre, of informing you by telegraph of my arrival. Thus if you have received no despatch before this letter reaches you, it will be because I shall not have been able to get through, in which case I shall be in Baghdad.

As my messenger found nothing in Ǧiddah of what I had taken the liberty of requesting from you to [enable me to] complete my expedition in Arabia, I fear that your ministry may not wish to continue its support for me in the future. So I am bold enough to beg you, M. le Ministre, to be good enough to confirm to me on receipt of this letter, whether to Ǧiddah or Baghdad, whether I must really return to Paris, and whether or not your support for me is to continue, as in the former case I shall leave part of my baggage in the East.

To pay my courier who is to deliver this letter to Baghdad, and to fund my own expenses from here to Ǧiddah or Baghdad, I am forced to draw a bill of 500 francs on my mother which, with the guarantee of the emir, an inhabitant of Mashhad [Mashhad ʿAlī, Naǧaf] is discounting for me. These are my last resources. So I am forced to beg you to be kind enough, in your despatch, to authorize me to draw on your bank the amount needed to pay my passage and to obtain a small set of clothes, without which I shall have to make my return to France dressed as a Bedouin, or rather a Shammari.

I had the timely honour to tell you about the journey of a M. Blunt and his lady[24] to Ǧabal Shammar. The emir has just told me that he has received a letter from him, from Ǧiddah, announcing his plan to make a journey in the Yemen, Wadi al-Dawāsir and al-Qaṣīm, and that he would return to visit the emir in Ḥāʾil. His letter is signed Blunt Bey. I have said previously that this individual was a political agent.

I have the honour etc.,
Ch. Huber
P.S. My address in Baghdad will be c/o M. Péretié, Consul of France.

Letter no. 15

This letter is the third of three comprising item no. 66 in Dossier F/17/2976/1:1.

Date: 20 February 1881
From: A. Péretié, French Consulate, Baghdad
To: HE M. Jules Ferry,[25] Minister of Public Education, Paris

[24] For the journey of Wilfrid and Lady Anne Blunt through northern Arabia, see Translation Part I, note 137.

[25] Jules François Camille Ferry (1832–93) was a prominent republican statesman. Born in the Vosges, he opposed the declaration of war against Germany in 1870, and administered Paris during the siege. He became prime minister of France from 1880 till 1885, with two short interruptions as Minister of Public Education (1881–82)

M. le Ministre,

I am in receipt of the letter that you have done the honour of writing to me dated 31 December 1880, inviting me to provide M. Cohun, director of a scientific expedition in the Euphrates Basin, with the sum necessary for his repatriation, should the exhaustion of his resources oblige him to break off from his journey and return to France.

I shall carry out Your Excellency's instructions to the letter.

But I beg you to allow me to respectfully observe that the immediate return of M. Cohun will make a very unfortunate impression in the city. M. Cohun having been recommended to me by my father, I took steps to accommodate him in my house. So he will not have to concern himself with his upkeep. Under these conditions, a small sum will perhaps enable him to complete his work. Would there not therefore be an advantage, from every angle, in not refusing him this credit?

In any case, I hope that Your Excellency will pardon these observations, which are dictated by my patriotism and my devotion to the Government of the Republic.

I have the honour to transmit to you, enclosed herewith, a letter from Dr Hubert [*sic*]. This intrepid traveller is due shortly to arrive in Baghdad. The shaykh Ibn Rashīd has declared war on a nomadic tribe, and M. Hubert has been obliged, at least temporarily, to change his plans.

Accept etc.
Your humble servant,
A. Péretié

LETTER NO. 16 AND REPORT OF MARCH 1882

This letter and its accompanying 65-page report comprise item no. 79 in Dossier F/17/2976/1:1. Huber wrote this important document on his return to Strasbourg in early 1882. Only the first ten pages are presented here in translation. This is, first, because of the report's length; and, second, because these ten pages comprise the only extensive part of the handwritten report that does not appear in Huber's published travelogue: they usefully cover the eight months Huber spent between October 1879 and May 1880 in

and Minister of Foreign Affairs (1882–83). He was a keen secularist as well as a colonialist, and granted much official support to scientific exploration.

Syria, together with two printed maps of Syria on which Huber traced his journeys there before setting out for Arabia. These routes also appear on the folding map that was published with Huber 1884b and which is reproduced at the end of this volume. The contents of the remainder of the report were expanded later into the articles in the *Bulletin de la Société de Géographie* that are presented in the Translation section of this volume (Huber 1884a, 1884b, 1885a). Any significant items of information that Huber chose not to include in those articles are quoted in the footnotes to the Translation. It is noteworthy that in this handwritten report, as in the printed articles, there is no mention of the Taymāʾ Stele.

Date: 27 March 1882
From: Charles Huber, Strasbourg
To: the Minister of Public Education

M. le Ministre,

I have the honour to send you a report on the expedition to explore central Arabia that you were good enough to commission me to carry out.

If the results of this expedition fall short of all that scholars and experts might have expected, please, M. le Ministre, attribute this in part to the explorer, but also take into account the novelty and the difficulty of the venture. For lack of adequate means he was able to explore only the most thankless part of the Peninsula and the one least covered in documentary sources of all kinds.

I have nevertheless done my utmost to bring back, from that part of the land that I travelled through, the materials that will enable a satisfactory description to be made of it.

If, upon examination, this report enables you to recognize the correctness of what I have told you, I would be happy if you would be kind enough to continue your support for me to accomplish the exploration of the remainder of central Arabia, and to carry out that of the south.

I have the honour to beg you to accept etc.

Charles Huber
Place du Temple Neuf, Strasbourg

The report

M. Charles Huber's expedition in Arabia

From the outset, my expedition ran into delays and difficulties which I must quickly recount at the outset of this report.

M. Delaporte, Consul-General of France at Beirut, whose entire career has been spent in the East, declared from the start that my project was unrealizable and only let me hope for his support and for the request for the Turkish *firmān*,[26] which I would need were I to touch upon Ottoman territory in Arabia, on condition that I gave him a written declaration stating that he had advised me against making my journey, and that whatever happened to me would be outside his responsibility.

M. Gilbert, French Consul at Damascus, whom I had asked to put me in contact with one of the great shaykhs of the Ḥamād[27] to hire one or two Bedouins whose job it would be to guide me to al-Ǧawf, replied that my project was impossible under such conditions and that I was acquainted with neither the Arabs nor the desert. According to him, I would have to be placed under the protection of a well-known shaykh who would undertake to have me conducted safe and sound as far as al-Ǧawf, and who would only let me go on from there once I had obtained a similar undertaking from the governor, charged with arranging the onward stage of my journey.

Though only half-trusting in the success of this manner of proceeding, I accepted the support of our consul. M. Gilbert's eye fell on Muḥammad Ṭūkhī, one of the great shaykhs of the Wuld ʿAlī,[28] to get me started on my journey. Ṭūkhī was then just five days away from Damascus. The divisional commander, Ǧamīl Pasha,[29] today military governor of Aleppo, conducted the negotiations.

---

[26] *Firmān*: originally a decree issued by a sovereign of an Islamic state. It came to mean a written permit issued by local or national authorities in the Ottoman empire, particularly, in the case of Europeans, a permit to travel.

[27] The Ḥamād: the vast region of the Syrian desert stretching between Syria/Jordan and Iraq. Starting south of Palmyra, it extends all the way to northern Saudi Arabia, and is characterized by mostly flat and stony topography with few wells or hilly areas, and by expanses of gravel, dry wadis leading to shallow depressions, coarse vegetation and, in the west, areas of *ḥarrah* (basalt boulders) running about 90 km to the east of Ǧabal Druze.

[28] Muḥammad Ṭūkhī was shaykh of the Wuld ʿAlī, a tribe of the northern ʿAnizah confederation.

[29] Huber writes 'Djamil Pacha'. This appears to be Ǧamīl Nāmiq Pasha, Ottoman governor of Aleppo at the time.

There were still going on when the Druze uprising broke out, soon to be suppressed by force. It nevertherless had the effect of causing all the nomads then in the Ḥamād to flee into the desert, Muḥammad Ṭūkhī among them.

The route via the Ḥawrān thus being closed, and for a long time, the only tribe remaining in the vicinity were the Ruwalah, a section of whom were to be found just then between Qaryatayn and Palmyra. From persons who knew them I obtained letters of recommendation to their paramount shaykh, Saṭṭām ibn Shaʿlān: as well as one from the French consul, I had letters from the emir ʿAbd al-Qādir,[30] from Midḥat Pasha,[31] then Wali of Damascus, from Saʿīd Pasha, the Amīr al-Ḥağğ, etc.

Full of confidence, I left Damascus on 27 October 1879 in the company of Fuʾād, shaykh of Qaryatayn, whose influence is greater than most and stretches beyond Palmyra. I had made his acquaintance in Damascus where he had spent a fortnight on business. He had then invited me to go along with him as far as Qaryatayn, where we arrived on 29 October 1879 at six o'clock in the evening.

We learned straight away that since just the day before Saṭṭām's tents were to be found no more than six hours from Qaryatayn. So despite Shaykh Fuʾād's efforts to keep me there for a few days, I left him during the afternoon of the following day and reached the Ruwalah encampment and the tent of Shaykh Saṭṭām at six o'clock that evening. The latter was away, and it was his deputy, a big black man named Addessem [*sic*], who welcomed me in the most cordial fashion.

On the next day and the days following we moved camp. I followed my hosts while waiting for the arrival of Saṭṭām, which was announced from one day to the next but which was still being awaited until 11 November.

On the next day, I submitted my letters of recommendation and, on the day after that, my gifts. He had wished me welcome on his arrival, and promised me 'on his head' to conduct me to al-Ğawf. He just asked me to be patient for a few days, as all his enemies, as he told me, were at that moment on the route.

So the days went by in constant outings, with me reminding Saṭṭām of his promise from time to time, and him prescribing patience all the time. On 2 December, there arrived from Damascus a Ruwalī who delivered a letter from M. Gilbert. It appears that a few days after his arrival at camp,

---

[30] For the emir ʿAbd al-Qādir, see Translation Part II, note 155.
[31] For Midḥat Pasha, see Translation Part I, note 136.

Saṭṭām had written to the various people who had given me letters for him, to the effect that 'just then he was surrounded by all his enemies, that it was impossible for him to get me to al-Ǧawf, and that besides I was in great danger while with him and that I ought to be made to return to Damascus'. This being the situation, M. Gilbert begged me to return.

The shaykh must have written these letters after a conversation we had had shortly after his arrival, in which he had argued that my project was impossible, painted a picture of the dangers that awaited me, and advised me to renounce the whole thing. Faced with me declaring my firm resolve to pursue the journey, he promised once again to conduct me to al-Ǧawf, and it was doubtless very shortly afterwards that he wrote to Damascus to have me recalled.

I had a discussion with Saṭṭām straight away and reproached him with his duplicity. He replied that he was sorry for not being able to keep his word, that he had not been able to do anything about it, that it was God who had interposed his enemies between us and my goal, etc. etc. – in short, he resorted to all the fine oriental expressions which a Bedouin never lacks when he is trying to put one off the scent.

I left the next day and was back in Damascus by the evening of 6 December. I had lost two and a half months, the gifts I had brought for him, two revolvers that he had begged me for, and finally 200 francs that I had lent him and that he never repaid.

Note: Map no. 60 in the Stieler Atlas, which I have appended to the present report, indicates the areas that I covered during my travels with the Ruwalah.[32]

I immediately set about preparing to leave once more following my original plan, via the Ḥawrān and the south. But the terrible winter of 1879–80 made itself felt all the way over here, and within a few days all the routes had been rendered impassable by two feet of snow.

It was only possible to resume my journey on 2 March [1880], and this time I went straight to the encampment of Muḥammad Ṭūkhī, which I reached after four full days on the march, at Ǧarāsh[33] to the east of the River

[32] These journeys and the next ones to Ǧarash and the Druze shaykhs are marked on Huber's folding map appended to Huber 1884b, and reproduced at the end of this volume.

[33] Ǧarāsh: the famous city of the Decapolis dating to the Hellenistic and Roman eras, located 48 km north of ʿAmmān in present-day Jordan.

Jordan. Bad news awaited me: of my camels, sent on here to pasture on my return from the Ruwalah, two had died of cold and a third was sick, and it was completely impossible to replace them as all the Arabs' camels were sick or too weak to march. I would not be able to leave, Ṭūkhī told me, before a month had passed, that is to say before the Sharārāt arrived.

Determined not to be defeated, I paid successive visits to Shaykh Muḥammad Khalīl at Boṣra, Shaykh Aṭrash at Ṣalkhad, Shaykh Nağm [al-Aṭrash] at ʿUrmān[34] etc. etc., but was met everywhere with the same response: 'No *dhalūl*s (dromedaries) available before a month is up.' On 13 March I was back in Damascus, cursing the ill-fortune that had dogged me since my departure.

Note: Map no. 61 in the Stieler Atlas, which I have appended to the present report, indicates the routes I took to the camp of Muḥammad Ṭūkhī and the Druzes.

More than a month had rolled by before I received news that at last all the routes were open and the animals ready. So I set off for the third time from Damascus on 28 April 1880, thoroughly determined not to come back again; and yet I came close to being forced to do so once more, as we shall see.

The shaykh of the Druzes, Nağm Ibrāhīm, had undertaken to find me the two or three Bedouin needed to act as my guides as far as Kāf. To this end he had made arrangements with Shaykh ʿAlī al-Qurayshī (the same man whom Lady Anne Blunt calls Ali el Kreysheh[35]), of the Banī Ṣakhr, who had given him his word. I reached the encampment of the latter on 7 May and he repeated the promise he had made to Shaykh Nağm. Every day I demanded to leave, and every day he put me off until the morrow. On 11 May, I took him aside and told him about the trick that Saṭṭām had played on me, adding that if he too had so few scruples about keeping his word he should tell me straight away. Put on notice like this, he reeled off the same laments and the same apologies for having enemies along the route, etc. etc. So I was faced with a second Arab shaykh going back on his word.

[34] Shaykh Ibrāhīm al-Aṭrash and Shaykh Nağm el-Aṭrash were the two leading Druze shaykhs of Ğabal Ḥawrān. Huber would revisit them with Euting at the start of his second Arabian journey in 1883.

[35] From this it can be deduced that Huber must have read Lady Anne Blunt's *Pilgrimage to Nejd* (Blunt 1881), which was first published in 1881, immediately on his return from his first journey. Huber had heard in detail about the Blunts' visit to Ḥāʾil in January 1879 from the Emir Muḥammad al-Rashīd himself. See Translation Part I, p. 132 and note 137.

First thing next morning I took leave of him, directing my steps towards Boṣra, which I reached the same day, for the second time.

Note: Map no. 61 in the Stieler Atlas, which I have appended to the present report, indicates the route I took to the Druzes, then to Shaykh ʿAlī al-Qurayshī, from there to Boṣra, and finally to Kāf by way of ʿAnz.

To go back to Damascus again for the third time was out of the question. I would rather have left all my baggage behind, and gone on my way alone, like a dervish.

First thing on the day after my arrival at Boṣra, I had the good fortune to find two Bedouin who agreed to serve me as guides and to take my animals as far as Kāf. I closed the deal with them, despite the advice of the Shaykh of Boṣra, who told me that these two men were *bawwāq*s.[36] Our departure was fixed for Friday 14 May.

For being forced to follow the advice of people full of good will but poorly informed about the Arabs and the desert, I had squandered eight months spent suffering fatigue and vexations; I had spent almost 2,000 francs and the greater part of my gifts; and, finally, I was finding myself having to leave on my own, with no guarantee of safety, and in the company of two *bawwāq*s into the bargain.

[From this point on, Huber's story of his first Arabian journey is given in full detail in the Translation, Parts I, II and III.]

LETTER NO. 17

This letter is item no. 86 in Dossier F/17/2976/1:1. It sheds light on Huber's activities in Iraq in 1881, after his first journey in Central Arabia.

Date: 13 May 1882
From: Charles Huber, Strasbourg
To: Xavier Charmes,[37] Director of the Secretariat and Accounts Department, the Ministry of Public Education and Fine Arts, Paris

---

[36] For the meaning of *bawwāq*, see Translation Part I, note 5.

[37] Xavier Charmes (1849–1919), was director of the Secrétariat et de la comptabilité du Ministère de l'Instruction publique et des Beaux-Arts, and General secretary of the Comité des travaux historiques et scientifiques, and as such was responsible for paying Huber's fees and expenses. He was a member of the Académie des sciences morales et politiques. He also contributed to the creation of the Institut français d'archéologie orientale in Cairo in 1880, and invited Gaston Maspero to be its first director. (MG)

Monsieur,

I note that I have omitted to reply to you on the subject of excavations that could be undertaken in Babylonia with a high chance of satisfactory results.

My information on this topic is the fruit of numerous excursions among the nomads as well as among the settled peasant population living between the Tigris and Euphrates, from ten or so places to the south of Baghdad almost as far as Qurnah, at the junction of the two rivers. Thanks to my bedouin clothing, my contacts, and my status as a brother of the Shammar, I was able to travel around freely and on my own among these virtually independent Arabs, who pay taxes only to the extent that the *Mutasarrif*-Pashas[38] of Ḥillah, Dīwāniyyah or Samāwah are prepared to visit them with troops to collect them. I had occasion to observe a large number of tells there, particularly in the territory ranged over by the Lemlum Arabs to the south-east of Dīwāniyyah, some of them as large as that of Muğallibah at Babylon, which have never been excavated at all. The Arabs go that way every spring and just pick up the alabaster or porphyry stamp seals and little cylinders of which there are so many in the British Museum, and which are brought to light by the winter rains washing away the ground. Some of these tells that are very exposed to the winds, which blow especially violently at Dīwāniyyah, and that are washed by the rains, give one sight of sections of wall, proving that these tells are of the same type as the three at Babylon.

Furthermore, the Arabs report how they sometimes find tablets and objects of gold and marble, which goes to prove that they are identical to the tells at Babylon, except that the latter have been investigated several times over the last century, by [Claudius] Rich, [Robert] Ker Porter, [Austin Henry] Layard, etc., and currently by the British Museum. It is only the difficulty of penetrating the district of the Lemlum Arabs and staying there that has preserved these tells from being excavated up until now, because Mr [Hormuzd] Rassam, the British Museum's agent, is perfectly aware of them and the riches they contain.[39]

I believe that a sum of 10,000 francs would suffice for a preliminary attempt at excavation, but it would be necessary to allocate double that

[38] *Mutasarrif*: the governor of an Ottoman *sanjak* or province.

[39] For Hormuzd Rassam and Huber's part in the British Museum excavations, see Translation Part III, note 140. For further information on Huber's time in Iraq, see Appendix 5, Letter no. 3.

amount, or 20,000 francs, half to be made available straight away, and the second half to be paid once a ministerial decision has been taken based on the report detailing the first excavation. It would be vital to authorize this second half in advance, so that it could be allocated immediately should the need arise, because if the preliminary works turn out well it would not be necessary for them to be stopped for lack of funds – a situation that would not be sustainable in the country.

For now I would wish to be authorized to carry out excavations in south-west Arabia, in those places where I believe they would produce results and provide facilities, that is, in Nağrān and Mā'rib, in the ruins of the ancient Himyarite cities, and to be able to avail myself of all or part of the first half of this budget, that is, 10,000 francs.

The possibility of carrying out excavations in Mā'rib is obviously uncertain. To do so I would have to be down there under the same conditions as those that I experienced in the Shammar country, which I could hardly dare hope for. In the latter event, the above budget would remain intact for the forthcoming excavations in Babylonia.

Please accept etc.
Charles Huber
10 Place du Temple Neuf

LETTER NO. 18

This letter is the first of two comprising item no. 87 in Dossier F/17/2976/1:1. Together these form Huber's formal request for the support of the Minister of Public Education to return to Arabia to continue his expedition to explore the whole Peninsula.

Date: 11 May 1882
From: Charles Huber, Strasbourg
To: the Minister of Public Education and Fine Arts, Paris

M. le Ministre,

Following my letter of 27 March last, sending you the Report on the expedition to explore Arabia that you were kind enough to entrust me with, I now have the honour to beg you to be kind enough to consider my request for the continuation of this project.

My first journey covered the exploration of the part of the Peninsula lying between 35° and 25° of latitude, and 36° and 46° of longitude. The southern portion, which remains to be explored, lies roughly between 25° and 15° of latitude and 40° and 55° of longitude.

The reasons for the support of my first expedition remain unchanged. But today I possess even better data on the points at issue, I shall proceed with more confidence, and shall follow my itineraries with greater certitude. I am now familiar with the people and the conditions.

Experience having taught me the danger of penetrating Arabia under the auspices of the Turks, my point of departure would not be any place on the west coast, and I shall even shun any advantages that Ǧiddah might afford for the initial stages. I shall leave again from Damascus, but follow a route more to the west of the one I followed before, going through Taymāʾ, Madāʾin Ṣāliḥ, al-ʿUlā, Khaybar etc. in the Ḥiǧāz, where more than a hundred large Himyaritic inscriptions remain to be copied at great height, and which I was unable to survey during my previous journey for lack of adequate means.

I am all the more eager to return to these regions because on my first journey my aneroid barometers were no longer registering and as a result the physical description of the country would be lacking in accuracy. In future I shall be better equipped and am even thinking of being able to bring two mercury barometers with me.

This time, when I leave Khaybar my plan is to march farther south almost to al-Madīnah, and from there go back up to Ḥāʾil, crossing the desert between these two towns, in such a way as to cut across Wadi al-Rimah, or rather Wadi Ermek, near the mountain of Abbān [*sic*] through which it must go.[40] By fixing this point I shall have a good idea of the line of this watercourse, the origin of which I identified on my last expedition. The notes I compiled then in this area between Khaybar, al-Madīnah and Ḥāʾil indicate the existence of ancient ruins, metalliferous mines, and inscriptions.

I want to go back to Ḥāʾil so as to take advantage of the Emir Muḥammad ibn Rashīd's favour towards me, and his promise to facilitate my further projects should I return to Arabia. Travelling under his auspices to Riyadh, I think I shall be on a fairly good footing to be able to explore the provinces of al-Washm, Sudayr, al-Aflāǧ, etc., just as I was able to explore those of the north, and even to find there the means to enable me to travel beyond. I must

[40] On Wadi al-Rimah/ Ermek, see Translation Part II, note 58; Part III, notes 15 and 17. It is not clear what Huber means by the 'mountain of Abbān'.

remark here that I am under no illusion about the security of the country and the difficulty of crossing Nağd, especially in view of the current weakness of Ibn Saʿūd's government.[41] But I think I can assure you that I shall achieve my aims even so, given prudence and my previous experience.

I find it harder to say how I plan to leave Nağd than to get there. Should I wish to go from there to the Persian Gulf coast, nothing could be easier: Sadleir[42] in 1819 and Palgrave in 1863 went in this direction, and trade routes too exist. But there are more interesting regions to explore. My itinerary includes going south-westwards via Wadi al-Dawāsir and the territory of the Qaḥṭān Arabs to reach Nağrān, and farther south into the ancient Himyarite kingdom. You are aware, M. le Ministre, of all the interesting things there are to carry out in this region, even after the [visit of the] scholar M. Halévy,[43] who was unable to record all the plentiful inscriptions he came across and could do still less in terms of describing the country. From there I want to go to the northern part of Ḥaḍramawt to check the phenomenon of the Baḥr al-Sāfī,[44] and to survey the surroundings.

Having thus reached the extremity of the Arabian Peninsula, I hardly dare tell you that I shall continue my journey eastwards, as I wish to do, across Mahra territory and towards Oman, and to go back northwards from there along the Persian Gulf, keeping between the most inland localities and the desert all the way so as to trace the limits of the latter with complete accuracy. All that will depend on the time of year at which I shall be in these low latitudes (though I know that high plateaux already begin at a short distance from the sea), and on the extent of my own ability to endure the fatigues and hard life of this land. But my heart is set

[41] Ibn Saʿūd: at that time this was the Imām ʿAbdullah b. Fayṣal b. Turkī (r. 1865–87).

[42] It is interesting that Huber knew about George Forster Sadleir's trans-Arabian journey in 1819, but he is in error about Sadleir's direction of travel: he went from the Gulf coast to al-Dirʿiyyah, al-Qaṣīm, al-Madīnah, and the Red Sea coast at Yanbuʿ (Sadleir 1866/1977; Facey 1992: 118–19).

[43] Joseph Halévy (1827–1917) was an Ottoman-born Jewish-French Orientalist, traveller and prominent member of the AIBL. He crossed Yemen during 1869–70 in search of Sabaic inscriptions, making a valuable collection of 800 copies of them. He also made major contributions to the deciphering of the Ancient North Arabian scripts. (MCAM)

[44] Al-Baḥr al-Sāfī, 'the Pure Sea', the sea of waterless sand north of Ḥaḍramawt, i.e. the southern Rubʿ al-Khālī, which had the reputation of swallowing up people and their herds (Meulen 1947: 101, 201). One wonders how Huber had heard about this region – perhaps from hearsay reported by Halévy.

on attaching my name to the first scientific exploration of Arabia, and I shall be desirous of doing more and better than we shall be able to do for a long time.

During the entire course of my explorations I shall make the same scientific observations as on the previous expedition that you were kind enough to entrust me with. My route will be plotted according to astronomical altitudes; climatic conditions will be recorded daily as before; as will the flora and fauna, geology and the products of the country, always with samples and specimens to support my findings.

I have the honour etc.,
Charles Huber

LETTER NO. 19

This letter is the second of two comprising item no. 87 in Dossier F/17/2976/1:1. It is a covering letter for the above proposal, addressed to Xavier Charmes.

Date: 11 May 1882
From: Charles Huber, Strasbourg
To: Xavier Charmes, Directeur du Secrétariat et de la Comptabilité au Ministre de l'Instruction Publique etc., Paris

Monsieur,

It is with the greatest pleasure that I received your honoured letter of the 8th of this month, and I thank you sincerely for your goodwill towards me. I hope to justify it by what follows and, Monsieur, whatever the outcome of my request may be, I shall be eternally grateful to you.

I have the honour to enclose for you my official request for the continuation of my mission to explore Arabia. I do not need to tell you that you can have every confidence in me for the success and sound results of the expedition. I shall perhaps appear presumptuous to some members of the [Expeditions] Committee for proposing my project to explore Nağd, Nağrān, Māʾrib and the Mahra country, but I am nonetheless very sure of my business. I have spent five years doing nothing but studying the [Arabian] Peninsula, I know all the literature on it almost by heart, and I can say that I am almost as familiar with it as I am with my own apartment. Besides, I do not need to plead my case before you, as you know what motivates me and that success must be mine, and that I could never be content with the empty glory of just crossing Arabia, but that I must bring back serious, precise and complete documentation.

I reckon that two years should be assigned to the execution of my plan and estimate that a sum of 35,000 francs would be needed. You will perhaps find this amount a little high. However, when I tell you that this time I plan to bring along two chronometers, that would already account for 3,000 francs, added to 2,000 francs for other instruments, and that when my caravan is ready I would scarcely have 25,000 francs left, you will perhaps recognize, as I do, that it is doubtful whether even that amount would suffice.

On the matter of funds, please allow me to remind you that you were kind enough to let me hope that the Ministry would reimburse me the sum of 2,900 francs, representing the overspend on my last expedition. If this payment can be made without prejudicing my current request, and if it is in your power to arrange for me to obtain it, I shall be grateful to you, as it will allow me to allay the hardship of my next journey.

As for the meeting of the [Expeditions] Committee, I venture to ask you to convene it as quickly as possible, and then to do me the honour of letting me know straight away what its decision is, since, as I have already had the honour of telling you, if the continuation of my expedition is agreed, I would not have a minute to lose to get ready to depart during the first days of September next, which would be absolutely vital for success.

My thanks to you once again, Monsieur, for your kindness towards me, and please accept etc.

Charles Huber
10 Place du Temple Neuf

LETTER NO. 20

This is item no. 88 in Dossier F/17/2976/1:1. It is not a letter but a note in Ernest Renan's handwriting describing Huber's epigraphic finds on his first Arabian journey. It is noteworthy that there is no mention of the Taymāʾ Stele. According to the list of documents at the start of this dossier, this piece was published in the *Séances de la Commission* [*des missions*] of 21 June 1882, along with a report by Charles Maunoir on the geographical aspects of Huber's journey (for Huber's report of March 1882, see Letter no. 16 above).

Date: 20 June 1882
By: Ernest Renan

The inscriptions collected in Arabia by M. Huber belong to the group already known from the inscriptions of the Ṣafā region, to the east of Damascus, on which M. Halévy has published various works in the *Journal Asiatique*.[45] We had already foreseen that these inscriptions would be found in large numbers in Arabia properly so called, and that one day we would have to consider them as representing the ancient Arabian script, as opposed to the script of Yemen, or Himyaritic. The texts discovered by M. Huber completely confirm this conjecture. In the present state of knowledge, the best thing to do would be to reproduce the texts brought back by M. Huber in facsimile, while also keeping as closely as possible to the original drawings which must exist in his notebooks.[46] Such a publication would, I believe, find a completely appropriate place in the Archives of Scientific Expeditions.

E. Renan

LETTER NO. 21

This is item no. 91 in Dossier F/17/2976/1:1. It is Huber's response to what appears to have been a false allegation about money owed by him in Damascus.

Date: 17 July 1882
From: Charles Huber
To: not named, but possibly Xavier Charmes

Monsieur,

I have been extremely ill following your communication, which explains the lateness of this letter. My immediate thought was to give up the honour of a

[45] These inscriptions are today known as Safaitic, after the basaltic Ṣafā region of southern Syria and northern Jordan. It was used by the nomads of that area to carve rock inscriptions in various dialects of Ancient North Arabian and Old Arabic. The Safaitic script belongs to the Ancient North Arabian (ANA) subgroup of the South Semitic family, which as well as the scripts of ancient Yemen also includes the indigenous variants of northern and north-west Arabia, such as Taymanitic, Dadanitic and other related scripts that used to be known as Thamudic.

[46] These copies of Huber's inscriptions were published in the *Bulletin de la Société de Géographie* in 1884a (Huber 1884a), and are reproduced in this volume in Appendix 1.

second expedition in Arabia. However, the certitude that I feel, in addition to all the other discoveries to be made, of bringing back this time several hundred unpublished inscriptions that are unknown even as to their language, gives me the courage to struggle on to the end.

So here is what happened in Damascus. When I returned from my wanderings with the Ruwalah I fell ill with a deadly fever, and so as to obtain the necessary medical care I lodged with the Lazarites in Damascus.[47] The freezing cold of the winter of 1879–80 which had made all the Arabs leave for the Wadi al-Sirḥān, and the snow which had interrupted all communication between Damascus and the desert, prolonged my stay there. When at last I was able to leave, I paid my bill to the Lazarites by sending them a draft on my mother for the amount which, if I remember rightly, was 500 or 550 francs. But, on the very day of my departure from Damascus, the courier brought me, among other things, a letter from my mother telling me that she was leaving for the country. Fearing that as a result of her absence my draft for the Lazarites might be delayed, I sent a second draft four or five days later from ʿUrmān (Ǧabal Druze) for the same amount as the first, payable by M. Flüry-Hérard, and asking them to cancel the first one.[48] Everything must have happened like that, because the draft on M. Flury-Hérard has been presented and paid, whereas the first one has never been presented to my mother.

I should add that on going through Damascus once again in December last, I paid a visit to the Lazarites, and their superior, Father Najean, confirmed that the payment had been made.

In Damascus, I only had dealings with Dr Selim Mokachen [*sic*] and Selim Ayoub, a member of the Mağlis, and at Beirut with M. Selim Azar, a silk spinner, and I believe that they will be able to say nothing but good about me. In any event, I am quite sure I owe not a cent to anybody over there.

Please accept etc.
Charles Huber

---

[47] Lazarites: a Roman Catholic order of priests and brothers founded in France in the 17th century by Vincent de Paul, a priest who dedicated himself to serving the poor. Their church, seminary and hospital in Damascus was known as the Couvent des Pères Lazaristes.

[48] This is probably Paul Flüry-Hérard (1836–1913), a banker in Paris and formerly French consul in Japan (1866–69). (MG/WF)

LETTER NO. 22

This is item no. 92 in Dossier F/17/2976/1:1.

Date: 8 August 1882
From: Charles Huber, Strasbourg
To: not named, but possibly Xavier Charmes, or Charles Maunoir at the Société de Géographie

Monsieur,

I do not know whether, since I had the honour of seeing you, you have been able to learn something about the accusations brought against me in the East which you told me about at the time. For my part, I have written to various people over there since my return here, and here is the information I have received:

> At the beginning of the year 1880, a Monsieur Bastard, [agent for] litigation and recovery, rue Ganneron (he no longer remembered the number), Paris-Batignolles, sent a letter to the French consul in Larnaca stating that he had in his possession a claim against M. Hüber [*sic*] by the lady Veuve Jolly-Dautel, previously owner of a hotel in Mézières and currently resident in Paris, for breach of trust and theft of an item of furniture worth 8,000 to 10,000 francs, and in addition of an advance payment of the sum of 9,741 francs; and that the aforesaid Hüber must be in Larnaca; and he demands his address so that he can institute proceedings against him.

It is thus a matter of a crime committed in Europe and not in the East, and if I find myself mixed up in this it can only be because of a confusion of names, as none of this has anything to do with me.

I have been suffering a little from fever for a few days and were it not for that I would come to Paris straight away, but perhaps you would be kind enough to write to this Bastard to obtain his information and let me know once you and the Ministry have shed light on the matter.

In following your advice to make use of the protractor to trace my routes on the map, I have obtained a much better result than by plotting my position at each change of direction. The circuit of my journey from Ḥāʾil to al-Qaṣīm and back is finished but for about 5 kilometres, with a total distance of 700 kilometres. I think I shall be able to send you the whole map from here in a fortnight.

I await with impatience your news on this Bastard affair, and beg you to accept etc.

Charles Huber
Place du Temple Neuf

LETTER NO. 23

This is item no. 96 in Dossier F/17/2976/1:1. Huber rebuts another, unspecified, allegation against him.

Date: 20 October 1882
From: Charles Huber, Strasbourg
To: Xavier Charmes, Directeur du Secrétariat et de la Comptabilité at the Ministry of Public Education, Paris

Monsieur,

During my last trip to Paris, M. Maunoir told me about the strange accusation against me that had reached you by diplomatic means. I was so troubled and overwhelmed by this new misfortune that I was unable to summon up the courage to request the honour of a meeting with you to plead my case. But I did urge M. Maunoir to do his utmost to hasten the enquiry which he told me had begun. I have written to him twice since then in the same vein. I have had no reply to my last letter, dated the 6th of this month.

Bearing in mind now the goodwill that you showed me on my arrival in Paris when I returned from the East, I am taking the liberty today of addressing myself directly to you in order to assure you that no dishonest deed can be laid at my door during the entire course of my expedition, and that I await the result of the enquiry with complete equanimity.

Apart from your certainty that I am worthy of your benevolence being a great advantage in my favour, I am on the other hand well aware that the continuation of my expedition depends on a good outcome of the enquiry. So for these two reasons I am taking the extreme liberty of asking you to issue the necessary instructions to set it in motion, as it is of the greatest importance to me to see this done as soon as possible, so that I can still take advantage of the rainy season to get started on my journey.

You are aware, Monsieur, of the motive that makes me lobby so strongly for the continuation of my expedition to Arabia. It is not through hope of profit or reward, as I am fortunate in not being in need. Nor is it through any thought of ambition, as I have no other than the desire to be the first person to penetrate central Arabia as a Christian and with scientific instruments, and the wish to complete my work by accomplishing the exploration of the southern part of Arabia, a task at which I reckon I can succeed better than anyone else.

You will probably have learnt that Dr Langer,[49] who was charged by the Austrian government with carrying out a scientific expedition into Arabia – and about whom I had a conversation at the time with M. Maunoir, at the same time telling him of the reasons which, in my opinion, would surely prevent the success of the expedition – that Dr Langer, I say, had actually been murdered almost at the start of it.

I shall end by begging you, Monsieur, to persevere in your goodwill towards me by not abandoning me because of an absurd allegation, and to do me justice. You are well aware of the good you can do me in that way and, as a consequence, of the gratitude that I shall owe you.

In expectation of that, and of the honour of reading your reply, please accept etc.

Charles Huber
10 Place du Temple Neuf

Letter no. 24

This is item no. 97 in Dossier F/17/2976/1:1. It is a rough draft of a letter to Huber from Xavier Charmes.

Date: 28 October 1882
From: Xavier Charmes, Ministry of Public Education, Paris
To: Charles Huber, 10 place du Temple Neuf, Strasbourg

Monsieur,

I have read your last letter [i.e. Letter no. 23 above] with all the interest that it deserves, and I am happy to respond to it by informing you of the result of the enquiry opened into your matter. Not only does none of the official information

[49] Siegfried Langer (1857–82) was an Austrian Orientalist and colleague of Eduard Glaser and David Heinrich Müller, who travelled to Yemen in 1881 to collect ancient inscriptions. He was murdered in the hinterland of Aden in 1882.

that we had set about collecting provide any foundation for the allegations brought against you, but everything coalesces to demonstrate that you have not ceased to show yourself entirely worthy of the government's trust.

The favourable outcome of this enquiry contains nothing, moreover, that might surprise me, and I would certainly hope that it will not in the least diminish the esteem in which the Ministry of Public Education has for long held you. …

The state of our finances, currently so overburdened, does not allow me for the present to give consideration to your plan to explore Arabia, to which you have applied yourself so doggedly. But I need not assure you that I am not losing sight of your projects, and that I intend to support it in front of the Expeditions Committee when the time comes.

Please accept etc.
Directeur du Secrétariat
Charmes

Letter no. 25

This is item no. 98 in Dossier F/17/2976/1:1.

Date: 30 October 1882
From: Charles Huber, Strasbourg
To: Xavier Charmes, Directeur du Secrétariat et de la Comptabilité at the Ministry of Public Education, Paris

Monsieur,

I have just received your honoured letter of the 28th of this month [i.e. Letter no. 24 above], and wish to inform you immediately of the pleasure and delight that it has brought me. Despite my conscience being clear, I was not without apprehension, having already once fallen innocent victim to people's malice.

You overwhelm me with your kind words in sharing with me the results of the enquiry. It would be fruitless for me to tell you how touched I was by your tact and attention, and how great is my gratitude to you.

On the subject of resuming my mission to Arabia, you were good enough to inform me that the financial situation does not enable you to attend to it just now; but that at the opportune moment you mean to lend your support to my projects before the Expeditions Committee.

We are actually almost at the end of the year, and the expeditions budget must be all used up. However, might we not proceed as we did with my first expedition? That is to say, to take the decision charging me with continuing my expedition in Arabia as from now, even if it means authorizing the cost at a later date? Indeed, the order relating to my first expedition was made on 18 December 1878 and, when he sent me the further details in his letter of 23 December 1878, the Minister added: 'A further order will determine the amount of your remuneration and the time for it to be paid by the Treasury.' And thus it was arranged.

Proceeding in this manner would be of great utility to me just now, as certainty about my expedition would enable me to get on with some of my preparations straight away. Knowing the extent of your kind interest in me, I would not venture to insist on the matter, relying as I do completely on you to decide the timing and whatever it may be possible to do.

But perhaps you may not find it an inconvenience, if such a small sum is available in the budget, to issue an order for the payment of the 2,900 francs that I spent from my own funds during my last expedition, and about which I had the honour to speak to you at the time.

This sum would enable me to acquire a multitude of small precision instruments essential for carrying out my future assignment, and which require numerous preliminary tests and trials, not to mention adaptations enabling them to be carried in regions where journeys can only be made on camelback. Chief among them are mercury barometers, as experience has shown me how little trust can be placed in aneroid barometers. But most important of all would be the theodolite which, among other uses, will enable me to shoot the altitudes of the sun at midday, when the noon altitude of this star is higher than the number of degrees marked on my sextant, which is reached in Arabia below 30° of latitude[50] as early as the end of the month of April.

I shall not expatiate further on this topic as I know that you will recognize that it is well founded and that, if at all possible, you will once again give evidence of your kindness by arranging the order of the above-mentioned sum of 2,900 francs.

I express once again my feelings of profound gratitude, and beg you to accept etc.

---

[50] 30° of latitude: i.e. the latitude of Sakākā in al-Ǧawf, northern Arabia.

Charles Huber
10, Place du Temple Neuf

Letter no. 26

This is item no. 99 in Dossier F/17/2976/1:1.

Date: 6 November 1882
From: Ministry of Public Education

Expedition to Central Asia [*sic*]

Order as follows:
The sum of 2,900 francs
To be authorized to the name of M. Charles Huber, 10 Place du Temple Neuf, Strasbourg, by way of remuneration for the expedition to Central Asia with which he was entrusted.

Letter no. 27

This is item no. 101 in Dossier F/17/2976/1:1.

Date: 11 November 1882
From: Charles Huber, Strasbourg
To: the Minister of Public Education, Paris

M. le Ministre,

I have received the letter that you have done me the honour of sending me on the 6th of this month, stating that by an order of the same date you have been kind enough to allocate the sum of 2,900 francs to me, in reimbursement of expenses incurred during the expedition in Arabia that I was commissioned to undertake.

I offer you my most sincere thanks for this payment, as well as for the assurance that you have been kind enough to give me that you will respond at a later date to my new request for an expedition.

I have the honour to beg you to accept etc.

Charles Huber
10 Place du Temple Neuf

LETTER NO. 28

This is item no. 104 in Dossier F/17/2976/1:1.

Date: 17 February 1883
From: Charles Maunoir, Secretary-General, Société de Géographie, Paris
To: the Minister of Public Education and Fine Arts

M. le Ministre,

It is the duty of the Société de Géographie to inform you that, on the report of its Prize Committee, it is conferring a Gold Medal on M. Charles Huber this year, in recognition of the results of his journey in Arabia.

The Society is delighted to be able once again to crown one of these Ministry of Public Education explorers, to whom the science of geography is so indebted for their precious achievements.

Please accept etc.
Charles Maunoir
Secretary-General

APPENDIX 4

Twenty-five letters from Huber to Maunoir and Weisgerber, 1882–84

THESE ARE among the Huber papers in the Archives du Cabinet of the *Corpus Inscriptionum Semiticarum* (*CIS*), Académie des Inscriptions et Belles-Lettres (AIBL), Institut de France, Paris. Correspondence with Charles Maunoir and Dr Weisgerber, classified under Ref. Armoire A, Boîte 'Correspondance H–K'.

Thanks go to Prof. Maria Gorea for making these letters available, for the information on their background she has provided, and for contributions to the footnotes identified by (MG). They have been translated by Barbara Newton, and edited and annotated by William Facey and Michael Macdonald (MCAM). Interpolations by the editors are shown in square brackets.

LETTER NO. 1

Date: 21 March 1882
From: Charles Huber, Strasbourg
To: Charles Maunoir, Secrétaire général de la Société de Géographie

Sir,

I have the honour to send you today at the Société de Géographie the report on my mission.[1] I have attached an outline of my itineraries. This outline probably will leave much to be desired as a map, but knowing that it was

[1] For this report by Huber on his first expedition, see Appendix 3, Letter no. 16 and the accompanying 65-page report of March 1882. It is the same as the one he sent to the Ministère d'instruction publique (see Letter no. 2, note 5 below).

based on the map in the work by Lady Blunt,[2] I think that by placing it over that map it will be a simple matter for your cartographers to complete it as it should be. I have reproduced the course of the journey firstly of Blunt in pencil, and then of my own in ink.

I must make one important remark about this map and that is that Taymāʾ, Madāʾin Ṣāliḥ, al-ʿUlā, Khaybar and al-Ḥāʾiṭ are too far north, and Taymāʾ and Khaybar are too close to each other. Consequently my line, which I should have made to go through Taymāʾ, Madāʾin Ṣāliḥ and Khaybar, which are already marked on the map, does not run where it ought to go.

Obviously, I have not been able to put any geographical detail on this sketch, which is on too small a scale. That will be for the definitive map, about the creation of which I shall take the liberty of writing to you shortly.

I had already noted as desiderata whatever I may be able to discover about the journey of Mr Doughty. I am therefore very happy that you drew my attention to it and that you promised me the *Globus* that gives a brief account of it.[3] Now I am first going to make a copy of the inscriptions that I have brought back, and then carry out a review of my rock samples to prepare a mineralogical map. Next, I shall begin an extensive account of my journey.

Before this, however, I shall take the liberty of sending you a few lines which could be used as a conclusion to my report.[4]

Please have the goodness to let me know that you have received my report and be assured, dear Sir, of my highest consideration.

Charles Huber

---

[2] Lady Anne Blunt, author of *A Pilgrimage to Nejd*, London 1881.

[3] Huber, not having previously realized that the 'Khalīl' about whom he had heard in Ḥāʾil was in fact Doughty, had become aware of the Englishman's journey on his return to Strasbourg. Doughty's *Travels in Arabia Deserta* was not published until 1888, but accounts of his 1877–78 journeys were first published in the German periodical *Globus: Illustrierte Zeitschrift für Länder- und Völkerkunde* in 1880–82:

- Doughty's Forschungen im nördlichen Arabien. By Prof. A. Sprenger. *Globus* no. 37, 1880, pp. 201–3.
- Reisen in Arabian. *Globus* no. 39, 1881: Part I, pp. 7–10; Part II, pp. 23–30.
- Khaibar in Arabien. *Globus* no. 40, 1881, pp. 38–41.
- Wanderungen zwischen Teimâ, Ḥâil, Khaibar und Bereida. In *Globus* no. 41, 1882: Part I pp. 214–18; Part II pp. 249–52.

[4] Huber sends these lines in Letter no. 2, 3rd paragraph from the end, see below.

Letter no. 2

Date: 28 March 1882
From: Charles Huber, Strasbourg
To: Charles Maunoir

Sir,

In reply to your esteemed letter of the 26th inst., I have the honour to enclose with this present letter the one accompanying my report to the Minister of Education.[5]

Under a separate cover I am also sending you:

1) a list of the astronomical altitudes taken to determine the latitudes;
2) a similar list for the determination of the longitudes.

Since the calculations have not as yet been done, and consequently the positions have not yet been precisely determined, I am not enclosing the drawing that you asked for with the points marked on it.

Kindly let me have more time for all that. It will be necessary for me first to make an estimate for each observation before being able to calculate it, and for that I need my notebook of calculations, which is in a box that I shall only receive in a few days' time. The main thing is for me to have everything that is necessary. The rest is a question of time.

As for my map, up until a few days ago I thought that I would not need to trouble you, at least in order to begin it, but it is precisely for this that I need your help.

In order to mark out all my documents [i.e. to mark all the places whose positions I have documented], I need a sheet which only has the lines of latitude and longitude on it, spaced one decimetre to one degree, which means a scale of 2 mm to one geographic mile. I thought I would be able to have this blank map made here but I have just found out that it cannot be done. So, if this task is not too onerous, I would be very grateful if you could have it carried out by your specialist technicians, and in that case to have two or three sheets sent to me. It could even be done at 3 mm to 1 mile to enable me to properly mark all the little details around the bigger places such as Ḥāʾil, Buraydah etc. We shall be able to reduce it for the engraving later.

[5] For this report by Huber on his first expedition, see Appendix 3, Letter no. 16 and the accompanying 65-page report of March 1882.

Along with the two lists mentioned above, which are being sent under a separate cover, I am also sending you a copy of the inscriptions discovered in the course of my expedition and of which I have just finished the transcription from my diary. Probably these sheets will be handed to M. Halévy[6] to be deciphered, and in that case please have the goodness to tell him that I paid the closest attention to the copy I made *in situ* as well as to the transcriptions I made from my diary. If, however, there were to be any doubt about the form of a character, he should notify me of it and I shall rectify it if need be. To make things easier, I have marked each inscription with a letter of the alphabet and I shall only need to be informed of this with the date of the diary entry which is to be found at the foot of each page.

In all there are 11 sheets of which one is double. Please have the goodness to let me know of their safe arrival.

Here is what I would have wanted to add as a conclusion to my report:

Personally I am not satisfied with the result of my mission, above all if I consider what remains to be done and what I am sure of being able to do in Arabia, and which I would have done if I had been given a small subsidy. I do not need to demonstrate to you, dear Sir, the interest there would be in resuming and carrying on with my original itinerary, continuing my journey on foot from ʿUnayzah to al-Riyāḍ via Sudayr, al-Washm and al-ʿĀriḍ, and reaching Nağrān through the Wādī al-Dawāsir, and from there going round and exploring the immense desert of the Dahnāʾ, which is a blank covering half of our maps of Arabia and perhaps wrongly so.[7] I was told of ancient ruins and inscriptions in al-ʿĀriḍ and Wādī al-Dawāsir, and even in the province of Sudayr. Apart from this I shall be able to record things that were unknown to M. Halévy or that he was prevented from copying.[8] The continuation of my mission would surely be of immense benefit as regards geographical and other scientific questions.

---

[6] For Joseph Halévy (1827–1917), see Appendix 3 note 43. These are the inscriptions presented in Appendices 1 and 2 of this volume.

[7] By the Dahnāʾ, Huber means the great Rubʿ al-Khālī or Empty Quarter, a confusion that Palgrave also made (1865, folding map and *passim*). The actual Dahnāʾ is the 1,000+ km zone of longitudinal sand strips running from the Nafūd to the Rubʿ al-Khālī and separating Nağd from Eastern Arabia.

[8] To the best of our knowledge, the only time Halévy travelled in what is now Saudi Arabia was on his journey from al-Ḥudayda via Ṣanʿāʾ to Nağrān in 1869–70 (Halévy 1873, 1877). All but the final paragraph of his account is concerned with that journey, ninety-nine percent of which was in what is now Yemen. (MCAM)

If I was not practically certain of success I would not make this request to continue my mission because I know what the risks are in Arabia, but my knowledge of the country and the contacts I enjoy there now enable me to be more ambitious. Moreover, as I have said above, what I have done is only a part, and it is only by completing the entire project that that part will have any value.

If you share my point of view, I know that I shall have won my case; and if I am needed in Paris to enable the decision to be made in principle, I shall come there as soon as I hear from you. The sooner I can be sure of this the better, because if my assignment is to be continued, I shall need from now until the autumn to make my preparations. So, one word from you, I beg you.

In that expectation, I assure you of my highest consideration.

Charles Huber

LETTER NO. 3

Date: 18 May 1882
From: Charles Huber, Strasbourg
To: Charles Maunoir

Sir,

It was with great pleasure that I received the letter which you did me the honour of writing to me yesterday, because I was worried that I had not heard from you since my letter of the end of March.

Since then, I have hardly been out and have been working day and night. Despite this, I am not making very fast progress. There are days when I do not find the work at all easy.

At first I intended to write the report of my journey and to draw up the map at the same time, but I can see that I shall be unable to do that as my narrative is too extensive. However, I intend to continue this way of working until the end of June, when I shall leave my narrative aside in order to apply myself exclusively to the map. The latter, I think, will be finished, as well as a geological map and a supporting geographical explanation, during the month of August, and I shall send it all to you immediately, because in September I intend without fail to set off again for the Orient, with or without the continuation of my mission.

If I am authorized to continue, I shall take up the exploration of Arabia again; if not, I shall set off for Persia at my own expense.

With regard to the calculations of my observations, I have to inform you of a misfortune of which I only became aware a few days ago. It is that all the estimates of altitude that I took to calculate longitude are useless because of my chronometer which, besides stopping at ʿUnayzah, was defective in its working. I have just received the proof that it did not run at a constant rate, sometimes going too fast and sometimes too slow.

In order to fix the longitude of the places on the map, all that I have are my estimates which fortunately were made very precisely. I certainly always took great care over them.

The altitudes that I took for the latitudes retain their value.

Thank you for your offer to have my calculations done for me. I shall probably take you up on it when I have reached that point, if only as a check and also for your peace of mind and that of the geographical world, which has the right to interrogate me about what the elements of my map are based on. But for that I shall take advantage of my imminent journey to Paris.

You say that I shall have to put my notebooks of observations at the disposal of the Commission,[9] but I do not have any special observation notebooks. I only have my diary. It is there that I have noted everything in chronological order, and I would be grateful if you could spare me from having to place it before the members of the Commission. You will understand that the notes that I took on my lap in the desert with the cold and the heat, and with the exhaustion and the myriad annoyances that accompany journeys in these countries, are not models of style or order.

I received the two sheets enabling me to compile my map in good time, and I think that their scale is adequate. For those parts where it is not, I shall be able to help myself by following your advice.

In numbers 14 and 16 of the *Globus* of this year,[10] I saw an article by Mr Doughty about his journeys between Khaybar, Ḥāʾil and Buraydah, and I noted with pleasure that my observations do not duplicate his at almost any point. My observations were everywhere more accurate and my intelligence more detailed. Moreover, the disadvantageous conditions under which that

---

9 This is the Commission centrale de la Société de Géographie. (MCAM)

10 Doughty, C.M., Wanderungen zwischen Teimâ, Ḥâil, Khaibar und Bereida. In *Globus* vol. 41, 1882: no. 14, pp. 214–18 and map on p. 225; no. 16, pp. 249–52. (MCAM/WF)

traveller found himself, and the scant consideration or rather the complete lack of consideration that attended him, prevented him from garnering all the fruit necessary from his journey.

One word more about me. – I don't know if you are aware that a few days ago M. Charmes[11] did me the honour of writing to me on the subject of my desire to continue the exploration of Arabia, a letter that gave me much pleasure and which invited me to make an official application, and promised me his support in bringing it before the Commission des missions [Expeditions Committee]. My application has been sent off and he must already have it in his hands.

I have had the honour of discussing it with you already both verbally and in my last letter, and I must confess that I would have liked to have your opinion about it. If I am allowed to continue my mission, I intend to go back quickly through all the places I visited before and take astronomical measurements again with more precise instruments. Furthermore, I shall take squeezes of the inscriptions this time instead of just copying them.

I am all the more insistent on continuing my mission because I am so certain of success, and also because in order to fulfil its possibilities both a great number of people and a great deal of time would be needed. Will it be long before the Expeditions Committee convenes?

I thank you again for your good wishes for me and I beg you, dear Sir, to be assured of my highest and most respectful consideration.

Charles Huber
Place du Temple Neuf

LETTER NO. 4

Date: 13 June 1882
From: Charles Huber, Strasbourg
To: Charles Maunoir

Sir,

I have disagreeable news for you. I am not getting on very well with my cartographical work. Since receiving your last esteemed letter I have clarified

[11] For Xavier Charmes, see Appendix 3 note 37. Charmes had written to Huber on 8 May 1882 inviting him to submit an application for a second Arabian expedition. Huber sent his application off on 11 May 1882 (see Appendix 3, Letters nos. 18 and 19).

and calculated my itinerary from the Ḥawrān to Ḥā'il, and not only do these calculations not fit with my predictions, but even when I plot them stage by stage on the map I get a quite different result from that produced by the figures indicated by the calculations.

I have searched in vain over recent days and am unable to identify where the error lies. Ḥā'il is approximately one degree too far north and one degree too far west.

I am therefore forced to have recourse to your obliging aid. If you would kindly authorize me to do so, as soon as I receive your reply I shall send you a fair copy of my itinerary from Boṣra to Ḥā'il with the heights of the sun at its zenith taken on this trip. Next at intervals of three to four days I shall send you successively the fair copy of my itineraries from Ḥā'il to Baghdad; from Ḥā'il to al-Qaṣīm and back; from Ḥā'il to the Ḥiǧāz and back; and then from Baghdad to Damascus. It is probable that your experts will do better than I.

Once my outline is traced onto the map it will be easy for me then to add my other geographical information.

If you could have another sheet drawn up with the degrees marked on it, I shall keep the one that has been sent to me.

Please be assured of my highest consideration,

Charles Huber

LETTER NO. 5

Date: 1 July 1882
From: Charles Huber, Strasbourg
To: Charles Maunoir

Sir,

I had the honour to send you a letter on 14th June last about my cartographic work, to which I have not yet received a reply.

Might it be that your workload has prevented you from replying? Or perhaps I have had the misfortune to make you ill-disposed towards me by the aforementioned letter. I would be very grateful if you would honour me with a line about this as I am very worried.

Tomorrow I am sending a crate to M. de Quatrefages[12] at the museum with the most recent objects brought back from my expedition:

1) A skull from Khaybar. The only one I could get hold of in Central Arabia (the Maronite, Syrian and Babylonian skulls are already in Paris.)
2) My mineral samples, each one in a little labelled bag.
3) Bottles of insects, lizards, and snakes from the whole of Arabia.

Along with your reply, which I await with the keenest impatience, please have the goodness to tell me if the Expeditions Committee has yet made a decision about my application to mount a new expedition, and whether or not a decision will soon be made.

Please be assured of my highest consideration.

Charles Huber
10 Place du Temple Neuf

LETTER NO. 6

Date: 6 July 1882
From: Charles Huber, Strasbourg
To: Charles Maunoir

Sir,
I am extremely worried that I have had no reply from you to my last two letters, and I beg you urgently to honour me with a note.

If, in order to make up for the delay that my map will now incur, I have to come to Paris, I shall do so.

In that case it would be important for me to ascertain in advance the decision of the Expeditions Committee, if there has been one, relating to the continuation of my expedition.

Please, I beg you, dear Sir, allay my anxiety by a word of reply. Assuring you of my highest consideration.

Ch. Huber
Place du Temple Neuf

---

[12] For Jean Louis Armand de Quatrefages de Bréau, see Appendix 3 note 1. Huber had written to him from Khaybar (Huber 1881).

Letter no. 7

Date: 17 August 1882
From: Charles Huber, Strasbourg
To: Charles Maunoir

I have the honour of confirming to you that my letter of 8th inst. is still without a reply.

Since then I have finished the following maps of my journeys:

- From Damascus to Ḥā'il
- From Ḥā'il to al-Qaṣīm and back
- From Ḥā'il to the Ḥiğāz and back

Those from Ḥā'il to Baghdad and from Baghdad to Damascus will be finished in five or six days but, in order to do that, I will need the *Connaissance des Temps*[13] for 1881, which cannot be found here, in either the town library or the university library. I only have years 1879 and 1880. Your library probably has the volume for 1881 and, if so, please would you be so kind as to have one of your clerks copy for me the following data:

1) The angle of the sun and variation of one hour on average at midday in Paris on:
   - 6 and 26 January
   - 13 and 14 February
   - 2, 8 and 14 March
2) Half the diameter of the sun during the months of January, February and March.

With that information I shall be able to do without the volume itself.

So that you will be in a better position to judge the value of my astronomical altitudes, I have the honour to send you by this same post, but unsealed, my readings of the sun's altitude at its zenith taken at Ḥā'il and calculated. The average of these altitude measurements gives me the latitude of the Shammar

---

[13] The *Connaissance des Temps ou des mouvements célestes, à l'usage des astronomes et des navigateurs* was an annual French publication listing the astronomical events expected for the year in question. It was started in 1679 and continues to this day. (MCAM)

capital as 27° 30' 7". As you will see, the altitude that deviates the most from this average only does so by 1' 12", i.e. 2,220 metres, which I think is not a great deal. But the majority of the altitudes only deviate from the average by 200 to 300 metres.

I dare to hope that you will be pleased with my maps, which have turned out well and which will be the first accurate maps of the interior of Arabia.

Please be assured, my dear Sir, of my highest and most respectful consideration,

Charles Huber

The figures copied from the *Connaissance des Temps* will need to be verified before they are sent, and above all it needs to checked that the angle of the sun is taken at 'average midday' rather than 'actual midday'.

LETTER NO. 8

Date: 28 August 1882
From: Charles Huber, Strasbourg
To: Charles Maunoir

Sir,

This morning I received your esteemed letter of yesterday and I thank you heartily, because the lack of news from you concerns me more than I can say.

I am also grateful to you for pursuing the enquiry in question with the Ministry. I hope therefore that light will soon be shed on it.

Being without a reply to my letter of 17 August, I turned to Geneva to get the relevant data from the *Connaissance des Temps* of 1881, which I still needed to calculate the altitudes of the sun taken in that year, and which I took the liberty of asking you for. Thus my map was completed three days ago, and this morning, as soon as I received your letter, I sent it straight off to the Société de Géographie, so you will receive it tomorrow.

The map is on four sheets:

I) Journeys with the Ruwalah tribe in the Ḥamād to the east of Damascus and at Palmyra

II) Between Damascus, Baghdad and Ḥāʾil, mapping three journeys:

    1) From Damascus to al-Ǧawf and Ḥāʾil

    2) From Ḥāʾil to Baghdad

3) From Baghdad to Damascus

III) Itinerary from Ḥāʾil to al-Qaṣīm and back

IV) Itinerary from Ḥāʾil to the Ḥiğāz and back via Taymāʾ, al-ʿUlā, Khaybar, al-Ḥāʾiṭ etc.

This last sheet contains the course of the Wadi Ermek [Wādī al-Rimah] (not Wadi e'Rumem [*sic*] as it has been called up to now, or Wadi er Rummah (as Doughty calls it), from its source to beyond ʿUnayzah.[14] This course modifies considerably those accepted up to now.

I do not need to tell you that this map is entirely my own work[15] and the result of my expedition. I have borrowed nothing from anyone, so it contains only my own personal observations. I have left out anything that my journeys did not reach. If, when the engraving is made, it would be useful to include other information, I await your suggestions as to what they should be.

There remains the geographical note to add to this map, a note that will be strictly topographical. I would not want to publish my [full] account of the journey until after my second expedition, i.e. when I have it all complete.

To help me with this explanatory information would you please kindly send me:

1) The part of my report (the rough draft) to the minister which you still have.[16]

2) The *Bulletin* with the map of Guarmani's journey, published I think in 1865.[17]

3) The map (only) from 'The Mountain of Ansariés and the Pashalik of Aleppo' published in 1873.[18]

[14] On Wadi al-Rimah/Ermek, see Translation Part II, note 58; Part III, notes 15 and 17.

[15] This was not quite true. As Julius Euting later pointed out (see Appendix 10, Letter to Philippe Berger dated 2 November 1885), he had supplied the calligraphic title, the table of transliteration, and the two sketches of Khaybar.

[16] This seems to be a reference to Huber's preliminary report of March 1882 to the Ministry of Public Education (see Appendix 3, Letter no. 16, and note 5 above).

[17] This is a reference to Carlo Guarmani's report of his 1864 journey into central Arabia entitled 'Itinéraire de Jérusalem au Neged septentrional', and first published in the *Bulletin de la Société de Géographie*, 5ᵉ série, tome 8ᵉ, September 1865 and following.

[18] I have been unable to identify this map.

I am pleased with what you are kind enough to tell me about M. Renan's[19] opinion of the value of the inscriptions recorded in Arabia, but I too am aware of their importance and it is perhaps greater than he thinks because, although they are written in a Himyarite alphabet,[20] they are conceived in a new language that could perhaps be called Thamudean [Thamudic].[21] But I beg you not to say anything to anyone about this opinion, for, even if true, it could do me harm.[22] What is urgent is the publication of the text of my inscriptions, since Doughty's are not yet published.[23]

If I am so insistent about the continuance of my expedition, it is mostly in connection with these inscriptions, the importance of which I recognize today and which I know how to turn to considerable advantage.[24]

Before I last left Paris, M. Daubrée[25] received all the mineralogical samples brought back from Arabia. Their analysis must be finished by now. Would you kindly ask for the results so they can be added to your report?

Dare I also ask you to arrange for complimentary copies of the *Bulletins de la Société de Géographie* to be sent to me, which have been published since the beginning of this year? Thanking you in advance.

---

[19] Ernest Renan (1823–1892) was a French scholar with a prodigious output on Semitic languages and inscriptions, Biblical studies, the history of religion, philosophy, and political theory. He had written an initial assessment of Huber's epigraphic finds in June 1882: see Appendix 3, Letter no. 20. He was an influential member of the Académie des Inscriptions et Belles-Lettres in Paris and wrote the introduction to the publication by the AIBL of the squeezes and copies of inscriptions Doughty had made on his journey to Arabia in 1877–78 (Doughty 1884). (MCAM/WF)

[20] 'Himyarite' is an incorrect term here, since it refers to the scripts of ancient *South* Arabia, whereas Huber is writing about the scripts of ancient *North* Arabia later identified as Lihyanite (now 'Dadanitic'), Taymanitic, Hismaic and Thamudic B, C, and D. For Huber's use of the term 'Himyarite', see also Translation Part I, note 158. (MCAM)

[21] 'Thamudic' is not in fact a language, but a collection of different Ancient North Arabian scripts which have not yet been completely deciphered (see Macdonald 2000: 32–5). It is therefore not possible to know what language(s) is/are recorded in these inscriptions. (MCAM)

[22] It is not clear what Huber means by this. (MCAM)

[23] In fact, Doughty's copies and squeezes were published by the Académie des Inscriptions et Belles-Lettres three years later in 1884, the same year in which the Société de Géographie published Huber's report on his 1880–81 journeys in Arabia and the inscriptions he had copied (see note 33 below). (MCAM)

[24] It is not clear what Huber meant by this, but see note 106 below. (MCAM)

[25] Gabriel Auguste Daubrée (1814–96) was professor of mineralogy at the École des mines, Inspecteur général des mines, and a member of the Académie des sciences. (MG)

Please be assured, my dear Sir, of my greatest and most respectful consideration,

Charles Huber
Place du Temple Neuf

LETTER NO. 9

Date: 14 November 1882
From: Charles Huber, Strasbourg
To: M. Charles Maunoir, Secrétaire générale de la Société de Géographie, Paris

Sir,

I have not yet received any communication whatsoever from M. Hansen.[26] I shall not fail to respond to anything he might ask me, in accordance with the desire you expressed in the letter you did me the honour of writing me yesterday.

Indeed the enquiry made by the Ministry has produced results, and M. Charmes informed me of it in such terms as touched me deeply.[27]

Without a reply to the last letter that I had the honour to send you, I was very discouraged and have laid aside the Explanatory Information which is to be attached to my map. I have since been working to complete the notes on my journeys and to gather together materials for a full publication of my expedition. But I am going to redo the first task taking into account the points you have made.

I am most grateful to you for the help you are again willing to offer me, and I will do everything to make your task less irksome.

I am very sensible of your offer, which is a great honour, for me to give a paper at a session of the Société de Géographie, but I am obliged to turn

---

[26] Jules Hansen (1849–1931) was a cartographer, collaborator of Charles Maunoir and member of the Société de Géographie. He reproduced Huber's drawings for publication in Huber 1891. He was undoubtedly Huber's main adviser in the preparation of his maps and calculations, as it is he who is credited with drawing the big folding map that accompanies Huber 1884b, and is reproduced at the end of this volume. (MG)

[27] Huber is referring to unspecified allegations made against him, into which the Ministry of Public Education had instituted an enquiry. Huber was cleared by the enquiry: see Appendix 3, Letters nos. 23 and 24 of October 1882.

it down. That which would have filled me with joy at another time would be impossible for me at the present. I have been too worn down by recent events and I shall be in no state at all to do justice publicly to the results of my expedition, however good they may be.

If, apart from that, my presence in Paris would make it easier for you to do what you propose to do for me, you need only tell me so and I shall set off immediately, despite the fact that my situation here is deteriorating, and it is only with great difficulty that I can any longer obtain travel and residency permits.[28]

Concerning my observations, about which you wish to question me, they have all been calculated and their results set down on the map.

I am going to start on the text to be added to the map and I think I shall be able to finish it in a week or ten days' time.

With feelings of profound gratitude, please be assured, my dear Sir, of my deep and most respectful consideration.

Charles Huber
10 Place du Temple Neuf

LETTER NO. 10

Date: 25 November 1882
From: Charles Huber, Strasbourg
To: not specified, but certainly Charles Maunoir

Sir,

I received your esteemed letter of the 18th of this month the other day. Before that I had also received from M. Hansen the drawing in reduced format of my map with a questionnaire. I filled in the latter, completed the map and returned everything two days ago. I found no omissions on the map. There are only two names that M. Hansen quotes, Kalaat el Burkua [possibly Qalʿat al-Burqūʿ][29] and Tourdaïn [*sic*; unidentified] which are not mentioned, but I do not know whether they exist in Arabia.

[28] On the reason for this, see Letter no. 10 and note 30 below.

[29] If this is Qaṣr Burqūʿ, then it is in what is now north-eastern Jordan. It was visited by Gertrude Bell on 24–25 December 1913 en route to Ḥāʾil during her crossing of northern Arabia. (MCAM/WF)

As for my situation here, I must tell you that I have two younger brothers whose choice of French nationality has not been recognized by Germany, and as they did their military service in France they are in breach of the law here and have been condemned in the past to prison and fines. As for myself, I was expelled in 1878 as a member of the Alsace League[30] and all the rest of our family is viewed in the same unfavourable light. When I returned from my expedition [in early 1882] it was only with great difficulty that, despite the conciliatory feelings of the Governor of Alsace-Lorraine,[31] I obtained the authorization to stay in Strasbourg at my mother's home. All the members of parliament and city councillors of Strasbourg had to speak up for me. Every Monday I have to present myself at police headquarters. If I want to leave town and return, I have to obtain authorizations and declarations. On my last return from Paris I had to undergo a real interrogation about what I had been doing there.

So if I want to stay here, at least until my next departure for the Orient, I have to keep a low profile and not give them any cause to expel me. I have another motive for this: because of the judgements against my brothers, part of the money we inherited from my late father's estate has been sequestered for the last seven years. Now, at this very moment, my mother is negotiating an agreement with the government of Alsace-Lorraine aimed at getting the funds released.

I am so sorry to weary you with these extraneous matters but you need to know why I do not have personal freedom of movement here. If possible I would like to come to Paris only once my [new] expedition has been decided upon, and then to stay there for the time necessary to complete all my preparations. If at that juncture I were not allowed to come back here, no great harm would have been done since I would be ready to leave for the Orient.

---

[30] In 1878 Huber had joined Léon Gambetta's Ligue d'Alsace, an anti-German organization set up in the wake of the German takeover of Alsace-Lorraine in 1871, urging Alsace-Lorrainers to retain their French citizenship – a move that served to exacerbate his difficulties with the authorities.

[31] This governor was Edwin Freiherr von Manteuffel (1809–85), one of the successful German generals of the 1870–71 Franco-Prussian War, who in 1879 had been appointed governor of Elsass-Lothringen by Bismarck. Huber would thus have had no reason to like him, but von Manteuffel had a reputation as a fair and cultivated man. In 1883, he put up the funds enabling Julius Euting to go to Arabia with Huber (see Introduction pp. 29–30).

I am going to start straight away writing the text to accompany my map and I shall send it to you as soon as it is done.

In that regard, allow me one more important observation. – I would like to transcribe all the Arabic proper names according to the spelling adopted by Orientalists and especially the Académie des Inscriptions et Belles-Lettres, but in that case, the following special characters would be needed: ḍ, Ḍ, and š, Š (both letters with upside-down circumflex over them), as well as the sign to be placed above some letters. – Is this possible and, if so, may I write up my text using them?

Could you please have the *Bulletins de la Société de Géographie* published since last January sent to me as well as the *Bulletin* containing the map and the narrative of M. Guarmani's journey published in 1865?[32] I would be most grateful.

I have taken the liberty of telling M. Hansen that I would like to have some copies of the map but without the names on them, i.e. blank. These maps, on which I shall fill in the names in Arabic script, are destined for Emir Mohammed ebn Reschid [Muḥammad Ibn Rashīd, ruler of Ḥā'il], to whom I promised one, as well as for some other important personages, and they would facilitate my onward expedition. I would therefore be very much obliged if you would consider my request. I would need eight such maps.

In the assurance, my dear Sir, of my highest and most respectful consideration.

Charles Huber
Place du Temple Neuf

LETTER NO. 11

Date: 29 December 1882
From: Charles Huber, Strasbourg
To: not specified, but certainly Charles Maunoir

Sir,

I have the honour to confirm to you my letter of November last.

In this present letter I am taking the liberty of sending you the map of Arabia from the *Ğihan-numâ*, the Turkish Geography of Hadji Khalfâ

[32] For Guarmani's article, first published in the *Bulletin* in 1865, see note 17 above.

[Ḥāǧǧi Khalīfā or Kātip Çelebi] printed at Constantinople in 1732, which is extremely rare.

As I am trying to assemble all that has been published about Arabia for my library, and as I have not yet been able to find this work to buy, as an interim measure I have had the map of Arabia photographed and coloured according to the original. The few names that have been distorted on the photograph have been pencilled in on the copy.

I beg the Society to accept this copy for its library.

I am still working on the text destined to accompany my map in the *Bulletin*.[33]

Four days ago I received the *Bulletin* containing the map of Guarmani's journey, and also the scientific minutes of 1882, for which I offer my most sincere thanks.

So that you will not have a year missing, I will return the *Bulletin* with Guarmani's map to the Society when I no longer need it.

I am still awaiting, and not without apprehension, news of the renewal of my mission, as I see the season advancing.

Allow me, dear Sir, at this season of New Year to offer you my best and most respectful wishes. Assuring you of my highest consideration,

Charles Huber

LETTER NO. 12

Date: 6 January 1883
From: Charles Huber, Paris
To: not specified, but certainly Charles Maunoir

[33] This is the text published in translation in this volume. It first appeared as two articles published in three issues of the *Bulletin de la Société de Géographie* in 1884 and 1885, after Huber's death on 29 July 1884:

- (1884a), Inscriptions recueillies dans l'Arabie centrale (1878–1882). *Bulletin de la Société de Géographie* 7ème série, 5, pp. 289–303
- (1884b), Voyage dans l'Arabie centrale (1878–1882), Hamâd, Šammar, Qaçîm, Hedjâz. *Bulletin de la Société de Géographie* 7ème série, 5, pp. 304–63 and 468–530
- (1885), Voyage dans l'Arabie centrale (1878–1882), Hamâd, Šammar, Qaçîm, Hedjâz (suite et fin). *Bulletin de la Société de Géographie* 7ème série, 6, pp. 92–148.

Sir,

I have the honour to enclose a draft letter to the Minister for War. Kindly have the goodness to look through it and let me know when I can have it back.

M. Charmes has let me know this morning that he will receive me on Wednesday from 1 to 3 o'clock.[34]

Should everything be concluded on that day, I would like to set off again that very evening for Nancy, where my mother is impatiently awaiting me.

Assuring you, dear Sir, of my highest and most respectful consideration,

Charles Huber
18 rue de la Harpe

LETTER NO. 13

Date: 20 May 1883
From: Charles Huber, Strasbourg
To: Charles Maunoir

M. Maunoir,

I think that a few words about the political situation in those parts of Syria and Arabia that I have traversed may interest you.

I suppose that you are aware that our diplomats have lost all the influence in Syria acquired by France by the expedition of 1860.[35] Moreover, from the

[34] This meeting was to discuss Huber's application to continue his exploration of Arabia, which he had sent to Charmes on 11 May 1882 (see Appendix 3, Letters nos. 18 and 19, and 24 and 25). See also Appendix 4, Letter no. 4 above. Charmes was keenly in favour of the expedition, but unsure about the funds requested (see Appendix 3, Letters nos. 24 and 25 dated 28 and 30 October 1882).

[35] Traditionally, the French had supported the Christians, and particularly the Maronites, in what is now Lebanon, while the British had supported the Druze. In late 1859 and early 1860 a series of conflicts broke out between Christians and Druzes in Lebanon. By the end of May 1860, a major civil war had begun between large Christian and Druze militias. This spread to other parts of Syria with major massacres of Christians by Druze, particularly that in Damascus on 9–11 July in which between 7,000 and 11,000 Christians were killed. In August 1860, Napoleon III sent a French expeditionary force of 6,000 men to Syria (with smaller numbers contributed by other European countries). Although the Civil War was already over, this force stayed in Syria until June 1861 and led to the establishment of an autonomous, mainly Christian region on Mount Lebanon. (MCAM)

start, this influence has never been what it ought to have been and this is the fault of Napoleon III who, in order not to ruffle English susceptibilities, gave them almost all the concessions they asked for. The first effect of these concessions has been the constant nomination of mountain pashas [local governors under the Ottomans] hostile to the Maronites[36] and to France and entirely devoted to England. The most recent example is Rustem Pasha[37] who, despite loans, concessions, presents and even decorations, has remained the declared enemy of French interests and of the Maronites. At this time when his mandate has expired we cannot even get a temporary replacement.

If the Maronites, with all the persistent nuisances they suffer despite French protection, still remain faithful to France, it is obvious that this faithfulness must be attributed to a feeling other than self-interest, even though it is conventional for the French General Consulate in Beirut to cast doubt on this.

Our diplomacy being over-honest or else lacking sufficient cunning to grapple with English diplomacy, one ought only to send energetic men to Constantinople and Beirut, who could at least compensate for the impotence and inferiority of our French representatives.

The English, so as to be able to justify their involvement in the affairs of Syria, have started protecting the Druze, who massacred Christians in

---

[36] The Maronites are an Eastern Catholic group, adhering to the West Syriac rite (with an Aramaic liturgy) but in communion with the Roman Catholic church and accepting the leadership of the Pope. Traditionally, Maronites have been considered (not always correctly) to be the most numerous religious group in what is now Lebanon. After the civil war between Christians and Druzes in 1860, an international commission made up of France, Britain, Austria, Prussia, Russia and the Ottoman Empire forced the Ottoman Sultan to agree to making Mount Lebanon a semi-autonomous *mutasarrifate* (an administrative district) under a Christian (but not necessarily Maronite) *mutasarrif* (governor) with an administrative council made up of two members each from the different religious groups: Maronites, Greek Orthodox, Melkite, Druze, Sunni, and Shiʿah. (MCAM)

[37] Rustem Pasha was governor of Mount Lebanon from 1873 to 1883. He made great efforts 'to improve the conditions necessary for a peaceful, stable, and just order in Mount Lebanon, and his achievements in this regard were widely acknowledged and appreciated by its inhabitants' (Akarli 1993, p. 45, quoting a contemporary Ottoman report by Ahmad Hamdi Pasha). However, the same report also points out that: 'The French view the uninterrupted intensification of their influence in Mount Lebanon as a crucial investment toward acquiring the whole of Syria as a cardinal principle of their policy in the region. The fulfilment of this [objective] depends upon the intensification of the power and influence of the Maronite clergy, who nourish desires for independence and feel strongly attached to the French.' (ibid. 44–5). (MCAM)

1860; and they have established a large number of schools and charitable institutions for them.

The Druze, however, are not a power in Syria. Their population is certainly no greater than 40,000 souls, i.e. scarcely a tenth of even the Maronites, without counting the other Christian ethnic groups. But they compensate for this inferiority by their belligerence. In this respect they are true mountain-dwellers.

If the Egyptian origin which they claim for themselves is true,[38] they will have acquired their turbulent and independent character in their mountains, the Ǧabal Druze,[39] an entirely isolated volcanic range in the direction of the desert. They are never nomadic and live in ancient stone villages which today are in ruins, and which were built formerly by Aramaean people[40] towards the beginning of our era. What might justify their origin are their occupations: they are all farmers.

Their lands are as rich and fertile as those of the Ḥawrān and the Célésyrie [Coele Syria, i.e. south-western Syria] and they would have been able to attain the same level of prosperity and wealth as the peoples they dispossessed were it not, in my opinion, for the feudal system that still governs them, and above all in the past the Turkish government, which more than once must have made them feel its ruinous influence, inimical to all development.

Moreover, abandoned Druze villages at the foot of the mountain in recent years lead me to believe that the population is in decline, perhaps under the influence of that still unknown factor which causes a large number of populations to die out as soon as they come into contact with modern civilization, just as we also see with our Algerian Muslim population other than the Berbers.

Apart from the Christians and the Druze, there is a third element in Syria: the Muslim population. It is the most numerous. For a long time its sympathies have drifted away from the Ottoman government, to which it is no longer attached except by religion, for in general they are very fanatical

[38] Although the Druze faith was first preached in what is now Afghanistan and Iran, it became an organized movement in Egypt under the Fatimid caliph al-Ḥākim (AD 996–1021). (MCAM)

[39] This is the ancient Ǧabal Ḥawrān, now known as Ǧabal al-ʿArab. (MCAM)

[40] The Aramaeans were a people in Syria and Mesopotamia in the first half of the 1st millennium BC. It is unlikely that the stone houses used by the Druze dated from that time, but it is impossible to date them accurately. It is likely that Huber is referring to people whose language was Aramaic. (MCAM)

and the title of Caliph of the Believers[41] has more value among them than among the Muslim populations of the west [i.e. North Africa].

Leaving aside the philosophies of the powers that be in Syria, if one wanted to engage the affections of the populations described above more closely – apart from the Christians whose self-interest invariably compels them to throw in their lot with France – I offer here some brief suggestions as to how we should proceed.

The Druze have been divided for many years into two more or less equal sections which are not at enmity, and whose leaders are Shaykh Ibrāhīm al-Aṭrash and Shaykh Nağm al-Aṭrash at ʿUrmān, the latter being the noblest and most generous, and consequently the more influential. He is also the more independent.

The first, Ibrāhīm al-Aṭrash, has a rather haughty character. He has lost a great deal of his influence as a result of his questionable conduct during the last Druze uprising in autumn 1879.[42] He is also, as far as one can gather, the most committed or the one closest to the English Consul.

As for Nağm al-Aṭrash, although sedentary he has all the qualities of the Bedouin without having their faults. He is brave. His conduct was irreproachable during the 1879 war. But above all he is just, which is a very rare thing in the Orient.

The means by which one might influence these two shaykhs if one did not want to address them directly would be through the emir ʿAbd al-Qādir[43] in Damascus. There is one thing that is not widely known but which the

[41] The Ottoman sultans had taken the title 'Caliph' in 1517, thus claiming religious as well as secular authority. (MCAM)

[42] In 1878, the Ottoman government appointed Midḥat Pasha as governor of Damascus and he launched a military expedition to enforce direct Ottoman rule in Ğabal Ḥawrān (= Ğabal al-Druz = Ğabal al-ʿArab), which had been relatively autonomous for the previous ten years. In October 1879 he appointed Saʿīd Talhuq, a Druze from Mount Lebanon, as governor of Ğabal Ḥawrān and instigated many reforms. However, he also demanded that the Druze shaykhs pay 10,000 Turkish lira to compensate the Ottoman government for the cost of the military expedition. After a number of conflicts between the Druze and Sunni Muslims, the Druze shaykhs were forced to pay large sums in blood money. Ibrāhīm kept out of these conflicts, which led many Druze to regard him as a collaborator with the Ottoman government. This belief was only increased by his appointment as *mudīr* (very roughly 'mayor') of al-Suwaydah, the chief town on Ğabal Ḥawrān, and then as *Kaymakam* (governor of a third-level province) of the region in January 1883, four months before this letter was written. (MCAM)

[43] For ʿAbd al-Qādir (1808–83), emir of Mascara, see Translation Part II, note 155.

Quai d'Orsay should be aware of: that is that in the past, ʿAbd al-Qādir, seeing how easy it would be to take advantage of the lack of cohesion in the Ottoman empire, thought at one time of carving out a new principality for himself in Syria to compensate for the one he lost in Algeria. To this end he forged good relations with the Druze shaykhs. For reasons which it would take too long to go into here, he did not carry out his plan but he nevertheless kept up his good relationship with them as well as his great influence over the whole nation.[44] During the 1879 uprising he was one of the intermediaries for concluding the peace and, aided by the English, obtained from the Ottoman government exceptionally favourable conditions. All the Druze shaykhs visiting Damascus are his guests.

In addition, his reputation for sanctity has brought ʿAbd al-Qādir great prestige and considerable influence among the Muslim population of Damascus and part of Syria. (The Druze are not Muslim and have their own religion).

At the time of writing, the news has arrived in Europe of the illness and probably the imminent demise of the emir ʿAbd al-Qādir. None of his sons will inherit his prestige. I know them all personally. There is only one who has the slightest intelligence. He is the eldest, Emir ʿAlī; but he is blind, and the others are just fond of having a good time.

At Beirut our position is very strong. At Damascus, thanks to a Christian population of about 15,000 souls, it is still quite strong but it has nevertheless been greatly disrupted by subversive English activities targeting rich Muslim families and all the government officials.

The Syrian desert with its nomadic population is no threat, because the Arab of Arabia bears no comparison either in tribal organization or in bravery with the nomad of Algeria. I know most of the tribes of the Ḥamād[45] and I cannot see a single one – including the most powerful like the Ruwalah or the Wuld ʿAlī – who, faced with a common danger, could assemble a thousand rifles.

The authority of the Turks over the Bedouin is in effect nil. They can only get them to pay tax when, after a winter without rain and when there is no more pasture in the desert, the nomads are obliged to lead their flocks to graze among the villages of Syria.

---

[44] Huber is almost certainly referring to the Druzes here. (MCAM)

[45] The Ḥamād: the Syrian desert; see Appendix 3 note 27.

The Bedouin of the Syrian desert are not very observant of their religion and are not fanatics. Although their tribes share a common origin – they are almost all ʿAnizah Arabs[46] – they are in a continuous state of hostility.

Their forces must never have been much greater than they are now, judging by the smallness of the forts whose remains one still finds scattered in the desert and which were surely used in the past to contain them.

Everything that I have just told you concerns in particular the populations situated between Homs, Hamah and the Dead Sea and between the Mediterranean and the desert; but I have reason to think that the same also applies to those to be found farther south and farther north than these limits.

Despite the difficulty and the novelty of the question, allow me now to add a note about the interior of Arabia.

This region has always been considered by the [Sublime] Porte[47] as belonging to them despite the fact that until recently they had only possessed the two holy cities of the Ḥiǧāz, Mecca and al-Madīnah. At the beginning of this century, driven out by the Wahhabis, they even lost these two for a few years.

Ibrāhīm Pasha,[48] having destroyed the power of the Wahhabi sect, conquered the Ḥiǧāz and re-established the authority of the sultan there. It is only recently that the sultan subjugated ʿAsīr[49] as well, and part of the Yemen. The conquest of al-Ḥasāʾ in the Persian Gulf is even more recent.[50]

At the time when the Wahhabi power collapsed, its dominion reached throughout the whole Peninsula and, for the provinces of the centre, this state of affairs had already been in existence for half a century.

After the destruction of al-Dirʿiyyah, the capital city of the Wahhabis, the empire created by the successors of Ibn Saʿūd broke up and the various provinces resumed their independence.

---

[46] Huber here is using 'Arabs' in the sense of 'Bedouin'. The ʿAnizah is a large confederation of Bedouin tribes, including those he has just mentioned. (MCAM)

[47] That is, the central Ottoman administration. (MCAM)

[48] Ibrahim Pasha (1789–1848) was the son of Muḥammad ʿAlī, the de facto ruler of Egypt, which was theoretically part of the Ottoman empire. In 1816, Ibrahim Pasha succeeded his brother in command of the Egyptian army in Arabia which was fighting the Āl Saʿūd dynasty, a successful campaign that led to the collapse of the First Saudi State (1744–1818). (MCAM)

[49] The mountainous region in the south-west of what is now Saudi-Arabia. (MCAM)

[50] The oases of al-Ḥasāʾ and al-Qaṭīf, in today's Eastern Province of Saudi Arabia, were incorporated into the Ottoman Empire by Midḥat Pasha in 1871.

Subsequently, various fluctuations modified this state of affairs and today Central Arabia is divided into two sovereign states. The northern one includes the provinces of al-Ǧawf, the Shammar and al-Qaṣīm under the rule of a prince of the main tribe of the Shammar Arabs. Those in the south – Sudayr, al-Washm and Alladj [*sic*; al-Kharǧ or al-Aflāǧ must be meant] under the authority of the successors of Ibn Saʿūd.

The first has its capital at Ḥāʾil, at the foot of the Shammar mountain range, and the second at al-Riyāḍ.

Between the two states lies ʿUnayzah [in al-Qaṣīm], a rich and populous city with a small independent territory.

The Shammar emirate, which stretches from 26° of latitude to the mountain of the Druze to the north-west, and to near the Euphrates to the north-east, is very extensive but includes much barren desert. It is more sparsely populated and also less fertile than Naǧd to the south, but it is more unified and, as a result, also more powerful and more strongly constituted than Naǧd, which has exhausted itself in civil wars in recent years.

The current ruler, Muḥammad Ibn Rashīd, is forty-eight and has been emir since 1874.[51] He enjoys a great reputation for justice and is loved by the Shammar as much as he is feared by their enemies. He loves literature and is himself a poet. His generosity is renowned throughout the whole of Arabia.

The Wahhabi doctrines that he still professes did not, however, prevent him from offering me, an infidel, a cordial welcome.

The forces of the Shammar emir amount to a troop of about 300 riders who form his bodyguard and a Bedouin contingent of about 5,000 men. The latter can increase to 8,000 and even under certain circumstances to double that number, with the addition of tribes which are his allies but not his subjects.

Relations with the ruler of Naǧd, the former suzerain of the Shammar,[52] are good and they offer each other presents at least once a year; the currency of these civilities usually being horses.

---

[51] Actually 1872.

[52] The Rashīdī dynasty had come to power in Ǧabal Shammar with the backing of the Saudi rulers of Riyadh in the 1830s and continued to owe them technical allegiance even as they rose to dominance in central Arabia at the expense of Āl Saʿūd. The Emir Muḥammad al-Rashīd of Ḥāʾil was related by marriage to his counterpart in Riyadh, the Imām ʿAbd Allāh ibn Fayṣal Āl Saʿūd, and recognized the latter as his suzerain even as the balance of power in Naǧd tilted in favour of Ḥāʾil.

Muḥammad Ibn Rashīd also maintains good relations with the Sharif of Mecca, whose religious supremacy he partly recognizes.[53]

Relations with Egypt go back a long way and are likewise very good.[54]

Those with the Ottoman empire are frankly hostile, especially since the government of al-Madīnah a few years ago wrested from him the oasis of Khaybar, five days' journey to the north of the holy city.[55]

Until recently, the interior of Arabia remained free from all foreign influence, but I think that this has changed in the last few years. I am led to this opinion by the numerous expeditions by English nationals in Mesopotamia, that of Lady Blunt in this very region and in the Shammar,[56] as well as those of the agents sent by the Indian government to al-Riyāḍ and the Arab shaykhs of the south with presents.[57]

This latter enterprise had already been recounted at ʿUnayzah in the province of al-Qaṣīm and very recently in Paris by M. Flüry-Hérard,[58] who had probably learned of it through contact with India. I cannot however see that the English have managed to create serious alliances up to now in Nağd, for the simple reason that for half a century there has been no stable government, nor any lasting authority. Moreover, I am much inclined to think that they have their eyes more on the provinces along the coast like Oman than on the central provinces; but I think they have recognized the need to be on good terms with the inland population.

As far as the Emir Muḥammad Ibn Rashīd is concerned, I think he is still untouched by any foreign influence, and I would add that in order to make,

---

[53] The Wahhabis were and remain highly suspicious of any religious hierarchy. (MCAM)

[54] The Rashidis had benefited greatly from the Egyptian defeat of the Āl Saʿūd in 1818; see note 48 above. (MCAM)

[55] On the question of Khaybar, see Appendix 5, Letter no. 2 from Huber to the Emir Muḥammad al-Rashīd.

[56] Lady Anne Blunt and her husband Wilfrid Blunt travelled in Mesopotamia in 1877–78 and in northern Nağd in 1878–79. Their journey was not intended to advance British interests in the region – in fact Wilfrid Blunt was a vociferous anti-imperialist – but to acquire first-class Arabian horses for their stud at Crabbet Park in Sussex.

[57] Presumably a reference to Col. Lewis Pelly's visit to Riyadh in 1865. Huber does not mention (though he must have known) that the Englishman William Gifford Palgrave's journey across Arabia in 1862–63, during which he spent several weeks in Riyadh, was actually sponsored by the French emperor Napoléon III.

[58] For Paul Flüry-Hérard, see Appendix 3 note 48. It is not clear what British intrigues in central Arabia are being referred to, though vague reports of the journeys of Sadleir (1819), Palgrave (1862–63) or Pelly (1865) may have given rise to such rumours.

should we need to, a firm ally of him, we would only need to use diplomatic channels to restore to him the oasis of Khaybar, which the Turks took from him in a time of peace.

As for Mesopotamia, one can apply to it all that I have said relative to Syria. For a long time there has been no love lost between the entire population and the Ottoman government.

Such is the succinct summary of my observations about the countries through which I travelled during my first expedition; during the second expedition, for which the government has just graciously given permission,[59] I will try to complete them and fill in more details.

Assuring you, Monsieur Maunoir, of my highest consideration,

Charles Huber

LETTER NO. 14

Date: 25 June 1883
From: Charles Huber, Beirut
To: not specified, but certainly Charles Maunoir

Sir,

I received this morning your letter of 12th of this month, and I have the honour to confirm to you mine of the 15th of this month.

Professor Euting is a great scholar, one of the best authorities on Semitic languages, but he is as much a wild enthusiast[60] as a scholar, and before he suggested travelling with me to Arabia – a plan which he had long been contemplating but which grew ever more pressing on the news of my epigraphic discoveries in the Ḥiǧāz – he had already announced more or less *urbi et orbi* [to the whole world] that he would go with me.

[59] Hence the Ministry of Public Education had at last given permission for Huber's second expedition in May 1883, a whole year after he had submitted his proposal (see Appendix 3, Letters nos. 18 and 19 of 11 May 1882). The date of this letter, 20 May 1883, was just two days before Huber and Euting's departure from Strasbourg for Marseille and the East.

[60] It should be noted that in 19th-century French the term 'enthusiaste' had distinctly negative connotations, suggesting fanaticism, zealotry, lack of judgement, etc. (Littré 1873). This letter is in reply to Maunoir, who had written to Huber deploring the plan for Euting to accompany him on the Arabian expedition. See Letter no. 16 below; and Appendix 6, Letters nos. 1, 2 and 3. (MCAM/WF)

However, I had never offered him much hope, for the simple reason that I saw more advantage in it for him than for me, and when last January I spoke with you about it in Paris and you expressed your disapproval of it, I told him straight away on returning to my country, where he had come to find me, to contemplate it no further.

He was distinctly less quick to publish the fact that he was setting off on his own than he had been to state the contrary. Some reporter or other, having heard the first version, must have used this false story to fill his column.

But it is not my business to know the source of this article. What I can assure you is that it does not come from M. Euting. What I can affirm is that I have no closer relationship with him than with anyone else, that we are not travelling together and that, as a consequence, there can be no question of being travelling companions or of one of us being subordinate to the other.

One of these days you will perhaps read in some leaflet that I am leaving with Dr Landberg,[61] about whom I had the honour to speak to you in my last letter; at least that is the rumour that is spreading here. Indeed, on my arrival here he did ask me but, when I declined, he confined himself to asking me to recommend him to the Emir Muḥammad Ibn Rashīd at Ḥāʾil, as he will be going there in six months' time.

If you lend credence to this rumour and any others that may be spreading with the same virulence as that of my departure with Euting, I do not think my second expedition will turn out well, and I have been wondering for a few hours now whether I would not do better to go home and leave the trouble of finishing my work to others. Even as things are I am not so full of hope. I still have no passport nor any recommendation to any consul, and I see myself thus deprived of the only advantage that I might expect from a difficult mission, that is to say diplomatic support. I am extremely disheartened.

I need encouragement and I am getting more or less the opposite. You do not know what it is to penetrate into Arabia and to explore it. Three expeditions destroyed and murdered[62] in eighteen months can scarcely give you an idea.

---

[61] Count Carlo de Landberg (1848–1924) was a Swedish orientalist with a special interest in the languages of southern Arabia.

[62] One of these was doubtless that of Siegfried Langer, who was murdered in the Aden hinterland in 1882. We do not know what other failed expeditions Huber is referring to here.

I am aware of what I owe you; I have already told you so and am happy to repeat it, and nothing would give me greater joy than sometime to prove the sincerity of my gratitude to you. For as a result of the obligations which I have towards you, I recognize your right to ask more of me than anyone else; but please, I beg you, do not do so in such harsh terms.

As far as my situation is concerned, I confirm completely my last letter. I would add only that the news that I received from the desert makes me doubt whether I shall be able to stop at Ǧiddah and consequently to receive the money from Europe.[63] From Ḥāʾil I shall probably have to continue my journey to al-Riyāḍ and from there through the Dawāsir to Ṣanʿāʾ or Aden, so that as soon as I leave Damascus I would need to have all my resources available.

The question of the four Gras rifles is still of great importance to me.[64]

The squadron is to arrive here today, tomorrow I will do my time comparisons, and in the evening I shall leave for Damascus.

I announce to you a new competitor for Arabia. It is Dr Hartmann,[65] the author of various Arabic works, who says he will come in the spring or in autumn 1884. He has just written to ask me for information.

Assuring you of my highest consideration,

Charles Huber
[Contactable] at the French Consulate in Damascus

I am still waiting for the proof copy of my map.

LETTER NO. 15

Date: 27 June 1883
From: Charles Huber, Beirut
To: not specified, but certainly Charles Maunoir

[63] Huber was at this stage planning to have 5,000 francs of his 10,000-franc subsidy from the Ministry of Public Education sent to Ǧiddah, but this plan was soon abandoned. See Appendix 4 below: Letter no. 18 dated 19 July 1883 from Huber to Maunoir, stating that arrangements could not be made for delivery to Ǧiddah; Letter no. 21, penultimate paragraph; Letter no. 24 note 154.

[64] Huber wanted these as a gift for the Emir Muḥammad al-Rashīd. See note 87 below.

[65] Martin Hartmann (1851–1918), a German Arabist. (MCAM)

Sir,

I have the honour of confirming to you my letters of 15th and 25th of this month.

In the 28th May [18]83 issue of the *Revue Critique et Littéraire* [*sic*] under the heading 'Germany', I have just this minute read the announcement of M. Euting's expedition, which can only mean that he will undertake it by himself.[66]

I would have asked M. Euting for the meaning of the article that you brought to my attention, but at the German Consulate where he is staying and where I have just sent word, they told me that he left a few days ago on a trip into Lebanon with the German consul-general.

A quarantine period of ten days has been imposed today on all those coming from Egypt, and consequently from France, because of the cholera that has been reported in the Delta. I quote this fact to you with regard to the Gras rifles,[67] which will therefore take ten days longer to arrive, if they arrive at all.

The squadron[68] only got here yesterday evening, I will have my [time] comparison[69] shortly, and I shall leave for Damascus tomorrow.

Assuring you of my highest and most respectful consideration,

Charles Huber

LETTER NO. 16

Date: 3 July 1883
From: Charles Huber, Beirut (see final paragraph)
To: not named, but most probably Dr Weisgerber

My dear friend,

Yesterday's steamer brought me your letter of 18 June as well as the planisphere, for which my liveliest thanks. Please, always note down all expenses

[66] Huber is referring to the *Revue critique d'histoire et de littérature*, vol. XV, no. 22 of 28 May 1883, pp. 436–7: 'M. Euting, librarian of the University Library of Strasbourg, has to leave for central Arabia where he will stay for two years and collect Arabic inscriptions.' (MG)

[67] Gras rifles: see note 64 above and 87 below.

[68] See the last paragraph of Letter no. 16 below.

[69] See the end of Letter no. 14 above.

incurred on my behalf, purchases, journeys, transport costs etc., so that I can reimburse you later.

You will have seen, concerning Euting, in my last letter of 26 June I think, that Maunoir had written to me on the subject and that I replied that there is no question and there has never been any question of an association between Euting and me, and that nothing is more ridiculous than to suppose that I, who have been appointed by the French government, should make myself subordinate to a German appointed by his government. Where would be the advantage, what benefit would there be for me? – I would understand if it were the other way round because I do not need anyone with whom to go to Arabia, whereas anybody else would need me. I am surprised that this has not been taken into consideration and that Maunoir swallowed such a ridiculous story so easily.[70]

On receiving his letter, I was ready to have nothing more to do with the Ministry or Maunoir, and that is still not beyond the bounds of possibility. I shall take up again my initial idea of setting off on my own account. Apart from the question of money, for me, being officially accredited would only have the advantage of diplomatic support. Up to now the latter has been completely lacking and in a few days I shall no longer have any need of it.

What vexes me is when I think how unpleasantly surprised you must have been when Maunoir spoke to you of all this, with you not knowing what to reply. You already need a strong dose of friendship, I realize, to look after my affairs, but you are a pearl among friends if such annoyances do not cause you to give up on me.

I still intend to set off at the end of July, by which time I think everything will be ready, but I continue to nurse the hope that I shall receive the funds from the Ministry before that date.

For now I would ask you, in case the decision comes through suddenly and the order for payment is given to Flüry-Hérard, to go and find him and ask him if I can use his funds,[71] in which case you are to wire them to me straight away – in this way I shall gain ten to fifteen days. My telegraphic address will be:

---

[70] Again, this implies that Maunoir had written to Huber expressing his displeasure at the 1883–84 journey being a joint Franco-German enterprise between Huber and Euting without his knowledge, and even suspecting Euting to be the senior partner in their association. See Letter no. 14 above, and Appendix 6, Letters nos. 1, 2 and 3.

[71] For Flüry-Hérard, see note 58 above and Appendix 3 note 48. He was responsible for transferring the Ministry of Public Education's subsidy to Huber in Damascus.

Huber
French Consulate
Damascus

I am writing to Schmidt[72] by this same post to send me more zinc phosphate granules, then some dye for my beard, and am telling him that you will pay for it all. You will put in a pocket compass of the size of a pocket watch (from 5 to 7 francs). One of mine has already been damaged by seawater. Get me one with a metal lid. In my next letter I shall send a letter of credit drawn on Flüry-Hérard to cover your expenses.

The Mediterranean squadron has left Beirut this morning for Candie[73] – as for me, I am setting off for Damascus in two days' time. My postal address remains the same.

Thank you, dear fellow, for all your trouble and your cordial aid, and hearty handshakes.

Charles Huber

LETTER NO. 17

Date: 13 July 1883
From: Charles Huber, Damascus
To: Charles Maunoir

Sir,

I have the honour to confirm to you my letters of 15th and 25th last.

This morning I received the letters of recommendation promised by ʿAbd al-Raḥmān Pasha Rushdī,[74] the friend of M. Duveyrier.[75] There are two for the Sharif of Mecca and one for the Grand Mufti of the Yemen. M. Gilbert, the French consul in Damascus, kindly telegraphed a few days ago to the Marquis de Noailles, our ambassador at the Porte, to remind him of my request for a *firmān*;[76] this document too will therefore reach me by one of the next posts.

---

[72] Schmidt: see Letter no. 24. It is not at present known who Schmidt was.

[73] Candia, Crete; modern-day Iraklion.

[74] We have been unable to identify ʿAbd al-Raḥmān Pasha Rushdī.

[75] This must be Henri Duveyrier (1840–92), the well-known geographer and explorer of the Sahara, and contributor of articles to the *Bulletin de la Société de Géographie*. See e.g. Duveyrier 1883.

[76] A *firmān*: a permit to travel (see Appendix 3 note 26). It is clear from this paragraph that Huber was still making contingency plans to travel as far as Yemen. T. Gilbert

As far as official documents go, I shall only need the letters for Arabia which I have requested from the Khedive through our diplomatic agent in Cairo, M. Raindre.[77] However, he will only put in the request when he receives the official notification of my expedition from the Ministry of Foreign Affairs, which seems not to have come through yet.

Have my explanations about M. Euting convinced you and can I hope that you will be willing to continue to interest yourself in my expedition? – If so, please let me know, and act so that I can still take advantage of it. – If not, still kindly let me know, because the uncertainty and indecision in which I find myself, apart from being very painful to me, is costing me a great deal of time and money.

I spoke to M. Gilbert about the four Gras rifles,[78] and he has agreed, in order to avoid all difficulty with the Turkish authorities, for them to be sent direct to him. You may issue the relevant instructions.

Please be assured, my dear Sir, of my highest and most respectful consideration,

Ch. Huber
[Contactable] at the French Consulate, Damascus

Letter no. 18

Date: 19 July 1883
From: Charles Huber, Damascus
To: not specified, but certainly Charles Maunoir

Sir,

I have the honour to confirm to you my letters of 15 and 25 June last and of the 13th of this month.

Since my last letter, I have received from M. Raindre, the agent of the Cairo consulate, a letter informing me that the Khedive did not think himself able to authorize the delivery of letters of recommendation for Arabia. This matter is now closed, therefore, and I shall manage without this help.

was French consul in Damascus: see Appendix 3, Letter no. 9 from him to Charles Maunoir dated 29 October 1879, and Letter no. 16 from Huber to the Ministry of Education dated 27 March 1882.

[77] De Raindre was French agent and consul-general in Cairo.

[78] For the Gras rifles, see notes 64 above and 87 below.

It now remains for me to wait for the documents or the negative reply from our ambassador to the Porte.

I shall set off in three days' time to visit the Druze, with whom I have arrangements to make about my journey on foot to the Wādī al-Sirḥān. I shall be back a fortnight later and my preparations will by then be almost complete.

I permit myself therefore for a last time to ask you to honour me with a reply to my previous letters, because time is pressing.

Please be assured, my dear Sir, of my highest and most respectful consideration,

Ch. Huber
French Consulate, Damascus

Letter no. 19

Date: 17 August 1883
From: Charles Huber, Damascus
To: Huber's 'dear friend', most probably Dr Weisgerber

My dear friend,

I told you in my last letter that I was setting off for Palmyra where, at the desire of the Académie des Inscriptions et Belles-Lettres, I was to make a squeeze of the inscription of the duty tariff of Palmyra discovered there a year ago by Prince Lazaref.[79] – I returned from there on the 10th of this month with the desired object.

Very important news about Central Arabia was waiting for me here. You know that I contacted my friend M... in Constantinople to get in touch there with ʿAbdullah Pasha,[80] who is a member of Ibn Saʿūd's family, the

[79] The Tax Law of Palmyra is an edict concerning the taxation of the city of Palmyra in the early Roman imperial period, dated to the year AD 137 in the reign of Hadrian. It is embodied in an inscription in Greek and Palmyrene, which was discovered in 1881 in a place known as the Tariff Court. Its discoverer, Prince Simon Abamelek Lazareff, first published the text in the 1880s, and the inscription was removed to the Hermitage Museum in St Petersburg. See Lönnqvist 2008.

[80] Huber appears to be confusing this man with his namesake, the actual ruler of Riyadh, the Imām ʿAbdullah ibn Fayṣal (r. 1865–89). This ʿAbdullah Pasha was a cousin and claimant to the rule of Naǧd who had decided to petition the Ottoman Sultan to promote his cause. His full name was ʿAbdullah ibn Ibrāhīm ibn ʿAbdallah ibn Thunayyān Al Saʿūd, and his father had been briefly ruler of Riyadh in 1841–43. He

shaykh of the Wahhabis and ruler of lower Nağd – who since his wars with Turkey in the province of al-Ḥasā' on the Persian Gulf is kept prisoner at Yildiz Kiosk.[81] My aim was to contrive to obtain from ʿAbdullah Pasha one or more letters of recommendation for notable people in Nağd to facilitate my expedition into this region.

ʿAbdullah Pasha, without refusing M… my request, has put off replying to it on various pretexts until now.

A few days ago, M… received a visit from ʿAbdullah Pasha, who told him he had received a very important letter from Nağd, which he communicated to him and authorized him to make a copy of it. It is this letter that M…. has just sent me, and of which a faithful translation is given here.

The letter, with no indication of the town where it was written, is dated 20 Shaʿban (25 June) and was posted in Baṣrah.

> We write to inform Your Highness that your son, Emir Ibrāhīm Bey, in league with the Emir Muḥammad Al Saʿūd have attacked Muḥammad Ibn Rashīd, the Shammar emir in the High Nağd (*fī ʿaliyyat Nağd*) near to a water course called Khuff and Khufayf. It was a hot day. Saʿūd (that is Ibn Saʿūd, Ibrāhīm Bey and Muḥammad al-Saʿūd) had 3,500 horsemen, all from the ʿUtaybah tribe, and their footsoldiers amounted to as many as 10,000 men. This was the preamble [?].
>
> Muḥammad al-Saʿūd had with him 1,500 cavalry and 6,000 footsoldiers, the remainder of his troops being under Ibrāhīm.
>
> Ibn Rashīd had 4,000 cavalry or even more, and 12,000 footsoldiers. The clash was terrible. Ibn Rashīd was defeated after losing 1,000 horsemen killed and many footsoldiers. Also, many were taken prisoner. He was forced to flee and take refuge in his own country.
>
> He was not pursued on the day of the battle, but the victors stopped at the Nafūd al-Sirr, waiting to gather up all their forces from the various regions of Nağd, to be able then to proceed to the lands of Ibn Rashīd. This is the narrative of how things happened.

---

arrived in Istanbul in 1880. His claim was futile and his influence in Riyadh would have been nil. See Winder 1965: 266.

[81] Yıldız Palace (Turkish: *Yıldız Sarayı*) is the vast complex of former imperial Ottoman pavilions and villas in Istanbul, built in the 19th and early 20th centuries. It was used as a residence by the sultan and his court in the late 19th century.

> Of livestock, Sa'ūd lost approximately 100 mares and 200 cattle [i.e. camels], as well as 40 of his soldiers – the camels were taken back after Ibn Rashīd had fled.
>
> The other members of Sa'ūd's family and their troops did not take part that day.

According to a second letter written to the same 'Abdullah Pasha, the *ibn 'amm* [lit. 'son of a paternal uncle', i.e. first cousin] of Ibn Rashīd was reported to have been taken prisoner. I only know of one '*ibn 'amm*' of the Shammar emir: that would be Ḥamūd al-'Ubayd.

On first reading this letter and under the influence of initial emotion I did indeed think that there had been an attack by the Wahhabis against the young Shammar empire and that the latter had been defeated. But, on reflection and on analysing the letter, I think we can be assured that the one who provoked the fight and who came out the victor is Muḥammad Ibn Rashīd. What proves this to me is that the location of the battle, Khuff and Khufayf,[82] as well as the Nafūd al-Sirr (Nafūd is a desert of pure sand), where the Wahhabis encamped after the battle, are both situated to the south of Ouadi Ermek [*sic*; Wādī al-Rimah, the main wadi running through al-Qaṣīm] and consequently outside Shammar territory. And the letter itself confirms this by saying that the 'Utaybah camped in the Nafūd al-Sirr to gather their forces together and then move on to the territory of Ibn Rashīd.

I also have my doubts as to whether Ibn Rashīd was the vanquished party, because a battle in which the defeated side manages to get away with 100 mares in Arabia is the equivalent of a victory. – I will not dwell on the 1,000 riders of Ibn Rashīd who were killed nor on the 40 lost by Ibn Sa'ūd; that is too much like the reports of European battles. Nor do I believe in the 16,000 men that Ibn Rashīd supposedly had. I am familiar enough with his country to know that it would be extraordinarily difficult for him to muster such a force, and even more difficult to lead them to the south in the month of June, a time of year when the wells would no longer have sufficient water to serve such an army.[83]

[82] Khuff is approximately 50 km south-west of Shaqrā in al-Washm, just west of the Nafūd al-Sirr. Khufayf is a diminutive form of Khuff.

[83] Huber's instinct about the outcome of this raid being in Ibn Rashīd's favour was correct. It seems to have taken place at midsummer 1883 in the wake of a defeat inflicted by Ibn Rashīd on a coalition of Saudi and 'Utaybah forces at 'Arwā', 75 km south of Dawādimī and 125 km south of Khuff. In the hostilities that followed, the

I think therefore that in this case it was just a Ṟazou [*sic*; *ghazū*] (we say Razzia in Algeria), a raid such as the Shammar emir makes once or twice every year on the ʿUtaybah tribes, only this time the latter would have probably been warned and would have concentrated their forces and fought hard for their herds. There would have been a fight, and this is proved by the capture of Ḥamūd al-ʿUbayd by the ʿUtaybah.

What surprises me most in all this is the capture of a hundred mares by Ibn Rashīd. I know that the main aim of all his raids is to steal mares but I have never heard of a single raid in Arabia in which such a large number was taken. These are the possessions that the Bedouin usually defend most fiercely.

What I find personally disagreeable in this news is that it shows that the dynasty of al-Riyāḍ, Ibn Saʿūd [*sic*; i.e. Āl Saʿūd], has finally taken the side of the ʿUtaybah against Ibn Rashīd, who up till now has made at least one campaign every year against this powerful tribe without Ibn Saʿūd getting involved.

This upsets all my plans because, apart from the fact that it is not very prudent to enter Central Arabia, I am now no longer able to get to al-Riyāḍ via Ḥāʾil and the territory of the Shammar. Not only do I thus lose a powerful protector, but I am also greatly perplexed to know which route to take, as I know that I absolutely have to go through the Ḥiǧāz to make squeezes of the inscriptions discovered on my first expedition to Taymāʾ, Madāʾin Ṣāliḥ and al-ʿUlā.[84]

I suppose that the news from Naǧd must already have reached the Syrian desert, so in order to find out about this as soon as possible I am setting off tomorrow for the Wādī al-Sirḥān to glean from the nomads who are there at the moment what they have been able to discover about it. I will be back in Damascus in ten to twelve days and I shall let you know the result of my enquiries straight away.

By then I shall also find here the letter that the minister mentioned to me in his last telegram, and I will probably then be able to make a decision with all the facts at my disposal.

Goodbye for now, my dear friend.

Cordially yours,
Charles Huber

Saudi coalition consistently came off worst, and their fortunes reached their nadir at the battle of Ḥamādah in the spring of 1884 (Winder 1965: 268–9).

[84] These inscriptions had already been discovered by Doughty in 1877–78. (MCAM)

LETTER NO. 20

Date: 24 September 1883
From: Charles Huber, Damascus
To: Charles Maunoir, 14 rue Jacob, Paris

Sir,

Here is the explanation for the telegram which I had the honour to send to you on the 21st of this month.

I left Damascus on the 27th[85] [of August] to go to Ḥā'il when, arriving at Kāf, I met four horsemen from the Emir Muḥammad Ibn Rashīd, whom the latter had sent to Damascus to look for me. They carried letters from the emir and from my other friends in Ǧabal Shammar, which were all very affectionate towards me.

I have many presents for the emir this time and especially many rifles (31);[86] nevertheless Ḥamūd al-Miqrād, the officer commanding the escort, asked me if I had the two or three rifles used by the French army,[87] the only thing that the emir had previously asked me for.

Fearing that the outcome of my expedition could suffer from this omission, I did not hesitate to make a forced march back from Kāf to here with Ḥamūd to ask you by telegram whether these rifles, which you kindly allowed me to hope for previously, are going to be delivered to me. I have awaited your reply for four days and I now see that it will not come. As it is not possible for me to stay here any longer and to leave my servant alone in Kāf with my luggage,[88] I am setting off from Damascus again tonight.

[85] Although he never says so, this was the beginning of his journey with Euting. The date presumably was 27 August (the original letter is torn after '27th') though in fact Huber was visiting Druze villages on that date and only caught up with Euting at the small fort of Brāq on 4 September to start their journey together (Huber 1891: 19–21). (MCAM)

[86] Huber fails to acknowledge here that twenty-seven of these firearms were in fact brought along by Euting. See also note 139 below.

[87] These were the Gras rifles, four of which Huber was anxious to obtain. The Fusil Modèle 1874 or Gras was the French Army's primary service rifle from 1874 to 1886. See Letter no. 24 below.

[88] Huber had left not just his servant Maḥmūd behind in Kāf to await his return, but also Julius Euting.

Had you not previously led me to hope for these rifles, I would have bought something equivalent. From here, I can no longer do this, so I am much perplexed as to how I shall satisfy the emir.

Your silence to all my letters since I left Paris proves to me that you have completely lost interest in my mission. I hope therefore that you will not hold it against me if in future I do not tire you with my correspondence.

Assuring you of my highest and most respectful consideration,

Charles Huber

Letter no. 21

Date: 30 November 1883
From: Charles Huber, Ḥā'il, Ǧabal Shammar
To: Charles Maunoir, Secrétaire générale de la Société de Géographie, Paris

Monsieur Maunoir,

I take the liberty of begging you to excuse my bad temper in my last letter. Even if you are unwilling to do anything more for me or my expedition, I cannot forget that you have done a great deal for me in other circumstances, and you have my gratitude. Once again, therefore, please excuse me.

I have moreover been able to forestall the harm which might have resulted from my not bringing the guns I promised to the Emir Muḥammad Ibn Rashīd, by ordering them direct from a supplier of firearms who will send them to Ǧiddah, where I will go to fetch them at the beginning of next March.

Since I left Arabia two years ago, great events have occurred there. War broke out between Ibn Rashīd and ʿAbdullah Ibn Saʿūd [Imām ʿAbdullah ibn Fayṣal Āl Saʿūd, r. 1865–87], the inheritor of the Wahhabi throne.[89] The struggle only ended last August with the almost complete submission of the Arabs [i.e. Bedouin] (ʿUtaybah and Muṭayr) who were on Ibn Saʿūd's side.

The letter I sent from Paris[90] to the emir Ibn Rashīd to announce my impending arrival found him in the theatre of war north of the Ǧabal Ṭuwayq. He immediately ordered three mounted warriors to proceed to Damascus to fetch me.

[89] The raid on which Huber reports in Letter no. 19 of 17 August 1883 was part of this war. See notes 80 and 83 above.
[90] See Appendix 5, Letter no. 2 dated *ca.* 10 April 1883.

I arrived in Ḥā'il with this escort on 27 October last. The emir, who received me in the most cordial way, had had one of the finest houses in the capital prepared for me.[91]

Since then I have made two short excursions, one into Ǧabal Aǧā, the second to Ǧabal Ǧildiyyah. From both I have brought back, as well as much geographical information, more than a hundred new Thamoudian [Thamudic] inscriptions.[92]

In a few days' time I shall set out to travel round the whole of Ǧabal Aǧā and the surrounding area; after that I hope that the last word will have been said about the true orientation of this mountain range.

When I return from this trip I shall set off immediately for the Ḥiǧāz, all of which I hope to traverse this time from Tabūk as far as Ǧiddah, where I shall stop off to pick up my correspondence and the presents for the emir that I have had sent there. From there too I shall send to Paris the squeezes of the Nabataean inscriptions from Madā'in Ṣāliḥ.

From Ǧiddah I shall return to Ḥā'il, where most of my luggage still is. Depending on the remaining means available to me, I shall make a trip to the south or else go back to Europe via Iraq. As for crossing al-ʿĀriḍ [the area around Riyadh], the Dawāsir and Naǧrān, I shall have to relinquish this plan once again this time, as M. Charmes, as you probably know, has made me an allowance of only 10,000 francs; now, on the day of my departure from Damascus, having paid for my camels and everything else, I had [already] spent 9,600 francs.

Please be assured, M. Maunoir, of my highest and most respectful consideration,

Charles Huber
[Contactable] at the French Consulate in Ǧiddah

---

91 Huber nowhere mentions, here or in his other writings, notably *Journal d'un voyage en Arabie* (Paris 1891), that he was travelling with Julius Euting, from whom he did not part until 27 March 1884, at Madā'in Ṣāliḥ (see Euting 1914: 222–3, 230, 254–8).

92 'Thamudic' is the modern name for a collection of Ancient North Arabian scripts which have not been sufficiently studied to be given distinct names (Macdonald 2000, pp. 32–5). For the Thamudic inscriptions mentioned here, see Huber 1891: 79–82, 84, 87–90. (MCAM)

Letter no. 22

This letter is a brief report by Huber on his second Arabian expedition, sent to an unnamed government minister in Paris – almost certainly the Minister of Public Education who had commissioned his expedition: see the second and penultimate paragraphs, and note 111 below. This version is a copy in copperplate handwriting of Huber's original letter, which was sent from Ǧiddah with Huber's four notebooks and squeezes not to Baghdad, as stated, but by steamer to Marseille (see note 130 below).

Date: 20 June 1884
From: Charles Huber, Ǧiddah
To: the French Consulate, Baghdad [*sic*; for the Minister of Public Education, Paris]

I have the honour to inform you that I arrived in Ǧiddah yesterday evening, having left Mecca the previous day, ʿUnayzah in al-Qaṣīm on 1 June, and Ḥāʾil on 25 May last.[93]

I hasten to submit to you a quick report on the Expedition in Arabia that you have been kind enough to entrust me with, but I beg all your indulgence for the brevity of this account because, apart from the fact that I am unwell, I can only stay here for the time strictly necessary for seeing to my correspondence, otherwise I risk seeing the routes for my return to the interior being cut.

Expeditions on this side of Arabia are much more dangerous than my information had led me to believe and, had it not been for the inscriptions that I had to leave in Ḥāʾil and that I want to bring back to France, I would have abandoned all the effects that I still possess in Naǧd and would have returned to France by now.

All my preparations were completed at the beginning of September 1883 and I left Damascus on the 4th of that month. A week later, in the little oasis of Kāf, I met an escort which the Shammar emir, Muḥammad Ibn Rashīd, whom I had forewarned of my departure two months previously, had sent to fetch me.

On 21 October following I arrived in Ḥāʾil, the Shammar capital, where the emir received me in the most cordial manner and with the greatest honour.

[93] Huber's departure from Ḥāʾil on 25 May 1884 is confirmed by his journal (Huber 1891: 677–8).

Various circumstances, which I shall wait to inform you about later, prevented me from making my trip into the Ḥiǧāz within the schedule that I had fixed for myself. I only left Ḥāʾil to go to that province on 29 January 1884.

On 27 January, I went to Ǧabal Sarrā, where I made another copy of the great Tamoudean [Thamudic] inscription which is there, and I can assure you that this copy no longer contains a single doubtful character.[94] On 6 February, I reached Ǧabal Mismāʾ, which I explored until the 9th of the same month. There I recopied the inscriptions already recorded during my first mission[95] and I discovered some new ones, among which were three Aramaean [Aramaic] ones.[96]

From Ǧabal Mismāʾ I proceeded towards Taymāʾ, exploring en route the country between these two points. In this way I recorded new Thamudic and Aramaic inscriptions in the deserts of al-Rukhum,[97] Qamrah,[98] al-Maḥaǧǧah,[99] Laqaṭ,[100] al-Kabād,[101] etc.

I reached Taymāʾ on 15 February. I had promised myself this time that I would acquire the inscriptions that I had discovered on my first mission, in order to bring them back to France.

---

[94] This is in fact seven short 'Thamudic' inscriptions carved close to each other. Huber first copied them on his 1880 journey (see Translation Part I, pp. 140–3), and copied them three times on this 1883–84 journey with Euting who also copied them twice. See Appendix 1, no. 1 (Huber 1884a: no. 1); Huber 1891: 221–2 nos. 1 and 2, and 626; Euting 1914: 116–17 (Notebook IV, 27–28 January 1884, pp. 44r, 45 r). They have since been photographed and edited by F.V. Winnett (Winnett and Reed 1973: 86–9, 112–13, no. 203 a–f). (MCAM)

[95] These were Huber 1884a, nos. 75–84, of which all but nos. 76 and 79 (a tribal mark) were recopied (see Appendix 1; Huber 1891: 254 no. 1; 253 no. 8; and 265 nos. 59–60, 61b–63). (MCAM)

[96] See Huber 1891: 254, no. 1 (copied three times = *CIS* ii 340); 263, nos. 2 (= *CIS* ii 342) and 3 (= *CIS* ii 343). These were all also copied by Euting and published by him as nab 34, and nab 35 (he read the two texts as one), respectively (1885: 7). (MCAM)

[97] Huber 1891: 275–6, nos. 1–5 = HU 281–286 = Eut 328–332. (MCAM)

[98] Huber 1891: 278, nos. 1–4 = HU 287–290 = Eut 335–339. (MCAM)

[99] Huber 1891: 280–290, nos. 1–55 = HU 291–348 = roughly Eut 341–406 but see Jamme 1974: 122. As Huber himself writes, the shapes shown on p. 290 do not seem to be either letters or *wusūm* (tribal marks). (MCAM)

[100] Huber 1891: 291–305, nos. 1–124 = HU 349–470 = roughly Eut 501–651 but see Jamme 1974: 122. Still within what he calls 'the territory of Laqāṭ' he copied the inscriptions on pp. 307–11 (unnumbered) = HU 471–494 = Eut 651bis–653, 656. (MCAM)

[101] Huber 1891: 308–11 (unnumbered) = HU 472–494 = Eut 652–675. Note that it is not clear in Huber 1891 that these were at al-Kabād, but Euting marked his copies of the same texts as coming from there (Jamme 1974: pl. 31A). (MCAM)

First of all, I acquired from its owner the large Phoenician stele to which I propose to give the name 'Stele of King Shazab',[102] since it was this ruler who had it erected.[103]

This stele is of a very hard limestone and bears 24 lines of inscriptions[104] in relief, each one of 20 to 22 letters. Had it not unfortunately been damaged in its upper third it would be the biggest Phoenician text that we have, including that of the tomb of king Echmunazar [Eshmunazar].[105]

The monument is precious not only from the epigraphic point of view but also from a historical one, for it proves irrefutably what nobody would have dared to suppose up till now, that the Phoenicians did not just trade in Arabia but that they were partly the rulers of it and precisely in the region in which up till now the Nabataeans had been located.[106] The Nabataeans therefore

[102] This is the famous 'Taymāʾ Stele', now in the Musée du Louvre (AO 1505). It is not Phoenician but Imperial Aramaic, probably dating to *ca.* 500 BC, and records the introduction of a new cult into Taymāʾ. It was actually found and paid for by Euting (1914: 156–61), not Huber, and Euting was the first to recognize its script and its importance when he saw it in February 1884. It is clear that Huber did *not* see it on his 1880 journey since he did not publish a copy of it in his 1884a article (see Appendix 1), and he makes absolutely no mention of it until after he and Euting saw it in February 1884. He would not have neglected so large and clearly important an inscription, even though he was unable to read it. Huber persisted in calling it 'Phoenician' even after Euting had realized it was Aramaic (see Introduction, note 181), given him a rough preliminary translation and, at Huber's request, made a copy of it in Huber's diary. While the Middle Phoenician and Imperial Aramaic scripts are in many ways not dissimilar, it was quite clear to Euting that it was Aramaic as soon as he started studying it. Huber was in no way a Semitic epigraphist and so was incapable of telling the difference between the Phoenician and Aramaic scripts. (MCAM)

[103] This is a complete misrepresentation by Huber. The man he calls 'King Shazab' is actually a priest of the new cult called Ṣalmshazab. Moreover, he did not erect the stele; it was put up by the existing priests of the temple. Euting had already explained this to Huber while they were in Taymāʾ (see Appendix 10, Letter no. 4 dated 1 August 1885 from Euting to Philippe Berger), but it seems that Huber thought that a 'Phoenician' stele 'set up' by a previously unknown 'Phoenician king' would be more sensational. (MCAM)

[104] It is of course all one inscription. (MCAM)

[105] Probably a reference to the sarcophagus of Eshmunazar II, king of Sidon in the 5th century BC.

[106] This is of course complete nonsense, based on Huber's obsession with the script of the stele being Phoenician despite being told by Euting that it was Aramaic. It is possible that he felt that evidence for a 'Phoenician presence' in Arabia would be far more sensational than simply another Aramaic inscription. One wonders if this is what he meant when in Letter no. 8 above, dated 28 August 1881, he refers to 'these inscriptions whose importance I recognize today and which I know how to turn to considerable advantage.' But this is speculation. (MCAM)

surely only made their appearance in the north-west of Arabia after the 5th or 6th century before our era[107] (dates between which is placed the Stele of King Shazab), or they must have had much less importance than that which has been attributed to them up until now.

From the linguistic or ethnographic point of view, just as from the geographical one, this monument raises many interesting topics which I shall address later.

I also acquired two Nabataean inscriptions and two Aramaean [Aramaic] ones,[108] but these are smaller and less important than the Stele, as well as a beautifully carved bas relief representing, I think, a priest sacrificing in front of an altar.[109]

Apart from one of the Nabataean inscriptions,[110] all the inscriptions from Taymā᾽ have this characteristic, that they are in bas relief and carved with great care.

I have packed all these stones and transported them from Taymā᾽ to Ḥā᾽il, and my intention was to bring them with me to Ǧiddah and send them on to Paris, but to my great regret this has not been possible because of the current situation in the interior of Arabia and my lack of adequate resources.

This last reason will explain to you also why once again I have not been able to fulfil my intention of carrying out some archaeological excavations at Taymā᾽.

I therefore left these epigraphic monuments in my house at Ḥā᾽il, from where I shall take them with me later when I leave Arabia, but I have made squeezes which I have the honour to send from here to your Ministry[111] at the same time as this letter.

---

107 It is not known where the Nabataeans originated, but they are first heard of in southern Jordan at the end of the 4th century BC. Their kingdom gradually expanded into southern Syria but they did not conquer north-west Arabia until the 1st century BC. (MCAM)

108 The Nabataean inscriptions are Huber 1891: 322 no. 3 (= *CIS* ii 336) and 323 no. 5 (= *CIS* ii 337). The Aramaic are p. 320, no. 2 (= *CIS* ii 114) and p. 323, no. 4 (= *CIS* ii 115). (MCAM)

109 This is Musée du Louvre AO 29143, see Potts 1991 which has a photograph. Euting published his drawing of it in 1885, pp. 11–12, and (posthumously) 1914, p. 155. (MCAM)

110 This is Euting 1885, p. 12, nab. 12 = *CIS* ii 337 which is incised. Huber's copy is on 1891, p. 323, no. 5. (MCAM)

111 Huber means the Ministry of Public Education in Paris, rather than the Ministry of Foreign Affairs which was responsible for the consulate in Baghdad.

On 21 February, I left Taymāʾ to go to Tabūk, one of the stopping places on the Darb al-Ḥaǧǧ [the pilgrim route from Damascus to Mecca], which I reached on the 27th. On 6 March I was back ạt Taymāʾ.

This trip only provided geographical information. I discovered the existence of two ancient cities, one to the west and the other to the north of Tabūk, but I no longer had the means to get there.[112]

However I found more Kufic, Aramaean [Aramaic] and Tamoudean [Thamudic] inscriptions, close to Tabūk on the rock called al-ʿArayq;[113] in the narrow pass of Ḥaṣāt al-Qanīṣ in Ǧabal Farwah;[114] near the little ruined Qasr of Hilāl Surayḥān;[115] and finally at Ghār al-Ḥamām near Teimâ.[116]

On 13 March, I left Taymāʾ for the last time to go to al-Ḥiǧr, the ancient Madāʾin Ṣāliḥ of the Qurʾān,[117] a stopping place on the Ḥaǧǧ pilgrimage, and

[112] This statement appears to be exaggeration – if not invention – by Huber and is not supported by his *Journal* or by Euting's *Tagbuch*. What they *did* find, some three or four hours *south* of Tabūk, was an apparently ancient graveyard on the plateau of Ruǧm Shohar consisting of large numbers of small, low buildings with stone slabs for roofs. Huber and Euting are both quite clear that these are 'family tombs' (Huber 1891: 344, 353–4; Euting 1914: 179, 185–6), not a city. The only other possible site to which he might be referring is 'the small hill to the *east* of Tabūq [MCAM's italics]' which he was told was the site of the ancient town. However, on visiting it he found the remains to be 'too insignificant to have been ancient Tabūk, though in view of the shards of glass and pottery, I would be willing to believe that there must have been one or more dwellings there from earlier times' (1891: 349–50). (MCAM)

[113] Of these he copied only two Thamudic (1891: 347 = HU 496–497). (MCAM)

[114] Huber 1891: 365–366 = HU 498 (= Eut 686) and 499+500 (= Eut 687). (MCAM)

[115] Huber 1891: 368–369 = HU 501 = Eut 689–690 (which Huber took away and which is now in the Musée du Louvre, AO 5010), HU 501a, and some others which he took to be Aramaic but which are more likely to be simple geometrical shapes. (MCAM)

[116] Huber 1891: 372–376, 378 = Eut 692–718 including the famous mirror-written Arabic text in relief (see Al-Moraekhi 2002: 123–5, 131 Fig. 1). (MCAM)

[117] This is, of course, the wrong way round. The ancient name is Aramaic Ḥegrā, Arabic al-Ḥiǧr, and the mediaeval and modern name is Madāʾin Ṣāliḥ, though the name al-Ḥiǧr has also remained in use. It was a magnificent Nabataean city, and like Petra has huge tombs carved out of the rock. Although, *contra* Huber, the name Madāʾin Ṣāliḥ 'The cities of [the Prophet] Ṣāliḥ', is not found in the Qurʾān, it derives from the site's association in the minds of Muslims with two peoples who 'used to hew out dwellings from the mountain' (Qurʾān 7: 74, 15: 82), i.e. assuming the tombs of al-Ḥiǧr to have been houses. Both of these peoples had rejected earlier prophets and had been punished. It is tempting to believe that these are, in fact, references to the same people (i.e. the Thamūd living in al-Ḥiǧr) but this is never made clear in the Qurʾān. One of these peoples is called 'the men of al-Ḥiǧr' (15: 80–84) who 'were destroyed by a Shout' (15: 83). The other was the tribe of Thamūd (a well-known ancient people in north-west Arabia). Their story is alluded to several times in the Quʾrān. Like 'the men of al-Ḥiǧr', they 'hewed the mountains into houses' (7:

to al-ʿUlā. On the way I discovered another thirty or so inscriptions in the desert of Umm Ruqaybah.[118]

At al-Ḥiǧr I made squeezes or copied sixty-nine Aramaean inscriptions and one Phoenician,[119] either above the doors of the mortuary chambers or on the rocks all around.

Although my trips to al-Ḥiǧr were full of difficulties and dangers, the details of which I cannot go into here, I think nevertheless that I can affirm that I copied everything and that I have unveiled the mystery of the ancient Aramaean city.[120]

In the same way as at Taymāʾ, I regretted not being able to dig in the little mounds that cover the more than twenty-centuries-old ruins of ancient Egra [the Greek form of Ḥegrā = al-Ḥiǧr]. Nevertheless I am bringing back from there a marble slab with sculpted decorations in relief,[121] which will demonstrate the level of civilization that it had attained.

I also found four Greek inscriptions at al-Ḥiǧr, the first ones to be noted, I think, in Arabia.[122]

On 27 March I left al-Ḥiǧr to return to Ḥāʾil, making a few detours to revisit several places where I had been told there were inscriptions. Thus I

---

74) and so became associated with al-Ḥiǧr. Allāh sent them a prophet, Ṣāliḥ, who brought them a miraculous she-camel and calf. But they hamstrung the camel and rejected Ṣāliḥ's message and so Allāh destroyed them by an earthquake (7: 78), or by a thunderbolt (51: 44) or by 'a Shout' (54: 31). From the combination of all these elements the ruined city of al-Ḥiǧr came to be known as 'the cities of Ṣāliḥ', Madāʾin Ṣāliḥ. (MCAM)

[118] See Huber 1891: 389–92 (and 393 for the provenance) = HU 523–551 = Eut 719–754+753b. (MCAM)

[119] Again, this is wrong. There are no Phoenician inscriptions at al-Ḥiǧr. Huber was not a Semitist or an epigraphist and could not distinguish between the Imperial Aramaic and Phoenician scripts. But see notes 102, 103 and 106 above for his possible motivation in insisting on having found 'Phoenician' inscriptions. (MCAM)

[120] Madāʾin Ṣāliḥ was, of course, in no way an 'Aramaean city'. Its inhabitants were not ethnically 'Aramaean' and, being Nabataean, almost certainly the vast majority spoke Arabic, only using Aramaic as their *written* language. It should also be said that Doughty had been the first Westerner to see Madāʾin Ṣāliḥ and record inscriptions there, and his squeezes (Doughty 1884) and Euting's (1885) were the first records of the inscriptions to be published, though Huber would certainly have tried to have his squeezes published at the same time had he not been murdered. (MCAM)

[121] This is probably the relief mentioned earlier (note 109 above), though the stone is not marble but sandstone. (MCAM)

[122] These were at the large rock north of Madāʾin Ṣāliḥ known as Makhzan al-ǧindī (see Huber 1891: 407, 409 and the text which is in fact Latin on p. 408). This makes only three not four, and it is possible that he counted one of them as two texts. (MCAM)

arrived the following day at the Khubbat al-Thumāthīl pass 20 kilometres to the north of the stopping-place of Dār al-Ḥamrā᾽ on the Darb al-Haǧǧ, where I found Aramaean, Kufic and Thamoudean inscriptions.[123]

On 30 March I was at al-Mukattabah, where I copied about sixty Thamoudean inscriptions.[124]

I discovered some more on 31 March at Abraq al-Sbāʿ;[125] on 1 April in the Ǧabal Abū Mughayr;[126] on 2 April in the Ǧabal ʿArnān/ʿIrnān.[127]

On 3 April, I crossed Ǧabal Mismā᾽ once again, and on 7 April I was back at Ḥā᾽il.

From 28 April to 5 May, I made a trip to the south-south-east of Ḥā᾽il to reconnoitre the region between there and the Wādī al-Rimah.[128]

It was only on the 25th of May last that I was able to leave Ḥā᾽il to go to Ǧiddah, from where I have the honour to send you at the same time as this letter the squeezes I have made up to now.

I enclose with this letter a note containing the classification of the inscriptions apart from the Thamoudean ones, of which I have so far made copies or squeezes.[129] The numbers of the items in this note correspond to those on the squeezes.

As I am short of time to copy from my diary the inscriptions that I was unable to take squeezes of and that I was only able to copy, I enclose in the crate containing the squeezes the first four notebooks of my Journal de Voyage [Travel Diary],[130] so that, if need be, the gentlemen of the Academy des Inscriptions et Belles-Lettres can consult it. But until then, Monsieur le

---

[123] See Huber 1891: 459–466 = HU 593–615, as well as (p. 463) an Arabic and a Nabataean (Huber's 'Aramaean') inscription (= *CIS* ii 331). By this time he and Euting had already parted company. (MCAM)

[124] See Huber 1891: 472–483 = HU 616–671. (MCAM)

[125] See Huber 1891: 490–491 = HU 672–679, plus a supposed Aramaic inscription no. 99 = *CIS* ii 330. (MCAM)

[126] See Huber 1891: 496–505 = HU 680–717, plus Nabataean texts which he numbered 100–105 = respectively *CIS* ii 327, 326, 325, 324, 329, 328. (MCAM)

[127] See Huber 1891: 513–522 = HU 719–768. (MCAM)

[128] This was Huber's round trip from Ḥā᾽il to al-Ṣulayliyyah, 28 April–5 May 1884 (Huber 1891: 594–632).

[129] This is very probably the same list as that recorded in Huber 1891: 651–9. He did not make squeezes of the Thamudic graffiti. (MCAM/WF)

[130] In his diary entry dated 22–27 June 1884 (Huber 1891: 753), Huber states that he sent this crate containing his squeezes and four notebooks by Dutch steamer from Ǧiddah to Marseille, not to Baghdad.

Ministre,[131] please would you kindly have these four notebooks deposited with Monsieur C. Maunoir, Secrétaire général de la Société de Géographie in Paris, until my return.

I cannot tell you exactly where I shall be travelling on leaving here. I am going to al-Ṭāʾif from where, if I can make arrangements with the Qaḥṭān Arabs [Bedouin] to provide safe guides, I shall make my way to al-Riyāḍ. If not, I shall return to Ḥāʾil from where I shall once more make an attempt to get to al-Riyāḍ or at least to Sadūs.[132] After this I shall return home to Europe via Baghdad. I can be in Baghdad in January or February 1885.

[Unsigned][133]

LETTER NO. 23

Date: 3 July 1884
From: Charles Huber, Ǧiddah
To: Charles Maunoir, Secrétaire générale de la Société de Géographie, Paris

Sir,

I have the honour to confirm my letter of 20 June last.

As M. de Lostalot,[134] our French Consul here, is returning to France on furlough, I am taking advantage of his kindness to send you the fifth notebook of my Travel Diary which goes up to my arrival in Ǧiddah, and which was not yet up to date when the first four notebooks were sent off.

I enclose with this notebook two smaller ones containing rough notes and I would ask you to kindly keep them for me too, because if I later come across a transcription error, these rough notes will provide a check. My other rough notes are in Ḥāʾil.

[131] Huber does not specify which minister he was addressing, though it must have been the Minister of Public Education.

[132] Sadūs: in the Maḥmal district 60 km north-west of Riyadh, where there was a famous ancient column, since destroyed. See Winder 1865: facing p. 59, for an engraving of it as it was in 1865.

[133] This document is in a fine copperplate script and not in Huber's hand, and so must have been done by a ministry copyist in Paris.

[134] Jacques Félix de Lostalot-Bachoué, the French vice-consul in Ǧiddah who, after Huber's death, would be instrumental together with Sī ʿAzīz b. al-Shaykh al-Ḥaddād in recovering from Ḥāʾil the Taymāʾ Stele and other inscriptions acquired by Euting and Huber, and ensuring their transit to Paris. He left Ǧiddah on 5 July 1884 for almost four months' leave in France.

I feel a lively sense of annoyance at the moment as I am about to set off again from here. M. de Lostalot has been notified by an Algerian shaykh in exile in Mecca, a pensioner and on the best of terms with the authorities of the holy city, that the governor of the Ḥiǧāz, who is at the moment staying on vacation in al-Ṭāʾif with the Grand Sharif, had just sent the order to the governor of Ǧiddah to have me watched and, should I wish to return to the interior, to prevent me by force. The shaykh Sī ʿAzīz came here himself to communicate this information.[135]

As a result, through circumstances which would take too long to explain to you, the route to the east, i.e. through the territories of the ʿUtaybah, is completely closed to me. As I absolutely have to go back to Ḥāʾil there is only the northern route left across the territory of the Ḥarb Arabs.[136] This will involve long negotiations which will cause me to waste precious time and, unfortunately, money, because, by the report of the *rafīq* [guide], the Ḥarb are the most demanding Arabs in the whole of Arabia. I am not downhearted, however, and I hope that the good luck that has been on my side up till now will continue to follow me.

I cannot praise M. de Lostalot highly enough. He received me here like a brother and set everything in motion to help and promote my expedition. I am infinitely grateful to him.

You will come across a blank page in my travel diary from time to time. These are for sketch maps which I have not had time to trace and which I shall draw later.

Apart from my diary, I beg the Société de Géographie, should some misfortune befall me, to look for the notebook which contains the lists of the Arab tribes with their numerous subdivisions. This, after my diary, is the most valuable item in my luggage. I have not been able to enclose it with my diary because I need it by me all the time to make corrections and additions to it.

I would be very grateful if you would honour me with your news, if only a few lines.

---

135 Sī ʿAzīz b. al-Shaykh al-Ḥaddād was a worldly Berber refugee resident of Mecca and a pensioner of the French government. He had taken part in revolts in Algeria during the Franco-Prussian war; after their suppression he had led a varied life and was finally settled by the French government in Mecca, with a monthly stipend of 400 francs. See Introduction pp. 73–6.

136 The Ḥarb tribe controlled the desert between Mecca and Medina and were much-feared predators on the pilgrim caravans. Huber was not to know it, but his murderers on 29 July, just over three weeks after this letter, would be members of the tribe.

Assuring you of my highest and most respectful consideration,

Charles Huber
[Contactable] at the French Consulate, Baghdad

Letter no. 24

Date: 6 July 1884
From: Charles Huber, Ǧiddah
To: Dr Weisgerber (not named but addressed as 'Weis' at the end)

My dear friend,

I hope that you received my little note of the 1st.

I am going to quickly go through your three letters, then I will talk to you a little about me. In the first letter (of 17th September [lit. 7bre)] you said that you went to the *Temps*[137] about my article and that objections were raised about its insertion. You don't mention it again.

The letter of the 3rd of October [lit. 8bre] was almost entirely devoted to Euting – so you will be happy to hear that Euting succeeded in reaching the town of Ḥā'il but that once there I was able, with the help of the emir, to make him go off towards [*le faire filer par*] the west. He must have taken ship in al-Wağh on the Red Sea. I knew he was intending to call in at Ǧiddah, to which he had his mail forwarded, but on my arrival here I found that he had not shown up. I was unable to prevent him reaching Ḥā'il, any more than I could have prevented anyone else![138] Please could you pass this on to those entitled to know. But, once he had arrived, I could do no more than send him onwards, and that was not easily accomplished, as he was not commissioned by France and had very different means at his disposal from mine – even in the matter of guns, he brought twenty-seven to Ibn Rashīd.[139]

---

[137] *Le Temps* was a major Paris daily newspaper. It was founded in 1861 and ran until 30 November 1942 when it closed following the German invasion. On 19 December 1944, at the request of Charles de Gaulle, *le Monde* was founded to replace it. (MCAM)

[138] Huber is not telling the truth here to his friend Weisgerber. So far from making Euting leave Ḥā'il on his own, the two men travelled together westwards to Taymā', Madā'in Ṣāliḥ and al-ʿUlā, not separating till 27 March 1884, when Euting went back to al-ʿUlā and then al-Wağh while Huber returned to Ḥā'il (see Euting 1914: 222–3, 230, 254–8). See Introduction pp. 42–3, 50–1.

[139] Here Huber does acknowledge Euting's contribution of firearms. Compare note 86 above.

– At last he is far away, may the devil break his neck for the annoyances he has caused me.

I found a letter here from the Ministry dated 21 November 1883, informing me that the four guns[140] and the 4,000 cartridges had been agreed. It is a bit late but it will still be a help to me.

It is Dr Landberg, a Swede, that M. Maunoir wants to speak about.[141] Don't worry. I know this bird from having heard him being talked about at the consulate-general in Beirut.

Your last letter, of 21 April 1884, is in reply to mine of 30 November 1883 and tells me of your trip round the Mediterranean – which gave me much pleasure.

I was supposed to find six crates here but there were only five; the missing crate is the one that Schmidt sent to Beirut and it will arrive after my departure. I had left instructions with M. Palais, the director of the '*station*' [most probably the post office] in Damascus, to have it sent off again as soon as it arrived in Ǧiddah, so either he did not take any notice of my recommendations or the parcel did not reach him. Unfortunately I do not have time to look into the matter.

A month ago, my sister wrote to me that a letter had arrived from Paris with a bill for 200 francs for medicines, and that she had replied that it would have to await my return. I hope that Schmidt will not have taken offence at this stupid way of dealing with people. I straight away sent him a bill of exchange for 200 francs drawn on my mother; but as it is probable that what she owes is more than this, I would be very much obliged if you could let her have the amount. Repeat again to Schmidt how grateful I am to him for the care he has taken over my expeditions. You are not forgotten. I hold you in my heart.

You tell me that according to M. Maunoir 'it is more than probable that they will continue to support my mission but that it will be necessary to give signs of life to the ministry by sending a provisional report and by requesting a new grant.'

I have just done that, without asking for money. What can I do? It is beyond me. I cannot bring myself to beg in this way. So I have preferred, despite the fact that my meagre resources are running out, to draw 7,000 francs on my mother's credit. The French consul very kindly formally

---

[140] i.e the Gras rifles. See Letters 14, 15, 17, 20 and note 87 above.

[141] Landberg: see note 61 above.

opposed this, claiming to have the power to give me funds in the name of the ministry. But I held out and now the deal is done. I think that this money will allow me to make my trip to Sadūs[142] and to reach Baghdad.

If I reach that place with no more money in my pocket, then you will start a fund-raising drive in Alsace to repatriate me. I am certain that it will succeed.

The excavations to be carried out in Taymāʾ and al-Ḥiǧr/Madāʾin Ṣāliḥ are in the same situation. But I have talked about this twice at length with M. Charmes and submitted a special report to him eighteen months ago; what has happened to it? I have hardly received more than a few pence for my expedition and even then under what conditions! No, I have had enough – I am bringing back the Phoenician stele of King Shazab[143] for them, to prove that I have not made anything up. If this does not speak loudly enough, how else do you want me to act? I know that it will break my heart when the English get there, but what more can I do? If I were wealthy, my love for Arabia and science is such that I would carry out the digs at my own expense, but I am not.

Since I have been in Naǧd, I have made four trips from Ḥāʾil:

1) to Ǧabal Ǧildiyyah[144]
2) to Taymāʾ, Tabūk, al-Ḥiǧr and al-ʿUlā[145]
3) to al-Ṣulayliyyah to the SSE of Ḥāʾil [146]
4) to al-Qaṣīm, Mecca and Ǧiddah[147]

From Taymāʾ I am bringing back two Nabataean and three Aramaic inscriptions,[148] as well as the great Phoenician stele of King Shazab. Unfortunately the top third of the latter is slightly damaged, but were this not so, it would represent the most significant (Phoenician) text that we know today, including the tomb of king Echmunazar in the Louvre. I must

---

[142] See note 132 above.

[143] Actually the 'Taymāʾ Stele' which is in Aramaic not Phoenician and makes no reference to a 'King Shazab', see notes 102 and 103 above. For the text and references, see most recently Stein (in press); Macdonald and Al-Najem forthcoming, Appendix. (MCAM)

[144] See note 166 below.

[145] See Huber: 1891: 341–69.

[146] See note 128 above.

[147] See Huber: 1891: 677–753.

[148] In Letter 22, he says two Nabataean and two Aramaic, see note 108 above. (MCAM)

mention the enormous difficulty we had in transporting this very large stone from Taymāʾ to Ḥāʾil, and then the difficulty we face in transporting it on camelback to Baghdad. But I will not be deterred by the effort and hardships, as I am only too delighted to be handing over this beautiful stone to France.[149]

Tabūk has given us nothing. From al-Ḥiǧr I am bringing back squeezes of the famous Aramaic[150] inscriptions which are installed above the monumental doorways of the mortuary chambers. From al-ʿUlā I am bringing back about forty long Thamoudean [Thamudic] inscriptions.[151] This is only an estimate of the numbers of the latter from memory because at the present time I have several hundred of them.[152]

All the squeezes were sent off a few days ago in a crate addressed to the Ministry together with a report.[153] I have also sent a short report to M. Renan. You remember that he had the Académie des Inscriptions et Belles-Lettres award me 5,000 francs.[154] I would add that the inscriptions from Taymāʾ are to be found packed up in my house at Ḥāʾil.

To these squeezes I have added the first four notebooks of my travel diary and a request to hand them to M. Maunoir to keep them until my return. M. de Lostalot, our French consul here, who left yesterday on furlough for four months,[155] has taken with him the fifth notebook of my diary which goes up to my arrival here. He will be in Paris around 5 August and he will give it to M. Maunoir with a letter from me. I have also given him a letter for M. Renan whom he will also see. In addition, he will communicate with these two people privately on his own account about me.

[149] In this he succeeded posthumously. After Huber's murder on 29 July 1884, it was collected from Ḥāʾil by the French consul Félix de Lostalot with the help of Sī Azīz b. al-Shaykh al-Ḥaddād and taken to France where it is in the Musée du Louvre, registration no. AO 1505. See Introduction pp. 72–7 (MCAM)

[150] Aramaic: specifically Nabataean Aramaic. (MCAM)

[151] Here he is confusing Dadanitic (formerly called 'Lihyanite') and Thamudic inscriptions. The monumental inscriptions of which he made squeezes and copies are Dadanitic (Huber 1891: 393–8, nos. 1–4, 6–14), many of which had already been recorded by Doughty in 1878, though Huber could not know this at the time of writing since they were not published until later that year. The short graffiti are Thamudic. (MCAM)

[152] These were from many different places. (MCAM)

[153] This is the report represented by Letter no. 22 above.

[154] These 5,000 francs from the AIBL plus the 10,000 francs from the Ministry of Public Education made up the total of public support that Huber received for his 1883–84 journey.

[155] De Lostalot thus left for his four months' leave on 5 July 1884.

I have been forced to take this decision about my diary because, although I kept quiet about it, during my last trip here across the territory of the ʿUtaybah Arabs I risked my life ten times a day.[156] At least in this way if my water is cut off all will not be lost.

On the other hand, I was not so unhappy about showing M. Maunoir how my diary was kept and about him seeing that it is of some value.

While making my way here I had an adventure that I shall tell you about in detail another time. I was making a detour to avoid Mecca when I was picked up 40 kilometres to the north by thirteen individuals from a kind of urban guard and led forcibly into the holy city, where I arrived at midnight. I shouted so loudly in the morning that those who had arrested me were forced to give up forthwith, and I was showered with excuses and watermelons and other melons too; and, as I refused to walk any further that day, I was escorted on the following day all the way to Ǧiddah by a guard of honour of two Sharifs who were descendants of the Prophet, and two soldiers of the guard of the Grand Sharif.[157]

If I had found even a single word of encouragement here from the minister or M. Maunoir I would have gone on to al-Riyāḍ, but risking my life for nothing, not even a good word, means I shall leave the glory to others.

My next plans are:

1) to return from here to Ḥāʾil, which is not easy.
2) from Ḥāʾil to make a trip round the Nafūd.
3) from Ḥāʾil to Sadūs, four days' journey to the NE of al-Riyāḍ, where there are standing columns with inscriptions.[158]
4) from Ḥāʾil to Baghdad, veering to the east.

If all goes smoothly I shall be in Baghdad in February/ March and in Paris in April/May.[159]

---

[156] During these years the powerful ʿUtaybah tribe of western and central Naǧd was aligned with Āl Saʿūd and at enmity with Huber's friend and protector, the emir of Ḥāʾil, Muḥammad al-Rashīd (Winder 1865: 267–9) – hence Huber's fears for his safety while travelling through their territory.

[157] This was 17–18 June 1884. See Huber 1891: 747–9. (MCAM)

[158] See note 132 above.

[159] This, of course, was not to be since Huber was murdered on 29 July 1884 on his way from Ǧiddah to Ḥāʾil.

Thank you for everything you have done for me up till now. Don't bother Maunoir now. I have taken money from my own account. It is no longer necessary to beg.

I am setting off tonight on a hazardous trip and shall be back in ten days' time, so before my final departure I shall send you a few more lines to tell you what I have just been doing.

See you soon, dear friend Weis, salem [*salām*] and a warm handshake,

Charles Huber

Letter no. 25

Copy of a letter from Charles Huber, traveller in Arabia, to Dr Weisgerber: extracts in another's handwriting.[160]

Date: 30 November 1883
From: Charles Huber, Ḥāʾil, Ǧabal Shammar (Central Arabia)

First of all and so that I do not forget, go as soon as you can to the Société de Géographie and ask them to hand over my manuscript.[161] You will read it from the place where I approach the Nafūd, and everywhere where you find the word 'foulg' [fulǧ < *fulq*] you will erase it and replace it with the word 'q'ar' [*qaʿr*], and on the first page where you find it you will put a footnote such as the one below:

Note 1. Q'ar is what Lady Anne Blunt refers to in error under the name of Foulg.

On the map the word 'foulg' also appears twice.[162]

I hope that you have received my last letter from Damascus informing

[160] This letter is preserved in this position rather than in the proper chronological sequence of letters probably because it is not in Huber's own hand. It is only a partial copy, perhaps because the original was damaged. (MG)

[161] This must refer to the manuscript of Huber's account of his 1880 journey in Arabia, translated in this volume. It would appear posthumously in the *Bulletin de la Société de Géographie* in 1884 and 1885 (Huber 1884a, 1884b and 1885a).

[162] This is a confusion on Huber's part. Fulǧ is the local pronunciation of the Arabic word *fulq* which is the horseshoe-shaped depression in the sand dunes of the Nafūd desert. *Qaʿr* is the bottom of such a depression. Huber's request for these changes were ignored and fouldj [*fulǧ*] remains in his report, which was published posthumously (1884b: e.g. 327–8) and on the map published with it, though misspelt as *foûlgj* near Al-Beïdhâ, but *Foulg* in the 'Traduction de quelques termes géographiques'. (MCAM)

you that the Emir Muḥammad ibn Rashīd, sultan of the Shammar, had sent me an escort to take me to Damascus. So I crossed the Ḥamād desert, Wādī al-Sirḥān and the Nafūd without incident. We only had three or four cold nights and no days hotter than 36°. So I had a pleasant journey.[163]

We arrived here on 21 October last and I was received exceptionally warmly by the emir, who had reserved one of the largest and most beautiful houses in the capital for me. Moreover he assured me that he would do all he could to favour my scientific trips and if possible even as far as the lands of the famous Ibn Saʿūd, the current chief of the Wahhābī empire. In this regard I am therefore not worried. All is going to plan.

A few days after my arrival, the emir left for a razzia [*ghazū*, raid] to the south on the Ḥarb Arabs at Muṭayr.[164]

He remained absent for twenty-four days and returned as usual with considerable booty (a hundred camels and 1,500 sheep), and nobody had been injured. The raided tribes had about twenty people killed.[165]

While the emir was on his raid I made a trip of four days into the Ǧabal Aǧā and a second one of eight days to Ǧabal Ǧildiyyah.[166] From this second trip I brought back some interesting information from a geographical point of view and a fine harvest of new Thamoudean [Thamudic] inscriptions.

On arriving back a few days ago from this last trip I unfortunately caught a raging high fever which still has me in its grip although it is fading. I think it will be over in three or four days.[167] It is the first time I have been ill on my travels.

---

[163] Although Huber does not say so, this and the rest of his journey until 19 March 1884 was made with Euting. (MCAM)

[164] Ḥarb Arabs at Muṭayr: The copyist should have written 'Ḥarb Arabs *and* Muṭayr'. The raid was in fact against the Muṭayr tribe alone, according to Euting's report of it (Euting 1914: 6–7).

[165] This is not the same raid as the one described in Letter no. 19 which took place in the summer of 1883. This one took place from 28 October to 19 November 1883, and Huber gives a very full, day-by-day account of it as recounted by one of the participants and later by the emir (Huber 1891: 106–9; see also Euting 1914: 6–7).

[166] These journeys were from 31 October to 3 November and from 9 to 16 November 1883 respectively (1891: 68–103). The inscriptions he mentions are on pp. 80–82, 84, 87–90, 95–99, 101–102, and are HU 83–186. Although Huber never mentions it, Euting was with him on these journeys (Euting 1896: 216–240) and also copied these inscriptions which are Eut 99–224. (MCAM)

[167] This does not seem to be mentioned in his published diary. Indeed, he describes his many activities during these days (1891: 103–10). (MCAM)

So much for the past. For the future I shall set off in five or six days from here to circumnavigate the Aǧā mountains, and shall capture it completely in a network of triangles, after which the last word will have been said, I hope, for those who make this range run from NE to SW on their maps instead of from N to S as it does on my map. This trip will take me a month.

As soon as I get back to Ḥāʾil I shall make preparations for my journey to the west in the Ḥiǧāz. I shall probably go as far as Tabūk, and from there head to Taymāʾ, to Madāʾin Ṣāliḥ where I shall make squeezes of the inscriptions discovered on my first expedition,[168] and then to al-ʿUlā, Khaybar, and from there go past al-Madīnah to Ǧiddah. From this trip I shall bring back, apart from the squeezes of the inscriptions that I know of, new ones from Tabūk and stones covered in inscriptions that I shall take from Taymāʾ. In this last locality, for about 100 francs I shall carry out some excavations. If I am lucky I shall find some fine things, because all the ancient Thema of the Bible is there, covered by two or three metres of sand and all built of dressed stonework.

When I reach Ǧiddah I shall send what I have with me to the Ministry, then I shall go back to Ḥāʾil where the greater part of my luggage remains.

I shall make a few more trips to the south and east, and then come home to Europe via Baghdad, unless I stupidly take another few thousand francs out of my own pocket and go instead via al-Riyāḍ, the Wādī al-Dawāsir and Najrān, from which may God preserve me because risking one's money and one's head is not sensible.

What will perhaps keep me here next summer is the following fact: the emir has told me three times already that in his last campaign against Ibn Saʿūd, once summer was over, he made camp for a few days near a little town in Ǧabal Ṭuwayq called Sadūs, outside which he had seen, he and all his men, an upright column of marble 4 to 5 metres high completely covered in inscriptions.[169] Many of his men have confirmed this to me. If I do not return to Europe by the south-west, I want at least to get to this famous column.

However that may be, and despite the fact that I have only had from the Ministry a quarter of what I thought I would receive,[170] I am still sure that my

[168] The Madāʾin Ṣāliḥ inscriptions were not of course first discovered by Huber but by Doughty in 1878. It is also noteworthy that in this paragraph Huber makes no mention of the Taymāʾ Stele. (MCAM)

[169] See note 132 above.

[170] Huber had originally requested 35,000 francs from the ministry: see Appendix 3, Letter no. 19 dated May 1882 to Xavier Charmes.

mission will be a fine achievement, and I dare to hope that people will not be too unhappy on my return.

You will also tell me if they have decided at the Société de Géographie to publish my article on my first journey, but do not insist on it with anyone, because once again I am not satisfied with this work. If you see M. Hansen and the work on the map allows it, ask him to erase Qenâ [Qanāʾ] or Qenah to the north of Ḥāʾil and to place it two kilometres to the west of Umm el Goulbân [Umm al-Qulbān].[171] I was wrongly informed about it the first time.

* The emir has asked me for the vaccine as soon as possible. He saw 1,000 souls carried off by smallpox in the capital last year.

[171] On the map published in Huber 1884b and included as a fold-out at the end of this volume, 'Qenâ' is actually placed *ca.* 20 km south-south-west of 'Umm el-Qouilbân'. (MCAM)

APPENDIX 5

Letters from Huber to the Emir Muḥammad Ibn Rashīd and others in Arabia, April 1883

THESE ARE held among the Huber papers in the Archives du Cabinet of the *Corpus Inscriptionum Semiticarum* (CIS), Académie des Inscriptions et Belles-Lettres (AIBL), Institut de France, Paris. Correspondence with Charles Maunoir and Dr Weisgerber, classified under Ref. Armoire A, Boîte Correspondance H–K.

The French originals, in Huber's handwriting, are accompanied by draft translations in Arabic. Thanks go to Prof. Maria Gorea for making them available, and to Barbara Newton for help with translation.

It is not known whether the four letters to Ḥā'il and Ǧabal Druze reached their destinations, but they are none the less valuable as they shed light on Huber's plans for his second Arabian journey in 1883–84. Huber implies that these Arabic versions (see Letter no. 4, paragraph 3) were written by Julius Euting, though the handwriting does not closely match Euting's more fluent and stylish Arabic hand in his Notebooks. If true, however, it would show how closely the two men were collaborating in preparing for their journey before setting out for the Near East. Another interesting aspect of the letters is that Huber not only acknowledges his collaboration with Euting and his intention to travel with him into Arabia, but presents it in an entirely positive light.

Letter no. 1

Date: 10 April 1883 (given at end of letter)
From: Charles Huber, Paris
To: Ḥamūd al-Ibrāhīm ibn Ǧawād.[1]

From Charles Huber ibn Ǧirǧīz [Georges; full name given in Arabic script] to the most respected, honoured and beloved emir Ḥamūd al-Ibrāhīm ibn Ǧawād [name in Arabic script]. May the greeting and the benediction of God be upon you. May you always be well protected.

My Shammarī brother, the subject of this letter is to send you my greetings and to ask for news of you. May nothing unpleasant befall you, nor any misfortune, and may God keep you always under His protection, for He alone is powerful.

If you are kind enough to ask how I am, I thank the living God that I am well.

After which: I have not had any further news from you for a very long time since the month of Shaʿbān 1298 [= July 1881], and unfortunately it is only recently that I learned that you have not received the letters that I wrote to you and that are still in Damascus, because nobody could be found to take them to the Ǧabal [*viz.* Ḥāʾil, Ǧabal Shammar]. Faced with my silence, you may perhaps have thought that I had forgotten you, but God the All-knowing is my witness that I have not ceased for a single day to think of you, of the emir [*viz.* Muḥammad Ibn Rashīd], of Ḥamūd al-ʿUbayd, and all the friends that I know amongst you. I also know your heart well enough to be sure that you will not have doubted me and that you did not think that I had forgotten you.

But I had already written to you previously, from Iraq, that after my journey I would have a lot of work to do. This has proven to be true and, furthermore, I suffered many annoyances[2] – wicked men having tried to harm me – which caused me great unhappiness. God alone is just and our

---

[1] This is Huber's Shammarī friend and guide, Ḥamūd al-Ibrāhīm al-Miqrād, who played an important role in Huber's Arabian explorations, as he had helped Huber in 1880 (Huber 1884b: 354; see Introduction p. 40; and Translation Part I, note 144), and would be assigned by the emir to assist Huber and Euting on their 1883–84 journey through northern Arabia. See e.g. Euting 1896: 60–1, 64, 66. See also Letter no. 2 below, 4th paragraph; Letter no. 3 below, penultimate paragraph.

[2] No doubt a reference to Huber's troubles at the hands of the German authorities in Alsace, and to various other allegations about him (see Introduction pp. 11–12).

great consolation. My conscience also is clear because I do not know evil. I talk to you as my brother because you know me and you love me.

Next, I shall inform you that one month after sending off this letter I shall be leaving for Cairo, where I shall stay half a month, to speak with the Khedive. Then I shall go to Damascus and, having visited Baʿalbak, Tadmur and other ruined towns, I shall set off, God willing, for the Ǧabal, and therefore I shall soon once again have the happiness of seeing you. So I shall be in Damascus at the end of May. I am bringing you all the things that you asked me for when I left Ḥāʾil, as well as other items that will please you. I also have the rifles and all the things that Ḥamūd al-ʿUbayd requested.

Now I am asking you for a service. When I arrive in Damascus it will already be very hot and there will no longer be any Arabs in Wādī al-Sirḥān, so I am afraid of not being able to find the men I shall need as guides for me and my luggage as far as al-Ǧawf. Therefore I need you to send me two Shammarīs with four or five [amended to five or six] camels and two *dhalūls*, the hire of which I shall pay. You will set the price of hiring them. If the camels are good I shall buy them. Even were I to find Arabs still in Wādī al-Sirḥān, I would prefer even so to buy my camels in Ḥāʾil.

It would be best if you could send Ṭrād [given in Arabic], who was with me in al-Qaṣīm, rather than ʿAǧlān [given in Arabic], who has a timorous nature. As for me, you know that I fear only God, and not men. I am besides well-armed and I have a friend [*viz.* Julius Euting] who is coming with me and who is worth even more than I in every respect. You told me in your letters, as did the emir, that anything I wished for would be done. You will therefore do me this service that I am asking of you. If you cannot do it on your own, you will speak to the emir, and as you are a man of intelligence, courage and nobility, I know that the emir loves you and will help you to do me this service.

When you have obtained the men and the camels, you will instruct them to go to Shaykh Naǧm al-Aṭrāsh in ʿUrmān [given in Arabic] in Ǧabal Druze. As for me, I am writing to tell Shaykh Naǧm what is needed for him to receive your envoys and their camels and to safeguard them, and he will notify me straight away.

You are to do all this without delay, so that I am not obliged to wait for a long time in Damascus and because I am in haste to get to the Ǧabal. It would be the height of felicity for me if you came to fetch me yourself. In any case, you will give the men going to ʿUrmān a letter for me and you will write to me what I still need to bring to you from Damascus.

May salvation be on your house. You will also give my greetings to your brother ʿAlī, then Māğid al-ʿUbayd, also Naṣr al-ʿAtiq, Naṣr Sabhān, Ḥamad al-Zeher [Zuhayr?], ʿAbd al-Raḥmān al-Ḥumayd, Ghānim, and ʿAbdullah al-Muslimānī.

Let me know your state of health and your affairs so that I may be happy and my mind put at rest. May your life be long.

Paris
10 April 1883 [Date in Arabic: 10 Jumāda al-Akhir 1300]

Letter no. 2

Date: *ca.* 10 April 1883
From: Charles Huber, address not stated, but like Letter no. 1 it must be from Paris
To: Emir Muḥammad ibn ʿAbd Allāh al-Rashīd, Ḥāʾil

From Charles Huber ibn Ğirğīz to the most respected, most honoured, most noble Muḥammad ibn ʿAbd Allāh al-Rashīd, Shaykh al-Shuyūkh ['Shaykh of the Shaykhs'], Emir of Ğabal Shammar.

May God bless you and keep you. May you be always kept safe. May you attain all happiness. The subject of this letter is to send you my greetings and to ask for news of your health. May nothing unpleasant befall you nor any misfortune and may God keep you always under His protection, for He is the All-powerful. The Lord will surely protect you for you are just, and God loves the just.

If you would like to ask how I am, I thank the living God that I am well. After which: If you have not received my letters since I left Baghdad, it is through no fault of mine and you must not have any doubts about me. When I set off from Damascus a year ago, I wrote a letter to you, to Ḥamūd al-ʿUbayd and to my friends in Ḥāʾil. I handed all these letters to Salīm Mukashin [in Arabic script], a doctor in Damascus, to send them on to you, but he has written to me recently saying that he could not find anyone to go to Ḥāʾil. So the letters are still in Damascus along with other items.

Now I want to tell you some news, and I pray God that this reaches you at an opportune moment. Since my return to France, I have been longing for

Arabia and I am dying to see the Ǧabal again and the friends I have there. I have therefore made all my preparations and, God willing, I shall set off in a month's time, and after the 15th of the month of Raǧab [22 May 1883] I shall be in Damascus. In a letter that I am writing to Ḥamūd al-Miqrād [in Arabic script], I am asking him to send me some camels and men to the Ǧabal Druze to the house of my friend Shaykh Naǧm al-Aṭrāsh – I shall pay for the hire, and later I shall buy the camels that I need at Ḥā'il.

I ask you to do one thing: help Ḥamūd to do this for me, for I know that on his own he can do nothing. You on the other hand have only to say one word and everyone will obey. I want to tighten the bonds of our friendship and stay a few days more in the Ǧabal under the protection of your government and of your justice, and to enjoy your society. Afterwards, God willing, and if you allow it, I would then like to visit other lands.

Now I want to speak to you of a matter that has often occupied my mind since returning here, and which you probably thought I had forgotten about. It concerns Khaybar [in Arabic script]. When I left Egypt a year ago, I first went to Stamboul before returning to France, and there I explained the whole Khaybar affair to the French ambassador to the Porte. He understood it very well but, as I had supposed, and as I had already told Ḥamūd, I would have needed a letter from you. Nonetheless, he would have addressed the matter straight away if France had not at that very moment been experiencing a slight disagreement with the Sultan over Tunisia, which is now a French possession. But he told me to be patient and to wait for things to calm down once more between France and Turkey, and that then at an opportune moment we shall ask for Khaybar to be restored to you. Later, when at last I got back to Paris, thank God, I spoke about this affair with the Minister for Foreign Affairs and he made me the same promises. You shall have Khaybar back again ['God willing' in left margin], but you will have to wait until we find the right moment. God will bring it about because your request is just. I for my part shall not cease to remind them about this affair, for I have given you my promise and I am compelled to do so because I do not want you to doubt me.

I do not speak here of other political matters because, God willing, I shall soon be in Ḥā'il [in Arabic script] and then I shall bring you newspapers which will tell you what you want to know.

I shall not leave for Naǧd on my own. My friend [*viz.* Julius Euting], who is a better man than I, will accompany me. He has spent his whole life studying everything to do with the Arabs and like me he loves them greatly.

I told him about all your goodness to me and, God willing, you will look favourably upon him.

I hope that you will write to me soon about your state of health and about your affairs so that I may be happy and reassured. If you send your letter to Shaykh Nağm al-Aṭrāsh in ʿUrmān he will pass it on to me.

God willing be well, and may your life be long. Greetings.

LETTER NO. 3

Date: not stated, but same as Letters 1 and 2 above, i.e. *ca.* 10 April 1883
From: Charles Huber, probably in Paris
To: Ḥamūd ibn ʿUbayd al-Rashīd, Ḥāʾil

From Charles Huber ibn Ğirğīz to the most respected, most honoured, most noble Ḥamūd ibn ʿUbayd al-Rashīd [in Arabic script].

May God bless you and keep you. May you be always well protected. May you attain all happiness. The subject of this letter is to send you my greetings and to ask for news of your state of health. May nothing unpleasant befall you nor any misfortune, and may God keep you always under His protection, for He is the All-powerful. The Lord will surely protect you for you are just, and God loves the just.

If you are kind enough to ask how I am, I thank the living God that I am well.

After which: I received in good time your last letter of the month of Rabīʿ 1298 [i.e. February–March 1881] while I was in Iraq, but this letter was carried to Baghdad by your men while I myself was in Ḥillah[3] [in Arabic script], for you will probably have learned that I was held up for nearly a year in Iraq, on the orders of my government, in order to study the plague raging there at that time. When I finally received your letter, your men had already set off again for the Ğabal. I would have liked to send the rifle to you while I was still in Iraq as proof of my good faith, and also because we have a proverb at home that runs: To give quickly is to give twice. But that has not been possible in my case. The mail route from Iraq to France is a long one, especially when there are quarantines, *qarantīnah* [in Arabic script],

[3] Huber also took part in the British Museum excavations at the ancient site of Sippar in Babylonia. See Introduction p. 21. For his time in Iraq in 1881, see also Appendix 3, Letter no. 17.

and my letters have not always been well understood. Later, after my return to France, I had a lot of things going on that caused me much trouble and distress,[4] and I have been forced to postpone until now the errand that you entrusted me with.[5] There has been yet another impediment, which is the situation of the Ǧabal [Shammar], surrounded as it is on all sides by Turkish territory, so that it has not been easy to get weapons of war across the border, relations recently between France and Turkey having not been very good.

Since my return to France I have twice received news from the Ǧabal: once through Ḥāǧ Rasūl in Baghdad, and again some time ago through Sayyid Ǧawād Effendi Kalīdadāī in al-Naǧaf al-Ashraf [written in Arabic: سيّد جوَاد افندي كليدداي، نجف اشرف. Kalīdadāī is a doubtful reading]. I also recently learned that the last Ḥaǧǧ caravan coming back from Mecca had suffered many deaths from the plague in its midst, and that the Emir Muḥammad ibn Rashīd (may happiness always be his) did not allow the pilgrims to pass through Ḥāʾil, instead making them take their way through Mustaǧiddah and Fayd.[6] If that is the case, he did well to do so, and it is proof of his wisdom.

You will probably have heard of the war taking place in Egypt because of the rebellion by ʿArabī [*sic*; ʿUrābī] Pasha against the Khedive. But it has all come to an end now, and the English soldiers charged with punishing the traitor and restoring order in Egypt are going to leave the country in a few days and return to England.[7]

Now I want you to know that, God willing, I shall leave here again in a month's time to go to Cairo, and then from Cairo to Damascus, and after that from Damascus, God willing, to the Ǧabal. I shall be happy indeed on the day that I see you again, because of my love for you and because you have always been good and generous to me. Besides which you are a god-fearing man and you respect those who fear God and who pray to the one true and living

[4] Huber is again referring to his and his family's problems with their nationality as French citizens of Alsace-Lorraine, and to allegations against him. See note 2 above.

[5] Huber is referring to the acquisition of firearms: see Letter no. 1 above; also Appendix 4, Letters nos. 14, 15, 17, 20 and notes 64 and 87.

[6] i.e. the pilgrim caravan was made to avoid Ḥāʾil by reverting to the route of the mediaeval Darb Zubaydah back to Iraq.

[7] This refers to the nationalist uprising in Egypt from 1879 to 1882 against the Khedive Tewfiq, in protest at the extent of British and French influence over the country. It was led by Col. Aḥmad ʿUrābī, and was defeated by the military intervention of the British and the bombardment of Alexandria during the summer of 1882. The British did not then go home, as Huber says they were going to do, but stayed on and effectively ruled Egypt as a quasi-independent colony until 1954.

God. I am also happy to see the Arab lands again because I enjoy travelling so much, as you know, and above all I love the mountains and the desert. But I especially love the Shammar, who are the foremost and the bravest of the Arabs. I am asking Ḥamūd al-Miqrād [in Arabic script], to send me for hire men and camels to ʿUrmān in the Ğabal Druze to fetch me with my luggage. I beg you to help him so that he will be able to do me this service. I shall be most grateful to you.

If God wills, be in good health and be happy. My greetings also to Māğid, ʿAbd al-ʿAzīz, Fayd and their brothers. But above all give my greetings to Sulaymān and Shaykh Šāliḥ. I greet you once again, and may your life be long.

LETTER NO. 4

Date: not stated, but in April 1883
From: Charles Huber, Paris
To: Muḥammad ibn Ḥāğ Raḥīm Shayrawānī in Nağaf, Iraq

From Charles Huber ibn Ğirğīz to the most respected, most honoured, most noble friend Muḥammad ibn Ḥāğ Raḥīm Shayrawānī [in Arabic script], in al-Nağaf al-Ashraf.

May God bless you and keep you. May you be always well protected. The subject of this letter is to send you my greetings and to ask for news of you. May nothing unpleasant befall you nor any misfortune, and may God keep you always under His protection, for He alone is All-powerful. If you would like to ask how I am, I thank the living God that I am well.

After which: I wrote to you about four months ago, addressing my letter to Lūbiğ [in Arabic script], the governor at Ḥillah [in Arabic script]. I hope you received it and that you understood it. This current letter is now to let you know that in a few days' time I am leaving Paris once again to travel to the Orient. I will go first of all to Egypt and then to Syria, where I shall stay for a month. Then I will set off again for Ğabal Shammar and Ḥāʾil. I intend next to visit the Ḥiğāz and al-Qaṣīm once again and perhaps to go as far as Riyadh to the Emir Ibn Saʿūd. When I have completed all these journeys, I shall return, God willing, to Baghdad, and then I shall also spend a few days with you at al-Nağaf al-Ashraf. This time I shall not stay in Iraq as long as I did the first time because I also want to visit Persia on this occasion, God willing, and to go on pilgrimage to the tomb of the Imam Riza in Mashhad in Khurasān. On my way there I shall pass through Isfahan, and on my way back through Teheran. I shall not be alone on all these journeys. I have with me one of my friends [*viz.* Julius Euting], a learned man from my country; it is he who is writing this letter and who will accompany me and I hope, God willing, that you will accompany us too. We shall make a fine journey!

Now I want to know if you have thought about what I asked you to do: to make a list of all the tribes (Arabs, *fellaḥ*s, bedouins) great and small that are in Iraq, from the north as far as Baṣrah; and also whether you have thought to buy me all the beautiful carpets that you have come cross. For my part I have not forgotten you, and I shall bring what you asked me for. Write to me without delay. Put your letter into the envelope that I am enclosing for you and send it to Ḥāǧ Rasūl in Baghdad, instructing him to give it to the English post office. But straight away. I greet your father and Ḥāǧ Raḥīm and also Sayyid Ǧawād, and tell them that I kiss their hands. Tell me also if you have any news from the Russian Consul in Baghdad.

Regards.

Letter no. 5

Date: not stated, but *ca.* 10 April 1883 as Letters nos. 1–4
From: Charles Huber, Paris
To: Shaykh Naǧm al-Aṭrāsh in ʿUrmān, Ǧabal Druze

From Charles Huber ibn Ǧirǧīz, French doctor, to the most respected, most honoured and most noble Naǧm al-Aṭrāsh, Shaykh in ʿUrmān in Ǧabal Druze.

May God bless you and keep you. May you be always well protected. The subject of this letter is to send you my greetings and to ask for news of you. May nothing unpleasant befall you nor any misfortune and may God keep you always under His protection. If you would like to ask how I am, I thank the living God that I am well.

After which: When I left your hospitable house more than two years ago to go to stay in the desert with ʿAlī al-Khurayshī, who was to be my guide to Kāf, you remember that ʿAlī failed to keep his word to me or to you, for he left me at Boṣra. God be praised, I was able to set out even so. I wrote to you all about it and I hope that you understood it.

Having been well received by your friend the Emir Ibn Rashīd in Ḥāʾil, who honours you greatly, I visited the whole of the Ǧabal, the Ḥiǧāz, al-

Qaṣīm and Iraq. Now I want to let you know that I want to return to stay with Muḥammad Ibn Rashīd to take things to him that he asked me for, and I am writing to him to send me men and camels from where he lives to fetch me, to near where you are at ʿUrmān, because the Arabs of the Ḥamād and Wādī al-Sirhan cannot be trusted. I am sending you letters for him and I am asking you to send them by the route that you know as far as Ḥāʾil, but very quickly, because in a month's time, if God wills, I shall already be in Damascus, and I want to get the reply immediately because I am in haste to set off for Nağd.

I greet you and beg you to let me know the state of your health and your affairs so that my mind is at rest. May you live long. I greet also your son Ibrāhīm and Shaykh Ḥasan at Melekh, and also your secretary.

If you write to me, send your letter to the Emir ʿAbd al-Qādir[8] in Damascus or to the French Consul in Damascus. Tell them that I will come to collect it. I am writing to them too.

Regards.

[8] For the Emir ʿAbd al-Qādir, see Appendix 4, Letter no. 13 dated 20 May 1883 from Huber to Maunoir, and Translation Part II, note 155.

APPENDIX 6

Letters from Huber and Maunoir to the Ministry of Public Education, 1883

THESE ITEMS are held in the archives of the Ministère de l'Instruction publique et des Beaux-Arts, at the Archives nationales at Pierrefitte-sur-Seine, Paris. They are included in Dossier F/17/2976/1: 2, Mission en Arabie. 1883, containing 141 items between May 1883 and July 1886.

Thanks go to Prof. Maria Gorea for finding and making these documents available.

LETTER NO. 1

This letter is item no. 11 in Dossier F/17/2976/1:2. It reveals that Charles Maunoir had no knowledge of Huber's plan to travel to Arabia with Julius Euting.

Date: 12 June 1883
From: Charles Maunoir, Secretary of the Société de Géographie in Paris
To: not specified but most probably the Minister of Public Education

Dear Sir,

You will find enclosed a copy of a newspaper excerpt which has just been communicated to me. I have this instant written a stern personal letter to M. Huber, asking him to send me an immediate explanation. The *Journal d'Alsace Lorraine* has managed to inject a boastful tone. But it emerges from this article that M. Huber would be in subordination to M. Euting, who is funded by the German authorities. There are three points in all this that pain me. First, that M. Huber, having himself been commissioned by the

Seen by M. Cogordan[1]

He will send M. Raindre[2] a dispatch inviting him to investigate whether M. Huber is associated with the German mission led by Dr Euting.

28 June 1883

LETTER NO. 3

This letter is item no. 16 in Dossier F/17/2976/1:2.

Date: 7 July 1883
From: Charles Maunoir, Secretary of the Société de Géographie in Paris
To: not specified, but most probably the Minister of Public Education

Sir,

Here is a letter from M. Huber.[3] Unless it represents a duplicity so appalling that it would beggar belief – and which besides would contradict the closeness of dates [*viz.* of Huber and Maunoir's exchange of letters] – it must have been written before he had received mine. It establishes first of all that M. Huber is very keen on the Gras rifles and, secondly, that Dr Euting, the learned scholar sent by the government of Alsace-Lorraine, is a nuisance to M. Huber, who feels threatened, as he puts it, by having 'the grass cut from beneath his feet'.[4] Expressed in that way, the situation would be sufficiently at variance with that presented to us by the article in the *Gazette* [*sic*] *d'Alsace Lorraine*, of which I sent you a copy. Next, without a doubt, M. Huber will reply to my letter, and my fervent hope is that his answer will restore him to our good graces. We shall take up again the business of the rifles, which could be vigorously followed up. While waiting, I am going to acknowledge receipt of M. Huber's letter, while urging him to consider whether his travelling companion is not doing him a disservice from the sole point of view of Himyaritic epigraphy. Perhaps he will then succeed in making him understand that a venture possible for one person becomes

[1] Georges Cogordan was a deputy director of the Ministry of Foreign Affairs.

[2] M. de Raindre was the chargé d'affaires at the French consulate in Cairo.

[3] We have been unable to locate this letter by Huber. But it sounds as if it was similar in tone to, and sent shortly before, Letter no. 14 dated 25 June 1883 from Huber to Maunoir, quoted in Appendix 4.

[4] 'Having the grass cut from beneath his feet': a metaphor for being deprived of the advantages he might otherwise had enjoyed.

difficult when two people are involved, and that it would be better to go their separate ways.

I would be grateful, Sir, if having read the enclosed letter and – it goes without saying – having communicated it to M. Charmes,[5] you would be good enough to send it back to me. In my possession it will remain always at your disposal. I am going to write to M. Charmes on the subject of two free expeditions requested and for which it would be important for a decision to be taken …

[Letter continues on the subject of two non-Arabian expeditions.]

LETTER NO. 4

This letter is item no. 17 in Dossier F/17/2976/1:2.

Date: 16 July 1883
From: Charles Maunoir, Secretary of the Société de Géographie in Paris
To: not specified, but most probably the Minister of Public Education

Sir,

A letter (no. 3) from M. Huber reached me some days ago.[6] Today there arrived letter no. 2, which had been delayed, all larded with efforts to clear the air [*toute lardée pour les fumigations*].[7] It does not seem to me that the case of our expeditioner is as serious as I at first took it to be. It even seems to me that we can apply ourselves once more to facilitating his assignment. If this is your view of it, I shall ask you to be kind enough to discuss this business with M. Charmes, with a view to fulfilling the request submitted by M. Huber to have four Gras rifles, with ammunition. The cost would be deducted from the sum agreed for the expedition. Commandant Langlois has assured me that the thing can be quickly done, and that here there is an important point: a word will have to be written to the French consul in Damascus, so that he can give advice on how to send these arms to M. Huber's party.

Please accept, Sir, the expression of my most distinguished sentiments,

Ch. Maunoir

---

[5] Xavier Charmes, Director of the Secretariat and Accounts, Minister of Public Education in Paris, was the person responsible for allocating Ministry funds (10,000 francs) to Huber in Syria.

[6] This probably refers to Letter no. 15 dated 27 June 1883, in Appendix 4 above.

[7] This probably refers to Letter no. 14 dated 25 June 1883, in Appendix 4 above.

Letter no. 5

This is item no. 19 in Dossier F/17/2976/1:2.

Date: 19 July 1883
From: Charles Huber, Damascus
To: Xavier Charmes, Director of the Secretariat and Accounts, Ministry of Public Education

Sir,

I have the honour to confirm to you my letters of 14 and 19 June last.

M. Maunoir, in the only letter that he has done me the honour of writing to me since I left Paris, has told me about the person of Dr Euting, of the University of Strasbourg, whom a newspaper article described as my companion on my expedition in Arabia. I replied to him on 25 June last[8] that this article was a canard, and that I was and shall be absolutely alone on my Arabian expedition, just as I was on the first one.

You will surely be acquainted with this fact and will probably have understood the unlikelihood of such an association, quite apart from the fact that it would be morally repugnant to me, that it would have no advantage for me, and in any case would bring me into your utter disfavour. Nonetheless, for my peace of mind, I am taking the liberty of asking you if you would be kind enough to tell me whether you have made up your mind as to the genuineness of my declaration.

I am taking this opportunity to let you know that my preparations are in their final stages, and that all I have to do now is to pay a visit to Druze country to make arrangements for my crossing of Wadi al-Sirḥān. That will take me a fortnight. As soon as I get back I shall have more than few days to rest and thus shall be able to set off on the journey.

I have explained in a previous letter to M. Maunoir that the news that has come in from the desert makes me doubtful about being able to get to Ǧiddah at any given moment to draw funds from Europe. This doubt has since accrued a greater degree of certitude, by means of a letter of the 8th of this month from M. de Raindre, chargé of the Agency and Consulate-General of France at Cairo, informing me that the Khedive did not believe it possible

[8] See Appendix 4, Letter no. 14 dated 25 June 1883 from Huber to Maunoir.

for him to deliver letters of recommendation for me, which I had requested, to various notables in the Ḥiǧāz. It would therefore be necessary for me to be able to have the entirety of my funding at my disposal before my departure [for Arabia].

Before my departure from Paris, you had the kindness to allow me to hope that after six weeks you would be in the process of arranging the funds for my expedition. Two months have since elapsed and, if all has proceeded as planned, the order must have been able to have been signed. In view of the point that I have reached with my preparations, I need to know about this, and as soon as possible; allow me therefore to request a word in reply on this matter, and to say that you would enable me to gain much time and as a result much money by advising me by telegram. I take the liberty of asking you to be kind enough to let me have express notice if the order has been signed and is in the hands of M. Flüry Hérard. I should then be able to make use of the funds straight away and set forth to complete one of the finest expeditions ever carried out under your auspices.

I have the honour, Sir, to beg you to accept the assurance of my feelings of high and respectful consideration.

Charles Huber
Consulate of France
Damascus

LETTER NO. 6

This item is a letter item no. 28 in Dossier F/17/2976/1:2.

Date: undated, but from internal evidence on 21 August 1883. Received at the Ministry in Paris on 1 September 1883.
From: Charles Huber, Damascus
To: M. le Ministre de l'Instruction publique et des Beaux-Arts, Paris

I have just received the letter that you did me the honour of sending me on 16 August last. It has reached me just a few hours before my departure, as I am leaving Damascus tonight[9] to go to Ǧabal Druze and from there to al-Ǧawf by way of Wadi al-Sirḥān.

[9] Huber left Damascus on 21 August 1883 for Ǧabal Druze, but returned to it on the 27th. Euting then left Damascus for Ǧabal Druze on 31 August, and Huber followed him on 4 September.

I am grateful to you, M. le Ministre, for the grant of 10,000 francs[10] that you have been kind enough to make me. However small it may be, I have hopes that it will enable me, together with my own funds, to complete the exploration of Arabia.

Regarding the wishes of the Académie des Inscriptions et Belles-Lettres [AIBL], I travelled a few days ago to Palmyra to make the squeeze of the inscription of the Tax Law of that city,[11] discovered a year ago. This squeeze, along with ten Palmyrene skulls, all packed in a single crate, will be dispatched to your department as soon as the Marseille quarantine is lifted. The skulls are destined for Dr Quatrefages.[12]

I have the honour, M. le Ministre, to beg you to accept the assurance of your devoted servant's feelings of high and respectful consideration.

Ch. Huber
[Contactable] at the French consulate at Ğiddah

LETTER NO. 7

This letter is item no. 30 in Dossier F/17/2976/1:2.

Date: 24 September 1883
From: Charles Maunoir, Secretary of the Société de Géographie
To: not specified, but probably the Minister of Public Education

Here, my dear Sir, is a telegram from M. Huber. I would have brought it to you myself had I not been detained by my work at the Dépôt de la Guerre.[13] How should I reply? If the steps have not already been taken, could they not be taken straight away and I will write to M. Huber, after having telegraphed a 'Yes' to him? Commandant Langlois, at the Artillery, told me a little time ago that this dispatch could be made immediately on receipt of your order. It could without doubt be done even right now. If it has been dispatched, I cannot understand M. Huber's telegram.

---

[10] Flüry-Hérard actually sent 9,500 francs to Huber: see Dossier F/17/2976/1:2 'Mission en Arabie. 1883', item no. 26: letter dated 18 August 1883 from Flüry-Hérard. Huber had originally requested 35,000 francs from the ministry: see Appendix 3, Letter no. 19 dated 11 May 1882 to Xavier Charmes.

[11] On the Tax Law of Palmyra, sce Appendix 4, note 79.

[12] For de Quatrefages, see Appendix 3, note 1.

[13] The Depôt de la Guerre was a special department of the War Ministry where maps and topographical and military data were archived. (MG)

From a letter from M. Gilbert, our consul of France in Damascus, I have learnt that M. Huber had already done a good job at Palmyra in collecting the inscriptions ordered by M. Renan. M. Gilbert did say that the German professor was a nuisance to M. Huber, but did not seem to establish any connection between them, except that of a desire of the professor to follow in M. Huber's footsteps and to profit from his experience. Knowing M. Huber, I believe him to be a man who would escape from his own shadow, and also a man given to travelling on his own account, and capable of succeeding even if he believed himself to have been abandoned by the Ministry. I have no hesitation in thinking that we must support him here, seeing that he is engaged in bringing us the results of this expedition.

Please, Sir, receive once again my excuses for not having gone myself to see you, and accept the expression of my most devoted sentiments.

Ch. Maunoir

Letter no. 8

This letter is item no. 52 in Dossier F/17/2976/1:2.

Date: 30 November 1883
From: Charles Huber, Ḥā'il, Ǧabal Shammar.
To: Monsieur le Ministre de l'Instruction publique et des Beaux-Arts à Paris

Dear Minister,

The Persian hadj [Ḥağğ] (pilgrim caravan) that crosses central Arabia each year to go to the holy cities of the Ḥiğāz, with an escort provided by the Shammar emir, Muḥammad Ibn Rashīd, and which is coming back from the pilgrimage at this very moment on its return journey to Iraq, is today passing through the Shammar capital. I am taking this opportunity to send you, M. le Ministre, a news report of the expedition which you have been kind enough to entrust to me. But I beg you in advance to excuse its brevity, because I am unwell and have been suffering from a fever for the last eight days.

I finally left Damascus on 25 September with an escort which the emir Muḥammad Ibn Rashīd had been kind enough to provide me with. Hence the crossing of the deserts of the Ḥamād, the Wadi al-Sirḥān and the Nafūd was accomplished without incident. I reached Ḥā'il on 21 October, and the emir welcomed me with the utmost cordiality before assuring me of his support for all my undertakings. He had arranged for one of the most beautiful houses in Ḥāʾil to be prepared for me.

A few days after my arrival, the emir left on a raid [*ghazū*] (razou, razzia) to the south, from which he only returned after an absence of twenty-four days.

During this interval I made two excursions, one of four days in Ǧabal Aǧā, the other of eight days around Ǧabal Ǧildiyyah. These two trips enabled me to take numerous magnetic bearings which will give us all the precision we need for the geography of this region. On the trip to Ǧabal Ǧildiyyah I also collected more than a hundred new Thamudic inscriptions.[14]

As soon as I am slightly recovered from my fever, maybe in five or six days' time, I shall carry out an exploratory tour of Ǧabal Aǧā which will take me about a month, and immediately after that I shall set forth to complete the exploration of the Ḥiǧāz and to make squeezes of the Nabataean inscriptions at Madāʾin Ṣāliḥ.

On the rocks at Ǧubbah, the ancient Aïna of Ptolemy, two days to the north of Ḥāʾil, I found in addition to numerous Thamudic inscriptions two in Hebrew characters. In view of their importance, I am sending you with this letter a squeeze, in a tube made of welded tin, and including a manuscript copy to facilitate its decipherment.

I have the honour, M. le Ministre, to beg you to accept the assurance of your devoted servant's feelings of high and respectful consideration.

Ch. Huber
Sent to the French Consulate at Ǧiddah
[Enclosure: 1 sheet containing transcription of the Hebrew text]

[14] Both these trips, like the entire journey from Damascus to Ḥāʾil, were made in the company of Julius Euting, though Huber nowhere says so, either here or in his diary of the 1883–84 expedition (Huber 1891).

APPENDIX 7

Letter from Huber to Renan, 8 April 1883

THIS IMPORTANT document (see no. 2) is a copy of a letter that Charles Huber wrote to Ernest Renan on 8 April 1883 at the Académie des Inscriptions et Belles-Lettres (AIBL). It is an abridgement of Huber's original, in a clerk's copperplate hand and on AIBL notepaper. It was sent to the ministry with a covering letter (no. 1) from Ernest Renan, also translated below. It sets out the aims of his second Arabian journey, defines his understanding that Euting's participation was 'unofficial', and records that he and Euting had agreed that all epigraphic finds should be the property of the AIBL, save only a single unspecified inscription to which Euting would be entitled. It proves that Huber and Euting had indeed agreed to travel together to Arabia, despite Huber's protestations to Charles Maunoir at the Société de Géographie that he intended to travel alone.

The two documents are preserved among some Huber papers in the Archives of the Ministère des Affaires étrangères, held at La Courneuve, north of Paris. The 52-page file, no. 75ADP entitled 'Mission en Arabie, Assassinat, Stèle de Theima', is in Affaires diverses politiques Box 47, 'Archaeological excavations 1875–1896'. The items are arranged chronologically. Thanks go to Prof. Maria Gorea for finding it and making it available.

LETTER NO. 1

Date: 14 December 1884
From: Ernest Renan, AIBL, Paris
To: the Minister of Foreign Affairs

Dear Monsieur le Ministre,

I have the honour to send you the copy of the last report by M. Huber of which we possess the original,[1] as well as the copy of the first letter that M. Huber sent to us.

The report, as confirmed elsewhere by several other letters from M. Huber, demonstrates as clearly as could be that the Taymā' Stele, and the other Taymā inscriptions transported by him to Ḥā'il, are indeed his property and had been prepared for dispatch to France. The letter of 30 April [*sic*; actually 8 April, see below] 1883 proves, should there be any doubt in this respect, that M. Huber acquired these objects for our museums, and that after his death they belong to us.

Please accept the expression of my most respectful feelings,

Ernest Renan

LETTER NO. 2

Date: 8 April 1883
From: Charles Huber, Strasbourg
To: not stated, but to Ernest Renan at the AIBL

Sir,

I am taking the liberty of informing you that my preparations to leave once more for central Arabia are nearing completion and that I am planning to leave Strasbourg during the final days of this month.

The aim of this second journey is:

1. To make squeezes of all the Himyaritic, Nabataean, Aramaic and Thamudic inscriptions discovered in the course of my first journey in Ǧabal Shammar, and at Taymā', Madā'in Ṣāliḥ, al-ʿUlā, Khaybar, and in al-Qaṣīm, etc.
2. Following that, to explore the mountains of the Balī Arabs between the Darb al-Ḥajj and the Red Sea, and then Naǧd

[1] This is the report dated 27 March 1882 that Huber wrote on his return from his first Arabian journey (see Appendix 3 above, Letter no. 16 and report of March 1882). Contrary to Renan's assertion in the next paragraph, there is no mention of the Taymā' Stele in this report.

and the [Wadi al-] Dawāsir, from the geographical and epigraphic point of view.

.... [Passage omitted] Having M. Euting as companion should pose no obstacle because, since for his part he has no official assignment, we had made special arrangements that completely protect my rights and as a consequence those of France, and it has been agreed that the Académie des Inscriptions [AIBL] in Paris will take exclusive delivery of all the squeezes, even in the case of my not receiving any financial aid.

The same goes for the dressed stones bearing inscriptions that are at Taymāʾ, which I plan to remove and arrange to transport to France. M. Euting has only asked me for a single one for his personal collection. The others will come to the Académie.

[Unsigned]

APPENDIX 8

Huber's letter to Theodor Nöldeke, 3 September 1883

THIS LETTER is held in Tübingen University Library archives, shelfmark Md 782 A 65. It provides further evidence that Huber had been planning all along to travel with Euting, and that Nöldeke was fully aware of this.

With thanks to Prof. John Healey for making this item available.

Date: 3 September 1883
From: Charles Huber, Damascus
To: Theodor Nöldeke

Dear and honoured Sir,

I hope that Dr Euting will have passed on the greetings that I asked him to add to each of his letters, and that he will also have told you how busy I have been with our preparations, the responsibility for which has devolved upon me alone.

You will probably have been told of our trip to Palmyra and its results. It is there that M. Euting had his initiation to life in the desert, but still with a certain amount of comfort such as tents, a bed, good food, etc. He suffered a great deal from the heat and from the fatigue of the forced marches, but what he found hardest to bear on this trip was the lack of sleep. It was hard.

Already at Palmyra I had picked up rumours of a war between Muḥammad Ibn Rashīd and Ibn Saʿūd, his former suzerain, when a letter from Dr Mordtmann in Istanbul confirmed it. Therefore, having only just got back to Damascus, I set off for Ğabal Druze and the south to gain certain news of it.

Everything turned out to be true, so in order not to make the situation worse, I resolved to set off immediately for the centre [of Arabia]. I had got back to Damascus on 28 August and today everything is completed. All the loads have been sent off this morning and I will be following them tonight. Dr Euting left four days ago.

I had the good fortune in the Ḥawrān to meet some Ǧawfis who had come for the fair at Muzayrib. One of my friends, Shaykh Naǧm [al-Aṭrāsh], was able to delay them so that I would be able to go with them. In this way I shall very easily be able to cross that zone of the Wādī al-Sirḥān which is always so dangerous.

We are going in the first instance as far as al-Ǧawf, and there we shall take circumstances into consideration before going any farther. In any case, we think we shall be at Ǧiddah towards the end of the year.

I wish you, dear and honoured Sir, continued good health, and assure you of my highest consideration along with my cordial greetings.

Ch. Huber

APPENDIX 9

Letters from Félix de Lostalot Bachoué, August 1884 – November 1885

THESE LETTERS are among the Huber papers in the Archives du Cabinet of the *Corpus Inscriptionum Semiticarum* (*CIS*), Académie des Inscriptions et Belles-Lettres (AIBL), Institut de France, Paris. Correspondence classified under Ref. Boîte 'Dossiers 48': A. Lettres au sujet de Charles Huber.

This group includes twelve letters from de Lostalot to Charles Maunoir, and two (nos. 13 and 14) to Philippe Berger.

With thanks to Prof. Maria Gorea for making these documents available, and to Barbara Newton for translating them.

LETTER NO. 1

Date: 12 August 1884
From: de Lostalot, while on leave at Salies-de-Béarn, Basses-Pyrénées. On notepaper of the French Vice-Consulate, Ǧiddah.
To: M. [Charles] Maunoir, Secrétaire Général, Société de Géographie de Paris

My dear Sir,

It is with satisfaction that I can tell you that I have just received a letter from M. Huber from Ǧiddah dated 26 July 1884. 'The journey to Mecca did not take place,' our friend says, 'as a result of obstacles that presented themselves at the last minute. The business got off to a bad start. I shall take it up again later.'[1]

[1] It was as the result of this late change of plan, probably caused by his fear of problems with the ʿUtaybah, that Huber decided to return to Ḥāʾil via al-Madīnah.

Despite my keen desire to see a Frenchman add new and detailed information to what has already been published about this town, I have no choice but to approve the decision that M. Huber has taken, for in spite of the great care and secrecy surrounding the attempt he was going to make when I left Ǧiddah,[2] I will not conceal from you that I was seriously worried. The adventure was very risky indeed. The dangers will be less while the pilgrims are flooding into the holy places of Islam, i.e. during the first days of October. Perhaps M. Huber will be able to take advantage of that circumstance.

Nevertheless, he tells me that he is leaving Ǧiddah during the night of 26–27 July, without giving any further details. But looking at the study that we did together of the least dangerous routes to get back to Ḥāʾil (you know that he wants to bring back a stele[3] which he found and which he was not able to carry away for lack of the necessary means of transport), I think he must have set off from Ǧiddah towards al-Madīnah with a recommendation to the Bedouin tribe of the Ḥarb, who live on the outskirts of that town and who are in part independent and in part tributary to Muḥammad Ibn Rashīd, sultan [*sic*] of Ḥāʾil, the friend and protector of our dear fellow-countryman. I do not doubt that the latter will arrive safely and that he will be in Syria next spring on his way to Paris, according to what he told me he intended to do. He ends his letter by asking me to write to him at Ǧiddah so that his friends the Shammar can bring him his mail, as they are returning from their pilgrimage to Mecca (i.e. around 4 October next). 'In this note,' he says, 'you will tell me a little of what you have heard about your humble servant (i.e. Huber).' I did not hesitate to write to him; I did so a while ago but I do not think that he will have received my letter before he left.

So there is the news I had to tell you. It would be good of you, and I would be personally very grateful, if you would yourself write to M. Huber and send him, officially if possible, an expression of sympathy and encouragement on behalf of the Ministry of Education. Our friend would be very touched and would draw renewed strength from it to accomplish his mission, which is as dangerous as it is valuable.

Please accept, my dear Monsieur Maunoir, the expression of my devoted and respectful feelings.

---

[2] De Lostalot left Ǧiddah to go on leave in France on 5 July 1884: see Appendix 4, Letter no. 24 dated 6 July 1884 from Huber to Weisgerber.

[3] i.e. the Taymāʾ Stele.

Ministry of Public Education, has set out with a German, whatever merits the latter may possess; secondly, that he is considered to be a subordinate of his travelling companion; and third that he forewarned nobody of this part of his plan. On this last point, M. Huber had indeed broached it with me a few months ago, but I had responded with the very formal advice that he should travel alone. Since then, he had not spoken with me again about his plans for a companion. Perhaps you will judge, my dear Sir, that there are grounds to institute an enquiry into this matter, either in Strasbourg or Damascus. My support hitherto for M. Huber will be matched by my opposition to him, unless the explanations he provides are absolutely satisfactory, and unless he places himself in a situation that cannot give rise to any ambiguity.

Please communicate this letter to M. Charmes in due course, and accept, my dear Sir, the expression of my most devoted sentiments.

Maunoir

Enclosure

Extract

Le *Journal d'Alsace Lorraine* announces that Professor Euting, accompanied by M. Charles Huber, has just set off via Marseille on a two-year journey of exploration in the Syrian and Arabian desert. Professor Euting, whose expertise is well known, has been long preparing himself for this expedition, for which the necessary resources have been granted by His Excellency the Governor (Général de Manteuffel, Governor of Alsace Lorraine), from the funds of Alsace Lorraine. His companion, M. Huber, is a Strasbourgeois who has studied medicine and natural sciences; having opted for France after the events of 1870, M. Huber has already made, at the expense of the French government, several journeys in Syria and North Africa.

LETTER NO. 2

This note is item no. 13 in Dossier F/17/2976/1:2.

Date: 28 June 1883
From: the Ministry of Public Education
To: not specified

Félix de Lostalot de Bachoué
French Vice-Consul on leave in Salies-de-Béarn, Basses-Pyrénées

---

LETTER NO. 2

Date: 16 August 1884
From: de Lostalot, while on leave at Salies-de-Béarn, Basses-Pyrénées. On notepaper of the French Vice-Consulate, Ǧiddah.
To: M. [Charles] Maunoir, 14, rue Jacob, Paris

My dear Sir,

It is with a very heavy heart that I am sending you (enclosed) the telegram from Ǧiddah that has just reached me.

It is true that the news is not certain, and I know how easily unfounded rumours are spread abroad in Arab circles: nevertheless, I have very serious fears because there is no more dangerous a route than the one that our friend has already travelled, and that he wanted to take again so as to obtain the famous stele about which we were speaking recently.

I am writing immediately to Muḥammad Ibn Rashīd, sultan [*sic*] of Ḥāʾil, to ask him to get some definite information about the rumours that are currently circulating, to avenge the murder of our unfortunate compatriot if there is reason to do so, and above all to collect up as much as he can of the remains that may have been left behind by the murderers, so that they can be sent on to the French consulate in Ǧiddah or Damascus.

My letter will arrive in that district as securely as possible but we will not be able to count on getting a reply before a minimum of three months. That is a really long time, but let us hope that there is no truth in this terrible news.

Please accept, my dear Monsieur Maunoir, the expression of my best feelings of affection and devotion.

Félix de Lostalot

LETTER NO. 3

Date: 19 August 1884
From: de Lostalot, while on leave at Salies-de-Béarn, Basses-Pyrénées. On notepaper of the French Vice-Consulate, Ǧiddah.
To: M. [Charles] Maunoir, Paris

My dear Monsieur Maunoir,

The telegram that you have in your hands, although signed by my chief *cawas*,[4] certainly does not come from him but rather from a friend who, not wanting his name to be known at the telegraph office in Ǧiddah (which is very indiscreet), has sheltered behind an authorized subordinate. I have written to him to thank him and to ask for details in the unlikely event that he had not written as soon as he knew of the terrible misfortune that hangs over us.

I have besides written to three other people in a position to enlighten us; none of them is aware of the mission I have entrusted to the others, and in this way I am counting on arriving at an accurate version of events, which is extremely difficult to obtain by other means. In this way we shall have the information, and I am making efforts, in the event of the tragedy being confirmed, to ensure that the objects belonging to our compatriot are returned to us.

I am sending you the letter that M. Huber wrote to me on leaving Ǧiddah. Perhaps on reading it you will find clues that I have not discovered. I beg you to send it back to me after you have made notes, if necessary, on anything you find of interest.

Although I have not lost all hope of meeting M. Huber again, I am very anxious about his fate and I think constantly about what might have happened to him. He set off in the night of 26–27 July. If I am not greatly mistaken, he set off from Ǧiddah heading towards al-Madīnah.

> From Ǧiddah to al-Madīnah – eight days
> From al-Madīnah to Ḥāʾil – ten days, if I am right

The telegram left Ǧiddah on 15 August at about 5 o'clock in the evening.

From 27 July to 15 August – 20 days. Ten days for the arrival in Ǧiddah of the Bedouin bearing the sad news. It would therefore be ten days after his departure from Ǧiddah that M. Huber would have been murdered.

In that time he must have got beyond al-Madīnah, so the murder must have been committed between al-Madīnah and Ḥāʾil; two days beyond al-Madīnah.[5] And yet M. Huber told me that he had nothing to fear three or four days out from Ǧiddah!

---

[4] *cawas*: de Lostalot seems to mean a kavass or cavass, a Turkish term for a courier or guide.

[5] In fact de Lostalot was soon to learn that Huber had been murdered on 29 July, near Rābigh, well before al-Madīnah: see next letter.

I am kept alive by one hope: it is said that anyone who is falsely reported killed will be vouchsafed another ten years of life. Let us accept this prediction until we get more information. I shall keep you carefully informed about everything new that I learn, and meanwhile I beg you, my dear Monsieur Maunoir, to accept the expression of my most devoted feelings.

F. de Lostalot

I have been careful to ask for information about the attitude of ʿAlī,[6] M. Huber's servant, before, during and after the events.

LETTER NO. 4

Date: 7 September 1884
From: de Lostalot, while on leave at Salies-de-Béarn, Basses-Pyrénées. On notepaper of the French Vice-Consulate, Ǧiddah.
To: M. [Charles] Maunoir, Secrétaire Général, Société de Géographie de Paris

My dear M. Maunoir,

It is with great sadness that I have to inform you that I have just received from Ǧiddah the confirmation of our poor Huber's murder. The crime was committed, they tell me, by the camel drivers who were accompanying him, close to Rābigh, four days north of Ǧiddah, at a place called Kassar alia [*sic*; Qaṣr ʿAlia], near 'Hafna' [Ḥafnah]. It was motivated by the desire of these Bedouins of the Ḥarb tribe to steal the arms and money in M. Huber's possession. Their suspicions of him had been aroused by his incessant questions about the names of the mountains, the villages and even the rocks that he came across. His faithful servant Maḥmūd was murdered at the same time,[7] and M. Huber's sabre has just been publicly sold (I do not yet know where) for the sum of about 150 francs.

Unfortunately I have no doubt of the accuracy of this information, so I am asking my superiors, by this courier, for permission to cut short my furlough and set off immediately for Ǧiddah in order to take a closer look into this sad business and to establish beyond doubt the responsibilities incurred.

[6] De Lostalot is mistaken here about the name of Huber's servant, whose actual name was Maḥmūd.

[7] This information was incorrect. Maḥmūd was captured but escaped with his life and eventually made his way back to Ǧiddah, where he was suspected by some of complicity in the murder, and detained by de Lostalot as a witness.

I am deeply saddened by this misfortune, but I swear on my honour that I shall exact a resounding vengeance for our friend, if I have the support to do so.

Accept, my dear Monsieur Maunoir, the expression of my respect and devotion.

F. J. de Lostalot

I am informing the Ministry of Education and the Ministry of Foreign Affairs directly. I intend to go to Paris in a few days and I shall not fail to come and report to you.

Letter no. 5

Date: 15 September 1884
From: de Lostalot, Mont de Marsan, near Paris. On private notepaper.
To: M. [Charles] Maunoir, Secrétaire Général, Société de Géographie de Paris

My dear Monsieur Maunoir,

I have received the last two letters that you have done me the honour of writing to me about our poor Huber; unfortunately, I have no reason to doubt, as I have already told you, the accuracy of the reports that have reached me. Therefore, in my opinion, we must, and that without delay, turn our thoughts to avenging him. I do not underestimate the difficulties that will face us in doing this, but I intend to attempt the impossible to achieve it. But I think first we shall have to play our cards close to our chests to bring about the recovery of the poor traveller's personal effects, among which is the list of the Arab tribes of the interior that you spoke to me about. I have already written to Ǧiddah in this vein, and I shall be more specific as soon as I have the honour and genuine pleasure of shaking your hand.

You tell me that you will be in Paris around the 20th; so I shall come and see you at the War Ministry on Wednesday 24th between 9 o'clock in the morning and midday. Then we can agree on a time for a longer meeting enabling us to speak fully about this matter that so occupies our minds, and to decide on a suitable course of action.

I have not yet received a reply to the request I sent to my superiors to return to my post as soon as possible so as to report back. I am no further on today than I was a week ago. I shall see in Paris how things stand, and it is with this in mind that I am going there.

You have twice given me the address in Nancy of M. Emile Huber, the brother of the unfortunate traveller. I toyed with the idea of writing a letter of condolence to him but refrained, not thinking myself in a position to do so unless directly instructed, as my official position demands the greatest discretion, above all when it comes to writing letters.

However, I shall not fail, if you think it appropriate, to write to the family of our late compatriot. They would perhaps be touched to have the few personal details that the one who saw him for the last time would be able to give them.

Accept, my dear Sir, the expression of my most devoted feelings.

Félix de Lostalot

Letter no. 6

Date: 24 October 1884
From: de Lostalot, after his return to Ǧiddah from France. On notepaper of the French Vice-Consulate, Ǧiddah
To: M. [Charles] Maunoir, Secrétaire Général, Société de Géographie de Paris

My dear Sir,

I have arrived in Ǧiddah, I hope in time to outwit the Germans who are trying to get hold of the scientific documents and valuables left behind by our poor compatriot and friend Charles Huber.

I found on arrival M. C. [Christiaan] Snouck Hurgronje, a Dutchman and doctor of Semitic Studies from the University of Leiden, who has not tried to hide from me the fact that he has received letters from Strasbourg[8] wrongfully laying claim to the objects, so they say, forming part of the baggage of the victim, among them the famous Stele of Taymāʾ, of which a drawing was produced for me to see and a photograph of the characters covering it.

I replied that I had no authority to look into this matter; that I would only try to recover the whole of M. Huber's baggage, and that the only place to which it would be sent was Paris, where such claims, along with the proofs justifying them, could be produced. At the same time, I mobilized people to

[8] Letters no doubt from Julius Euting, who claimed that he had a prior agreement with Huber that he would be entitled to a single inscription from the journey, and that that inscription was the Taymāʾ Stele. See Introduction p. 70.

search for the coveted objects and I hope to succeed in having them in our possession shortly. I have written all this in detail to the Ministry of Foreign Affairs and to M. Renan. The head of the Collège de France will be satisfied I think for the moment, and I intend to announce to him in one or two months' time that the Stele is with me. In any case I will do everything I can to attain this end.

The murder of M. Huber is moreover beyond all doubt. His servant Maḥmūd, who saw his body, is here with me, and I am keeping him as a prosecution witness in case of the arrest of, and court proceedings against, the murderers, whom I am currently pursuing.

Accept, dear Sir, the expression of my affection and devotion.

F. J. de Lostalot de Bachoué

P.S. 1 November. Two influential persons who will be of great use to us in seeking out M. Huber's baggage, have asked me, against repayment, for two nice pairs of marine binoculars capable of night-time use. The offer of repayment is certainly a cloak for their desire to be given them as a gift. I believe it will be to our advantage to do this for them.

I have spoken about it to M. Renan in the letter that I have just written to him, and have asked him, if he shares my point of view, to request M. Charmes to dispatch these two field-glasses with their cases at the expense of the Ministry of Public Education, to be deducted from the funds that have been promised to me. These binoculars can be sent to me care of M. Tholozan, Shipbroker, 6 rue Bauvau [*sic*; Beauvau], Marseille, for onward despatch to M. de Lostalot in Ǧiddah.

I shall release these two items, gratis, only if genuine service is rendered us.

Please would you be good enough to refresh the memory of M. Charmes and M. Renan on this matter at the earliest opportunity.

Yours, F.J. de Lostalot

Letter no. 7

Date: 3 December 1884
From: de Lostalot, Ǧiddah. On notepaper of the French Vice-Consulate.
To: M. Maunoir, Paris

My dear Sir,

Just a quick note written in haste to let you know what progress we have made.

As far as the murderers are concerned, I hope we shall manage to bring them to justice [*raccourcir*, lit. 'shorten', a euphemism for beheading], but when? They are fugitives, and as we cannot use force we must get the better of them by cunning. All that could well take a long time. But if that is what it takes, so be it.

As for the documents left behind by Huber, and above all the Stele of Taymāʾ, we shall hunt them down vigorously. I say 'we' because our opponents[9] have wasted not a moment.

Through the intermediary of the Dutch Consulate-General they have prevailed on the Vali (Governor-General) of the Ḥiǧāz to act on their behalf, and he is searching on his part, but what a difference there is in the resources he can mobilize!

However, I do not lose heart. I feel supported, the ministry having notified me on 30 November last that I could lay out 3,000 francs in order to achieve a result.

I have manoeuvred myself into a position where I can be at least warned about everything that happens: I have a friend close to the Vali himself who sends me information and, when the psychological moment arrives, if the Stele is in the Vali's possession, I shall buy it from him with a substantial bribe, of 3,000, 4,000 or even 5,000 francs. I shall stake the whole amount; however, I shall not do so without first getting your unofficial opinion. I should be very grateful if you would kindly let me know, just between ourselves, how far I can go.

It may not perhaps be necessary, because I do in fact hold some good trump cards in my hand. Whatever the situation, I am a little anxious and I am saying this to you as I would to a good friend. I am not writing to M. Renan about this because it is actually futile to worry him. I only want to give him good news. When? At the end of this month, perhaps.

I would be very grateful if you could hasten the dispatch of the two pairs of fine binoculars that I requested: by fine I mean of especially superior quality.

With an affectionate shake of your hand,

F. J. de Lostalot

---

[9] A reference to Snouck Hurgronje, allegedly acting on behalf of Euting and Germany.

Letter no. 8

Date: 25 January 1885
From: de Lostalot, Ğiddah. On notepaper of the French Vice-Consulate.
To: M. Maunoir, Secrétaire Général, Société de Géographie de Paris

My dear Sir,

I waited before sending you my best wishes for the newly dawned 1885 until I had news from the interior of Arabia about the late Huber's luggage and the Stele of Taymāʾ.

I have just received this news and have just written it all down in a long letter to M. Renan. Everything that our unfortunate compatriot left in Ḥāʾil is now safely in the hands of the emir of the Shammar, including six inscribed stones (five small, one large) and they will be sent to us under the greatest secrecy at the first favourable opportunity, at the latest during the next pilgrimage, i.e. in September.

Ibn Rashīd has suffered for the hospitality he so generously gave to Huber, and he would be afraid of complications were it to become known now that he was corresponding with us. That is the cause of the caution he is showing, but he sent word to me that he is still on our side.

If ever Arabia becomes independent from the Turks it will be because of Ibn Rashīd, and the Turks are well aware of this. Because of this he is closely watched. Nevertheless, he is making [campaign] preparations, and he is counting on us to guard his rear while he attacks in the south. I have taken care not to disillusion him.

Whatever happens, I hope successfully to complete the mission entrusted to me. In the same way I have not given up hope of having the murderers punished. After a Homeric struggle against the obstruction and apathy of the Ḥiğāz authorities, I have at last obtained formal assurances that the murderers will be vigorously pursued, and I have no reason for the present to doubt the truth of the promises made to me.

Now all we can do is wait, and it will not be my fault if the wait is a long one.

Accept, my dear Sir, the expression of my absolute devotion.

F.J. de Lostalot

Dr Snouck Hurgronje, about whom I have already spoken, has become a

Muslim (from head to toe)[10] and is at present in Mecca in order to undertake a study there of the religious laws of Islam and the Qurʾān.

LETTER NO. 9

Date: 16 March 1885
From: de Lostalot, Ǧiddah. On notepaper of the French Vice-Consulate.
To: M. Maunoir, 14 rue Jacob, Paris

Marginal note: Communicated to M. [Ernest] Renan, at the Institut [i.e. the AIBL], 2 April 1885.

My dear Sir,

My special batch of letters is about to leave at any moment for Europe; I am writing this short note in all haste to tell you that after much trial and error, the time for action has come in the search for the late M. Huber's baggage and its recovery. It has started well, because I have just today been brought, in a crate, the bones of our unfortunate compatriot, collected by one of my emissaries[11] from the scene of the crime. If nothing happens to hinder our operation, the rest of the baggage, including the famous Taymāʾ Stele, will be with me on the first day of May, and my plan is to bring it all back to France myself.

Now that I have in my possession the remains of what a few months ago was a man in full vigour and energy, I find myself very much at a loss. To whom should I send these remains? And how can I get them into France? Do I have to stick to the usual protocol and thus to inopportunely advertise their return to France? Or else, seeing that they are absolutely harmless from the point of view of public health, can I bring them back to Paris myself, either to the Ministry of Public Education or the Ministry of Foreign Affairs, to be handed on to the family or close friends?

There are so many questions which put me very much in a quandary, and I have been counting on your benevolence to help me to find answers. Would you please have the kindness to see Messieurs Renan and Charmes and let them know of my uncertainties. Perhaps you will glean a few clues from them for me to follow. I beg you to kindly do me this service by notifying these gentlemen that I am very much afraid that the credit of 3,000 francs that was

---

[10] Meaning that Hurgronje had undergone circumcision.
[11] *viz.* Sī ʿAzīz ibn Shaykh al-Ḥaddād, see Introduction pp. 75–6.

made available to me is now overdrawn. You cannot imagine the rapacity of these wretched Arabs, for whom nothing is sacred except the god called 'dollar'. I have already spent more than 2,000 francs, and I still have to pay the expenses of getting the luggage and the Stele back from Ḥā'il to Ǧiddah. If they fail to reach their destination I would not have to pay anything more, of course, but I have grounds for hoping that they will arrive soon.

I am not writing directly to the Ministry of Public Education because I have already received observations about this. All official correspondence with other departments is forbidden to us by the regulations but I shall soon be speaking face to face, I hope, and the information that I bring will certainly interest those willing to lend an ear.

I intend to be in Paris on about 15 June. Send me a reply as soon as possible so that I may act according to the instructions that I am awaiting.

Please accept, dear Sir, the expression of my best feeling.

F.J. de Lostalot

If the present situation continues much longer I shall be fretful indeed. The authorities are giving me good grounds to hope that the arrest of the murderers, who they declare to be in the vicinity of al-Madīnah, is imminent. During this time, one of them, as I learned too late, was actually in Ǧiddah five or six days ago. I learned this too late!

The Muslims are laughing at us, but it doesn't matter. He who laughs last laughs longest. If one can use such expressions in such a sad affair.

Letter no. 10

Date: 28 May 1885
From: de Lostalot, Ǧiddah. On notepaper of the French Vice-Consulate.
To: Charles Maunoir

My dear M. Maunoir,

It is with immense satisfaction that I can announce to you that the late M. Charles Huber's baggage is at my house, including the famous Taymā' Stele. But at the same time, to my great annoyance, I have overspent the credit allocated to me by approximately 2,000 francs. When I requested a credit of 3,000 francs, my calculations were accurate but I had not foreseen, as indeed I could not have done, the succession of infuriating twists and turns that would unfold throughout the transport of this baggage and which would often endanger the lives of those who had been assigned the task of bringing it back to Ǧiddah. The Stele was well known and pursued from Damascus by M. Euting,[12] and from Mecca by Dr Snouck Hurgronje, who had converted to Islam under the name ʿAbd al-Ghaffār. Even the Ottoman government, knowing the value of this monument, probably through the indiscretions of those two gentlemen, was trying to get hold of it. Thus, despite its weight, it was the subject of a real steeplechase during the thirty days of its journey to Ǧiddah. In al-Madīnah the luggage was almost seized by the governor. They came at night to my messenger's house, fruitlessly as it turned out, for he had taken care to leave everything outside the town in a secluded garden. He was nevertheless arrested for twenty-four hours and he was only released when he gave the governor to understand that what they were looking for had been in Baghdad for a long time.

The weight of these objects is such that it needs the five or six men in attendance to handle them, and to load and unload them. These men, seeing that some mystery surrounded these packages, and that they could not travel in broad daylight, apparently became outrageously demanding, and it became necessary either to give up the whole enterprise or else to satisfy their demands.

When I saw the bill that had to be paid I protested loudly. Back came the cold but cunning reply: 'If you want to leave us the great stone, we shall let you have the rest of the baggage without asking for a penny, and we shall even give you some money.'

Those people knew the value of the Stele! What was to be done? I resolved to pay up, and I guaranteed the money from my own finances in order to please M. Renan and you too, my dear Sir, and so that poor Huber's memory should be honoured for ever.

We buried his mortal remains on Wednesday 27 March, and I drew up an official report on the inhumation which I shall bring to Paris at the same time as his costly but precious baggage.

I intend to be in Paris from the 20th to the 25th of June at the latest. I hope to be able to rest from my tiring exertions and from the countless anxieties that the murder of our unfortunate compatriot has put me through. I shall bring a small quantity of Moka,[13] which we shall savour together.

---

[12] This was a wild rumour. Euting had returned to Germany long before. See Introduction p. 44.

[13] i.e. Mocha coffee, exported from Mukhāʾ in the Yemen.

In expectation of the pleasure of shaking your hand, please accept the expression of my affectionate devotion.

F.J. de Lostalot

LETTER NO. 11

Date: 23 June 1885
From: de Lostalot, Mont de Marsan, near Paris. On private notepaper.
To: Not stated, but to Charles Maunoir

My dear Sir,

I shall be in Paris next Tuesday, the 30th of this month, and shall have the honour of going to the Ministry of War to shake hands with you during the morning.

I am bringing with me the Taymāʾ Stele and the baggage of the late M. Charles Huber. I am alerting M. Renan by this same post.

Respectfully and devotedly yours,

Félix de Lostalot
French Vice-Consul on furlough

LETTER NO. 12

Date: 12 November 1885
From: de Lostalot, Ǧiddah. On notepaper of the French Vice-Consulate.
To: not named, but to Charles Maunoir

My dear Sir,

I think that all the upheavals caused by the recent and extraordinary elections that we have had in France will have finished by the time you read these lines. So in my opinion now is the moment to send forth a sign of life, and that is what I am doing by sending you a greeting as splendid as the light of dawn, gentle as musk and the most enticing perfumes, graceful as beautiful flowers in full bloom and tossed by the breeze, gentle as a morning dream. You see, we are in the Orient; but reality is far from living up to the poetry of words.

On my return here, I found everyone in turmoil. The Europeans were very hurt at M. Snouck's expulsion from Mecca, for which they held me responsible, not without some justification. The local authorities were furious at the way I had treated them and looked on me with disapproval. It became intolerable. M. Snouck was expelled from Mecca in the wake of the hasty publication of *Le Temps* newspaper. He set off back to Europe and I expect unpleasant articles to start appearing about me. I am not frightened of them because what I say is true, right and just, whereas what he says is false, perfidious and wrong. I have placed myself in a position to prove it so, whatever happens, by having a deposition made before the Dutch consul who is the official and unofficial defender of M. Snouck: by having a deposition, I say, made by the person to whom M. Snouck promised 10,000 francs for the Stele in the name of M. Euting, it seems. The Dutch consul will bear witness to this if need be. Therefore I have said nothing that is untrue.

This situation, however, has made my life in Ǧiddah intolerable. This is why I am asking you, and I am asking M. Renan by this same post, to work towards getting me a change of residence without delay. They promised me this at the Ministry, but in the more or less distant future – I would not want to wait any longer; my service comes to an end this year; it is my wish to be replaced.

I am counting on you, my dear Sir, to enable me to be no longer forgotten. Please, I beg you, get me transferred as soon as possible.

I cordially shake your hand.

F.J. de Lostalot

Letter no. 13

Date: 18 December 1885
From: de Lostalot, Ǧiddah. On notepaper of the French Vice-Consulate.
To: Philippe Berger, at the AIBL, Paris

My dear Sir,

I am sending you, in strict confidence, the draft of my reply [see next letter] to the article from the *Allgemeine Zeitung* of 16 November last, published by Dr Snouck Hurgronje against me.[14]

The whole business is in the hands of my superiors who appreciate, as you read these lines, the timeliness of my reply. I do not need to tell you how

[14] See Introduction note 242, on Snouck Hurgronje's article in the *Münchener Allgemeine Zeitung* of 16 November 1885 (Snouck Hurgronje 1923).

careful we must be. I have written to M. Renan to warn him that he will very probably be consulted and, if he is not, to bring about an honourable solution to this business, which is really unpleasant for me.

You will understand that I require satisfaction. Were it to be decided that far too much fuss has already been made about the Stele and that it is a good idea for it to be brought to an end, I am counting on you, my dear Sir, to persuade M. Renan, the instigator of this business, to allow me at all events to obtain redress that will place my honour completely above reproach. My superiors need to prove publicly to everyone that I have done nothing discreditable. It is not up to me to say what that redress should be; but our governors are so busy that they may well forget about me, which it would not be proper for me to accept. If my replies are not published just as I have written them and submitted them to the ministry, could not a short announcement be made to appear in the Paris newspapers, *Le Temps* at the head of them, along the following lines: 'M. de Lostalot, French Vice-Consul in Ğiddah, has just been appointed Consul and retained in Ğiddah', or, better still: 'Sent to Ğiddah newly appointed. This unusual promotion is in recompense for the distinguished service that he has rendered in Arabia, and we congratulate him publicly etc etc.' It is up to M. Renan to bring about the promotion that I think I have deserved, and it is up to your friendship for me, my dear Sir, to persuade him that he must do it.

Would you very kindly lend me your good offices in this business, my dear Sir, and I shall repay you if the opportunity arises?

Yours sincerely,
F.J. de Lostalot

Letter no. 14

Dated (at end): 12 November [*sic*; December must be meant] 1885
From: de Lostalot, Ğiddah. On notepaper of the French Vice-Consulate.
To: probably Philippe Berger, as the enclosure referred to in Letter no. 13 dated 18 December 1885, though this is not stated.

In Arabia.
Response.[15]

[15] *viz.* to the allegations against de Lostalot first published by Snouck Hurgronje in Leiden on 5 November 1885, and then in the *Münchener Allgemeine Zeitung* of 16 November 1885 (see Snouck Hurgronje 1923).

In a long article published by the *Allgemeine Zeitung* of 16 November last [1885], under the heading 'Aus Arabien' (from Arabia), Dr Snouck Hurgronje of Leiden does us the honour of mentioning us in terms that render it impossible for us not to respond. Naturally we shall not follow him along the unspeakable path that he has chosen and we shall not resort to his style and manner, which are worthy of something that has escaped from M. Pasteur's laboratory; our tastes and our habits, which are nothing like those of Muslim society, which is so highly appreciated by him, are entirely antipathetic to it. We shall simply leave it to our readers to evaluate his arguments in both their content and their form – above all in their form, which is as unfitting as the content is inaccurate.

Of all his allegations, each one more deliberately erroneous than the last, notably the one about the excuses made to the authorities of the country, which we deny formally and absolutely – (Those who have knowledge of the official documents are well aware of this) – we shall discuss only two, which seem useful to explain for the edification of our readers.

First: Was M. Snouck Hurgronje involved, yes or no, in the search for the Taymāʾ Stele, which is currently in the Louvre in Paris, despite his written promises?

Secondly: Was M. Snouck Hurgronje expelled from Mecca following the publication of a French newspaper report which was supposedly reproduced by the Turkish and Arab press?

I affirm without hesitation that M. Snouck, despite his written promises, tried to get possession of the Stele, and my proofs are as follows. Last January, following several interviews between M. Kruyt, Consul-General of the Netherlands, and M. Snouck on one side, and ourselves on the other, interviews [took place] in which M. Snouck himself told us that he had been charged with the task of seeking the Stele on someone else's behalf. M. Snouck, I say, on his own initiative, sent us a letter in which he formally promised no longer to be concerned with the aforementioned Stele. And whatever he said about it, we did not for one moment suspect him to be capable of breaking his promises. He was then leaving for Mecca at the end of January or beginning of February. On our side, we were actively employed in seeking the monumental inscription in question, and those charged with this task went about it in the belief that this stone was destined to decorate a funerary monument that we intended to erect in honour of our unfortunate compatriot, the late M. Charles Huber. (The monument has been erected in the non-Muslim cemetery in Ǧiddah, under the auspices of the Ministry of Public Education in Paris.) They were completely unaware of the quality and the value of the object they were seeking; only we and M. Snouck were in the know about this.

When our agents,[16] who had set off from Mecca in March on their special mission [*viz.* to Ḥā'il], and not to look for the late M. Huber's baggage [*viz.* in the Rābigh area and al-Madīnah], brought the Stele to our house at the end of May, they presented us with a very exorbitant claim for expenses, which we contested, and we even refused to pay the whole sum they were demanding. It was then that one of them said to us: 'We shall reimburse you all the money you have paid already, i.e. 1,800 francs, and we shall even let you have all the objects that we have collected, if only you will leave us the great stone!' 'And what do you want to do with it?' we asked, with unfeigned astonishment. 'We shall take it to M. Snouck Hurgronje, who in Mecca promised us 10,000 francs on the day that it was brought to his house.' 'That is not possible,' we added. 'Let us have the stone, Sir,' came their reply.

M. Snouck Hurgronje denies having made the offers with which we reproached him at the time, and with which we still reproach him. Well! In order to convict him, we had our principal agent[17] make a deposition before the consul of the Netherlands, his protector and natural defender, in which he said that he had received *in Mecca* – let us not lose sight of this – the promise of ten thousand francs; thus, between the end of January and the beginning of March, and therefore *after* the undertaking he [*viz.* Hurgronje] had made to us. – Were we not therefore justified in thinking then and only then, that M. Snouck Hurgronje had had only one aim in writing to us: to lull us into a false sense of security in order to have more freedom to carry out his ulterior designs?

And even if we do not know the Arab, the Turk or Muslim society as well as M. Snouck Hurgronje does, and we humbly admit this, we do nonetheless know that it would never occur to an Arab, however intelligent he might be, if he had not been alerted to it, to put such a high price as ten thousand francs onto a derelict old stone like the Stele in question – and, what is really amazing, exactly the sum that the Taymā' Stele is worth! We shall let all impartial observers judge for themselves; but we shall insist no further and leave it to our readers to reach their own conclusions.

[16] *viz.* Sī ʿAzīz ibn Shaykh al-Ḥaddād and his party, see Introduction pp. 75–6.
[17] Sī ʿAzīz ibn Shaykh al-Ḥaddād.

Was M. Snouck expelled from Mecca for the reasons that he gave?

M. Snouck is no more telling the truth here than in everything else that he has written. Here are the real motives that caused him to break off his studies. It is known to everyone around here that the Vali of Mecca and the Qaïmaqam of Ǧiddah did not get on, both of them just waiting for the moment for one to depose the other. Now M. Snouck was not in the governor of Ǧiddah's good books for the simple reason that he had been received favourably by the governor of Mecca. Then came one fine day last July, when another European presented himself in Mecca who had sacrificed a tiny part of his epidermis so as not to jeopardize the whole, in a word who had embraced Islam (as everyone knows, circumcision is obligatory for all Muslims). (M. Huber did not do it, Sir, and that is what cost him his life!) The Vali had him expelled immediately, seeing which, the Qaïmaqam of Ǧiddah let it be known in Constantinople that the Vali had two weights and two measures, arbitrarily expelling one European convert while fawning on another; and the Vali, duly reprimanded, could not get out of applying to M. Snouck Hurgronje a measure that he had just applied to another. – These are the reasons for the expulsion of M. Snouck, and not some fatuous journalistic fantasy or other which is as apocryphal as it is unknown.

To sum up, M. Snouck Hurgronje, in publishing his diatribe inserted in the *Allgemeine Zeitung*, has once again committed a very wicked act. Not content with the unprecedented scandal to which his self-interested conversion to Islam has given rise in the European community in Ǧiddah, he has taken great pleasure in spreading undeserved slander and calumny about good people who are without exception held in universal high regard. We have to say that his activities leave us cold, and that whatever he may achieve in the future will never match the scale of our disdain.

M. Snouck screams, shouts and rages because he played a game against us that he was not able to win. At the very least it is in deeply poor taste. As far we are concerned, we give not a fig for it and propose to dwell upon it no further. But we shall be heartily glad to let the reading public discern for themselves where, in all this, are to be found truth, honour and loyalty!

Ǧiddah, 12 November [*sic*; December must be meant] 1885
Dr F.J. de Lostalot

APPENDIX 10

Letters from Julius Euting, 1884–86

THE FIRST five of these letters and postcards are from Julius Euting to French scholars. They are held in the Archives du Cabinet of the *Corpus Inscriptionum Semiticarum* (CIS), of the Académie des Inscriptions et Belles-Lettres (AIBL), Institut de France, Paris. Correspondence classified under Boîte Correspondence Do–E.

They demonstrate that Julius Euting continued to maintain warm relations with members of the AIBL despite his own claim to ownership of the Taymāʾ Stele. They also shed valuable light on Huber's unattributed use of Euting's initial sketch of the inscription on the Taymāʾ Stele, on how Huber came to believe that the inscription was Phoenician rather than Aramaic, and on the extent of Euting's contributions to Huber's diary of the 1883–84 Arabian journey.

Letter no. 6 was written by Euting in early 1886 to the Minister of Public Education in Paris. It is held in the archives of the Ministère de l'Instruction publique et des Beaux-Arts at Pierrefitte-sur-Seine, Paris, as item no. 128 in Dossier F/17/2976/1:2 Mission en Arabie. 1883. It is an important first-hand source for the arrangements and funding for the 1883–84 Huber–Euting expedition, and for the recovery by Euting of his belongings.

With thanks to Prof. Maria Gorea for making these items available, and to Barbara Newton for translating nos. 1–5.

LETTER NO. 1

Date: 21 November 1884

From: Julius Euting, Rohan-Schloss, Strasbourg

To: unidentified recipient, but probably Philippe Berger (1846–1912), the

Hebrew scholar who was secretary to Ernest Renan at the AIBL, and librarian at the Institut de France, Paris.

My dear Sir and friend,

I received your friendly letter dated the 17th yesterday evening, and hasten to reply to you.

First of all the main matter:

I have discovered no fewer than fifty mostly well-preserved Himyaritic[1] inscriptions from el-ʿÖlā [al-ʿUlā] (commonly written العلى \ العلا \ العله on maps, and in Doughty's version also el-Alli[2]) from which I also managed to get quite good squeezes, first because the wind was not so troublesome as in Madâïn Sâlih [Madāʾin Ṣāliḥ], and secondly because my personal security required no particular attention. I had leisure and time for a ten-day stay in el-ʿÖlā. As regards Madâïn Sâlih, we only stayed four days and my guides (two Balī [tribesmen]) threatened to leave me stranded should I fail to finish. And so in four days I copied as much as Doughty had done in almost as many months.

I reserved the Nabataean inscriptions for myself. As regards the Himyaritic ones, I had no plans at all for them; and when David Heinrich Müller in Vienna, whom I myself had previously initiated into epigraphy, wrote to [me in] Cairo from Jerusalem that he had heard from my letters that I had brought some Himyaritic inscriptions with me, and asked whether I would let him have them for publication, I did not hesitate for a moment to hand the material over to a specialist.

If you had expressed the same desire before he had, I would have handed the same material over to you just as willingly and cheerfully. He will of course soon publish his work in the memoirs of the Viennese Academy. Once that has been done, I intend to hand over to the Commission du *Corpus* [*viz.* the *Corpus Inscriptionum Semiticarum* in Paris] a squeeze of every inscription, provided I have not already offered them through my poor

[1] For the incorrect use of the term 'Himyaritic' by Euting and Huber at this period, see Translation Part I, note 158, and Appendix 4 note 20. The so-called 'Himyaritic' inscriptions that Euting collected at al-ʿUlā (ancient Dadan) were in Minaic and also in the script later known as 'Lihyanite' in English, now known as Dadanitic (see Macdonald 2000: 33). On the Lihyanite kingdom, see most recently Rohmer and Charloux 2015. (MCAM)

[2] In fact Doughty calls it el-Ally. Euting added a note to 'el-Alli' at this point in the letter: 'Written thus in the stupid phonetic transcriptions by Joseph von Hammer Purgstall in his translation of the pilgrim route in the Djehan numa.'

travelling companion, the late Herr Huber. I think there were nineteen of those; so there are approximately an additional thirty. Many are identical to Doughty's, but I think they are perhaps somewhat clearer. (Of the fifty, twenty-four are probably Minaic, as David Heinrich Müller writes.)

I do not yet know how long my work on the Nabataean inscriptions will take, but I shall work on them as carefully as I can, without hurrying, and shall be in a position to bring very substantial completions and corrections to the descriptions and explanations that have so far been made. The language is more closely related to Arabic than we thought.

So once again I can only repeat how sorry I am that I was not previously aware that you were equally familiar with the Himyaritic area of study, otherwise I would have taken great pleasure in handing this material over to you.

Should you ever come to Strassburg, I would be delighted. I think you would derive great enjoyment from my journals and, quite apart from those, there would be lots of other interesting things for you to see as well.

With friendly greetings.

Your devoted
J. Euting

Letter no. 2

Postcard to Charles Simon Clermont-Ganneau (1846–1923), the French Orientalist and archaeologist.

Date: 2 February 1885
From: Julius Euting, Str. Schloss (*viz.* Strassburg, Rohan-Schloss)
To: Charles Clermont-Ganneau, 44 Avenue Marceau, Paris

My dear Herr Ganneau,

Hearty thanks for your previous few lines and the brochures that you kindly sent. I have received comments from various sides about the great Taymāʾ inscription (even from Ge. Hoffmann[3] in Kiel) which are in accord with your views, namely that צלם [Ṣalm] denotes the name of God. For the moment at least I can only say that this opinion is quite probably correct. I will come back to this when I get to work on my squeeze again, when I shall try to

[3] Johann Georg Ernst Hoffmann (1845–1933), a friend of Theodor Nöldeke, was a German Orientalist and Semitist who worked at the University of Kiel.

prepare a life-size, hand-done drawing. For the present, I am completely taken up with my Nabataean inscriptions and I can spare no time for any other task.

With friendly greetings, also to Messrs Renan and Berger.

Your devoted
J. Euting

LETTER NO. 3

Postcard to Philippe Berger.

Date: 24 July 1885
From: Julius Euting, Str. Schloss (*viz.* Strassburg, Rohan-Schloss)
To: Philippe Berger

Most esteemed Sir!

Many thanks for your friendliness in sending me your most recent work, *L'Arabie avant Mahomet* [Arabia before Muḥammad].[4] You will understand that I am astonished to see published a drawing of the Taymāʾ Stele from Huber's journal which I myself had drawn in it, as a favour.[5] I would have thought that even without the J.E. you would have recognized my hand! Since Huber had no particular skill in drawing, I drew dozens of difficult inscriptions, pictures (and also maps) at his request, and likewise your title-page picture of the south-east corner of Maḥággeh.[6]

With the most humble respect,

J. Euting

---

[4] *L'Arabie avant Mahomet, d'après les inscriptions: conférence faite à la Sorbonne*, was a 30-page offprint from the *Bulletin hebdomadaire de l'Association scientifique*, nos. 271 and 272, published by Maisonneuve in Paris in 1885.

[5] Euting's sketch of the Aramaic inscription on the Taymāʾ Stele appeared on p. 29 of the offprint. The initials J.E. are nowhere to be seen on it, so they must have been removed from the original sketch in Huber's journal. The same sketch appeared again in 1891, likewise unattributed, in the published edition of Huber's journal of the 1883–84 journey (Huber 1891: 319). See Illustration no. 11 in this volume.

[6] This sketch by Euting of long-necked camels appeared on the title page of Berger's offprint, and again later in the published edition of Huber's journal of the 1883–84 journey (Huber 1891: 286–7).

Letter no. 4

Date: 1 August 1885
From: Julius Euting, Str. Schloss (*viz*. Strassburg, Rohan-Schloss)
To: Philippe Berger

My dear Herr Berger,

I was not able to answer your friendly letter of 25 July any sooner because I was completely taken up by the visit of Professor David Heinrich Müller from Vienna, who stayed with me for ten days.

The drawing in Huber's journal is in conformity with the drawing in my journal of 17 February 1884,[7] and is just a quick sketch of the appearance of the [Taymāʾ] Stone. For comparison's sake, on 12 and 13 June 1884 in Jerusalem I sent off a drawing which was as far as possible at the time more complete and, to the best of my ability, more accurate, based on my squeeze (to Nöldeke, intended for publication[8]).

Moreover, I noticed that the numbers on the drawing in Huber's journal stemmed from me: compare the dot above the 1 in the number 21, and my 5.[9]

Equally, I can see on the title-page picture [of Berger's *L'Arabie avant Mahomet*] that the camels and the inscriptions running behind them were drawn by me.

I did my friend Huber this favour dozens and dozens of times when he wanted something drawn, especially for example on 18 October '84 [*sic*; 1883 is meant]: the transcription of the Hebrew inscription that I discovered in Góbbeh [Ğubbah] into the usual square script comes from me. Furthermore, every one of the mountain panoramas without exception, and also the complete map of ʿAḳdeh [ʿUqdah] and the surrounding area in the Gebel Aga [Ağā], were done by me in colour based on Huber's notes and jottings, and at his direction.[10] I therefore ask that, at least from now on, somewhat more care may be taken in future publications; alas, I am now very sorry not to have been more careful myself.

---

[7] This first sketch by Euting is in his unpublished diary: Md 676-22, Notebook V, folio 8r. See Illustration no. 9 in this volume.

[8] Theodor Nöldeke was the first scholar to publish the inscription on the Taymāʾ Stele, from the squeeze and drawing sent to him from Jerusalem by Euting in June 1884 (Noldeke 1884). See Illustration no. 10 in this volume.

[9] The dot above the 1, and Euting's distinctive 5, both appear in his original diary, Md 676-22, Notebook V, folio 8r. See Illustration no. 9 in this volume.

[10] See Huber 1891 for all these items.

From 16 August to about 8 September I shall of course be absent from here: letters and suchlike will however always reach me at my present address.

In the hope of more favourable circumstances,

Yours sincerely,
J. Euting

I would just add that it was not Huber but I who, on the first evening, thought that the [Taymāʾ Stele] inscription was Phoenician (Huber could not possibly have come up with this), because on line 21 I thought I saw (בן) and not (בר). When the stone was brought into the house I had leisure to convince myself of my initial error and to recognize the language as Aramaic. Where would Huber have acquired the ability to make this distinction in the desert, and overnight into the bargain?

Even if various inhabitants of Taymāʾ told Mr Doughty that there was a 'similar' inscription to be found elsewhere, I can only say that I have been told hundreds and hundreds of times about inscriptions by people who had not the faintest notion whether they were even inscribed characters, let alone whether they were 'similar'.

LETTER NO. 5

Postcard to Philippe Berger.

Date: 2 November 1885
From: Julius Euting, Str. Schloss (*viz.* Strassburg, Rohan-Schloss)
To: Philippe Berger, Institut de France, Paris

Most highly esteemed Sir,

My best thanks for being so kind as to send me the two copies of the heliogravure[11] of the Taymāʾ Stele, which has come out very well. Could you please send me a copy of Huber's article about his journey in the *Bulletin de la Société de Géographie* in 1884? At the time, Huber promised that one would be delivered to me because I had drawn the Arabic title, the transcription list, and the picture of Khaybar for him.[12]

[11] Heliogravure: the earliest method of reproducing photographs for printing, by which the photographic image was etched onto a copper plate.

[12] Euting is referring to the sketch map and the panorama of the Khaybar oasis, which he himself had not visited but where Huber spent time on his first Arabian journey in

My baggage has still not arrived at Mme Huber's house. I hope that you will get some explanation via Herr Leblois.

With best greetings,

Your completely devoted
J. Euting

Have you not yet received my Nabataean Inscriptions?[13] I sent it to you five weeks ago via Leipzig.

LETTER NO. 6

Date: no date, but received on 6 January 1886
From: Julius Euting, presumably from Strasbourg
To: Monsieur le Ministre de l'Instruction publique et des Beaux-Arts, Paris

Dear Minister,

In reply to your esteemed letter of 26 November 1885,[14] I have the honour to acknowledge to Your Excellency receipt of the eleven objects which you have had the kindness to arrange to be sent to me by means of M. Barack, director of the Imperial Library at Strasbourg, and I thank you sincerely for dispatching them. As for the books sent in the same consignment and addressed to Mme Huber care of M. Béguin's address,[15] that lady has immediately restored to me those among them that belong to me.

December 1880 (Huber 1884b: 525–30). These sketches, which he must have done for Huber in 1882 while the two men were discussing possible collaboration on the 1883–84 Arabian journey, appeared as vignettes on the large fold-out map of Huber's 1880–81 journey (reproduced at the end of this volume), which was published with the first of the three parts of Huber's account in the *Bulletin de la Société de Géographie* (Huber 1884b). They appear in this volume on p. 205. As he points out to Berger, Euting had also drawn the handsome calligraphed Arabic title of the map, and the Arabic letters for the list of transliterations. See Appendix 4, Letter no. 8 dated 28 August 1882 from Huber to Maunoir, in which Huber fails to acknowledge Euting's contribution.

[13] Euting's seminal publication, *Nabatäische Inschriften aus Arabien* (Berlin: Reimer, 1885), was fresh from the press.

[14] This letter is listed as no. 117 in the Ministry of Public Education archives, Dossier F/17/2976/1:2 Mission en Arabie. 1883.

[15] Béguin was the Strasbourg bookseller who auctioned off Huber's library and other effects on 20 June 1885. See Appendix 12, Item no. 3, p. 477 below.

The items received represent only a tiny part of the effects that I left in Arabia and which had been sent to France as part of M. Huber's estate. I am therefore taking the liberty, M. le Ministre, of asking you with the greatest respect whether I may nurture the hope of recovering the remainder of my possessions.

When, on 22 May 1883, M. Charles Huber left with me for the East, he had not yet received the financial assistance confirming his official mission. For my part, I was in possession of the sum of 17,800 marks (= 22,250 francs) that the government of Alsace-Lorraine had granted for my expedition. Furthermore M. Huber, whose entire baggage comprised some instruments, some books and three almost empty chests, had contributed nothing at all to the costs of the expedition. Not only did I purchase all the items required for the journey, at a cost of 2,772 marks and 54 pfennigs (= 3,465 francs and 80 cents) – I have kept all the receipts for Your Excellency to see – but I also brought, thanks to the munificence of His Majesty the King of Württemberg, twenty-four rifles, as well as some books and instruments that various savants in Germany had spontaneously placed at my disposal. All of this was packed in fourteen chests, each bearing my initials J.E., while one of them carried my complete name, Dr Julius Euting, stamped on leather.

Just as we were leaving, M. Huber expressed the hope that he would shortly receive an adequate subsidy from the French government side. I have since learned from M. Renan that at the point of our arrival at Marseille (on 23 April 1883) he had received 2,500 francs granted him by the Académie des Inscriptions [*viz.* the AIBL].[16] But to me he maintained the most complete silence about this missive, and it was at my expense that he travelled all through the months of May, June, July and August 1883 from Strasbourg to Marseille, Alexandria, Cairo, Beirut, and finally from Damascus to Palmyra and back. It was only in August 1883 that he shared with me a telegram from the Ministry of Public Education in Paris, informing him that a sum of 10,000 francs had been granted to him, with the observation that he should not expect any more. From this sum, according to what he told me, he deducted in advance only 5,000 francs at Damascus, biding his time before drawing the remainder in Ǧiddah the following year.[17]

---

[16] See Appendix 11, Letter no. 1 dated 8 July 1885 from Renan to Euting.

[17] As it turned out, the remainder could not be sent to Ǧiddah and Huber would have had to take the full amount (in the event, 9,600 francs) in Damascus. See Appendix 4, Letter no. 21 dated 30 November 1883 from Huber to Maunoir; Letter no. 24

After a three-month sojourn in Ḥā'il, where I left the majority of my baggage, we travelled together until 19 March 1884. Having arrived at al-ʿUlā (el-Ōla), he suddenly announced his intention to continue on his way alone, in a different direction from me.

Our relationship having remained very affectionate, I left him with my Lefaucheux rifle and almost all the utensils and possessions I had brought from Ḥā'il, and gave him the authority, as he asked, to make use of the things I had left there. Besides the items I had brought from Strasbourg and various valuable objects that I had bought either in Egypt or in Arabia itself, as well as the gifts to me with which the emir had reciprocated mine to him, my chests remaining in Ḥā'il still contained a sum of at least 450 francs.

Since then I have settled the bill for two Mauser rifles (repeaters) that M. Huber had asked me to order for him. I have kept the letter that he addressed to me, informing me that he had received the rifles and asking me to pay the account (369 marks = 461 francs) and to wait until he was able to reimburse me.

During the months of July and August 1885, I wrote to M. Renan asking him if he would be kind enough to intervene in order to arrange for my remaining possessions to be sent to M. Huber's mother, his next-of-kin. As she knew what her son had taken with him, she would be able to restore my belongings to me without difficulty, as she had just done with the books that she had received. As these approaches have so far yielded no result, I am presuming, M. le Ministre, to address the same request to you. Once Mme Huber is in possession of the baggage regarded as belonging to her son, I shall be able to reclaim my property from her. As I am aware of this lady's precarious situation, I still hesitate to present her with the above-mentioned letter from her son on the matter of the Mauser rifles, and the note confirming that I paid for them on his behalf. Please allow me, M. le Ministre, to respectfully enquire whether, for the reimbursement of this sum, I may apply to Your Excellency and send to you the items confirming that I disbursed this sum at M. Huber's request, while he was in the service of France.

Please accept, M. le Ministre, the expression of my most respectful feelings.

Dr Julius Euting
Professor at the University of Strasbourg

---

note 154; Letter no. 18 dated 19 July 1883 from Huber to Maunoir, stating that arrangements could not be made for delivery to Ǧiddah.

APPENDIX 11

Correspondence between Ernest Renan, Julius Euting and Philippe Berger, 1885–91

THESE FIVE letters are preserved among the Renan papers in the Archives du Cabinet of the *Corpus Inscriptionum Semiticarum*, Académie des Inscriptions et Belles-Lettres (AIBL), Institut de France, Paris. Correspondence with Julius Euting and Philippe Berger, classified under Ref. Boîte 'Dossiers 48'.

Renan's letters are interesting mainly for showing the extent of his misapprehensions about Huber and Euting's 1883–84 journey through Arabia. With thanks to Prof. Maria Gorea for making these letters available, and to Barbara Newton for translating them.

LETTER NO. 1

Date: 8 July 1885
From: Ernest Renan, in Rosmapamon, near Perros (Côtes du Nord), on notepaper of the Académie des Inscriptions et Belles-Lettres, Commission du *Corpus Inscriptionum Semiticarum*.
To: Julius Euting

Dear M. Euting,

I received your letter in the depths of Brittany where I am taking some time off to rest. I left Paris on 30 June, the very day on which the Taymāʾ Stele arrived. I was only able to glance at it briefly an hour before catching a train. In order to reply to you with a complete and fully documented letter, I would need to be in Paris to confer with my colleagues and with M. de Lostalot. However, I want for now to repay your confidence and to tell you, from a purely personal point of view (the Ministry of Education alone is in a position to speak officially), how the matter should proceed from this point on.

We possess a very voluminous file of letters from M. Huber,[1] from all stages from before his departure to almost the day before his death. The Ministry of Foreign Affairs possesses reports which corroborate this absolutely. M. de Lostalot is in possession of all kinds of documents. These papers provide the proof that Huber did not cease for a single moment to regard himself as a person commissioned by the French and therefore obliged to hand over to France all the objects he had brought back. He repeats this assertion many times. As far as you in particular are concerned, M. Huber declares that you were not [officially] commissioned, that for him you were only a travelling companion, and that you have no right to remove anything from the resultant finds. In the light of these texts, the exact copy of which I regret not being able to send you today, the Ministry of Public Education and Fine Arts would certainly not concede that you had any share in the ownership of the objects of scientific interest resulting from Huber's assignment. For the Taymāʾ Stele in particular, apart from the sketch that Huber made of it during his first journey, and which was published by the Geographical Society, I have to say that Huber, before his departure, spoke to me about it saying that he viewed this monument as his main discovery, that it was above all with the aim of getting the Stele that he undertook his second journey, that it was to get the Stele that we principally commissioned him.[2]

It is not true to say that Huber received no subsidy before August in Damascus. I myself had 2,500 francs sent to him to Marseille from the Académie des Inscriptions et Belles-Lettres.[3] We have the receipt from M. Huber.

Another consideration which I submit to you is this: you admit that it would be fair to pay your share of the transport costs from Ḥāʾil to Europe. These expenses, as was to be foreseen, have been very considerable. Half of these costs would certainly exceed whatever you would be able to claim as co-owner of the objects of scientific interest.

---

[1] This file of letters has not been located and studied. But the gist of Renan's claims about Huber's entitlement is contained in Huber's letter to him of 8 April 1883, see Appendix 7.

[2] For the many erroneous claims made in this paragraph, see Introduction, p. 80.

[3] The AIBL made Huber a grant of 5,000 francs in total, and Euting was only aware of the 2,500 francs that Huber collected in Damascus, presumably because the latter had concealed the first tranche of 2,500 francs from him.

There remain the personal effects, that is, everything that does not pertain to the scientific goals of the journey. Here I am assured that you will find a more generous response from the Ministry and M. de Lostalot. Everything will have to be sent to M. Huber's mother in Strasbourg.[4] It will be easy for you to recover what belongs to you. You know that poor Huber's bags were ransacked. I heard M. de Lostalot speak of money stolen, and that criminal proceedings have been brought against a servant.

I will do everything I can for the piece of rock crystal which holds personal memories for you to be allocated to you, and the same with the chamois head.

I regret, dear Sir, given the distance, that I cannot write to you in more detail. Do get in touch with M. de Lostalot (in Salies de Béarn, Basses-Pyrénées) or, better still, with M. Philippe Berger, who has had long conversations recently with M. de Lostalot. I am very keen that everything should be concluded to your satisfaction; you know how much I prize the services you have rendered to science. I am confident that our relations will remain in the future what they have been up until now, i.e. governed by the love and interest which we share in our studies. I am sending your letter to M. Berger, so it is not necessary for you to repeat the contents to him.

Believe me to be your most devoted

E. Renan

LETTER NO. 2

This is a rough draft on AIBL notepaper of a letter from Philippe Berger to Ernest Renan, dated 10 July 1885, describing the first inspection of Huber's effects brought to Paris from Ǧiddah by de Lostalot. It is in Berger's handwriting and is peppered with crossings-out and insertions, rendering some passages difficult to interpret. In such cases we have tried to convey the general meaning as accurately as possible.

Date: 10 July 1885
From: Philippe Berger, Académie des Inscriptions et Belles-Lettres, Commission du *Corpus Inscriptionum Semiticarum*, Paris.

[4] As Euting wrote to Philippe Berger in November 1885, he was kept waiting for his baggage to be delivered to Mme Huber's house; see Appendix 10, Letter no. 5 dated 2 November 1885.

To: Ernest Renan

Sir [*viz.* E. Renan],

M. de Lostalot proceeded, in my presence, to open the crates containing the results of M. Huber's expedition and his personal effects. As well as the one containing the great Stele of Taymā', which you have seen, M. de Lostalot brought back four crates. The fifth contained four inscriptions and a fragment of bas-relief, likewise from Taymā', which had been announced by M. Huber either in the letters that he wrote to you or in his report to the Ministry. These five stones were placed in the Cabinet of the *Corpus*, while waiting to be placed around the Taymā' Stele. In the same crate, there was also a collection of mineralogical samples from the various parts of Arabia. It is among these samples (wrapped in small bags and with captions in M. Huber's hand) that there is the fragment of rock crystal that M. Euting claims for his personal collection. I have stored all these samples provisionally in the drawers of the *Corpus* Cabinet.

The three other crates contained for the most part the personal luggage of M. Huber. These bags were not in the same condition that M. Huber left them in Ḥā'il. They have been opened and ransacked after his death. Out of fifteen crates, cases or bundles making up the whole at the outset, there remains only enough to fill ['valeur'] three crates. The greater part of their contents was made up of coverings and utensils. There were notably four oriental carpets, silk (or not) embroidered robes, shoes, metal vases, linen underwear, boxes of cigars.

The objects are in two suitcases marked J.E. [Julius Euting] and bearing also the label Charles Huber in Damascus. They were open. The locks had been broken and the leather had been cut. One contained medicines and the other books, papers and personal effects all jumbled together. One could see that it had all been rifled through.

We found no trace of money or valuables in it all. Neither did we find any sort of ladder, nor any apparatus. The only precision measuring instrument that came back was an aneroid barometer. The ibex head claimed by M. Euting is also missing.

Perhaps on emptying the crates some of these objects will be found. We restricted ourselves to a cursory examination just to get an idea of the state of the things and to set aside anything that could be directly linked to M. Huber's scientific mission.

From all of this we only put to one side a single roll of squeezes and the rough copies of the travel notebooks that M. Huber had directed to the Ministry. The rest has been sent to the Ministry of Education.

LETTER NO. 3

Date: 18 July 1885
From: Ernest Renan, Rosmapamon
To: Philippe Berger, Académie des Inscriptions et Belles Lettres, Commission du *Corpus Inscriptionum Semiticarum*, Paris.

Dear M. Berger,

Your brochure is excellent. Circulate it without fear. Let us get a tight grip on the Euting question. The reserving of 'one inscription' is of course only valid if the Huber–Euting partnership had lasted. The break at Ḥā'il put an end to their agreement ['pacte'].[5] Euting was so conscious of this that he freed himself from the obligations contained in his letter by sending the copies of the inscriptions to Nöldeke alone. Lastly, in Palmyra Euting acted completely outside the agreement because he took everything for himself. In good conscience, I do not think that this clause about reserving an inscription should be taken into consideration. What we have to do is to avoid scandal. In any case the question of State ownership and the credit for the discovery must be kept completely separate. We scarcely need to bother about the first of these. As for the question of who discovered the Taymā' inscription, there are abundant proofs quite aside from Huber's letter.

I received the enclosed despatch from Sousse. See if the inscription is the same as the one M. Reinach had sent you. Give M. Collignon a word from me in reply and file his document in Hadrumète [Hadrumetum, an ancient port in Tunisia].

Affectionately yours,

Renan

---

[5] There was no 'break' at Ḥā'il between the two men: Renan had swallowed Huber's story about sending Euting ahead without him. Huber and Euting did not separate until they had reached al-ʿUlā and Madā'in Ṣāliḥ. See Introduction pp. 42–3 and 51.

LETTER NO. 4

Date: 20 July 1885
From: Ernest Renan, Rosmapamon
To: Philippe Berger, Académie des Inscriptions et Belles Lettres, Commission du *Corpus Inscriptionum Semiticarum*, Paris.

Dear M. Berger,

Here is the proof copy which seems to me to be the best for the time being. If Vogüé is in Paris, consult him. Oh! what a fine monument! How well we did to defend it tooth and nail!

I received a nice letter from Euting. Without Delaunay the affair would have gone smoothly. The incident must be confined to rectifying the stupid account in *Le Temps*. I think Euting will be easily satisfied. If we can give him back his rock crystal, I admit that I do not see any great objection to this.

We are so lucky to have you because you are so industrious and so wise, such a friend to truth.

Yours affectionately,

E. Renan

LETTER NO. 5

Date: 24 March 1891
From: Philippe Berger, Darmstadt
To: Ernest Renan

Dear Sir and very dear Maître [*viz*. Ernest Renan],

I saw Euting yesterday and the day before. He told me that Huber must have been about thirty-six but he could not tell me his exact age. I am writing a note to M. Maunoir to ask him to send it to you if he has more precise information.

He [Euting] stayed with him from September [1883] to April [1884].[6] So they separated before Huber came back to Ǧiddah. As for the drawings, there can be no doubt; Euting showed me the whole series of his copies, drawings and watercolours. The same distinctive hand is recognizable from start to finish.

[6] In fact the two men parted on 26 March 1884, at Madāʾin Ṣāliḥ.

He repeated to me that it was he who had done the majority of the drawings in Huber's notebook, but he added that he would want it to be said only that the bigger watercolours and the drawing of the Taymāʾ Stele were by him because that, he said, 'is my own work and Huber would never have been capable of doing it'.

His drawings and his copies of all sorts are of great interest but he told me that he will not publish them for a while. He lacks the time and is having difficulty finding a publisher.

He also showed me the inscriptions from Sinai. They will appear in three months at the latest. The plates are already done. He has only 750 of them but he has found some interesting things, dates on two or three occasions, even in the inscriptions published by Lepsing and translated by Lévy! It is very strange.

Finally, for the inscriptions from Madāʾin Ṣāliḥ, he forestalled me in what I was going to say to him. He told me that he would be willing to lend the Academy his whole collection of squeezes; he just added that he would like to be asked officially by the Permanent Secretary. He would like a sort of official recognition of the services he has rendered to the Academy, he said, for so long without quibbling. His ambition would be to be appointed the Institute's correspondent. Of course I told him that I was in no position to respond to this, and that he knew better than anyone all the difficulties that he would encounter on that side. As for the request to be made by the Permanent Secretary, I told him that that was another matter, and that I would convey his proposal to M. de Vogüé, who would in any case be very grateful for his offers.

Here, as imperfectly as a letter can express it, is the result of our conversations. Next Tuesday I hope to see you and give you more details.

Please accept, dear Sir, the homage of my deep and respectful attachment.

M. Berger

APPENDIX 12

Charles Huber by two of his friends

ITEM NO. 1
Letter from M. A. Sauval, Nancy

This item is a letter to the Ministre de l'Instruction publique, sent by a close friend of Huber having heard of the latter's death. It is held in the archives of the Ministère de l'Instruction publique et des Beaux-Arts, in the Archives nationales at Pierrefitte-sur-Seine, Paris, where it is item no. 74 in Dossier F/17/2976/1:2 Mission en Arabie. 1883. It sheds interesting light on the French attitude to Huber travelling with a German, as well as on the warmth of his friendships. The underlinings are by the author of the letter.

Date: no date, but received on 1 October 1884
From: A. Sauval, Nancy
To: Monsieur le Ministre de l'Instruction publique et des Beaux-Arts, Paris

Monsieur le Ministre,

I have just learnt from the newspapers of the death of my poor friend, Charles Hubert [*sic*].

I was still living in Strasbourg when he left for his second expedition. This friend, who used to confide in me about everything he was doing, said to me one day: 'You know, I have found a travelling companion, Professor Euting of Strasbourg.' But Euting, he said, had to obtain permission from his government, from which he had also requested funds for his journey; but his request having been denied, there being no financial support for explorers, he was granted leave and several years' salary, and in addition M. de Manteuffel gave him a grant of 5,000 marks.[1]

[1] Gen. Edwin Freiherr von Manteuffel, governor of Alsace-Lorraine, actually gave

As I was thoroughly familiar with the Germans, having lived amongst them for thirteen years, I had a far from positive opinion of this companion, and said so to my friend, making it clear that he could well make enemies, and that one could not expect any good to come from people of that sort. 'Indeed,' he replied, 'you could well be right.' But he argued at the same time that this man had a certain experience of travel and familiarity with it that certainly no [ordinary] volunteer would have. Then he added that in any case Euting would not be able to send anything back without it passing through his hands.

Finally, M. le Ministre, as far as I could see this was an ill-omened journey, and I had a presentiment of various misfortunes befalling my dear friend from then on, especially when he told me that the minister was not particularly inclined to let him leave with him [*viz.* Euting].

Before his departure, we went to have dinner together, and then I embraced him and told him how troubled I was that he was flying off with this bird, and that I would not stop worrying until his return. I made him promise that he would write to me frequently, and so he did, as he did not forget me, this dear friend.

A month or so after his departure, the *Bas-Rhin Courier*[2] published an article about the two travellers that seemed to me very droll, because it spoke of nothing but the professor and only made a very vague reference to my friend.

When I received the first letter, dated 1 September 1883, I was very grieved to learn of annoyances having arisen in connexion with Euting, as he wrote. So there they were fulfilled, my forebodings, which I had never stopped reminding him about. And though my dear friend did not complain too much about it, he accused his ministry of being surprised. Poor boy; he was always too good and too trusting.

It is a great misfortune and a great loss for all of us, his friends who loved and valued him.

I have no wish to accuse Professor Euting, nor am I able to, because I do not know how my friend was murdered. But what I would like to know is

---

Euting a grant of 17,200 marks (see Appendix 10, Letter no. 6 received 6 January 1886, from Euting to the French minister of education).

[2] The *Courier du départment du Bas-Rhin*, also known as the *Niederrheinischer Kurier*, was an Alsace newspaper published during the second half of the 19th century. The article to which Sauval refers sounds very similar to that reproduced above in Appendix 6, Letter no. 1 dated 12 June 1883 from Charles Maunoir to the Minister of Public Education.

how the professor behaved, if he was with him, and what actually happened, as the newspapers do not say anything at all about the professor.

I have the honour, M. le Ministre, of sending you one of the two letters in my possession for your information, and beg you to be kind enough to return it to me, because my firm intention is to keep them along with the photograph that I own of him as souvenirs of our happy relations.

Please accept, M. le Ministre, my respectful greetings.

A. Sauval
rue Guerrier de Dumast 16
Nancy

Items nos. 2 and 3
Biographical note on Charles Huber, 1891

This anonymous 8-page biographical note on Charles Huber is held in the Archives du Cabinet of the *Corpus Inscriptionum Semiticarum*, Académie des Inscriptions et Belles-Lettres (AIBL), Institut de France, Paris: Boîte 'Dossiers 48', Carnets 1. It is preserved with a covering letter, also translated below, from Charles Maunoir to an unidentified recipient who appears to have been writing an obituary notice on Huber.

The piece is a vital source of first-hand information on Huber's background and personality, his scientific interests, and especially his bibliophilia. It is by an unnamed author, someone who from internal evidence had known Huber personally. It is probable that it was Ferdinand Reiber (1849–92) or his brother Paul Reiber (1850–1934), Alsatian artists who had collaborated with a friend, a Charles Streissguth, in the production of *Insignia Civitatis Argentoratensis: Les armes de la ville de Strasbourg* (J. Noiriel, Strasbourg 1878), a limited-edition work mentioned at the end of this piece.[3] Huber had in some way been involved in this project, and it is therefore possible, since he felt the necessity to adopt pseudonyms during the 1870s, that he was the 'Charles Streissguth' of the threesome.

With thanks to Prof. Maria Gorea for making these two documents available and for her helpful comments.

---

[3] See note 14 below.

Covering letter

Date: 20 April 1891
From: Charles Maunoir, Ste. Marguerite sur Mer, by Offranville [Seine-Maritime], on notepaper of the Académie des Inscriptions et Belles-Lettres, Commission du *Corpus Inscriptionum Semiticarum.*
To: an unidentified recipient

Sir,

In response to approaches that have so far failed to yield results, I am now in receipt of a biographical note on Charles Huber. It is of interest in that it shows Charles Huber to have been a bibliophile almost to the point of bibliomania – and this side of our traveller's personality should not be overlooked in the notice that you are being kind enough to devote to him.[4] Hopefully there may still be time to make use of the note in question, which I have the honour to send to you as registered business documents.

Please accept the expression of my most distinguished feelings,

Maunoir

NOTICE ON CHARLES HÜBER [*SIC*], EXPLORER (1847–1884)

Charles Hüber[5] was born in Strasbourg on 19 December 1847 to very indigent parents. His father was a workman on a railway gang, his mother a washerwoman.[6] His father died a few years after the war [*viz.* of 1870], crushed between the buffers of two carriages. The surviving members of the family comprised a brother,[7] a mechanic at Nancy; and a sister, the widow of a German employed at the Strasbourg arsenal.

[4] It is not known what this notice was, nor by whom. If it was the introduction to Huber 1891, then this material arrived too late for inclusion therein. If it was another obituary notice, we have failed to find it.

[5] The author in most cases, though not consistently, spells the name Hüber, so I have standardized it thus throughout this piece.

[6] Huber's father, Georges, was born in 1821, and other sources (e.g. Weyl 1991: 1678; Appendix 3, Letter no. 3 dated 12 April 1879) state that he was a shoemaker, not a railwayman; he could of course have been both, in sequence. Huber's mother, Elisabeth (née Stapfer; see Weyl 1991: 1678; Appendix 3, Letter no. 3), died in about 1887 (see below).

[7] Huber himself mentions that he had *two* younger brothers, who in *ca*. 1875 had been sent to prison in Alsace for performing their military service in France: see Appendix 4, Letter no. 10, paragraphs 2 and 3.

Having attended the Fossé des Tanneurs municipal school, he went on to the school of Christian doctrine in the rue des Soeurs, and as things turned out, though he sometimes took time off from his studies, he did not altogether neglect them. Taking a position with a bailiff (Maître Moch),[8] he came by sufficient means to pursue courses of study in physics and anatomy at the Strasbourg Academy.

In this first phase of his life, Hüber was very assiduous in attending the services of the Trappists in the rue Ste. Elisabeth. His piety, whether real or simulated, endeared him to these religious men, who also provided him with the means to study. Despite all his efforts, his instruction always felt lacking in direction and consistency. He wanted to cover too much all at once.

Very clever and highly ambitious, Charles Hüber sought early on to raise himself above the class he was born into; and in that he fully succeeded. Despite his far from alluring exterior and his pronounced Alsatian accent, he possessed an ability to turn on the charm. This, coupled with a certain boldness, enabled him to mesmerize those in his circle. At a very young age violent passions entangled him in troublesome and more or less impolitic romantic adventures, the memory of which obsessed him. He spoke of them only rarely and with regret, and his most intimate friends were never able completely to dispel the aura of mystery with which he liked to enshroud them. Just occasionally he used to insist that fate held a grudge against him, and indeed his tragic end seemed to confirm this.

The war of 1870 made a maverick [*franc-tireur*] of Charles Hüber, as he used to say. He seems even to have been wounded in the leg, and a slight limp that afflicted him from time to time would have been as a result of this. Shortly after and perhaps even during the war, he went to Algeria, where he gained his first experience of Arabic, all the while without suspecting the importance that this language would one day have for him. Hüber, if we are not mistaken, made another visit to Algeria before his second journey [*viz.* to Arabia].[9]

---

[8] Weyl (1991: 1678) also states that Huber was a 'comptable', i.e. a bookkeeper or clerk of accounts.

[9] Claude Lorentz says Huber's first journey to Algeria took place in 1874 (Kurpershoek and Lorentz 2018: 109). Weyl (1991: 1678) also confirms that he made two trips to Algeria in the 1870s. The second was made in 1879 as part of his route to the East for his first Arabian journey. See Introduction pp. 11 and 14, and Appendix 3, Letters nos. 3 and 4.

Having returned to the city of his birth, he lived a life of quiet obscurity totally immersed in his books, after the hours devoted to a certain amount of account-keeping, which aggravated him but which provided him with a livelihood. Hüber had other dreams. He wanted to accomplish some great feat, on a stage better suited to his ambition than offered by German Strasbourg. While awaiting a wider theatre of operations, Hüber set about book-collecting with zeal. Most of all he collected books about Alsace, which he loved with a mad passion, but beautiful books in general were equally cherished by him. On the slender means of a bookkeeper he performed wonders in amassing a library. He would rather go without food than do without books! Once we saw him hand over a purchase order amounting to 1,600 francs to a bookseller, when he had not a penny to settle the account. 'I shall have to end up finding the money, and the bookseller will have to wait if necessary. I'm counting on the future and putting my faith in that!' That was typical of the man.

Ardent, impassioned, reckless, counting on getting things done tomorrow that could not be done today, he also possessed the requisite diplomatic qualities for a future Oriental explorer. His courage was unequalled, his health excellent, and his sobriety astonishing. As inquisitive as a ferret, and with a patience equal to every challenge, he usually ended up finding what he was looking for. He had inexhaustible stores of sagacity and insight, and achieved his ends slowly but surely.

At Strasbourg, Hüber was above all remarkable as a bibliophile, and he really was an accomplished amateur booklover. He favoured only the finest copies and would sacrifice the others when the best opportunity arose. He looked after his printed works with touching care. It was as a booklover that we became acquainted with him, and we enjoyed pleasant, friendly relations. In 1878, some escapade once again led to him finding the ground too hot for him in Alsace and he took the road to Paris.[10] There he obtained a job at the Nogent-le-Rotrou[11] limited company for chemical products, whose headquarters are at 24 rue Montaigne. At this time Hüber was calling himself M. Paul or M. Rémond. It is only then that he openly

[10] The 'escapade' was perhaps Huber's membership of Léon Gambetta's Ligue d'Alsace, for which he was expelled from Alsace by the German authorities in 1878. See Introduction p. 12; Appendix 4, Letter no. 10, paragraph 2.

[11] Nogent-le-Rotrou: a town in the Eure-et-Loir département, 150 km south-west of Paris.

came up with schemes of far-flung travel and submitted a request for an expedition – though in Strasbourg he had mentioned to us several times that he wanted someday to make an exploratory journey to Tibet, but only as an impossible dream. (His first journey took place in 1879. From that date until his death, which overtook him in 1884, his career is no longer familiar enough for us to be able to speak about it with any authority.) After his first expedition [1879–82] he stayed for some time in Strasbourg and resumed his bibliophile habits. In 1885, the bookseller Béguin of Strasbourg bought her late son's book collection from Mme Hüber (who died four years ago).[12] We ourselves bought his Alsace engravings comprising a collection of the most remarkable examples.

It was on 20 June 1885 that M. Béguin sold the books as well, at public auction. The catalogue of this sale comprised 1,411 items. (I possess just a single copy of this catalogue and do not wish to part with it. In case of need, ask for it at the bookseller J. Noiriel, rue des Serruriers, Strasbourg, who will probably be able to provide a copy.) We wrote the preface. Here is our appreciation of the bibliophile:

> Despite his varied occupations as an explorer, Hüber always remained a keen bibliophile even so, and while in the Orient he was still collecting books and precious manuscripts. Was he not also behaving like a bibliophile in copying, tracing and making squeezes along his entire route of inscriptions left by vanished peoples? In his letters from the depths of the desert this lost child of science never forgot to speak with tenderness of his beloved books, which his tragic end has caused to be prematurely dispersed.

A touching attachment to his mother was equally characteristic of the man.

The basis of Hüber's library was formed of books relating to Alsace, but noticeable too was a goodly component of Orientalia and Arabic and Syriac manuscripts, acquired for the most part by the University of Strasbourg. Some copies of Béguin's catalogue include the lithographic portrait of the ill-starred traveller by a brother of Béguin.

In 1878, in collaboration with Charles Hüber, we had published an album of twenty plates representing the arms of the town of Strasbourg according to documents from various periods (*Les Armes de la Ville de Strasbourg*, large

[12] Mme Elisabeth Huber, née Stapfer, would thus have died in 1887.

quarto, on papier de Hollande,[13] 100 numbered copies, Strasbourg 1878, published by J. Noiriel.[14])

In sum, Hüber was someone of humble origin who was seeking to overcome all the obstacles in his path by achieving renown as a great explorer. He was a daredevil and adventurer in the old sense of the word. The manner of his end was apt proof of this.

[13] *Papier hollande* was a de luxe paper commonly used for limited editions.

[14] *Insignia Civitatis Argentoratensis: Les armes de la ville de Strasbourg*, by Ferdinand Reiber, Paul Reiber and Charles Streissguth (possibly an alias of Charles Huber). Large 4[to], 20 plates, printed by R. Schultz & Co., Strasbourg. Published by J. Noiriel, Strasbourg, 1878.

APPENDIX 13

Concordance of Arabic place names, personal names and words as used by Huber

HUBER'S SYSTEM of transliteration was an old-fashioned French one that can present difficulties for the modern reader and, as the list of names below shows, he did not always apply it consistently. In note 1 to Part I, Huber's editors ('La Rédaction') listed its main features, as follows:

> ç renders the sound of *ṣād* in Arabic; q that of *qāf*; ghr and rh that of *ghaïn*. These three consonants have no equivalents in French.
>
> Š is to be pronounced *ch* [anglice *sh*].
>
> ÿ is to be pronounced *ī*.
>
> g before a vowel is to be pronounced *dj* [anglice *ğ*] (Gebel = Djebel, Gobbah = Djobbah etc.)
>
> n̆, m̆, r̆, simply indicate that *n*, *m* and *r*, even when they are found at the end of a syllable, must always preserve the sound that they have in Italian, English and German, i.e. *enne*, *emme*, *ère* [anglice *en*, *em* and *ar*].
>
> The apostrophe before a vowel represents the Arabic consonant *'aïn* [*ʿayn*], a phoneme that occurs in no European language.
>
> *ah*, *at*, is the silent final *a*, or *ta marbouta* [*tāʾ marbūṭah*] of feminine nouns.

However, they omitted other useful tips for guiding readers through the maze, for example:

> dh stands for both ḍ (*ḍād*) and ẓ (*ẓāʾ*).
>
> dz stands for dh (*dhāl*).

th stands for ṭ (*ṭāʾ*).

k stands for k (*kāf*) and sometimes also q (*qāf*).

ts stands for th (*thāʾ*) and sometimes even k (*kāf*).

h stands for both h (*hāʾ*) and ḥ (*ḥāʾ*).

z stands for both z (*zāʾ*) and ẓ (*ẓāʾ*).

Some of these are set out in the box entitled 'Transcription des lettres arabes' on the folding map at the end of Huber 1884b.

In this translation, Huber's spellings of Arabic words and names have been replaced according to a standard English system, as follows.

	This translation	***Huber***
ا	ā	â
ب	b	b
ت	t	t
ث	th	ts
ج	ǧ	dj or g, according to locality
ح	ḥ	h
خ	kh	kh
د	d	d
ذ	dh	dz
ر	r	r
ز	z	z
س	s	s
ش	sh	š
ص	ṣ	ç
ض	ḍ	dh
ط	ṭ	th
ظ	ẓ	dh
ع	ʿ	'a
غ	gh	ghr
ف	f	f
ق	q	q (pronounced ts in Ǧabal Shammar)

ك	k	k (pronounced tz in Ǧabal Shammar)
ل	l	l
م	m	m
ن	n	n
ه	h	h
و	w, ū	ou, oû
ي	y, ī	ï, î, eî
ء	ʾ	–
ى	a (*alif maksūrah*)	a
ة	-ah, -at (*tāʾ marbūṭah*)	ah, a

Initial short vowels:

أَ	a
إِ	i
أُ	u

In alphabetizing, the definite article as presented by Huber is standardized in all its variants (al- el, el-, E', A' etc) as al-.

Place names and other Arabic terms

A further complicating issue is that Huber did not always record names correctly. This edition has given me the opportunity to correct many of his renderings. The full list of words and names given here will enable readers with good local knowledge to check these corrected versions against the reality on the ground. I would be delighted to receive any such contributions. An asterisk before a name (e.g. *Drelha) marks those names for which I have retained Huber's spelling because I have been unable to identify a correct rendering.

This edition	***Huber***
al-ʿĀʿah	El 'Aâ'aa
ʿabāʾ	*'aba*
Abā al-Dūd	Abâldoud
Abā al-Krūsh	Aba el Krouš

Abā al-Ruwāth	Âbârouâts
Abā al-Ṣīrān	Âbâleçrâň
ʿAbd al-ʿAzīz	'Abd el'Azîz
ʿAbd Allāh al-Khamīs	'Abd-Allah el Khamîs
abadan	*abedèň*
ʿAbd al-Ghānī	'Abd el Ghrany
ʿAbd al-Raḥmān	'Abd e'Rahmâň
ʿAbd al-Wahhāb	'Abd el Ouahab
ʿAbdah	'Abtah
al-ʿAbīd	El 'Abîd
al-ʿAbr	El H'abr
ʿAbrayt	'Abreït
Abū	Aboû
Abyaḍ	Âbïath
*Abū Fahat	Aboû Fahat
Abū Shaqrah	Abou Šeqerah
ʿĀda	'Adah
al-ʿAdam	al-'Adm
Ādhaybah	Âdzeïbah
ʿādhir	*adr*
al-ʿAdwah	El 'Adoûah
al-ʿAfāyif	El 'Afâïf
Ağā	'Agâ, Âgà, Âga
ʿAğayb	'Ageïb
al-Agharī	El Ghrary
ʿAğlān	'Agelâň
aḥmar	*ahmar*
al-Akhḍar	El-Ekder
ʿAlāq	'Alâg
Alayd	Aleïd
ʿalayk al-salām	*'aleïk e' salâm*

al-ʿAlaym	El'Aléïm
ʿalī	*'aâly*
ʿAlī	'Ali, 'Aly
al-ʿAliyyā	El 'Alïâ
ʿAmārāt	Amarrat
ʿĀmiǧ	'Aâmeq, 'Amed
ʿAmr	'Amar
al-ʿAmrī, ʿAmarī	El 'Am̆ri, 'Ameri
ʿĀnah	'Anâ
ʿAnāmah	Ânemâr
ʿAnaybar	'Anber
ʿAnbar	'Añbar
ʿAnizah	'Anezah, 'aneïzah
al-ʿAnqarī	el 'Añqry
ʿAnz	'Añz
al-ʿAqabah	'Aqabah
ʿAqar-Qūf	'Aker-Koûf
ʿAqaylah	Akeile
ʿAqīl	'Aqîl
ʿAqlat al-Ghunaymī	'Aqelâ El-Renemy
al-ʿArabī	el 'Araby
al-ʿArādāt	El'Aredat
ʿarfaǧ	*'arfedj*
al-Arḫābiyyīn	É'Rahêbîn
Arkān	Ergâñ
Armāl	Armâl
armash	*ârmaš*
arṭā	*yertâ*
al-Aṣafāt	El Açefât
Aṣb	Âṣb
Aṣfar	Asfař

Ashabah	Ašabah
ashhadu	*ašhed*
Ashhīb	Ašhîb
al-ʿAshshār	El 'Ašak
al-ʿAṣmiyyah	El 'Asmïah
ʿaṣr	*'açr*
al-Aswar, al-Zawar	El Asouar, el Azouar
al-ʿAṭayfāt	El'Atheïfât
ʿAthāmīn	'Atsâmîň
ʿAthmān	'Atsemâň
al-Athqab	Āçeqâber
ʿAṭiyyah	'Athïah
ʿAwaḍ	'Awad
Āl ʿAwāǧī	El 'Aougy
al-ʿAwāmirah	El 'Aouâm̌erah
al-ʿAwǧā	El Aougâ
Awlād	Oulâd
al-ʿAwshaziyyah	el 'Aoušzïah
ʿAwthat	'Aouthat
al-ʿAyāriyyah	El 'Aïârïah
ʿAyn, pl. ʿUyūn	Aïn, 'Aïn, pl. 'Ayoûn
ʿAyn Ibn Fuhayd	'Aïn ebn Feyd
al-ʿAyẓar	El 'Ạïtsa
al-Azraq	El Ezraq
al-Baḥr	El Beheř
Bālarāk	Bâlerak
al-Bān	El Bân
Banī	Beny
Baqʿāʾ	Beq'aâ
baqr al-waḥsh	*baqrat el ouahas*
Bārzān	Berzaň

al-Baṣr	Boṣr
al-Bassām	El Bessam
baṭḥā’	*bathhâ*
Bātil Aṭūl	Bâtel Athoul
al-Baṭn	el Bathn
Bā‘ūr	Bâour, Bâ’aoûr
Bawṣ al-Thu‘aylibī	Bouç e’S’aïleb
bawwāq	*baowak*
al-Bayḍā	El Beîdha, Beïdhâ
Bid‘	Bed’a
al-Bikār	El Bekâr
Bilağbiyyah	Belegbïah
Bint	Beňt
birnī	*berny*
al-Bisāsah	el Besâsah
Bishr	Bîšr
Boṣra	Bosrah
Budayr	Bedeîr
al-Bukayriyyah	Bekerîah
Bulṭiyyah	Boulthīt
Buraydah	Bereîdah’, Bereïdah
Buraydisiyyah	Bereïdisïah
al-Buraykah	El Bereîkah
burğ, pl. *burūğ*	*bordj*
al-Buṭayn	El Betheïn
al-Buwayb	el Bouèb, el Boûeb, el Boûeîb
al-Buwayrah	El Boûeîrah
al-Ḍabaṭ	Âdhdhebath
al-Dahām	Dehâm̆
al-Ḍāḥī	E’Dhahi
al-Dahnā’	Dahnâ

al-Dalhāmiyyah	Delhemïat
Daqaya	Deqïah
Dār	Dâr
Darb	Derb
darwīsh	*derouîš*
al-Ḍāy'a	El Dhâï'a
Dayr	Deîr
dhalūl	*dzeloûl*
dhalūl Sharārī	*dzeloûl serâry*
*Dheïeth 'Aïaš	Dheïeth 'Aïaš
al-Dhība	Âdzeïbah
dhura	*dourra, houra'*
Ḍibīy	El Deby
al-Dinān	Addenâñ
al-Dir'	E' Der'a
al-Dir' Mārid	Edr'a Mârid
*Drelha	Drelha
al-Drūb	Âdroub
Druze	Druse
al-Ḍubayb	El Dhebeïb
Dughayrī al-Khamīs	Deghrery el Khamis
Dūmat al-Ğandal	Doumat el Djañdal
Ḍumayr	Dhemeîr
al-Dumğān	El Deñdjâñ
Duwayrah	Douîrah
al-Ḍuwiy'a	El Dhouï'a
*El Eslé	El Eslé
Fad'ān	Fedhâñ
al-Fahdah	el Fehadah
Falayt ibn Qanat	Feleît ibn Qenet

fallāḥ	*fellâh*
al-Falūḥ	Feloûh
Fardād	Fredâd
Farḥān	Farhân
Fataq	Fetet
Fayd	Feyd
Fayṣal	Feîçal
Fikal	Fekah
al-Fira'īn	El Fer'aïn
Firdaws	Ferdoûs
firmān	firmân
al-Fray'āt	El Fraï'aâ
fulūǧ, sing. *falǧ*	*foûldj*, *foûlg*
Fuqarā'	Fouqerâ, Fouqerah
al-Furaydisah	El Feredesah
furaysī	*fresy*
al-Furs	Fers
al-Fuwāḍlah	El Foûathlah
Āl Fuẓayl	El Fadhîl
al-Ǧa'āfrah	El G'aâferah
Ǧa'ārī	G'aâry
Ǧabal	Gebel, Djebel
al-Ǧabārah	El Gebârah
al-Ǧadīdah	Lağdeïdah
al-Ǧafrah	El Gferah
Ǧahannah	Gehennah
Ǧahannam	Gehennem̆
Ǧāl	Gâl
al-Ǧam'āt	El Djem'aât
ǧāmi'	*djâm'a*, *gâm'a*
al-Ǧarād	El Gerâd

al-Ǧarāwī	El Geraouy/Geraoui
Ǧarāyah	Geraïah
Ǧāwā	Djâwâ, Gâwâ
Ǧawā	Gouâ
al-Ǧawf	le Djouf, Djoûf
Ǧawhar	Djoûhar
Ǧaww	Gou
Ǧāzī	Gazy
Ǧiddah	Djeddah
Ǧildiyyah	Djildïah, Gildïah
al-Ǧill	El Gil
Ǧisr	Gâser
al-Ǧithāmiyyah	El Gedzsâmïah
Ǧubbah	Gobbah
Ǧudhām	Godzâm̌
Ǧufayfā	Gefeîfâ, Gefeïfâ
Ǧuhaynah	Geheînah
al-Ǧumāmah	El Gemâmah
al-Ǧumaymah	El Gemeïmâ
al-Ǧuraydah	Gereïdah
al-Ghabiyyah	El Ghrebeïa
ghaḍā	*ghadâ*
ghadīr	*ghradîr*
al-Ghaḍyān	El Ghredhïâň
al-Ghāf	El Ghrâf
Ghāfil	Ghrafîl
Ghalghal	Ghralghral
Ghamr	Ghrameř
Ghānim	Ghrânem
Gharbī	Ghrarbi
Ghārī	Râry

al-Ghatār	El Ghratâr
Ghaṭṭī	Ghroththy, el-Gotti
al-Ghawāṭ	El Ghrauât
Ghaynāt	Ghreïnât
Ghazāl	Ghrazâl
al-Ghaẓawrah	El Fadhâouarah
Ghaẓwar	Ghrathaouar, Ghadhouar
al-Ghazzālah	Ghrazâlah
ghazū	*ghrazoû*
al-Ghumaysah	El Ghremeïsah
Ghumayz	Ghremeïz
Ghunaym	Ghreneïň, Ghreneïm̌
al-Ghuzayzah	El Ghrezeïzah
al-Ḥaʿb	El-H'ab
al-Ḥabbuh	el Habbuh
Ḥabūb	Haboûb, el Heboub
al-Haḍab	El Hadhab
Hadanah	Hedenah
al-Hadar	El Hedeř
al-Ḥağarah	El Hegerah
ḥağğ	*hadj*
Ḥāʾil	Hâïl
al-Ḥāʾiṭ	El Hâïeth
Ḥalab	Haleb
Ḥalwān	Helouâň, Helouân
Ḥalwiyyat al-ʿAliyyah	Heloûïet El 'Alïâ
Ḥamad	Hamed
al-Ḥamād	Hamād
Ḥamādah	El Hamâdah
al-Ḥamḍ (Wadi)	El Ham̌dh
ḥamḍ armash	*hamedh ârmaš*

al-Hamdānī	Ham̌dāny
al-Ḥāmī	El Hâmeî
al-Ḥāmiyyah	El Hâmieh
al-Ḥammām	El Hamâm̌
Ḥammāmiyyah	Hamâmïah
ḥamrā'	*hamrâ*
al-Ḥamrān	El Hamraň
Ḥamūd	Hamoûd
al-Ḥamūdiyyah	El Hamoudïah
al-Hamūr	El Hemour
Ḥanayẓil	Haneîdhil
Ḥaqiy	Haqeî
Haql	Haqel
al-Harashī	El Herašy
al-Ḥarḍah	al-Hardhah
al-Ḥarīm	El Harîm
ḥarrah	Harrah'
al-Ḥarrī	El Hery
al-Harūfā	El Haroûfâ
Hārūn	Âroûn
al-Ḥasā'	Hasa, Hasâ
Ḥasan	Hasen
Ḥashab	Hašab
al-Hāshimah	El-Hâšma
Ḥasiyyah	Hasïâ, Hasïah
ḥaṭab	*hathab*
al-Ḥawrān	Haourân
al-Hayl	El Heîl
Ḥayzān	El Haîzâ
al-Ḥayāniyyah	El Heïânïâ, El Heïânïah
Ḥaẓawẓā	El Haçotah

al-Ḥazil	El-Hâzel
Ḥibrān	Hebrâñ
al-Ḥiğāz	Hedjâz
al-Ḥiğr	El Hegeř
Hiğrah	Hégire
al-Hilāliyyah	El Halâlïah
al-ḥilwah	*hellouah*
al-Ḥimād	El Hemâd
Hīt	Hît
Ḥsinnah	Hesseré
al-Ḥufaynah	Al-Hefeïnah
al-Ḥufayrah	El Heferah
al-Ḥufnah	El Hefenah
al-Huğūr	El Hedjoûr
al-Ḥulayfah	Heleïfah
Ḥumayd	Hemeîd
Huṣnā	Haçnah
Hutaym	Houteïm̆
al-Ḥuwaykim	El Houeîkem
Ḥuwaylān	Houîlâñ
al-Ḥuwaymil	El Houeïmel
al-Ḥuwayyiṭ	El Houeîth
ibn	Ebn
Ibrāhīm	Îbrâhim, Ibrâhim
al-Idrīsī	Edrisi
ʿifrīt	*'afrîts*
ʿiqāl	*aqâl, 'aqâl*
ʿIrāq	Irak
ʿIrnān	Arnâñ, 'Arnâñ
ʿIrq	'Areq
ʿĪsā	'Aïsa

ithl	*ithel*
Ithrah	Ittra, Etsrah
al-Kabīr	El Kebîr
Kabūd	Keboût
Kāf	Kaf
al-Kahfah	El Kehafah
Kalb	Kelb
kālib	*kalb*
Kanāt	Kenât
Karbalāʾ	Kerbelâ
Karsh	Qers
al-Khabb	El Khab
al-Khabrāʾ	Khabrâ
Khaḍar	Khatar
al-Khadhmāʾ	Khadzmà
al-Khādīd	El Khâdîd
Khaḍrāʾ	Khadhrâ
Khaḍrān	Khadrâň
Khālah	Khâlah
Khālid	Khâled
al-Khamʿalī	El Khemâ'alah
al-Khamashah	El Remešah
Khamsāt	Khaňsât
al-Khanaqah	El Kheneqah
al-Khanẓuwa	Kheňloûah
Kharāb	Kharâb
al-Kharābah	El Kherâba
Kharāsh	Kherâš
al-Kharğ	Khark, Kharg
al-Khashabah	el Khašabah
al-Khāṣirah	El Hâçerah

Khathāl	Khetsâl
al-Khathʿamī	El Khats'amy
khaṭīb	*khatîb*
Khaṭṭ Abū Zayid	Khatt Aboû-Zeéïd
Khawr	Khoûr
Khaybar	Kheïbar, Kheïbeř
al-Khayl	El Kheïl
al-Khishmāyah	El Khešamâïah
al-Khubbāz	Khebâz
al-Khuraymī	El Khereïm
khurǧ	*kherdj, kherg*
Khuwaymah	Khoueïmah
Khuwaymāt	Khoûeïmât
Khuwayt	Khoueït
Kindah	Kiňdâ
Kubaysah	Kebeïsah
Kuffār	Kouffâr
Kufic	coufique
kūfiyyah	*qefïah*
al-Kutayfah	El Keteifa
Lā Kalīl	Lâ Kalîl
al-Laǧāh	Ledjâ
al-Laqīṭah	El Laqîthah
Laqṭah	Laqethah
Lawqah	Louqah
Lazzām	Lezâm̆
Līdiān	Lîdiâň
Lubdah	Loubdah
lughuf	*loghrf*
al-Luwaymī	El Oueîmy

al-Maʿā	El M'aâ
al-Maʿāqlah	El M'aâqlah
al-Maʿāṣir	El M'aâçr, El Mâzer
Mabī	Mabï
Madāʾin Ṣāliḥ	Médaïn Salekh, Medaïn Saleh
al-Madīnah	Médine
Mafraq	Mefreq
Māğid	Madjid
Maghniyyat al-Āsūdah	Meghrenïah el Âsoûdah
al-Maḥāsh	El Mehâš
Makhīd	Makhîd
al-Mālayk	El Mâleïk
al-Malūṣah	El Meloçah
al-Maqnaʿ	El Meqen'a
Marbuṭ al-Ḥisān	Merboth el Haçâň
Marḥabā	Marhabâ
Mārid	Mârid
Marzī	Merzy
masğid	*mesdjid*
Mashkūk	Maškoûk
Mashrifah	Mašrefah
al-Mashṭaʾ	E'Mešetheh
al-Matāyīh	El-Metseîâha
al-Matnah	El Metnah
al-Maṭradah	El Methredah
Mawqaq	Mouqeq, Maûqaq
al-Maysarī	El Méïsery
Maẓhūr	Matsoûr
Mecca (Makkah)	la Mecque, El Makkah
*Mehaňtah	Mehaňtah
*El Mes'ad	El Mes'ad

al-Milḥāt	El Melkhhat
Miqrād	Miqrâd
Miqraṭ al-Dabūs	Meqrath e' deboûs', Miqrath el Deboûs
Miqwaʿ	Mîqou'a
Mirbaṭ	Mirbat
Mishʿal	Mešel
al-Mismāʾ	el Mismâ
Mitʿab	Met'ab
al-Muʿayshir	El M'aïšeř
Mubaḥil	Mebehel
al-Mubārak	El Mebârek
al-Mudhābirah	El Medhaberah
mudīr	moûdîr, moûdir
Mufayḍah	Mefeîdhah
al-Mughāṣīb	El Meghrâçîb
Mughayrāʾ	Mereîrah
Mughīthah	Meghritsah
Muǧiyān	Mougïân
Muḥammad	Mohammed
Muhannā	Nehanna
Muḥārib	Mehârib
al-Muhaymizāt	El Mehîmezat
Muḥaywir	ʿAywir
Muḥsin	Mahsin
mullah	*mollah*
al-Muraydīsiyyah	Bereïdisïah
Āl Murayḥim	El Mereîhem
Murayqib	Mereîqeb
al-Murayr	El Mereïd
al-Murrah	El Merrah
al-Murtʿad	El Mert'ad

al-Musayyib	Meseïeb
al-Mushāsh	El Mešâš
al-Mushrif	El Mešref
Muslim	mouslim, musulman
Mustağiddah	Mestaggedt, Mestağedt
Muṭlaq	Mothelaq
al-Muwāhīb	El Moû'aïb, El Mouahib
Muwaysin	Mouéiseñ
al-Nabaytah	Ânebeïtah
Nabhāniyyah	Benhânïâh
al-Nabk Abū Qaṣr	A' Nebek Aboû Qaçr
al-Nabqiyyah	El Nebqïah
al-Nafīd	El Nefîd
al-Nafūd	Nefoûd
Nağaf	Nedjef
Nağd	Nedjd
al-Naʿqah	El N'aqah
Nağm al-Aṭrash	Nedjem el Adraš
Naṣāra	Naçâra, Naçârâ
Naṣrānī	naçrâni
Nāyīf	Nâïf
al-Niʿayy	'Anéaï
al-Nibāğ	E' Nebay
al-Nihāt	El Nehât
al-Nuqṭah	Noqtah
nuṣī	*noçy*
al-Nuwāmasah	El Noumesah
*Ourdemy	*Ourdemy
al-Qabal	El Qebel
Qafīʿa	Qefi'a

al-Qahd	El Qahed
qahwah	qahwah
al-Qaʿīd, al-Qaʿayyid	El Q'aïd
qalʿah	*qel'a*
Qalanqūwah	Qalañqouah
Qanāʾ	Qenâ
al-Qanī	El Qeny
Qārā (in al-Ǧawf)	Qârâ
al-Qaʿrāʾ (mountain range)	El G'arâ
al-Qarʿāʾ (NW of Buraydah)	Qer'a
Qarāthīn	Qerâthîñ
Qarn	Qern
al-Qarqar	Korâkir/Qerâqer
Qaryah	Qarïah
Qaryatayn	Qarïeteîn
Qāsayyim	Qâsayem
qasb	*gesb*
al-Qaṣīm	Qaçîm
Qaṣr	Qaçr/Qàsr
Qaṣr al-Sayyid	Qaçr e' Seïed
al-Qawr ʿAṭiyyah	El Qoûr 'Athïah
al-Qudayr	Gedair, El Qedair
Qufayl	Qefaïl
Qufār	Qefâr
qulbān	*qoulbân, qoulbâñ*
qūm	*goûm*
Qurayshī	Qoréïšy
al-Quṣayʿah	Qeçeî'aah
Quṣaybāʾ	Q'eçeïbah, Qoçeïbâ
Quṣaybah	Q'eçeïbah
al-Quṣayfah	El Qeçeîfah

al-Quṣayr	el-Qeçeir, El Qçeîr
Quṭayān	Qetheïâň
al-Quwārah	Qouârah
Quwayʿān	Qoûeî'aâň
rabāb	*rebâb*
Radhmā	Rhadzmâ
Rāḍī	Radi
al-Radiyyah	E'Redeïah
Rafīʿah	Rafïah
Rağāʾ	Redjâ
Rağīʿa	Regï'a
al-Rāḥ	El Râh
raʾīs	Raïes
Rakhah	Rakkah
al-Rakiyyah	El Rekeïah
Ramādah	Remâdah
Ramaḍān	ramadhâň
al-Ramādī	Remâdy
Ramāhah	Remâhah
Ramīḍ	Remîdh
raml	ramel
al-Ramūṭ	El Remoût
al-Ranamī	El Renemy
Rāʾs	Râs
al-Rashd	Ârašd
Rashīd	Rešîd, Rachîd
rashrāsh	*restres*
al-Rass	Rass
al-Rawḍah	Ghroudah', Ghroudah, El Roûdhah
Rawḍān	Roudhâṅ
al-Rayal	e' Rayel

al-Rāyāt	Rayāt
al-Rayyā	El Reïâ
Rīʿat al-Salf	Rî'a e' Self
Riğm	Riqm
al-Riyāḍ	El Rïâdh, El Râïd
riyāl	*riâl*, réal
al-Rubʿ al-Khālī	Rob'a el-Khâli
Rubāḥ	Roubakh
al-Rubaylāt	El Rebeïlat
al-Ruğūm (sing. al-Riğm)	e' Redjoûm, e' Regoûm, Ergoûm
Ruḥaybah	Ruheïba
Ruhaym	Reheïm̆
al-Ruhaymāt	Erhéïmât
Rummān	Remâñ
al-Ruqqab	e'Rekob, e'rekob
al-Ruwalah	Rou'ala
Ruwayḍiyyah	Rouedïah
Ruwaysah	Roueïsah
al-Ṣaʿaynīn	El Seneïeñ
al-Sabʿān	El Sab'aâñ
sabaṭ	*çobath*
sabkhah	*sebka, sebkha*
Ṣābūn	Saboûñ
saʿd	*s'ad*
al-Safābī	Asefeby
Saʿfan	S'afañ
ṣafrāʾ	*safrâ*
Ṣafṣāfah	Çafçafah
Saghīr	Sereîr
al-Saḥamah	El Sehamah
Saḥārā	Sehârâ

Ṣaḥbī	Çeheby
Saʿīd	S'aïd
al-Saʿīdān	E' Saïdàn̆
al-Saʿīdīn	E' S'aïdîn
Sakākā	Sekâkâ
Ṣakhr	Sokhr
Salālīm	Selâlîm̆
salām ʿalayk	*salâm 'aleïk*
Salāmī	Salâmy
al-Ṣaʿlikah	'Çaïlizah, El Ç'aïlîdzah
Sālim	Sâlem
Salmā	Selmâ
Sālmī	Sâlmy
Samāḥ	Semâh
al-Samāwah	Semâoûah
al-Samḥah	El Sam̆hah
Samḥān	Sem̆hân̆
Samīrā	Semîrâ
Samrā	Som̆râ, Sam̆râ
Sanabayn	Sen̆bîn̆
Ṣanbūrah	Çan̆boûrah
Sanūd	Senoud
al-Sāqah	El Sâqah
Ṣaqlāwiyyah	Saqlâwïah
al-Ṣarīf	El Çérîf
Sarrāʾ	Serrâ
Saṭām	Sattam
Saʿūd	S'aoûd
al-Ṣawrah	el Çourah
Sayil	Saïel
Sayqal	Seîqal

Sbāʿ	Sebâ
Sennacherib	Sin-akhi-irib
al-Silmān	E'Selmâň
Sinğārah	Siňgârïah
Sinn	Senn
al-Ṣirāwān	el Çirâouâň
Sirdab	Serdab
al-Sirḥān	Sirhâň
al-Sirḥānī	Serhâny
Ṣubayḥ	Çebeîh
Ṣubayḥah	Çebîhâ
al-Ṣufayrī	El Çefeîrey
al-Ṣuhbān	El Çohbâň
al-Suhūl	El Sehoual
Sukhnah	Sokhnah
al-Sulaymah	El Seleîmah
Sulaymān	Selîmâň
al-Sulaymī	El Seleîmy
Sulṭān	Soultâň
Sulṭānī	Çoulthâny
Ṣulubah	Saloby
Sumayḥah	Semaïhah
Sumayr	Smeîr
Sumayrah	Semerah
sūq	*soûq*
Ṣuwāb	Çoûâb
Ṣuwayb	Çoûeïb
Suwayd	Soueîd
Suwayflah	Soueîflah
Suways	Soueîs

al-Shafaqah	El Šefeqah
al-Shaḥamī	El Š'amy
sha'īb	*ša'ïb, š' aïb*
al-Shalālah	El Šelâlah
Sha'lān	Šalâň, Š'alâň
al-Shāmah	El Šâma
Shamās	Šemâs
al-Shamāsiyyah	El Šemâsïah
al-Shāmī	El Šāmy
al-Shamlān	El Šeṁlâň
Shammar	Šammar
Shaqīq	Šeqîq
Shaqīr	Šeqîr
Shaqrā'	Šakra
*El Šer'abah	El Šer'abah
al-Sharāfah	El Šarâfah
Sharārāt	Šerârât
Sharqī	Šerqii, Šerqy
Shatawī	Šetaouy
Shaṭṭ	Šatt
shaykh	šeîkh
al-Shibībiyyah	'Ašbîbïah
al-Shifah	Ašefah
Shighār	Šeghrar
al-Shīḥiyyah	Šeîhïah
Shilīl	Šeleîl
al-Shinānah	Šenânah
al-Shu'aybah	Š'aïbah
al-Shubaykah	Šebeïkah, Šebîkah
al-Shubrum	El Šebroṁ
al-Shuqqah	Ešeqah

al-Shurayf	Ašreîf
Shuwaymah	Šoueïma
Ṭābah	Tabah
Ṭafīlah	Thafîlé
Ṭā'iyy	Thaï
Ṭakīl	Thakîl
Ṭalāl	Telâl
al-Ṭalḥāt	Âthelahât
Tamīm	Tamîm̆, Temîm, Temîm
al-Ṭa'miyyah (Ṭu'miyyāt?)	Althamïah
Tarbiyyah	Terbïah
al-Ṭarfiyyah	Athrefïeh
al-Ṭawīl	Toueïl, Theouï
Taymā'	Teïmah', Teïmâ
Thakīl	Thakîl
Thamad	Tsemed, Themed
Thamūd	Tsemoûd
thawb	*tsoûb*
al-Thu'aylibī	e'S'aïleb
al-Ṭibiq	El Thebeq
Tīn	Tîn
al-Tinf	El Tenef
al-Tinifāt	el Tennefât
al-Tiyāq	El Tiâg
Ṭrād	Thrâd
Ṭūkhī	Toukhî
al-Ṭulūḥ	El Thelouh
Tūmā	Toûmâ, Toumâ
Tūmān	Toûmân̆
al-Ṭu'miyyah (Ṭa'miyyah?)	El Th'amïah

al-Tunayf	El Teneîf
Turabah	Trobah
Turmuṣ	al-Termoç
Ṭuʿūs	Taous
al-Tuwāliʿah	El Thoual'ah
Tuwārin	Touarine, Touârin
Ṭuwayl	Thouaïl
al-Ṭuwayyah	Touïah
ʿUbayd	'Abeïd
al-ʿUbaysah	El 'Abeïsah
Ukaydir	Okéïdiř/Ukéïdir
al-ʿUlā	El 'Alâ
Umm	Oumm
Umm Ādhan	Āmâdzen
Umm Kīdah	Makîdah
Umm al-Misk	Oumm el Mesk
Umm Qurūn	Ouâmeqroûn
Umm al-Rūğ	Umm e'Roug
Umm al-Rummān	Umm e' Remâň
Umm al-Silmān	Umm e' Selmâň
ʿUnayzah	'Anéïzah
ʿUqdah	'Aqdah
ʿUqlah	'Aqela
Urfa	Orfa
ʿušūb (sing. *ʿušb*)	*'ašoûb*
ʿUtaybah	'Ateïbah
Ūthāl	Outsâl
Utraymiyyah	Outreïmïah
ʿUwayriḍ	'Aouarah
Uwaysiṭ	Wîçeth
al-ʿUyūn	Ayoun, 'Ayoûn

al-Wābṣah	El Ouabçah
Wadd	Woudd
Wādī	Ouâdy/Wady
al-Wağh	Oueg
Wahhāb	Ouahab
Wahhābī	Ouahâbi
al-Wahlān	El Ouahlâñ
al-Waḥshah	El Ouahšah
wālī	*vâly*
al-Wāliğ	El Ouâleg
Wallah	Ouallah
Walmā	Ouelmâ
Wāqiṣah	Ouaqçat
Warbiyʿah	Ouarbaï'aah
Warkdiyyah	Ourekdïah
Washrāf	Ouašrâf
al-Washwāsh	El-Uscevuasce
al-Waṣīd	El Ougîd, El Oueçîd, Ouçîd
wasm	*wesm*
Wasmah	Ouesma
al-Waybār	El Oueïbâr
Widyān	Oûdïâñ
al-Withr	Outseř
Wuld	Ould
Wuqayyān	Oüqïïañ
al-Wurayk	Oueraïk, Ouraïk, Ouréîtz
al-Wusayṭah	Ousétah, El Ouçeîthâ
Yabrīn	Yabriñ
Yahūdī	Yehoûdy
Yanbuʿ	Yañbo
Yāqūt	Yâqoût

Yūsuf al-Milkī	Ioûsef el Milky
al-Ẓafīrī	Âdhafiry
al-Zaḥlānī	Azehelâny
al-Zalf	El Zelf
Zāmil	Zâmil
al-Zarb	El Zerb
Zarghaṭ	Dheraghrath, Thaghrat
Zarqa	Zerqah
Zayd	Zeïd
al-Zayyād	Âzeïâd
Zubālah	El Zebâlah, Zebâlâ
Zubaydah	Zobeïdah
al-Zuhayrī	El Zhéry, Zehery
al-Ẓuhūr	el Dhehoûr
Zumurrud	Smourred

Sources and References

Sigla

CIS ii: *Corpus Inscriptionum Semiticarum. Pars II Inscriptiones Aramaicas continens.* Paris: Imprimerie nationale, 1889–1954

Eut: inscriptions copied by Euting on the 1883–84 expedition

Hub: inscriptions in Huber 1891

HU: van den Branden's (1950) renumbering of all the inscriptions copied by Huber on the 1883–84 expedition

HuIR: inscriptions in Huber 1884a

IG 12 (3): *Inscriptiones Graecae Insularum Maris Aegaei. Fasciculus Tertius. Edidit Fridericus Hiller de Gaertringen*, Berlin: apud Georgium Reimerum, 1898

JSLih: Dadanitic (formerly 'Lihyanite') inscriptions published by Jaussen and Savignac 1909–22, vols. I and II

JSMin: Minaic inscriptions published by Jaussen and Savignac 1909–22, vols. I and II

JSNab: Nabataean inscriptions published in Jaussen and Savignac 1909–22, vols. I and II

JSTham: Thamudic inscriptions published in Jaussen and Savignac 1909–22

Müller, D.H: Müller, D.H. 1889

vdB: refers to the page number in van den Branden 1950, in which all the so-called 'Thamudic' inscriptions known at that time were collected and republished by provenance

WHI: inscriptions in Winnett and Reed 1973

Unpublished archives

1. Archives du Cabinet du *Corpus Inscriptionum Semiticarum* of the Académie des Inscriptions et Belles-Lettres, Institut de France, Paris

Armoire A, Boîte 'Correspondence Do–E'

- Five letters from Julius Euting to Philippe Berger and Charles Clermont-Ganneau, dated 21 November 1884, 2 February 1885, 24 July 1885, 1 August 1885, and 2 November 1885. See Appendix 10.

Armoire A, Boîte 'Correspondence H–K'

- 25 letters from Charles Huber to Charles Maunoir, Dr Weisgerber, and the French consulate in Baghdad, between 21 March 1882 and 6 July 1884. See Appendix 4
- Five letters in Arabic, with French versions, from Charles Huber to friends in Ḥāʾil, 1883. See Appendix 5:
    - to Ḥamūd Ibrāhīm ibn Ǧawād in Ḥāʾil, dated Paris 19 April 1883
    - to the Emir Muḥammad ibn ʿAbdallāh al-Rashīd in Ḥāʾil, undated (but *ca.* August 1883), from Damascus
    - to Ḥamūd al-ʿUbayd in Ḥāʾil, undated (but *ca.* August 1883), from Damascus
    - to Muḥammad ibn Ḥāj Raḥīm al-Shirwānī in Nağaf al-Ashraf, Iraq, undated (but *ca.* May 1883 before Huber's departure for Arabia)
    - to Shaykh Nağm al-Aṭrāsh at ʿUrmān in Ǧabal Druze, undated (but summer 1883 before Huber's departure for Arabia), probably from Damascus

Boîte 'Dossiers 48': A. Lettres à ou au sujet de Ch. Huber

- Letter from T. Gilbert, French consulate in Damascus, to Charles Maunoir dated 10 October 1883
- Thirteen letters from Félix de Lostalot Bachoué to Charles Maunoir, dated 12, 16 and 19 August 1884, 7 and 15 September 1884, 24 October 1884, 3 December 1884, 25 January 1885, 16 March 1885, 28 May 1885, 23 June 1885, 12 November 1885, 12 December 1885. See Appendix 9.
- Letter from Félix de Lostalot Bachoué to Philippe Berger dated 18 December 1885. See Appendix 9.

- Five letters from Ernest Renan to Philippe Berger dated 19 August 1884, 16 November 1884, 8 December 1884, 18 July 1885, and 20 July 1885. See Appendix 11 for the latter two.
- Letter from Ernest Renan to Julius Euting dated 8 July 1885. See Appendix 11.
- Two letters from Philippe Berger to Ernest Renan dated 10 July 1885 and 24 March 1891. See Appendix 11.
- Carnets 1: Anonymous 8-page biographical note on Huber, 1891. See Appendix 12.

2. Archives nationales, Pierrefitte-sur-Seine, Paris

Archives of the Ministère de l'Instruction publique et des Beaux-Arts

- Dossier F/17/2976/1:1. 'M. Huber (Charles), Mission au Thibet et dans l'Asie centrale (recherches scientifiques, anthropologique et géographiques)'. 107 items between 3 December 1878 and early 1883. See Appendix 3.
- Dossier F/17/2976/1:2. 'Mission en Arabie. 1883'. 141 items between May 1883 and July 1886. See Appendices 6 and 12.

3. Archives of the Ministère des Affaires étrangères, La Courneuve

Affaires diverses politiques Box 47, 'Archaeological excavations 1875–1896'

- 52-page file, no. 75ADP entitled 'Mission en Arabie, Assassinat, Stèle de Theima'. See Appendix 7.

4. Bibliothèque Nationale de France

ID/Cote: SG Carton HI-HY (564)

- Charles Huber, manuscript of 1880–81 journey. 'Voyage dans l'Arabie centrale …', s.d. (180 pages); relevés de positions astronomiques afin d'établir latitudes et longitudes durant son voyage en Arabie.

5. Euting Archiv, Universitätsbibliotek, Eberhard Karls Universität Tübingen

Euting MSS diaries, sketchbooks and correspondence

(http://idb.ub.uni-tuebingen.de/diglit/Md676)

Notebook I	Md 676-18. Tagebuch der Reise nach Syrien, Band 1: 1883, May 22 [Strassburg] – 1883, Juli 24 [Damascus]
Notebook II	Md 676-19. Tagebuch der Reise nach Syrien, Band 2: 1883, Juli 27 – 1883, September 22
Notebook III	Md 676-20. Tagebuch der Reise nach Syrien, Band 3: 1883, September 22 – 1883, November 27
Notebook IV	Md 676-21. Tagebuch der Reise nach Syrien, Band 4: 1883, November 28 –1884, Februar 15
Notebook V	Md 676-22. Tagebuch der Reise nach Syrien, Band 5: 1884, Februar 15 – 1884, April 20
Notebook VI	Md 676-23. Tagebuch der Reise nach Syrien, Band 6: 1884, April 20 – 1884, August 11
Sketchbook I	Md 676-24. Skizzen- und Notizbuch zur Reise nach Syrien: 1884, Januar 9 – 1884, März 25
Sketchbook II	Md 676-25. Skizzen- und Notizbuch auf der Reise nach Syrien: 1883, Dezember 7 – 1883, Dezember 20
Sketchbook III	Md 676-32. Skizzenbuch 6 (Reise nach Syrien): 1883, September 10 – 1883, November 14
Sketchbook IV	Md 676-33. Skizzenbuch 7 (Reise nach Syrien): 1883, Oktober 28 – 1884, Februar 27
Sketchbook V	Md 676-34. Skizzenbuch 8 (Reise nach Syrien): 1883, Meptember 25 – 1884, Februar 6
Inscription Book I	Md 676-26. Inschriftenbuch zur Reise nach Syrien: 1883, Oktober 11 – 1884, März 25
Correspondence	Md 782 A 65. See Appendix 8.

UNPUBLISHED THESIS

PEARSON, H.L. (1993), Relations between Julius Euting and Charles Huber in Arabia. Unpublished MA thesis, University of Manchester

Official print

Burdett, A. (ed.) (1995), *Records of the Hijaz, 1798–1925*. 8 vols. Cambridge University Press: Archive Editions

—— (ed.) (2013), *The Expansion of Wahhabi Power in Arabia, 1798–1932*. 8 vols. Cambridge University Press: Archive Editions

Published references

Abū Duruk, Ḥ.I. (1986), *Introduction to the Archaeology of Taymāʾ*. Riyadh: Department of Antiquities and Museums

Akarli, E. (1993), *The Long Peace: Ottoman Lebanon, 1861–1920*. Berkeley: University of California Press

Allan, M. (1972), *Palgrave of Arabia*. London: Macmillan

Bagnold, R.A. (1941), *The Physics of Blown Sand and Desert Dunes*. London: Methuen

Beaulieu, P.-A. (1989), *The Reign of Nabonidus, King of Babylon, 556–539 bc*. New Haven: Yale University Press

Béguin, J. (1885), Catalogue des livres composant la bibliothèque du feu M. Charles Huber. Strasbourg

Berger, P. (1884), Nouvelles inscriptions nabatéennes de Medaïn Salih. *Comptes rendus des séances de l'Académie des Inscriptions et Belles-Lettres*, vol. 28, no. 3, pp. 377–93

—— (1885), *L'Arabie avant Mahomet, d'après les inscriptions: conférence faite à la Sorbonne*. Offprint from the *Bulletin hebdomadaire de l'Association scientifique*, nos. 271 and 272. 29 pp. [including drawing by Euting of the Taymāʾ Stele.] Paris: Maisonneuve

Bilkadi, Z. (1984), Bitumen: A History. *Aramco World Magazine*, vol. 35, no. 6 (November/December 1984)

Blunt, A. (1879), *Bedouin Tribes of the Euphrates*. New York: Harper & Bros.

—— (1881), *A Pilgrimage to Nejd, the Cradle of the Arab Race. A Visit to the Court of the Arab Emir, and "Our Persian Campaign"*. 2 vols. London: Murray

—— (1882), *Voyage en Arabie. Pélerinage au Nedjed, berceau de la race arabe*. Tr. M. Derome. Paris: Hachette

Borger, R. (1956), *Die Inschriften Asarhaddons, Königs von Assyrien.* Graz: im Selbstverlage der Herausgebers

Boyer, D. (2017), Guilty or Innocent? The Buckingham vs. Bankes Libel Trial of 1826. *Lost and Now Found: Explorers, Diplomats and Artists in Egypt and the Near East.* Ed. N. Cooke and V. Daubeny, pp. 183–204. Oxford: Archaeopress

Brinner, W.M. (tr.) (1987), *The History of al-Tabari.* vol. 2. SUNY series in Near Eastern Studies. New York: State University of New York

Burckhardt, J.L. (1822), *Travels in Syria and the Holy Land.* London: John Murray

—— (1829), *Travels in Arabia, comprehending an Account of those Territories in Hedjaz which the Mohammedans regard as Sacred.* 2 vols. London: Colburn

—— (1831a), *Notes on the Bedouins and Wahábys, collected during his Travels in the East.* Published by Authority of the Association for Promoting the Discovery of the Interior of Africa. 2 vols. London: Colburn & Bentley

—— (1831b), *Bemerkungen über die Beduinen und Wahaby, gesammelt während seinen Reisen im Morgenlande.* Herausgegeben von der Gesellschaft zur Veförderung der Entdeckung des innern Africa. Aus dem Englischen. (Neue Bibliothek der wichtigsten Reisebeschreibungen zur Erweiterung der Erd- und Völkerkunde, 57). Weimar: im Verlage des Grossh. S. pr. Landes-Industrie-Comptoirs

Burton, R.F. (1893), *Personal Narrative of a Pilgrimage to al-Madinah and Meccah.* Memorial Edition, 2 vols. London: Tylston & Edwards

Butler, S.S. (1909), Baghdad to Damascus via El Jauf, Northern Arabia. *Geographical Journal*, vol. XXXIII, no. 5 (May), pp. 517–35. London: Royal Geographical Society

Carruthers, D. (1922), Captain Shakespear's Last Journey. Part 1 in *Geographical Journal*, vol. LIX, no. 5 (May), pp. 321–34; Part 2 in *Geographical Journal*, vol. LIX, no. 6 (June), pp. 401–18, with map following p. 400. London: Royal Geographical Society

—— (1935), *Arabian Adventure: To the Great Nafud in Search of the Oryx.* London: Witherby

Chesney, F.R. (1850), *The Expedition for the Survey of the Rivers*

Euphrates and Tigris, Carried on by Order of the British Government in the Years 1835, 1836 and 1837, Preceded by Geographical and Historical Notices of the Regions. 2 vols. London: Longman, Brown, Green, and Longmans

CHRASTIL, R. (2014), *The Siege of Strasbourg*. Cambridge: Harvard University Press

ÇIÇEK, M.T. (2017), The Tribal Partners of Empire: The Ottomans and the Rashidis of Najd. *New Perspectives on Turkey*, vol. 56, pp. 105–30

CORANCEZ, L.A.O. de (1810), *Histoire des Wahabis, depuis leur origine jusqu'à la fin de 1809*. Ed. Sylvestre de Sacy. Paris: Crapart

CRAWFORD, M. (2014), *Ibn ʿAbd al-Wahhab*. London: Oneworld

DICKSON, H.R.P. (1949), *The Arab of the Desert*. London: George Allen & Unwin

DIDIER, C. (1857), *Séjour chez le grand-chérif de la Mekke*. Paris: Hachette

—— (1985), *Sojourn with the Grand Sharif of Makkah*. Tr. R. Boulind. Cambridge: Oleander Press

DOUGHTY, C.M. (1881a), Reisen in Arabien. *Globus: Illustrierte Zeitschrift für Länder- und Völkerkunde*, no. 39: Part I, pp. 7–10; Part II, pp. 23–30

—— (1881b), Khaibar in Arabien. *Globus: Illustrierte Zeitschrift für Länder- und Völkerkunde*, no. 40, pp. 38–41

—— (1882), Wanderungen zwischen Teimâ, Ḥâil, Khaibar und Bereida. *Globus: Illustrierte Zeitschrift für Länder- und Völkerkunde*, no. 41: Part I, pp. 214–18; Part II, pp. 249–52

—— (1884), *Documents épigraphiques recueillis dans le nord de l'Arabie*. Intr. E. Renan. Paris: Imprimerie nationale

—— (1888), *Travels in Arabia Deserta*. 2 vols. Cambridge: Cambridge University Press

—— (1891), *Documents épigraphiques recueillis dans le nord de l'Arabie*. Ed. E. Renan. (Notices et extraits des manuscrits de la Bibliothèque Nationale et autres bibliothèques, 29). Paris: Imprimerie nationale

—— (1923), *Travels in Arabia Deserta*. 2nd edition; 2 vols. New York: Boni & Liveright / London: Cape & The Medici Society

—— (1936), *Travels in Arabia Deserta*. 3rd edition; 2 vols. London: Jonathan Cape

Duveyrier, H. (1883), M. Charles Huber – Médaille d'Or. *Bulletin de la Société de Géographie*, 7ème série, vol. 4, pp. 212–20

Edgell, H.S. (2006), *Arabian Deserts: Nature, Origin and Evolution.* Dordrecht: Springer

Égal, F. (2018), Images d'un voyage en Arabie en 1883–1884 : sur les pas de Charles Huber et Julius Euting. *Comptes rendus des séances de l'Académie des Inscriptions et Belles-Lettres*, 3rd trimester, October, pp. 1299–1311

Eph'al, I. (1982), *The Ancient Arabs: Nomads on the Borders of the Fertile Crescent, 9th–5th Centuries BC.* Jerusalem: Magnes / Leiden: Brill

Euting, J. (1885), *Nabatäische Inschriften aus Arabien.* Berlin: Reimer

—— (1896), *Tagbuch einer Reise in Inner-Arabien.* vol. I. Leiden: E.J. Brill

—— (1914), *Tagbuch einer Reise in Inner-Arabien.* vol. II, ed. Enno Littmann. Leiden: E.J. Brill

—— (1993), *Tagebuch einer Reise in Inner-Arabien.* Ed. and abridged by Uwe Pfullmann, with an Epilogue by Kerstin and Uwe Pfullmann. Hamburg: SOLDI-Verlag

—— (1420/1999), *Riḥlah dākhil al-ǧazīrah al-ʿarabiyyah.* Tr. Saʿīd Fayz al-Saʿīd. Riyadh: Dārat al-Malik ʿAbd al-ʿAzīz

Facey, W. (1992), *Riyadh: The Old City, from Its Origins until the 1950s.* London: Immel

—— (1997a), *Dirʿiyyah and the First Saudi State.* London: Stacey International

—— (1997b), *Back to Earth: Adobe Building in Saudi Arabia.* Riyadh: Al-Turath

—— (2013), Pilgrim Pioneers: Britons on Hajj before 1940. Chapter 16 in *The Hajj: Collected Essays*, ed. V. Porter and L. Saif, pp. 122–30. London: The British Museum

Facey, W. and Grant, G. (1996), *Saudi Arabia by the First Photographers.* London: Stacey International

G.E. (1884), Explorateur Strasbourgeois. *Journal d'Alsace et de Lorraine*, 25 December 1884. Strasbourg

Gervais-Courtellemont, J. (1896), *Mon voyage à la Mecque.* Paris: Librairie Hachette

Gilmore, M., Al-Ibrahim, M. and Murad, A.S. (1982), Preliminary Report on the Northwestern and Northern Regions Survey 1981 (1401). *Atlal*, vol. 6, pp. 9–23. Riyadh: Department of Antiquities and Museums

Grant, C.P. (1937), *The Syrian Desert: Caravans, Travel and Exploration*. London: A. & C. Black

Grimme, H. (1926), Ein Felspsalm aus altarabischer Heidenzeit. *Orientalistische Literaturzeitung*, vol. 29, col. 13–33

Groom, N. (1983), *A Dictionary of Arabic Topography and Placenames. A Transliterated Arabic–English Dictionary with an Arabic Glossary of Topographical Words and Placenames*. London: Longman / Beirut: Librairie du Liban

Guarmani, C. (1865), Itinéraire de Jérusalem au Neged septentrional. *Bulletin de la Société de Géographie*, 5ème série, vol. 10 (July–December), pp. 241–91, 365–423, 486–515

—— (1917/1938), *Northern Najd: A Journey from Jerusalem to Anaiza in Qasim*. Translated from the Italian by Lady Capel-Cure with an Introduction and Notes by D. Carruthers. London: Argonaut Press. [Original Italian edition: *Il Neged settentrionale. Itinerario da Gerusalemme a Aneizeh nel Cassim*. Jerusalem: Franciscan Press, 1866. First English edition: 'For Official Use Only': Cairo, 1917; first published English edition: London: Argonaut Press, 1938; Reprinted: New York: Da Capo, 1971]

Halévy, J. (1873), Voyage au Nedjran. *Bulletin de la Société de Géographie*, 6ème *série,* vol. 6, pp. 5–31, 249–73, 581–606

—— (1877), Voyage au Nedjran (suite). *Bulletin de la Société de Géographie*, 6ème *série,* vol. 13, pp. 466–79

—— (1882), *Essai sur les inscriptions du Safa*. L'ouvrage couronné par l'Institut en 1878. (Extrait du *Journal Asiatique*). Paris: Imprimerie nationale

—— (1884), Une inscription araméenne. Report of a lecture by Joseph Halévy at the session of 22 August 1884. *Comptes rendus des séances de l'Académie des Inscriptions et Belles-Lettres* (CRAIBL), 28e année, no. 3, 1884, p. 332

Hamaker, H.A. (1820), *Specimen Catalogi Codicum Mss. Orientalium Bibliotecae Academiae Lugduno-Batavae*. Leiden: Luchtmans

Harrison, D.L. and Bates, P.J.J. (1991), *The Mammals of Arabia*. 2nd edition. Sevenoaks: Harrison Zoological Museum

Hausleiter, A. (2010), The Oasis of Tayma. In *Roads of Arabia: Archaeology and History of the Kingdom of Saudi Arabia*, ed. A.I. Al-Ghabban, D. André-Salvini, F. Demange, C. Juvin and M. Cotty, pp. 219–61. Paris: Musée du Louvre

—— (2011), Das antike Taymāʾ: eine Oase im Kontaktbereich der Kulturen. Neue Forschungen an einem Zentralort der Karawanenstraße. In *Roads of Arabia: Archäologische Schätze aus Saudi-Arabien*, ed. A.I. Al-Ghabban, D. André-Salvini, F. Demange, C. Juvin and M. Cotty, pp. 102–23. Berlin/Tübingen: Wasmuth

—— (2021), On the iconography of the 'Great Nephesh' TA 10277 from Taymāʾ. In M.C.A. Macdonald, *Taymāʾ II. Catalogue of the Inscriptions Discovered in the Saudi-German Excavations at Taymāʾ 2004–2015*, with contributions by A. Hausleiter, F. Imbert, H. Schaudig, P. Stein. F. Tourtet, and M. Trognitz, pp. 105–9. Oxford: Archaeopress

Hausleiter, A. and Schaudig, H. (2016), Rock Relief and Cuneiform Inscription of King Nabonidus at Ḥāʾiṭ (Province of Ḥāʾil, Saudi Arabia), ancient Padakku. *Zeitschrift für Orient-Archäologie* 9, pp. 224–40

Healey, J.F. (2004), 'Sicherheit des Auges': The Contribution to Semitic Epigraphy of the Explorer Julius Euting (1839–1913). *Biblical and Near Eastern Essays: Studies in Honour of Kevin J. Cathcart*, eds. C. McCarthy and J.F. Healey, pp. 313–30. London: T&T Clark International

al-Ḥelwah, S., Aal al-Shaikh, A. and Murad, A.S. (1982), Preliminary Report on the Sixth Phase of the Darb Zubaydah Reconnaissance 1981 (1401). *Atlal*, vol. 6, pp. 39–62. Riyadh: Department of Antiquities and Museums

Henty, G.A. (1872), *The Young Franc-tireurs and their Adventures in the Franco-Prussian War*. London: Griffin & Farran

Hilden, J.T. (2010), *Bedouin Weaving of Saudi Arabia and Its Neighbours*. London: Arabian Publishing

Hogarth, D.G. (1904), *The Penetration of Arabia: A Record of the*

Development of Western Knowledge concerning the Arabian Peninsula. London: Lawrence & Bullen

—— (1917), *Hejaz before World War I: A Handbook*. Cairo: Arab Bureau [reprinted 1978, Cambridge: Falcon-Oleander]

—— (1928), *The Life of Charles M. Doughty*. London: Oxford University Press

Holt, A.L. (1923), The Future of the North Arabian Desert. *Geographical Journal*, vol. LXII, no. 4 (October), pp. 259–71, with folding map at end. London: Royal Geographical Society

Huber, C. (1879), Extrait d'une letter de M. Hubert [*sic*]. Published in *Comptes-rendus des séances de la Société de géographie et de la commission centrale*, séance du 6 juin 1879, p. 195

—— (1881), Voyage en Arabie: lettre de M. Charles Huber à M. de Quatrefages [from Khaybar, dated 6 December 1880]. *Bulletin de la Société de Géographie*, 7ème série, vol. 1 (January–June), pp. 269–70

—— (1883), letter from Ḥāʾil dated 30 November 1883. Published in *Comptes-rendus des séances de la Société de géographie et de la commission centrale*, séance du 7 mars 1884, pp. 151–2

—— (1884a), Inscriptions recueillies dans l'Arabie centrale (1878–1882). *Bulletin de la Société de Géographie*, 7ème série, vol. 5, pp. 289–303

—— (1884b), Voyage dans l'Arabie centrale (1878–1882), Hamâd, Šammar, Qaçîm, Hedjâz. *Bulletin de la Société de Géographie*, 7ème série, vol. 5, pp. 304–63 and 468–530

—— (1884c), letter from Ǧiddah dated 20 June 1884 to the Ministry of Public Education. Published in *Comptes rendus des séances de la Société de géographie et de la commission centrale*, séance du 18 juillet 1884, p. 433

—— (1885a), Voyage dans l'Arabie centrale (1878–1882), Hamâd, Šammar, Qaçîm, Hedjâz (suite et fin). *Bulletin de la Société de Géographie*, 7ème série, vol. 6, pp. 92–148

—— (1885b), *Voyage dans l'Arabie centrale. Hamâd, Šammar, Qaçîm, Hedjâz. 1878–82*. Extrait du *Bulletin* de la Société de Géographie (1884–1885). [Huber 1884b and 1885a published as a monograph.] Paris: Société de Géographie

—— (1891), *Journal d'un voyage en Arabie (1883–1884)*. Paris: Imprimerie nationale

—— (2003), *Riḥlah fī al-Ǧazīrah al-ʿArabiyyah al-Wusṭa, 1878–1882: al-Ḥamād, al-Shammar, al-Qaṣīm, al-Ḥiǧāz*. [Arabic translation of Huber 1885b.] Tr. Elissar Saadeh. Beirut: Kutub

Hunziker-Rodewald, R. (2020), Squeezes, Fleas and 'a Beautiful Clay Head of Egyptian Style': Julius Euting in Petra (March 7–23, 1898). *Jordan Journal of History and Archaeology*, vol. 14, no. 4, pp. 375–91

Ingham, B. (1986), *Bedouin of Northern Arabia: Traditions of the Al-Dhafir*. London: KPI

Irwin, R. (2006), *For Lust of Knowing: The Orientalists and Their Enemies*. London: Allen Lane

Jamme, A. (1974), *Miscellanées d'ancient* [sic] *arabe V*. Washington, DC: privately produced

Jaussen, A. and Savignac, A.R. (1909–22), *Mission archéologique en Arabie*. 5 vols. Paris: Ernest Leroux/Librairie Paul Geuthner

—— (1914 [appeared 1920]), *Coutumes des Fuqarâ. Mission archéologique en Arabie*: supplément au volume II. Paris: Librairie Paul Geuthner

Jolly, R. (1893), Les missions françaises. Voyages de Charles Huber. Arabie. *Journal des Voyages et des Aventures de Terre et de Mer*, no. 856, 3 décembre 1893, pp. 362–3

Kay, S. (1978), Some Ancient Dams of the Hejaz. *Proceedings of the Seminar for Arabian Studies* 8, pp. 68–73

Kiernan, R.H. (1937), *The Unveiling of Arabia: The Story of Arabian Travel and Discovery*. London: George G. Harrap

Kloss, M.M. (2016), Benjamin Reilly, *Slavery, Agriculture and Malaria in the Arabian Peninsula*. Review in *Arabian Humanities* [Online], 6, 2016. Consulted 10 October 2020. URL: http://journals.openedition.org/cy/3095; DOI: https://doi.org/10.4000/cy.3095

Knop, C. and Hausleiter, A. (2016), Tayma, Saudi-Arabien: Bauforschung am Qasr al-Radm. *e-Forschungsberichte des Deutschen Archäologischen Instituts* 2, pp. 155–60

Kurpershoek, P.M. (2001), *Arabia of the Bedouins*. London: Saqi Books

—— (2005), *Oral Poetry and Narratives from Central Arabia*. Vol. 5:

Voices from the Desert. Glossary, Indices, and List of Recordings. Leiden: Brill

Kurpershoek, P.M. and Lorentz, C. (2018), Charles Huber, voyageur en Arabie: sur deux manuscrits de poésie bédouine de la Bibliothèque nationale et universitaire de Strasbourg. *Revue de la BNU*, vol. 17, pp. 100–11

Lawrence, T.E. (1935), *Seven Pillars of Wisdom*. London: Jonathan Cape

Leachman, G. (1911), A Journey in North-east Arabia [in 1910]. *Geographical Journal*, vol. XXXVII, no. 3 (March). London: Royal Geographical Society

—— (1914), A Journey through Central Arabia [in 1912]. *Geographical Journal*, vol. XLIII, no. 5 (May), pp. 500–20; map on p. 604. London: Royal Geographical Society

Littmann, E. (1904), *Zur Entzifferung der thamudenischen Inschriften. Eine Untersuchung des Alphabets und des Inhalts der thamudenischen Inschriften auf Grund der Kopieen von Prof. J. Euting und unter Benutzung der Vorarbeiten von Prof. D.H. Müller, nebst einem Anhange über die arabischen Stammeszeichen*. Mitteilungen der Vorderasiatischen Gesellschaft, 9. Berlin: Peiser

Littré, E. (1873), *Dictionnaire de la langue française*. 2ème édition. Paris: Hachette

Lönnqvist, K. (2008), The Tax Law of Palmyra and the Introduction of the Roman Monetary System to Syria – A Re-evaluation. *Jebel Bishri in Context: Introduction to the Archaeological Studies and the Neighbourhood of Jebel Bishri in Central Syria*. Proceedings of a Nordic Research Training Seminar in Syria, May 2004, ed. M. Lönnqvist, pp. 73–88. Oxford: BAR International Series 1817

Lostalot, F. de (1885), M. Charles Huber: les circonstances de son assassinat. La stèle de Teïma. Récit de M. Félix de Lostalot de Bachoué, vice-consul à Djeddah. Séance du 3 juillet 1885, in *Comptes rendus des séances de la Société de Géographie et de la commission centrale*, 1885, pp. 430–1, 441–7

Lozachmeur, H., and Briquel-Chatonnet, F. (2013), Charles Huber und Julius Euting in Arabien nach französischen, auch heute noch nicht veröffentlichen Dokumenten. *Anabases* [online], 12, pp. 195–200

Lyall, C. J. (1913), Julius Euting. *Journal of the Royal Asiatic Society of Great Britain and Ireland* (Cambridge), April 1913, pp. 505–10

Macdonald, M.C.A. (2000), Reflections on the Linguistic Map of Pre-Islamic Arabia. *Arabian Archaeology and Epigraphy* 11, pp. 28–79. [Reprinted as article III in Macdonald 2009a]

—— (2009a), *Literacy and Identity in Pre-Islamic Arabia*. Variorum Collected Studies Series, CS906. Farnham: Ashgate

—— (2009b), Wheels in a Land of Camels: Another Look at the Chariot in Arabia. *Arabian Archaeology and Epigraphy* 20, pp. 156–84

—— (2010), Ancient Arabia and the Written Word. In *The Development of Arabic as a Written Language*, ed. M.C.A. Macdonald. Supplement to volume 40 of the *Proceedings of the Seminar for Arabian Studies*. Oxford: Archaeopress, pp. 5–28.

—— (2012a), Goddesses, Dancing Girls or Cheerleaders? Perceptions of the Divine and the Female Form in the Rock Art of Pre-Islamic North Arabia. In *Dieux et déesses d'Arabie: images et representations*, eds. I. Sachet et Ch. J. Robin. Actes de la table ronde tenue au Collège de France (Paris) les Ier et 2me octobre 2007. Orient & Méditerranée, 7. Paris: De Boccard, pp. 261–97

—— (2012b), Wheeled Vehicles in the Rock Art of Arabia. In *The Arabian Horse: Origin, Development and History*, ed. M. Khan. Riyadh: Layan Cultural Foundation, pp. 357–95

Macdonald, M.C.A. and King, G.M.H. (2000), Thamudic. *The Encyclopaedia of Islam* (New Edition), vol. 10, pp. 436–8. Leiden: Brill.

Macdonald, M.C.A. and al-Najem, M. (forthcoming), *Taymāʾ III. Catalogue of the Inscriptions in the Taymāʾ Museum and Other Collections*. With contributions by F. Imbert, J. Norris and P. Stein. Oxford: Archaeopress

MacGregor, N. (2014), *Germany: Memories of a Nation*. London: Allen Lane

Mackenzie, N. and al-Ḥelwah, S. (1980), Darb Zubaida Architectural Documentation Program: a. Darb Zubaida – 1979: A Preliminary Report. *Atlal*, vol. 4, pp. 37–50. Riyadh: Department of Antiquities and Museums

McMeekin, S. (2010), *The Berlin–Baghdad Express: The Ottoman Empire and Germany's Bid for World Power, 1898–1918*. London: Allen Lane

Mandaville, J.P. (1990), *Flora of Eastern Saudi Arabia*. London: Kegan Paul International / Al-Riyadh: National Commission for Wildlife Development and Conservation

—— (2011), *Bedouin Ethnobotany: Plant Concepts and Uses in a Desert Pastoral World*. Tucson, AZ: University of Arizona Press

Maunoir, C. (1880), Rapport sur les travaux de la Société de Géographie et sur les progrès des sciences géographiques pendant l'année 1879. *Bulletin de la Société de Géographie*, 6ème série, vol. 19, pp. 193–253

—— (1883), Rapport sur les travaux de la Société de Géographie et sur les progrès des sciences géographiques pendant l'année 1882. *Bulletin de la Société de Géographie*, 7ème série, vol. 4, pp. 55–7

—— (1885), Rapport due les travaux de la Société et sur les progrès des sciences géographiques. *Bulletin de la Société de Géographie*, 7ème série, vol. 6, pp. 149–250 [pp. 169–72 is a summary of Huber's Arabian journey]

Mawsūʿat ismāʾ al-amākin al-Mamlakah al-ʿArabiyyah al-Suʿūdiyyah. 2003/1424. 6 vols. Riyadh: Dārat al-Malik ʿAbd al-ʿAzīz

Mengin, F. (1823), *Histoire de l'Égypte sous le gouvernement de Mohammed-Aly*. 2 vols. plus Atlas. Paris: Arthus Bertrand

Meulen, D. van der (1947), *Aden to the Hadhramaut: A Journey in South Arabia*. London: John Murray

Al-Moraecki, M. (2002), A New Perspective on the Phenomenon of Mirror-image Writing in Arabic Calligraphy. In *Studies on Arabia in honour of Professor G. Rex Smith*, eds. J.F. Healey and V. Porter, pp. 123–33. *Journal of Semitic Studies* Supplement 13. Oxford: Oxford University Press on behalf of the University of Manchester

Müller, D.H. (1889), *Epigraphische Denkmäler aus Arabien (nach Abklatschen und Copien des Herrn Professor Dr. Julius Euting in Strassburg). Borgelegt in der Sitzung am 9. Mai 1888*. Denkschriften der (kaiserlichen) Akademie der Wissenschaften in Wien. Philosophisch-historische Klasse, 37.2. Vienna: Tempsky

Musil, A. (1926), *The Northern Ḥeǧâz: A Topographical Itinerary*. Oriental

Explorations and Studies, 1. New York: American Geographical Society

—— (1927), *Arabia Deserta: A Topographical Itinerary*. Oriental Explorations and Studies, 2. New York: American Geographical Society

—— (1928a), *Northern Neğd: A Topographical Itinerary*. Oriental Explorations and Studies, 5. New York: American Geographical Society

—— (1928b), *The Manners and Customs of the Rwala Bedouins*. Oriental Explorations and Studies, 6. New York: American Geographical Society

—— (1928c), *Northern Arabia*. Map in four sheets at 1:1,000,000 scale accompanying the author's works on northern Arabia. New York: American Geographical Society

Al-Najem, M. and Macdonald, M.C.A. (2009), A New Nabataean Inscription from Taymāʾ. *Arabian Archaeology and Epigraphy* 20: 208–17

Nehmé, L. (ed.) (2015) *Les tombeaux nabatéens de Hégra*. Épigraphie & Archéologie, 2 vols. Paris: Académie des Inscriptions et Belles-Lettres

Nolde, Baron Eduard von (1895), *Reise nach Innerarabien, Kurdistan und Armenien, 1892*. Braunschweig: Vieweg

Nöldeke, T. (1884), Altaramäische Inschriften aus Taimâ (Arabien). *Sitzungsberichte der königlichen preussischen Akademie der Wissenschaften* 1884, pp. 813–20

Oppenheim, M.A.S. von (1939–1968), *Die Beduinen*. 4 vols. Leipzig/Wiesbaden: Harrassowitz

Palgrave, W.G. (1865), *Narrative of a Year's Journey through Central and Eastern Arabia (1862–63)*. 2 vols. London: Macmillan

—— (1866), *Une année de voyage dans l'Arabie centrale (1862–1863)*. Paris: Hachette

Parr, P.J., Harding, G.L. and Dayton, J.E. (1971), Preliminary Survey in NW Arabia, 1968. Part I: Archaeology (continued), and Part II: Epigraphy, by G.L. Harding, A.F.L Beeston and J.T. Milik. *Bulletin of the Institute of Archaeology* 10, pp. 23–61 and plates 1–31

PESCE, A. (1986), *Makkah a Hundred Years Ago: C. Snouck Hurgronje's Remarkable Albums*. London: Immel

PETRAGLIA, M.D. *et al.* (2012), Hominin Dispersal into the Nefud Desert and Middle Palaeolithic Settlement along the Jubbah Palaeolake, Northern Arabia. *PLOS ONE* 7:11, pp. 1–21

PFULLMANN, K. and U. (1993), Nachwort [Epilogue] to abridged edition of Euting's *Tagebuch einer Reise in Inner-Arabien*. Hamburg: SOLDI-Verlag

PHILBY, H. St J. B. (1923), Jauf and the North Arabian desert. *Geographical Journal*, vol. LXII, no. 4 (October), pp. 241–59 (map by Philby and A.L. Holt after p. 320)

—— (1928), *Arabia of the Wahhabis*. London: Constable

—— (1930), *Arabia*. New York: Charles Scribner's Sons

—— (1948), *Arabian Days: An Autobiography*. London: Robert Hale

—— (1955), *Sa'udi Arabia*. London: Benn

—— (1957), *The Land of Midian*. London: Benn

PIRENNE, J. (1958), *À la découverte de l'Arabie: cinq siècles de science et d'aventure*. Paris: Le livre contemporain

POTTS, D.T. (1991), Tayma and the Assyrian empire. *Arabian Archaeology and Epigraphy* 2, pp. 10–23

PTOLEMY, CLAUDIUS (1991), *The Geography*. Tr. and ed. Edward Luther Stevenson. New York: Dover Publications

RALLI, A. (1909), *Christians at Mecca*. London: Heinemann

AL-RASHEED, M. (1991), *Politics in an Arabian Oasis: The Rashidi Tribal Dynasty*. London: I.B. Tauris

AL-RASHID, S. (1980), *Darb Zubaydah: The Pilgrim Road from Kufa to Mecca*. Riyadh: Riyadh University Libraries

RASWAN, C. (1935), *The Black Tents of Arabia: My Life amongst the Bedouins*. London: Hutchinson

RAWLINSON, H.C. *et al.* (1861), *The Cuneiform Inscriptions of Western Asia*. II: *A Selection from the Miscellaneous Inscriptions of Assyria*. London: British Museum

REALLEXIKON DER ASSYRIOLOGIE UND VORDERASIATISCHEN ARCHÄOLOGIE. Berlin/New York: De Gruyter

Reiber, F., Reiber, P., and Streissguth, Ch. (1878), *Insignia Ciuitatis Argentoratensis. Les armes de la ville de Strasbourg*. Strasbourg: Noiriel

Reilly, B. (2015), *Slavery, Agriculture, and Malaria in the Arabian Peninsula*. Athens, GA: Ohio University Press

Renan, E. (1885), [Report to the AIBL of a] Lettre de M. de Lostalot relative à la stèle araméenne de Teïma, at the session of 26 June 1885. *Comptes rendus des séances de l'Académie des Inscriptions et Belles-Lettres* (CRAIBL), 29ème année, no. 2, p. 107

Rentz, G. S. (2004), *The Birth of the Islamic Reform Movement in Saudi Arabia. Muḥammad b. ʿAbd al-Wahhāb (1703/04 – 1792) and the Beginnings of Unitarian Empire in Arabia*. Intr. W. Facey. London: LCAS

Ritter, C. (1847), *Die Erdkunde im Verhältnis zur Natur und zur Geschichte des Menschen, oder allgemeine vergleichende Geographie, als sichere Grundlage des Studiums und Unterrichts in physicalischen und historischen Wissenschaften*. Vols. XII and XIII [on Arabia]. (2nd improved and revised edition). Berlin: Reimer

Rohmer, J. and Charloux, G. (2015), From Liḥyān to the Nabataeans: Dating the End of the Iron Age in North-west Arabia. *Proceedings of the Seminar for Arabian Studies* 45, pp. 297–320

Rosenfeld, H. (1965), The Social Composition of the Military in the Process of State Formation in the Arabian Desert. *Journal of the Royal Anthropological Institute*, vol. 95, pp. 75–86 and 174–94

Rutter, E. (2015), *The Holy Cities of Arabia*. Ed. and intr. W. Facey and S. Sharpe. London: Arabian Publishing

Ryckmans, G. (1951), Review of Van den Branden 1950. *Vetus Testamentum* 1, pp. 149–55

—— (1952), Trois mois de prospection épigraphique et archéologique en Arabie. *Comptes rendus des séances de l'Académie des Inscriptions et Belles-Lettres*, 96, no. 3, pp. 501–10

Rzewuski, Comte W.S. (2002), *Impressions d'Orient et d'Arabie: un cavalier polonaise ches les Bédouins, 1817–19*. Ed. B. Lizet et al., from the MS conserved in the Polish National Library. Paris: Librairie José Corti/Muséum d'Histoire Naturelle

Sadleir, G.F. (1866, repr. 1977), *Diary of a Journey across Arabia (1819).* Bombay: Education Society's Press, Byculla / Cambridge: Oleander

Said, E. (1991), *Orientalism: Western Conceptions of the Orient.* London: Penguin

Seetzen, U.J. (1854), *Reisen durch Syrien, Palästina, Phönicien, die Transjordan-Länder, Arabia Petraea und Unter-Aegypten.* Ed. and comm. Fr. Kruse, G. Hinrichs, G.Fr. Hermann Müller, and H.L. Fleischer. 4 vols. Berlin: Reimer

Snouck Hurgronje, C. (1923), Aus Arabien. *Verspreide geschriften* ['Scattered Writings'], vol. III. Leiden/Bonn/Leipzig: E.J. Brill

—— (2007a), *Mekka in the Latter Part of the 19th Century*, tr. J.H. Monahan (London: Luzac 1931). Introduction by J.J. Witkam. Leiden: Brill

—— (2007b), *Mekka in de tweede helft van de negentiende eeuw. Schetsen uit het dagelijks leven.* Vertaald en ingeleid door Jan Just Witkam. Amsterdam/Antwerpen: Uitgeverij Atlas

Sprenger, A. (1865), *Die alte Geographie Arabiens als Grundlage der Entwicklungsgeschichte des Semitismus.* Bern: von Huber

—— (1880), Doughty's Forschungen im nördlichen Arabien. In *Globus: Illustrierte Zeitschrift für Länder- und Völkerkunde*, vol. 37, no. 13, pp. 201–3. Braunschweig

Steen, E. J. van der (2009), Tribal States in History: the Emirate of Ibn Rashid as a Case Study. *Al-Rāfidān*, vol. 30, pp. 119–34

Stein, P. (2014), Ein aramäischer Kudurru aus Taymāʾ? In *Babylonien und seine Nachbarn in neu- und spätbabylonischer Zeit.* Wissenschaftsliches Kolloquium aus Anlass des 75. Geburtstags von Joachim Oelsner Jena, 2. und 3. März 2007, ed. by M. Krebernik and H. Neumann unter Mitarbeit von G. Neumann, pp. 219–45. (Alter Orient und Altes Testament, 369). Münster: Ugarit-Verlag

—— (in press). Musée du Louvre AO 1505. In M.C.A. Macdonald and M. Al-Najem, *Taymāʾ III. Catalogue of the inscriptions in the Taymāʾ Museum and other collections.* With contributions by F. Imbert, J. Norris, and P. Stein. Oxford: Archaeopress

Stretton, H. (1871), *Max Krömer: A Story of the Siege of Strasbourg.* London: The Religious Tract Society

al-Sudairī, A.A. (1995), *The Desert Frontier of al-Jawf through the Ages.* London: Stacey International

Tamisier, M. (1840). *Voyage en Arabie. Séjour dans le Hedjaz. Campagne d'Assir.* 2 vols. Paris: Louis Desessart

Taylor, A. (1999), *God's Fugitive: The Life of Charles Montagu Doughty.* London: HarperCollins

Trüper, H. (2019), Epistemic Vice: Transgression in the Arabian Travels of Julius Euting. *Scholarly Personae in the History of Orientalism, 1870–1930*, ed. C. Engberts and H. Paul, pp. 64–98. Leiden: Brill

Twitchell, K.S. (1953), *Saudi Arabia, with an Account of Its Natural Resources.* New Jersey: Princeton University Press

van den Branden, A. (1950), *Les inscriptions thamoudéennes.* Bibliothèque du Muséon, 25. Louvain: Publications Universitaires de Louvain

Vassiliev, A. (1998), *The History of Saudi Arabia.* London: Saqi Books

Veccia Vaglieri, L. (1978). Khaybar. In *Encyclopaedia of Islam*, vol. IV, 2nd edition, pp. 1137b–43a. Leiden: Brill

Vrolijk, A. (2013), An Early Photograph of the Egyptian *Mahmal* in Mecca: Reflections on Intellectual Property and Modernity in the Work of C. Snouck Hurgronje. Chapter 25 in *The Hajj: Collected Essays*, ed. V. Porter and L. Saif, pp. 206–13. London: The British Museum

Wallin, G.A. (1850), Notes Taken during a Journey through Part of Northern Arabia, in 1848. *Journal of the Royal Geographical Society*, vol. XX, pp. 293–344. [Reprinted in Wallin 1979]

—— (1854), Narrative of a Journey from Cairo to Medina and Mecca, by Suez, Arabá, Tawilá, al-Jauf, Jubbé, Háil, and Nejd, in 1845. *Journal of the Royal Geographical Society*, vol. XXIV, pp. 115–207. [Reprinted in Wallin 1979]

—— (1864–1866), *Reseanteckningar från Orienten åren 1843–1849. Dagbok och bref, efter resandens död utgifna af S.G. Elmgren.* 4 vols. Helsingfors: Frenckell

—— (1979), *Travels in Arabia (1845 and 1848).* With introductory material by W.R. Mead and M. Trautz. Cambridge: Oleander

Ward, P. (1983), *Ha'il: Oasis City of Saudi Arabia.* Cambridge: Oleander Press

Weyl, R. (1987), Huber, Charles. *Nouveau dictionnaire de biographie alsacienne*, vol. 17 (Hoc à Hug). Strasbourg: Fédération des Sociétés d'Histoire et d'Archéologie d'Alsace

Winder, R.B. (1965), *Saudi Arabia in the Nineteenth Century*. London: Macmillan

Winnett, F.V. (1937), *A Study of the Liḥyanite and Thamudic Inscriptions*. University of Toronto Studies – Oriental Series, 3. Toronto: University of Toronto Press.

Winnett, F.V. and Reed, W.L. (1970), *Ancient Records from North Arabia*. Near and Middle East Series, 6. Toronto: University of Toronto Press

—— (1973), An archaeological-epigraphical survey of the Ḥāʾil area of northern Saudi Arabia. *Berytus* 22, pp. 53–113

Winstone, H.V.F. (1976), *Captain Shakespear: A Portrait*. London: Jonathan Cape

—— (1978), *Gertrude Bell*. London: Jonathan Cape

Witkam, J.J. (2007), Christiaan Snouck Hurgronje's Description of Mecca. Introduction to reprint of C. Snouck Hurgronje, *Mekka in the Latter Part of the 19th Century*, tr. J.H. Monahan (London: Luzac 1931). Leiden: Brill

—— (2020), Snouck Hurgronje's Consular Ambitions. In *Scholarship between Europe and the Levant: Essays in Honour of Alastair Hamilton*, ed. J. Loop and J. Kraye, pp. 349–73. Leiden: Brill

—— (forthcoming/a), Before Mecca: The Jeddah 'Diary' of Christiaan Snouck Hurgronje, 1884–1885. In *Scholarship in Action: Studies on the Life and Work of Christiaan Snouck Hurgronje (1857–1936)*, ed. L. Buskens and J.J. Witkam, assisted by A. van Sandwijk. Leiden: Brill

—— (forthcoming/b), Christiaan Snouck Hurgronje: Lives and Afterlives. In *Scholarship in Action: Studies on the Life and Work of Christiaan Snouck Hurgronje (1857–1936)*, ed. L. Buskens and J.J. Witkam, assisted by A. van Sandwijk. Leiden: Brill

—— (forthcoming/c), Meccan Voices: Proverbs and Sayings from Mecca. Collected and explained by Christiaan Snouck Hurgronje. Translated and annotated by Jan Just Witkam. In *Scholarship in Action: Studies on the Life and Work of Christiaan Snouck Hurgronje (1857–1936)*, ed. L. Buskens and J.J. Witkam, assisted by A. van Sandwijk. Leiden: Brill

WEBSITES

fr.wikipedia.org, entry 'Charles Huber (explorateur)', consulted November 2019

fr.wikipedia.org, entry 'Julius Euting', consulted November 2019

Euting's notebooks and sketchbooks: http://idb.ub.uni-tuebingen.de/diglit/Md676

GeoNames: http://geonames.nga.mil/ggmaviewer/default.asp

Gertrude Bell's archive and photographs: www.gertrudebell.ncl.ac.uk. Consulted September 2020

MAPS AND CARTOGRAPHIC DATA

Arabian Peninsula (1973). Scale 1:200,000. London: Director of Military Survey, Ministry of Defence, United Kingdom

Baghdad (1928). Scale 1:1,000,000. Geographical Section, General War Staff, GSGS no. 2555. London: War Office, United Kingdom

El Djauf (1918). Scale 1: 1,000,000. Geographical Section, General Staff, No. 2555. Compiled at the Royal Geographical Society. Drawn and printed at the War Office. London: War Office, United Kingdom

Geographic Map of the Northeastern Hijaz Quadrangle, Kingdom of Saudi Arabia (1378 AH/AD 1959). Scale 1: 500,000. Miscellaneous Geologic Investigations Map 1-205. Compiled by Brown, G.F. and Jackson, R.O. United States Geological Survey/Arabian American Oil Company. Washington DC: US Department of State

Geographic Map of the Northwestern Hijaz Quadrangle, Kingdom of Saudi Arabia (1378 AH/AD 1959). Scale 1: 500,000. Miscellaneous Geologic Investigations Map 1-204 B. Compiled by Brown, G.F., Jackson, R.O., and Bogue, R.G. United States Geological Survey/Arabian American Oil Company. Washington DC: US Department of State

Geographic Map of the Wadi as Sirhan Quadrangle, Kingdom of Saudi Arabia (1381 AH/AD 1962). Scale 1: 500,000. Miscellaneous Geologic Investigations Map 1-200 B. Compiled by Bramkamp, R.A., Brown, G.F., Holm, D.A., and Layne, N.M. United States Geological Survey/Arabian American Oil Company. Washington DC: US Department of State

Al Jauf (1956). Scale 1:1,000,000. Series GSGS 4646, Sheet NH-37, Edition 5-GSGS. London: D Survey, War Office and Air Ministry, United Kingdom

Medina (1921). Scale 1: 1,000,000. Geographical Section, General Staff, No. 2555. Drawn and printed at the War Office. London: War Office, United Kingdom

Medina (1960). Scale 1:1,000,000. Series 1301, NG-37 and part NG-36, Edition 4-GSGS. London: D Survey, War Office and Air Ministry, United Kingdom

Northern Arabia (1928c). Musil, A. Map in four sheets at 1:1,000,000 scale accompanying the author's works on northern Arabia. New York: American Geographical Society

Travellers' Routes in the Country around Teima, 1876–1914 (1914). Scale: 1:270,000. Unpublished. London: Royal Geographical Society, RGS-IBG Collections, Map Room, mr Saudi Arabia S.7

Index

In alphabetizing, al-, Āl, el and ibn are ignored.

first Arabian journey (1880–81) 2–3, 13–23, 87–272 (The Translation), 314, 327–33, 349–63, 365, 403
dating of first Arabian journey 88n
Voyage dans l'Arabie centrale. Hamâd, Šammar, Qaçīm, Hedjâz, 1878–82 (Huber 1884a, 1884b, 1885a, and 1885b) publication history 83–4, 406
narrative style 3–4, 21–2, 59–60
award of Gold Medal (1883) 23, 348
second Arabian journey (1883–84) 2–3, 6, 23–4, 28–9, 39–44, 335–9, 352–3, 355, 357, 361–2, 367, 375–406, 407–16, 424–5
Journal d'un voyage en Arabie (Huber 1891) 6, 38–9, 44–5, 57, 62–3
mapping 3n, 4, 187n, 342, 350–1, 353–6, 358–60, 362–3, 365–6
longitude inaccuracy 187n, 354
scientific exploration, use of instruments 4, 6, 14, 18, 22–5, 29, 121, 127, 155, 306, 314, 321, 324, 336–9, 343–4, 346, 355, 380, 425, 466
birth, family and working-class background 5, 7, 26, 310, 474–5
Catholic education 7–8, 42, 475
character and interests 8–12, 18, 21–3, 45–8, 316–17, 418, 424, 473–8
early career 7–12, 310, 475–6
early travel plans 12
interest in physical anthropology, skulls 11, 12, 196, 249n, 311–12, 317, 319, 323–4, 357, 423
convicted of theft 8, 19, 310, 313, 315, 321
criminal record 14–15, 17–19, 313, 315–16, 321
allegations of dishonesty 25–6, 341–5
medical expertise 8
war injury 9
lack of cultural snobbery 5
patriotic Frenchman 5, 7, 10, 312
and French and German nationality 10–12, 26, 311–12, 317, 364, 418
relations with German authorities 26, 311–12, 363–4, 408n, 413n
in Algeria 8–9, 11, 311, 313–14, 316–17, 475
relations with Arabs, Arabic 5, 11, 12, 15, 47–8, 133–4, 475
archaeological collecting 249n
bibliophilia and manuscript collecting 11–12, 23n, 473–4, 476–7
epigraphic recording and collecting 22–4, 41, 50–1, 55, 57–8, 142–3, 149, 160, 165, 179–80, 185, 193, 199–200, 211, 299n, 301n, 352, 355, 385, 388–95, 400–1, 404–5, 425, 428
fauna collecting 357
geological collecting 15, 319, 324, 357, 361, 466
watershed of N. Arabia, identification of 20–2
funding of expeditions 13, 17, 18–21, 23–5, 31–3, 36, 39, 46, 49, 60–1, 306, 321–2, 324–6, 334–5, 338–9, 345–7, 377, 379, 388, 399–401, 403, 405–6, 421–3, 453, 460, 464
and Taymāʾ Stele 64–82, 463–6
relations with Julius Euting 26–55, 64–71, 375–6, 398–9, 407, 409, 411–12, 415, 417–21, 424, 427–9, 431–2, 453, 456–8, 467–9, 471–3
erasure of Euting 38–40, 44–6, 386n, 388n, 425n
firearms 40, 49, 57. *See also* Gras rifles
travels 'as a Muslim' 59
plans to go through Mecca disguised as a woman 60n, 73n
intercedes over Khaybar 203n, 411

activities in Iraq during 1881 249n, 333–4, 412–13
murder 2–3, 6, 38, 61–4, 72–4, 76–7, 435–45
remains and tomb in Ǧiddah 6, 64, 443, 445, 449–50
travel diary/notebooks 395–7, 401–2, 467
biographical notice 474–8
sale of Huber's books and manuscripts 477
See also Euting; Streissguth
Huber, Elisabeth (*née* Stapfer; Huber's mother) 7, 61, 77, 310, 326, 341, 364, 367, 399, 459, 461, 465, 474, 477
Huber, Émile (brother of Huber), and unnamed brother and sister 7, 439, 474
Huber, Georges (Huber's father) 7, 310, 474
al-Ḥufaynah 266n, 267, 270
al-Ḥufayrah, basin 182
al-Ḥufnah 266, 270
Ḥulayfah, Ǧabal 222
al-Ḥumayd, ʿAbd al-Raḥmān 410
Hurgronje, Snouck *see* Snouck Hurgronje
Ḥusayn ibn ʿAdī (Ḥarbī guide) 76
Hutaym, tribe 21, 129n, 213–14, 216, 220, 322
Ibn Samrah subtribe 214
status 214
Ḥuwaylān (near Buraydah) 169–70, 175, 272
Ḥuwayṭāt, tribe 197
al-Ḥuwayyiṭ/Yadīʿ 219n, 268, 271

ibex 42
Ibrāhīm Pasha, of Egypt 103n, 163n, 308n, 372
al-Idrīsī, geographer 102
iḥrām 59
inscriptions/graffiti and rock art 142–3, 149, 165, 193, 211, 277–304, 352, 388, 390–5, 400–1, 404–5, 425, 442. *See also* Ancient North Arabian; Ancient South Arabian; Aramaic; 'Himyaritic'; Nabataean; Sarrāʾ, Ǧabal; Taymāʾ Stele; Thamudic
Iraq 2, 13, 21, 51, 58, 119, 154n, 231n, 246–7, 333–4, 388, 408, 412–16, 424
ʿIrnān, Ǧabal 20, 54, 116, 185, 187, 395
Islam, conversion to 48, 102
Israelites 204
Babylonian captivity 204
Istanbul 21, 431. *See also* Constantinople
Italy 44, 95n
ithl, *Tamarix aphylla* 92, 125, 144, 164
Ithrah 90, 94–6, 264, 270

Jaffa 33
Jago, Thomas 4, 44n, 60
Jaussen and Savignac 293
Jerusalem 44, 71, 95n, 454
Jews 48, 102, 195–6, 204, 206, 215, 221
Jordan 16, 82, 331–2, 363
Journal d'Alsace Lorraine 33–4, 417–19, 472n

al-Kabād, Ǧabal 54, 390
Kāf 17–18, 40–1, 88–9, 91–6, 264, 270, 332–3, 386, 389, 415
Kafiristan 13, 309
al-Kahfah 58, 156–9, 178, 187, 269, 271
Kalb, Banī 218
Kanāt/Abū Zayd, Ǧabal 219, 222
Karbalāʾ 245n, 246, 255
Karsh, Ǧabal 215
al-Khabb (near Buraydah) 169–70, 272
al-Khabrāʾ 175